The Colonial Merchants and the American Revolution, 1763-1776

The Colonial Merchants and the American Revolution, 1763-1776

Arthur Meier Schlesinger

BeardBooks
Washington, D. C.

New York: Frederick Unger

copyrighted 1939 by Arthur Meier Schlesinger
ISBN 1-58798-108-4
Reprinted 2001 by Beard Books, Washington, D.C.

Printed in the United States of America

PREFACE

A greater number of investigations of the American revolutionary epoch have been made in the last three or four decades than in all the preceding years. This diligence has been the outgrowth of the modern spirit of historical research and has been productive of results which completely discredit the simple formulae by which the earlier historians explained the colonial revolt. In the light of these studies it is now almost universally agreed that the revolutionary movement was the product of a complexity of forces, governmental and personal, British and colonial, social, economic, geographical and religious. No definitive history of the American Revolution can be written until it becomes possible to appraise each one of these factors at its true value.

In the present work attention is focused on the part which the colonial merchants played—willingly and unwillingly—in bringing about the separation of the thirteen colonies from the mother country. This has rendered necessary some discussion of the evolution of the radical party, with its shifting program, membership and methods; but the latter theme, so fascinating in its possibilities, is entirely incidental to the main purpose of the book.

The most distinctive activity undertaken by the merchants was the formation of non-intercourse agreements. These agreements, because of the peculiar part they played in the development of revolutionary sentiment, receive extended consideration in the present work. No reader will leave these pages without perceiving the source of inspiration for the Jeffersonian policy of commercial coercion adopted in the early nineteenth century. If the latter years of the revolutionary movement be taken for the purpose, the similarity will be seen to be more than superficial. In each case the non-mercantile elements holding the reins of power were driving a reluctant minority of merchants into a sacrifice of trading interests for a good desired only by the former.

John Adams once wrote that the great problem of the revolutionary movement was to get the thirteen clocks to strike at the same time. My own belief is that instead of thirteen revolutionary movements, as Adams suggests, there were fundamentally only two, one functioning along characteristic lines in the northern provinces, and the other developing in a characteristic way in the southern provinces. This view of events has furnished the mode of attack which has been utilized in dealing with the multitudinous happenings of the individual provinces.

This volume appears deep-freighted with my obligations to many fellow-workers in the field of history. In particular I am greatly indebted to Professor Herbert L. Osgood, of Columbia University, who first directed my attention to the subject of colonial non-intercourse and whose constructive criticism has improved my work in content and form. To my colleague, Professor Henry R. Spencer, I am deeply grateful for many helpful suggestions made in the course of reading the manuscript. Indirectly I owe much to the example of certain inspiring teachers, particularly to that of Dean George Wells Knight, of Ohio State University, who in my undergraduate days first awakened in me a scholarly interest in history. I wish to acknowledge my indebtedness to

Mr. John Bennett, of Charleston, S. C., for kindly gathering material for me in the *Loyalist Transcripts*. I desire also to say that Professor C. M. Andrews' splendid essay on "The Boston Merchants and the Non-Importation Movement" (*Col. Soc. Mass. Pubs.*, vol. xix) did not reach my hands in time to be of assistance to me; but I have availed myself of the opportunity to make footnote references to it from time to time. I could not conclude these personal acknowledgments without registering the deep sense of my obligation to my wife, Elizabeth Bancroft, who has been of great assistance to me at every stage of my labors.

Through the generosity of the editors of the *Political Science Quarterly* I have been enabled to make free use of material which appeared in an article entitled "The Uprising against the East India Company," in vol. xxxii, no. 1. Finally, I take great pleasure in recording my appreciation of the untiring courtesy and unfailing helpfulness of the officers and assistants of the following libraries: Library of Congress, Massachusetts Historical Society, Massachusetts State Library, Boston Public Library, New York Public Library, Columbia University Library, New York Historical Society, Historical Society of Pennsylvania, Maryland Historical Society, Charleston Library Society, Ohio State Archaeological and Historical Society, Greene County (Ohio) Library Association, Ohio State University Library, and Ohio State Library,

A. M. S.

OHIO STATE UNIVERSITY,
OCTOBER, 1917.

CONTENTS

CHAPTER I

THE OLD ORDER CHANGETH

	PAGE
Effects of British commercial and financial supervision on the colonies	15
Economy of commercial provinces	22
Dominance of merchant class in commercial provinces	27
Economy of plantation provinces	32
Leadership of planting class in plantation provinces	34
Survey of colonial smuggling to 1763	39

CHAPTER II

THE FIRST CONTEST FOR COMMERCIAL REFORM (1764–1766)

Restrictive acts of 1764	50
Sectionalization of discontent	54
First stage of industrial depression	56
Beginning of organized opposition on part of merchants	59
Broadening the basis of protest	62
Early movement for retrenchment in commercial provinces	63
Stamp Act (1765) and its economic burden	65
Popular demonstrations in commercial provinces	71
Contrast with plantation provinces	73
Union of commercial and plantation provinces in Stamp Act Congress	75
Organized efforts for economic relief in commercial provinces	76
Remedial legislation of Parliament (1766)	82

CHAPTER III

THE SECOND MOVEMENT FOR COMMERCIAL REFORM (1767–1770)

Position of merchant class early in 1767	91
Townshend legislation (1767)	93
General modes of opposition	96
Opposition to regulations against smuggling (1767–1770)	97
General character of non-importation movement	105

CONTENTS

	PAGE
New England town movement for non-consumption (October, 1767—February, 1768)	106
Efforts for a tri-city mercantile league of non-importation (March—June, 1768)	113
Independent boycott agreements in chief trading towns (August, 1768—March, 1769)	120
Attempt to extend scope of mercantile agreements (October, 1769)	131
Non-importation movement in plantation provinces	134
In Virginia	135
In Maryland	138
In South Carolina	140
In Georgia	147
In North Carolina	148
Boycott agreements in minor northern provinces	149
In Delaware	149
In New Jersey	150
In Connecticut	150
In Rhode Island	152
In New Hampshire	155

CHAPTER IV

ENFORCEMENT AND BREAKDOWN OF NON-IMPORTATION (1768-1770)

Difficulties of judging execution of non-importation	156
Enforcement at Boston	156
Enforcement at New York	186
Enforcement at Philadelphia	191
Enforcement in other northern provinces	194
Accession of New Hampshire to non-importation	194
Uncandid course of Rhode Island	195
Enforcement in Delaware, New Jersey and Connecticut	196

CHAPTER V

ENFORCEMENT AND BREAKDOWN OF NON-IMPORTATION (*Continued*)

Operation of non-importation in plantation provinces	197
Situation in Virginia	198
Situation in Maryland	199
Enforcement in South Carolina	202
Enforcement in North Carolina	208
Early defection of Georgia	209
General trend toward relaxation of non importation	209

CONTENTS

Movement of great trading towns to terminate non-importation (April—October, 1770) 217
Collapse of non-importation in plantation provinces (October, 1770—July, 1771) 233
Coercive effects of non-importation in England 236

CHAPTER VI

Colonial Prosperity and a New Peril (1770–1773)

Alienation of merchant class from radicals. 240
Return of prosperity 241
Widespread acquiescence in tea duty. 244
Continuance of smuggling 246
Attempt of radicals to revive agitation (November, 1772—July, 1773). . . 253
Cause for renewal of opposition: tea act of 1773 262
Analysis of literature of protest 265

CHAPTER VII

The Struggle With the East India Company (1773–1774)

Inauguration of movement of opposition at Philadelphia 279
Development of Boston opposition to tea shipments 281
Course of opposition at Philadelphia 290
Course of opposition at New York 291
Course of opposition at Charleston 294
Effect of Boston Tea Party on colonial opinion 298

CHAPTER VIII

Contest of Merchants and Radicals for Dominance in the Commercial Provinces (March—August, 1774)

Passage of coercive acts of 1774 305
Effect of coercive acts on American opinion 306
Movement in commercial provinces for non-intercourse 311
    In New England 311
    In New York 327
    In Pennsylvania 341
    In New Jersey 356
    In Delaware 357

CHAPTER IX

CONTEST OF MERCHANTS AND RADICALS FOR DOMINANCE IN THE PLANTATION PROVINCES (MAY—OCTOBER, 1774)

	PAGE
Factors conditioning the non-intercourse movement in plantation provinces	359
Action of Maryland	360
Measures of Virginia	362
Attitude of North Carolina	370
Course of South Carolina	373
Backwardness of Georgia	379
Indications of rising tide of radicalism in British America	386
Combination of workingmen at Boston and New York against Gage	386
Destruction of the *Peggy Stewart* at Annapolis	388

CHAPTER X

THE ADOPTION OF THE CONTINENTAL ASSOCIATION
(SEPTEMBER—OCTOBER, 1774)

Genesis of First Continental Congress	393
Factors determining the policy of Congress	396
Proceedings of First Continental Congress	410

CHAPTER XI

RATIFICATION OF THE CONTINENTAL ASSOCIATION
(NOVEMBER, 1774—JUNE, 1775)

Position of moderates after First Continental Congress	432
Literature of protest	435
Establishment of Association in commercial provinces	440
In Massachusetts	440
In New Hampshire	442
In Rhode Island	444
In Connecticut	444
In New York	447
In New Jersey	455
In Pennsylvania	456
In Delaware	460
Establishment of Association in plantation provinces	460
In Maryland	461
In Virginia	461
In North Carolina	462
In South Carolina	464
Failure of Georgia to ratify	469

CONTENTS

CHAPTER XII

FIVE MONTHS OF THE ASSOCIATION IN THE COMMERCIAL PROVINCES
(DECEMBER, 1774—APRIL, 1775)

	PAGE
General conditions affecting operation of Association	473
Workings of Association in Massachusetts	476
Workings of Association in New Hampshire	483
Workings of Association in Rhode Island	485
Workings of Association in Connecticut	486
Workings of Association in New York	489
Workings of Association in New Jersey	493
Workings of Association in Pennsylvania	495
Workings of Association in Delaware	502

CHAPTER XIII

FIVE MONTHS OF THE ASSOCIATION IN THE PLANTATION PROVINCES
GENERAL CONCLUSIONS

Contrast with commercial provinces	504
Workings of Association in Maryland	504
Workings of Association in Virginia	509
Workings of Association in North Carolina	519
Workings of Association in South Carolina	525
Employment of provincial boycott	529
Regulation of coastwise trade	534
General conclusions as to non-importation regulation in all provinces	535
Effects of Continental Association on Great Britain	536

CHAPTER XIV

TRANSFORMATION OF THE ASSOCIATION (APRIL, 1775—JULY, 1776)

Cause of transformation of Continental Association	541
Widespread adoption of defense associations	542
Belated accession of Georgia to Continental Association	546
Changing functions of committees of observation	552
Early adoption of non-exportation for military purposes	559
Modifications in Continental Association made by Second Continental Congress	563
Advent of non-exportation	570

CHAPTER XV

TRANSFORMATION OF THE ASSOCIATION (*Continued*)

	PAGE
Nullification of acts of navigation and trade	576
Relaxation of tea non-consumption	581
Removal of restraint on prices	584
Merchant class and the supreme decision	591
APPENDIX	607
BIBLIOGRAPHY	614
INDEX	631

CHAPTER I

THE OLD ORDER CHANGETH

THE century closing with the treaty of Paris of 1763 was the Golden Age of commerce for the merchants of the thirteen continental English colonies. The location of these colonies in the temperate zone and the relative newness of some of them had caused the mother country to accord to them a treatment different from that extended to the tropical colonies. In particular they had been enabled to escape most of the injurious restraints which a thorough application of the mercantilist theory would have involved—a theory dear to the economic writers of the times and to the Board of Trade, and one which would have converted the colonies into mere sources of supply and markets for the English merchants and manufacturers. Under these favoring circumstances, the colonists acquiesced without serious complaint in the British commercial system, and found the burdens which it imposed counterbalanced by corresponding benefits.[1]

The foundation stone of the commercial system was

---

[1] The summary of the effects of the British commercial policy, which follows, is based principally upon the anonymous pamphlet, *The Interest of the Merchants and Manufacturers of Great Britain in the Present Contest with the Colonies Stated and Considered* (London, 1774); and upon the following monographic studies: Ashley, W. J., "The Commercial Legislation of England and the American Colonies, 1660-1760," in *Surveys Historic and Economic* (New York, 1900), and Beer, G. L., *The Commercial Policy of England toward the American Colonies* (Col. U. Studies, vol. iii, no. 2).

the navigation act of 1660, which confined the colonial carrying trade wholly to English and colonial shipping. Under operation of this monopoly, ship building had become a lucrative source of wealth for colonial capitalists and of employment for colonial artisans and sailors.

The most comprehensive regulation affecting the distribution of goods was the requirement that European commodities imported into the colonies must be laden and shipped in England.[1] The hardship which this restriction imposed on the colonies was theoretical rather than actual. For one thing the Americans generally found it more profitable to buy British manufactures than foreign wares because of the superior quality and lower price of the former. This position of superiority, enjoyed by the English merchant and manufacturer independent of any legal advantage, made it possible for them to retain their American market even after the colonies had established independence.[2] Furthermore, England

[1] There were a few exceptions; e. g., wines from Madeira and the Azores; salt from any port of Europe for the New England fisheries, and, at a later time, for Pennsylvania and New York; provisions, horses and servants from Ireland and Scotland; and later, linen from Ireland.

[2] Lord Sheffield, by comparing the prices of standard British manufactures with foreign-made wares, made it apparent that "the preference formerly given [by the American colonists] was not the effect of our restrictions . . ." *Observations on the Commerce of the American States* (London, 1783), p. 234. So; also, a London merchant in the American trade testified before the House of Commons in 1775 that printed calicoes and other colored and striped goods, and probably also muslins and silk handerchiefs, could be procured on better terms in England than in Holland. All these were important articles of American consumption. Stevens, B. F., *Facsimiles of Mss. in European Archives etc.* (London, 1889-98), vol. xxiv, no. 2037, p. 16. Madison wrote in 1785 that "our trade was never more compleatly monopolized by G. B., when it was under the direction of the British Parliament than it is at this moment." Madison, James, *Writings*, (Hunt, G., ed.), vol. ii, p. 147.

was, by virtue of her geographical position with reference to continental Europe, the natural entrepôt for most of the outgoing European trade to the colonies. In the case of non-English manufactures, usually the the greater portion of the English import duty was refunded, or "drawback," upon re-shipment of the goods to America, with the result that certain goods, such as German linens, sold more cheaply in the colonies than in the home country.[1] If the parliamentary regulations did sometimes tend to cramp American commercial opportunities, the colonists were apt to ignore the restrictions and, as Lord Sheffield says with a large measure of truth, "it is well known that from the first they uniformly did evade them whenever they found it to their interest."[2]

As for the colonial export commerce, little or no restraint was imposed on the trade of the northern colonies with foreign countries, except in so far as the law governing imports compelled the colonial shipmasters to take their return cargoes back to America by way of England. They might send their articles of commerce the world over, wherever a market could be found, with the exception during the eighteenth century of naval stores, which, being confined to the English market, were favored with governmental bounties. Only on their trade with the mother country were the restrictions on exports of any apparent importance. By the terms of the so-called corn laws, English ports were closed, either absolutely or by heavy duties, to colonial cereals and meats; and a discriminatory duty was laid on oil and blubber imported in colonial vessels. This deprived the

[1] The drawback amounted to all but one-half of the "Old Subsidy" of 1660, or about 2½%. *Vide Va. Mag. Hist. and Biog.*, vol. xi, p. 142.
[2] *Op. cit.*, p. 234.

northern colonists of convenient articles of exchange for British manufactures and would have proved a serious restraint had they not been free to seek elsewhere commodities that could be marketed in England.

Like naval stores, the staple of Virginia and Maryland was an "enumerated" article, and thus the tobacco of these colonies could be exported only to the home country; but careful provision was made that colonial tobacco should enjoy a monopoly of the home market even at the expense of English farmers and foreign importers. In the case of South Carolinia and Georgia, the exportation of rice was early in the eighteenth century confined to Great Britain where it also was given a monopoly of the market. After 1730 this staple, upon payment of one-half of the British duties, was admitted directly to the southern countries of Europe, whither nearly one-fourth of the exported crop went. North Carolina was affected by the regulations as to tobacco and rice and, more largely, by the restraint on the exportation of naval supplies; but, as has been noted, this last industry was subsidized by the British government, and without such help it could not have maintained itself against the competition of Sweden.

Notwithstanding that colonial tobacco and rice could under most circumstances be sent only to the home country, these products enjoyed fairly free access to the continental European market, for on re-exportation from England the whole or the greater part of the import duty, as the law at any given time provided, was remitted as a "drawback." Thus, toward the end of the colonial era four-fifths of the tobacco carried to England was re-shipped by British merchants to the continent, and nearly three-fourths of the American rice was re-exported to the North German and Dutch manufacturing towns. As England was on the direct route between the colonies and the European ports north of Cape Finisterre, the additional freight charge was not high. Even if colonial vessels had gone directly to the continental ports and thus deprived the British middlemen of their profits, they would have found it difficult to secure return cargoes.

So far as the regulations of exports and imports were concerned, the colonies north of Maryland were not seriously affected; and the restraints on the southern colonies were balanced by governmental subsidies and vested privileges in the English market. But other features of the commercial system bore a somewhat closer relation to the industrial life of the northern colonies. Most notable in this connection was the Molasses Act of 1733, which was designed by means of prohibitive duties to compel the rum distillers and dealers of New England and elsewhere to buy molasses, sugar and rum of British, instead of foreign, colonies in the West Indies. But, as we shall see, this law, oppressive in intent but not in execution, had its chief effect in increasing the volume of colonial smuggling.

Restraints were also placed upon the exportation of certain manufactures. If the British merchants and the Board of Trade could have had their way, these restrictions would have been sweeping and effectual; but as it was, no earnest effort was made either to prevent manufactures generally or to prohibit any manufacturing for private consumption within a colony. In 1699 it was enacted that no woolen manufactures should be exported from the colonies, transported from one colony to another or from one place to another in the same colony. In 1732 the exportation of locally-made hats from a colony was forbidden. In the middle of the century a third law forbade the erection of any new steel furnaces or slitting mills, although country forges where nails and farm implements were wrought were not in any wise affected. This last restriction worked some hardship on the colonies north of Maryland; but the ill wind blew favorably for Virginia and Maryland, for these colonies profited by the special encouragement which the act granted for the American production of bar iron and pig iron.

The three laws against manufacturing may, in general, be considered as having had little effect, for the reason that even the northern colonies showed small promise of developing important manufacturing interests. Causes unconnected with the British commercial system operated against the establishment of manufacturing, except for household purposes: the abundance of land in proportion to the population; the resulting high price of labor; and the want of sufficient capital.[1] The thousands of British workingmen who migrated to America in the last quarter-century of the colonial era found it more profitable and congenial to become farmers or seafarers than to labor at their old occupations. Colonial capitalists found a better investment for their capital in commerce

---

[1] Gallatin assigned the same reasons for the natural industrial backwardness of the country in 1810 in his "Report on Manufactures." *Am. St. Papers, Finance,* vol. ii, pp. 425-426. Colonists and Englishmen at home widely appreciated that natural conditions in the colonies were unfavorable to the development of manufacturing. *E. g., vide* "An Essay on the Trade of the Northern Colonies" in *Bos. Eve. Post,* Jan. 30, Feb. 6, 1764; article by "A North American," copied into *N. Y. Merc.,* June 10, 1765; article in *Conn. Cour.,* Aug. 17, 1767; the pamphlet, *The Int. of Merchants and Mfrs.,* pp. 20-21; reports of following governors to home government: Moore, of N. Y., *N. Y. Col. Docs.,* vol. vii, pp. 888-889; Wentworth, of N. H., *British Papers* ("*Sparks Mss.*"), vol. i, p. 6; Sharpe, of Md., *Md. Arch.,* vol. xiv, pp. 496-497; Franklin, of N. J., *1 N. J. Arch.,* vol. x, pp. 31-32; Macpherson, D., *Annals of Commerce* (London, 1805), vol. iii, pp. 186-191; Franklin, Benj., *Writings* (Smyth, A. H., ed.), vol. v, p. 116.

or agriculture and refused to hazard their resources in manufacturing enterprises of any size, even in later times when non-importation agreements were creating an artificial demand for colonial wares.[1]

An act of Parliament of 1732 sought to safeguard British investments in colonial businesses by protecting creditors at home against discriminatory colonial legislation designed to impede the collection of their debts. The act was passed upon petition of some London merchants. It provided that the affidavit of a British subject at home should have the same force as evidence given in open court in the colonies and that the lands, tenements and negroes owned by the colonists should be liable for the payment of debts in much the same manner as real estate was in England. The undoubted effect of the law was that colonial merchants and planters of substance were enabled to secure a more generous credit; the chief hardship of the regulation fell on the unthrifty and unfortunate in the colonies.

Another regulation of Parliament, aimed solely at New England, prohibited the issue of legal-tender paper money after 1751. Beginning in 1690, Massachusetts had been beguiled into the use of paper currency through the heavy expenses entailed by the successive French and Indian wars. Merchants of substance and the royal officials in the colony viewed this deluge of paper money with dismay. Other colonies followed the example of Massachusetts, with varying degrees of good faith. The upshot was the act of 1751 directed against the New England governments where the evil was worst.[2] This

---

[1] "A. Z." in *Bos. Gaz.*, Feb. 20, 1769.
[2] Davis, A. McF., *Currency and Banking in Massachusetts Bay* (3 Am. Econ. Assn. Pubs.), vol. i, pp. 253-265; Russell, E. B., *The Review of American Colonial Legislation by the King in Council* (Col. U. Studies, vol. lxiv, no. 2), pp. 120-124.

law, though failing to meet the need which undoubtedly existed for a more abundant circulating medium, insured a safe currency and stabilized business conditions to the satisfaction of the men of means and the creditor class generally in New England.

It would appear, then, that the business men of the colonies north of Maryland had little reason to quarrel with the British commercial and financial regulations as they actually operated prior to the reign of George III. Indeed, under parliamentary supervision, the colonies had made such progress in wealth and population as to attract the attention of all Europe. There were besides, as we shall see presently, other powerful ties of interest that bound the colonial business and planting class to the mother country. It was a perception of these facts that prompted Franklin to say in 1754 of the restrictive regulations of Parliament: "These kind of secondary taxes, however, we do not complain of, though we have no share in the laying or disposing of them;"[1] and caused James Otis to declare in 1764: "The act of navigation is a good act, so are all that exclude foreign manufactures from the plantations, and every honest man will readily subscribe to them."[2]

From north to south, the colonial economy revealed marked contrasts which were destined to have far-reaching consequences. Fundamentally, the provinces fell into two clearly differentiated groups.[3] North of Mary-

[1] Franklin, *Writings* (Smyth), vol. iii, p. 236.
[2] *The Rights of the British Colonies Asserted and Proved* (Boston, 1764), pp. 54-55.
[3] Viewing the matter from a somewhat different angle, Professor C. M. Andrews has made this luminous remark: "The real difference between the north and the south in colonial times lay not in politics, law, religion, education, in manners, customs, or mental attitudes. It

land were the *commercial provinces*, regions in which the economic life centered chiefly in marine activity, as in New England, or else depended very largely upon trading, with agriculture as an important local feeder, as in the Middle Provinces.[1] In the commercial provinces the most influential men were merchants or lawyers allied with them, and political life radiated from the trading centers. South of this group lay the *plantation provinces*, where the native economic interests were almost exclusively agricultural along specialized lines and the trading relations were managed by merchants of the mother country or coastwise by northern merchants. Here towns were small and for the most part unimportant, and political leadership fell to the owners of the great plantations.

Each group of provinces displayed a wide diversity of industry and trade within itself.[2] A facetious member of the South Carolina Assembly was heard to remark when a proposal for a Stamp Act Congress was under consideration: "If you agree to the proposition of com-

is to be found in the fact that the southern colonies from the beginning to the end of the colonial period represented a purely agricultural form of life without towns, trading communities, variety of industrial interests and competition, and consequently without that ingenuity and scientific skill which is essential to the spread of democratic ideas and the increase of wealth." *The Colonial Period* (New York, 1912), pp. 105-106.

[1] One New England writer said: "'Tis not difficult to prove clearly, the whole Product of the Lands to the Northward of Maryland is not equal in Value to the fourth Part of our Imports from Great Britain." *Bos. Post-Boy,* Nov. 28, 1763.

[2] The subject of colonial economic conditions had been treated in innumerable places. For excellent general discussions, *vide* Ford, W. C., "Colonial America," *Col. Soc. Mass. Pubs.*, vol. vi, pp. 340-370; and Johnson, E. R., *History of Domestic and Foreign Commerce of the United States* (Washington, 1915), vol. i, pp. 3-121.

posing a Congress of deputies from the different British colonies, what sort of a dish will you make. New-England will throw in fish and onions. The middle states flax-seed and flour. Maryland and Virginia will add tobacco. North-Carolina, pitch, tar and turpentine. South-Carolina, rice and indigo, and Georgia will sprinkle the whole composition with saw-dust. Such an absurd jumble will you make if you attempt to form a union among such discordant materials as the thirteen British provinces."[1] The ingredients of the continental dish were even more variegated than the South Carolinian asserted.

Of the commercial provinces, the enterprising merchants of New England developed a network of trade routes that covered well-nigh half the world. Possessing within themselves no staple with which to make returns for their vast consumption of English drygoods and other wares, the main resources of trade of these provinces were the fisheries, the molasses-rum trade, the marketing of slaves and the coastwise traffic.[2] All these sources were vigorously exploited in order to pile up a favorable balance of specie to send as remittance to England.

[1] Ramsay, D., *History of the Revolution of South Carolina* (Trenton, 1785), vol. i, pp. 12-13.

[2] This statement of New England conditions is based largely upon the following materials: representation of R. I. Assembly in *R. I. Col. Recs.*, vol. vi, pp. 378-383; "Essay on Trade of Northern Colonies," in *Bos. Eve. Post*, Jan. 30, Feb. 6, 1764; Postlethwayt, M., *The Universal Dictionary of Trade and Commerce* (London, 1751), vol. i, pp. 366-367; Macpherson, *Annals of Commerce*, vol. iii, pp. 397-398, 570; *Commerce of Rhode Island* (7 *M. H. S. Colls.*, vols. ix and x); Weeden, W. B., *Economic and Social History of New England* (Boston, 1890), and *Early Rhode Island* (New York, 1910); statistics of fisheries, *1 M. H. S. Colls.*, vol. viii, pp. 202-203; examination of merchants before Parliament, *4 American Archives* (Force, P., ed.), vol. i, pp. 1638-1652, 1663-1670.

In 1764 forty-five thousand tons of shipping and upwards of three thousand men were employed in the fisheries. After the fish had been caught and cured, the merchants exported the "merchantable" variety to Spain, Portugal and Italy, where it was sold for cash or bills of exchange, save a small portion which was exchanged for salt, lemons and raisins for the return voyage. Such fish as was unfit for the European market was exported for slave consumption in the West Indies in exchange for more cash and for molasses.

The circuit of trade based upon West Indian molasses brought even more generous returns and indeed constituted the chief source of specie supply. The molasses became marketable when it was distilled into rum, for throughout British America it had great popularity as a tipple and as an article in the Indian trade, and it also played an important part in the African trade. Most of the output of rum was carried by coasting vessels to other provinces and exchanged for products which might be used as remittances to England or as cargoes to the West Indies. The remainder—about one-seventh in the case of Rhode Island—was sent to Africa where it was sold for slaves or for gold-dust and ivory. The last two articles served directly as remittances to England; the slaves were sold for hard money in the West Indies and the proceeds used to pay English debts.

Under the stimulus of this ceaseless round of activity, trading communities sprang up in many parts of New England, with Boston and Newport as the chief centers. Ship building leaped into prominence as a leading industry, so that New England built annually twice as great a tonnage of vessels as all the other continental provinces. The rum industry grew apace, being represented in Rhode Island in 1763 by nearly thirty distilleries "erected at vast expense," with hundreds of persons dependent upon them for subsistence, and in Massachusetts in 1774 by sixty distilleries producing two million seven hundred thousand gallons annually. "In short," declared Macpherson, "their earnest application to fisheries and the carrying trade, together with their unremitting attention to the most minute article which could be made to yield a profit, obtained them the appellation of *the Dutchmen of America.*" Connecticut alone seemed to stand apart, possessing no first-rate ports, having resources of grain and stock more like the Middle Provinces, and confining its trading activities chiefly to coasting voyages and West Indian trade. Its trans-Atlantic trade was for many years handled through Boston, but after the parliamentary act of 1751 prohibiting the emission of legal-tender money in New England, the merchants diverted their trade to New York.[1]

The provinces next to the southward had the advantage of possessing both staples of export and a mercantile population equal to the opportunity.[2] The great ports of New York and Philadelphia possessed a hinterland of large and small farms producing a wealth of grain and livestock. New York was the commercial capital

[1] Referring to this dominant position of New York, "A Connecticut Farmer" expressed the pious wish that "the plumes of that domineering city may yet feather the nests of those whom they have long plucked." *New London Gaz.*, Aug. 17, 1770. *Vide* also *Conn. Journ.*, Jan. 19, 1770.

[2] This statement of conditions in the Middle Provinces is based largely upon the following materials: petition of the New York merchants to House of Commons, in Weyler's *N. Y. Gaz.*, May 4, 1767; Tryon's report to Board of Trade, *N. Y. Col. Docs.*, vol. viii, pp. 434-457; Postlethwayt, *Dict. of Com.*, vol. i, p. 366; Kalm, P., *Travels into North America* (Warrington and London, 1770-1771), vol. i, pp. 31, 49-50, 253-258; reports of Gov. Franklin, *1 N. J. Arch.*, vol. ix, pp. 402-404, 442-444.

of Connecticut and old East Jersey, just as Philadelphia was the entrepôt of West Jersey and the Delaware Counties. Less dependent than New England on circuitous trading for remittances to England, nevertheless the West Indian trade was essential to the prosperity of these provinces, also. The wheat, lumber and meat of the farmers were sent by the merchants to the West Indies, where they were, in part, bartered for sugar, cotton and indigo, which served directly as remittances to Great Britain, and, in part, for rum and molasses. The last two commodities were converted into cash through the triangular trade with Africa and the West Indies, or, by being exchanged for New England fish or South Carolina rice, served indirectly as a means of drawing coin from Spain, Portugal and Italy. The fur trade with the Indians produced a commodity acceptable to English merchants, also. The exportation of colonial flaxseed to Ireland brought a favorable balance of trade with respect to that article; and the carrying to Europe of logwood obtained from the Bay of Honduras proved another means of procuring specie.

Throughout New England and the Middle Provinces, the merchants and their lawyer-allies constituted the dominant element in colonial society, an ascendency shared in the case of New York with the landed gentry. The chief trading communities of the commercial provinces were: Philadelphia, which by 1760 with a population of almost nineteen thousand had usurped the place of Boston as the greatest emporium of British America; Boston, which ranked second with more than fifteen thousand population; New York, a city somewhat smaller than Boston but destined to outstrip her in a few years; and Newport, the fifth city on the continent with more than seven thousand people.[1] In each center, wealthy merchant families had come into existence. Who were better or more favorably known than the Whartons, Pembertons, Willings and Morrises of Philadelphia; the Amorys and Faneuils, the Hancocks and Boylstons of Boston; the Livingstons and Lows, Crugers and Waltons of New York; the Wantons and Lopezes of Newport, or the Browns,—"Nicky, Josey, John and Mosey," —of Providence?

Dependent upon the merchants for a livelihood were great numbers of petty shopkeepers, vendue-masters, ropemakers, sailmakers, sailors, coopers, caulkers, smiths, carpenters and the like. These men "were that numerous portion of the community in republics, styled the People; in monarchies, The Populace, or still more irreverently The Rabble, or Canaille," as a contemporary said;[2] and they were, for the most part, unenfranchised, unorganized, and unaware that in their numerical superiority they possessed a vast potential power in the community.

At Philadelphia, the merchant-aristocracy ruled the city with a rod of iron; their methods of harrying the price-cutting vendue-masters and of discouraging country peddling were similar in kind to those which modern business integration has rendered familiar.[3] The same was true, in lesser degree perhaps, at New York, Boston and Newport.

In their business activities, the merchants showed a capacity for joint undertakings that revealed their kinship with the race that had built up the great East India

---

[1] *A Century of Population Growth* (Washington, 1909), pp. 11-15.

[2] Graydon, A., *Memoirs of His Own Time* (Philadelphia, 1846), p. 122.

[3] Lincoln, C. H., *Revolutionary Movement in Pennsylvania* (U. of Pa. Pubs. in Hist., no. 1), pp. 80-89.

Company and the Hudson's Bay Company. The New York company "for Settling a Fishery in these parts," established in 1675, the Free Society of Traders, a Pennsylvania corporation founded in 1682, and the Philadelphia Contributionship for the Insuring of Houses from Loss by Fire were a few instances of their aptitude for organization.[1] The New-London Society United for Trade and Commerce, formed in 1732, was an example of a promising enterprise that was soon wrecked through the opposition of a farmer-controlled legislature to its plan to issue bills of credit.[2] Mercantile organizations sometimes crossed provincial boundaries and it is not altogether improbable that the historian of the future will cite such an enterprise as the spermaceti candle combine of 1761–1769 as revealing an interprovincial solidarity of interest perhaps as great as the more pretentious New England Confederation of earlier times.[3]

Less intent on politics than business, the merchants as a class did not ordinarily concern themselves with political questions. But when their interests were jeopardized, they entered politics with a vim, and might be expected to carry things their own way. Thus, the merchants of Boston contributed powerfully toward defeating the land bank project of 1740, which was being pushed by the farmers and debtor class generally in the province.[4]

[1] Baldwin, S. E., "American Business Corporations before 1789," *Am. Hist. Assn. Reps.* (1902), vol. i, pp. 253-274; Clark, V. S., *History of Manufactures in United States* (Washington, 1916), pp. 182-185.

[2] *Col. Soc. Mass. Pubs.*, vol. v, pp. 96-111; vol. vi, pp. 6-11.

[3] *R. I. Commerce*, vol. i, pp. 88-92, 97-100; Mason, G. C., "The United Company of Spermaceti Chandlers, 1761," *Mag. N. Engl. Hist.*, vol. ii, pp. 165-169; Weeden, *Early Rhode Island*, pp. 328-329; Hunt's *Merchants' Magazine*, vol. xxxii, pp. 386-387.

[4] Davis, *Currency and Banking in Mass. Bay*, vol. i, pp. 406-412; vol. ii, pp. 130-235.

No one understood better than the merchants that the rock of their prosperity was the maintenance of the British empire. The system of parliamentary regulations had yielded benefits without great corresponding disadvantages in actual practice. Furthermore, American commerce had prospered under the protection of the British flag and British navy,[1] and colonial merchants saw their potential world market widening with each new conquest. These were advantages that the colonial merchant received in common with his brother at home and to an extent at the latter's expense. Of great importance, also, were the liberal credits which the English merchants extended to the colonial merchants. The Americans could not have secured such favorable terms from foreign houses; and without such indulgence they would have found difficulty in financing their undertakings.[2]

---

[1] For example, there were the advantages which came to American merchants from the presents of Great Britain to the Barbary States, amounting to nearly $300,000 annually. At the outbreak of the War for Independence, it was estimated that one-sixth of the wheat and flour exported from British America, and one-fourth of the dried and pickled fish, and a quantity of rice, found their best market in the ports of the Mediterranean. In this commerce, there were employed eighty to one hundred ships. Moore, J. B., *American Diplomacy* (New York, 1905), p. 65.

[2] The slow development of Canada and Grenada before they came under British control was attributed to the short credits granted by the merchants in France. *The Int. of Merchants and Mfrs.*, pp. 32-36. The British merchant usually granted twelve months' credit without interest and thereafter made an annual charge of 5%. Collins, Stephen, *Letters* (L. C. Mss.), vol. xvii, Feb. 18, 1774; Stevens, *Facsimiles*, vol. xxiv, no. 2037, pp. 11-12, 17. As late as 1810, Gallatin spoke of "the vastly superior capital of the first manufacturing nation of Europe which enables her merchants to give very long credits, to sell on small profits, and to make occasional sacrifices." *Am. St. Papers, Finance*, vol. ii, pp. 425-426.

This business *entente* between the mother country and the merchant class in the colonies was a centripetal force of great importance in the last century of colonial history, making for imperial stability and union when other influences were tending toward disruption. It was with a fine appreciation of these impalpable, but sinewy, bonds that the Committee of Merchants of Philadelphia wrote to the Committee of Merchants of London at a critical juncture of the revolutionary movement: "We consider the Merchants here and in England as the Links of the Chain that binds both Countries together. They are deeply concerned in preserving the Union and Connection. Whatever tends to alienate the Affections of the Colonies or to make them averse to the Customs, Fashions and Manufactures of Great Britain, hurts their Interests. While some, therefore, from ambitious Views and sinister Motives, are labouring to widen the Breach, we whose private Interest is happily connected with the Union or, which is the same, the Peace and Prosperity of both Countries, may be allowed to plead for an End to these unhappy Disputes . . . by a Repeal of the offensive Acts . . ."[1]

On the other hand, the merchants were sensitive and articulate with regard to their interests as members of the British empire. They were ever on the alert to obtain the best terms possible from the home government. Thus, the merchants of Boston and Portsmouth endeavored in 1710 to introduce improvement into the administration of the bounty on naval stores;[2] and in 1731 the Philadelphia merchants and many others re-

[1] Letter of Nov. 25, 1769, *Lon. Chron.*, Mch. 3, 1770; also *Pa. Gaz.*, May 10.

[2] Lord, E., *Industrial Experiments in the British Colonies* (J. H. U. Studies, extra vol., 1898), pp. 69-70.

monstrated against the passage of the proposed molasses act.¹ They also knew the passages to governmental favor in Great Britain, as Bellomont testified when he wrote in 1698 that twenty-eight merchants of New York had contributed one hundred pounds for use in obtaining royal approval for an indemnity bill.²

To understand rightly the agitation against Parliament after 1763, it is important to note that a century of exceptional opportunities had given to the colonial merchants a sense of power in dealing with Parliament and had developed between the chief trading towns in America a consciousness of a fundamental identity of interests. Therefore, when Parliament in 1764 began to pass legislation injurious to their commerce, the merchants of Boston, New York and Philadelphia undertook to create a public opinion favorable to preserving the conditions that had brought them prosperity. Their object was reform, not rebellion; their motives were those of a group of loyal subjects in any country intent upon securing remedial legislation.

The plantation provinces, stretching from Maryland to Georgia, had an industrial and mercantile system in sharp contrast with that of the northern provinces. Virginia and Maryland, almost from their first settlement and under persistent encouragement by Great Britain, had made tobacco their staple; and it long continued to constitute the most valuable export not only of these

---

¹ Channing, E., *History of United States* (New York, 1909 in progress), vol. ii, pp. 517-518.

² Later, Bellomont informed the British authorities that, on the third reading of a bill before the New York Council, a member declared that there would be £40,000 available " to stop the King's approbation in England." Russell, E. B., *Review of American Colonial Legislation by the King in Council*, p. 220.

THE OLD ORDER CHANGETH

provinces but of all the continental colonies as well.[1] The exportation of tobacco was confined by law to Great Britain; and by the middle of the eighteenth century, two hundred sail of ships were employed in the trade, most of them owned in England. Sweet-scented tobacco from the region of the York River was highly esteemed by English epicures, and thus only the inferior varieties, like the "Oronoac," were re-exported to Holland, Germany and Sweden. The planters invested their capital solely in the growing of the weed; and on man's weakness for smoking and snuffing was built up a great agricultural and social system.

In South Carolina and Georgia, almost as great attention was devoted to the culture of rice, although Georgia, as a newer settlement, was backward agriculturally as compared with South Carolina.[2] Not of indigenous growth, the plant nevertheless became the staple of these provinces in the eighteenth century; and American rice

[1] This statement of conditions in the tobacco provinces is based largely upon the following materials: Postlethwayt, *Dict. of Com.*, vol. i, p. 364; Macpherson, *Annals of Com.*, vol. iii, p. 569; Burnaby, A., *Travels through the Middle Settlements in North America* (London, 1775), pp. 15-17, 26-30; *American Husbandry* (London, 1775), vol. i, pp. 225-231, 237-238, 244-245; report of Lt. Gov. Sharpe, *Md. Hist. Mag.*, vol. ii, pp. 354-362; article on Md. commerce in *Pa. Chron.*, Feb. 5, 1770; Morriss, M. S., *Colonial Trade of Maryland, 1689-1715* (J. H. U. Studies, vol. xxxii, no. 3); Bruce, P. A., *Economic History of Va. in the Seventeenth Century* (New York, 1896); report of Gov. Fauquier of Va., *British Papers* ("*Sparks Mss.*"), vol. iii, p. 212.

[2] This statement of conditions in the rice provinces is based very largely upon the following materials: *Political Magazine* (1780), p. 172; Macpherson, *Annals of Com.*, vol. iii, pp. 570-572; table of rice and indigo exports from Charleston, 1748-1773, *S. C. Gaz.*, June 21, 1773; McCrady, E., *S. C. under the Royal Government* (New York, 1901), pp. 262-271, 388-398; report of Gov. Wright of Ga., *Ga. Hist. Soc. Colls.*, vol. iii, pp. 164-167; *Brit. Mus. Addl. Mss.*, no. 8133B (*L. C. Transcripts*), pp. 164-165.

had the reputation of being the best in the world. Although an "enumerated" article, it monopolized the Dutch, German and Portuguese markets and had gained a foothold in Spain. Near the middle of the eighteenth century, another plant was introduced, which quickly gave promise of pushing rice for pre-eminence. This was indigo, the production of which was greatly stimulated by parliamentary bounties. Though its exportation was confined to the mother country, many of the indigo planters, it was said, were able to double their capital every three or four years.

North Carolina, by virtue of her midway geographical position, displayed some characteristics of both adjoining provinces, growing tobacco in her northerly parts and indigo and rice in the southern counties.[1] Her chief articles of export, however, were the products and by-products of her forested areas—tar, pitch, turpentine and many varieties of lumber. In 1767, there were on the Cape Fear River and its tributaries fifty saw-mills, cutting annually a total of seven and one-half million feet of boards.

The most striking feature of the southern economy was the fact that native capital, in its larger aspects, was invested almost exclusively in plantation production. Out of these large landed estates there grew up a great social and political system, with its aristocracy of birth and leadership and its vital distinction between slave labor and gentlemanly leisure. Towns in the plantation provinces were neither large nor numerous. Charleston, possessing a population of almost eleven thousand in 1770, was the chief port of the South and the fourth city in British America. Each province had some place of

---

[1] *American Husbandry*, vol. i, pp. 331-351; report of Gov. Tryon, *N. C. Col. Recs.*, vol. vii, pp. 429-430.

which it could be said that "trade is more collected here than in any other place . . . ";[1] thus, Baltimore in Maryland, Norfolk in Virginia, Wilmington in North Carolina and Savannah in Georgia.

Native Americans did not ordinarily become merchants, and commerce was handled in British bottoms in one of two ways, each of which was uneconomical for the planter.[2] The wealthy planter employed the London or Bristol or Glasgow merchant as a sort of commission merchant, to dispose of his tobacco or rice and to lay out the probable proceeds in goods of one kind or another, to be delivered at the planter's wharf in the following season. This system resulted in careless and wasteful management on the part of the merchant in England, high commissions and freight rates, and chronic overbuying on the part of the colonist.

For ordinary trading purposes, the British merchant maintained an agent or "factor" in the colonies, who kept up a stock of merchandise the year round, worked up business, and acted as financial agent and confidential adviser of his employer. The factors were almost altogether "foreigners," as the local vernacular termed them—that is, natives of Scotland. They had the reputation of being shrewd, hard business men, veritable Shylocks; and from the point of view of their patrons they undoubtedly were, for they demanded, from as wasteful a race of gentlemen-farmers as ever lived, punctual payment for goods sold or money loaned.[3]

---

[1] *4 Am. Arch.*, vol. i, pp. 371-372.

[2] Bassett, J. S., "The Relation between the Virginia Planter and the London Merchant," *Am. Hist. Assn. Reps.* (*1901*), vol. i, pp. 551-575; Schaper, W. A., "Sectionalism in S. C.," *ibid.* (*1900*), vol. i, pp. 287-288, 297; Sioussat, St. G. L., "Virginia and the English Commercial System," *ibid.* (*1905*), vol. i, pp. 71-97.

[3] For an able defense of the Scotch merchants, *vide* "A Scotchman" in Pinkney's *Va. Gaz.*, Mch. 23, 1775.

Here again, there were large profits for the British dealers and shipowners, and lavish buying on the part of the colonist.

The British capitalist advanced money and gave generous credit to the planter, but this merely served to complicate matters; the planter continually operated on borrowed capital and found his next crop mortgaged before it was planted. For more than a quarter of a century, Colonel Byrd of Virginia, struggled to repay indebtedness contracted with a London firm for the sake of enlarging his plantations. In 1736, he was "selling off land and negroes to stay the stomach" of his hungry creditors; and he asserted that they allowed him twenty-five per cent less for tobacco than they gave to other people, knowing that they had him for a customer until the debt was discharged.[1]

The result of this financial system, in its various ramifications, was the economic bondage of the planting class to the British merchants. The planter, Thomas Jefferson, declared that in Virginia "these debts had become hereditary from father to son, for many generations, so that the planters were a species of property, annexed to certain mercantile houses in London."[2] When the statute of 1732 was enacted by Parliament to protect the debts of British creditors in the colonies, the Virginia Assembly drew up a memorial, the "whole aim and intent" of which, says Professor Sioussat, was "expressive of a revolt against the domineering and 'grafting' rule of the combination of merchant creditors," in its various manifestations. From time to time, the

[1] Bassett, J. S., *Writings of Colonel William Byrd* (New York, 1901), pp. li, lxxxiv.
[2] Jefferson, *Writings* (Ford, P. L., ed.), vol. iv, p. 155. *Vide* also "A Planter" in Dixon & Hunter's *Va. Gaz.*, Apr. 13, 1774.

colonists tried to improve their situation by passing lax bankruptcy laws and other legislation prejudicial to non-resident creditors; but their efforts were usually blocked by the royal veto.[1] Toward the close of the colonial era, their condition was becoming well-nigh insupportable.

The situation was especially acute in Virginia.[2] In 1748, the Virginia Assembly provided that, in actions for the recovery of sterling debts, the amount adjudged could be settled in currency at twenty-five per cent advance, notwithstanding the fact that exchange fluctuated and was at times as high as forty per cent. Seven years later, the Assembly was induced to modify the law to the extent that the Virginia courts should be empowered to fix the rate of exchange. This law was hardly more satisfactory to the British merchants than the earlier one; and their dissatisfaction was sharpened by the fact that, about this time, Virginia began to issue legal-tender paper money. This money depreciated steadily; and, as a large portion of the debts of the British merchants was in paper, the action of Virginia had the effect of partial repudiation.

But the resourcefulness of Virginia was not yet exhausted. In 1758, a law was passed, permitting persons, who owed tobacco for debts, contracts, fees or salaries, to discharge their obligations during the following year in money at the rate of twopence a pound. This "Two-Penny Act" was passed because of a sharp rise in the price of tobacco; and it aroused the bitter opposition,

---

[1] The plantation provinces displayed much greater activity along these lines than the commercial provinces. This legislation is conveniently summarized in Dr. Russell's *Review of American Colonial Legislation*, pp. 125-136.

[2] Beer, G. L., *British Colonial Policy, 1754-1765* (New York, 1907), pp. 179-188.

not only of British creditors, but also of the Virginia clergy. In 1759, the merchants of London interested in Virginia trade presented a memorial against the act, showing that large quantities of tobacco were owing to them in Virginia, and that under this law the debts could be commuted in money at the rate of twopence per pound notwithstanding that at the time the market price of tobacco was considerably higher. The act thus had the effect of annulling contracts that had turned out unfavorably to the planters; and in August, 1759, an order in council disallowed it, as well as others of a similar nature enacted prior to 1758.

The local clergy were in a similar dilemma, since an earlier law had established their salary at a fixed quantity of tobacco. They believed that they should reap the benefit of any advance in the price inasmuch as they had always suffered by its decline. One of the suits, brought by the "parsons" to recover the full market price of the tobacco, gave opportunity for the first grandiose declaration of the rights of the colonists in the matter. The question of justice had already been decided in favor of the "parson"-plaintiff, when young Patrick Henry was called in by the vestry to exhort the jury to scale down the amount of the verdict which should be assessed. Arguing vigorously for the natural right of the community to govern for itself in the matter, he persuaded the jury to award nominal damages of one penny.[1]

The peculiar economic situation in the plantation provinces shaped the developments of the decade 1764-1774 in fundamental contrast with those of the commercial provinces. Whereas, in the latter, financial power

[1] Henry, W. W., *Patrick Henry* (New York, 1891), vol. i, pp. 30-46; Maury, A., *Memoirs of a Huguenot Family* (New York, 1872), pp. 418-423.

and political power were vested in the hands of the same class in the early years of the decade, in the plantation provinces financial control and political leadership belonged to two classes, dissimilar in nativity, social manners and political sympathy. The important result was that when the new policy of Parliament adopted in 1764 threatened to inflict serious injury on the merchants of the North, the planters of the South felt an instinctive affinity for their oppressed brethren and were moved to join them in their demands for remedial legislation and a larger measure of colonial autonomy. Oliver Wolcott went so far in later years as to say with reference to the chief plantation province: " It is a firmly established opinion of men well versed in the history of our revolution, that the *whiggism* of Virginia was chiefly owing to the *debts of the planters.*"[1]

Thus far it has not been necessary to distinguish between legal commerce and illicit commerce, for the reason that the mother country failed to draw sharply the distinction until the closing years of the colonial era.[2] The

[1] *British Influence on the Affairs of the United States Proved and Explained* (Boston, 1804), quoted by Beard, C. A., *Economic Origins of Jeffersonian Democracy* (New York, 1915), pp. 297-298. It will be recalled that the question of payment of the pre-Revolutionary private debts to British merchants occupied the attention of the British and American governments in the treaties of 1783 and 1794 and in the convention of 1802. The claims presented against the commercial provinces amounted to £218,000; those against the plantation provinces, £3,869,000. The former figure consisted, in large part, of claims on behalf of American loyalists for compensation, while this was not true in the latter case. *Ibid.*

[2] This summary of smuggling is based largely upon the following materials: Postlethwayt, M., *Great Britain's Commercial Interest Explained and Improved* (London, 1759), vol. i, pp. 485-498; "An Essay on the Trade of the Northern Colonies," *Prov. Gaz.*, Jan. 14, 21, 1764; report of commissioners of the customs, *Brit. Mus. Addl. Mss.*, no.

business of smuggling was made easy and attractive by several favoring circumstances—the extensive and irregular coastline, the distance of the colonies from England, the inefficient system of administration, and, it must be said, the practice of custom-house officials "of shutting their eyes or at least of opening them no further than their own private interest required."[1] Smuggling was almost exclusively a practice of merchants of the commercial provinces. "The Saints of New England," wrote Colonel Byrd of Virginia acridly, ". . . have a great dexterity at palliating a perjury so well as to leave no

---

8133c (*L. C. Transcripts*), ff. 85-86; Hutchinson, *History of Mass. Bay*, vol. iii, pp. 160-163; and other sources noted from time to time. The conclusions presented do not differ materially from those given in: Andrews, C. M., "Colonial Commerce," *Am. Hist. Rev.*, vol. xx, pp. 61-62; Ashley, W. J., "American Smuggling, 1660-1760," *Surveys Historic and Economic*, pp. 336-360; Beer, G. L., *British Colonial Policy, 1754-1765*, pp. 235-246, and *Commercial Policy of England*, pp. 130-143; McClellan, W. S., *Smuggling in the American Colonies* (New York, 1912), chap. iii; Root, W. T., *Relations of Pennsylvania with the British Government* (New York, 1912), pp. 61-76. As to the quantity of illicit trade, every student will agree with Professor Andrews that "it is doubtful if satisfactory conclusions can ever be reached . . . owing both to the lack of evidence and to its unsatisfactory character."

[1] "Essay on Trade of Northern Colonies," *Prov. Gaz.*, Jan. 14, 21, 1764. Surveyor General Temple accused Governor Bernard of sharing in such illegal gain. Quincy, S. L., *Mass. Reports, 1761-1772*, pp. 423-424. Hutchinson wrote on Sept. 17, 1763: "The real cause of the illicit trade in this province has been the indulgence of the officers of the customs, and we are told that . . . without bribery and corruption they must starve." *Ibid.*, p. 430. On Feb. 8, 1764, Governor Franklin of New Jersey reported to the Board of Trade that the custom-house officers entered "into a Composition with the Merchants and took a Dollar a Hogshead, or some such small matter, in Lieu of the Duties imposed by Act of Parliament," and he had no knowledge that they ever remitted the "Composition Money" to England. *1 N. J. Arch.*, vol. ix, pp. 403-404. It should be noted that by law the collectors had a discretionary power to accept partial payment of duties as full payment (13 and 14 Charles II, c. 11).

taste of it in the mouth, nor can any people like them slip through a penal statute."[1]

For the most part, colonial smuggling took two forms.[2] First, there was a direct traffic, back and forth across the Atlantic, between the British provinces and foreign countries. The outgoing commerce was likely to infringe the regulation which confined certain colonial exports to Great Britain alone; and the incoming trade unavoidably violated the requirement that practically all products of Europe and Asia should reach the colonies *via* England. The illicit traffic in colonial exports was apparently very small. Of much larger proportions was the clandestine importation of foreign commodities and manufactures, although its relation to the total volume of legitimate trade was not important. Colonial merchants carrying legal cargoes to Holland, Hamburg and France sometimes returned with drygoods, tea, wines and gunpowder, which they had not troubled to enter at a British port.[3] Or these wares found a more circuitous entrance into the colonies by way of the foreign islands in the West Indies. Or New England merchants, having disposed of their fish in Portugal, Spain or Italy and having, in accordance with the law, loaded all the salt they wished, completed their cargoes with fruit, oil and

[1] Letter of July 12, 1736, *Am. Hist. Rev.*, vol. i, p. 88.

[2] One form of smuggling disappeared after the seventeenth century and is not discussed here. This was the direct exportation of colonial tobacco to Scotland. The illegal character of this traffic was removed when the acts of trade were extended to Scotland in 1708. Morriss, *Colonial Trade of Maryland*, pp. 116-120.

[3] *E. g., vide* reports of Lt. Gov. Colden of New York, Colden, *Letter Books, 1760-1775* (*N. Y. Hist. Soc. Colls.*, vols. ix and x), vol. i, pp. 257-259, 375-376; letter of William Bollan, Feb. 26, 1742, *Col. Soc. Mass. Pubs.*, vol. vi, pp. 299-304. The letter of an Amsterdam commission house to a Rhode Island merchant, dated Jan. 31, 1764, is interesting first-hand evidence on this point. *R. I. Commerce*, vol. i, pp. 105-106.

wine, and made straightway for America. Governor Bernard of Massachusetts spoke of "an Indulgence time out of mind allowed in a trifling but necessary article, ... the permitting Lisbon Lemons & wine in small quantities to pass as Ships Stores";[1] and, acting upon the same understanding, Peyton Randolph, attorney general of Virginia, drew upon himself the withering wrath of Governor Dinwiddie, for dismissing a case involving this breach—"inconsistant with Justice, the Sense and Spirit of the Laws that were produc'd on the Tryal," as Dinwiddie declared.[2]

By far the greatest mass of contraband trade consisted in the importation of unduticd molasses, sugar and rum from the foreign West Indies, particularly molasses. The heavy restrictions of 1733 had been imposed regardless of the protests of colonial merchants, the avowed purpose of Parliament being to give to the British planters in the West Indies a monopoly of marketing their molasses in the commercial provinces. The act had been passed at the behest of the "West India interest" in Parliament;[3] and to colonial merchants, it appeared a sinister piece of exploitation intended to enable "a few pamper'd Creolians" to "roll in their gilded

[1] He added: "I have always understood that this was well known in England,—allowed, as being no object of trade, or if it was, no way injurious to that of Great Britain." Quincy, *op. cit.*, pp. 430-431. *Vide* also article in *Bos. Eve. Post*, Jan. 2, 1764. S. Toovey, clerk to the customs collector at Salem, described, in convincing detail, how the customs entries were manipulated for this purpose, in a deposition of Sept. 27, 1764. *Bos. Gaz.*, June 12, 1769.

[2] *Official Records of Robert Dinwiddie* (Richmond, 1884), vol. ii, pp. 679-681. Gov. Fauquier of Virginia reported on Nov. 20, 1764, that ships returning from Lisbon generally brought a small quantity of fruit and sometimes wine. *Brit. Papers* ("*Sparks Mss.*"), vol. ii, p. 43.

[3] About forty members were usually so classified. *Bos. Eve. Post*, Nov. 21, 1763; *Bos. Post-Boy*, Aug. 4, 1766.

THE OLD ORDER CHANGETH 43

equipages thro' the streets" of London, at the expense of two million American subjects.[1]

If any serious attempt had been made to enforce the statute, the prosperity of the commercial provinces would have been laid prostrate. It was the West India trade, more than anything else, which had enabled them to utilize their fisheries, forests and fertile soil, to build up their towns and cities, to supply cargoes for their merchant marine, and to liquidate their indebtedness to British merchants and manufacturers. The entire molasses output of the British islands did not equal two-thirds of the quantity imported into Rhode Island alone, and was estimated to amount to only about one-eighth of the quantity consumed annually by all the provinces.[2] Moreover, the prices of the British planters were twenty-five to forty per cent higher than those asked at the foreign islands; although the foreign planters would accept business only for cash.[3] That smuggling with the foreign islands was extensive and important, the evidence is plentiful and uncontradicted. It is to be found in such a variety of sources as letters of colonial

[1] *Bos. Eve. Post*, July 8, 1765, quoting an article by "Anti-Smuggler" in the London *Public Ledger*. *Vide* also *ibid.*, Jan. 2, 1764. For the best explanation of the motives of Parliament in passing this law, *vide* Andrews, C. M., "Anglo-French Commercial Rivalry," *Am. Hist. Rev.*, vol. xx, pp. 761-780.

[2] Of the 14,000 hogsheads of molasses imported into Rhode Island each year, 11,500 hogsheads came from the foreign West Indies, paying no duty. Representation of R. I. Assembly, in *R. I. Col. Recs.*, vol. vi, pp. 378-383. Of the 15,000 hogsheads imported into Massachusetts in 1763, all but 500 came from the foreign islands. Bernard, F., *Letters on Trade*, p. 7; evidence of William Kelly before a committee of Parliament, *Brit. Mus. Addl. Mss.*, no. 33030 (*L. C. Transcripts*), f. 135

[3] Postlethwayt, *Great Britain's Interest*, etc., vol. i, p. 494; letter from New York in *London Chronicle*, Oct. 2, 1764. There were also heavy duties levied on the products of the British sugar plantations at exportation. Channing, *op. cit.*, vol. ii, p. 511.

governors and customs officials, newspaper articles and merchants' letter books, instructions to governors, and the writings of economists.[1]

Although of decided economic advantage to the commercial provinces, the non-enforcement of the Molasses Act proved a serious political blunder for the home government. As British statesmanship should have foreseen, it gave to colonial smuggling every aspect of respectability. Numbers have become "reconciled to it by example, habit, and custom," declared a contemporary observer, "and have gradually consented to amuse themselves with some very superficial arguments in its favour, such as, that every man has a natural right to exchange his property with whom he pleases, and where he can make the most advantage of it; that there is no injustice in the nature of the thing, being no otherwise unlawful than as the partial restrictions of power have made it; arguments which may be . . . adopted in extenuation of many other disorderly and pernicious practices."[2]

"There is no error in a commercial nation so fruitful of mischief," was the keen observation of another writer, "as making acts and regulations oppressive to trade [without enforcing them]. This opens a door to corruption. This introduces a looseness in morals. This destroys the

---

[1] *E. g.*, the commissioners of the customs in England reported on Sept. 16, 1763, that "it appears to Us, from the Smallness of the Sum Collected from these Duties and from other Evidence, that they have been for the most part, either wholly evaded or Fraudulently Compounded . . ." *Brit. Mus. Addl. Mss.*, no. 8133c (*L. C. Transcripts*). A writer in the *Bos. Eve. Post*, Nov. 21, 1763, voiced the current colonial opinion when he averred: "The sugar act has from its first publication been adjudged so unnatural that hardly any attempts have been made to carry it into execution."

[2] "A Tradesman of Philadelphia" in *Pa. Journ.*, Aug. 17, 1774. *Cf.* Bollan's letter, *Col. Soc. Mass. Pubs.*, vol. vi, p. 300.

reverence and regard for oaths, on which government so much depends. This occasions a disregard to those acts of trade which are calculated for its real benefit. This entirely destroys the distinction which ought invariably to be preserved in all trading communities between a merchant and a smuggler. But the sugar act has thrown down all distinction: Before this was published, a merchant disdain'd to associate with the unfair trader."[1] The truth was that the income of many wealthy families in the North—yea, the prosperity of whole provinces—depended upon a trade which was approved by a robust public opinion but forbidden by parliamentary statute. The "Smuggling Interest" became a factor of great potential strength in public affairs in the trading towns of the North.[2]

Colonial smugglers felt the first impact of an opposing imperial interest during the last intercolonial war, when, covetous of large profits, they supplied the French belligerents in America with foodstuffs, whereby they were enabled to prolong the war.[3] In defiance of patriotic duty, acts of Parliament, and the efforts of the British and provincial administrations, not only was the old illicit intercourse with the French continued but many new routes were opened up. The early efforts of the British government to suppress the traffic resulted in more than doubling the average annual revenue from the Molasses Act during the war, at a time, however,

[1] *Bos. Eve. Post*, Nov. 21, 1763.

[2] *Vide* the important letters of Richard Oswald to Lord Dartmouth in Stevens, *Facsimiles*, vol. xxiv, nos. 2032, 2034, 2037; *Sagittarius's Letters and Political Speculations* (Boston, 1775), nos. i and iii, *passim*.

[3] The present account is based largely upon the excellent treatment in Beer, *Brit. Col. Policy, 1754-1765*, pp. 72-131, and Root, *Rels. of Pa. with Brit. Govt.*, pp. 76-84.

when the volume of smuggling had probably trebled or quadrupled.[1] In 1760 and 1761, a vigorous employment of the navy resulted in disturbing the centers of smuggling in the West Indies and in further diminishing its volume.

The experience of the British government during the war sharply revealed the strength, sordidness and energy of the forces supporting the contraband trade. Provincial governors had been bought out by the smugglers in one or two instances; and from Massachusetts to South Carolina, the Americans managed pretty successfully to control the vice-admiralty courts in their favor. Governor Hamilton, of Pennsylvania, reported in 1760 that the most eminent lawyers of that province were retained by the smugglers. In New York, Lieutenant Governor Colden complained in 1762 that his efforts against illicit trade had failed of the desired effect because the enforcement of the law rested largely with persons who had connections with smugglers or who feared their resentment.[2] A prominent Rhode Island lawyer averred that the courts of vice-admiralty had become " subject to mercantile influence; and the king's revenue sacrificed to the venality and perfidiousness of courts and officers."[3]

In Massachusetts, the smuggling merchants struggled

---

[1] The extent of this partial enforcement is indicated by the aggregate amount of the revenue derived from the Molasses Act. The total duties paid on molasses from 1734 to the close of 1755 amounted to £5,686, or a yearly average of £259. In the seven years, 1756-1762, £4,375 was collected, the yearly average being £625. For the years 1760 and 1761 the amounts were £1,170 and £1,189. Beer, *op. cit.*, pp. 115-116 and f. n.

[2] *Letter Books*, vol. i, pp. 195-196.

[3] Howard, M., *A Letter from a Gentleman at Halifax to his Friend in Rhode Island* (Newport, 1765).

hard to impair the efficiency of the customs collection by instituting damage suits against customs officials in unfriendly common-law courts. Toward the end of the war, the services of James Otis, recently prosecuting officer for the local vice-admiralty court and the most eloquent lawyer of the province, were retained by the merchants of Boston and Salem, in an attack on the legality of the general search warrants, or "writs of assistance," which had proved an effective means of locating contraband goods. Like Henry in Virginia, Otis made a perfervid plea for the "inherent, inalienable, and indefeasible" rights of the colonists and particularly for the privacy of one's home and warehouses from prying customs officers acting under general search warrants.[1] But he lost his case. This failure led the Massachusetts General Court to pass an act, which, if Governor Bernard had not vetoed it, would have drawn the teeth from the writs. This bill, the governor assured the Board of Trade, was "the last effort of the confederacy against the custom-house and Laws of Trade."[2]

The suppression of smuggling had been originally undertaken by the British government as a war measure; but before the war had terminated, it became apparent that a strict enforcement of the acts of trade was to be a permanent peace policy. Pitt's circular dispatch of August 23, 1760 marked the transition;[3] the year 1763 brought a succession of unqualified steps in this direction. An act of Parliament of that year authorized the

[1] For a bibliography of Otis's speech, *vide* Green, S. A., *2 M. H. S. Procs.*, vol. vi, pp. 190-196.

[2] Palfrey, J. G., *Compendious History of New England* (Boston, 1884), vol. iv, p. 313.

[3] Text in Quincy, *Mass. Reports*, p. 407.

use of the navy against smuggling in the colonies.¹ The vicious practice of absenteeism in the customs service was terminated: all colonial customs officials residing in England were ordered to repair to their stations in America.² In July, special instructions were sent to colonial governors and naval commanders to suppress illicit trade, especially the clandestine traffic carried on directly with continental Europe.³ In the last days of the year, strict orders were issued from all the custom houses in the northern district, requiring masters of vessels to conform to the old Molasses Act "in all its parts."⁴ Early in 1764, American newspapers recorded the arrival of warships at various ports. The frequency of seizures increased.⁵

The publication of the orders to enforce the Molasses Act "caused a greater alarm in this country than the taking of Fort William Henry did in 1757," declared Governor Bernard, of Massachusetts.⁶ He reported that it was common talk among Boston merchants that the trade of the province was at an end, "sacrificed to the West Indian Planters," and that every prudent man should resort to farming and homespun. Lieutenant

¹ 3 George III, c. 22.

² Kimball, G. S., ed., *Correspondence of the Colonial Governors of Rhode Island, 1723-1775* (Boston, 1902), vol. ii, p. 355.

³ *Md. Arch.*, vol. xiv, pp. 102-103; *Prov. Gaz.*, Sept. 24, 1763, also *Mass. Gaz. and News-Letter*, Sept. 29.

⁴ *Bos. Post-Boy*, Jan. 2 and 9, 1764, contained such orders, under date of Dec. 26, 1763, from the custom houses of the ports of Boston, Salem, Piscataqua and Falmouth; Newport; New London and New Haven; New York; Perth Amboy, Burlington and Salem, N. J.

⁵ Hutchinson, *Hist. of Mass. Bay*, vol. iii, pp. 160-163.

⁶ Bernard, *Letters*, p. 9. Commenting on this comparison, John Adams declared in 1818: "This I fully believe and certainly know to be true; for I was an eye and an ear witness to both of these alarms." *Works* (Adams, C. F., ed.), vol. x, p. 345.

THE OLD ORDER CHANGETH

Governor Colden at New York warned the Board of Trade that the stoppage of trade with the foreign West Indies would reduce importations from England and force the people to do their own manufacturing. The legislature of that province granted a bounty on hemp, with the hope of providing a staple commodity for export to England in place of commodities from the foreign West Indies.[1] Governor Franklin, of New Jersey, informed the Board of Trade: "At present there are great Murmurings among the Merchants, and others, in North-America, on account of the Stop put to" the trade with the foreign West Indies.[2] "Trade [is] very dull," wrote a smuggling merchant of Philadelphia as early as November 12, 1763, after noting the presence of two men-of-war in the river. "I suppose the number of Vessells in this harbour, at this time, exceeds any that ever was Knowne here & people not knowing what to do with them." At various times in the next twelvemonth he lamented the great scarcity of cash and the vigilance of the warships. They " are so very strict that the smallest things don't escape their notice," he complained.[3] There was, beyond question, a gloomy prospect ahead for the smuggling merchants.

[1] Colden, *Letter Books*, vol. i, pp. 312-313; Weyler's *N. Y. Gaz.*, Apr. 2, 1764. "The intercourse between the Dutch &c, & the Colonies (I mean Dry Goods everywhere) ought to be entirely suppress'd, but the rigorous execution of the Sugar [Act] is injurious," wrote Jonathan Watts, a member of the New York council. *4 M. H. S. Colls.*, vol. x, p. 507.

[2] *1 N. J. Arch.*, vol. ix, p. 404.

[3] "Extracts from the Letter-Book of Benjamin Marshall, 1763-1766," *Pa. Mag.*, vol. xx, pp. 204-212.

CHAPTER II

THE FIRST CONTEST FOR COMMERCIAL REFORM
(1764-1766)

EVENTS were shaping themselves in England to accentuate the economic distress which the commercial provinces had already begun to feel. The Peace of Paris of 1763 marked a turning point in the relations of Great Britain to her colonies. The mother country faced the complex task of recasting her imperial policy, of safeguarding her newly-acquired world empire, of readjusting the acts of trade to meet the new situation and of improving their administration.[1] The particularistic course of the colonial legislatures during the recent war had shown that the requisition system could not be depended upon to furnish a permanent revenue for a colonial military establishment; and the lawlessness of the colonial merchants had revealed the need for reforming the machinery of administering the trade laws. Forced to action by these conditions, Parliament, under the leadership of George Grenville, proceeded to adopt an imperial policy which in its main principles conformed to the views long maintained by the British mercantile interests and their apologist, the Board of Trade.

In the light of subsequent history, the most important

[1] " The several changes of territories, which at the last Peace took place in the Colonies of the European world, have given rise to A NEW SYSTEM OF INTERESTS; *have opened a new channel of business; and brought into operation a new concatenation of powers, both commercial and political.*" Pownall, T., *The Administration of the British Colonies* (London, 1768), vol. i, p. 1.

feature of the legislation of 1764 was the fact that, for the first time, Parliament provided specifically for the raising of a revenue in America. But as watchful colonists at the time viewed the unwonted legislative activity, they were impressed almost solely with the idea that their business interests were being vitally affected. It goes without saying that they did not perceive or appreciate the problem of imperial reorganization with which Parliament was wrestling. They stood for a Ptolemaic conception of the empire, with England as the sun and America the earth about which the sun revolved; while the statesmen at home justified their course in the terms of the Copernican theory.[1]

The program of Parliament, therefore, so far as the colonists were concerned, had to stand or fall upon its merits as legislation dealing solely with colonial interests. The group of enactments thus readily divided itself into two parts, those provisions favorable to American commerce and industry, and those detrimental.

The beneficial portions were of minor importance and affected chiefly the plantation provinces where relief was not particularly needed. South Carolina and Georgia were allowed, upon payment of a slight duty, to export rice to any part of America to the southward of those provinces, in order that they might continue to dominate the markets which they had entered during British occupation of certain West India islands in the recent war.[2] As a means of encouraging the indigo industry, a protective duty was placed

[1] *Vide* Beer, *British Colonial Policy, 1754-1765*, pp. 193-251, 274-286, for an excellent presentation of the imperialistic point of view. *Vide* Macpherson, *Annals of Commerce*, vol. iii, pp. 395-399, for a well-balanced statement of the colonial view; also *Col. Soc. Mass. Pubs.*, vol. xiii, pp. 431-433.

[2] 4 George III, c. 27. This liberty was extended to North Carolina in the following year. 5 George III, c. 45.

on foreign indigo imported into the provinces.¹ On the other hand, New England fishermen received concessions in England, by which American whale-fins succeeded in securing a practical monopoly of the home market;² and colonial rum distillers were favored by an absolute prohibition of the introduction of foreign rum.³

The detrimental features of the acts were far-reaching and fundamental in their influence upon American prosperity.⁴ Resolute measures were taken against smuggling. Customs officials were granted ampler authority, and the powers of the admiralty courts were enlarged. In order to protect customs officials from damage suits in common law courts, it was provided that, in cases where the court held there had been a probable cause for making a seizure, the officers should not be liable for damages. In addition, the burden of proof was placed on the owner of the seized goods or vessel; and all claimants of such goods had to deposit security to cover the costs of the suit. Stricter registration of vessels was required. Because of the amenability of vice-admiralty courts to local opinion in the various provinces, a vice-admiralty court for all America was authorized, in which an informer or prosecutor might bring his suit in preference to the local court, if he so chose.

Equally alarming to the commercial provinces was the plan to make the old Molasses Act really productive through a reduction of rates. The former duty on molasses im-

---

¹ 4 George III, c. 15.

² 4 George III, c. 29. Instead of employing eighty or ninety sloops in the whale fishery as prior to this time, New Englanders were employing one hundred and sixty before 1775. Macpherson, *op. cit.*, vol. iii, pp. 401, 567-568.

³ 4 George III, c. 15.

⁴ 4 George III, c. 15. Only the main provisions are noted here.

ported from the foreign West Indies was reduced from sixpence per gallon to threepence, with the understanding that the new rate would be collected. The old duty on raw sugar was continued; and an additional duty was levied on foreign refined sugar.

Other changes were made, which affected colonial merchants only in lesser degree. The purpose of certain of these was to enlarge the market for British merchandise in America by enhancing the price of foreign manufactures. Thus, the amount of the duty withheld in England upon reshipment of foreign goods to the colonies was doubled.[1] Import duties were placed, for the first time, upon certain varieties of Oriental and French drygoods when they were landed in America. Wines, which hitherto had been imported directly from Madeira and the Azores without duty, were now required to pay a high tariff, while Spanish and Portuguese wines, which as before were to be imported by way of Great Britain, were to pay only a low duty.[2] Import duties were also imposed on foreign indigo and foreign coffee brought into the colonies. The list of articles which could be sent to Great Britain alone was increased by the addition of iron, whale-fins, hides, raw silk, potashes and pearlashes. Slight duties were placed on coffee and pimento when shipped from one colony to another.

The only regulation that directly concerned the plantation provinces in any unfavorable way was the prohibition of further issues of legal-tender currency in the provinces outside of New England. This restraint was imposed upon the complaint of some British merchants engaged in Vir-

[1] Prior to this time, the amount had been about 2½ per cent.
[2] The colonists had desired to obtain permission to make direct importations of wine, fruit and oil from Spain and Portugal. *Pa. Journ.*, June 7, 1764; *Bos. Gaz.*, June 11.

ginia trade and was merely an extension of the principle which had been applied in 1751 to New England.¹

Dissatisfaction with the acts of 1764 was thus largely a sectional matter, affecting chiefly the commercial provinces. It is not surprising that the chief polemic efforts of the colonists came from provinces such as Massachusetts, Rhode Island and Pennsylvania; or that, in the one instance, the author was a lawyer, who time and again had been employed by smugglers and who sympathized with them temperamentally;² in the next instance, a merchant, who was largely concerned in illicit trade with the West Indies;³ in the third, a gentleman-farmer and lawyer, fully cognizant

---

¹ 4 George III, c. 34; Franklin, *Writings* (Smyth), vol. v, pp. 85-86, 187-189; Russell, *Review of American Colonial Legislation*, pp. 120-124.

² Otis, James, *The Rights of the British Colonies Asserted and Proved* (Boston, 1764). This pamphlet, largely speculative, made the novel assertion that the duties of 1764 were as truly a fiscal measure as taxes on real estate would be. It should be remembered that Otis had been retained by the merchants of Boston and Salem to attack the legality of the writs of assistance in 1761. Otis, wrote Peter Oliver in 1781, " engrafted his self into the Body of Smugglers, and they embraced him so close, as a Lawyer and an usefull Pleader for them, that he soon became incorporated with them." *Brit. Mus. Egerton Mss.*, no. 2671 (*L. C. Transcripts*). Leading merchants of Boston, like Thomas Hancock and his nephew John, lost no opportunity to recommend Otis as a lawyer to commercial houses in England. Brown, A. E., *John Hancock His Book* (Boston, 1898), p. 33 *et seq*. *Vide* also Hutchinson, *Mass. Bay*, vol. iii, p. 201.

Closer to the economic roots of the troubles was the forceful pamphlet, *The Sentiments of a British American* (Boston, 1764), written by Oxenbridge Thacher, who had been Otis' colleague in the writs of assistance case. Thacher died in 1765, before his usefulness to the anti-parliamentary party had fully developed. For a characterization of the two men, *vide* Adams, John, *Works*, vol. x, pp. 284-292.

³ Hopkins, Stephen, *The Rights of the Colonies Examined* (Providence, 1764). Hopkins also had three sons and four nephews, all captains of vessels. Weeden, *Econ. and Soc. Hist. of New Engl.*, vol. ii, pp. 584, 656, 658.

of the sources from which the prosperity of his community arose.[1]

For the most part, this literature of protest contained a cogent presentation of the economic springs of mercantile prosperity. The prevailing note was sounded by a comment in Thacher's pamphlet on the recent action of Parliament: "Does not this," he asked, "resemble the conduct of the good wife in the fable who killed her hen that every day laid her a Golden Egg?" The new measures for enforcing the acts of trade were roundly denounced, especially the provisions for protecting customs officers from damage suits in case of mistaken seizures, and the provisions granting to the informer or prosecutor the right to choose the court in which he wished to sue. These regulations were termed a denial of the common law and of trial by jury. The new duties on foreign wines were complained of, on the ground that wines had now to be brought to America by a roundabout and expensive route. The restricting of iron exports to Great Britain caused protest, especially in Pennsylvania, because cargoes of iron had always found a ready market in Pŏrtuguese ports.

The chorus of denunciation rose loudest on the subject of the new molasses duties. This appeared to the pamphleteers a species of economic strangulation by which the colonies were cut off from the source of their specie supply. "The duty of 3d. per gallon on foreign molasses is well known

---

[1] Dickinson, John, *The Late Regulations respecting the British Colonies . . . considered* (Philadelphia, 1765). Though published after the passage of the Stamp Act, attention was given almost exclusively to the economic effects of the acts of 1764. Note the striking similarity of Dickinson's views to Charles Thomson's arguments, urged in a letter of November, 1765, to a London mercantile house. Thomson. *Papers* (*N. Y. Hist. Soc. Colls.*, vol. xi), pp. 7-12. Thomson was an importer and also had interests in iron manufacturing and in rum distilling. Harley, L. R., *Life of Charles Thomson* (Philadelphia, 1900), *passim*.

to every man in the least acquainted with it to be much higher than that article can possibly bear and therefore must operate as an absolute prohibition," declared Hopkins. If the merchants and distillers suffered losses, the provincial farmers would become deeply involved, because their surplus stock and products had been sent to the foreign islands in exchange for molasses. If there were no specie in circulation, debts could not be paid to England, importations must be reduced, and local manufacturing undertaken. With the volume of money rapidly shrinking, it was charged that the prohibition of further issues of legal-tender money was calculated to heighten the distress, since paper money had generally served a useful purpose as a circulating medium within provincial boundaries. Finally, some warmth was displayed in referring to the commercial system as a whole, and the question asked whether the disadvantages which the colonies suffered under it and the enhanced prices which the colonists paid for British importations loaded with British taxes at home were not equivalent to a tax directly levied in America.

The assumptions and arguments, urged by the pamphleteers, received substantial confirmation from the prostration of industry which began to be apparent throughout the commercial provinces. This period of economic depression was not, as they contended, produced entirely by the restrictive legislation of 1764. The beginning of the change was traceable to the more vigorous enforcement of the old Molasses Act in 1763. A more important cause was the collapse of the artificial war-time prosperity which the provinces had enjoyed.[1] The presence of British forces in

[1] Franklin, *Writings* (Smyth), vol. v, pp. 71-73; speech of P. Cust, M. P., in *Bos. Chron.*, June 11, 1770; Colden, *Letter Books*, vol. ii, pp. 77-78; article in *Pa. Journ.*, Mch. 21, 1765; Burke's "Observations on the Right Honourable Mr. Grenville's State of the Nation," *Bos. Chron.*, June 26, 1769; "A Friend to the Colony" in *Prov. Gaz.*, Mch. 26, 1768; "The Citizen" in *Pa. Journ.*, Jan. 26, 1769.

America had caused a great influx of coin for the paying and provisioning of the troops; and the high cash prices paid by the French for foodstuffs added to the supply of specie. Under such stimulus, prices soared; merchants increased their stocks and undertook speculative risks; farmers enlarged their operations; people generally began to adopt more luxurious modes of living. The close of the war and the disbanding of the greatest part of the army dried up these sources of abundant specie. Merchants and farmers found themselves deprived of their profitable markets, with an overplus of supplies on hand. An especially serious blow was administered to those merchants who had succeeded during the war in monopolizing the trade of Havana and the French West Indian islands, after these colonies had fallen into the possession of England. The restoration of these islands at the conclusion of peace greatly diminished this trade. The rice planters of South Carolina and Georgia would have shared in the distress, had not Parliament enabled them by the act of 1764 to continue to export their staple to these new markets.

But the chief cause of the hard times was the restrictive legislation of 1764. The *Boston Post-Boy* of June 3, 1765 declared that not one-fifth as many vessels were employed in the West Indian trade as before the regulations of the preceding year, and that cash had practically disappeared from circulation. The mercantile community experienced "a most prodigious shock" at the failures of Nathaniel Wheelwright, John Scollay, Joseph Scott and certain other Boston merchants of note. John Hancock, whose own trading connections were with many parts of the world, wrote that "times are very bad, . . . the times will be worse here, in short such is the situation of things here that we do not know who is and who [is] not safe." [1]

[1] *John Hancock His Book*, pp. 61-62. He concluded: "The affair of

Conditions were bad at Newport, also.¹ A statement, issued by leading citizens of New York, lamented the dwindling of trade, the extreme scarcity of cash, the prohibition of paper money and the recent restrictions placed on commerce.² A New York merchant of twenty years' standing withdrew from trade because he was apprehensive of the effects of the new regulations. He testified before a committee of Parliament that, whereas the price of molasses at New York had formerly been 1s. 6d. to 1s. 9d. per gallon, the threepenny duty had increased it by one or twopence, and the price of the rum distilled from it had advanced sufficiently to enable Danish rum to undersell the American on the Guinea coast. The ten or a dozen New York vessels, formerly engaged in the slave trade, were now idle.³ In Pennsylvania, it was complained that "Trade is become dull, Money very scarce, Contracts decrease, Law-Suits increase so as to double the number of Writs issued in every County within two Years past . . ."⁴ The farm-

Wheelwright's failure with such aggravated Circumstances is the greatest shock to trade that ever happened here." In another letter he wrote: "Money is Extremely Scarce & trade very dull. If we are not reliev'd at home we must live upon our own produce & manufactures." *Ibid.*, pp. 63-64. Hancock had taken over his uncle's business upon the latter's death in August, 1764; and, according to Thomas Hutchinson, old Thomas Hancock had amassed great wealth by "importing from St. Eustatia great quantities of tea in molasses hogsheads, which sold at a very great advance." *Mass. Bay*, vol. iii, pp. 297-298.

¹ *Newport Merc.*, Feb. 25, 1765.
² Statement of the Society of Arts, Agriculture and Oeconomy, Weyler's *N. Y. Gaz.*, Dec. 10, 1764.
³ Testimony of William Kelly, Feb. 11, 1766, *Brit. Mus. Addl. Mss.*, no. 33030 (*L. C. Transcripts*), ff. 130, 134-135, 137.
⁴ "The Farmer" in *Pa. Journ.*, Aug. 23, 1764. The Philadelphia merchant, Benjamin Marshall, wrote on Oct. 22, 1764: "Cash Monstrous scarce (I believe we must learn to Barter), as the Men of War are here so strict that nothing can escape them . . ." *Pa. Mag.*, vol. xx, p. 208. *Vide* also the business correspondence of S. Rhoads, Jr., at this period. *Ibid.*, vol. xiv, pp. 421-426.

ers of the commercial provinces were involved in the general distress. "Merchants and Farmers are breaking and all things going into confusion," wrote a New Englander despondently.[1] "What is your City without Trade, and what the Country without a Market to vend their Commodities?" queried a Pennsylvania writer.[2]

The merchants did not remain idle while their profits evaporated and their debts accumulated. They had been excited to activity by the first rumors that the old Molasses Act might again be renewed in 1764. A keen observer declared in retrospect, several years later, that the union among the colonies had derived " its original source from no Object of a more Respectable Cast than that of a Successful practice in Illicit Trade, I say contrived, prompted and promoted by a Confederacy of Smuglers in Boston, Rhode Island and other Seaport Towns on that Coast."[3] These gentry were aided and abetted by the rum-distillers, who were particularly powerful in New England.[4] John Adams was franker than most historians when he reflected in his old age: "I know not why we should blush to confess that molasses was an essential ingredient in American independence."[5]

The first move was made by the merchants of Boston in April, 1763, when they organized the " Society for encouraging Trade and Commerce within the Province

[1] *N. H. Gaz.*, Dec. 7, 1764.

[2] "The Farmer" in *Pa. Journ.*, Aug. 23, 1764.

[3] Letter of Richard Oswald, a native American and a Londoner in the American trade, to Dartmouth, Feb. 9, 1775; Stevens, *Facsimiles*, vol. xxiv, no. 2032, pp. 3-4.

[4] In another portion of his letter Oswald alluded to "the great Rum Distillers of Boston who began all this disturbance." *Ibid.*

[5] He added sagely: "Many great events have proceeded from much smaller causes." *Works*, vol. x, p. 345.

of Massachusetts Bay."¹ There was to be a standing committee of fifteen to watch trade affairs and to call a general meeting of members whenever occasion demanded. A memorial was drawn up for presentation to the General Court; and accounts of their activities were sent to the merchants in other provinces. The committee also corresponded with influential members of Parliament.²

Further action was called for by an article in the *Boston Evening Post*, November 21 and 28, 1763. The writer proposed that, at the instance of the Boston merchants, a provincial committee of merchants representing the maritime towns should urge the General Court to petition Parliament for a revision of the acts of trade, particularly for the removal or substantial reduction of the duties on foreign molasses and sugar. Perhaps in response to this suggestion, a sub-committee of the Boston merchants requested a meeting with committees of the merchants of Marblehead, Salem and Plymouth; and the result was that the merchants of these ports also presented memorials to the General Court.

The merchants of New York were the next to take action. Of these merchants, Lieutenant Governor Colden said: " Many of them have rose suddenly from the lowest Rank of the People to considerable Fortunes, & chiefly by illicit Trade in the last War. They abhor every limitation of Trade and Duty on it, & therefore gladly go into every Measure whereby they hope to have Trade free."³ They

---

¹ *M. H. S. Ms.*, 91 L, pp. 23-25. The rules of organization were signed by one hundred forty-seven merchants. For a more detailed account of this organization, *vide* Andrews, C. M., "The Boston Merchants and the Non-Importation Movement," *Col. Soc. Mass. Pubs.*, vol. xix, pp. 161-167.

² *Bos. Gaz.*, Jan. 16, Oct. 29, 1764.

³ *Letter Books*, vol. ii, p. 68. *Vide* also *Parliamentary History of England* (Cobbett, W., ed.), vol. xvi, p. 125.

met at Burn's Long Room on January 27, 1764 and took under consideration the declining state of trade. A committee was appointed to memorialize the legislature on the situation and to ask their interposition with Parliament. The committee later established regular meeting nights.[1] A communication in the *New York Gazette and Post-Boy* of February 2 commended the rational action of the merchants and declared riotous opposition would be "seditious and injurious to Government" when redress might be obtained by dutiful petition. At the suggestion of the New York Committee of Merchants, the merchants of Philadelphia became active, and appointed a committee to urge the Pennsylvania Assembly to solicit Parliament to discontinue the molasses duties of 1733.[2]

In every case the legislatures took the desired step, although little was done until after the new duties of 1764 had become a law.[3] Only Rhode Island had been forehanded enough to petition for the repeal of the old Molasses Act prior to the new legislation of Parliament. In June, the Massachusetts House of Representatives ordered its agent in London to press for a repeal of the new duties and also to protest against the Stamp Act, which was on the government's program for 1765. A committee was appointed to urge the other legislatures on the continent to join in the movement. In July the Rhode Island Assembly appointed a committee for the same purpose; and a committee of the New York Assembly began a similar propaganda in October.[4]

[1] Weyler's *N. Y. Gaz.*, Jan. 30, 1764; *N. Y. Gaz. & Post-Boy*, Feb. 2; *N. Y. Merc.*, Mch. 5, 1764. The memorial was read in the provincial assembly on Apr. 20, 1764.

[2] *Bos. Post-Boy*, Mch. 26, 1764.

[3] Frothingham, R., *The Rise of the Republic of the United States* (Boston, 1881), pp. 173-174.

[4] The New York committee was instructed to correspond "on the

The problem of the commercial provinces was to enlist the support of the plantation provinces in their campaign for remedial legislation. In this way, a united front could be shown to Parliament and the chances for success greatly increased. The tobacco provinces were readier of response than any of the others, because of the unsatisfactory condition of crops and crop prices and because of the scarcity of money. " The Courts are filled with Law-Suits, and many People are obliged to sell their Estates," wrote a Virginian.[1] George Washington, one of the large Virginia planters, was forced to explain to a creditor that he had fallen " so much in arrears " because he had not had " even tolerable crops " for three straight years, and when he had one, it did not sell well.[2] But these conditions could not be attributed to the acts of 1764, and did not seem to prevail in the more southerly provinces.

The position of the commercial provinces was greatly strengthened strategically by the fact that the Stamp Act was on the boards for active consideration by Parliament in 1765. A stamp tax was clearly a departure from the ancient custom of the home government. It was more purely a fiscal measure than was the so-called Sugar Act of 1764, its incidence was more obvious and it fell on people in all the provinces. Thus, the proposed stamp duty afforded an opportunity to the mercantile interests to stir up a

Subject Matter of the Act, commonly called the Sugar Act; on the Act restraining Paper Bills of Credit in the Colonies from being a legal Tender; and of the several other Acts of Parliament lately passed, with relation to the Trade of the Northern Colonies: And also on the Subject of the impending Dangers which threaten the Colonies, of being taxed by Laws to be passed in Great-Britain." Note the sequence. *Pa. Gaz.*, Nov. 28, 1764.

[1] Virginia and Maryland news in *Prov. Gaz.*, Jan. 19, 1765; *Bos. Post-Boy*, June 10, July 29.

[2] *Writings* (Ford, W. C., ed.), vol. ii, pp. 200-202.

general discontent as well as to increase local dissatisfaction. Consciously or not, the northern legislatures made the most of the occasion. In their official utterances, they dovetailed in with their economic indictment of the Sugar Act a protest against the proposed Stamp Act as an inexpedient and unconstitutional measure.[1] Their efforts to secure continental co-operation were successful: petitions and remonstrances were sent from Virginia, North Carolina, South Carolina, and, with considerable reluctance, from Georgia.[2]

Meantime, the hard times had been causing people in the commercial provinces to retrench expenses; and in some cases this object was accomplished by concerted effort. A clear-seeing writer in the *Providence Gazette*, October 6, 1764, proposed a continental agreement to suspend trade with the British West Indies, in order to strike a body blow at the West India interest in Parliament; but it was ten years too soon for such a proposal to win favorable response. Fifty merchants of Boston set an example in August, 1764, by signing an agreement to discard laces and ruffles, to buy no English cloths but at a fixed price, and to forego the elaborate and expensive mourning of the times for the very simplest display.[3] The mourning reso-

[1] As Oswald observed to Dartmouth in 1775, the disgruntled merchants had had "the art to interweave in their System of Grievances . . . some others of a political nature and apparently of a more liberal cast than do[e]s really lye at the bottom of their designs." Stevens, *Facsimiles*, vol. xxiv, no. 2032, p. 5.

[2] Of the commercial group, Connecticut and Pennsylvania now joined in with the others. The southern legislatures generally included a complaint against certain restrictions placed in 1764 upon the exportation of lumber, a matter that was satisfactorily adjusted by Parliament in 1765. South Carolina also complained of the Currency Act. *Documentary History of the American Revolution* (Gibbes, R. W., ed.), vol. ii, pp. 1-6. The Virginia Committee of Correspondence expressed alarm at the duties on Madeira wine but seemed pleased at the Currency Act. *Va. Mag.*, vol. xii, pp. 6-11.

[3] *Newport Merc.*, Aug. 20, 1764; also *N. Y. Gaz. & Post-Boy*, Aug. 30.

lutions were so well kept by the people generally that it was reported that there had been only one or two violations after four months' trial, although almost one hundred funerals had occurred; and it was estimated that the saving would be more than £10,000 sterling a year.[1] Burials " according to the new mode " were recorded by the newspapers in New Hampshire, Rhode Island, New Jersey and New York.

In September the tradesmen of Boston followed in the path of the merchants, by agreeing to wear only leather of Massachusetts manufacture for their work clothes.[2] In November the students of Yale took unanimous action to abstain from the use of foreign liquors.[3] The people of New York apparently took no formal action; but five fire companies of Philadelphia attempted to counteract the high price of mutton by agreeing to refrain from the purchase of lamb.[4] One company added a pledge against the drinking of imported beer.

The logical counterpart of the efforts for the disuse of imported superfluities was the encouragement of domestic manufactures. This movement had greatest vitality in New York, where a number of prominent men in December, 1764, organized the " Society for the Promotion of Arts, Agriculture and Oeconomy," and proceeded to award premiums for a great variety of local productions, to print informing pamphlets, and to promote the formation of similar societies throughout the province.[5] In other provinces, the news-

---

[1] *Bos. Eve. Post*, Jan. 21, 1765; *Bos. Post-Boy*, Oct. 1, 8, 1764, July 1, 1765.

[2] *Ibid.*, Oct. 1, 1764.

[3] *N. Y. Gaz. & Post-Boy*, Nov. 22, 1764.

[4] *Pa. Gaz.*, Feb. 28, Mch. 7, 14, May 16, 1765.

[5] Files of Weyler's *N. Y. Gaz.* and of the *N. Y. Merc.* from Dec. 3, 1764, to June 1, 1767. The notice of Dec. 3, 1764, declared that the society was formed upon a plan " wholly detached from all Party

papers teemed with instructive articles on the methods and opportunity of American manufactures; and the provinces north of Maryland showed many instances of increased production of linen and woolen homespun. Outside of New York, greatest progress seems to have been made at Boston, where the "Linen Manufactory" produced four hundred yards of "Bengals, Lillepusias and Broglios" in a period of three months, and "Lynn Shoes" won a merited popularity.[1]

On March 22, 1765, the Stamp Act received the royal assent, and by its terms was to go into effect on November the first of that year. The act was an integral part of the taxation program inaugurated by Grenville in 1764. Stamp duties were placed on commercial papers of various kinds, on deeds, bonds, leases and other legal documents, on pamphlets, newspapers and advertisements, and on articles of apprenticeship, liquor licenses, etc. Heavy fines and forfeitures were provided for infractions of the law, and these might be collected through the vice-admiralty courts at the option of the informer or prosecutor.[2]

In view of the later revolutionary movement, it is not too much to say that the Stamp Act derived its chief importance from the fact that it lifted the controversy from the profit-and-loss considerations of the northern colonists and furnished a common ground on which the planting provinces might join with the commercial provinces in protest. The eighteenth century Anglo-Saxon liked nothing better than

---

Spirit, personal Interest, political Views or private Motives." The next week, it was stated that the severe times had caused the formation of the society.

[1] *Bos. Post-Boy*, Oct. 8, 1764, Jan. 24, 1765. John Hancock's wealthy uncle had bequeathed £200 to this society on his death on Aug. 1, 1764. *Ibid.*, Aug. 13, 1764.

[2] 5 George III, c. 12.

the expansive phrases of the natural rights theory; and the Stamp Act readily lent itself to protests against " taxation without representation " and " trial without jury." [1]

The economic burden of the new law, as in the case of the duties of 1764, fell very largely on the commercial provinces. The merchants, lawyers and printers were the classes particularly affected; and these classes, as we shall see, felt impelled to take a leading part in instigating popular demonstrations against the measure.

The taxes on commercial documents threatened to paralyze such business as had survived the restrictive legislation of the preceding year. " Under this additional Burthen of the Stamp Act," wrote one of the merchant princes of Boston, " I cannot carry it [trade] on to any profit and we were before Cramp'd in our Trade & sufficiently Burthen'd, that any farther Taxes must Ruin us." In another letter, Hancock declared that if the act were carried into execution, it " will entirely Stagnate Trade here, for it is universally determined here never to submit

---

[1] Colonel George Mercer, of Virginia, told a committee of Parliament in Feb., 1766: "I have heard the Complaints of Right and oppression blended together. But the thinking people don't speak so plainly on the right as others; they complain of the oppression " ; he apprehended that " the Idea of Oppression awakened the Idea of Right." *Brit. Mus. Addl. Mss.*, no. 33030 (*L. C. Transcripts*), ff. 126, 129. A letter from a New Yorker to an English friend said: "It is thought the stamp act would not have met with so violent an opposition if the colonies had not previously been chagrined at the rigorous execution of the laws against their trade." *Bos. Eve. Post*, Feb. 17, 1766. Dean Tucker wrote in his pamphlet, *A Letter from a Merchant in London to his Nephew in North America* (1766): " What is the Cause of such an amazing Outcry as you raise at present? Not the Stamp Duty itself; . . . none can be so ignorant, or so stupid, as not to see that this is a mere Sham and Pretence. What, then, are the real Grievances . . . ? Why, some of you are exasperated against the Mother Country on the Account of the Revival of certain Restrictions laid upon their Trade." *Pa. Mag.*, vol. xxvi, p. 86.

to it, and the principal merchants here will by no means carry on Business under a Stamp." Early in October, he told Governor Bernard that he would rather perform the severest manual labor than continue business under the burden of the pending Stamp Act, and that " I am Determin'd as soon as I know that they are Resolv'd to insist on this act to Sell my Stock in Trade & Shut up my Warehouse Doors." In a letter a few days later, he protested that " there is not cash enough here to support it." Hancock's commercial correspondence of this period sounded a genuine note of despair; and only as an afterthought did he allude, once or twice, to the unconstitutionality of the act.[1]

Voicing the apprehensions of the merchants of Pennsylvania, John Dickinson questioned whether, under present panic conditions, a merchant's commerce could bear " the payment of all the taxes imposed by the Stamp Act on his policies, fees with clerks, charter parties, protests, his other notarial acts, his letters, and even his advertisements." He showed that hard times were having a cumulative effect. Money, where any remained, had gone into hiding. When creditors took out executions, they discovered that the lands and personal estates could be sold only at a fraction of their value. The records of the courts attested that the number of debtors had increased enormously; at the last term, no less than thirty-five persons from Philadelphia County alone had sought relief under the insolvency act, although the law applied only to those who owed no single debt above £150. This being the situation, said Dickinson, " from whence is the silver to come, with which the taxes imposed by this act, and the duties imposed by other late acts, are to be paid? "[2]

---

[1] Brown, *John Hancock His Book*, pp. 83, 87, 88, 90. *Vide* also pp. 69, 70, 81, 86-90, 103-104, 115.

[2] *The Late Regulations* etc., Dickinson, *Writings* (Ford, L., ed.), pp. 227-230. *Vide* also pp. 440-441.

Jonathan Watts, a member of the New York Council, was writing home in the same strain: " I cannot conceive there will be silver or gold enough to carry this Act and the high duties that are laid, through, and what shall people then do in a new country where property so frequently changes hands, must everything stagnate, and will not a universal discontent prevail? Man is man, and will feel and will resent, too . . . "[1] The Philadelphia merchant, Stephen Collins, repeated the plaintive note in many letters to London creditors, alleging that, owing to the stagnation of trade, " I have not been able to Forward your Remittances more timely."[2]

Benjamin Franklin believed that the new act would fall " particularly hard on us lawyers and printers."[3] The lawyers throughout British America were affected by the duties imposed on all important legal documents. " It is well known," commented a writer in the *New York Gazette and Post-Boy*, February 20, 1766, " that some of the Lawyers in the several Provinces have been, and still continue, the principal Writers on the Side of American Liberty." Indeed, one of the ablest pamphlets against the Stamp Act was written by Daniel Dulany, the foremost lawyer of Maryland, a man who opposed no subsequent tax of Great Britain and who eventually became a loyalist.[4]

[1] *4 M. H. S. Colls.*, vol. x, p. 576. " N " claimed in the *Pa. Journ.*, Sept. 5, 1765, that there was not nearly enough money in America to pay the current debt to British merchants, let alone the new taxes. " Publicola " calculated in the *N. Y. Gaz. & Post-Boy*, May 30, 1765, that all the gold and silver would be drained off in two years at most.

[2] *Letter Book, 1760-1773* (L. C. Mss.), May 18, June 24, 1765; Aug. 14, Nov. 10, 1766.

[3] *Writings* (Smyth), vol. iv, pp. 361-363.

[4] *Considerations on the Propriety of imposing Taxes in the British Colonies* (October, 1765), reprinted in *Md. Hist. Mag.*, vol. vi, pp. 376-406. Dulany was largely responsible for the nullification of the Stamp

Although he based his opposition largely on constitutional grounds, he did not fail to show that the tax fell on a province, "not in proportion to its wealth, but to the multiplicity of juridical forms, the quantity of vacant land, the frequency of transferring landed property, the extent of paper negotiations, the scarcity of money, and the number of debtors," and he argued that "the principal part of the revenue will be drawn from the poorest individuals in the poorest colonies, from mortgagers, obligors, and defendants." Lieutenant Governor Colden of New York had "the strongest presumption from numerous Circumstances to believe that the Lawyers of this Place are the Authors, Promoters & Leaders" of the local opposition to the stamp duties.[1]

Printers were directly involved in the new act as publishers of newspapers and pamphlets. The foremost printer of the continent, Benjamin Franklin, wrote to his fellow-publisher of the *Pennsylvania Gazette* that he believed the Stamp Act "will affect the Printers more than anybody, as a Sterling Halfpenny Stamp on every Half Sheet of a Newspaper, and Two Shillings Sterling on every Advertisement, will go near to knock up one Half of both. There

---

Act in Maryland. Latrobe, J. H., "Daniel Dulany," *Pa. Mag.*, vol. iii, pp. 4-5. *Vide* also the views of William Smith, Jr., a New York lawyer whom Colden characterized as "a violent republican independent" and an organizer of mobs. *4 M. H. S. Colls.*, vol. x, pp. 570-571.

[1] *Letter Books*, vol. ii, pp. 61-62. He continued: "People in general believe it, and many must with certainty know it. I must add that all the Judges have given too much Countenance to their Proceedings . . ." *Vide* also *ibid.*, p. 92. The lawyers of New York were discontented with other matters besides the Stamp Act; and Colden claimed that they were more powerful there than anywhere else in America. "Nothing is too wicked for them to attempt which serves their purposes—the Press is to them what the Pulpit was in times of Popery." *Ibid.*, p. 71.

is also Fourpence Sterling on every Almanack."[1] The twenty-odd newspapers of America carried on a tremendously effective propaganda against the Stamp Act,[2] and in no later crisis exhibited such unanimity of protest.

Aside from their influence as directors of popular opposition, the merchants, lawyers and printers were faced with the problem of making a living while their business was legally subject to the use of stamps. The merchants refused to use stamps in their business transactions and usually succeeded in keeping the ports open for commerce, when it became apparent to the authorities that the sale of stamps was impracticable or impossible.[3] The lawyers, in first instance, agreed that all legal business should be suspended until the Stamp Act should be repealed; but when their purses began to grow lean from lack of clients' fees and the merchants and creditors clamored for the opportunity to collect their debts, they generally induced the courts to open for business without stamps.[4] " This long interval of indolence and idleness will make a large chasm in my affairs," wrote the lawyer John Adams in the period before the courts were re-opened. He added: " I have groped in dark obscurity, till of late, and had but just known and gained a small degree of reputation, when this project was set on foot for my ruin as well as that of America in general, and

[1] *Writings* (Smyth), vol. iv, pp. 363-364.

[2] *E. g.*, Jonathan Watts, of New York, wrote on Sept. 24, 1765: " You will think the printers all mad, Holt particularly, who has been cautioned over and over again, and would have been prosecuted, but people's minds are so inflamed about this stamp act, it would only be exposing Government to attempt it." 4 *M. H. S. Colls.*, vol. x, p. 576. Holt published the *New York Gazette and Post-Boy* at this time.

[3] *E. g., vide* Hutchinson, *Mass. Bay*, vol. iii, p. 141; 4 *M. H. S. Colls.*, vol. x, p. 587.

[4] *E. g., vide* 1 *N. J. Arch.*, vol. ix, pp. 540-548; *N. Y. Merc.*, Dec. 9, 23, 1765; Hutchinson, *op. cit.*, vol. iii, pp. 138, 141-142.

of Great Britain." [1] All but a few newspapers continued publication without stamps; and most of those few reappeared when it became evident that infractions of the law would entail no penalty.

The period between the enactment of the Stamp Act and the date of its operation was marked by a series of popular demonstrations, designed to coerce the colonial stamp agents into resigning. Distressed by non-employment and temperamentally inclined to boisterous forms of expression, the rougher elements in the leading seaports responded readily to the leadership of the classes disaffected by the legislation of 1764 and 1765.

This appeared clearly in the case of Boston, where the most serious disturbances occurred.[2] In the first of the August riots, the stamp office was razed by a mob, and Hutchinson declared: " It is said that there were fifty gentlemen actors in this scene, disguised with trousers and jackets on." [3] In the succeeding riots, the mob, led by a shoemaker named Mackintosh, secured a promise of resignation from Oliver, the stamp collector, and showed its animus by attacking the houses of the registrar of the admiralty and the comptroller of the customs and by destroying the records of the admiralty court. Lieutenant Governor Hutchinson's house was also visited and despoiled. Hutchinson believed that this last outrage was inspired by certain smuggling merchants who had just learned of certain depositions sworn against them before him several months before. We have it on the word of one merchant writing to another that Oliver's promise was not deemed decisive enough, and that therefore the " Loyall Nine " repaired

[1] *Works*, vol. ii, pp. 155-156.
[2] Hutchinson. *op. cit.*, vol. iii, pp. 120-125; *Parliamentary History*, vol. xvi, pp. 126-131; Palfrey, *History of New Engl.*, vol. iv, pp. 389-394.
[3] Letter of Aug. 15, to Halifax; Palfrey, *op. cit.*, vol. iv, p. 391.

to "Liberty Hall" and planned a public resignation under oath, which was duly carried out on December 17. "We do everything," added the merchant a little anxiously, "to keep this and the first affair Private; and are not a little pleas'd to hear that McIntosh has the Credit of the whole Affair. We Endeavour to keep up the Spirit which I think is as great as ever."[1] The Sons of Liberty, composed of Boston workingmen, performed the actual work of violence. It is perhaps not without significance that their regular meeting-place was the counting-room of a distillery; and John Adams records that, when he was invited to attend one night, he found there two distillers a ship captain, the printer of the popular organ and four mechanics.[2]

[1] Henry Bass to Samuel P. Savage, Dec. 19, 1765. *M. H. S. Procs.*, vol. xliv, pp. 688-689.

[2] Chase and John Avery; Joseph Field; Benjamin Edes, a publisher of the *Boston Gazette;* John Smith and Stephen Cleverly, braziers, Thomas Crafts, painter, and George Trott, jeweler. *Works*, vol. ii, pp. 178-179.

Hutchinson's own analysis of mob government at this period was as follows: "It will be some amusement to you to have a more circumstantial account of the model of government among us. I will begin with the lowest branch, partly legislative, partly executive. This consists of the rabble of the town of Boston, headed by one Mackintosh, who, I imagine, you never heard of. He is a bold fellow, and as likely for a Masaniello as you can well conceive. When there is occasion to burn or hang effigies or pull down houses, these are employed; but since government has been brought to a system, they are somewhat controlled by a superior set consisting of the master-masons, and carpenters, &c., of the town of Boston. . . . When anything of more importance is to be determined, as opening the custom-house on any matters of trade, these are under the direction of a committee of merchants, Mr. Rowe at their head, then Molyneux, Solomon Davis, &c.: but all affairs of a general nature, opening all the courts of law, &c., this is proper for a general meeting of the inhabitants of Boston, where Otis, with his mob-high eloquence, prevails in every motion, and the town first determine what is necessary to be done, and then apply either to the Governor or Council, or resolve that it is necessary the General Court correct it; and it would be a very extraordinary resolve indeed that is not carried into execution." Quoted by Hosmer, J. K., *The Life of Thomas Hutchinson* (Boston, 1896), pp. 103-104.

Conditions probably were not greatly different at Philadelphia. Although the stamp collector there was inclined to lay the popular outbreak to the machinations of the " Presbyterians and proprietary minions," it seems rather more significant that the committee which asked him to resign was composed of five merchants, one attorney and one printer.[1] In New York, as we have seen, the lawyers seemed to be at the bottom of the tumults, aided beyond a doubt by the merchants and printers.

Popular outbreaks also occurred in the plantation provinces; but, lacking the multiplied resentments accumulated by two years of hostile legislation, the demonstrations were neither as frequent nor usually as violent as in the commercial provinces. The planters generally were wedded to the notion of dignified protests by representative assemblies; and a compact working-class element was non-existent, except at Charleston. The agitation of the newspapers aided in spreading the tumultuous spirit of the northern trading towns to the South. Governor Bull, of South Carolina, testified that the people of Charleston were generally disposed to obey the Stamp Act, " but by the artifices of some busy spirits the minds of men here were so universally poisoned with the principles which were imbibed and propagated from Boston and Rhode Island (from which Towns, at this time of the year, vessels very frequently arrive) that after their example the People of this Town resolved to seize and destroy the Stamp Papers . . ."[2] There was indeed a shortage of currency, chiefly in Virginia and South Carolina, which bore hardly on men owing money and which

---

[1] Robert Morris, Charles Thomson, Archibald McCall, John Cox and William Richards; James Tilghman; and William Bradford, editor of the *Pennsylvania Journal*.

[2] Smith, W. R., *South Carolina as a Royal Province, 1719-1776* (New York, 1903), p. 351.

the Currency Act of 1764 made it difficult to relieve. "This private distress which every man feels," wrote Governor Fauquier, of Virginia, "encreases the general dissatisfaction at the duties laid by the late Stamp Act, which breaks out and shews itself on every trifling occasion."[1] However, the inconvenience was not great enough to cause the people to take part in the efforts to establish domestic manufacturing or to boycott British goods.

The merchants and factors generally lent the weight of their influence against popular demonstrations. Henry Laurens, of Charleston, was a representative of the best that the class had to offer. Wealthy, of an excellent American family and a disapprover of the Stamp Act, he did all he could to discourage "those infamous inglorious feats of riot and dissipation which have been performed to the No'ward . . ." He believed that "the Act must be executed and . . . that if a stamp officer were so timid as to resign and a Governor so compliant as not to appoint another in his stead— we should in one fortnight . . . go down on our knees and pray him to give life to that law. What, else, would become of our estates, particularly ours who depend upon commerce?" The searching of houses by mobs he regarded as "burglary and robbery" and he saw in the zeal of the rioters only a desire to postpone the payment of their debts.[2] Lauren's attitude, although consistent in itself, aroused popular suspicion and brought the mob down on his own ears.

---

[1] *Brit. Papers* ("*Sparks Mss.*"), vol. ii, p. 44. Other evidence of money stringency in the various plantation provinces may be found in: *Bos. Post-Boy*, Mch. 17, 1766; *N. C. Col. Recs.*, vol. vii, p. 144; Gibbes, *Doc. Hist.*, vol. ii, pp. 1-6; *S. C. Gaz.*, Dec. 17, 1765; *Ga. Hist. Soc. Colls.*, vol. vi, pp. 44-46.

[2] Wallace, D. D., *Henry Laurens* (New York, 1915), pp. 116-122. Laurens's business was that of factor and, to a lesser extent, independent trader, importing and exporting on his own account. He also had planting interests. *Ibid.*, pp. 16, 21, 44-47, 69, 123-136.

In Georgia, some of the merchants, who at first had talked against the act, drew off and even endeavored to suppress the spirit of opposition by converting the majority of the shipmasters to their change of view. In the latter part of December they circulated a petition asking the governor to appoint a new stamp agent. When the mob got wind of this and protested to the governor, he declared he would act as he thought best; and forty merchants, with their clerks, and several ship captains evinced their approbation by arming and guarding the governor until danger of violence subsided.[1] Some stamps were actually used in Georgia.

Christopher Gadsden, a Charlestonian possessing large mercantile and planting interests, represented a different spirit. A radical by temperament, he was, for years, to be a contradiction of anything that might be said of the factors who managed most of the trade of the South. He employed his talents on the present occasion in instructing the leaders of the mob, meeting with them frequently under Liberty Tree for that purpose.[2]

The two groups of provinces met on common ground in the Stamp Act Congress at New York in October, 1765. This event, so important in light of the subsequent trend toward union, received scarcely any contemporary mention in the newspapers, even at New York. The lower houses of the various provincial legislatures had been invited by Massachusetts to send committees to a continental congress to confer on "the difficulties to which they are and must be reduced by the operation of the acts of parliament for levying duties and taxes on the colonies" and to unite on petition for redress.[3] Delegates from nine provinces appeared.

[1] Letter from Georgia in *Newport Merc.*, Feb. 10, 1766. *Vide* also *S. C. Gaz.*, Feb. 25.
[2] Gibbes, *op. cit.*, vol. ii, pp. 10-11; Wallace, *op. cit.*, p. 120.
[3] *Bos. Eve. Post*, Aug. 26, 1765.

It was clearly the design of the Massachusetts House of Representatitves that the congress should remonstrate chiefly against the restrictive and revenue measures passed by the Parliament in the years 1764-1765. When the members of congress assembled, they found it necessary to make certain alterations in their ideas before a common ground could be reached. In particular, there was much skirmishing as to the form in which the various arguments and views should be presented. Gadsden, the South Carolina radical, displayed great political acumen in insisting that all sections could harmonize in their opposition by urging their views "on the broad, common ground" of natural rights.[1] The official utterances of the congress show the result of this plan. A great deal was said about the theoretical rights of the colonists, and the stamp tax and the laws enabling admiralty courts to try breaches of the trade laws were roundly denounced as heinous invasions of such rights. Nevertheless, all trace of the spirit of the Massachusetts summons was not obliterated: each memorial, with varying degrees of emphasis, set forth the alarming scarcity of hard money and requested the repeal of the laws restricting trade and enlarging the jurisdiction of the admiralty courts, as well as the act imposing the stamp duty.[2]

Meantime, in the commercial provinces, the increasing evidences of economic distress had stimulated the people to multiply their efforts to retrench expenses. Leading citizens of New York and Boston, as well as of Philadelphia, signed resolutions not to purchase or eat lamb, and to boycott any butcher who sought to counteract the resolutions.[3]

[1] Frothingham, *Rise of Republic*, p. 188.

[2] *Authentic Account of the Proceedings of the Congress held at New York, in MDCCLXV, On the Subject of the Stamp Act (1767)*. The petition to the House of Commons is especially explicit on these points.

[3] Weyler's *N. Y. Gaz.*, Feb. 10, 17, 1766; *Bos. Post-Boy*, Apr. 8, 1765, Mch. 10, 1766; *Pa. Gaz.*, Feb. 13, 1766.

The movement for simpler mourning, so popular farther north, now spread to Philadelphia.¹ Articles in newspapers advocated the superiority of sage, sassafras and balm to the enervating beverage of tea.² The New York Society for the Promotion of Arts, Agriculture and Oeconomy now reached the zenith of its activity, increasing its list of premiums for local manufactures, establishing spinning schools, and conducting a fortnightly market for the sale of New York manufactures. The service of the society in encouraging flax culture and linen manufacture was of more than temporary importance. In the making of linen, more than three hundred persons were employed from the middle of 1765 to the close of 1766.³ Philadelphia took over the idea of a market, and three times a week linens, shalloons, flannels, ink-powder and other wares of Pennsylvania fabrication were offered for sale. Nearly two hundred poor women were employed in spinning flax in the factory.⁴ In Rhode Island the thrifty maids and matrons improved the shining hours by gathering in groups and spinning, usually "from Sunrise to Dark." The maids of Providence and Bristol displayed the extent of their resolution by bravely agreeing to admit the addresses of no man who favored the Stamp Act.⁵

It did not take the Americans long to perceive that their measures of economic self-preservation might be capitalized to good advantage as political arguments for the repeal of the obnoxious laws. In face of the fact that British imports were rapidly diminishing from natural causes, news-

¹ *Pa. Journ.*, May 16, Sept. 12, 1765; *Pa. Gaz.*, Jan. 9, 1766.
² *Pa. Journ.*, May 9, 1765; *N. Y. Gaz. & Post-Boy*, May 30.
³ *N. Y. Journ.*, Dec. 17, 31, 1767.
⁴ *Pa. Journ.*, Nov. 28, 1765, Jan. 23, 1766; *The Record of the Celebration of the 200th Anniversary of the Birth of Franklin* (Hays, I. M., ed.), vol. ii, p. 57.
⁵ *Newport Merc.*, Apr. 14, May 12, 1766; *N. Y. Gaz. & Post-Boy*, Apr. 3, 1766; *A Prov. Gaz.*, Aug. 24, 1765.

paper writers in New York and Connecticut urged in September, 1765, that the people should abstain from the use of British manufactures until the trade restrictions and taxes were removed.[1] About the same time, a number of Boston merchants, in writing for spring goods, ordered them to be sent only when the Stamp Act should be repealed.[2] But to New York belongs the credit of taking the first formal action for the boycotting of British goods.

Four days before the Stamp Act was to go into operation, most of the gentlemen of New York signed an agreement to buy no European wares until the Sugar Act should be altered, trade conditions relieved and the Stamp Act repealed. Three days later the merchants held a general meeting and agreed to make all past and future orders for British merchandise contingent upon the repeal of the Stamp Act. Such merchants as were shipowners were to be permitted to bring their vessels back to port with cargoes of coal, grindstones or other bulky articles. Two hundred merchants affixed their signatures to the agreement. In order to protect the merchants from the unrestricted importers of other provinces, the retail dealers of the city bound themselves to buy no goods whatsoever which should be shipped from Great Britain after January 1, 1766, until the repeal of the Stamp Act.[3] The merchants of Albany agreed unanimously to accept the New York resolutions.[4]

[1] *N. Y. Gaz. & Post-Boy*, Sept. 12, 1765; *Conn. Gaz.*, Sept. 13.

[2] *Bos. Eve. Post*, Sept. 23, 1765; also *N. Y. Gaz. & Post-Boy*, Sept. 26.

[3] *N. Y. Merc.*, Oct. 28, 31, Nov. 11, 1765; *N. Y. Gaz. & Post-Boy*, Nov. 7. A London newspaper of Dec. 17 noted: "We hear that the merchants upon 'change on Wednesday last received upwards of one hundred letters from New-York, countermanding their orders for goods." *Newport Merc.*, Feb. 24, 1766. Colden said of the non-importation agreement, that "the people in America will pay an extravagant price for old moth eaten Goods, and such as the Merchants could not otherwise Sell." *Letter Books*, vol. ii, p. 78.

[4] Weyler's *N. Y. Gaz.*, Jan. 27, 1766.

The merchants of Philadelphia got under way about a week after New York. With a prefatory statement that the trading difficulties were due to " the Restrictions, Prohibitions, and ill advised Regulations, made in the several Acts of the Parliament of Great-Britain, lately passed " and that they regarded the Stamp Act as the last straw, they united in an agreement similar to that of the New Yorkers.[1] More than four hundred merchants and traders signed the agreement, and a committee was appointed to observe its execution and to report violations to the body of subscribers. Printed forms for countermanding former orders were distributed to every local merchant.[2] The merchants also sent a memorial to the merchants and manufacturers of Great Britain, urging their assistance in the repeal of the Stamp Act and the removal of commercial restrictions, particularly the restraints on paper currency, the molasses duty, the prohibition of the exportation of bar iron to foreign ports in Europe, the heavy duties on Madeira, and the requirement that European wines and fruits must be imported by way of Great Britain.[3] The retailers of Philadelphia supported the merchants by refusing to buy any goods, shipped from Great Britain after January 1, 1766, except those approved by the merchants' committee.

---

[1] Local shipowners were permitted to include in the return cargo of their vessels from abroad dye-stuffs and utensils for manufacturing, as well as bulky articles. The agreement was limited to May 1, 1766, when another meeting should consider the advisability of continuing it. *Pa. Journ.*, Nov. 14, 21, 1765; also *N. Y. Merc.*, Nov. 25. The original copy of the agreement, in the library of the Historical Society of Pennsylvania, contains the signatures of all the subscribers.

[2] For samples of conditional orders of Philadelphia merchants, *vide* letters of Benjamin Marshall, *Pa. Mag.*, vol. xx, pp. 209-211, and of Charles Thomson, *N. Y. Hist. Soc. Colls.*, vol. ix, pp. 6-8.

[3] *Pub. Rec. Off.*, C. O. 5, no. 114 (L. C. Transcripts), pp. 161-169; *Pa. Gaz.*, Nov. 28, 1765; *Pa. Mag.*, vol. xx, p. 211.

The principal backcountry dealers cheerfully acquiesced in this regulation.

On December 9, 1765, the merchants of Boston drew up a formal agreement to import no goods from England until the Stamp Act should be repealed, except utensils for manufacturing, certain bulky articles, and articles absolutely necessary for the fishery. Two hundred and fifty merchants and traders quickly signed.[1] Salem and Marblehead, the ports of next importance, came into the same measure, and, soon after, Plymouth and Newbury.[2]

Only a few instances of enforcement are recorded in the case of the several provinces, a fact which indicates lack of infraction and not an absence of zeal. Money was tight; business men in Great Britain and America were retrenching. It has already been suggested that the non-importation agreements derived their importance less as economic measures than as political protests. Indeed, more than three months before the first non-importation agreement had been signed, London houses had begun to notice a sharp falling-off of American orders, due to the hard times from which the colonies were suffering. Thus, a London concern stated on July 5, 1765 that "so few and so small are the orders from America . . . that the ships lately sailed thither have not had half their lading."[3] It was estimated in England that, for the entire summer, American commissions for English goods were £600,000 less than had been known for thirty years, and that the fall orders had not been so small " in the memory of man."[4] British

---

[1] The agreement was limited to May 1, 1766, when it might be renewed. *Bos. Post-Boy*, Dec. 9, 16, 23, 1765. For orders of Hancock in accordance with this agreement, *vide* Brown, *John Hancock His Book*, pp. 103, 106, 108, 112, 114, 115, 117.

[2] Adams, J., *Works*, vol. ii, p. 176.

[3] *Pa. Gaz.*, Sept. 12, 1765. *Vide* also *ibid.*, Oct. 24.

[4] *Ibid.*, Jan. 2, 1766. *Vide* also *ibid.*, Feb. 27; *Bos. Eve. Post*, Feb. 17.

merchants in comparing accounts were alarmed at the extent of their debts, and, knowing the precarious state of colonial commerce, they contracted their credits to the serious embarrassment of their American correspondents.[1] In November, a London house declared that more bills from America had been protested within six months than in the preceding six years.[2] On the other hand, the *Boston Post-Boy* of December 23, 1765 declared: " A Merchant of the first Rank in the Town Re-ship'd in one of the last Vessels for London above £300 Sterling worth of Goods on Account of Money's being so scarce that they would not vend." The adoption of non-importation agreements added no new difficulty to the situation already existing.

The first attempt to introduce forbidden British merchandise occurred at Philadelphia. A Liverpool brig arrived there with goods debarred by the merchants' agreement. The Committee of Merchants took the matter in hand and ordered that the goods be locked up until news of the repeal of the Stamp Act should arrive.[3] A little later the *Prince George* arrived at New York with goods from Bristol, shipped on account of the British owners. At the demand of the " Sons of Liberty," the goods were delivered into their care, to be returned to Bristol at first opportunity.[4]

---

[1] " A Merchant " in *Public Ledger*, Apr. 1, 1765; letter from London, *N. H. Gaz.*, Nov. 22; Burke in *Bos. Chron.*, June 26, 1769; *R. I. Commerce*, vol. i, pp. 168-169, 172-173. On the basis of statements from the merchants of London, Bristol, Glasgow, Liverpool and Manchester. Trecothick, a leading London merchant in American trade, told a committee of Parliament in February, 1766, that the American debts to those cities amounted to more than £4,450,000. *Brit. Mus. Addl. Mss.*, no. 33030 (*L. C. Transcripts*), ff. 88, 104.

[2] *Pa. Gaz.*, Feb. 6, 1766. *Vide* also petition of London merchants to House of Commons, Jan. 17, 1766. *Parl. Debates*, vol. xvi, pp. 133-135.

[3] *Pa. Gaz.*, Apr. 24, 1766.

[4] *N. Y. Merc.*, Apr. 28, 1766.

Two other ports, one of which was not bound by any formal agreement of non-importation applied the principle of the secondary boycott to ports where the stamp tax was being paid. The country people at Newburyport attempted to prevent the sailing of a schooner for Halifax; and when other means failed, they informed the customs officers of irregularities in her cargo and occasioned a seizure of the vessel.[1] At Charleston, S. C., the fire company, composed of radicals, agreed that no provision should be shipped "to that infamous Colony Georgia in particular nor any other that make use of Stamp Paper," on penalty of death for the offenders, if they persisted in error, and the burning of the vessel. A schooner, laden with rice for Georgia, attempted to put to sea by night; but the master and the owner were stopped by a threat that the letter of the resolution would be carried out, and they discharged the cargo.[2]

About the middle of 1766, official news reached the colonies that Parliament had given heed to the American situation and had made sweeping alterations in the trade and revenue laws of 1764-1765. This had come as the result of a combination of circumstances, fortuitous and natural, which had spelled victory for the colonists.[3] Leading among these circumstances were the distress of the British merchants, manufacturers and workingmen, and the examination of Dr. Franklin before the House of Commons. Figures at the London custom house showed that English exportations to the commercial colonies had declined from £1,410,372 in 1764 to £1,197,010 in 1765; and from £515,-

---

[1] *N. H. Gaz.*, Jan. 10, 1766.

[2] *Newport Merc.*, Mch. 17, 31, 1766; *S. C. Gaz.*, Feb. 25; *Pa. Journ.*, Mch. 20.

[3] Hodge, H. H., "Repeal of Stamp Act," *Pol. Sci. Quar.*, vol. xix, pp. 252-276.

192 to £383,224 to the tobacco colonies—a loss which was far from being offset by an increase from £324,146 to £363,874 in the exportations to North Carolina and the rice colonies.[1] Dr. Franklin had laid bare the economic reasons for the American commotions, declaring them to be " the restraints lately laid on their trade, by which the bringing of foreign gold and silver into the Colonies was prevented; the prohibition of making paper money among themselves; and then demanding a new and heavy tax by stamps; taking away, at the same time, trials by jury, and refusing to receive and hear their humble petitions." [2]

Whether or not Franklin's analysis was a complete statement of the case, the remedial legislation of Parliament followed generally the lines indicated by him. The first step taken was the total repeal of the Stamp Act, upon an understanding, embodied in the accompanying Declaratory Act, that Parliament, nevertheless, possessed authority to bind the colonies " in all cases whatsoever." [3] When Secretary Conway communicated this news to the colonial governors in a letter of March 31, 1766, he assured them that Parliament would at once undertake to " give to the Trade & Interests of America every Relief which the true State of their Circumstances demands or admits." [4] A second letter of June 12, signed by the Duke of Richmond as secretary, announced the accomplishment of this latter object—that " those Grievances in Trade which seemed to be the first and chief Object of their Uneasiness have been taken into the most minute Consideration, & such Regulations have

[1] *Bos. Chron.*, Jan. 30, 1769.
[2] *Writings* (Smith), vol. iv, p. 420.
[3] 6 George III, c. 11 and c. 12.
[4] *1 N. J. Arch.*, vol. ix, pp. 550-552. As early as Feb. 14, Henry Cruger had written with the assurance of one who knew the facts that the molasses duty would be reduced to one penny. *R. I. Commerce*, vol. i, p. 143.

been established as will, it is hoped, restore the Trade of America . . ."[1]

The new regulations of Parliament did indeed remove the chief economic objection to the restrictive act of 1764.[2] The threepenny duty on foreign molasses was taken off, and in its place a very low duty of one penny a gallon was substituted upon all molasses, whether imported from British or foreign possessions. The high duties on foreign sugar were retained; but the cost of British West Indian sugar was reduced by removing the long-established export duties at the islands. It was provided, for the discouragement of smuggling, that all sugars exported to Great Britain from the continental colonies should be classed as "French" and charged with higher duties accordingly.

It was further enacted that all colonial products, whether "enumerated" or not, must thereafter be entered at an English port, if destined for a European port north of Cape Finisterre (other than the Spanish ports in the Bay of Biscay). The imposts on foreign textiles that had been collected upon importation into America were in the future to be collected at the time of exportation from England. The export duties on British colonial pimento and coffee were replaced by low duties upon their importation into other British colonies.

The new duty on molasses met the wishes of the agents of the continental colonies; and it would appear that the merchants of Boston, so vitally concerned, had intimated

---

[1] *1 N. J. Arch.*, vol. ix, pp. 553-554.

[2] 6 George III, c. 52. The British West Indies had been suffering hard times also, and Parliament passed special legislation at this time with a view of relieving the distress there; 6 George III, c. 49, for the establishment of free ports at Jamaica and Dominica. *Vide* Edwards, B., *The History, Civil and Commercial, of the British Colonies in the West Indies* (London, 1793), vol. i, pp. 239-243.

in advance their willingness to accept such a reduction.[1] It was understood that the rum business of the commercial provinces could easily support a small tax. Franklin believed that the new regulations afforded "reasonable relief . . . in our Commercial grievances "[2] and the Rhode Island agent wrote, even more exuberantly, to the governor of Rhode Island that "every grievance of which you complained is now absolutely and totally removed, — a joyful and happy event for the late disconsolate inhabitants of America."[3]

If the colonists had been more intent on their theoretical rights than on immediate business concessions, the keener minds would have perceived that rejoicing was premature. Far more ominous to American liberties than the Declaratory Act was the fact that the new molasses duty applied to all molasses imported, British as well as foreign. By no possible interpretation could it be construed in any other light than a tariff for revenue. It was an unvarnished contradiction of the colonial claim to "no taxation without representation."

However, the remedial legislation of 1766 was received in America with great popular satisfaction. Measures

[1] Beer, *British Colonial Policy, 1754-1765*, p. 279; *1 M. H. S. Colls.*, vol. vi, p. 193; Hutchinson, *Mass. Bay*, vol. iii, p. 261 n.; Quincy, *Mass. Reports*, p. 435; *Brit. Mus., Egerton Mss.*, no. 2671 (*L. C. Transcripts*); *Sagittarius's Letters*, no. xix, pp. 84-88. Dennys de Berdt, agent of the Massachusetts House of Representatives, informed Lord Halifax that a duty of one penny on molasses, "colected with the good will of the people, will produce more neat money than 3 pence collected by the dint of Officers." *Col. Soc. Mass. Pubs.*, vol. xiii, p. 430. Dickinson had said in his powerful arraignment of "the late regulations" that "we should willingly pay a moderate duty upon importations from the French and Spaniards, without attempting to run them." *Writings* (Ford), vol. i, p. 224.

[2] *Writings* (Smyth), vol. iv, p. 411.

[3] *R. I. Col. Recs.*, vol. vi, pp. 491-493.

against the use and importation of British goods collapsed. The widespread enthusiasm for local manufacturing greatly diminished or entirely vanished. The New York Society for the Promotion of Arts, Agriculture and Oeconomy declined temporarily into a comatose state.[1] The majority of the people again bowed to the custom of expensive funerals and lavish mourning. At a public entertainment in Philadelphia, the citizens resolved unanimously to give their homespun to the poor and on June the fourth, the king's birthday, to dress in new suits of English fabrication.[2] When news of the repeal of the Stamp Act reached Boston, Hancock wrote: "You may rest assured that the people in this country will exert themselves to show their Loyalty & attachment to Great Britain" and he promised his "best Influence & endeavors to that purpose."[3] Charles Thomson, of Philadelphia, wrote to Franklin of "a heartfelt joy, seen in every Eye, read in every Countenance; a Joy not expressed in triumph but with the warmest sentiments of Loyalty to our King and a grateful acknowledgment of the Justice and tenderness of the mother Country."[4]

The generality of the merchants in the commercial provinces were not so unreservedly gratified by the action of Parliament. Important concessions had been made in response to the American propaganda; indeed, the leading grievances had been removed. Yet trade had not been restored to the footing which it had enjoyed before the pass-

[1] *N. Y. Journ.*, Dec. 17, 24, 1767. During the Townshend Acts, as we shall see, the society revived its activities, and traces of its proceedings may be found in the *Journal* as late as Mch. 29, 1770.

[2] *Pa. Gaz.*, May 22, 1766; *Franklin Bicentennial Celebration*, vol. ii, pp. 58-59. Weyler's *N. Y. Gazette*, May 26, 1766, suggested that this action proceeded from the desire of the anti-proprietary party to curry favor with the king.

[3] Brown, *John Hancock His Book*, pp. 124-125.

[4] *N. Y. Hist. Soc. Colls.*, vol. xi, p. 16.

age of the laws of 1764 and 1765. To that extent, the merchants had fallen short of their goal.

In November, 1766, the New York merchants summed up their outstanding grievances in a petition to the House of Commons, containing two hundred and forty signatures.[1] In the following January, the merchants of Boston followed their example.[2] These two papers covered substantially the same ground. The Bostonians seized this early opportunity to deny that rum could be profitably distilled from molasses that bore a duty amounting to practically ten per cent *ad valorem,* as did the one-penny duty. They also protested against the administrative regulations of 1764, declaring that one part of them made the proper registration of a vessel an expensive and tedious process, and that another part granted naval officers autocratic powers of seizure, together with protection from damage suits.[3] The

---

[1] Weyler's *N. Y. Gaz.*, May 4, 1767; Pitt, Wm., *Correspondence* (London, 1838), vol. iii, p. 186. *Vide* also the statement of "Americus," copied into Weyler's *N. Y. Gaz.*, Jan. 19, 1767, from a London newspaper.

[2] *M. H. S. Mss.*: 91 L, pp. 27, 31; *Col. Soc. Mass. Pubs.*, vol. xiii, pp. 451-452.

[3] The New Englanders had a special grievance, which was of first importance while it lasted. In 1765 Governor Palliser, of Newfoundland, had prevented American fishermen from taking cod off Labrador and in the Strait of Belle Isle. His action was based upon a narrow interpretation of the statutes relating to the Newfoundland fisheries, and upon a belief that a smuggling trade was being carried on with the French of Miquelon and St. Pierre. A petition of the Massachusetts House of Representatives, presented about this time, asked for an act of Parliament to prevent such restraints in the future. The ministry would not concede this; but in March, 1767, they agreed to revise Palliser's instructions so as to preclude any further interruption of the legitimate fishing-trade. This action apparently settled the matter satisfactorily. *Ibid.*, pp. 447-448, 451-452; 4 *M. H. S. Colls.*, vol. iv, pp. 347-348; 5 *M. H. S. Colls.*, vol. ix, pp. 219-220; Andrews. " Boston Merchants and Non-Importation Movement," *Col. Soc. Mass. Pubs.*, vol. xix, pp. 173-174.

New Yorkers, on the other hand, stood alone in their contention that the exclusion of foreign rum from the colonies was a hardship, averring that it was a necessary article of exchange at the Danish West Indies particularly.

On most points the two petitions were in essential agreement. The high duty on foreign sugar was said to eliminate it as an article of trade, although it was a commodity frequently used to fill out a return cargo. This excessive duty, said the New York merchants, " had induced the Fair Trader to decline that Branch of Business, while it presents an irresistable Incentive to Smuggling to People less scrupulous." The requirement that all sugars exported to Great Britain from the continental colonies should be classed as "French" was said to prevent a valuable return to Great Britain for her manufactures. The high duty on Madeira wine was objected to as a discouragement to its importation into America and, therefore, to the exportation of American foodstuffs and lumber to the Wine Islands. The requirement as to the importation of fruit and wine from Spain and Portugal was again held up as a grievance.[1] The new regulation, which required all outgoing commodities to be entered at a British port before going on to European ports north of Finisterre, was said to increase the cost of voyages unduly and preclude the competition of colonial merchants in European markets. The exportation of foreign logwood and of colonial lumber, provisions and flaxseed was especially affected by this restriction.

Of the grievances here enumerated, the regulations against smuggling had already begun to prove less irksome

[1] In 1767, Townshend desired to remove this grievance, but was unsuccessful. It was urged that a direct trade between Portugal and America would be a hazardous relaxation of the acts of trade. 5 M. H. S., vol. ix, pp. 231, 236; Pa. Gaz., July 16, 1767.

FIRST CONTEST FOR REFORM 89

in practice than they appeared on paper.[1] Thus, in 1764, the Rhode Island legislature had forbidden the governor to administer the oaths to British customs officials, and the latter had been forced to suspend operations. In 1765, a customs collector in Maryland had been violently assaulted; and in Massachusetts and New York, the officials were afraid to execute the laws after the Stamp Act riots. For the future, the necessity for smuggling seemed somewhat lessened by the radical reduction of the molasses duty.

One grievance had not been included by the petitioners— the failure of Parliament to provide relief for the currency situation. The colonial merchants had probably placed reliance upon the assurance of the London merchants, communicated the preceding June, that the government, after much deliberation, had concluded to postpone a regulation of colonial paper money until the colonies could be consulted upon a scheme for a general paper currency upon an intercolonial basis.[2] Unfortunately, however, nothing was to come of this plan;[3] and the money stringency, though some-

---

[1] Beer, *British Colonial Policy, 1754-1765*, pp. 301-302; Arnold, S. G., *History of Rhode Island* (New York, 1860), vol. ii, pp. 257-259; Colden, *Letter Books*, vol. ii, p. 124.

[2] *Pa. Gaz.*, Aug. 21, 1766, also Weyler's *N. Y. Gaz.*, Aug. 25; *Newport Merc.*, Sept. 1; *Bos. Post-Boy*, Sept. 1; *N. H. Gaz.*, Sept. 4. Franklin had confidently expected action from Parliament on this subject while revision of the trade laws was being undertaken. *Writings* (Smyth), vol. iv, p. 411.

[3] The dilatory course of the British government in this matter seems scarcely excusable. The British merchants in the American trade, with the backing of the colonial agents, worked for the repeal of the Currency Act of 1764, and proposed a plan by which colonial bills of credit should be legal tender for everything except sterling debts payable in Great Britain. The ministry refused in 1767 to listen to this plan, partly because of irritation over New York's cavalier treatment of the Quartering Act. *Pa. Gaz.*, Apr. 9, 1767; *Pa. Journ.*, Apr. 23, July 30. In the same year Grenville proposed in Parliament a plan for a general paper currency which was intended as a means of increasing the

what relieved by the reopening of trade with the foreign West Indies, was to become increasingly distressing in the next three or four years as the redemption periods of the outstanding paper money arrived and the volume of legal tender thereby became greatly contracted. Thus, the real trial in New York began with the redemption of its paper money in November, 1768.[1] In these later years, complaints of the scarcity of money came chiefly from the provinces outside of New England, and were voiced by governors, newspaper writers and legislative petitions.[2] Many sagacious men of the time believed that the British government was guilty of grave injustice, particularly in the case of those provinces where the power to issue legal-tender money had never been abused.[3]

American revenue. This did not receive serious consideration. *5 M. H. S. Colls.*, vol. ix, p. 231. New York was given relief from the severe money stringency by a special act of 1770: 10 George III, c. 35. Finally, an act of 1773 (13 George III, c. 57) permitted colonial paper money to be received as a legal tender for payment of colonial duties, taxes, etc. *Vide infra*, pp. 243-244.

[1] Becker, C. L., *The History of Political Parties in the Province of New York, 1760-1776* (Univ. Wis. Bull., no. 286), pp. 65-71, 77-79, 88, 95, and references.

[2] *E. g., N. Y. Col. Docs.*, vol. viii, pp. 175-176; *1 N. J. Arch.*, vol. xviii, p. 46; "Mercator" in *Pa. Journ.*, Sept. 14, 1769; *Brit. Papers* ("*Sparks Mss.*"), vol. ii, pp. 184-186, 220-225, 263-267. *Vide* also Franklin, *Writings* (Smyth), vol. v, pp. 71-73.

[3] For a statement of the case of New York, *vide 4 M. H. S. Colls.*, vol. x, pp. 520-521; of Pennsylvania, Franklin, *Writings* (Smyth), vol. v, pp. 1-14.

CHAPTER III

THE SECOND MOVEMENT FOR COMMERCIAL REFORM
(1767-1770)

Although the colonial merchants had won their chief demands in their contest with Parliament, they had yet fallen short, in several respects, of attaining their ultimate goal, *i. e.* a restoration of the commercial system as it existed in the days before 1764. This purpose was the objective of the mercantile provinces in the subsequent years, and was relinquished by them only when it became apparent that their agitation for commercial redress was unloosing social forces more destructive to business interests than the misguided acts of Parliament. The typical merchant cared little about academic controversies over theoretical right; but he was vitally concerned in securing every practicable concession he could without endangering the stability of the empire. Paul Wentworth, in writing his "Minutes respecting political Parties in America" in 1778, took care to differentiate the merchant class from all other groups of malcontents in the period leading to the Revolutionary War. After showing their purpose, he made it clear that their influence controlled a very large majority of the people throughout the provinces at the outset.[1] The ultimate success of the merchants depended upon their ability to retain this position of leadership, to control public opinion in America, and to direct the course of opposition.

The experience of the years 1764-1766 gave the merchant class food for sober reflection. Intent on making out a

[1] Stevens, *Facsimiles*, vol. v, no. 487.

complete case for themselves, they had, in their zeal, over-reached themselves in calling to their aid the unruly elements of the population. These unprivileged classes had never before been awakened to a sense of their muscular influence in community affairs; and, under the name of "Sons of Liberty," they had instinctively stretched out for alliance with their brethren in other cities.[1] Dimly the merchants began to perceive the danger of an awakened self-conscious group of the radical elements; well might they be apprehensive, as Colden recorded, "whether the Men who excited this seditious Spirit in the People have it in their power to suppress it."[2] Men of large propertied interests were undoubtedly more sensitive to the danger than were the smaller merchants; some of the former had exhorted the people of New York city against "mob government" while the Stamp Act riots were still under way.[3]

The violence of the colonial propaganda had alienated from the mercantile side such influential men as Governor Bernard and Lieutenant Governor Hutchinson, of Massachusetts,[4] and had cooled the ardor of such important figures as Dulany, of Maryland, and Joseph Galloway, of

[1] Ramifications of the Sons of Liberty were to be found in New York, Albany and other New York towns, in Philadelphia, Boston, Providence, Portsmouth, several towns of Connecticut and New Jersey, and in Baltimore and Annapolis. Becker, *N. Y. Parties*, pp. 46-48.

[2] *Letter Books*, vol. ii, p. 99. *Vide* also p. 111. Even Charles Thomson, the Philadelphia merchant, hoped that the whole people would not be credited with the "acts of some individuals provoked to madness and actuated by despair." *N. Y. Hist. Soc. Colls.*, vol. xi, p. 16. The merchants of Brunswick, N. J., apologized to the Committee of Merchants of London for the "riots or tumults" as being "the follies of less considerate men" than themselves. *1 N. J. Arch.*, vol. xxv, pp. 235-237.

[3] Becker, *N. Y. Parties*, chap. ii.

[4] An excellent modern example of the same type of mind may be found by reading Peabody, A. P., "Boston Mobs before the Revolution," *Atl. Monthly*, vol. lxii, pp. 321-333.

Pennsylvania.¹ For the future, the merchants as a class were resolved to rely upon orderly methods of protest—memorials and the boycott. A first step had been taken by the merchants of New York and Boston, in accordance with this new policy, by the sending of petitions to Parliament for trade redress in the winter of 1766-1767.²

Such was the situation when Parliament made its next attempt to reorganize British imperial policy. The new plan found its justification in the fact that colonial theorists had, as yet, discovered nothing " unconstitutional " or " tyrannical " in revenue duties collected at American ports. The recent molasses duty was the best, but not the only, example of the willingness of Americans to pay an " external tax " without protest.³ Charles Townshend was, thus, acting within the best traditions of British practical statesmanship, when he proposed to build a revenue act based upon the colonists' own views of the powers of Parliament.

Townshend's policy, enacted as the will of Parliament about the middle of 1767, not only dealt with taxation, but also proposed to strengthen the customs service where recent experience had shown it to be inadequate. A third measure, designed to meet a temporary emergency, was the suspension of the legislative functions of the New York Assembly until that body should comply with all the provisions of the Quartering Act.⁴

---

¹ Galloway's biographer analyzes the character of his propertied interests and then adds: "He feared the tyranny of mob rule more than the tyranny of Parliament." Baldwin, E. H., "Joseph Galloway," *Pa. Mag.*, vol. xxvi, pp. 163-164, 289-294.

² *Vide supra*, pp. 87-88.

³ The colonists also paid revenue duties on enumerated goods imported from another British colony (25 Charles II, c. 7), on coffee and pimento imported from British possessions (6 George III, c. 52), and on imported wines (4 George III, c. 15).

⁴ It is not necessary to recount here this familiar episode. The mer-

The revenue feature of Townshend's policy was accomplished by adding a list of port duties to those already in force. The following articles were to be taxed at the time of their landing in America: five varieties of glass, red and white lead, painters' colors, sixty-seven grades of paper, and tea.[1] All these articles were British manufactures, except tea, which was handled by the greatest British monopoly of the times, the East India Company. The imposition of the three-penny tea tax in America was accompanied by the remission of the duty paid at the time that the tea was imported into Great Britain, the object being to enable dutied tea to undersell any tea that was smuggled into the colonies.[2]

One portion of the revenue act was designed "for more effectually preventing the clandestine running of goods. . ." With this purpose in view, it was provided that the revenue produced by the duties should be used to free the judges and civil officers in such colonies as "it shall be found necessary" from financial dependence on the local legislatures. More immediately to the point, express legalization was given to the hitherto questionable practice of the colonial supreme courts in issuing writs of assistance to customs officials. By means of these writs, customs officers were to receive power to search for contraband goods in any house or shop, and, in case of resistance, to break open doors, chests, etc., and seize the goods in question.

Other regulations were designed to strengthen the administrative side of the customs service.[3] These made

chant class were not interested in this act of Parliament; and in the various non-importation agreements adopted later, this law was not once named for repeal.

[1] 7 George III, c. 46.

[2] 7 George III, c. 56. The East India Company was required to make good any deficiency in the revenues which might result from the discontinuance of certain tea duties. Farrand, Max, "Taxation of Tea, 1767-1773," *Am. Hist. Rev.*, vol. iii, pp. 266-269.

[3] 7 George III, c. 41.

possible the establishment of a board of commissioners of the customs at Boston, with entire charge of the collection of customs throughout the continent as well as at Bermuda and the Bahamas. The commissioners were given power to place the customs service on a basis of comparative efficiency. Disputes, which had hitherto been carried to the Commissioners of the Customs at London for settlement, were to be determined by this new American board with much less trouble, delay and expense to the parties concerned.

Certain changes in the interest of greater efficiency were also made in the system of colonial courts of vice-admiralty.[1] In addition to the courts already existing in the several provinces, vice-admiralty courts of large powers were established at Boston, Philadelphia and Charleston with original jurisdiction over the capture of vessels in their respective districts and with appellate jurisdiction over the subordinate vice-admiralty courts.

The situation in which the merchants of the commercial provinces found themselves in the latter months of 1767 was not unlike their situation in the latter part of 1764, save that on this later occasion Philadelphia did not seem to be as greatly affected as the other ports. Again, the merchants were confronted with trade restrictions—some of them hanging over from 1764—which reduced business profits. Again, they faced new and rigorous regulations against smuggling, regulations which betokened a seriousness of purpose on the part of the government which was not open to misconstruction. And again, they perceived that the burden of seeking redress must fall upon their own shoulders, the planters of the South being involved less directly and less obviously in the new legislation.

[1] 8 George III, c. 22. *Vide* also *N. C. Col. Recs.*, vol. vii, pp. 459-460.

The determination of the merchants to conduct their campaign for redress along legal and peaceable lines was at once made manifest. On November 20, 1767, the day the Townshend acts became effective, James Otis, the lawyer of the Boston merchants, presided over a town meeting; and after telling the people that relief should be sought " in a legal and constitutional way," he roundly denounced mob riots, even to the extent of declaring that " no possible circumstances, though ever so oppressive, could be supposed sufficient to justify private tumults and disorders . . ." The selectmen, most of whom were merchants by trade, appealed to the people a few days later, in an article over their signatures, to avoid " all outrage or lawless proceeding " and stand firm " in a prudent conduct and cautious behaviour." [1] In a similar spirit, John Dickinson, the wealthy Pennsylvania lawyer, in his " Letters from a Farmer in Pennsylvania," published serially during the subsequent three months, took frequent and emphatic occasion to condemn " turbulence and tumult " and to laud " constitutional modes of obtaining relief."[2] This was the spirit in which the second contest for commercial reform got under way. Had the conflict been of shorter duration, the desires of the leaders might have been realized. But the length of the contest, with the increasing restlessness and self-confidence of the radical elements, made the introduction of mob methods inevitable.

The course of opposition pursued by the merchants par-

[1] *Vide Bos. Post-Boy*, Nov. 30, 1767, and Frothingham, *Rise of Republic*, pp. 206-208, for these and other instances. *Vide* also Hutchinson, *Mass. Bay*, vol. iii, pp. 180-181.

[2] The twelve articles appeared originally in issues of the *Pa. Chronicle* from Dec. 2, 1767 to Feb. 15, 1768. For Dickinson's views on "hot, rash, disorderly proceedings," *vide* in particular Letter III; *Writings* (Ford), vol. i, pp. 322-328.

took of a double character. On the one hand, there were the activities of the smuggling merchants, protected by popular opinion and bent upon the pursuit of gain in defiance of parliamentary restrictions. On the other hand, there stood the whole merchant class, confident of their power to coerce the nation of shopkeepers into concessions through exercise of the boycott, and prepared to develop this instrument beyond anything dreamed of during Stamp Act times.

Smuggling proved to be the first channel through which violence was injected into the struggle. There occurred the usual vicious sequence: evasion of the law leading to defiance of the law, and defiance of the law breeding violence. After the revision of the trade laws in 1766 and the passage of the new acts of 1767, the character of colonial contraband trade changed greatly. The running of molasses, which had formerly formed the great bulk of illicit traffic, had been rendered considerably less profitable by the reduction of the duty.[1] The Townshend duties, with a single exception, fell on articles manufactured in Great Britain; and instead of encouraging smuggling in these articles, served as a stimulus to their production in the colonies.

The exception noted, the duty on tea, was so ingeniously

[1] Since the duty has been reduced, "the whole, tho' grievous, has been regularly paid." *Observations of the Merchants at Boston upon Several Acts of Parliament*, etc. (1770), pp. 29-30. It should further be noted that, beginning with the year 1768, a succession of temporary acts removed the prohibition from the exportation of American meats and butter to Great Britain, and sometimes from cereals and raw hides as well. *E. g., vide* 8 George III, c. 9; 9 George III, c. 39; 10 George III, c. 1, c. 2; 11 George III, c. 8; 13 George III, c. 1, c. 2, c. 3, c. 4, c. 5; 15 George III, c. 7. The passage of these acts made it less necessary for colonial merchants to seek in foreign markets commodities which might serve as remittances to England and thus reduce the temptation to smuggling.

contrived as to have the immediate effect of lowering the price of customed tea in America below that of any that could be smuggled from Holland or elsewhere.[1] This condition lasted until 1769 when the East India Company, hard pressed by creditors and seeking to recoup some of its losses, advanced the upset price of tea at the public auctions in Great Britain. This caused the exporting merchant, who bid in the tea, to raise the price to the American merchant, and the American merchant to raise the price to the colonial retailer. So that the colonial consumer thereafter found it advantageous to drink Dutch tea; and tea smuggling began to thrive.[2]

Until that time, it would appear that the chief concern of the smugglers was the running of wine from Madeira and the Azores, a traffic vastly stimulated by the high duty demanded for legal importation.[3] In view of the commotions that resulted, one might add in supplementation of John Adams' remark concerning molasses that wine was another essential ingredient of American independence. The importation of Dutch, French and German manufactures without stoppage at Great Britain, as required by

[1] Tea imported from Great Britain became ninepence cheaper per pound. *Bos. Gaz.*, Aug. 15, 1768; *Mass. Gaz. & Post-Boy*, Dec. 19, 1774.

[2] Hutchinson to Hillsborough, Aug. 25, 1771, *Bos. Gaz.*, Nov. 27, 1775. *Vide infra*, p. 250.

[3] This duty was no less than seven pounds per tun under the act of 1764. As Kelly, the New York merchant, told a committee of Parliament, "wherever there is a great difference of Price, there will be a Daring Spirit to attempt [smuggling] notwithstanding all Preventions." *Brit. Mus. Addl. Mss.*, no. 33030 (*L. C. Transcripts*), f. 136. For example, an official report, made evidently for the Customs Board, stated that thirty vessels, entering at New York from Madeira and the Azores, had not entered sufficient goods to load one vessel. *Ibid.*, no. 15484, f. 6. Colden said that few New York merchants were not engaged in contraband trade and that "Whole Cargoes from Holland and Ship Loads of Wine" had been brought in without the payment of duties. *Letter Books*, vol. ii, pp. 133-134.

COMMERCIAL REFORM

law, probably continued much as before; and there may have been a slight increase in the volume of the illicit export trade, due to the fact that after 1766 all American commodities, shipped for European ports north of Cape Finisterre, must first be entered at a British port.

The continuance of smuggling after 1767 should not be made to argue the total failure of Townshend's endeavor to reform the customs administration. The Board of Customs Commissioners at Boston performed a vastly creditable service in reducing peculation and laziness on the part of officials and in establishing a stricter system of coast control. The number of customs employees was greatly increased—in the case of Philadelphia, trebled in the years 1767-1770.[1] Writs of assistance were more generally and more effectively used than at any earlier period. Revenue cutters were stationed at leading ports; and smaller vessels, belonging to the navy and acting under deputation of the commissioners, searched out suspected ships in the numerous rivers and inlets. A representation of the Boston merchants, made in 1770, declared that the Customs Board had employed upwards of twenty vessels that year, and that some of the captains had purchased small boats of their own to search in shallow waters.[2] Undoubtedly the total volume of illicit trade was smaller after 1767 than at any period subsequent to the enactment of the Molasses Act in 1733;[3] and this was due, in some degree, to the activities of the Customs Board.[4]

[1] Channing, *History of United States*, vol. iii, pp. 88-89.

[2] *Observations of the Merchants at Boston*, etc., pp. 24-25.

[3] On the other hand, Colden claimed, in November, 1767, and repeatedly in the following months, that at New York "a greater quantity of Goods has been Run without paying Duties since the Repeal of the Stamp Act than had been done in ten years before." *Letter Books*, vol. ii, pp. 133-134, 138, 148, 153, 163, 172.

[4] Note the table of penalties and seizures, quoted by Professor Chan-

Two conditions militated against the success of the Customs Board in wiping out smuggling. One was the extent of the coastline to be watched. The other was the active sympathy which the populace extended to the smugglers. The importance of this latter factor was shown by the peremptory treatment of those who were reckless enough to reveal to a customs officer the secret of their neighbors' prosperity. Thus, an informer cowered before a gathering of merchants and inhabitants of New Haven in September, 1769, and humbly acknowledged his iniquity in attempting to inform against Mr. Timothy Jones, Jr., for "running of goods."[1] During the following month an informer at Boston was tarred and feathered and paraded through the principal streets;[2] and three others of his kind in New York received similar treatment—"to the great Satisfaction of all the good Inhabitants of this City, and to the great Terror of evil doers," as one loyal New Yorker averred.[3]

Popular sympathy also produced collisions with the customs officials. While in discharge of his duty, Jesse Saville, a tide waiter of the custom house at Providence, was viol-

ning, *op. cit.*, vol. iii, p. 89 n. Eloquent evidence of the prevalence of smuggling as late as 1770 is shown in a survey of the customs districts and ports, made, it would appear, for the Customs Board. This report is entitled, "Ports of North America." It shows clearly that wide stretches of coast were free from proper customs supervision and makes detailed recommendations for stricter oversight. Considerable smuggling is also alleged in the plantation provinces at this period *Brit. Mus. Addl. Mss.*, no. 15484 (*L. C. Transcripts*).

[1] *New London Gaz.*, Sept. 29, 1769; also *Mass. Gaz. & News Letter*, Oct. 5.

[2] *Ibid.*, Nov. 2, 9, 1769; Hutchinson, *Mass. Bay*, vol. iii, pp. 259-260.

[3] *Mass. Gaz. & News Letter*, Oct. 12, 1769. Colden wrote in January, 1768, to Grenville: "No man dare inform, so that whole cargoes have been run without entry in the Custom House." *Letter Books*, vol. ii, p. 153.

ently assaulted and then tarred and feathered, in 1769. A reward of fifty pounds sterling for the perpetrators of this act was vainly offered by the Customs Board.[1] In July of the same year, a mob at Newport dismantled and burnt the revenue sloop *Liberty,* which had just brought into the harbor two vessels suspected of smuggling.[2] "Both vessels that were seized have since proceeded on their respective voyages," noted the *Newport Mercury* laconically on July 22. At Philadelphia, the revenue officials attempted in April, 1769, to get possession of about fifty pipes of Madeira wine that had been imported without payment of duties. Their efforts stirred up a mob which stole away the booty from under their very noses and maltreated some of the officers. Later, the merchants offered to restore the wine; and, after some delay, they returned " not near the Quantity that was taken " and, instead of Madeira, " no better than mean Fyall [Fayal]." A revenue employee who had been active in this affair went to Boston to recuperate from his injuries, because, as he earnestly avowed, " I could not think of tarrying among a sett of People under my present circumstances whose greatest pleasure would be to have an oppo[rtunity] of burying me."[3]

Even from the plantation provinces came echoes of indignation against the officiousness of customs officers and the new powers of the vice-admiralty courts. Infringements of the acts of trade were comparatively rare in that portion of British America; and it was the boast of the

[1] Arnold, *Rhode Island,* vol. ii, p. 294.
[2] *R. I. Col. Recs.,* vol. vi, pp. 593-596; Gammel, W., *Samuel Ward* (*2 Libr. Am. Biog.,* vol. ix), pp. 288-290. For instances of forcible importation in Massachusetts and Rhode Island, *vide* Weeden, *Ec. and Soc. Hist. of New Engl.,* vol. ii, p. 762.
[3] *4 M. H. S. Colls.,* vol. x, pp. 611-617.

wealthy Charleston merchant and factor, Henry Laurens, that he had never intentionally violated them. Yet, in spite of the efforts of the Customs Board to secure higher administrative efficiency, the customs officers at Charleston were unprincipled and corrupt; and the merchants of that port were subjected to petty tyrannies, from which the local vice-admiralty court afforded no relief. Laurens himself was put to great expense through the seizure on technical charges in 1767 and 1768, of three of his vessels, two of which were eventually released. A conservative from temperamental as well as business reasons, his emotions were, for the first time, deeply stirred to the defense of so-called American liberties, and in 1769 he produced an able controversial pamphlet setting forth his new views under the title, *Some General Observations on American custom house officers and Courts of Vice-Admiralty.* Thoroughly academic and unemotional as he had been in his objections to the Stamp Act, he could write in 1769 to a London friend that " the enormous created powers vested in an American Court of Vice-Admiralty threatens future generations in America with a curse tenfold worse than the Stamp Act." [1]

The most important work performed by the Customs Board was the breaking of the power of the smugglers at Boston. This was accomplished only through a resort to extreme measures. In the years immediately following 1766, there were a number of cases at Boston of forcible landing of contraband goods, of rescue of lawful seizures, and of mobbing of revenue officers.[2] John Robinson, one of the Customs Board, in his testimony before the Privy

[1] For this incident, *vide* Wallace, *Henry Laurens*, pp. 137-149. *Vide* also *Prov. Gaz.*, Oct. 3, 1767, July 23, 1768.

[2] *Acts of the Privy Council, Colonial*, vol. v, no. 155. *Vide* also Hutchinson, *Mass. Bay*, vol. iii, p. 188.

Council in 1770, stated that he hesitated to say that "the Disturbances may be properly called Riots, as the Rioters appear to be under Discipline."

Feeling unable to cope with the situation, the Customs Board, in February, 1768, asked Commodore Hood at Halifax for a public vessel to protect them in the discharge of their functions. "We have every reason," they said, "to expect that we shall find it impracticable to enforce the execution of the revenue laws, until the hand of government is properly strengthened. At present, there is not a ship-of-war in the province, nor a company of soldiers nearer than New York."[1] In answer to repeated requests, the man-of-war *Romney* was stationed at Boston a few months later. The board now pressed for additional ships and for the presence of troops, but their requests failed of effect.

Affairs came to a crisis a few months later, when John Hancock's sloop *Liberty* arrived in port from Madeira with a quantity of wine. A tidesman went on board and objected to the landing of any wine until entry was made at the custom house; whereupon the fellow was heaved into the cabin and kept there while the cargo was expeditiously removed. On June 10, about a month later, the vessel was seized by order of the Customs Board. A crowd assembled and, in great uneasiness, watched the removal of the vessel to within gun-range of the *Romney*. Soon they lost their restraint; and, in the rioting that ensued, the custom-house officers were assaulted and the houses of several of them pelted, and other damage done.[2]

[1] Bancroft, G., *History of United States* (Boston, 1876), vol. iv, p. 75.
[2] The *Liberty* was condemned by the vice-admiralty court. *Bos. Chron.*, June 13, 1768; Sears, L., *John Hancock* (Boston, 1912), pp. 110-114; Brown, *John Hancock His Book*, p. 156; Hutchinson, *Mass. Bay*,

Alleging helplessness, the Customs Board retired to Castle William and again renewed their demand for troops. This time they had made good their case; two regiments arrived on the scene about four months after the riot, and the customs commissioners resumed their headquarters at Boston. From this time forward Boston lost its importance as a smuggling port; and the great centers of contraband trade became New York and Philadelphia, with Newport as a center of minor importance.[1]

However justfiable the action may have appeared from an administrative point of view, the British government made a bad tactical error in sending soldiers to Boston. The statesmanlike policy of maintaining a standing army to protect the empire from foreign enemies had degenerated into an employment of the troops as a military police to enforce hated laws on the people themselves. The worst fears of the radicals were vindicated. Their efforts and those of the merchants were used for the next two years to procure the removal of the troops. Sporadic outbreaks of resistance to customs officials continued to occur.[2]

Of greater interest and significance in the controversy

---

vol. iii, pp. 189-194. For Hancock's letters ordering the wine, *vide* Brown, *op. cit.*, pp. 149-150.

After referring to the *Liberty* affair, John Adams writes in his diary: "Mr. Hancock was prosecuted upon a great number of libels, for penalties upon acts of Parliament, amounting to ninety or an hundred thousand pounds sterling. He thought fit to engage me as his counsel and advocate, and a painful drudgery I had of his cause. There were few days through the whole winter, when I was not summoned to attend the Court of Admiralty. . . . this odious cause was suspended at last only by the battle of Lexington, which put an end, forever, to all such prosecutions." *Works*, vol. ii, pp. 215-216.

[1] Letters of Thomas Hutchinson; Hosmer, *Hutchinson*, p. 432; *Mass. Arch.*, vol. xxvii, p. 317. *Vide* also *infra*, chap. vi.

[2] *E. g., vide* 4 *Am. Arch.*, vol. i, p. 26.

with Parliament was the endeavor of the merchants to control the economic life of their communities and by use of the boycott to starve Great Britain into a surrender of her trade restrictions. This movement of a class-conscious group within the leading provinces constituted the one tremendous fact of the revolutionary movement prior to the assembling of the First Continental Congress. Striving for reform, not rebellion, the merchants, nevertheless, through the effect of their agitation and organized activity upon the non-mercantile population, found themselves, when they wished to terminate their propaganda, confronted with forces too powerful for them to control.

The efforts at combination from 1767 to 1770 suffered from all the disadvantages which inhered in an attempt to bind together thirteen disparate communities. The story of these endeavors is a long and devious one, bringing to light many instances of discord and harmony, of good faith and broken pledges, which should go far toward revealing the secret springs of human action.

The trading communities of New England and New York took the lead in the movement, Philadelphia hanging back at first; and it was not until 1769 that the co-operation of the plantation provinces was secured. In the trading centers of the commercial provinces several stages were clearly apparent in the development of organized efforts for boycott against Great Britain: the initial movement promoted by town meetings in New England for the purpose of effecting a non-consumption of certain imports from Britain; second, the efforts, futile in their outcome, for a non-importation league of the merchants of the great northern seaports; third, the period in which the merchants of the great towns entered into non-importation agreements independently of each other; fourth, the renewal, but without success, of efforts for a non-importation league of merchants along more comprehensive lines; fifth, the accession of the minor northern provinces to non-importation.

The first phase of the movement originated in the fall of 1767 in New England where evidences of hard times had at once become apparent, and had for its primary object a reduction of the cost of living.[1] The efforts took the form of agreements not to purchase a stated list of imported wares, and to lend all encouragement to domestic manufactures. In contrast to Stamp Act times, these agreements were not in first instance drawn up by importing merchants, but were adopted by town meetings and circulated among the people for general signing. It is clear that the framers of the agreements were not greatly concerned with the abstract question of the parliamentary right of taxation, since no town meeting placed more than one or two dutied articles on the blacklist. Indeed, the great merchant, John Hancock, ordered a consignment of dutied glass for his personal use as late as December 17, 1767, apparently without compunction.[2]

The movement received its first impulse from the action

[1] References to hard times were plentiful in New England after the passage of the Townshend Acts. The Newport merchant, George Rome, wrote to England in December, 1767, that creditors at home would lose £50,000 in Rhode Island, owing to "deluges of bankruptcies." *Bos. Eve. Post*, June 28, 1773. "A Friend to the Colony," writing in the *Prov. Gaz.*, Mch. 26, 1768, painted a doleful picture of the trade situation of Rhode Island. The *Mass. Post-Boy* of Oct. 26, 1767 spoke of "the present alarming Scarcity of Money and consequent Stagnation of Trade" and "the almost universally increasing Complaints of Debt & Poverty." It later adopted the popular slogan, "Save your Money and Save your Country." The *N. H. Gaz.*, in its issue of Nov. 13, 1767, referred to "this time of great distress and grievous complaining among tradesmen about the dullness of trade and uncommon scarcity of money."

[2] Brown, *John Hancock His Book*, p. 151.

of a Boston town meeting on October 28, 1767. A form of subscription was adopted, which attributed the prevailing commercial depression to the high war taxes, the loss of trade in late years and the many burdensome trade restrictions, the money stringency and the unfavorable balance of trade with England. The agreement pledged all who should sign it to the patronage of colonial manufactures, especially those of Massachusetts, and to the observance of frugal regulations about mourning; further, it bound all subscribers not to purchase, after December 31, 1767, a long list of imported articles.[1] In view of the Townshend duties, it was agreed that the colonial manufacture of glass and paper should receive particular encouragement. Considerable enthusiasm was aroused when townsmen present exhibited samples of starch, glue and hair powder, and of snuff equal to Kippen's best, all of which had been made in Boston. A committee was appointed to consider the feasibility of reviving the manufacture of linen in order to employ the poor of the town. Copies of the Boston agreement were ordered to be sent to every town in the province and to the chief towns of the other provinces. At Boston, the subscription rolls filled rapidly.

[1] *Bos. Post-Boy*, Oct. 26, Nov. 2, 23, 1767; also *Boston Town Records, 1758-1769*, pp. 220-225. This list was typical of a great many others, and was as follows: "Loaf Sugar, Cordage, Anchors, Coaches, Chaises and Carriages of all Sorts, Horse Furniture, Men and Womens Hatts, Mens and Womens Apparel ready made, Household Furniture, Gloves, Mens and Womens Shoes, Sole Leather, Sheathing and Deck Nails, Gold and Silver and Thread Lace of all Sorts, Gold and Silver Buttons, Wrought Plate of all Sorts, Diamond, Stone and Paste Ware, Snuff, Mustard, Clocks and Watches, Silversmiths and Jewellers Ware, Broad Cloaths that cost above 10s. per Yard, Muffs Furrs and Tippets, and all Sorts of Millenary Ware, Starch, Womens and Childrens Stays, Fire Engines, China Ware, Silk and Cotton Velvets, Gauze, Pewterers hollow Ware Linseed Oyl, Glue, Lawns, Cambricks, Silks of all Kinds for Garments, Malt Liquors & Cheese."

The Boston agreement faithfully reflected the general opinion of the community in favor of a retrenchment of expenses. Nevertheless, it did not escape without criticism. There were those who objected to the boycott of only certain enumerated articles and declared that all British imports should be included; furthermore, they urged that all persons who failed to sign the agreement should be boycotted. Others felt that at least all the duties articles should have been placed on the blacklist.[1] The chief objection was the failure of the agreement to provide against the drinking of tea, one of the duties articles.

Efforts were at once made to remedy this oversight. The newspapers teemed with articles urging the ladies, in spite of the silence of the agreement, to abandon the use of "the most luxurious and enervating article of Bohea Tea, in which so large a sum is spent annually by the American colonists."[2] A clever bit of verse, which went the rounds of the press of the commercial provinces, concluded with this appeal to the ladies:

> Throw aside your Bohea and your Green Hyson Tea,
> And all things with a new fashion duty;
> Procure a good store of the choice Labradore,
> For there'll soon be enough here to suit ye;
> These do without fear, and to all you'll appear
> Fair, charming, true, lovely and clever;
> Though the times remain darkish, young men may be sparkish,
> And love you much stronger than ever.[3]

" A Countryman " wrote piteously that in recent years he had found the expenses of living higher than ever before;

[1] "Pelopidas" and "A Friend to Britain and her Colonies," quoted by *N. Y. Journ.*, Nov. 19, Dec. 3, 1767.

[2] *Bos. Post-Boy*, Nov. 16, 1767. *Vide* quotations from the Boston press in the *N. Y. Journ.*, Nov. 12, 26, Dec. 10.

[3] *Bos. Post-Boy*, Nov. 16, 1767; *N. Y. Gaz. & Post-Boy*, Nov. 26; *Pa. Journ.*, Dec. 3.

for " there is my daughters Jemima and Keziah, two hearty trollups as any in town, forenoon and afternoon eat almost a peck of toast and butter with their Tea; and they have learned me and their mother to join them." On the authority of his doctor he held tea responsible for many modern complaints; " for you never used to hear so much of such strange disorders as people have now a days, tremblings, appoplexies, consumptions and I don't know what all." [1]

Early in December, 1767, a large number of the ladies agreed that they would use no foreign teas for a year beginning on the tenth of that month.[2] One tart dissent was entered to these proceedings. The fair writer expatiated on the depravity resulting from " hard drinking," and then asked " where the Reformation ought to begin, whether among the Gentlemen at Taverns & *Coffee Houses* where they drink scarcely any Thing but Wine and Punch; or among the Ladies at those useful Boards of Trade called Tea Tables, where it don't cost half so much to entertain half a dozen Ladies a whole Afternoon, as it does to entertain one Gentlemen only one Evening at a Tavern." [3]

The committee appointed by the town to propose measures for employing the poor reported in due time in favor of the establishment of the manufacture of duck (or sail) cloth, hitherto imported from Russia. This material could be made from either flax or hemp and thus held an advantage over linen. The committee proposed that the project be financed by public subscription; and they were authorized by the town to go ahead. Four months later, they had succeeded in collecting less than one-half of the amount

---

[1] *Bos. Gaz.*, Aug. 29, 1768. "Trahlur" in *Bos. Post-Boy*, Nov. 30, 1767, held the same view of modern ailments.

[2] *N. Y. Journ.*, Dec. 14, 1767.

[3] *Bos. Eve. Post*, Dec. 28, 1767; also *Newport Merc.*, Dec. 14.

that was necessary for making a beginning. Further efforts were unproductive; and the project was given up.¹

Reports filled the newspapers with reference to the increase and perfection of local manufactures. From grindstones and precious stones to shoes and shalloons, the gamut of praise was run. The man who made the paper which the *Boston Gazette* was printed on stated that the people of the province were so intent on saving rags for his mills that he now received more tons than he formerly did hundreds.² The theses of the graduates at Harvard were printed " on fine white Demy Paper manufactured at Milton " and the men received their degrees garbed in homespun.³ By 1770 a leading newspaper of the town declared that: " The extraordinary and very impoverishing custom of wearing deep Mourning at Funerals is now almost entirely laid aside in the Province." ⁴

The Boston plan spread rapidly to other towns of the province. By the middle of January, 1768, the names of twenty-four towns had been published, which had voted to conform to the Boston agreement.⁵ Salem alone was recorded as having refused to co-operate.⁶ At a town meeting on December 22, 1767, Boston had unanimously voted instructions to her representatives in the General Court, recommending bounties for the establishment of domestic

¹ *Bos. Town Recs.* (*1758-1769*), pp. 226-227, 230-232, 239-240, 249-250.
² *Bos. Post-Boy*, Jan. 18, 1768; *Bos. Gaz.*, Jan. 25.
³ *N. Y. Journ.*, Aug. 4, 1768.
⁴ *Bos. Gaz.*, May 7, 1770.
⁵ Abington, Ashburnham, Bolton, Braintree, Brookfield, Charlestown, Dartmouth, Dedham, Eastham, Grafton, Harwich, Holleston, Kingston, Leicester, Lexington, Middleborough, Milton, Mendon, Newton, Plymouth, Roxbury, Sandwich, Spencer, Truro. *Bos. Post-Boy*, Nov. 23, Dec. 14, 1767; *Bos. Gaz.*, Jan. 11, Mch. 28, 1768; *N. Y. Journ.*, Dec. 3, 24, 1767, Jan. 28, 1768; *Prov. Gaz.*, Dec. 26, 1767.
⁶ *Bos. Eve. Post*, Dec. 21, 1767.

COMMERCIAL REFORM 111

manufactures, and suggesting a petition to Parliament for the repeal of the recent duties.[1] On February 11, 1768, the House of Representatives adopted the famous circular letter to the other assemblies on the continent, suggesting concerted opposition in the way of constitutional discussions and petitions. In the latter days of the month, other resolutions were passed, reciting the decay of trade and pledging the support of all the members against the use of foreign superfluities and in favor of Massachusetts manufactures.[2] The House also sent resolutions of protest against the Townshend Acts to the king.

Two other New England provinces followed in the wake of Boston. The letter of the Boston selectmen, announcing the non-consumption agreement and suggesting like measures, convinced towns outside of Massachusetts of the wisdom of pursuing a similar course. The people of Rhode Island were in particularly hard straits, due to the diminished profits of rum production and the falling-off of the carrying trade.[3] Providence, the second port of Rhode Island, was the first town to act. At a town meeting on December 2, 1767, largely attended by merchants and persons of wealth, a more stringent agreement was adopted than that of Boston. In place of a resolution of mere non-consumption, it was agreed not to import, after January 1, 1768, a list of articles which exceeded the Boston list by twelve items. The agreement contained a pledge against the use of any teas, chinaware or spices, a resolution against expensive mourning, and one favorable to wool and flax production. The compact was to be enforced by a dis-

[1] *Bos. Post-Boy*, Dec. 28, 1767; also *Bos. Town Recs.* (1758-1769), pp. 227-230.
[2] These resolutions passed by a vote of eighty-one to one. *Bos. Gaz.*, Feb. 29, 1768; also *N. Y. Journ.*, Mch. 10.
[3] *E. g., vide* "A Friend to this Colony," *Prov. Gaz.*, Nov. 14, 1767.

countenancing, " in the most effectual but decent and lawful Manner," of any person who failed to sign or conform to these regulations. A few weeks later, the subscription rolls were reported to be filling rapidly.[1]

Two days after the action of Providence, a town meeting at Newport adopted an agreement of non-consumption, modeled very closely on that of Boston, save that it was to become effective one month later. Mourning resolutions were also adopted.[2] In the following two months, the Newport agreement was concurred in by other Rhode Island towns, including Middletown, Little Compton and Tiverton.[3]

" Liber Nov-Anglus," writing in the *Connecticut Journal,* December 25, 1767, was one of the first to urge the Boston agreement on the people of Connecticut. The larger towns soon began to take action, Norwich leading the way. In the subsequent weeks, non-consumption agreements, patterned more or less after the Boston plan, were adopted by town meetings at New London, Windham, Mansfield and New Haven.[4] In both Rhode Island and Connecticut, the newspapers gave abundant evidence of the wide drinking of " Labradore or Hyperion tea," and of increased activity in the production of homespun.[5] The *Newport Mercury* inserted, free of charge, all advertisements of Rhode Island textiles.

Owing perhaps to the fact that the movement in New England was engineered by town meetings, it did not spread

[1] *Prov. Gaz.,* Nov. 14, 28, Dec. 5, 12, 1767; *Newport Merc.,* Dec. 14.

[2] *Newport Merc.,* Nov. 30, Dec. 7, 1767; *Prov. Gaz.,* Dec. 12.

[3] *Newport Merc.,* Jan. 25, Feb. 29, 1768.

[4] *Prov. Gaz.,* Dec. 26, 1767; *N. Y. Journ.,* Feb. 11, Mch. 17, 1768; *Bos. Gaz.,* Feb. 15, Mch. 28; *Newport Merc.,* Feb. 15.

[5] *Newport Merc.,* Dec. 7, 1767, Jan. 11, 18, 25, 1768; *New London Gaz.,* Dec. 18, 1767; *N. H. Gaz.,* Mch. 11, 1768; *N. Y. Journ.,* Jan. 28, Feb. 18.

in its present form to any of the other commercial provinces, where those potent agencies of local opinion did not exist. The interest of the people at New York and Philadelphia was aroused, however. "A Tradesman," writing in the *New York Journal,* December 17, 1767, asked pertinently why the example of Boston had not been followed by New York. "Are our Circumstances altered?" he asked. "Is Money grown more plenty? Have our Tradesmen full Employment? Are we more Frugal? Is Grain cheaper? Are our Importations less?" On December 29, 1767, a public meeting was held, and a committee was appointed to report on a plan for retrenching expenses and for employing local tradesmen and the deserving poor. At a meeting on February 2, 1768, the report of the committee was approved, and instructions were given for carrying it into execution.[1] Contemporary records do not reveal the nature of the New York plan; but it is probable that it did not include an agreement of non-consumption. A public meeting, held at Philadelphia to discuss the action of Boston, did not venture further than to vote an expression of sympathy for that city.[2]

By the beginning of spring, 1768, it was apparent to all interested that the sumptuary regulations of the New England towns would fail to secure relief from the hard times. The non-mercantile elements of the population were not, as yet, sufficiently co-ordinated or self-conscious to secure obedience to their mandates; and the merchants hesitated to lend their support until they had assurance that their brethren down the coast would unite in the measure.[3]

[1] *N. Y. Journ.,* Jan. 23, 28, Feb. 4, 1768.
[2] Dickinson, *Writings* (Ford), vol. i, pp. 409-410.
[3] "Few of the trading part have subscribed," wrote Andrew Eliot, of Boston, with reference to the agreement on Dec. 10, 1767. *4 M. H. S.*

Without such an understanding, they felt that their own self-denial would have no other result than to deliver up their customers to their competitors at New York and Philadelphia. Meantime, importations continued as before, though in somewhat lessened degree.

The basis for an appeal for a non-importation plan of a wider geographical scope was supplied by "The Letters from a Farmer in Pennsylvania," which were published serially in the newspapers of the various provinces during December, 1767, and through the first two months of 1768.[1] The author, in language more legalistic than bucolic, reminded the Americans of the success of the legislative petitions and non-importation agreements in effecting the repeal of the Stamp Act, and exhorted them to revive those agencies of protest. These articles were read everywhere and helped to prepare the public mind for the mercantile opposition of the next few years.

The Boston merchants now took active steps to bring about a non-importation league of the leading ports. The body of the merchants were moved by the necessity of commercial reform; but individuals were not unmindful of the fact that a suspension of trade would enable them to clean out their old stock at monopoly prices.[2] At the instigation of Captain Daniel Malcom, a notorious smuggler, and a few others, the merchants and traders gathered at the British Coffee-House on the evening of March 1, 1768 "to consult on proper Measures relative to our Trade under its present Embarrassments."[3] At this and several subsequent meet-

Colls., vol. iv, p. 418. The leaders of the non-consumption movement consist "chiefly of persons who have no property to lose," declared "A Trader" in the *Bos. Eve. Post*, Oct. 12, 1767.

[1] The text has been reprinted in Dickinson, *Writings* (Ford), vol. i, pp. 305-406.

[2] *Bos. Post-Boy*, Sept. 28, 1767.

[3] *Bos. Gaz.*, Feb. 29, 1768. "This may be said to be the first Move-

ings, an agreement was drawn up and adopted, which pledged all merchants who should sign it, to refrain for one year from importing merchandise from Great Britain (save such as was absolutely necessary for the fisheries) in case the merchants at New York and Philadelphia should take like action. This conditional agreement was circulated about Boston and was almost universally signed by the merchants. The merchants of Salem, Marblehead and Gloucester concurred in the same measure.[1]

Events now awaited the action of the merchants at New York and Philadelphia. At the former port, several meetings of the merchants and traders were held early in April to consider the matter. About the middle of the month, an agreement was adopted to import no goods shipped from Great Britain after October 1, 1768 until the Townshend duties should be repealed, provided that Boston should continue and Philadelphia adopt similar measures by the second Tuesday of June.[2]

ment of the Merchants against the Acts of Parliament," Governor Bernard told Hillsborough in a letter of Mch. 21, 1768. *Bos. Eve. Post,* Aug. 21, 1769.

[1] The chief facts concerning this agreement of Boston and the other towns may be found in: *4 M. H. S. Colls.,* vol. iv, pp. 350-351; *M. H. S. Mss., 91 L,* p. 37, 70-74; *Bos. Gaz.,* Feb. 29, Mch. 7, 1768; Bernard to Hillsborough, *Bos. Eve. Post,* Aug. 21, 1769. The merchants of Portsmouth, N. H., refused to accede to this agreement. *Brit. Papers* ("*Sparks Mss.*"), vol. i, pp. 7-8.

[2] *N. Y. Gaz. & Merc.,* Apr. 18, 1768; *N. Y. Journ.,* June 28, 1770. The terms of this agreement had not been formulated without considerable difference of opinion. Some of the more radical merchants wished to include the Quartering Act with the Townshend duties as the object of the non-importation. But this proposal was rejected by the majority. Others insisted that the Boston plan of immediate non-importation should be followed, for the six months' interval would enable unscrupulous men to enlarge their orders and defeat the purpose of the agreement. This again met with little favor. Article by "G" in *ibid.,* Apr. 21, 1768.

The agreement was signed by every merchant and trader in New York, save two or three unimportant ones, within less than two days. Another outcome of the conferences of the merchants was the formation of the New York Chamber of Commerce, with the avowed purpose of encouraging commerce and industry and of procuring better trade laws.[1] The Committee of Merchants at Boston were informed of the New York agreement; and an answer was returned that, although the Boston merchants considered the New Yorkers mistaken in not stopping trade immediately, nevertheless, for the sake of unanimity, they would accept their proposal.[2]

In Philadelphia, the movement for co-operation with Boston and New York was devoid of any real vitality, notwithstanding that the great proponent of non-importation, John Dickinson, was an influential citizen of that place. The merchants as a whole did not yet suffer from the trade embarrassments, which the sea ports farther north were experiencing or which they themselves had experienced during the critical years 1764-1766.[3] "A. B." represented the merchants' point of view in a set of queries in the *Pennsylvania Chronicle*, July 25, 1768. The anonymous author, probably Joseph Galloway, questioned the wisdom of severing commercial connections with England except in

[1] *Bos. News-Letter*, Jan. 5, 1769; *Memorial History of the City of New York* (Wilson, J. G., ed.), vol. iv, p. 516.

[2] Letter of N. Y. Merchants' Committee to Philadelphia Committee, *N. Y. Journ.*, June 28, 1770. The Boston meeting to consider the New York proposal was probably held on May 2. *Bos. Gaz.*, May 2, 1768.

[3] Dickinson's "Farmer's Letters," in contrast to his pamphlet against "The Late Regulations" of 1764-1765, made no claim to severe times; and only a few articles in the newspapers spoke of business stagnation and currency stringency or advocated local manufactures, thus "Philo-Patriae" in *Pa. Chron.*, Dec. 2, 1767; "Lover of Pennsylvania" in *ibid.*, Jan. 4, 11, 1768; "Freeborn American" and "Monitor" in *Pa. Gaz.*, Feb. 9, Apr. 14, 1768.

cases of dire necessity, for he declared that all the wool in North America would not supply the colonists with hats and stockings alone. Among his queries were these: Had the merchants in their letters to England done all they could to induce the mercantile houses there to agitate for repeal? If the merchants should take action, ought not non-importation to be restricted to dutied imports alone? Was the provincial legislature not the proper body to take cognizance of the situation, and would anarchy not ensue from the adoption of other measures? Even if it were prudent for New England merchants to resort to non-importation, might it not be imprudent for Pennsylvania and other provinces where the circumstances differed widely? Was it consistent with the rights of mankind for one province to insist that another should adopt its measures, more especially for a people who called themselves " Sons of Liberty "?

" A Chester County Farmer " claimed that the farmers would be slow to be inveigled into local manufacturing again after their experience during Stamp Act days, for the " ill-timed Resolution," made at the time of the repeal, to cast aside all homespun, had dealt a staggering blow to the people who had invested their capital in pastures, sheep, looms, spinners, *etc.*[1] The situation was further complicated by the long-standing local controversy over the desirability of continuing the proprietary government.[2] A meeting of the merchants and traders of Philadelphia was held on March 26, 1768, to act upon the proposal of the Boston merchants. The Boston letter was not favor-

[1] *Pa. Gaz.*, June 16, 1768. It should be noted that the pseudonym was another one of Joseph Galloway's, according to Ford in his edition of Dickinson's *Writings*, vol. i, p. 435.

[2] " A. L." in *Pa. Chron.*, May 30, 1768. In this controversy Galloway and Dickinson were the local leaders of the royal and proprietary parties respectively.

ably received and, after a heated debate, the meeting adjourned without taking action.[1]

On April 25, John Dickinson addressed a merchants' meeting in order to induce favorable action. He first dwelt eloquently on the effort of Great Britain to check the industrial and commercial development of the colonies. He cited the prohibition of steel furnaces and slitting mills, the acts against the exportation of hats and woolens, the requirement of exporting logwood by way of England, and the heavy restraints on the wine trade. He maintained that the acts of trade compelled the colonists to pay twenty to forty per cent higher for goods from England than they could be gotten from other countries. He then reviewed the Quartering Act and the Townshend Acts and showed that their tendency was to diminish the control of the people over their provincial governments, *i. e.* their "Liberty." "As Liberty is the great and only Security of Property; as the Security of Property is the chief Spur to Industry," he urged the merchants to join with Boston and New York, to forego a present advantage, and to stop importation from Britain until the unconstitutional acts were repealed.[2]

Remaining unconvinced by these appeals to an alleged self-interest, the merchants were fiercely assailed from another angle. Under the signature of "A Freeborn American," Charles Thomson, himself not disinterested in his cause as an iron manufacturer and distiller, quoted the

---

[1] Dickinson, *Writings* (Ford), vol. i, p. 410; *Pa. Gaz.*, Mch. 31, 1768.

[2] *Pa. Journ.*, Apr. 28, 1768; also Dickinson, *Writings* (Ford), vol. i, pp. 411-417. On the same day as Dickinson's speech, the *Pennsylvania Chronicle* contained an able article entitled, "Causes of the American Discontents before 1768," written by Benjamin Franklin under the signature "F. and S." This was a trenchant analysis covering many of the same points, and had been published originally for English consumption in the *London Chronicle*, Jan. 7, 1768. Franklin, *Writings* (Smyth), vol. v, pp. 78-89.

words of the " Pennsylvania Farmer " to the effect that: " A people is travelling fast to destruction, when individuals consider their interests as distinct from those of the public." The merchants were told that the eyes of their customers, as well as of God, had been on them expectantly for a long time; and that eagerness for a few pence or pounds should not deter them from joining strength with Boston and New York.[1] A contributor in the *Pennsylvania Gazette* of June 2 urged that the people of the city take affairs into their own hands and agree to buy only American manufactures. A few days later, the merchants received a letter from the Committee of Merchants at New York, reminding them that, unless they adopted non-importation by June 14, the merchants of New York and Boston would be absolved from their agreements.[2] The Philadelphia merchants remained unmoved; the appointed day arrived and passed; and the project of a non-importation league of the great trading towns collapsed.

The delinquency of the merchants occasioned a most virulent attack on their motives by John Dickinson in the form of a broadside, entitled " A Copy of a Letter from a Gentleman of Virginia to a Merchant in Philadelphia." The manuscript copy, which the printer used in getting up the broadside, was in the handwriting of a third person, making it evident, so the editor of Dickinson's *Writings* thinks, that Dickinson desired to conceal his connection with it. The writer did not mince words in charging that the merchants were actuated by self-interest. During the Stamp Act, when their " Patriotism and private Interests "

[1] *Pa. Gaz.*, May 12, 1768. Ford, *op. cit.*, vol. i, p. 435, ascribes the pseudonym to Thomson.
[2] Letter of June 6, 1768; *N. Y. Journ.*, June 28, 1770.

were intimately connected, the merchants had entered into a non-importation agreement, he said. But they had been able to shift the burden of the Townshend taxes on their customers, and the abstract question of right did not concern them. The principle involved they considered of slight importance as compared with their personal comfort and profit.[1]

The failure to bring about a non-importation union placed the Boston merchants in the dilemma of either resigning themselves nervelessly to business depression or pursuing a vigorous course independently of the other great ports. After one or two meetings for discussion, the merchants chose the latter alternative in an agreement drawn up August 1, 1768.[2] The preamble attributed the commercial distress to money stringency—a condition growing daily more severe because of "the large Sums collected by the Officers of the Customs for Duties on Goods imported," to restrictions on trade laid by the recent acts of Parliament, to the heavy war taxes, and to bad success in the cod and whale fisheries. All subscribers of the agreement pledged themselves to send no further orders for fall goods, to discontinue all importations from Great Britain for one year beginning January 1, 1769,[3] except coal, woolcards, duck, cardwire, shot, and four or five articles necessary for carrying on the fisheries, and to cease the importation of tea, glass, paper and painters' colors until the duties on them should be removed. Several days later,

---

[1] *Writings*, vol. i, pp. 435-445.

[2] *Mass. Gaz. & News-Letter*, Nov. 17, 1769; *Bos. Gaz.*, July 25, Aug. 1, 8, 15, 1768; *Bos. Post-Boy*, May 8, 1769; *Bos. Eve. Post*, May 8, 1769; Hosmer, *Hutchinson*, p. 432; Brown, *John Hancock His Book*, p. 163.

[3] At a meeting on Oct. 17, 1769, the merchants removed the one-year limitation and made the period of operation contingent upon the repeal of the Townshend duties. *Mass. Gaz. & News-Letter*, Nov. 9, 17, 1769.

Hutchinson informed an English friend that all the merchants in town, save only sixteen, had signed the agreement.

The example of the Boston merchants stimulated the other trading towns of the province to emulation. Within the next few months, agreements were signed by the merchants of Salem, Plymouth, Cape Ann and Nantucket. Marblehead, somewhat belated, joined in October of the following year.[1] New vigor was also injected into the movement for the non-consumption of tea. The *Boston Gazette* reported " from the best Authority " that fifteen hundred families of Boston had relinquished the use of tea, and that most of the inhabitants of Charlestown, Lexington, Dedham, Weymouth and Hingham, as well as the students at Harvard, had done likewise.[2] The Boston town meeting revived its efforts to provide work for the poor of the town, " whose Numbers and distresses are dayly increasing by the loss of its Trade & Commerce." Rejecting the earlier plan of a popular subscription, the town, on March 13, 1769, voted a subsidy out of town funds for a free spinning school, and placed it under charge of William Molineux. The venture proved sufficiently successful for the town meeting, three years later, to vote thanks to the manager for the faithful performance of his duties.[3]

Within a year of the date of the merchants' agreement, news reached Boston that the ministry was prepared to yield up all the Townshend duties except the tax on tea;[4] and the merchants were forced to consider whether it was

---

[1] *Essex Gaz.*, Sept. 6, 1768; *N. Y. Journ.*, June 22, 1769; *Mass. Gaz. & News-Letter*, Nov. 2, 1769.

[2] Issues of Oct. 24, 1768; Mch. 27, 1769.

[3] *Bos. Town Recs.* (*1758-1769*), pp. 273-277; *ibid.* (*1770-1777*), p. 73.

[4] Hillsborough's circular letter of May 13, 1769. *N. Y. Col. Docs.*, vol. viii, pp. 164-165.

worth while to continue the controversy under the circumstances. On July 26, 1769, they voted unanimously that such a partial repeal would by no means relieve the trade situation and was designed to prevent the establishment of colonial manufactures. At this meeting and a succeeding one of August 11, they materially strengthened the enforcement feature of the non-importation agreement by providing for a boycott of all vessels and all merchants dealing in merchandise proscribed by the agreement. At the same time, the list of articles which might be imported was somewhat extended.[1] They agreed, further, on October 17, that, if any British merchandise should be consigned to them on commission, they would either refuse to receive it or ship it back at the first opportunity.[2] A paper was also circulated among the inhabitants of Boston, pledging them to buy no goods imported contrary to the merchants' agreement, and to support the merchants in any further efforts to render the measures effectual.[3]

Meantime, domestic manufacturing entered a new stage: spinning was taken up by women's circles in churches all over New England and thus popularized as a social diversion. The atrabilious Peter Oliver declared: " The female spinners kept on spinning six Days of the Week; and on the seventh, the Parsons took their turns and spun out their prayers and sermons to a long thread of Politics."[4] From

---

[1] *Mass. Gaz.*, July 31, 1769; *Bos. Gaz.*, Aug. 14. In a meeting on April 27, the merchants had already resolved to buy of no one articles which were imported, contrary to the agreement, from Great Britain or any province. *Ibid.*, May 1.

[2] *Mass. Gaz. & News Letter*, Nov. 9, 17, 1769.

[3] *M. H. S. Ms.:* 151, 1, 15. With a similar purpose in view, the vendue-masters and brokers signed an agreement not to handle any goods debarred by the merchants' agreement. *Bos. Gaz.*, Aug. 21, 1769.

[4] *Brit. Mus., Egerton Mss.*, no. 2671 (*L. C. Transcripts*).

January to September, 1769, twenty-eight spinning bees were noted in the newspapers; and this probably represented a fraction of the entire number held. Many instances of individual industry were cited; and the little town of Middletown, Mass., established a record of weaving 20,522 yards of cloth in the year 1769, an average of more than forty yards for every adult and child in the population.[1] Money prizes were occasionally offered for the making of textiles; and efforts were even made to foster silk culture in this way.[2] All this pother resulted in some progress toward a greater independence of imported textiles.[3]

Nevertheless, it is clear that the people were interested only in tiding over a difficult period and not in laying the foundations of permanent industries. It was an exceptional case when men, like Upham and his associates at Brookfield, Mass., " erected a Building 50 Feet in Length and two Stories high, for a Manufactory House," and installed looms and collected workmen for the weaving of woolens.[4] Manufacturing enterprises, which would, in all probability, collapse the moment trade with England was renewed, did not appeal as attractive investments to men of capital; and as a class they refused to lend support.[5] The news-

[1] *Mass. Gaz. & Post-Boy*, Mch. 12, 1770.

[2] *Bos. Gaz.*, Apr. 10, Oct. 16, 1769; May 1, 1770.

[3] Note, for example, the articles offered for sale by John Gore, Jr., in the *Boston Gazette*, June 12, 1769: " North-American Manufactures, viz Blue, black, claret coloured and mix'd Cloths, Whilton mix'd Cotton and Linnen, masqueraded ditto, superfine mix'd double Camblet for Mens Summer or Womens Winter Ware, half-yard and 3 qr Diaper, fine 7-8th Nutfield Linnen, fine Hatfield Thread, Mens ribb'd worsted Hose, white cotton and linnen Tow-cloth, Lynn Shoes, Pole Combs, Cards, &c. N. B. All sorts of Mens and Womens Ware manufactured in New England, taken in Exchange for English Goods."

[4] *Bos. Gaz.*, Oct. 3, 1768. For a similar enterprise, *vide* the advertisement of Thomas Mewse in *Bos. Post-Boy*, Sept. 11, 1769.

[5] *E. g., vide* article by " A. Z." and an advertisement of Charles Miller in *Bos. Gaz.*, Feb. 20, 1769.

papers of New England and elsewhere made a great fuss over local manufactures; and it was no doubt the propagandist character of such notices that caused many Americans to refer to them as "great puffs" and "newspaper manufactures."[1]

Not many days elapsed after the first merchants' agreement of Boston before the New York merchants decided to take a similar stand. On August 27, 1768, an agreement was signed by nearly all the merchants and traders, which was more stringent in its terms than the Boston agreement. The subscribers were obligated to countermand all orders sent to England after August 15 and to cease the importation of goods shipped from Great Britain after November 1, until the Townshend duties should be repealed.[2] Some concession was made to the criticism that the project was promoted chiefly by smuggling merchants, by providing that no goods should be imported from Hamburg and Holland, directly or indirectly, other than had already been ordered, except tiles and bricks.[3] Any goods sent over contrary to the agreement were to be stored in a public warehouse until the Townshend duties were repealed. Finally, it was provided that any subscribers who violated the agreement should be deemed "Enemies to their Country."

A few days later, the tradesmen of the city signed an agreement to withhold patronage from all merchants, who refused to sign or to obey the merchants' agreement, and

[1] Franklin, *Writings* (Smyth), vol. v, p. 116; "True Patriot" in *Bos. Eve. Post*, Nov. 23, 1767.

[2] *N. Y. Gaz. & Merc.*, Mch. 13, 1769; also *N. Y. Journ.*, Sept. 8, 1768. Excepted from this general prohibition were: coal, salt, sail cloth, woolcards, card-wire, grindstones, chalk, lead, tin, sheet-copper and German steel.

[3] This list of exceptions was later extended to include corn-fans, millstones, and all those articles which were permitted to be imported from Great Britain.

from any European mercantile houses that imported contrary to the agreement.[1] The importers at Albany concurred in the New York merchants' agreement, not, however, without protest from some of the merchants on the score that the importation of goods for the Indian trade should be continued.[2] Some of the small inland towns resolved to buy no British or Scotch goods.[3] On April 10, 1769, the provincial House of Representatives, on motion of Philip Livingston, an eminent merchant of the city, passed a vote of thanks to the merchants of the city and province for their patriotic conduct in declining importation from Great Britain.[4] Andrew Oliver, of Boston, wrote from New York on August 12, 1769, that, although his business there led him to associate with the best citizens, they universally approved of the non-importation combination, an attitude which appeared to him " little less than assuming a negative on all acts of parliament which they do not like." [5]

On September 1, 1768, the Committee of Merchants of New York sent a copy of their agreement to the Philadelphia merchants, explaining that it was " widely different " from the Boston plan, then in operation, in that its binding force extended to the repeal of the Townshend duties, and trusting that they would now feel free to enter into a similar compact.[6] Newspaper contributors at Philadelphia

[1] *N. Y. Journ.*, Sept. 15, 1768. This agreement was dated September 5.
[2] *N. Y. Gaz. & Merc.*, Aug. 14, 1769.
[3] *N. Y. Gaz. & Post-Boy*, July 31, 1769.
[4] *N. Y. Col. Docs.*, vol. viii, pp. 194-195.
[5] *N. Y. Journ.*, July 29, 1773.
[6] Ms. in Historical Society of Pennsylvania. The original Boston agreement was to last for one year beginning January 1, 1769. This clause was changed to correspond with the New York provision on October 17, 1769.

were again fired by the example of the trading towns to the north; and "Tradesman," "Agricola" and others lent their persuasive pens to pleas for non-importation and non-consumption regulations.[1] Letters from correspondents in London urged these steps, also.[2]

The great Quaker merchants dominated the situation; and they were determined not to resort to trade suspension until all ordinary means of obtaining redress had been exhausted. In accord with their wishes, the Pennsylvania Assembly, on September 22, 1768, sent petitions to the king and to the houses of Parliament, praying for a repeal of the Townshend Acts. They based their plea on their claim to constitutional exemption from parliamentary taxation; it was not deemed necessary to include arguments against the economic expediency of the British measures.

The merchants continued to betray no outward signs of activity. Their apparent callousness provoked a bitter article in the *New York Journal*, October 10, 1768, signed by "A North American," charging a few drygoods merchants of Philadelphia with preventing an agreement there. Shall a few selfish, dastardly merchants, it was asked, be permitted to defy the desires of the vast majority of the people and defeat a great public purpose? Under sting of this attack, the merchants began to grow restive. An inspired contributor, "Philadelphus," disclosed to the public the true condition of affairs.[3] As soon as they had been informed of the Boston agreement, the Philadelphia merchants had appointed a committee to canvass a similar proposal. The committee labored in vain to obtain a general concurrence, and then concentrated its efforts on enlisting

---

[1] *Pa. Chron.*, Oct. 10, Nov. 28, 1768; *Pa. Journ.*, Jan. 26, 1769.
[2] *Pa. Journ.*, Jan. 26, Apr. 6, 13, 1769.
[3] *Pa. Gaz.*, Oct. 20, 1768.

the support of eight or ten mercantile firms, whose backing would give prestige to the project. None of these firms would go further than to recommend a non-importation of dutied articles and certain luxuries; and this proposal was rejected by the committee as unsatisfactory. On September 22, the committee had called a general meeting of merchants and traders; but, as not one-fourth of the drygoods merchants attended, this was deemed conclusive that the majority disapproved of a general non-importation.

The disposition of the merchants and of conservative-thinking people generally was to await the result of the legislative petitions.[1] But, within two weeks after " Philadelphus " spoke, the merchants were moved to send a memorial of their own to the merchants and manufacturers of Great Britain, representing the deplorable situation of trade. The idea was to prod the British business interests to bring pressure to bear upon Parliament. The memorial was sent on November 1, 1768; it was conservative in tone. The British merchants and manufacturers were asked to solicit a repeal of the statutes imposing the anti-commercial and unconstitutional Townshend duties and to obtain " further relief from the other Burthens which the American trade has long laboured under." It was affirmed as " a Solemn Truth " that, if the various discouragements to trade continued unabated, the Americans must, " from necessity if not from Motives of Interest," establish their own manufactures and curtail importations. The memorial further stated that many of the present trade restrictions had been complained of by the Philadelphia merchants in their petition of November, 1765. The chief grievances, other than the Townshend duties, were declared to be: the

[1] Letter of Philadelphia Merchants' Committee to London Merchants' Committee, *London Chron.*, June 10, 1769; also *Pa. Mag.*, vol. xxvii, pp. 84-87.

prohibition of paper money as a legal tender; the heavy duty on Madeira wine which barred it as an article of exchange with England; the unnecessary trouble and expense incurred by the roundabout shipment of Portuguese wines and fruit to America through England; the prohibition against exporting American bar iron to continental Europe; and the regulation which classified all sugars imported from the American continent into England as foreign and thus deprived the colonists of an advantageous remittance.[1]

The transmission of the memorial was followed by a lull in public interest in the non-importation question, for the signers of the memorial pledged themselves to adopt non-importation in the spring, provided their appeal met with no success.[2] Early in February, 1769, various fire companies in the city adopted resolutions to abstain from buying mutton, as a measure to aid the woolen manufactures; and a number of citizens asserted their independence of English fashions by agreeing to wear leather jackets thereafter.[3]

Events now forced the commercial class to take more decisive action. Several merchants were planning to send orders for fall goods by a vessel which departed for England in the middle of February. As no information had yet been received of remedial measures by Parliament, the body of merchants apprehended that these orders might seriously complicate the non-importation agreement, to which they were conditionally pledged for the spring. Meeting together on February 6, they resolved that all orders, already sent for fall goods, should be cancelled unless the goods be

[1] *Pub. Rec. Office: C. O. 5*, no. 114 (*L. C. Transcripts*), pp. 161-169.
[2] *Papers of the Merchants of Philadelphia* ("*Sparks Mss.*," vol. lxii, sub-vol. vii), pp. 1-2.
[3] *Pa. Journ.*, Feb. 9, 16, Mch. 16, 1769; *Pa. Chron.*, Feb. 20.

shipped before April 1, and that no further orders be sent before March 10, by which time they expected to learn definitely of the outcome of their memorial.[1] News soon arrived that the hopes of the petitioners had been misplaced. The London merchants professed to be willing to use their influence for repeal; but, on the advice of Burke and other of their friends in Parliament, they had been convinced that it was an unpropitious time to press the matter. They regretfully informed the Philadelphia merchants of their determination.[2]

March the tenth arrived and the merchants took the final step. Justifying their action as a consequence of heavy debts and the ruinous effects of the revenue acts, and as the only means of stimulating their British creditors to activity for repeal, they adopted an agreement to import no goods shipped after April 1 from Great Britain, until the Townshend duties should be repealed, except twenty-two articles useful for local manufacturing, ship-ballast and medicinal and educational purposes. With the apparent purpose of denying special advantages to smugglers, these conditions were extended to include imports from the rest of Europe, except linens and provisions directly from Ireland. The subscribers of the agreement were pledged to buy no goods imported contrary to the agreement, and to discountenance " by all lawful and prudent measures " any person who defied the agreement. The agreement was to continue until the repeal of the Townshend duties or until

[1] *Papers of Phila. Merchants*, pp. 1-2. For a countermanding order of Stephen Collins under this agreement, *vide* his *Letter-Book 1760-1773* (L. C. Mss.) under date of February 6.

[2] *Col. Soc. Mass. Pubs.*, vol. xiii, pp. 355-356; *Papers of Phila. Merchants*, p. 7. For an explanation of their failure to urge the petition in the subsequent months, *vide Franklin Papers, Misc.* (L. C. Mss.), vol. i, no. 71; and *Pa. Journ.*, May 4, 1769.

a general meeting of the subscribers should determine otherwise.[1] The paper was circulated among the merchants and traders of the city and " a very great majority " signed in the course of the next few weeks. At a later meeting, it was determined that goods arriving at Philadelphia contrary to the agreement should not be stored but be sent back. The principle of the boycott was further extended: any person violating the word or spirit of the agreement should be stigmatized " an Enemy of the Liberties of America," and it was held proper that his name should be published in the newspapers.[2]

No conspicuous activity in local manufacturing was displayed until the high price of imported goods, produced by the non-importation regulation, caused people to turn their energies in that direction.[3] Even then their activity was not comparable with that of the provinces farther north. A report to the American Philosophical Society showed that, in the little town of Lancaster, fifty looms and seven hundred spinning-wheels were in constant use. In the twelvemonth beginning May 1, 1769, the net output was close to thirty-five thousand yards.[4] An effort was made to foster the production of domestic silks. In 1769 sixty-four families raised silkworms, many of them raising from ten to twenty thousand; but little benefit came of the venture because of the inexpertness of the people in reeling the silk. To overcome this obstacle, a number of citizens subscribed £250, in March, 1770, for the erection of a filature. Some of the

---

[1] *Papers of Phila. Merchants*, pp. 2-5, 19-21. For orders for all kinds of goods, to be shipped when the revenue acts were repealed, *vide* Stephen Collins's *Letter-Book 1760-1773*, under the dates Mch. 12, 15, Sept. 23, Oct. 14, Nov. 6, 25, Dec. 11, 12, 1769; Apr. 7, 1770.

[2] August 2, 1769. *Pa. Gaz.*, Aug. 3, 1769.

[3] *Pa. Chron.*, July 24, 1769. Article by "A Merchant."

[4] *Pa. Gaz.*, June 14, 1770; also *Gentleman's Magazine* (1770), p. 348.

leading merchants of the city were chosen on the board of managers; and by November, 1771, one hundred and fifty-five pounds of raw silk had been exported to England. The Society for the Promotion of Silk Culture offered annual premiums for silk production until the outbreak of the war.[1]

By the spring of 1769, the three great ports had finally united in non-importation measures against the mother country, Philadelphia acting tardily about six months later than the merchants of Boston and New York. This consummation soon prompted the progressive merchants of Boston to urge on their brethren more radical measures for trade redemption. The Townshend revenue acts, against which all the existing agreements were directed, represented only one source of mercantile distress. The wine duties and the revised duty on molasses drew from them considerably more cash than the imposts of 1767,[2] and violated as seriously the new American notion of the unconstitutional character of revenue tariffs. The New Englanders realized that the mere repeal of the Townshend duties would not restore their prosperity; and, despite the fact that they had failed to denominate the earlier taxes as unconstitutional in their petition of January, 1767, they now decided to take an advanced stand in conformity with the recent developments in colonial theory. In a letter of September 2, 1769, they pressed the merchants of Philadelphia to extend their agreement to comprehend the repeal of *all* revenue acts,

---

[1] *Pa. Gaz.*, Mch. 15, 22, 1770, and *passim* to 1775; *Franklin Bicentennial Celebration*, vol. ii, p. 126; *Pa. Mag.*, vol. xxvi, pp. 304-305.

[2] For all the colonies, the Townshend duties on tea, *etc.*, amounted to £17,912 in the period from September 8, 1767 to January 3, 1770. In the same length of time, the wine duties (6 George II and 4 George III) amounted to £20,130, and the molasses duty (6 George III) to £22,652. Channing, *History of U. S.*, vol. iii, p. 90 n.

including the molasses and wine duties; and they revised their own agreement on October 17 to incorporate the new demands.¹ A letter of October 25 carried the news of the new agreement to Philadelphia, with an urgent plea for similar action there. It was probably not a coincidence that John Hancock was in Philadelphia at this time for the express purpose of visiting the author of the "Farmer's Letters," who was also the great advocate of non-importation in that city.² If his visit had a political motive, his mission was a failure.

In reply to the Boston letters, the Committee of Merchants at Philadelphia admitted " that the acts of the 4th and 6th George 3rd, being expressly for the purpose of raising a revenue and containing many grievous and unreasonable burdens upon trade, are . . . as exceptionable as " the Townshend duties; and they agreed " that the design of the Merchants through the continent was not only to procure a repeal of any Single Act but to give weight to the petitions . . . of their representatives in Assembly met against the Parliament's claim to tax the Colonies and to prevent any future attempts of like Nature, that a precedent admitted will operate against us, and that an acquiescence under the acts of the 4th and 6th, even though that of the 7th of George 3d should be repealed, will be establishing a precedent." Nevertheless, they declared that, as this consideration " has unfortunately been so long neglected, our Merchants are extremely averse to making it now an object of their non-importation agreement." They refused, furthermore, to prohibit all incoming trade from Great Britain, for the reason that this restriction would simply

---

¹ *Mass. Gaz. & News-Letter*, Nov. 9, 17, 1769. This revised agreement was widely signed, only ten or twelve importers declining.

² Letter of William Palfrey; *M. H. S. Procs.*, vol. 47, pp. 2⁻1-212.

divert the trade to laxer ports. They did promise, however, that if Parliament failed to remove *all* the revenue acts, they would then be ready to unite with the other colonies " in any measure that may be thought prudent and practicable for obtaining a full redress of all grievances." [1]

The Boston proposal met with the same sort of treatment at the hands of the New York merchants;[2] and, at a meeting on December 4, the Boston merchants reluctantly yielded up their project upon a plea of the necessity for uniformity among the chief trading towns.[3]

The tangible outcome of this episode was the publication, in the same month, by the merchants of Boston, of a pamphlet, entitled *Observations on several Acts of Parliament passed in the 4th, 6th and 7th years of his present Majesty's Reign; and also on the Conduct of the Officers of the Customs since those Acts were passed, and the Board of Commissioners appointed to reside in America*.[4] This pamphlet was the clearest and strongest statement ever formulated of the position of the American merchant class, particularly that of New England. In the compass of some thirty pages

[1] These quotations are from letters of Sept. 21 and Nov. 11, 1769. *Papers of Phila. Merchants*, pp. 27-28, 37-42. In their next letter to the London Committee of Merchants, the Philadelphia Committee wrote: Though the merchants have confined their agreements to the repeal of the Townshend duties, " yet nothing less than a Repeal of all the Revenue Acts and putting Things on the same Footing they were before the late Innovations, can or will satisfy the Minds of the People." *London Chron.*, Mch. 3, 1770; also *Pa. Gaz.*, May 10.

[2] Colden, *Letter Books*, vol. ii, p. 193.

[3] *Mass. Arch.*, vol. xxvi, pp. 411, 413; *Am. Hist. Rev.*, vol. viii, pp. 313-314.

[4] *Mss. 1745-1770* (in M. H. S.), p. 15, contain the letter of the Committee of Merchants to Dennys de Berdt, explaining the inception of the pamphlet. The committee, which was appointed to draft the pamphlet, was composed of Arnold Welles, Henderson Inches, William Dennie, William Molineux and Isaac Smith. *Mass. Gaz.*, July 31, 1769.

a well-reasoned argument, buttressed with evidence, was presented for a restoration of American trade to the footing it had enjoyed before the passage of the old Molasses Act of 1733. This step, it was asserted, would unite Great Britain and the colonies on a lasting foundation and eliminate all clandestine trade. The repeal of the recent Townshend duties would not suffice; for the colonies must again enjoy the free importation of molasses, sugars and Madeira wine, and must obtain the right of a free and direct importation of fruit, wine and oil from Spain and Portugal. The acts of Parliament prior to 1764 had been intended merely as regulations of trade and, in one instance, a duty had been placed on foreign molasses in order to encourage the British West Indies; but the present statute could not be so construed, for it imposed duties on all molasses and expressly for the purpose of raising a revenue. According to the figures cited in the pamphlet, the various restraints on trade with the foreign West Indies, Africa, Madeira and Southern Europe had rendered unprofitable the employment of four hundred vessels in the fisheries, and of one hundred and eighty vessels in the lumber and provisions trade to the West Indies, not to mention the decrease in the coasting-trade and other channels of commerce. The shipbuilding industry had also been seriously affected, only one hundred vessels being built annually instead of three hundred as before the late restrictions on trade. In closing, a representation was made of the embarrassments to commerce, due to the unlimited amount of red tape required for trading voyages, and to the excessive power, officiousness and unlawful conduct of the customs officers and the Customs Board.

The non-importation movement ran a different course in the plantation provinces from that in the commercial provinces, due to the characteristic methods of doing business in each section. The marketing of the staples of the South was largely in the hands of English and Scotch merchants and factors, whose business had been very little affected by the parliamentary duties of 1766 and 1767. The planters constituted the chief discontented class, because of their losing struggle to pay the debts they owed to their mercantile creditors. Animated by a desire to curtail living expenses and to strike at their creditors, the planters assumed the initiative in promoting non-importation associations, while the southern trading class stood aloof or were actively hostile. These circumstances caused the non-importation movement to assume many of the characteristics of the non-consumption movement that had been promoted by New England town meetings in late 1767 and early 1768. As one contemporary said, the associations of the plantation provinces, besides being less restrictive than the northern agreements, " excluded a great number of articles which are mere luxuries, confin'd their importations from Britain to the necessaries of life, and thereby answered the purpose of a sumptuary law." [1]

George Washington, of Virginia, spoke of the peculiarities of the local trading situation when he transmitted a copy of the Philadelphia non-importation agreement, in a letter of April 5, 1769, to his neighbor, George Mason. He expressed approval of a non-importation plan for Virginia; but he pointed out that it could be made successful only by going over the heads of the factors and inducing the people throughout the province to buy no imported articles, except certain enumerated ones. He proposed the meeting of the Assembly in May as the best time for launching the project with any prospect of uniform action by the several counties.[2]

---

[1] *Bos. Gaz.*, Jan. 29, 1770; also *Pa. Journ.*, Feb. 15.
[2] *Writings* (Ford), vol. ii, pp. 263-267.

Mason agreed cordially with Washington's views, and yet made it clear that no plan could be enforced in the tobacco provinces unless it should be considerably more liberal in the number of importations permitted. Mason seemed to be aware of the lack of support for the measure in a well-fertilized public opinion, as in the North; and, like a good propagandist, he urged the necessity of publishing " something preparatory to it in our gazettes, to warn the people of the impending danger and to induce them the more readily and cheerfully to concur in the proper measures to avert it." He proposed also that the association should provide for the non-exportation of tobacco.[1]

The House of Burgesses convened at Williamsburg in May. Washington found ready backing for a non-importation measure among such men as Peyton Randolph, Richard Bland, Patrick Henry, Richard Henry Lee and Thomas Jefferson. But the house proceeded first to declare, in a set of resolutions, its official opinion that the sole right of taxing Virginians lay with that body and to state its objections to certain recent acts of the British administration; whereupon Governor Botetourt peremptorily dissolved the body. The members, though now divested of their legal character, met at a private house in town and, electing Peyton Randolph their chairman, promulgated a plan of non-importation.[2]

The association bore the date May 18, 1769. In the pre-

[1] Washington, *Writings* (Ford), pp. 267-268 n.
[2] *Pa. Journ.*, June 1, 1769; also *S. C. Gaz.*, July 20. This plan of association was presented by Washington; and in its essentials followed a draft, made several weeks before, by George Mason. One proposal of Mason's was rejected, however, viz., if the other measures proved ineffectual, a non-exportation of tobacco and naval supplies should go into effect. Washington, *Writings* (Ford), vol. ii, pp. 268-269 n.; Rowland, K. M., *Life of George Mason* (New York, 1892), vol. i, pp. 392-393.

amble, it was declared that the debt for British merchandise was very great and that the means of paying were becoming more and more precarious because of the restrictive legislation of Parliament, particularly the Townshend Acts. The subscribers pledged themselves never thereafter to import any goods, which were then or should thereafter be subject to a revenue duty, save paper not exceeding eight shillings per ream. They agreed, further, not to import thereafter a long list of luxuries and fineries from Great Britain or any part of Europe, this abstention to continue while the duties continued or until a general meeting of subscribers decided otherwise.[1] In all cases, orders already sent for goods might be received; and the subscribers were not restricted from buying such goods in local trade until September 1. They further agreed to buy no slaves imported after November 1. There were also resolutions to encourage frugality and to prevent the killing of lambs.

Copies of the association were carried back to the counties by the gentlemen who attended the Williamsburg meeting. One month later Washington was able to report from

[1] Certain Irish wares imported from Ireland were excluded. This blacklist was typical of similar lists in other of the plantation provinces and is here given in full: " Spirits, Wines, Cyder, Perry, Beer, Ale, Malt, Barley, Pease, Beef, Pork, Fish, Butter, Cheese, Tallow, Candles, Oil, Fruit, Sugar, Pickles, Confectionary, Pewter, Hoes, Axes, Watches, Clocks, Tables, Chairs, Looking Glasses, Carriages, Joiners and Cabinet Work of all Sorts, Upholstery of all Sorts, Trinkets and Jewellery, Plate and Gold, and Silversmith's Work of all Sorts, Ribbons and Millinery of all Sorts, Lace of all Sorts; India Goods of all Sorts, except Spices; Silks of all Sorts except Sewing Silk; Cambrick, Lawn, Muslin; Gauze except Boulting Cloths; Callico or Cotton Stuffs of more then 2s. per Yard; Linens of more than 2s. per Yard; Woollens, Worsted Stuffs of all Sorts of more than 1s. 6d. per Yard; Broad Cloths of all Kinds at more than 8s. per Yard; Narrow Cloths of all Kinds at more than 3s. per Yard; Hats; Stockings (Plaid and Irish Hose excepted); Shoes and Boots, Saddles and all Manufactures of Leather and Skins of all Kinds."

Fairfax county that "the association in this and in the two neighboring counties of Prince William and Loudoun is compleat, or near it."[1] In Dinwiddie county nearly one thousand people signed. Its reception generally was favorable, the merchants being the only class to hold aloof.[2] As we shall see, after a year's experience under the association it was found necessary to adopt a new plan, which the merchants evinced a willingness to support.

Meantime, a similar movement had been going forward in Maryland. In the middle of March, 1769, the Merchants' Committee of Philadelphia had transmitted their agreement to the merchants of Baltimore and Chester with the admonition that, "though the Merchants and traders here have entered into this agreement without any condition, yet many will be very uneasy under it if you do not come into the Like."[3] The result was that, on March 30, the merchants of Baltimore adopted an agreement.

Outside of this chief commercial center, there was total apathy among the traders and factors. "Atticus" came forward in the *Maryland Gazette*, May 11, 1769, with a plea to the inhabitants of the province not to wait on the factors to act—for they were powerless because of their English connections—but to take measures for themselves against the use of British fineries. The principal inhabitants of Annapolis and Anne Arundel county led the way on May 23 with an association for a limited importation. Soon similar associations had been entered into by most of the

[1] Washington, *Writings* (Ford), vol. ii, p. 269 n.
[2] *N. Y. Journ.*, Aug. 10, 1769; *S. C. Gaz.*, Sept. 12.
[3] *Papers of Phila. Merchants*, pp. 5-6. A letter of April 17 from Bristol, England, to Philadelphia affirmed: "Some People here are evading the Resolution of your Merchants. Large Quantities of Goods now are shipping for Maryland which are intended for your Place and New York." *N. Y. Journ.*, June 29, 1769.

counties of the province.¹ The promoters of the original Annapolis association now invited representatives from each county to meet at Annapolis and draw up a uniform association for the whole province. " Merchants, Traders, Freeholders, Mechanics and other Inhabitants " were represented at the meeting on June 22.

The association adopted closely resembled the Virginia agreement in its preamble of justification, its pledges against lamb consumption, and its resolutions against the importation of dutied articles and of foreign luxuries, save that in the latter case the Maryland list was more than twice as long. In providing machinery of enforcement, the Maryland association went beyond any plan yet formulated in any province. The subscribers, whether merchants, tradesmen or manufacturers, agreed not to take advantage of the prospective scarcity of goods but to maintain the prices usual during the last three years. Business relations were to be severed with any persons acting contrary to the spirit of the association; they were to be considered " Enemies to the Liberties of America " and treated " on all Occasions with the Contempt they deserve." The subscribers further pledged themselves not to purchase from any other province the articles that were debarred by the agreement. The association was to continue in force until the Townshend revenue act was repealed or until a general meeting of county representatives should decide otherwise. Twelve copies of the paper were sent to each county to be signed by the people.²

¹ *Md. Hist. Mag.*, vol. iii, p. 144.
² *Ibid.*, pp. 144-149; also *Md. Gaz.*, June 29, 1769. Again on December 21, a numerous meeting assembled at Annapolis, including many members of the county committees, and resolved unanimously that the association be "most strictly adhered to and preserved inviolate." *Ibid.*, Dec. 21, 1769; also *Pa. Gaz.*, Jan. 4, 1770.

The mercantile influence in South Carolina politics was stronger than in any of the other plantation provinces, although, of course, it was very different in character from that in the commercial provinces. Charleston was the most important trading town of the South; and its citizens dominated the politics of the province. The movement for non-importation was supported by the workingmen of Charleston, who, for some years, had been developing a degree of group consciousness, and by the planters of the province. In the election of the new lower house of the Assembly in October, 1768, the mechanics of the two town parishes ventured to make up a slate and succeeded in securing the election of three of their men, or one-half of their ticket.[1] In the same election, the planting representation in the legislature was vastly increased, because of the admission of four thousand freeholders to the electorate through the establishment of parish boundaries in the interior.[2]

The chief leader of the forces for non-importation was Christopher Gadsden, a native-born merchant who had learned business methods in the commercial provinces and who possessed large planting interests, also. His indomitable spirit was illustrated by his conduct upon the death of his wife in January, 1769, when he appeared in a suit of blue homespun at the funeral rather than wear imported black cloth.[3] His chief lieutenant among the mechanic class was Peter Timothy, printer of the *South Carolina Gazette* and correspondent of the Massachusetts Adamses. The members of the new Assembly lent moral support to the cause. The standing order for the wearing of wigs

[1] *S. C. Gaz.*, Oct. 3, 10, 1768.

[2] *Brit. Papers* ("*Sparks Mss.*"), vol. ii, pp. 193-195.

[3] "The whole expense of her funeral, of the manufacture of England, did not amount to more than 3l. 10s. our currency." *Bos. News-Letter*, Mch. 9, 1769.

and stockings was altered so as to permit members to transact committee business in caps and long trousers. If the Assembly had occasion to send a committee to greet a newly-arrived governor, wrote a shocked contemporary, " he would probably from their dress take them for so many unhappy persons ready for execution who had come to petition him for a pardon." [1]

In September, 1768, a letter arrived from the Boston Committee of Merchants, urging the Charleston merchants to adopt regulations of non-importation. The letter was handed about among several of the principal merchants but received no favor; and the body of merchants were not even called together to confer upon it.[2] Governor Bull wrote home approvingly of this " silent neglect;" but a great many people began to feel differently, especially when reports of the widespread adoption of agreements in the North continued to pour in and hope of relief from Parliament grew smaller. The *South Carolina Gazette* of February 2, 1769 published a form of agreement for the non-consumption of imports, which all people were advised to adopt unless news of the repeal of the Townshend duties should come speedily. A few days later, "A Planter" wrote in favor of an association to buy no newly-imported slaves until American rights should be restored.[3] In the latter part of May, another " Planter " urged his brethren to foster local manufacturing and to patronize non-importers only. " You cannot expect the merchants will begin this matter themselves," he wrote. ". . . Oblige them to it, by declaring you will deal with none that do import extra articles," and, by this method, you will bring about " a

---

[1] *S. C. Gaz.*, Nov. 2, 1769.
[2] *S. C. & Am. Gen. Gaz.*, July 10, 1769; *B. it. Papers* ("*Sparks Mss.*"), vol. ii, p. 195.
[3] *S. C. Gaz. & Country Journ.*, Feb. 7, 1769.

happy Coalition of our Interest and that of Merchants into *one immediate self-interest.*" ¹ These various pleas brought no satisfactory results.²

Evidently the time had arrived to force the issue on the merchants. Gadsden opened the hostilities on June 22 by writing an article, under the pseudonym, " Pro Grege et Rege," addressed to the " Planters, Mechanicks and Freeholders . . . no ways concerned in the importation of British manufactures." ³ The importers of European goods were stigmatized as strangers in the province, many of them of a very few years' residence. To listen to any more assurances that the revenue acts would be repealed if the people remained quiet, was declared to be folly. Had the people had enough real friends among the merchants to obtain even one meeting to consult what they could do to aid the general good, though every newspaper informed them of the generous actions of the merchants to the northward? On the contrary, had not the people been " affronted with numberless *weak* and *groundless reasons* . . . in order to frighten and deter " them from acting as they ought? Could it be prudent to entrust the public good to a body " whose *private interest* is *glaringly* against us? " Let the freeholders and fixed settlers resolve upon non-consumption, and the merchants would immediately decide not to import. A suggested form of agreement was appended to the article.

¹ *S. C. Gaz.*, June 1, 1769.

² It was claimed that a number of people in different parts of the province did come into the association, proposed on February 2, by a show of hands; but the evidence of this is not very satisfactory. *Ibid.*, June 8, 1769.

³ *S. C. Gaz.*, June 22, 1769. Replies were made by "The Merchants of Charles-Town," *S. C. & Am. Gen. Gaz.*, July 10, and by "Pro Libertate et Lege," *S. C. Gaz.*, July 13; but Gadsden's views were not effectively refuted.

The following week, the *South Carolina Gazette* published a non-importation agreement, which was being pushed by Gadsden and Peter Timothy and which had already been subscribed by a number of people, including twenty-five members of the Assembly. This form was recommended as one suitable for workingmen and planters; and it was announced that the present measure would supersede any earlier forms that might have been accepted. Necessity for this measure was attributed to the heavy and unconstitutional burden of the Townshend revenue acts and the failure of petitions to secure relief. The agreement was to be operative until the acts were repealed. By its provisions, the subscribers agreed to stop all importation from Great Britain thereafter, and to countermand all orders, wherever possible, except for negro cloth, osnaburgs and duffel blankets, workmen's tools, nails, woolcards, cardwire, canvas, ammunition, books, salt and coal. They agreed that prices should not advance; and that they would promote American manufactures and discard the use of mourning. The inhabitants were given notice to sign the subscription within one month, on pain of being boycotted.[1]

The mechanics of Charleston met under Liberty Tree on July 3 and 4 to act upon the agreement; and after inserting two new articles, the amended agreement was quickly signed by two hundred and thirty people. The added parts provided that no goods, usually imported from Britain, should be purchased from transient traders; and that no negroes should be bought who were brought into the province after January 1, 1770. A few days later, some of the mechanics began to make a list of the merchants who signed the agreement with the avowed purpose of trading only with such.[2]

The great body of the merchants would have nothing

---

[1] *S. C. Gaz.*, June 29, 1769.   [2] *Ibid.*, July 6, 13, 1769.

to do with these proceedings, objecting bitterly to the non-representative character of the meetings which had formed the agreement, and denouncing the measure as "an unjust attempt of one part of the community . . . to throw a burthen on the rest, more grievous than ever was conceived by the most arbitrary minister of the most despotic King." They charged that the agreement was so framed as to enable the planters and mechanics to import the articles that they deemed indispensable, while the merchants received no special favors; and they considered that their interests were assailed by the mourning agreement, since their stores were well stocked with mourning materials.[1] The merchants held their first meeting to consider the situation on Friday afternoon, June 30, and, after appointing a committee to draw up a report, adjourned to July 7, when final action was taken. Nearly eighty merchants were present at the adjourned meeting. The non-importation regulations, which the meeting adopted, were much less rigorous than those of the other inhabitants. The agreement was limited to January 1, 1771, unless the revenue acts should be repealed sooner; and a larger and different list of articles was permitted to be imported. All the other terms of the rival agreement were taken over by the merchants, except the pledges for promoting local manufacturing and for casting aside mourning apparel. In addition, it was specified that, because of the heavy duty, no wine should be imported or marketed during the year 1770.[2]

Affairs were now in a bad state of confusion. Two forms of agreement were being actively circulated for signatures; and the feeling of animosity between the classes was

[1] "The Merchants of Charles-Town," *S. C. & Am. Gen. Gaz.*, July 13, 1769.
[2] *S. C. Gaz.*, July 6, 13, 1769.

growing each day more acute. "A Mechanic" demanded of the public how the planters and mechanics could be expected to subscribe to an agreement which did not contain one syllable in favor of American manufactures or any provision against the use of mourning.[1] The intolerable situation was brought to an end by overtures from the merchants for a joint committee to draft a uniform agreement containing the essentials of the two forms. The joint committee completed its work on Wednesday, July 19. On the following day, the merchants unanimously accepted the plan that had been agreed upon, and appointed a committee of thirteen to act as an executive body for doing "whatever might be farther necessary to give Force to the new Association."[2] On Saturday, the twenty-second, a great meeting was held, under Liberty Tree, of the mechanics and such planters as happened to be in town. Christopher Gadsden read the new form, paragraph by paragraph, so that objections might be offered, but the whole was immediately voted satisfactory.[3] The association was quickly signed by two hundred and sixty-eight people, headed by the members of the House of Representatives who were in town. A committee of thirteen planters and of as many mechanics was appointed to serve with the merchants' committee as one General Committee of thirty-nine, for the purpose of supervising the enforcement of the association.[4] By the following Thursday, one hundred and forty-two merchants had signed the new resolutions.

[1] *S. C. Gaz.*, July 13, 1769.

[2] *Ibid.*, July 27, 1769; also *Bos. News-Letter*, Aug. 17.

[3] *S. C. Gaz.*, July 27, 1769; *Bos. Gaz.*, Aug. 14. The names of the members of the General Committee may be found in McCrady, *S. C. under Royal Govt.*, p. 651 n.

[4] Among the planters named were some who had mercantile interests as well. Before the vote was taken, Gadsden withdrew his own name, and induced the meeting to strike out of the planters' list all others who were similarly situated.

The new association represented a victory for the non-mercantile classes, in most respects, although it contained most of the provisions of both earlier associations. In one respect, it was the most comprehensive agreement on the continent, for it was to remain in operation until the various regulatory acts of Parliament, including the establishment of the Customs Board and the extension of vice-admiralty jurisdiction, were repealed. The subscribers contracted to import no European or East Indian goods from Great Britain or elsewhere, except such orders as it was too late to countermand and excluding a list of articles which comprehended all those of the earlier agreements. They engaged to maintain the usual prices; to foster provincial manufactures; to dispense with mourning apparel; to trade with no transient vessels for any goods after November 1, save salt and coal; to import no negroes from Africa during the year 1770 nor to import any wine after January 1, 1770. Finally a boycott was declared against every resident of the province, who failed to sign within one month; and any subscriber who became delinquent was to be treated with "the utmost contempt." Later in the year, the General Committee amended the association so as to include a non-exportation of tanned leather until the revenue acts were repealed, since saddlery and shoes were no longer to be imported from abroad.[1]

Effects of the mourning regulation were soon manifest; and by October the use of scarves and gloves at funerals was totally discarded at Charleston.[2] The practice of the wealthier families of educating their sons in Great Britain was, in a number of cases, given up, "now that the Mother Country seems unfriendly to us." Thus, in August, 1769,

[1] *S. C. Gaz.*, Oct. 26, 1769.
[2] *Ibid.*, Oct. 5, 1769.

seven youths sailed on the same vessel to Philadelphia to enter the college there.¹ Some sporadic interest was shown in manufacturing.

The situation in Georgia revealed the same discord between the merchants and the other inhabitants that existed elsewhere in the plantation provinces. Spurred on by a letter from the General Committee of South Carolina, a radical group, known as the "Amicable Society," met at Liberty Hall in Savannah, and issued a call for a meeting of all inhabitants on Tuesday, September 12, to consider methods of obtaining relief from the Townshend Acts. Notwithstanding the claim that "Merchants, Planters, Tradesmen and others" attended the public gathering, it is evident that the merchants, if any were present, formed an ineffective minority. A committee was appointed to submit a form of agreement to the inhabitants a week later.²

The merchants of Savannah now determined to head off the popular movement; and three days before the appointed time they assembled at a private house and adopted an agreement against the importation of dutied articles alone. In the preamble, the recent acts of Parliament were declared unconstitutional; and the particular grievance of Georgia was asserted to be the requirement that the duties should be paid in specie, this in face of the fact that the stoppage of the Spanish trade, some years before, had plugged the source of specie supply.³

Their efforts proved unavailing. The mass meeting of September 19 adopted a comprehensive agreement, patterned after that of South Carolina of July 20 and 22. The terms of the agreement were to expire with the repeal of the

¹ *S. C. Gaz.*, Aug. 24, 1769.
² *Ga. Gaz.*, Sept. 6, 13, 1769.
³ *Ibid.*, Sept. 20, 1769; also White, *Ga. Hist. Colls.*, p. 42.

Townshend duties. The subscribers engaged to import no European or East Indian goods, save thirty-seven varieties and such former orders as it was too late to countermand. They pledged themselves to sell goods at the customary rates; to promote provincial manufactures, and to discard mourning; to import no negroes from Africa after June 1, 1770 nor to import any wine after March 1 of the same year. All trade should be severed with inhabitants of the province and with transient traders who neglected to sign the agreement within five weeks; and every violator should be deemed "no Friend to his Country." [1] This agreement adopted, it remained for the future to reveal whether the merchants would deem themselves bound by an ordinance not of their own making.

All the southern provinces but North Carolina had now taken action. The excellent example of the neighboring provinces seemed to make little impression on North Carolina. Here, as elsewhere in the South, the merchants of the chief trading community used their influence to retard the movement.[2] Finally, on September 30, 1769, under the leadership of Cornelius Harnett, the "Sons of Liberty" of Wilmington and Brunswick adopted resolutions of non-importation.[3] The next step was the adoption of a provincial association; and this was accomplished under circumstances closely parallel to those in Virginia six months earlier. It was the *verbatim* adoption of the defiant resolutions of Virginia that caused Governor Tryon to dissolve the North Carolina Assembly. The members, in their private capacities, then held a meeting in the courthouse at Newbern; and

---

[1] *Ga. Gaz.*, Sept. 20, 1769; also *Ga. Rev. Recs.*, vol. i, pp. 8-11. Jonathan Bryan was suspended from the provincial council because he presided over this meeting. *Brit. Papers* ("*Sparks Mss.*"), vol. ii, p. 284.

[2] *S. C. Gaz.*, Oct. 26, 1769; *S. C. Gaz. & Country Journ.*, Sept. 12.

[3] *Cape Fear Merc.*, July 11, 1770; also *S. C. Gaz.*, Aug. 9.

on the next day, November 7, 1769, an association of non-importation was agreed upon and signed by the sixty-four members present. The first part of the association attributed the current depression to the revenue acts and other statutes depriving Americans of their rights as Englishmen, and called upon all inhabitants of the province to concur in the association until the oppressive acts should be repealed. Derelict subscribers were " to be treated with the utmost contempt;" the customary standard of prices for domestic goods was to be maintained; and the terms of the document were to go into effect beginning January 1, 1770. In other respects, the association was almost precisely like that of Virginia of May 18. The subscribers agreed not to import the same list of foreign wares, nor to buy newly imported slaves, nor ever again to import dutied goods, except paper. There were also similar regulations for encouraging economy and preventing the killing of lambs.[1]

While the non-importation movement was making headway in the plantation provinces, most of the minor provinces in the commercial group had expressed formal allegiance to the measure. Since these provinces were, in most cases, tributary commercially to the great trading-towns, their action was not of great importance. Only two provinces, Rhode Island and New Hampshire, held off for a while; and the course of Rhode Island created a situation of some perplexity because of the importance of Newport as a commercial center.

Delaware was the first of the minor provinces to act. At the August session of the grand jury of Newcastle county on the Delaware, a " compact " was entered into to conform to the spirit of the Philadelphia agreement, and to

[1] *S. C. Gaz. & Country Journ.*, Dec. 8, 1769; also *N. C. Booklet*, vol. viii, pp. 22-26.

boycott and publish any offenders against it. On Saturday, August 26, 1769, a meeting of the principal freeholders of the county approved and unanimously signed the compact.[1] Apparently no action was taken by the other counties on the Delaware.

On October 18, the members of the House of Assembly of New Jersey passed a vote of thanks to the merchants and traders of New Jersey, New York and Pennsylvania " for their disinterested and public spirited Conduct in withholding their Importations of British Merchandize."[2] The only other evidence of formal action on the part of the inhabitants came at mass meetings in Essex county and at New Brunswick in June, 1770, when loyalty to non-importation was pledged and a sentence of boycott pronounced upon all importers and their allies.[3]

On April 26, 1769, the Committee of Merchants at New York wrote a letter to the merchants at New Haven, the chief trading place in Connecticut, appealing to them to adopt the same measures that Boston, New York and Philadelphia had united upon.[4] The merchants of New Haven met for that purpose on July 10, and agreed neither to receive nor purchase any goods from Great Britain until the Townshend duties should be repealed, with the exception of certain specified articles and such commodities as were excluded by the Boston and New York agreements. Delinquent subscribers were to be boycotted as " enemies to their Country."[5] In August the merchants at New London and Groton adopted regulations of a similar tendency.[6]

[1] *Pa. Journ.*, Aug. 31, 1769; also *S. C. Gaz.*, Oct. 12.
[2] *Pa. Gaz.*, Oct. 26, 1769; also *1 N. J. Arch.*, vol. xxvi, p. 546.
[3] *N. J. Journ.*, June 7, 28, 1770; also *1 N. J. Arch.*, vol. xxvii, pp. 169-172, 186-189.
[4] *Conn. Cour.*, July 30, 1770; also *N. Y. Gaz. & Post-Boy*, Aug. 6.
[5] *Bos. Eve. Post*, Aug. 7, 1769; *Conn. Cour.*, July 30, 1770.
[6] *Bos. Chron.*, Aug. 28, 1769.

The support of the farmers of the province was manifested in a resolution passed, on October 12, by the House of Representatives, a body which they entirely controlled. High approval was expressed of the merchants of Connecticut and the other provinces for stopping importation from Great Britain.[1] On Christmas day, a town meeting at Wethersfield congratulated the merchants on their conduct, and voted to use no goods debarred by the merchants' agreement. Silas Deane, a local merchant in the West Indian trade, had worked actively for these resolutions and was made chairman of the committee of enforcement.[2] Norwich followed the example of Wethersfield a month later.[3]

Now occurred a movement to standardize the agreements of the various towns; and a call was sent forth for a meeting of the principal merchants and traders at Middletown on February 20, 1770, to take proper measures. The mercantile convention met at the appointed time and there were also "a Number of the respectable Inhabitants" in attendance. After a three days' session, the meeting formulated a program of action, designed to free the province from the economic domination not only of England but of the neighboring provinces as well. A uniform agreement of non-importation was drawn up.[4] Old prices were to continue; violators of the non-importation, whether merchants or others, were to be boycotted; and a similar treatment was to be visited on any provinces that did not observe non-importation. A project was launched for a "society for

[1] *N. Y. Gaz. & Merc.*, Nov. 20, 1769.
[2] *Bos. Eve. Post*, Jan. 22, 1770.
[3] *Ibid.*, Feb. 5, 1770.
[4] About thirty articles were permitted to be imported, most of which were useful for local manufacturing. This list was further extended at a general meeting of September 13. *Conn. Cour.*, Sept. 17, 1770.

the purpose of promoting and extending the arts, agriculture, manufactures, trade and commerce of this colony;" and a committee was appointed to float the enterprise by means of popular subscriptions.[1] Another committee was instructed to seek preferential treatment from the legislature for the exportation of Connecticut flour in Connecticut vessels, for local ships in the fisheries, and for the establishment of a glass factory. The convention further resolved that, in view of the extreme scarcity of cash, they would urge the legislature at its May session " to make notes of hand negotiable with us, under proper regulations, as they are in Great Britain, and in some of our sister colonies." [2]

At first thought, it may seem strange that the merchants of Rhode Island were not abreast of Boston and New York in opposition to the trade restrictions of Parliament. With the course of these greater towns their true interest undoubtedly lay; but the temptation in hard times to turn the self-denial of their neighbors to their own immediate advantage proved too great.[3] Moreover, they had so long

---

[1] This society was duly organized; and, at its first meeting, on May 22, 1770, it offered premiums for domestic wheat, wool, textiles, stockings and nails. *New-London Gaz.*, June 15, 1770. But the breakdown of the non-importation movement later in the year prevented this society from accomplishing its purpose.

[2] *Conn. Journ.*, Jan. 19, 1770; *Conn. Cour.*, Feb. 26.

[3] Thus, newspapers in New York and Boston alluded to recent "large Importations of British Goods into Rhode Island with Intent to take an Advantage of the Sister Colonies." *N. Y. Journ.*, June 29, Nov. 30, 1769; *Mass. Gaz.*, July 10. *Vide* also *R. I. Commerce*, vol. i, p. 246. In August, 1769, two British manufacturers, who had been expelled from Charleston, S. C., and later from New London, Conn., for trying to sell imported British wares, journeyed on to Newport and quickly disposed of their goods there. *Bos. Chron.*, Aug. 28, 1769; *N. Y. Gaz. & Post-Boy*, Aug. 28. In December, a trader in "a Country Town Southward of Boston" complained that the trade of the western part

accustomed themselves to defiances of the trade regulations of Parliament that it violated no moral scruple to ignore the extra-legal ordinances of nearby provinces. The merchants of Newport, the leading town, were the chief offenders. As one observer put it, the merchants there " have been pretty unanimous in disputing fees with their Collector &c." but have failed to adopt non-importation measures. " They have been busy in killing flies while they should have been destroying wolves and tygers! " [1]

After some preliminary agitation on the part of the local merchants, a town meeting at Providence on October 24, 1769 resolved not to import or purchase any of the commodities listed in the old town agreement of December 2, 1767.[2] This, it should however be noted, was an extremely liberal form of non-importation regulation in comparison with the agreements in the other commercial provinces. As the snow *Tristram* was soon expected from London with goods forbidden by the agreement, the various importers, some of whom had been unmoved before, arose in the meeting and agreed to store the goods with a committee of the town. Later, precaution was taken to prevent inhabitants from buying goods, which local merchants were forbidden to sell, from strolling vendors, all purchasers being warned that their names would be publicly advertised.[3]

of Massachusetts was being absorbed by Rhode Island merchants, because prices at Newport were twenty per cent cheaper than at Boston. *Mass. Gaz. & News-Letter*, Dec. 21, 1769. "A Bostonian" charged in the *Boston Chronicle*, Feb. 5, 1770, that Providence had developed a considerable trade with western Massachusetts. In like vein, the *Chronicle*, Dec. 11, 1769, reported that twenty chests of tea had been brought overland from Rhode Island within the fortnight.

[1] *N. Y. Journ.*, Nov. 9, 1769.
[2] *Mass. Gaz. & Post-Boy*, Oct. 16, 1769; *Bos. Gaz.*, Oct. 30; *Mass. Gaz. & News-Letter*, Nov. 2, Dec. 14. *Vide supra*, p. 111.
[3] *Mass. Gaz. & News-Letter*, Nov. 17, 1769.

The Newport merchants were more refractory. A letter of October 21, 1769 from the Philadelphia Merchants' Committee notified them that a plan was under way to sever commercial relations with them unless they united in the measures of the other provinces.[1] A Boston newspaper announced that "all intercourse with Rhode Island is nearly shut up, as if the plague were there;"[2] and the *South Carolina Gazette* of November 14 asserted that similar measures were about to be adopted at Charleston. Under this outside pressure, the body of Newport merchants met on October 30, and agreed to import no British manufactures or East India goods after January 1, 1770.[3] Their design was quickly detected. The Philadelphia Merchants' Committee informed them that the agreement was unsatisfactory in two respects: by confining themselves to British and East India goods, they still were at liberty to import from Great Britain German, Russian and other European commodities; and, by postponing the operation of the agreement until the first of January, they might import vast quantities of goods, ordered especially for the interval. Unless these matters were rectified and a "determinate answer" given by December 10, they were told that Philadelphia would boycott them.[4] At New York, the merchants instituted an immediate boycott, subject to removal when the Newport merchants conformed to conditions somewhat similar to those imposed by Philadelphia.[5] The Newport merchants now adopted a new agreement, which was acceptable in every respect, save that the imports lately arrived were not

[1] *Papers of Phila. Merchants*, pp. 31-34.
[2] *Mass. Gaz. & News-Letter*, Oct. 5, 1769.
[3] *N. Y. Gaz. & Merc.*, Nov. 13, 1769.
[4] *Papers of Phila. Merchants*, pp. 43-45.
[5] *Mass. Gaz. & News-Letter*, Nov. 23, 1769.

to be stored.¹ Although not entirely satisfied, the Philadelphia merchants, upon strong assurance of strict observance in the future, determined to continue trade relations; and, some weeks later, the New Yorkers re-opened trade with Newport.² Nevertheless, the equivocal course of the Newport merchants did not promise well for the future conscientious performance of pledges reluctantly given.

The inaction of New Hampshire was due, for the most part, to causes of a different character. The province was in the midst of a period of unusual prosperity, and taxes were lower than they had been for years.³ The predominant interests of the province were agricultural; and, lacking a first-rate trading-town, there was no aggressive mercantile class to disturb the general complacency. Moreover, most of the seats of power in the province were occupied by relatives of Governor Wentworth, the royal appointee.⁴ Under the circumstances, it is not surprising that Governor Wentworth was able to write to the home government as late as February 18, 1770: " There are not any non-importation committees or associations formed in this province, tho' daily solicited." He added that some Scotch merchants had now sent their European importations there and were carrying on their business " without the least molestation." ⁵ No steps were taken in New Hampshire to join the union of the other provinces until the alarming news arrived of the Boston Massacre.

¹ *Bos. Gaz.*, Jan. 29, 1770; also *Pa. Journ.*, Feb. 15.
² *N. Y. Journ.*, Jan. 25, 1770; *N. Y. Gaz. & Merc.*, Jan. 29.
³ Fry, W. H., *New Hampshire as a Royal Province* (Col. U. Studies, vol. xxix, no. 2), p. 420.
⁴ It would appear that, of the nine members of the council, eight were connected with the governor by blood or marriage ties; Judge Atkinson of the Superior Court was the governor's uncle; and the clerk of the Superior Court was the judge's nephew. *Bos. Eve. Post*, June 25, 1770.
⁵ *Brit. Papers* ("*Sparks Mss.*"), vol. iii, p. 205.

CHAPTER IV

ENFORCEMENT AND BREAKDOWN OF NON-IMPORTATION (1768-1770)

By the autumn of 1769 non-importation agreements had been adopted in every province save New Hampshire. But if these paper manifestoes were to accomplish their purpose of coercing the mother country, they must be accompanied by a firm enforcement. It is appropriate, therefore, to inquire to what extent the boycott against Great Britain was actually executed. Certain difficulties, inherent in the inquiry, will render dogmatic conclusions impossible. Thus, the agreements of the several provinces went into operation at different times, some being separated by long intervals of time. Their provisions varied widely in their comprehensiveness. Furthermore, the evidence, upon which conclusions must be based, is voluminous in the case of some provinces, and very scanty for others. Custom house figures are of doubtful assistance in gauging the earnestness of the non-importers, since they do not indicate whether the goods imported were allowed or proscribed by the agreements, and they do not at all take into account the peculiar obstacles with which the non-importers may have had to contend in any particular locality.

In no province were the difficulties of enforcement greater than in Massachusetts. The actual good faith of the merchant body of Boston was impugned by many people at the time; and the writers of history have found it easy to follow this example since.[1] But the story of the enforcement at Boston will show that the merchants were laboring earnestly, and with a large measure of effectiveness, to establish the non-importation against unusually heavy odds. "I wonder for my part," wrote a Boston merchant in 1770 to a New York friend, "how we have been able to continue and so strictly to adhere to the agreement as we have done." Besides the usual obstacles, "we have had a governor, together with a board of commissioners, with their train of officers and dependants who have exerted every nerve to render abortive the non-importation agreement," and they have had support from the military power. "We have had a government on each side of us who have imported as usual without the least restraint;" and "we have six or seven ports within our government to attend to besides our own."[2] The writer might have added that the Boston merchants were the first on the continent to adopt a non-importation agreement and had anticipated the action of most of the provinces by many months. Finally and not least, he should have noted that the opponents of non-importation had a giant of strength on their side in the person of the shrewdest and most pertinacious controversialist in British America, John Mein of the *Boston Chronicle*.

The merchants' agreement went into effect on January 1, 1769. On April 21, a meeting of the merchants appointed a committee to inspect the manifests, or official cargo lists, of vessels which were then arriving from

[1] *E. g.*, editorial note in Dickinson, *Writings* (Ford), vol. i, p. 436; Becker, *N. Y. Parties, 1760-1776*, p. 85.

[2] *N. Y. Journ.*, July 5, 1770.

Great Britain with spring shipments and to report back to the body the names of merchants who had imported in defiance of the agreement.¹ On the twenty-seventh, the merchants heard the report: six subscribers of the agreement had received a few articles, the residue of former orders, and six or seven, who were not signers, had imported small quantities of prohibited articles. The former had readily agreed to store their importations with the committee, while the committee was instructed to confer further with the latter.² An inspired statement a few days later informed the public that the merchants' agreement had been "strictly adhered to" by its signers, and that there had not been imported "in all the ships from England more Goods than would fill a Long-Boat." ³

A campaign that was destined to continue through many months was begun to discredit utterly those who violated the merchants' agreement. On May 8, the Boston town meeting expressed its high satisfaction over the scrupulous conduct of the merchants and recommended to the inhabitants to withdraw their patronage from "those few persons" who had imported goods contrary to the agreement.⁴ Within the next two weeks, some thousands of handbills were dispersed through Massachusetts and the neighboring provinces, advising

---

¹ *Bos. Gaz.*, Apr. 24, 1769; also *N. Y. Journ.*, May 4.

² *Bos. Gaz.*, May 1, 1769. This account contained no names. The complete report of the committee, with the names of the importers, *etc.*, may be found in *M. H. S. Ms.*, 91 L., p. 42. There were actually twenty-eight importers who were non-signers, but the contents of their orders were not known in most instances.

³ *Bos. Gaz.*, May 1, 1769; also *N. Y. Gaz. & Merc.*, May 8.

⁴ *Bos. News-Letter*, May 11, 1769; also *Bos. Town Recs. (1758-1769)*, p. 289.

all people to shun the shops of the following firms as men who preferred private advantage to public welfare: William Jackson, Jonathan Simpson, J. and R. Selkrig,[1] John Taylor, Samuel Fletcher, Theophilus Lillie, James McMasters & Co., Thomas and Elisha Hutchinson, and Nathaniel Rogers.[2] Thomas and Elisha Hutchinson, it should be noted, were sons of the lieutenant governor and carried on a business of tea importation in which the elder Thomas himself was interested.[3] Nathaniel Rogers, another of the proscribed men, was a nephew of the lieutenant governor. All these men were respected merchants of the city; and so far as any records would indicate, none of them were interested in illicit traffic or even in the West Indian trade. No doubt most of them, like the Hutchinsons, were conducting lawful businesses which throve best under the regulations of Parliament; and a number of them had friends and relatives among the official class. They were not Tories in any political sense, and neither then nor afterwards did they hold posts under the government. They were men who, however, objected as fiercely to a direction of their affairs by the populace as the smugglers of 1761 did to an interference with *their* business by a governmental writ of assistance.

The effort to inaugurate a boycott against these men brought to their defense the doughty champion, to whom reference has already been made, John Mein, a co-pub-

[1] Also spelled Selkridge and Selking.
[2] *N. Y. Journ.*, June 29, 1769.
[3] *Vide infra*, p. 282. I have found no evidence to support William Palfrey's allegation, made in a private letter to John Wilkes, October 30, 1770, that the elder Hutchinson, after graduation at Harvard, "was for many years in the Holland trade, where he constantly practised all the various methods of smuggling." Palfrey, J. G., *William Palfrey* (*2 Libr. Am. Biog.*, Sparks, ed., vol. vii), pp. 368–369.

lisher of the *Boston Chronicle*. Mein was a native of Scotland and had been a book dealer in Boston since his arrival in October, 1764. He had received a good education, he possessed a faculty for effective literary expression and made himself a useful citizen generally. He had established a circulating library; and in December, 1767, he founded, with John Fleeming, the *Boston Chronicle*, which quickly showed itself to be the most enterprising sheet on the continent in content as well as typographical appearance. After a time, he converted it from a weekly to a semi-weekly, without any addition in price, and it thus became the only journal in New England published with such frequency. Mein had hitherto avoided any part in the turmoil of the times and, with the other editors, he had published the entire series of the *Farmer's Letters*. In arousing the ire of John Mein, the merchants of Boston had stirred up a veritable hornet's nest.[1]

[1] For the facts of Mein's life, *vide* Thomas, I., *History of Printing in America* (Albany, 1874), vol. i, pp. 151-154, vol. ii, pp. 59-61; Ayer, M. F., and Mathews, A., *Check-List of Boston Newspapers 1704-1780* (*Col. Soc. Mass. Pubs.*, vol. ix), pp. 480-481. Thomas inclines to the contemporary opinion that Mein was in the pay of the government at this period. Hutchinson's correspondence in the *Mass. Archives* fails to give any hint of such a connection. Mein himself denied again and again that he was acting in behalf of "a Party," and he maintained that he was "unbiassed by fear or affection, prejudice or party." It is evident, of course, that he held the confidence of the Customs Board and had access to the information contained in their books. There are some reasons for thinking that Mein left America in November, 1769, and never returned. The present account has assumed, for good reasons, that he was not away from Boston for any perceptible length of time. *E. g., vide* Hutchinson, *Mass. Bay*, vol. iii, p. 260. After all, the chief consideration is that the articles in the *Chronicle*, of which he was universally reputed to be the author, continued to appear without interruption until the *Chronicle* ceased publication. Professor Andrews has recently brought to light some new facts concerning Mein's experiences in Boston in "The Boston Merchants and the Non-Importation Movement," *Col. Soc. Mass. Pubs.*, vol. xix, pp. 227-230.

Mein's first blast came in an unsigned article in the *Chronicle* of June 1, 1769. Declaring that the handbills, recently circulated, gave the impression that the firms named were the only importers of British goods in the city, the article asserted that it was only just to make known the truth. An exact account showed that twenty-one vessels had arrived from Great Britain at Boston from January 1, the date on which the agreement became operative, to June 1, 1769; and that one hundred and ninety different persons, many of them signers of the agreement, had imported 162 trunks, 270 bales, 182 cases, 233 boxes, 1116 casks, 139 chests, 72 hampers, and other quantities, all carefully detailed.

The attack elicited a quick response. A writer, evidently speaking for the Committee of Merchants, replied in the *Boston Gazette* of June 12. In the number of importers, he declared that Mein included almost one hundred belonging to other ports, also clergymen, masters of vessels and private persons who had imported only a single article for family use. He called attention to the fact that Mein had stated the quantity of goods without differentiating between those permitted and those debarred by the agreement and without noting the number of packages imported for army and navy use. Mein, he averred, included four vessels which, but for storms and other delays, would have reached Boston before the agreement went into effect, and three vessels from Scotland, belonging to strangers who had come over to build ships. These being omitted from the list, it was evident that the merchandise imported by the people of Boston in violation of the agreement was "trifling and of little Value." So far as signers were concerned, the report of the merchants' committee of inspection was cited to prove that they had imported, contrary to the agreement, only 14 cases, 27 chests, mostly of oil, 36 casks of beer, linseed oil and cheese, 50 hampers, chiefly of empty bottles, and 15 bundles; all of which had been immediately placed under direction of the committee. Not a single article of woolens nor any kind of piece-goods had been imported by the signers. The author of the earlier article was called upon to publish the names of the importers and to point out any signers who had failed to submit their goods to the committee of inspection.

Mein closed the discussion, for the time, simply by announcing in his issue of the nineteenth that a list of importers and manifests, from which his facts had been drawn, was now lodged at the *Chronicle* office, and could there be consulted by the candid and impartial public. Up to this point, the chief effect of Mein's pugnacity on public opinion concerning him was his expulsion from the Free American Fire Society, on grounds that he was an importer and was concerned in a " partial, evasive and scandalous" attack on the respectable merchants of the town.[1]

Realizing the necessity for more effective measures of dealing with importing merchants, the Boston trade proceeded to work out an ingenious system of boycott. At a meeting of July 26, 1769, they agreed to withhold their business from any vessel which should load at any British port with goods forbidden by the agreement. In addition, a committee was appointed to examine the manifests of any vessels which should arrive from Great Britain before January 1, 1770, and to insert in the public prints the names of violators of the agreement, unless they should deliver the goods into charge of the stand-

---

[1] *Bos. Gaz.* July 10, 1769.

ing committee of the merchants. Another committee was appointed to secure a subscription of Boston inhabitants to boycott those men whose names had been published in the handbills.¹ A few days later, a house-to-house canvass was made among the citizens for signatures to buy no goods debarred by the merchants' agreement, and to support any further measures of the merchants.² Lieutenant Governor Hutchinson, in a letter about this time, wrote angrily that merchants' meetings "are called and held by adjournments, whose resolutions are come into, Committees appointed, and other proceedings had in as formal a manner as in a body corporate legally assembled and known and established by the Constitution; and those meetings have had such effect that . . . most of the Traders who until now had firmness to stand out have joined in the subscription to import no goods."³ Indeed, of the importers who had been exposed by the handbill, Jackson, Simpson, the Selkrigs, Taylor and Fletcher now hastened to accept the agreement and to promise that their fall importations would be stored with the Committee of Merchants.⁴

Having made such headway, the merchants determined to press their advantage. At a meeting at Faneuil Hall on August 11, they voted that, whereas all the "Well Disposed Merchants" (note well the expression!) of almost every province on the continent had resolved on non-importation, local merchants who persisted in defying the agreement "must be considered as Enemies to

¹ *Mass. Gaz.* July 31, 1769; also *N. Y. Gaz. & Merc.*, Aug. 7.

² *M. H. S. Ms.*, 151, I, 15. This non-mercantile agreement, dated July 31, was soon signed by 113 persons.

³ Letter to Hillsborough, Aug. 8, 1769. *Brit. Papers* ("*Sparks Mss.*"), vol. i, p. 111.

⁴ *Bos. Gaz.*, Aug. 14, 1769; *N. Y. Journ.*, Feb. 8, 1770.

the Constitution of their Country, and must expect that those who have any Regard for it will endeavour in every constitutional Way to prevent their Building themselves up on the ruin of their Fellow-Citizens." Thereupon, the names of the following men were ordered to be inserted in the newspapers as objects of boycott: Theophilus Lillie, McMasters & Co., T. and E. Hutchinson and Nathaniel Rogers, all unrepentant though named in the original handbills, and, in addition, John Mein, John Bernard and Richard Clarke & Son. Richard Clarke was another nephew of Hutchinson. John Greenlaw, being called before the meeting upon charge of having bought goods of violators of the agreement, acknowledged his fault, and he surrendered the goods to the custody of the committee.[1] A few days later Clarke & Son, who had been published as importers, fully acceded to the agreement and were ordered to be reinstated in the public estimation.[2]

These new developments brought John Mein to the firing-line again. In the *Chronicle* of August 17, he devoted almost three entire pages to a vindication of his conduct and leveled a charge of dishonesty against the signers of the agreement. In his various occupations, he declared, he daily supported seventeen people, fourteen of whom lived under his own roof and most of whom would have lost employment if he had signed the agreement. In his two years as printer, he had purchased something like £400 worth of paper from the mill at Milton. He employed four or five people in his bookbindery and paid his foreman a yearly salary of £69 6s. 8d lawful money. Moreover, it was notorious, he continued,

[1] *Bos. Gaz.*, Aug. 14, 1769; also *N. Y. Gaz. & Merc.*, Aug. 28.
[2] *Bos. Gaz.* Aug. 21, 1769.

that the non-importation was not generally observed. In support of his statement, he announced his design to publish, in the course of the following months, a detailed account of the cargoes of the vessels which had arrived at Boston since the beginning of the year. He began by presenting the itemized manifest of the snow *Pitt*, which had arrived at Boston on June 1.

This was the opening gun of a bitter campaign, which continued at semi-weekly intervals, almost without interruption, until the event of the Boston Massacre in March, 1770.[1] Mein's usual course was to place at the head of the first column of page one of the *Chronicle* a copy of the merchants' agreement, with the allowed articles in enlarged black letters; then to follow with a trenchant attack on the good faith of signers of the agreement; and to conclude with a manifest, which purported to show, by name and item, that signers were continuing to import clandestinely. Mein revealed himself to be a keen and relentless disputant; he utilized every favorable point to the utmost, and was a past master of phrase and retort. For instance, inasmuch as the merchants' resolutions of August 11 had alluded to the advocates of non-importation as the "Well Disposed," Mein never lost a chance to apply the term to the Committee of Merchants; and he did it with many a satiric turn that must have entirely destroyed the peace of mind of those worthies.

The statement of "the Merchants of the Town of Boston" on August 28, with the fusillade of personal

---

[1] These articles were published during the period August 17, 1769 to March 1, 1770. After the issue of October 19, the publication of manifests, though not of jibes and queries directed at the Committee of Merchants, ceased until December 11, when they were resumed. Fifty-five cargoes were listed in all.

vindications that followed, was a fair example of the answering volleys which the supporters of the agreement delivered.[1] Taking the five manifests which had been published up to that time, they analyzed the figures carefully and showed that in no case had a signer deliberately sought to evade the spirit of the agreement, and that when a fault had been committed unintentionally, the goods had been stored. Their analysis of the manifest of the *Pitt* will suffice for purposes of illustration. Of the thirty-one importers interested in the cargo, only fifteen were Bostonians; and, of these, only four were signers: Timothy Newell, John Rowe, John Erving and the Hubbards. Newell had imported tin and iron plates, which, it was stated, though not inserted in the original agreement as permissible, were so understood from the beginning and had since been made so by express vote, and also several other articles open to importation in other provinces. Rowe had imported shot and lines, allowed by the agreement, and blankets and lines, consigned to him for use of the army. Erving had imported Irish linen and beer, which had been ordered prior to the agreement and were now under care of the committee. The goods sent to the Messrs. Hubbard had been directed to their care for Stephen Ayrault, the Newport merchant. Of the four other manifests discussed by the committee, three of the vessels, *Lydia*, *Last Attempt* and *Paoli*, were owned by John Hancock; and each cargo contained articles forbidden by the agreement. In one instance, that of N. Green, it was shown that the 34 casks of pork, which he had imported, had originally been sent by him to London and had failed of sale. In numerous cases, it was shown that the packages had been

---

[1] *Bos. Eve. Post*, Aug. 28, 1769; also *Bos. News-Letter*, Aug. 31.

wrongly labeled in the manifests. In conclusion, the committee reiterated their former position that the agreement was being closely obeyed, except by a few non-signers; and Mein was charged with an attempt to misrepresent and defraud.

Replies to Mein's attacks came from other sources as well, usually in the form of flat disclaimers from the individual merchants accused.[1] Mein again paid his respects to the Committee of Merchants in a lengthy reply in the *Chronicle* of October 9 and 12. He made much of the admission that Newell's importations were admitted on June 1 although not made an allowed article until July 26, a palpable injustice to other dealers. He had "good reason" to believe that Rowe's blankets were not for army use; and he demanded to know just where or how Erving's importations had been stored. As for N. Green's pork, even admitting the circumstances, was pork an allowed article? "Do the Public begin to suspect," he wrote on October 23 in his "Catechism of the 'Well Disposed'," "that a certain scheme is principally calculated to *crush* all the young Merchants and Importers, that the trade may still remain in the hands of *a few grave 'well disposed' Dons*, who are believed to be *exceedingly well* stocked with Goods?"

Perhaps the most interesting charge which Mein made was against John Hancock, merchant prince and

---

[1] Thus, John Avery denied absolutely that he had imported china and British linen from London in the *Sukey* and declared that he had imported nothing from Great Britain for two years. *Bos. News-Letter*, Aug. 31, 1769. *Vide* statements of F. Johonnot and Benj. Andrews in the same issue. Francis Green declared wrathily that he "did not deviate from the Agreement in any Instance, of Course did not import any Tea," and he dubbed Mein a "Mushroom Judge" and "conceited empty Noddle of a most profound Blockhead." *Ibid.*, Sept. 21. For examples of Mein's rejoinders, *vide Bos. Chron.*, Sept. 4, 25.

non-importer, for having imported five bales of "British Linen" in the *Lydia*, which arrived at Boston on April 18, 1769. As that gentleman was out of the city, his manager, William Palfrey, came to his defense in a sworn statement that the contents of the bales had been misrepresented by Mein, and that they were, in reality, "Russia Duck," allowed by the agreement. Mein replied by publishing a copy of the cocket, certified by the customs collector and comptroller, which attested the correctness of his description. This verbal exchange continued for some time,[1] and received some attention in the *Newport Mercury*, September 4, 1769, where it was observed that Hancock as "one of the foremost of the Patriots in Boston . . . would perhaps shine more conspicuously . . . if he did not keep a number of vessels running to London and back, full freighted, getting rich, by receiving freight on goods made contraband by the Colonies."[2] Hancock himself took no notice of Mein's attack until a letter from the New York Committee of Merchants made allusion to it; and in a signed statement he announced: "This is ONCE FOR ALL to certify to whom it may concern, That I have not in one single Instance, directly or indirectly, deviated from said Agreement; and I now publickly defy all Mankind to prove the CONTRARY."[3] The truth seems to be that the worst irregularity of which he was guilty was an occasional carelessness on the part of his ship-masters in receiving prohibited goods as freight; and this did not become an offense under the Boston

[1] For this dispute, *vide Bos. Chron.*, Aug. 21, 28, Sept. 4, 18, Oct. 9; and *Bos. News-Letter*, Aug. 31, 1769.

[2] "Civis" in the *N. H. Gaz.*, July 6, 13, 1770, expressed surprise that "Mr. Hancock would suffer a consignment of 35 chests of tea to a gentleman in this town, to come in a vessel of his from London . . ."

[3] Under date of January 4. *N. Y. Journ.* Jan. 18, 1770.

agreement until July 26, 1769.[1] The discrepancy between the description in the manifest and the actual contents of Hancock's bales was, in all probability, due to clerical carelessness or possibly to the notorious practice of merchants to doctor their freight lists in order to evade export duties in England.

In the *Chronicle* of October 19, Mein announced that, if the "'well disposed' Committee" did not discontinue "their abusive hints and publications either here or at New York, the Public shall be entertained with Anecdotes of the lives and practices of many of these *Worthies* as individuals; for all due pains shall be taken to unkennel them; and already ... a great store of materials has been collected." This promised exposé, however, never progressed further than a preliminary description, a week later, of "The Characters of some who are thought to be 'W. D.'," wherein much was said of "Deacon Clodpate, alias Tribulation Turnery, Esq.," "William the Knave,"[2] and other personages scarcely recognizable by readers of the twentieth century. A few weeks later, Mein collected the various controversial articles and published them in a pamphlet of one hundred and thirty

[1] Hancock's vessel, *Boston Packet*, arrived on August 10 with 54 chests of tea in her cargo. Hancock wrote on Sept. 6, 1769 to his London representatives, Haley & Hopkins: "The merchants of this town having come into a new agreement not to suffer any freight to be taken on board their vessels, I beg you would note the same, & prevent any of it, except Coals, Hemp, Duck & Grindstones being put on board any of my vessels. You will please to inform my ship masters that they may conform themselves accordingly." Brown, *John Hancovk His Book*, p. 166.

[2] Probably John Barrett and William Palfrey. Barrett had imported woolcards but had been credited on the manifest with "turnery." This labored performance gave "great offense" to the non-importing party, according to Hutchinson, *Mass. Bay*, vol. iii, p. 259.

pages, under the title, *State of the Importations from Great Britain into Boston, from Jan. 1769 to Aug. 17, 1769.*[1] Editions were gotten out the following year which tabulated the later importations. These pamphlets were widely read in the other commercial provinces and were frequently dispersed by employees of the Customs Board.[2]

The merits of the dispute between Mein and the merchants may now be sufficiently clear. The strength of Mein's position lay in being a literalist in his interpretation of the agreement; in failing to differentiate between permissible and prohibited importations; and in testing the efficacy of the agreement by examining the importations of non-signers as well as signers, of outsiders as well as Bostonians, of non-merchants as well as merchants. The success of the non-importation regulation, on the other hand, lay in the sagacious exercise of a rule of reason by the Committee of Merchants with regard to the interpretation of the agreement, meantime placing stress upon the performance of signers, and bringing all possible pressure to bear upon recalcitrant merchants. This was the course of action that was adroitly carried out by the merchants.

While Mein was the one unrelenting opponent of non-importation, it should not be thought that he was without earnest support. Opponents of non-importation began, after a time, to perceive the apparent contradiction between the methods of the merchants and their shibboleths. Shall we " still pretend to talk of LIBERTY, PROPERTY and RIGHTS without a blush?" demanded "Martyr." "Have we not . . . established courts of inquisition in the colonies unparalleled in any age or na-

---

[1] *Boston Chron.*, Nov. 20, 1769.   [2] *Pa. Journ.*, June 28, 1770.

tion? where . . . was there ever an instance of men, free men, being summoned by illegal and mock authority to answer for actions as offences, which are warranted by the laws of the land, the law of nations and the law of God?—'for he that will not provide for his family is worse than an infidel'." [1] Theophilus Lillie, one of the proscribed merchants, declared: "I had rather be a slave under one master, for if I know who he is, I may perhaps be able to please him, than a slave to an hundred or more who I don't know where to find nor what they will expect from me." [2] Another merchant, Colburn Barrell, placed his failure to re-ship certain goods, as he had agreed, partly on the ground that "it was an unlawful agreement made with what I must call an unlawful assembly; such an agreement as both the laws of my Maker and my Country forbid me to stand to." [3] He maintained, further, that the laboringmen in town and country could better afford to pay the Townshend duties the remainder of their lives than to pay the prices exacted by the merchants that winter for the necessary articles of baize and other woolens. [4] Another newspaper writer argued pleasantly that he thought all marrying should discontinue until the revenue acts should be repealed. "Those who marry," he observed, "may possibly have children; and if we have one spark of genuine Liberty animating our breasts, can we bear the thought of transmitting the most abject slavery to another generation? Besides, the Ministry at home, when they see

[1] *Bos. Chron.*, Jan. 15, 1770. *Vide* also "A Bostonian" in *ibid.*, Feb. 5.
[2] *Mass. Gaz.*, Jan. 11, 1770; also *Bos. Chron.*, Jan. 15.
[3] *Mass. Gaz. & News-Letter*, Nov. 17, 1769.
[4] *Bos. Chron.*, Dec. 11, 1769.

our fixed determination to depopulate the country, will be more shockingly mortified than . . . by any of our resolutions to impoverish by Non-Importation." In short, he confided that his plan was to have all the women stored and a committee appointed for keeping the keys, of which he himself should be chairman. "If any man should refuse to deliver up his wife or daughter upon such an interesting occasion, he must be deemed AN ENEMY TO HIS COUNTRY."[1]

Thomas Hutchinson got close to the root of the situation in frequent letters to the home government. He denounced "the confederacy of the merchants" as unlawful, and showed that statutes of Parliament would always be nullified in America "if combinations to prevent the operation of them and to sacrifice all who conform to them are tolerated, or if towns are allowed to meet and vote that measures for defeating such acts are legal." With the utmost persistence, he urged an act of Parliament for punishing all persons concerned in such confederacies.[2]

Meantime, in face of Mein's virulent efforts, more and more pressure was brought to bear upon the little band of obdurate importers.[3] On October 4, 1769, the town meeting, ruled by the non-importers, voted its indignation that

[1] *Boston Chron.*, Jan. 18, 1770.

[2] Letters quoted by Hosmer, *Hutchinson*, pp. 166-168, 437-438; Wells, *Samuel Adams*, vol. i, pp. 281, 301.

[3] Thus, the Seniors at Harvard College resolved never again to deal with John Mein. *Bos. Gaz.*, Sept. 4, 1769. The Committee of Merchants published the name of a storekeeper who, under false representations, had disposed of two chests of tea which had come from the store of T. and E. Hutchinson. *Ibid.*, Sept. 11. The merchants called before them three dealers who had imported tabooed goods and induced them to re-ship the goods. *Mass. Gaz. & News-Letter*, Oct. 5.

any citizens should persist in importation, and gave an appearance of legality to the merchants' boycott of August 11 by declaring that the seven men then proscribed (not counting the repentant Clarke & Son) should be entered by name on the town records " that posterity may know who those persons were that preferred their little private advantages to the common interest of all the colonies . . . "[1] Armed with this resolution, the merchants, who met the same day, sought again to convince the importers of the error of their ways. A committee of the merchants conferred with T. and E. Hutchinson, at their own request, and these gentlemen felt impelled to accede to every article of the agreement, and they agreed to surrender eighteen chests of tea, recently imported, as well as any goods which might arrive later. A letter of the lieutenant governor, written on the next day to an English friend, explained the action of his sons: " My sons tell me they have sold their T to advantage . . . tho' with the utmost difficulty; but the spirit rose too high to be opposed any longer, and besides the danger to their persons they had good reason to fear there was a design to destroy the T;" and he concluded by observing that: " It was one of the sellers of Dutch T who made the greatest clamour; and had they imported any other goods than T, they would not have submitted."[2] Theophilus Lillie entered into similar engagements with the merchants. McMasters, Rogers and Bernard returned answers " highly insolent;" and Mein, for obvious reasons, was not approached. The merchants

[1] *Mass. Gaz. & News-Letter*, Oct. 5, 1769; also *Bos. Town Recs.* (*1758-1769*), pp. 297-298.

[2] *Mass. Arch.*, vol. xxvi, p. 386. Lillie was likewise intimidated by popular clamor, according to his statement in the *Mass. Gaz.*, Jan. 11, 1770.

voted unanimously that these four men "were unworthy of the future countenance and favour of the public in any respect," and appointed a committee to publish the names of all persons who should thereafter deal with them.[1]

Several days later, Nathaniel Rogers gave up his opposition to the agreement; and the number of firms advertised as "*those* who AUDACIOUSLY continue to counteract the UNITED SENTIMENTS of the Body of Merchants thro'out North-America" was reduced to three.[2] The Committee of Merchants continued its work of supervising the enforcement of non-importation with great assiduity; and its transactions were made public from time to time. About the middle of December, the names of A. and E. Cummings, of Boston, and Henry Barnes, a Marlboro trader, were added to the list of those "audaciously" offending.[3]

Those importers, who had become eleventh-hour converts to non-importation, had yielded chiefly on the supposition that the agreement would expire on January 1, 1770. Imagine, then, their consternation when, on October 17, the merchants made the operation of the agreement contingent upon the repeal of the Townshend duties![4] Still other importers began to regard pledges that had been wrung from them through intimidation as having no binding force.[5] This was a situation pregnant with trouble. Late in December, the merchants' committee of inspection made an

---

[1] *Mass. Gaz. & Post-Boy,* Oct. 9, 1769; also *N. Y. Gaz. & Merc.,* Oct. 16.

[2] *Bos. Gaz.,* Oct. 9, 1769; *Mass. Gaz. & News-Letter,* Oct. 19.

[3] *Bos. Gaz.,* Dec. 11, 1769; also *Mass. Gaz. & News-Letter,* Dec. 14.

[4] *Ibid.,* Nov. 9, 17, 1769; Hutchinson, *Mass. Bay,* vol. iii, p. 266.

[5] *E. g., vide* statements of John Taylor and Theophilus Lillie, *Bos. Eve. Post,* Jan. 15, 1770, and *Mass. Gaz.,* Jan. 11.

examination of the goods which had been stored by the various merchants in their own shops in rooms for which the committee held keys. They found a considerable quantity wanting in the instance of John Taylor and Theophilus Lillie, and they heard several other merchants declare their intention to sell their stored goods after January 1, 1770. A meeting of the Boston merchants on December 28 voted a boycott against Taylor and Lillie and all those who should trade with them. The committee of inspection were directed to examine all stored goods at least once a week; and their diligence brought immediate result in placing Benjamin Greene & Company under the ban on the following day.[1] But, in spite of these measures, other merchants, the Hutchinsons among them, were not deterred from renewing the sale of their merchandise after January 1.

The merchant body was evidently facing another crisis. On Wednesday, January 17, 1770, a large number of the merchants gathered at Faneuil Hall to consider more drastic measures than hitherto had been employed, and they adjourned from day to day, increasing their numbers with each adjournment.[2] It was claimed by the *Chronicle* that pains had been taken to induce many workingmen to swell the attendance—men "who find it their interest to proscribe foreign commerce because they can better dispose of the articles they make at any extravagant price."[3] William Phillips acted as moderator. At the first day's session, the recreant merchants were summoned to appear before the meeting. When they refused, committees were sent to wait on them separately, but with no result save a verbal promise

[1] *Bos. Eve. Post,* Jan. 1, 1770; also *N. Y. Journ.,* Jan. 18.
[2] For these proceedings, *vide* letter of S. Cooper, *Am. Hist. Rev.,* vol. viii, pp. 314-316; *Bos. Eve. Post,* Jan. 22, 29, 1770; *N. Y. Journ.,* Feb. 1, 8, 15, Mch. 1; Hutchinson, *Mass. Bay,* vol. iii, pp. 266-267.
[3] *Bos. Chron.,* Feb. 5, 1770. Article by "A Bostonian."

from the Hutchinsons to turn over their teas to the committee of inspection. Even this slight advantage was lost when the Hutchinsons refused, on the next day, to perform their promise. The meeting now voted unanimously that the offending merchants, eight in number,[1] had forfeited all favor and confidence of their fellow-citizens. The whole body of more than a thousand persons then proceeded, in impressive and orderly array, to the houses or stores of each of these men; and, through William Molineux as spokesman, demanded that the goods, which had once been placed in store, should be immediately deposited with the committee of inspection. Only Cary made the concession demanded. At the Hutchinson home, no one was permitted to enter, but His Honor the Lieutenant Governor threw up the window and chose to regard the crowd as making a tumultuous and threatening application to him in his official capacity. Molineux insisted that they had come in peaceable fashion to confer with his sons about " their dishonourable Violation of their own contract;" whereupon Hutchinson replied angrily that " a contract without a consideration was not valid in law." But under the influence of cooler thought, he sent for the moderator early next morning and effected arrangements for his sons, by which the teas that remained unsold were delivered to the committee and the equivalent in money paid over for the balance. The body of merchants met later in the day and adjourned until the Tuesday following, in order to give the other delinquents further time to make their peace. In the interim, the Greenes repented of their ways; but Taylor, Lillie, Rogers and Jackson continued obdurate.

On Tuesday, January 23, the merchants voted to with-

[1] John Taylor, Theophilus Lillie, Greene & Son, T. and E. Hutchinson, Nathaniel Rogers, William Jackson and Nathaniel Cary.

hold from these four men " not only all commercial dealings but every Act and Office of common Civility." Then turning their attention to John Mein and the merchants who had been placed on the proscribed list prior to the recent unpleasantness, they voted that " they deserve to be driven to that Obscurity from which they originated and to the Hole of the Pit from whence they were digged." The proceedings of that day were spread upon handbills, distributed through the nearby provinces and pasted up over the chimney-pieces of the better known public houses.

The lieutenant governor took occasion, on this day, to make a trial of strength between the merchants and the government. For some months, he had been trying to convince his council that " the Confederacy of the Merchants and the proceedings of the town of Boston" were " unwarrantable," but he could not persuade a majority to his view.[1] He now decided to act without the consent of his council; and, while the merchants were in the midst of their discussions at Faneuil Hall, he sent the sheriff with a message denouncing their present meeting as unjustifiable " by any authority or colour of law," and their house-to-house marchings *en masse* as conducive to terror and dangerous in tendency. As representative of the crown, he required them to disperse and " to forbear all such unlawful assemblies for the future . . ."[2] Later, by dint of importunity, the lieutenant governor succeeded in getting the council to approve his action by a bare majority. As for the merchants, they merely paused long enough to vote their unanimous opinion that their meeting was lawful, and resumed their transactions.

[1] Letters of Hutchinson in *Brit. Papers ("Sparks Mss.")*, vol. i, p. 114, and *N. Engl. Chron.*, June 22, 1775.

[2] *Bos. Eve. Post*, Jan. 29, 1770; *M. H. S. Ms.*, 61J, 110; Hutchinson, *Mass. Bay*, vol. iii, pp. 267-268.

The renewed activity of the merchants drew another volley from Mein. The *Chronicle* of January 22, 1770, published an itemized list of the dutied goods imported into the port of Boston during the year 1769, with the names of the persons who had paid the duties. Tea, paper, green glass and painters' colors were the most frequent entries; and, although most of the goods had gone to notorious importers, the names of some of the "Well Disposed" were on the list also, especially for consignments of glass. These charges were answered by signed statements of the various merchants accused.[1] The glass was, in some instances, alleged to be bottles containing drugs, *etc.*; in others, consignments for persons in Rhode Island and New Hampshire addressed in care of local merchants. Mein replied in the *Chronicle* of February 1, analyzing these explanations, accepting some as satisfactory and rejecting others. The career of the *Chronicle* was fast drawing to a close. Its subscription list was depleted; its advertising columns were neglected by the non-importers; Mein himself was being prosecuted for debt by John Hancock in behalf of London creditors;[2] and his physical whereabouts were unknown. On June 25, the *Chronicle* closed its meteoric career with the commonplace statement to subscribers that "the *Chronicle,* in the present state of affairs, cannot be carried on, either for their entertainment or the emolument of the Printers . . ."[3]

Public opinion was thereafter entirely molded by the Committee of Merchants. Through a strange transposition

---

[1] *Bos. Eve. Post,* Jan. 29, 1770; *Bos. Gaz.,* Jan. 29.

[2] Brown, *John Hancock His Book,* p. 94; Murray, J., *Letters* (N. M. Tiffany, ed.), pp. 169-171, 173-174.

[3] In May, 1772, Mein petitioned Parliament for compensation for his losses while "endeavoring to support Administration at the time of the late American Revenue Acts." *Bos. Eve. Post,* Aug. 10, 1772.

of terms, people had come to speak of merchandise, legally imported but brought in contrary to the agreement, as "contraband." "Tea from Holland may lawfully be sold," wrote Hutchinson. "Its a high crime to sell any from England."[1] The Customs Board were now without an organ in Boston. However, on August 27, they succeeded in inserting in the *New York Gazette and Weekly Mercury* a statement of British importations to Boston from January 1 to June 19, 1770, filling five columns of that journal.

The high tension which public affairs had reached ripened the public mind for violence. Already in 1768, popular demonstrations in behalf of the smugglers had caused the stationing of troops in Boston. In September, 1769, had occurred the affray between James Otis and one of the customs commissioners at the British Coffee House—an affair which the radicals spoke of as "the intended assassination of Mr. Otis."[2] Sometime later, John Mein and his partner had been assaulted while walking along King Street; and before the mob would desist, the two regiments had to be ordered to their arms.[3] Thereafter, the customs officials and army officers occupied the barroom of the coffee house to the exclusion of the citizens of Boston, until the fact was noted, when a group of the radicals made it their business to frequent the place in order to assert their equal rights.[4]

The zeal of some school children over non-importation brought on the first death of a townsman.[5] On Thursday

[1] Letter to Hillsborough, Apr. 27, 1770; *Mass. Arch.*, vol. xxv, p. 391.
[2] Palfrey to John Wilkes; *M. H. S. Procs.*, vol. 47, p. 211.
[3] Hutchinson, *Mass. Bay*, vol. iii, pp. 259-261.
[4] Letter of Thomas Young, *Col. Soc. Mass. Pubs.*, vol. xi, p. 7.
[5] *Bos. Eve. Post*, Feb. 26, Mch. 5, 1770; Hutchinson, *op. cit.*, vol. iii, pp. 269-270.

morning, February 22, 1770, some boys placed a crude figure representing four importers, in front of Theophilus Lillie's door. Richardson, an "infamous Informer," remonstrated with the youths, and finally endeavored to destroy the effigy. Failing in this, he retreated to his house nearby to the shrill jeers of "Informer! Informer!" Here he was joined by his wife and a man; and the two sides pelted each other with rubbish until the better marksmanship of the children was clearly established. Then from inside the house, Richardson fired several times into the crowd, killing Christopher Snider, an eleven-year-old boy, and wounding the little son of Captain John Gore. Snider's funeral was made the occasion for a great demonstration; and the lad became the "little hero and first martyr to the noble cause."

Less than two weeks later occurred the unfortunate street-affray, which was glorified by the radicals as the "Boston Massacre." It was the inevitable result of the festering ill-feeling, which had been caused by the altercations over smuggling and non-importation and by the unaccustomed presence of troops in the midst of a civil population. The familiar story of the night of March the fifth need not be recounted here. Like earlier clashes, the trouble was begun by irresponsible youths on the street; but it closed with the fatal shooting of five men and the wounding of several others by the soldiers. It is possible that some of the shots into the crowd were fired from the windows of the custom house nearby.[1] While the bloodshed was wholly accidental, the radicals immediately made it a pretext for procuring the removal of the soldiers to Castle William in the harbor,

---

[1] On this point, *vide* Channing, *History of United States*, vol. iii, pp. 119-120 n. For a different view, *vide* Hutchinson, *Mass. Bay*, vol. iii, pp. 279-280. *Vide* also Murray, *Letters*, p. 165.

where the Customs Board found it prudent to join them for a time.¹

Resorts to mob violence now became more frequent. When Hutchinson sought to get a wealthy importer to promote an association in opposition to non-importation, he was told that such a project would only serve to expose the signers to "popular rage."² Nathaniel Rogers, the un-redeemed, was forced to flee the Boston mob only to find conditions equally bad in New York, his place of refuge: and he returned to Boston to sue humbly but fruitlessly for a restoration to public favor at the hands of the Committee of Merchants.³ One of the proscribed McMasters was carted about Boston by a mob on June 19 and saved from a "suit of the modern mode" only by his promise that he would at once depart the town.⁴ "Boston people are run mad," wrote Hutchinson on August 26. "The frenzy was not higher when they banished my pious great-grandmother, when they hanged the Quakers, when they afterwards hanged the poor innocent witches . . ."⁵

The intense feeling aroused by the Massacre undoubtedly put new life into the non-importation cause in New England at a time when sentiment in its favor was waning throughout the continent. On March 13, the town of Boston appointed a committee to circulate an agreement among the shopkeepers against the sale of any more tea until the duties should be removed; and more than two hundred and twelve dealers responded. On the nineteenth, the town, by unanimous vote, entered in the town records the

---

[1] Letters of S. Cooper, *Am. Hist. Rev.*, vol. viii, pp. 317, 319.
[2] *Mass. Arch.*, vol. xxv, pp. 393-394.
[3] *Ibid.*, vol. xxvi, pp. 488, 491; *Bos. Eve. Post*, May 21, June 11, 1770.
[4] *Ibid.*, June 25, 1770.
[5] *Mass. Arch.*, vol. xxvi, p. 540.

names of all those proscribed by the merchants on January 23. A week later it was decided by the town that three ships should be constructed in order to give employment to the poor.[1] In the following two months, the merchants rejected several offers of importers and Scotch merchants to construct ships because of the invariable condition that the latter should have the privilege of a free sale of goods.[2]

What degree of success did the non-importers attain in enforcing the agreement at Boston? As already stated, trade statistics are not satisfactory on this point, as no distinction was made between allowed and prohibited articles, or between importation into Massachusetts and into New England in general. And it should be recalled that two provinces of New England were admittedly dilatory or derelict in their professions of non-importation. Nevertheless, even such figures show a decrease of British imports of almost fifty per cent, the imports from Great Britain into all New England falling from £430,806 in 1768 to £223,694 in the following year.[3] It is certain that Lieutenant Governor Hutchinson believed that the non-importation agreement was well enforced, and that in contrast to the forces supporting it the powers of the government were insignificant.[4] The retired Governor Bernard informed a committee of the Privy Council in June, 1770, that "a sort of State Inquisition" had been erected in Boston and that the agreements " were intirely done by force and to this Hour

[1] *Bos. Town Recs. (1770-1777)*, pp. 12-13, 16-17, 20.

[2] *Bos. Gaz.*, Apr. 9, May 7, 1770.

[3] Macpherson, *Annals of Com.*, vol. iii, p. 486, 494-495. The figures for the year 1770 are even less informing, as trade was re-opened in October of that year. Nevertheless, only £394,451 was imported as compared with £1,420,119 in 1771. *Ibid.*, pp. 508, 518-519.

[4] Hosmer, *Hutchinson*, pp. 166-168, 437-438.

intirely effected by having a trained Mob."¹ It would seem that two friendly eye-witnesses of these events were singularly restrained in their judgments on the execution of the non-importation regulation. Wrote William Palfrey: "the agreement has been as generally and strictly adhered to as was possible from the nature of so extensive an undertaking, notwithstanding all the opposition it has met with from a few individuals."² And said Dr. Andrew Eliot in a private letter: "That there hath been deceit among some individuals cannot be doubted. But the Town in general has been honest, and has suffered incredibly; more, I am persuaded, than any Town on the continent."³ Even that exacting radical, Sam Adams, wrote to a congenial spirit: "Thro the Influence of the Com^{ers} & Tories, Boston has been made to *appear* in an odious Light. The Merchants in general have punctually abode by their Agreement, to their very great private loss."⁴ In view of all the evidence, these seem conclusions which the student of history may fairly accept.

Outside of the environs of Boston, the problem of securing enforcement of the non-importation in other ports and towns of Massachusetts also presented some difficulties. It proved difficult to scrutinize the conduct of Falmouth on remote Casco Bay; and this port probably provided entrance for some debarred goods into the province. The traders and inhabitants there did not formally adopt an agreement until June 26, 1770.⁵ Salem and Marblehead,

---

¹ *Acts of Privy Council, Colonial*, vol. v, no. 155.
² *Bos. News-Letter*, Aug. 31, 1769.
³ Letter of Jan. 26, 1771; *4 M. H. S. Colls.*, vol. iv, p. 457.
⁴ Letter of Nov. 21, 1770 to Peter Timothy; Adams, *Writings* (Cushing), vol. ii, p. 65.
⁵ *Bos. Gaz.*, Oct. 30, 1769, July 9, 1770.

the chief trading towns next to Boston, proved more faithful. The merchants of Salem adopted an agreement in September, 1768, similar to that of Boston of the preceding month.[1] On May 1, 1769, the *Essex Gazette* published an itemized account of the spring importations, and concluded: " There has not been any Goods imported here or expected that has been wrote for since the Agreement," save, of course, certain permitted articles. During the following year, public notices from time to time showed that the Salem Committee of Inspection was alert in detecting forbidden importations and in procuring the storing of goods.[2] In September, 1770, four dealers whose importations had been placed in store obtained possession of them through the assistance of a " process of law " and a doughty under-sheriff. These persons were proscribed, as were also the inhabitants who dealt at their stores. The town meeting solemnly resolved that an account of the dealers' defiant conduct should be publicly read at every annual meeting for the next seven years.[3]

The Marblehead merchants exhibited the first symptoms of joining with Boston and Salem on October 19, 1769, when a chest of tea, purchased of a Boston importer, was carted ceremoniously about the streets and then returned to its starting-point in Boston.[4] A week later the merchants of Marblehead signed an agreement to dispense with

[1] *Essex Gaz.*, Sept. 6, 1768; also *Bos. Gaz.*, Sept. 12.

[2] *Bos. Post-Boy*, July 4, 1769; *Essex Gaz.*, Aug. 15, 1769; *Bos. Gaz.*, Aug. 27, 1770. Upon news of the partial repeal of the Townshend duties, the town meeting on May 1, 1770 voted an agreement against the drinking of tea; and within a week three hundred sixty persons, almost all heads of families, attached their signatures. *Essex Gaz.*, May 8, 1770.

[3] *Ibid.*, Oct. 2, 9, 16, 23, 1770.

[4] *Bos. Gaz.*, Oct. 23, 1769.

British importations, save certain articles, until the repeal of the Townshend duties.¹ Under this agreement, importations were duly stored with the committee by all the merchants, except four whose names were published.² A signed statement of the committee of inspection, in the *Essex Gazette*, May 22, 1770, affirmed that a strict scrutiny of all importations since the adoption of the agreement had revealed only a few forbidden articles and these had been sent to Boston for re-shipment to London. As was to be expected, whispers began to reach Boston that Salem, Marblehead, Newbury and Haverhill had deviated from non-importation; and finally, on July 31, 1770, the merchants and inhabitants of Boston appointed a committee to visit the towns and make report of their observations. A week later the committee was able to report that the towns in question had honorably carried out their agreements and the assembled body passed resolutions congratulating them on their steadfastness.³

In addition to the places already mentioned, a host of inland towns joined, in 1770, in resolutions to boycott the Boston importers and to consume no more tea. Although Charlestown took this step in February, the vast majority adopted their measures coincident with the Boston Massacre

¹ *Mass. Gaz. & News Letter*, Nov. 2, 1769.

² The proscribed merchants entered a vigorous defense and promised future adherence to the agreement; but they won no lenience. *Essex Gaz.*, Dec. 19, 26, 1769; Jan. 16, 1770; *Mass. Gaz. & News-Letter*, Dec. 28, 1769. On learning of the partial repeal of the Townshend duties, the town meeting voted on May 10, 1770 a continuation of the agreement and ordered that, whereas 719 heads of families had signed an agreement to use no tea, the ten delinquents should be stigmatized in the newspapers. It was also voted that the town should pay the freight in sending back such goods as had arrived in consequence of the partial repeal. *Essex Gaz.*, May 15, 1770.

³ *Mass. Spy*, Aug. 14, 1770; also *N. Y. Journ.*, Aug. 23.

and the ensuing period of excitement. On the very day of that affair, nine towns entered such resolutions.[1] Before the first of April, seventeen more towns followed their example;[2] and in May, at least four other towns joined in the resolutions.[3]

The enforcement of non-importation at New York did not present any very unusual features. The agreement went into operation after November 1, 1768; and in the following March, before the spring shipments began to arrive, a committee of inspection was appointed by the merchants who were subscribers to the agreement, with Isaac Low at its head.[4] Low represented the best type of merchant-reformer, and was long to head merchants' committees in their efforts to obtain trade concessions from Parliament. He possessed wide commercial connections and was financially interested in a slitting mill.[5] The doctrinaire phrase of "no taxation without representation" meant to him merely a cover for carrying on business with a modicum of parliamentary restraint. In the stormy days of 1774-1775, he retained the confidence of both radicals and conservatives, but his own influence was thrown against the dismemberment of the empire; when war came, his choice lay with the home country.

[1] Acton, Dedham, Holliston, Littleton, Malden, Medway, Waltham, Watertown, Westford. Most of the resolutions of this period may be found in the *Bos. Eve. Post*, Mch. 19 to July 9, 1770.

[2] Abington, Attleborough, Billerica, Brookfield, Cambridge, Gloucester, Groton, Hingham, Lancaster, Medford, Milton, Pembroke, Plymouth, Roxbury, Salisbury, Sandwich, Sudbury.

[3] Andover, Boxford, Danvers, Taunton.

[4] *N. Y. Gaz. & Merc.*, Mch. 20, 1769. For names of the committeemen, vide Becker, *N. Y. Parties, 1760-1776*, p. 75, n. 106.

[5] P. Curtenius to Boston Committee of Correspondence, Aug. 26, 1774. *Bos. Com. Cor. Papers* (N. Y. Pub. Libr.), vol. ii, pp. 381-385.

The operations of the committee of inspection differed from those of its counterpart in Boston chiefly in requiring merchandise, imported contrary to the agreement, to be kept in a public store under the lock and key of the committee. This arrangement placed a stopper on a possible leakage of stored goods, and created public confidence in the good faith of the non-importing merchants. In the *New York Journal*, May 11, 1769, the committee stated officially that the several vessels which had lately arrived had brought some packages upon consignment, which were under ban of the agreement and which had been placed in the public store, in all but one or two instances.[1] The *New York Gazette and Weekly Mercury* of May 8 averred that the dutied goods imported in the preceding fall amounted to some hundreds of pounds sterling but that the amount did "not exceed 40s. this Spring." Later in the year, ship masters whose cargoes contained prohibited articles found it necessary to publish sworn statements, explaining and excusing their inadvertence.[2]

The most difficult problem that the committee of inspection dealt with was to prevent clandestine importations from neighboring provinces, Pennsylvania in particular. Since the Philadelphia agreement went into effect four months after New York, there was a constant temptation to introduce into New York goods that had been imported at Philadelphia later than was permitted by the local agreement. Such an instance caused " uneasiness " among the inhabitants in April, 1769, and the offending merchant

[1] The public were asked to boycott these delinquents and all those who traded with them. For the enforcement of the agreement upon the arrival of the *Britannia* from London, April 29, 1769 (probably the first case of enforcing non-importation), *vide N. Y. Gaz. & Merc.*, May 1, 1769; *Bos. Chron.*, May 15.

[2] *Vide* two instances in *N. Y. Gaz. & Merc.*, Nov. 20, 1769.

"voluntarily" returned the goods to Philadelphia.¹ Two months later, the committee commended to the public the action of Peter Clopper, for returning to Philadelphia, of his own accord, some fineries which he had purchased there for his family.² Alexander Robertson, another merchant, was not so tractable. Some New Jersey people examined his casks of goods in transit from Philadelphia and reported the nature of his shipment to the committee of inspection. With an air of injured surprise, he avowed to the committee his innocence of evil intent, implored the pardon of the public in a published statement, and agreed to send back the goods. It quickly developed that he did conscientiously return the casks, but their contents remained in the cellar of the ferry-house for a later introduction into New York. This duplicity brought upon him all the rigors of a boycott.³

The shopkeepers and other inhabitants had adopted an agreement which confirmed and buttressed the merchants' combination. This element of the population soon began to grow impatient with the deliberate measures of the merchants, and they recalled with relish the swift effective methods of Stamp Act days. When, therefore, the silversmith, Simeon Cooley, was proscribed by the committee on July 20, 1769, for insolent defiance of non-importation, it did not seem sufficient to the inhabitants in general that his behavior should be dismissed with a declaration of boycott. A mass meeting was held the following day in the Fields to treat with him; and when he refused to appear for fear of personal violence, the crowd moved *en masse* upon his house.

[1] *N. Y. Gaz. & Merc.*, Apr. 17, 1769.
[2] *N. Y. Journ.*, June 29, 1769.
[3] *N. Y. Gaz. & Merc.*, June 19, 1769; *N. Y. Journ.*, June 29, July 6; *Bos. News-Letter*, June 29. For Willett's offense of a similar character, *vide N. Y. Gaz. & Merc.*, July 17.

Fleeing to the fort, he prevailed upon Major Pitcairn to send a file of soldiers to guard the house; but these were suddenly withdrawn, apparently upon sober second thought of the military. Cooley agreed to meet the crowd the next afternoon; and there he "publickly acknowledged his Crimes; . . . engaged to store an Equivalent to the Goods he had sold, together with all those he had in Possession," and to conduct himself faultlessly in the future. The boycott remained; and two months later he disposed of his business and departed in disgust for Jamaica with a pocket-book much the lighter for his pertinacity.[1] On September 19, an assemblage of inhabitants again met to deal with a jeweller who had been proscribed by the merchants. A scaffold was erected near Liberty Pole; the culprit, Thomas Richardson by name, was then called before them; and, mounted on the rostrum, he discovered a readiness to ask the forgiveness of the public and to agree to store his goods.[2]

With each application of mob law the merchants as a class became more fearful. The employment of violence was not a part of their program for obtaining trade reforms; they had every reason to desire to hold the populace in leash. As events progressed, the rift between the merchants and the "Sons of Liberty" widened. As Colden remarked, at this time, of attempts to instigate violence, "People in general, especially they of property, are aware of the dangerous Consequences of such riotous and mobish proceedings."[3] On Tuesday, June 26, 1770, a transient named Hills was detected in the act of peddling wares debarred by the agree-

---

[1] *N. Y. Journ.*, July 20, 1769; *N. Y. Gaz. & Merc.*, July 24, Sept. 18. Cooley's version, first published in the *London Public Ledger*, may be found in *Mass. Gaz. & News-Letter*, Nov. 23.

[2] *N. Y. Journ.*, Sept. 21, 1769.

[3] Colden, *Letter Books*, vol. ii, p. 200.

ment, and on the demand of the committee of inspection he surrendered his goods, worth almost £200, to be stored. About one o'clock that night a number of persons in disguise took forcible possession of the goods and committed the whole to the flames. Without further warning, Hills fled the town. The committee of inspection made this the occasion for a solemn preachment and warning. In a signed statement, the midnight visitation was stigmatized as " a high Insult " offered to the committee and to the city by " some lawless Ruffians," and every good citizen was urged to do all in his power " to bring the Authors, Aiders and Abettors of so unwarrantable an Act to speedy Justice."[1] Naturally the offenders continued undiscovered; but these new instances of mob assertion had a controlling influence on the course of the merchants in the subsequent years.

There is every reason to believe that non-importation was exceedingly well enforced in New York. The committee had no difficulty to contend with, except the greed of those merchants who sought to import goods at the prevailing high prices. It was claimed in December, 1769, that every bit of goods brought in contrary to the agreement had been placed in the public store.[2] Although this high standard of perfection was not reached, the figures show that the importations from Great Britain in 1769 had fallen to £75,930, as compared with £490,673 in the preceding year, a record which was not equalled or even approached in any other province.[3]

---

[1] *N. Y. Journ.*, June 28, July 5, 1770.

[2] Letter from New York; *Mass. Gaz. & News-Letter*, Dec. 21, 1769.

[3] Macpherson, *Annals of Com.*, vol. iii, pp. 486, 494-495. The British importations into New York in 1770 amounted to £475,991. *Ibid.*, p. 508. It is, of course, impossible to know what proportion of the goods imported during these years was permissible under the agreement. It will be remembered that the agreement was also directed

In Philadelphia the opposition to non-importation, once that measure had been adopted, was even milder in character. The body of merchants were its hearty supporters, although there was a pronounced feeling on the part of the importers of British drygoods that the provisions of the local agreement discriminated unjustly against them. Their complaint was that their commerce was cut off, while the merchants who traded with the West Indies and the Wine Islands continued their business as before the agreement; and they pointed out that these prospering traders were paying duties upon importations of molasses and wines and thus counteracting the principle of home rule in taxation, for which the Americans professed to be fighting. Moreover, the merchants of Maryland and Albany, acting under more liberal agreements, were importing goods for the Indian trade, a privilege that was denied to the Philadelphia merchants.[1] Their dissatisfaction with the agreement took the form of efforts to modify it or repeal it rather than clandestine attempts to violate it.

The Society of Friends, in which some of the great merchants were very influential, found an early occasion to take an official stand against it. At the time of the Stamp Act, more than fifty of them, including such prominent Quakers as Israel and James Pemberton, had signed the agreement; and indeed the measure appeared to be a Quaker method of resistance. But the present agreement was more rigorous in its terms; and when the *Charming Polly* episode disclosed that the populace, most of whom "were incapable of judging prudently on a matter of so great importance," might

---

against smuggled importations from Hamburg and Holland. There were no published accounts of efforts to enforce these latter restrictions. "A. B." in the *N. Y. Journ.*, Nov. 23, 1769, made an incidental reference to the storing of large consignments from foreign merchants.

[1] *Pa. Gaz.*, Jan. 25, 1770; *Pa. Mag.*, vol. xiv, p. 42.

be called in to exert force in executing the agreement, the monthly meeting of Philadelphia advised Friends to have nothing to do with non-importation measures.[1] Nevertheless, many prominent Quakers were concerned in the agreement, including John Reynell who headed the committee of inspection.

The Philadelphia merchants established an excellent record of enforcement. On Monday, July 17, 1769, occurred the first effort to violate the agreement, when the *Charming Polly* with a cargo of malt arrived in port. Amos Strettell, the consignee, was able to show that he had not ordered the malt; and at a public meeting the following day the brewers of the city presented an agreement that they would have none of it. The meeting voted unanimously that any person who bought any of the malt or helped to unload it should be deemed an "Enemy to his Country." A week later, the captain of the brig, not perhaps lacking a sense of humor, sailed with his malt to Cork.[2] On July 29, the brig *Speedwell* arrived with some debarred goods, which had been ordered prior to the agreement; these were placed in a public store.[3]

The expeditious return of imports commended itself as a better device than the storing of them on either the New York or the Boston plan. The Philadelphia Committee believed it would defeat the scheme of "some monied people" in England "to buy up quantities of manufactures on easy terms and lodge them in the principal towns in America to be ready for the first opening of the markets after the repeal."[4] Therefore, at a meeting of August 2, the mer-

---

[1] Sharpless, I., *The Quakers in the Revolution* (Philadelphia, 1899), pp. 77-80; Lincoln, *Revolutionary Movement in Pa.*, p. 151.
[2] *Pa. Journ.*, July 20, 1769; also *N. Y. Gaz. & Merc.*, July 24.
[3] *Pa. Journ.*, Aug. 3, 1769.
[4] *Papers of Phila. Merchants*, pp. 29-31.

chants decided that all goods, which arrived from England on consignment or which had been ordered after February 6, should not be stored as other goods but should be sent back.¹ This plan was followed thereafter. A notable case of enforcement occurred when the *Friend's Good Will* arrived on September 30 with a great quantity of merchandise shipped by British merchants on speculation. These goods were said to have been offered to eighty-four merchants in vain; and the brig returned with her cargo intact.² In December, the signers of the agreement authorized the committee to auction off such stored goods as were likely to perish from prolonged storing, the profits of such sale to be devoted to some public use.³

The committee of inspection continued its activities far into the year 1770 and did not find it necessary to proscribe offenders by name until June of that year.⁴ Statistics show that British imports had been reduced in value from £441,829 in 1768 to £204,978 in the year 1769, and to £134,881 in 1770.⁵ Next to New York, this was the best record of any province for the year 1769, and the best record on the continent for the year 1770. The enforcement of non-importation was free from all exhibitions of mob violence,

¹ *Pa. Gaz.*, Aug. 3, 1769; also *Pa. Journ.*, Aug. 3.

² *Pa. Journ.*, Oct. 5, 1769; *S. C. Gaz.*, Nov. 16. The committee of inspection also had to be watchful to detect fraudulent practices on the part of British merchants. In one instance, Stephen Collins solemnly informed the London merchant, Samuel Elam, "thy Brother Emanuel was found to have antedated his Invoices and Letters in sutch a manner as to Lead people here [to] talke very freely of them." A few months later, he returned a bale of cloth sent by Samuel Elam himself contrary to orders, with the admonition: "I am realy sorry for thy sake it has happened, as many people seem mutch Disaffected." Collins, *Letter Book 1760-1773*, Sept. 18, Dec. 11, 1769.

³ *Papers of Phila. Merchants*, pp. 64-67.

⁴ *E. g., vide Pa. Journ.*, July 5, 12, 28, 1770.

⁵ Macpherson, *Annals of Com.*, vol. iii, pp. 485, 494-495, 508.

largely because goods violative of the agreement were immediately re-shipped to Great Britain.

Of the minor provinces in the commercial group, New Hampshire took a belated stand on the side of non-importation when the emotions of the people were deeply stirred by the news of the Boston Massacre. As late as February, 1770, Governor Wentworth had written that some Scotch merchants were plying a trade in imported wares undisturbed.[1] After the fateful fifth of March, all indifference vanished among the people. "The cry of Blood, reechoed from one to the other, seems to infuriate them," wrote the governor. "Upon this event the Assembly were prevailed upon to forward their petition, which would otherwise have slept forever; the people will not be persuaded but that the Commissioners of the Customs and the Revenue Acts are exerted to destroy the lives and absorb the property of the people."[2] The first action was taken by town meetings at New Ipswich and Exeter, two towns located not far from the Massachusetts line. New Ipswich was a sparsely settled township with trading relations solely with Boston; and on March 19, they resolved to purchase no articles forbidden by the Boston agreement and to boycott all importers.[3] The inhabitants of Exeter, notwithstanding the reputation they enjoyed of living up to "the tip top of the Fashion," agreed a week later to discourage the use of foreign luxuries and to stop totally the consumption of tea until the duty should be removed.[4] No action was taken by Portsmouth, the chief port, until McMasters, a proscribed importer of

---

[1] *Vide supra*, p. 155.

[2] *Brit. Papers* ("*Sparks Mss.*"), vol. i, p. 17. Letter of Apr. 12, 1770 to Hillsborough.

[3] *Bos. Eve. Post*, Apr. 9, 1770.

[4] *N. H. Gaz.*, Apr. 13, May 11, 1770.

Boston, sought to introduce his wares there. The town meeting, on April 11, resolved to have no dealings with McMasters or any other importer, and to boycott vendue masters and coasting vessels that were in any way connected with them. They even threatened to cancel the licenses of tavern-keepers who permitted such goods to be exposed for sale in their houses.[1] The movement in New Hampshire partook too much of the nature of an emotional revival to be lasting in its effects; and, as we shall see, the merchants at Portsmouth resumed importation as soon as the excitement subsided.

Of the remaining northern provinces, Rhode Island was the only province whose conduct resembled, in any respect, that of New Hampshire. Dragged into the non-importation league by threats of boycott by the great trading-towns, the merchants at Newport regarded their tardy agreement with keenest disrelish. Hutchinson voiced the common opinion of other provinces when he said: " Rhode Island professed to join but privately imported to their great gain."[2] When John Maudsley, a member of the Sons of Liberty, returned from London with goods forbidden by the agreement, which had been adopted during his absence, he " cheerfully submitted " the goods to be stored, according to the account in the *Newport Mercury*, April 9, 1770. But if "Americanus," of Swanzey, is to be believed in the *Boston Gazette*, May 7, the goods in question were placed in Maudsley's store on the wharf, and, after dark, were carted to his house, immediately opened and publicly sold to almost every shop in Newport, unnoticed by the Merchants' Committee. This tale bears the color of truth. Certain it is that the Merchants' Committee at Newport

---

[1] *N. H. Gaz.*, Apr. 13, 1770; also *Bos. Eve. Post*, Apr. 16.
[2] *Mass. Bay*, vol. iii, p. 261 n.

never displayed any noticeable activity in detecting tabooed importations.

All evidence would indicate that New Jersey, the Delaware Counties and Connecticut were true to their professions of non-importation and non-consumption. In the case of Connecticut, "A Freeman of Connecticut" wrote in July, 1770, with every assurance of truth, that the various agreements of the towns had been kept " save in three or four trivial instances, inadvertently and inconsiderately done; and in every instance, one excepted, public satisfaction has been given and the goods stored." [1] The exception was a small importation of tea from Boston.

[1] *Conn. Courant,* July 30, 1770. A case, which gained local notoriety, was the importation of some coarse woolens by Mr. Verstille, of Weathersfield, a man who had been in England when the non-importation agreement was adopted. As the merits of the case were not at all clear, some merchants cut the knot by buying the goods from Verstille and placing them in store at their expense. *Ibid.,* Mch. 5.

CHAPTER V

ENFORCEMENT AND BREAKDOWN OF NON-IMPORTATION
(*Continued*)

IN the plantation provinces, non-importation and the problems of its enforcement were much less a part of the fabric of everyday life than in the commercial provinces. The agreements and associations had been promoted by the planting class in opposition to the small, active mercantile class; and in the general absence of trading centres, it was difficult for the planting element to implant the fear of discipline in the hearts of the merchants. The geographical distribution of southern society deprived the planters of the opportunity of exerting their influence compactly, except at the periodical meetings of the legislative assemblies. Furthermore, since the economic discontent in the South was not directly traceable to the Townshend duties and restrictions, a literal obedience to the agreements did not always seem imperative to the planters themselves.[1] The result was that

---

[1] The conduct of George Washington probably typified the attitude of many of the planters toward the non-importation association. On July 25, 1769, he ordered a bill of goods from a London house, with instructions that: "If there are any articles contained in either of the invoices (paper only excepted) which are taxed by act of Parliament . . . it is my express desire . . . that they may not be sent." Washington ignored the fact that a long list of household luxuries and personal fineries were equally under the ban with the dutied articles. *Vide supra*, p. 137 n. A little more than a year later, however, he placed orders in London for goods, which seemed to correspond entirely with the provisions of the Virginia association. Washington, *Writings* (Ford), vol. ii, pp. 270 n., 284 n.

imports from England to the plantation provinces actually increased somewhat in the years 1769 and 1770, whereas, in the commercial provinces, they declined two-thirds in the year 1769 as compared with the year 1768, and fell below the level of 1768 even in the year 1770 when the agreements collapsed. Virginia appears to have been the worst offender quantitatively. To Maryland and South Carolina falls the distinction of having made the most honorable record.

Soon after the adoption of the Virginia Association of May 18, 1769, it became evident that the factors dominated the situation in the province and that, unless their aid was enlisted, the association could be hardly more than a glittering futility.[1] A new and even more liberal plan was therefore drafted; and on June 22, 1770, it was jointly adopted by the members of the House of Burgesses and the merchant body of Williamsburg. The new association was a lengthy document which covered the essential points of the earlier agreement. Several changes were made in the list of articles enumerated for non-importation. A regulation was added to boycott importers who defied the association or who bought goods imported into Virginia because rejected in other provinces; and a committee of inspection was authorized for each county with instructions to publish the names of all offenders. The association was signed by the moderator, Peyton Randolph, by Andrew Sprowle, chairman of the Williamsburg traders, and by one hundred and sixty-six others. Copies of the association were sent to the counties for signing.[2] Only one or two attempts to enforce the

---

[1] Bland, *Papers* (Campbell, C., ed.), vol. i, pp. 28-30; Washington, *Writings* (Ford), vol. ii, pp. 280-283.

[2] *Pa. Gaz.*, July 12, 1770; also *N. Y. Journ.*, July 19. A copy, signed by sixty-two inhabitants of Fairfax County, is in the Library of Congress.

association were noted in the newspapers. In one instance, Captain Spier of the *Sharpe*, whose conduct at Philadelphia had caused his proscription, arrived at Norfolk to ply his trade. Although the signers of the association took occasion to express their belief that the landing or storing of his goods would be an offense against the association, nevertheless the merchants, William and John Brown, received goods from him and defied the local committee. In Rind's *Virginia Gazette* of August 2, 1770, the committee published the facts of the affair, with the statement: " What is further necessary to be done .... is submitted to the Consideration of the Virginia Associators."

Considerably more pains were taken to enforce the association in Maryland and with greater success. The non-importation combination in that province gained much strength from the proximity of the Maryland ports to Philadelphia and from the fact that non-importation had received some local mercantile support from the beginning. The number of native merchants was greater than in Virginia; and indeed Baltimore was showing indications of becoming a commercial rival of Philadelphia.[1] The execution of the Maryland pact was jealously scrutinized by the merchants at Philadelphia, and for a time the good faith of the Baltimore merchants was suspected. This feeling took definite shape in November, 1769, when the Baltimore Committee of Merchants permitted two merchants to bring in goods, valued at £2600, that violated the local agreement of March 30. In the one case, the importer had satisfied a meeting of associators that he had received a special exemption covering the fall shipments; and, in the other, it had been shown that the goods were permitted by the general Maryland association which postdated the local agreement.

---

[1] Lincoln, *Revolutionary Movement in Pa.*, pp. 59-65.

These occurrences brought a sharp letter from the Philadelphia Committee of Merchants, with an intimation that the Marylanders were plotting to deflect trade from Philadelphia and a warning that their conduct would surely bring on them a rigorous boycott. When they got further light, however, the Philadelphia Committee freely admitted their error and expressed pleasure at the upright conduct of Baltimore.[1] In view of no evidence to the contrary, the merchants of Baltimore seem to have merited this good opinion. Thus, in May, 1770, a meeting of merchants refused to permit a shipment, valued at £1292, to be landed.[2]

In all Maryland, the best known case of enforcement was that of the brigantine *Good Intent* at Annapolis in February, 1770.[3] Courts of law have seldom sat on cases involving nicer points of interpretation; and few better examples could be found of the application of a rule of conduct against the wish and interest of individuals. The *Good Intent* arrived from London heavily laden with European goods for a number of mercantile houses of Annapolis. James Dick and Anthony Stewart, the largest importers and respected merchants of the town, admitted that their own shipment amounted to £1377, of which only £715 worth consisted of articles permitted by the agreement. Believing that the character of the importations was being widely misunderstood, Dick & Stewart requested a joint meeting

---

[1] *Md. Gaz.*, Dec. 28, 1769; *Papers of Phila. Merchants*, pp. 45-47, 62-63.

[2] *Pa. Gaz.*, June 7, 1770; also *N. Y. Journ.*, June 7.

[3] *The Proceedings of the Committee Appointed to examine . . . Brigantine Good Intent* . . . (Annapolis, 1770), reprinted in *Md. Hist. Mag.*, vol. iii, pp. 141-157, 240-256, 342-363; statement of minority of this committee in *Md. Gaz.*, Apr. 19, 1770. An abstract of the pamphlet was published in *ibid.*, Feb. 14, and copied into *N. Y. Journ.*, Mch. 8. *Vide* also Governor Eden's correspondence with reference to this affair in *4 M. H. S. Colls.*, vol. x, pp. 621-626.

of the committees of the counties of Baltimore, Prince George and Anne Arundel to render judgment in the matter, and agreed that no goods should be removed from the vessel for twelve days after its arrival. Before this joint committee a vast mass of evidence was laid by the various importers, consisting of correspondence, manifests, invoices, shop-notes, bills of lading and other papers. After careful consideration, "Abundant and satisfactory Proofs "[1] made it clear that the importers had ordered their goods before any association had been formed in Maryland; but the committee held that, long since, the orders had properly become "dead," because of the protracted delay of the London shipper in sending the goods after hearing of the Maryland Association, and because of countermanding orders in other cases. The shipper's belated performance of his orders was attributed to his " ungenerous Principle . . . in trumping up old Orders to colour a premeditated Design to subvert the Association." Therefore, the committee resolved that merchandise debarred by the association should not be landed, and that, as the allowable articles were packed in with them, no goods at all should be landed. The importers made several pointed protests, emphasizing that they had not violated the letter of the association and that many practical difficulties lay in the way of returning the goods. Nevertheless, they were forced to yield; and the *Good Intent* with all goods on board sailed for London on Tuesday, February 27. The principle upon which the committee acted was that, if the present cargo were admitted, " every Merchant in London, trading to this Province, might send in any quantities of Goods he pleased, under Orders that he must in Course of Business have refused to comply with."

Although Baltimore and Annapolis were the chief trading

---

[1] The committee's own expression.

centres, committees of inspection were established throughout the province; and a number of instances of enforcement were noted in the newspapers.[1]

The efforts to execute the non-importation association at Charleston, South Carolina, developed a situation which contained some unusual features. Sam Adams has been said to have had his counterpart in Chris Gadsden of South Carolina. Likewise, it may be said that the course of William Henry Drayton at this period reflected the stormy career of John Mein. Drayton was a young man scarce twenty-seven, a gentleman of independent wealth. Fearless, hotblooded, and of brilliant parts, he was by nature a conservative. His later conversion to the radical cause has been attributed to personal ambition, but can be more rightly ascribed to his intense Americanism and to a change of British policy in 1774 that outraged his sense of justice as deeply as the situation he faced in 1769. Drayton was the foremost adversary of non-importation in South Carolina; and unlike John Mein, his tendency was to place his opposition on legal and constitutional grounds, although he indulged in furious abuse upon occasion. Whether he knew of Mein or not is uncertain; but Mein knew of him and copied some of his most effective strictures into the columns of the *Boston Chronicle.*

Drayton opened the attack in an article in the *South Carolina Gazette*, August 3, 1769, under the signature "Free-man." Centering his attention on the clause of the association which proscribed all persons who failed to attach their signatures within one month, he likened it to "the Popish method of gaining converts to their religion by fire and faggot. To stigmatize a man . . . with the infamous

---

[1] Particularly in the counties of Prince George, St. Mary's, Talbot and Charles. *Md. Gaz.*, Apr. 12, May 24, July 12, 1770; *Pa. Gaz.*, Nov. 30, 1769.

name of *an enemy to his country* can be *legally* done by no *authority* but by *that* of the *voice* of the Legislature." Of Gadsden he declared, in a transparent allusion, "this man who sets up for a patriot and *pretends* to be a friend to Liberty, scruples not, like *Cromwell*, who was the *patriot* of *his day*, to break through and overthrow her fundamental laws, while he *declared* he would *support* and *defend* them *all*, and to endeavour to enslave his fellow-subjects, while he *avowed* that he *only contended* for the *preservation* of their *liberties*." Doubtful as to whether this patriot were " a traitor or madman," he proposed that, to avoid any ill consequences of his disorder, " he may be lodged in a certain brick building, behind a certain white house near the old barracks, and there maintained, at least during the ensuing change and full of the moon, at the public expence."

The next issue of the *Gazette* brought an answer from " C. G.", full of abuse and personalities; and he was answered in kind by " Freeman " the following week. On the afternoon of September 1, 1769, a general meeting of the inhabitants of Charleston was held under Liberty Tree to take counsel over the persistence of a few people in refusing to sign the agreement. It was voted that the delinquents should be given until September 7 to redeem themselves.[1] When that day arrived, handbills were distributed over the city containing the names of all non-subscribers. It appeared that, exclusive of crown officials, only thirty-one persons had withheld their signatures.[2] Among the names published were those of William Henry Drayton, William Wragg and John Gordon. All three men hastened to issue protests,[3] but the burden of the controversy clearly rested

[1] *S. C. Gaz.*, Sept. 7, 1769; also *N. Y. Gaz. & Merc.*, Oct. 30.
[2] *S. C. Gaz.*, Sept. 14, 1769; also *N. Y. Gaz. & Merc.*, Oct. 30.
[3] Gordon announced that he had signed the early merchants' agreement; but that in the profusion of agreements, attempted and signed,

with the energetic and caustic pen of Drayton. Drayton dwelt long and emphatically on the charge that the committee—"that Harlequin Medley Committee"—had violated the first principle of liberty while pretending to strive for it. He denounced "the laying illegal Restraints upon the free Wills of free Men, who have an undoubted Right to think and act for themselves;" and he declared: "The *profanum vulgus* is a species of mankind which I respect as I ought,—it is *humani generis*.—But I see no reason why I should allow my opinion to be controlled by theirs." [1]

Gadsden replied in an article bristling with insinuation and disparagement. He maintained that the proceedings of the association did not violate a single law of the land; and, turning Drayton's own phrase, he held that freemen had a right to associate to deal with whom they pleased.[2] The mechanic members of the General Committee, aroused by Drayton's supercilious allusions, expressed their gratification in print that he had "been pleased to allow us a place amongst human beings," and added reprovingly: "Every man is not so lucky as to have a fortune ready provided to his hand, either by his own or his wife's parents."[3]

"Freeman" returned to the controversy in two more articles, addressing himself largely to the task of refuting Gadsden's assertion that the association did not violate the law. He showed, to his own satisfaction, that the associa-

---

he would not be "bandyed from resolutions to resolutions" and, moreover, he would not adopt a measure of which he disapproved. *S. C. Gaz.*, Sept. 14, 1769. Wragg wrote that he had not signed, because he did not believe in subscribing to an agreement to starve himself; and he argued that the agreement would not accomplish the end desired. *Ibid.*, Sept. 21.

[1] *Ibid.*, Sept. 21, 1769; also *Bos. Chron.*, Oct. 30.
[2] *S. C. Gaz.*, Sept. 28, 1769.
[3] *Ibid.*, Oct. 5, 1769.

tion bore the legal character of a "confederacy" in that it was a voluntary combination by bonds or promises to do damage to innocent third parties, and that therefore the associators were punishable by law.[1] Gadsden now advanced to a truly revolutionary position. Passing over the charges of the illegal character of the association, and citing the history of England as his best justification, he affirmed that, whenever the people's rights were invaded in an outrageous fashion by a corrupt Parliament or an abandoned ministry, mankind exerted "those *latent*, though *inherent* rights of SOCIETY, which *no climate, no time, no constitution, no contract*, can ever destroy or diminish;" that under such circumstances petty men who cavilled at measures were properly disregarded.[2]

Drayton was precluded from seeking redress for his injuries in a court of law, as a majority of the common pleas judges were signers of the association and as the jury would probably consist entirely of signers, also. On December 5, 1769, he therefore had recourse to the legislature; but his petition was rejected by the lower house without a reading. The petition was afterwards published;[3] it contained a powerful summary of the arguments he had used in the *Gazette* as well as eloquent evidence of the efficacy of the boycott measures. He freely admitted that "his commodities which heretofore were of ready sale now remain upon his hands," and that possible purchasers, as soon as they learned of his ownership of the commodities, "im-

---

[1] *Ibid.*, Oct. 12, 26, 1769. William Wragg, maintaining the same point, argued that it did not follow that a number of persons associating together had a right to do what one man might do, and he said that Parliament had acted on this doctrine in punishing tailors for combinations to increase wages. *Ibid.*, Nov. 16.

[2] "A Member of the General Committee," *ibid.*, Oct. 18, 1769.

[3] *Ibid.*, Dec. 14, 1769; also *Bos. Chron.*, Jan. 11, 1770.

mediately declined any further treaty for the purchase of them, because of the Resolutions." Realizing that he was a beaten man, he sailed for England on January 3, 1770, in a ship that, appropriately enough, carried goods outlawed by the association.[1]

A vigorous execution of the association at Charleston was insured by the fact that two-thirds of the General Committee consisted of planters and mechanics, only one-third being merchants and factors. So successful was the enforcement that a recountal of even the striking instances would be tedious and purposeless.[2] The General Committee met regularly every Tuesday; subordinate to them was a vigilant committee of inspection, which saw to the storing of goods or their reshipment, as the importer preferred.[3] Almost every issue of the *South Carolina Gazette* contained statements of the arrival of vessels and of the transactions of the committee thereon. In only one instance was the good faith of the committee impugned. Ann and Benjamin Mathews having been publicly proscribed for selling goods stored by them, Mrs. Mathews retorted, in a printed article, that the goods had been ordered prior to the association, that her son had given the promise to store while she was lying very ill, and that stern necessity had compelled her to open the goods. She charged that individual members of the committee, whom she named, had been permitted to receive articles ordered before the association had been adopted, and that in one or two instances their articles had arrived after hers. The only difference between her offense and that of Mr. Rutledge, who had recently

---

[1] *S. C. Gaz.*, Jan. 4, 1770.

[2] An interesting account may be found in McCrady, *S. C. under Royal Govt.*, pp. 664-676.

[3] *S. C. Gaz.*, Nov. 14, 1769.

imported two horses in consequence of an old order, was, she averred, that he was a man who would not be trifled with, while she was a poor widow living within two doors of a leading man of the committee and thus in a position to take a little cash from some of his customers. By way of vindication, the committee was able to show that the importations of the Mathews' had been purchased after copies of the South Carolina Association had arrived in England, a fact not obtaining in the other cases. A few months later, the son appeared before the committee, acknowledged guilt and heartfelt contrition, and promised to deliver all goods, remaining unsold, into charge of the committee.[1]

The provision for the immediate reshipment of slaves was rigidly enforced. For instance, Captain Evans arrived on May 2, 1770, from Africa with three hundred and forty-five negroes; and after attending a public meeting held to consider his case, he filled his casks and set sail with his cargo for the more hospitable shores of Georgia.[2] It was estimated by friends of non-importation that Great Britain had lost not less than £300,000 sterling, at a moderate computation, through the South Carolina regulations against slave importation.[3] Some little difficulty was experienced in preventing violations of the association at Georgetown and Beaufort; but this was obviated when committees of inspection were appointed there early in February, 1770.[4]

Governor Bull wrote on December 6, 1769, to the home government that "the people persevere under much inconvenience to trade in the strict observance of the association;" on March 6 following, that the royal officials who

[1] *S. C. & Am. Gen. Gaz.*, June 15, 1770; *S. C. Gaz.*, May 31, June 28, Oct. 4.
[2] *Ibid.*, May 17, 1770.
[3] *Ibid.*, May 24, 1770.
[4] *Ibid.*, Feb. 1, 1770.

had declined the association " daily experience great losses thereby, as Subscribers are forbidden to purchase Rice, Indigo &c from non Subscribers;" and again on October 20, that the subscribers to the non-importation were " taking large strides to enforce the rigid observing of their Resolutions " through " the vigilance and industry of the leaders, whose impetuosity of behaviour and reproachful language deter the moderate, the timid and the dependent." [1] Trade statistics substantiate this view of the situation: English imports into the Carolinas dropped from £306,600 in 1769 to £146,273 in 1770.[2]

Facts throwing light on the observance of non-importation in North Carolina are meager; but it would appear that the province-wide association, inaugurated by the assembly in November, 1769, was generally ignored by the merchants. On June 2, 1770, a general meeting was called at Wilmington by the " Sons of Liberty " and was attended by "many of the principal inhabitants of six large and populous counties," mostly planters. The meeting agreed to boycott and publish all who imported or purchased goods contrary to the agreement. A letter, issued later by the General Committee of the Sons of Liberty upon the Cape Fear, expressed the hope that the merchants' " own interest will convince them of the necessity of importing such articles, and such only, as the planters will purchase." Committees of inspection were established in the six counties, and those for the towns of Wilmington and Brunswick were instructed to use particular vigilance.[3] Thereafter, the conditions of enforcement improved. The *Cape Fear Mercury* of July 11, 1770, presented some instances of the

[1] *Brit. Papers ("Sparks Mss.")*, vol. ii, pp. 202, 206, 217.
[2] Macpherson, *Annals of Com.*, vol. iii, pp. 494-495, 508.
[3] *Cape Fear Merc.*, July 11, 1770; Connor, *Harnett*, pp. 55-56.

activity of the Wilmington Committee of Inspection, although it admitted that some merchants were "daily purchasing wines and many other articles" prohibited by the agreement, a course of conduct which would surely lead to the publication of their names. At the town of Newbern no formal steps were taken to adopt an agreement; but it was claimed in September, 1770, that "the whole town cannot now furnish a single pound of Bohea Tea," and that "all the merchants here cannot produce for sale a single yard of osnabrigs, negro cloth, coarse linens or scarcely any European goods at all." [1]

In Georgia, the non-importation association, which had been so reluctantly adopted, was speedily disregarded.[2] Attempts were made to introduce slaves overland into South Carolina; but this clandestine trade was closely watched.[3] On June 27, 1770, a general meeting of Charleston inhabitants voted solemnly, without a dissenting voice, that Georgia ought "to be amputated from the rest of their brethren, as a rotten part that might spread a dangerous infection," and that all commercial intercourse should be severed, after fourteen days.[4] The desertion of Georgia had no important results, since Georgia had no trading relations of importance.

At first thought it may provoke surprise that the movement for a general relaxation of non-importation should be promoted by the merchants of two of the chief commercial provinces. The merchants of the northern provinces were certain to receive important material benefits from a repeal

[1] *S. C. Gaz. & Coun. Journ.*, Oct. 2, 1770.
[2] *Brit. Papers* ("*Sparks Mss.*"), vol. ii, p. 286.
[3] *S. C. Gaz.*, May 17, 1770.
[4] *Ibid.*, June 28, Aug. 23, 1770.

of the various trade and revenue statutes; and it was this purpose that had caused them to undertake the great non-importation union of the provinces at the outset. But as the months passed, they began to discover that the character of their utilitarian revolt was changing under their eyes; that self-styled "Sons of Liberty" conceived of them as bearing the standard in a great struggle for constitutional rights; and they were chagrined to realize that they had, in some instances, given grounds for such an interpretation.

Furthermore, the chief burden of the non-importation had fallen upon the commercial provinces, imports from England decreasing two-thirds in the year 1769 whereas they actually increased somewhat in the plantation provinces. In the early months, the checking of the stream of British manufactures had increased the demand for goods which had long cluttered their shelves; and the merchants disposed of much old stock to advantage.[1] Debts, long outstanding from their customers, were called in; and remittances were made to England at fifteen to twenty per cent advantage on the £100 sterling.[2] But when, after a time, their stocks became depleted, they began to feel the injustice

[1] The merchants obliged us at this time "to take old moth-eaten cloths that had lain rotting in the shops for years and to pay a monstrous price for them;" this was the statement made later by a bitter opponent of the non-importation movement of 1774. Seabury, S., *Free Thoughts on the Proceedings of the Continental Congress. . . . By a Farmer* (New York, 1774), p. 12.

[2] *Conn. Cour.*, July 30, 1770; *Pa. Gaz.*, May 31; *Mass. Gaz. & Post Boy*, Sept. 24. Governor Pownall declared in Parliament in March, 1770, that a monthly record of the rate of exchange for the last eight years at the three leading ports of America showed an average rate of 167½ for the £100 sterling at Philadelphia, 171⅘ at New York, and 133⅓ at Boston; while the current rate at the same ports was 145, 162 and 125-123. The rise and fall of exchange, he asserted, was the barometer of trade, a falling exchange signifying a doubly great loss of trade. *Parliamentary History*, vol. xvi, p. 860.

of bearing the brunt of a struggle, from which the whole populace expected to reap large benefits.

When they advanced their prices, they were accused by the populace of being "monopolists" and "extortioners;" and no countenance was given to their plea that high profits were necessary in order to offset the general falling-off of business. The storm centre of controversy was the price of Bohea tea. At Philadelphia a memorial was presented to the Committee of Merchants, in January, 1770, which complained that the price of Bohea had reached 5s. a pound and upward in face of an agreement of dealers to maintain it at 3s. 9d.; and "A. B.", writing in the *Chronicle*, declared he would post a list of all offenders in his shop and distribute it among his neighbors.[1] At New York, the Committee of Merchants advertised in the *New York Journal*, September 28, 1769, that a careful investigation had failed to disclose any enhancement of prices; but on February 24, 1770, they found it necessary to call the tea dealers before them and extract a promise to keep the retail price of Bohea down to 5s. 6d. and the wholesale price at 4s. 6d.[2] A few weeks later, the inhabitants of the city assembled, and called some of the delinquents before them.[3] Nevertheless, the price of tea continued its ascent. Bohea reached 10s. a pound at Annapolis by the middle of the year; and when Williams & Company, the worst offenders, refused to conform to the

---

[1] *Pa. Chron.*, Jan. 29, 1770. It was announced in the same issue that thereafter the size of the *Chronicle* would be smaller, because of the rise in the price of paper. In the issue of July 23, a writer claimed that tea had reached the "unconscionable sum of 10s.," a paper of pins had advanced from 10d. to 2s. 9d., and other articles were equally high in proportion.

[2] *N. Y. Gaz. & Merc.*, Feb. 26, 1770.

[3] *Ibid.*, Mch. 12, 1770; *N. Y. Journ.*, July 12.

demand of the committee of inspection, the firm was proscribed in the newspapers.¹ A few complaints were also heard at Boston against high prices, although apparently no attempts were made to regulate prices there.²

While the importing merchants were suffering a decline in trade and the radical class in the population was beginning to dominate the situation, a further affliction came in the form of a decrease in the export trade to England. An excessive exportation of American products to England in 1768 produced a slump in the export market in the year 1769, and there was only a slow recovery in the next few years. This condition bore proportionately more severely upon New York and Pennsylvania than upon New England.³ "Interest, all powerful Interest, will bear down Patriotism," predicted a Quaker merchant on December 9, 1769. ". . . Romans we are not as they were formerly, when they despised Riches and Grandeur, abode in extreme poverty and sacrificed every pleasant enjoyment for the love and service of their Country." ⁴

Thus, the seeds of discontent were pretty generously sown among the merchants when news reached America that Parliament had, on April 12, 1770, repealed the most important portions of the law against which their agreements were directed.⁵ This news did not come as a surprise, as the governors had been notified by a letter of May 13, 1769 that such a measure was under contemplation and that the taxes on glass, paper and colors had been laid " Contrary

---

¹ *N. Y. Journ.*, Aug. 2, 1770.

² *Bos. Chron.*, Dec. 11, 1769; *Mass. Gaz. & News-Letter*, Dec. 21.

³ There was some decrease in the export trade of the plantation provinces, also; but the merchants there did not dominate the non-importation movement.

⁴ Letter of Henry Drinker; *Pa. Mag.*, vol. xiv, p. 41.

⁵ 10 George III, c. 17. To be operative on December 1, 1770.

to the true principles of Commerce."¹ The reasons stated for the proposed repeal coincided exactly with those urged in the formal utterances of the merchant class in America.² When Lord North carried through the repeal bill on the plea that the duties affected were anti-commercial, the merchants throughout the commercial provinces, with the exception of the Bostonians, who had taken an advanced stand in their pamphlet of December, 1769, had a right to feel self-gratulatory. They had obtained all the remedial legislation that they had been specifically demanding, save only the rescinding of the tea duty which had been withheld because the king believed that "there must always be one tax to keep up the right."³

The only question before them was whether they, as practical men of business, would be justified in continuing their costly boycott against Great Britain for the sake of the one remaining tax.⁴ As in 1766, they felt it was no concern of theirs that the tea tax was retained as an assertion of the right of Parliament to tax the colonies for revenue

---

¹ *1 N. J. Arch.*, vol. x, pp. 109-110.

² North was primarily interested in the fact that the duties were anti-commercial from the standpoint of the home merchants, declaring "so many articles, the manufactures of Great Britain, are, by the Act in question, subject to taxation, that it must astonish every reasonable man to think how so preposterous a law could originally obtain existence from a British legislature." *Parliamentary History*, vol. xvi, pp. 853-855.

³ Donne, W. B. *Correspondence of George III with Lord North* (London, 1867), vol. i, p. 202.

⁴ *E. g. vide* letter of Phila. Comm. to N. Y. Comm., May 15, 1770, in *N. Y. Journ.*, Aug. 16, 1770. As "Cethegus" put it, "It is vain to think that we can hold Breath always . . . We have only to chuse whether to unite in maintaining an Agreement of a more restricted Nature, or to go on disputing about a Shadow which cannot longer be realized." *N. Y. Gaz. & Post-Boy*, Oct. 8, 1770; also *1 N. J. Arch.*, vol. xxvii, pp. 282-283.

only; or that earlier revenue duties remained on the statute books; or that the Declaratory Act continued in its pristine vigor as a part of the imperial constitution. To these generalizations, the merchants of Massachusetts constituted an exception, probably because the warp of their prosperity was woven so closely with the woof of an unrestricted foreign commerce.

Upon hearing that the bill for partial repeal of the Townshend duties was pending passage in Parliament, the South Carolina General Committee addressed a circular letter to the committees of the other provinces on April 25, 1770. The letter recounted that the provinces had adopted agreements differing " in Extent of Matter and Limitations of Time," and that South Carolina, being among the last to act, had been the most comprehensive in her plan, specifying among her *sine qua non* demands the disestablishment of the Customs Board and of the oppressive vice-admiralty jurisdiction. The committee asserted that, if any province should take advantage of the repeal of " these trifling duties " to re-open trade with Great Britain, it would have been infinitely better to have submitted to the yoke from the beginning.[1] In this letter and in a later one, the northern provinces were exhorted to extend their agreements to cover all the demands named in the South Carolina Association.[2]

Authentic news of the passage of the repeal bill reached America early in May, 1770. Outside of Boston and a few other places of minor importance, there ensued, throughout the commercial provinces, several perplexing months of indecision, interrupted only by the premature break of

[1] *N. C. Col. Recs.*, vol. viii, pp. 197-199; published at the time in *S. C. Gaz.*, May 17, 1770; *Pa. Gaz.*, May 24; *N. Y. Journ.*, May 17; *Bos. Gaz.*, May 28.

[2] The second letter was dated June 27; *S. C. Gaz.*, June 28, 1770; also *N. Y. Journ.*, July 12.

Albany, the Rhode Island ports and Portsmouth from the non-importation combination. The merchants of Albany rescinded their agreement on May 10 in favor of the non-importation of tea alone; but when, after a few weeks, they learned that Boston and New York remained steadfast, they hastened to resume their agreement and to countermand the orders which had been sent to England in the meantime.[1]

Only a few days behind Albany, the merchants of Newport and Providence cast aside their agreements and discharged their committees of inspection.[2] " They were dragged in the first place like an ox to the slaughter, into the non-importation agreement . . .," wrote a contemporary. "Adherence to the non-importation agreement in them would have been acting out of character and in contradiction to the opinion of the country." [3] Within a week the answer came from the great ports: mass meetings at Philadelphia and New York and a meeting of merchants at Boston declared an absolute boycott against the merchants of Rhode Island.[4] The town of Providence now took things in hand, and followed the prudent example set by Albany by scurrying back under cover of the agreement, announcing a boycott against any who should have dealings with the abandoned Newport importers.[5] The merchants of Newport re-enacted their agreement also; but their resolution to store rather than re-ship the goods recently arrived inclined the other provinces to believe that the action of Newport was merely a screen for clandestine importations. A wave

[1] Ms. in Hist. Soc. of Pa.; *N. Y. Journ.*, Aug. 23, 30, 1770; *N. Y. Gaz. & Merc.*, Sept. 24.

[2] *Bos. Gaz.*, May 28, 1770.

[3] "Rachel" in *New London Gazette*, June 22, 1770.

[4] *Pa. Gaz.*, May 24, 1770; *N. Y. Journ.*, June 7; *Bos. Eve. Post*, May 28.

[5] *Prov. Gaz.*. June 2, 9, 1770.

of anger swept up and down the coast; and by the early days of July trading relations had been suspended by the leading ports of eight provinces.¹ The Rhode Islanders began to perceive, as Stephen Collins had predicted, that where they gained a penny in the trade of British drygoods, they stood a chance of losing a pound in their coastwise trade.² The Boston trade sent a committee, headed by Molineux, to Newport and Providence to induce the merchants to enter new resolutions. Both towns acceded—the Newport merchants on August 20 ³—and, on a recommendation of the Boston merchants, the merchants of Philadelphia and Charleston now re-established trading connections with the city.⁴

In New Hampshire, the merchants had remained unsympathetic with the non-importation movement all along; but, it will be remembered, the inhabitants in general had been inflamed to resolutions of protest and non-importation by the event of the Boston Massacre. Several weeks later, the Boston trade learned that Portsmouth merchants were importing British merchandise on a larger scale than ever before; and on June 18, they instituted a boycott against that province.⁵ The trading towns on the Connecticut river followed the example of Boston.⁶ The inhabitants of the little parish of Rye, New Hampshire, near the Massachu-

¹ Mass., N. Y., Conn., Pa., Md., Del., N. C., S. C. *Vide* files of *N. Y. Journ.* Newport coasting-sloops were actually turned back at Marblehead, New Haven, New York, Philadelphia, Chester, Baltimore, Norfolk and Charleston, S. C.

² Collins, *Letter-Book 1760-1773*, June 8, 1770.

³ *Newport Merc.*, Aug. 27, 1770; *N. Y. Journ.*, Aug. 30.

⁴ *Mass. Spy*, Aug. 14, 1770; *Pa. Gaz.*, Sept. 20; *S. C. Gaz.*, Oct. 18, 25.

⁵ *Bos. Eve. Post*, June 11, 25, 1770. For an instance of enforcement, *vide ibid.*, July 9.

⁶ *Essex Gaz.*, July 2, 1770.

setts border, voted unanimously to unite with Boston in non-importation;[1] but Portsmouth, the chief centre of population, remained unmoved. "One of the Boston zealots was immediately dispatched here," wrote Governor Wentworth to the home government; and he carried with him a ready-prepared report, "expressed in the most abusive terms," for adoption by the town meeting. But his machinations were in vain; he "decamped precipitately for Boston" in fear of tar and feathers; and the town meeting, by a poll of ten to one, dismissed the whole matter and dissolved the meeting.[2]

After all, the bone and sinew of the non-importation movement were the agreements of the great trading towns of Boston, New York and Philadelphia. On the action of these towns depended the integrity of the commercial combination. Should the merchants of any of these towns accept the partial repeal as satisfactory and proceed to revoke their boycott of British importations, this breach in the non-importation dike would render the whole barrier useless. There was no indecision at Boston. When the merchants there learned, at a meeting of April 25, 1770, that some of their number had ordered goods to be shipped upon the passage of the partial repeal, it was agreed that this event would not justify a re-opening of trade, and it was voted that the goods should be re-shipped immediately upon their arrival.[3] But in both Philadelphia and New York, there was a sharp division of sentiment, the alignment being be-

[1] *N. H. Gaz.*, July 27, 1770; also *Bos. Eve. Post*, July 30.
[2] *Brit. Papers ("Sparks Mss.")*, vol. i, p. 18; *N. H. Gaz.*, July 13, 1770.
[3] Letter of Boston Comm. in *N. Y. Journ.*, May 10, 1770. Tea was excepted from this vote upon the belief that the act of 11 George I, c. 30, sec. 8, would thereby be violated. *Ibid.*, July 5. The merchants were later obliged to publish the names of five merchants who refused to obey. *Mass. Spy*, Aug. 14.

tween the leading merchants, who were willing to accept the remedial legislation of Parliament as the best that could be attained under the circumstances, and the non-mercantile, propertyless population, who were fired with the current political views and considered the issue of taxation unchanged until every one of the Townshend duties had been removed. In both cities, there was an active dispute over the merits of the situation, and a further controversy over the question of where the power lay to re-open importation. It was clear that the merchants had been the prime movers in non-importation; but they had depended upon the populace for endorsement and support. Could the merchants give up their agreement without the consent of the populace?

At Philadelphia, the importers of British goods had been nursing a particular grievance because the importers of wines and molasses remained undisturbed in their traffic, notwithstanding that duties derived from these sources were piling up in the British treasury. Moreover, the Maryland Agreement, differing from the Philadelphia Agreement, permitted the importation of coarse woolens, an article necessary for the Indian trade; and the Maryland merchants were running away with their trade.[1] As a protest, four members, including John Reynell, the chairman, resigned from the Committee of Merchants, and three others ceased to attend meetings; the committee was reduced to twelve members.[2] These ex-members, with other interested merchants, began to agitate a relaxation of the agreement, and quickly drew the fire of the newspaper writers.

An article in the *Pennsylvania Chronicle*, May 7, 1770, maintained that the merchants would be betraying the American cause, if importation were resumed, and that the

[1] *Pa. Mag.*, vol. xiv, pp. 42-43.
[2] Circular letter of the "late Committee," *Pa. Chron.*, Oct. 1, 1770.

consuming class would buy no goods from them in such a contingency.[1] Other writers denied that two or three hundred signers of the agreement had " the sole right to determine a question of liberty that most nearly concerns every freeman of this province."[2] A meeting of the subscribers of the non-importation was called for Monday afternoon, May 14. As many of the signers were not in the importing business and were thus likely to vote a continuance of the agreement, the importing merchants held several sessions in preparation for the occasion and agreed that each should be present promptly at the hour set and bring with him a friend. This scheme was detected at the last moment and exposed in a broadside, addressed to the artificers, manufacturers and mechanics, probably written by Charles Thomson.[3] As a result, the meeting, when it assembled, was prevailed upon to postpone definite action until June 5 and, in the meantime, to consult with the merchants of New York and Boston.[4]

The merchants of the sister ports, however, declared against any change in their agreements, Boston on principle, New York because of the hope that the tea duty would be repealed in the next few weeks.[5] On May 23, a meeting of the workingmen and tradesmen of Philadelphia resolved their unanimous determination " to render the non-importation, as it now stands, permanent," and agreed to support this action at the meeting of June 5.[6] About the same time,

[1] For similar arguments, *vide* " Tradesman " in *ibid.*, May 21, 1770; " Nestor " in *Pa. Journ.*, July 12, Aug. 9.

[2] " Cato " in *Pa. Chron.*, June 4, 1770; " Son of Liberty " in *Pa. Gaz.*, May 31; letter from Philadelphia in *N. Y. Journ.*, May 31.

[3] *Pa. Chron.*, May 14, 1770; *Pa. Mag.*, vol. xiv, pp. 43-44.

[4] *N. Y. Journ.*, Aug. 16, 1770.

[5] *Bos. Eve. Post*, May 28, 1770; *N. Y. Journ.*, May 24, Aug. 16.

[6] *Pa. Gaz.*, May 24, 1770; also *N. Y. Journ.*, May 31.

letters were received by Joseph Galloway and Charles Thomson from Doctor Franklin in England, urging Philadelphia to persist in the agreement; and his advice had "wonderful effects." [1] The trend of events was distinctly turning in favor of the opponents of change; and at the general meeting of inhabitants on June 5, the signers of the agreement, having first met by themselves, agreed, with only four dissenting votes, to make no alteration in it " at this time." [2]

The inhabitants of New York engaged in a similar controversy, although the outcome was different. The non-importation pact was there based upon an agreement of the merchants, confirmed and supported by a separate agreement of the tradesmen and workingmen. The issue between the two groups was made clear in the opening sentences of a broadside issued about the middle of May: " Nothing can be more flagrantly wrong than the Assertion of some of our Mercantile Dons that the Mechanics have no Right to give their Sentiments about the Importation of British Commodities. . . . What particular Class among us has an exclusive Right to decide a Question of General Concern?" [3]

At a meeting on May 18, prompted by the letter from Philadelphia, the merchants decided, as we have seen, " to wait a few Weeks longer in Hopes of hearing the Duty on Tea would also be repealed " before taking any action.[4] This brought about a meeting of the inhabitants of all ranks, who voted by a large majority to preserve the non-importation inviolate and to boycott all persons who should transgress it. They also issued a pronunciamento against the

[1] *Pa. Mag.*, vol. xiv, p. 45; Colden, *Letter Books,* vol. ii, p. 223.
[2] *Pa. Gaz.*, June 7, 1770.
[3] Broadside in N. Y. Pub. Libr., signed " Brutus."
[4] *N. Y. Journ.*, May 24, Aug. 16, 1770.

cargo of a Glasgow vessel then in the harbor, a matter already dealt with in regular manner by the Committee of Merchants.[1] The Committee of Merchants accepted the issue, resigned their seats because of the irregular proceedings of the mass meeting, and had the satisfaction of being re-elected at a public meeting of citizens.[2] On the strength of this vindication, the Committee of Merchants, now convinced that hope of a total repeal of the Townshend duties was illusory, determined to abandon the agreement and confine non-importation only to dutied articles; and for this purpose they invited the merchants of the non-importing commercial provinces to send delegates to a congress at Norwalk on June 18, " to adopt one general solid System for the Benefit of the Whole, that no one Colony may be liable to the Censure or Reproaches of another . . ."[3]

The invitation found the other trading towns in anything but a receptive mood. The Boston trade voted unanimously to have nothing to do with it, chiefly for the reason that any deviation from the present agreement would create an impression in England prejudicial to a further redress of grievances.[4] The merchants of Essex County, New Jersey, asked pointedly: " Shall we meet to consult whether we have Honour or Faith or public Virtue . . . If you had proposed a Meeting for strengthening . . . the Resolutions of the Colonies, we should have joined you."[5] Hardly less decisive were the answers of meetings at Newark and New

[1] This meeting occurred on May 30. *Ibid.*, June 7, 1770.

[2] The re-election occurred on June 1. *N. Y. Gaz. & Merc.*, June 4, 1770; *N. Y. Journ.*, June 7.

[3] Circular letter of June 2; *New London Gaz.*, June 15, 1770; also *N. Y. Journ.*, June 28, Aug. 16.

[4] The Boston meeting occurred on June 8. *Bos. Eve. Post*, June 11, 1770; also *N. Y. Journ.*, June 21.

[5] *Ibid.*, July 5, 1770; also *1 N. J. Arch.*, vol. xxvii, pp. 193-194.

Brunswick a few days later, although the people of the latter place agreed to accept the conclusions of the Norwalk congress.[1] Even the Philadelphia merchants, stiffened by the action of the public meeting of June 5, advised against precipitate measures, and refused to take part in the proposed congress.[2] Only at Hartford and Providence did the merchants actually appoint delegates; and the latter rescinded their action when they learned of Boston's declination.[3] The New Yorkers were thus forced to solve their problem according to their own lights.

It was probably the unfavorable action of the Boston merchants that determined the New York promoters of importation to abandon the project of a congress and to concentrate their efforts at once on the local situation. Their plan was to ascertain the sentiments of the inhabitants by a house-to-house poll. When "a number of selfish, mercenary importers and a few mechanicks" proposed this course to the Committee of Merchants, that body, while withholding official assent, made it clear that they would not discountenance the proceedings.[4] How deeply individual members of the committee were interested in this scheme was revealed on June 14 when the ultra-radical Isaac Sears and the shopkeeper Peter Vander Voort resigned membership on the ground that many of the committee were working to break through the agreement.[5] Beginning on June

[1] *N. Y. Gaz. & Merc.*, Aug. 6, 1770; *N. Y. Journ.*, June 28.

[2] Letter of June 18; *ibid.*, Aug. 9, 1770.

[3] *New London Gaz.*, June 15, 1770; *Prov. Gaz.*, June 16.

[4] *N. Y. Journ.*, June 21, 1770. The words quoted are taken from an account by "A Son of Liberty" in the same issue. *Vide* also *N. Y. Gaz. & Post-Boy*, July 2.

[5] *N. Y. Journ.*, June 21, 1770. Jacob Watson and Edward Laight were among those who worked openly for an alteration of the agreement. *Ibid.*, July 12.

12, the poll was taken by persons appointed in each ward, each inhabitant being asked if he approved of confining non-importation to tea and other dutied articles, provided Boston and Philadelphia concurred; or if he preferred the continuance of the present agreement. Now, as the promoters of the poll knew of the unfaltering resolution of Boston, it is clear, as the non-importers charged, that their motive was to feel the pulse of the people with a view of determining whether it would be safe to ask their support later when it was learned that the other two towns had refused to co-operate. The canvass showed that 1180 persons favored re-opening trade in concert with Boston and Philadelphia, about 300 were indifferent or unwilling to talk, and a minority, whose number was not stated, preferred the existing system. Colden noted that "the principal Inhabitants" voted for importation and that "few of any distinction declared in opposition to it."[1] The opposition protested that the voters for importation were hardly one-fourth of the city people entitled to vote, and that the country folks should have been consulted.

On June 16, letters were despatched to Boston and Philadelphia with news of the New York vote. The merchants in those places, however, saw no reason for revising their former decisions.[2] On July 4 a broadside, scattered about

[1] *Letter Books,* vol. ii, p. 223.
[2] *N. Y. Journ.,* July 5, 1770; *Bos. Eve. Post,* July 2. The Boston Committee of Merchants reminded the New York Committee that, as the preamble of the Townshend Act remained unrepealed, it was clear that the tea duty was retained expressly for raising a revenue. Furthermore, they asserted that the sentiment of Boston had been ascertained in the surest way, "that is, not by appointing Gentlemen to go thro' the several Wards, asking Persons singly, but by calling a Meeting and there coming to a Conclusion after fair Debate and reasoning upon the Point." *N. Y. Gaz. & Merc.,* July 30. From the merchants at Hartford, where Silas Deane was a member of the committee, came likewise a letter protesting against any alteration. *Conn. Journ.,* July 27.

New York, inquired of the public whether, in face of this uniform response, it would be just or politic or honorable for New York to undertake a measure "independent of the Approbation of those whose hearty Concurrence we have hitherto solicited?" New York was reminded of having originated non-importation at the time of the Stamp Act; "and shall New York be the first to disgrace an Expedient originally devised by itself . . . ?"[1]

But this appeal and others like it fell on deaf ears. The latter days of June brought to New York authentic news that an act of Parliament had been passed with the sole view of relieving business stringency in that province. This was the statute exempting New York temporarily from the operations of the general prohibition of legal-tender currency, enacted in 1764, and authorizing her to issue £120,000 in legal-tender paper money.[2] This event removed any remaining misgivings that the merchants may have felt; the body of the trade worked with precision and speed. The group solidarity of the merchants was clearly revealed by an article from New York in a Boston newspaper, containing the names of some of those who were working hardest for a re-opening of trade. Of the one hundred and twenty-eight persons named in the article, eighty-five were classed as merchants or importers; eighteen as dealers or shopkeepers; three as vendue-masters; two as brewers. Of workingmen (such as carpenters, blacksmiths, rope-makers, *etc.*), there were but twelve.[3] Fifteen of the one hundred and twenty-eight were members of the Committee of Mer-

---

[1] Signed "Fabius;" *N. Y. Journ.*, July 12, 1770.

[2] 10 George III, c. 35; Becker, *N. Y. Parties, 1760-1776*, pp. 69-71, 77-79, 88.

[3] "Bona Fide" in *Bos. Gaz.*, July 23, 1770. To complete the list, there were three lawyers, three royal officials, Hugh Gaine, editor of the *New York Gazette and Mercury*, and James DeLancey, Esq., member of the General Assembly.

chants (of which there were at that time twenty-two members in all); and among the fifteen was Isaac Low, the chairman. Colden is authority for the assertion that all the members of the governor's council, with a single exception, and the city representatives in the Assembly were zealous advocates of importation.[1] The merchants had an excellent talking-point in the exaggerated charges of violations of non-importation at Boston; and especially convincing for their purpose proved a timely pamphlet from John Mein's press, which purported to give an account of British importations into Boston from January 1 to June 19 of the current year.[2]

The first step taken by the New York Committee of Merchants, upon hearing from Boston, was to call a meeting of citizens and read the replies that had come from Philadelphia and Boston.[3] The crowd that assembled was not as small as the promoters of the meeting had apparently intended, for a large majority opposed the proposal for taking another poll of the city. A motion was then made that the letters read should be published, so that the people might better judge of the expediency of departing from the agreement; but the committee, through their chairman, declined to permit publication. A few days later, on Saturday, July 7, a number of merchants conferred privately with several members of the committee, and decided, notwithstanding the public vote, that a poll of the city should be taken at once. With the sanction of the committee, two persons, one

[1] *Letter Books,* vol. ii, p. 229.

[2] Reprinted in *N. Y. Gaz. & Merc.,* Aug. 27, 1770. For a pointed correspondence between the Boston and New York committees with regard to this pamphlet, *vide* the *N. Y. Journ.,* Aug. 9, and *Bos. Eve. Post,* Sept. 10.

[3] For this meeting and the troubles during the poll, *vide* two letters in *Bos. Eve. Post,* July 16, 1770; "A Citizen" in *N. Y. Gaz. & Merc.,* July 23; accounts in *N. Y. Col. Docs.,* vol. viii, pp. 218-220.

of each party, were therefore appointed to canvass each ward, presenting to the citizens, without comment, this proposition: as the people of Boston and Philadelphia are in favor of maintaining their agreements unchanged, is it your judgment " that we should also abide by our present Non-Importation Agreement; or to import every Thing except the Articles which are, or may hereafter be, subject to Duty?"

At noon the same day, the radicals, led by Isaac Sears and Alexander McDougall, met at the City Hall, declared unanimously against an importation, and agreed to use all lawful means to oppose it. In the evening a mob collected, parading the streets with a flag inscribed with the legend, " Liberty and no Importation but in Union with the other Colonies," hissing and hooting at the doors of those who favored importation. A crowd of the opposition gathered, and under the leadership of Elias Desbrosses, magistrate of the city and already slated for the next presidency of the Chamber of Commerce, they came in collision with the rioters in Wall Street, where stiff blows were exchanged with cane and club and the non-importers finally dispersed.

By Monday evening, July 9, the canvass was completed; and the vote resulted in a victory for the merchants. A protest signed by many inhabitants later declared that " only 794 Persons in this populous City, including all Ranks and both Sexes," signed for importation, notwithstanding " the Co-operation of Interest, Necessity and Influence."[1] It was further claimed that the great number of those entitled to vote had abstained because they considered the proceeding irregular.[2] Nevertheless, the merchants accepted the poll as

[1] *N. Y. Journ.*, July 26, Aug. 2, 1770.

[2] *Ibid.*, July 12, 1770. Another method employed to discredit the poll is illustrated by the recantation of Charles Prosser for signing in favor of importation when "too much in Liquor to be trusted with the common Rights of Mankind." *Conn. Cour.*, Aug. 20.

conclusive; and within two days a vessel departed for England with orders for a general importation of goods, except tea or any other dutied articles.¹

The late Committee of Merchants of New York made all haste to inform their brethren in Philadelphia and Boston of the new developments. When a copy of the letter reached Princeton, James Madison and his fellow-students, garbed in black gowns, solemnly witnessed the burning of the letter by a hangman, while the college bell tolled funereal peals.² This was an augury of the reception that the letter was to receive elsewhere. At Philadelphia, a great meeting of the inhabitants of the city and county adopted numerous resolutions, condemning the action of New York as " a sordid and wanton Defection from the common Cause " and declaring a boycott against that city except for five necessary articles.³ At Boston, a meeting of the trade at Faneuil Hall voted unanimously that the New York letter, " in just indignation, abhorrence and detestation, be forthwith torn into pieces and thrown to the winds as unworthy of the least notice;" which was accordingly done.⁴ The New York Committee received a scathing letter from the merchants of Albany, remarking on their " unaccountable Duplicity " and quoting cruelly from their recent letter of censure on Albany for wavering in their non-importation.⁵

¹ *N. Y. Journ.*, July 12, 1770; *N. Y. Col. Docs.*, vol. viii, pp. 220-221. On Nov. 26, Isaac Low advertised that, although he had lately been "distinguished as Chairman of a certain Committee," he had freshly imported goods in stock. *N. Y. Gaz. & Merc.*, Nov. 26.

² *N. Y. Journ.*, July 19, 1770; Madison, *Writings* (Hunt), vol. i, pp. 6-7.

³ Meeting of July 14; *Pa. Chron.*, July 16, 1770; also *Pa. Gaz.*, July 19. The excepted articles were: alkaline salt, skins, furs, flax and hemp.

⁴ Meeting of July 24; *Bos. Eve. Post*, July 30, 1770; also *N. Y. Journ.*, Aug. 2, 9. A New York sloop with a cargo of pork was turned away from Marblehead by the Committee of Merchants there. *Essex Gaz.*, Aug. 14.

⁵ *N. Y. Journ.*, Aug. 23, 1770. A town meeting at Huntington in

New Jersey was aflame with indignation. " Shall we be humbug'd out of our Liberty and enslaved only by a Sett of Traders?" wrote the committee of Somerset County.[1] Formal resolutions of censure and boycott were adopted by mass meetings in Woodbridge and New Brunswick and in the counties of Essex, Sussex and Burlington.[2] A New Yorker, daring to hawk fruit at Woodbridge, was " genteelly ducked to cool his courage."[3] The inhabitants of Sussex County, in the extreme northwestern corner of the province, resolved that, although they had hitherto patronized New York markets "by a long and tedious land-carriage," they would now turn their trade of wheat and iron " by the more natural and easy water-carriage down the River Delaware " to Trenton and Philadelphia.[4]

The people of Connecticut were equally incensed. The New Haven merchants and other inhabitants resolved to buy no British imports from New York and, when a general importation occurred, to exert their influence either to divert the trade of Connecticut to Boston or Philadelphia or to give preference to local merchants.[5] Before very many towns had followed this example, a public meeting at Hartford started a movement for a general meeting of " the mercantile and landed interest of the several towns " at

the eastern part of Long Island denounced the "mercenary and perfidious Conduct" of New York and resolved to maintain the non-importation inviolate. *Ibid.*, Aug. 30.

[1] *N. Y. Gaz. & Post-Boy*, Sept. 24, 1770; also *1 N. J. Arch.*, vol. xxvii, pp. 253-254.

[2] *N. Y. Journ.*, July 26, Aug. 9, Sept. 27, Oct.11, 1770; also *1 N. J. Arch.*, vol. xxvii, pp. 206-207, 215-217, 218-219, 252-253, 260-262.

[3] *N. Y. Journ.*, Aug. 9, 1770; also *1 N. J. Arch.*, vol. xxvii, p. 220.

[4] *N. Y. Gaz. & Post-Boy*, Sept. 24, 1770; also *1 N. J. Arch.*, vol. xxvii, pp. 252-253.

[5] Meeting of July 26; *Conn. Journ.*, Aug. 3, 1770.

New Haven on September 13 to adopt uniform measures in dealing with New York.¹ At this meeting, attended by delegates from a great majority of the towns, resolutions were passed to sever all intercourse with New York so far as the purchase of British imports was concerned.² From the plantation provinces, also, came expressions of indignation.³

The patriotic indignation of the other provinces at the defection of New York was splendid to behold. But the merchants throughout the continent realized in their hearts that the prostration of the stalwart pillar of New York would cause the whole great edifice to topple. The dry-goods importers at Philadelphia were stirred to re-open the agitation there. Some frankly placed their demand for alteration on the ground that a non-importation of tea would accomplish every desirable object, and that the defection of New York precluded any possibility of distressing British merchants at the same time that it made Pennsylvania traders a prey to the merchants of that city.⁴ Others re-

¹ *New London Gaz.*, Aug. 17, 1770; also *Mass. Spy*, Aug. 21.
² *Conn. Cour.*, Sept. 17, 1770; also *N. Y. Journ.*, Sept. 20.
³ Considerably less notice was attracted in the plantation provinces than in the commercial provinces. The inhabitants of Talbot County in Maryland resolved to cut off all trade relations with the province of New York. *Pa. Gaz.*, Aug. 23, 1770. A general meeting of merchants and inhabitants of Wilmington and Brunswick in North Carolina took occasion to renew their agreement "with great spirit and unanimity." *Mass. Spy*, Sept. [Dec.] 3, 1770. At Charleston, South Carolina the keenest interest was displayed. A general meeting of August 22 unanimously voted that the "scandalous Revolt from the common Cause of Freedom" should be punished by an absolute boycott; and in the subsequent months, New York skippers were actually forbidden trading rights in the port. *S. C. Gaz.*, Aug. 20, 23, Sept. 6, 27, Nov. 22, 1770.
⁴ "Philo-Veritas" in *Pa. Gaz.*, Aug. 2, 1770; "Philadelphian" in *ibid.*, Aug. 16; Collins, *Letter-Book 1761-1773*, Nov. 24.

vived the old complaint that the persons most violent in favor of the existing agreement were in general "Men little or not at all interested in the [drygoods] Trade" but who were cheerfully paying duties on molasses, sugar and wine in the course of their trade with the West Indies and the Wine Islands.[1]

To these arguments came the answer of "Juris Prudens" in exalted strain—that if the wine and molasses merchants were little affected, the glory of the drygoods merchants was all the greater; and he recalled that "the Weight of the Stamp Act fell upon the Lawyers, they generously bore it and desired not Partners in Distress."[2] Rather more pointed was the reminder given by "Amor Patriae" that the merchants had deliberately chosen to make the Townshend duties the sole object of repeal, even to the point of rejecting a proposition from Boston for including the wine and molasses duties as objects; that therefore reflections upon these latter merchants had no bearing upon the matter under discussion.[3] Other writers emphasized that the tea act was, in principle, just as much a violation of American rights as the duties that had been repealed, and that the material condition of the poor in Pennsylvania was better than it had been in years.[4]

Matters came to a head when the seven ex-members of the Committee of Merchants joined with seven other mercantile firms, on September 12, 1770, to request the committee to canvass the sentiments of the subscribers of the agreement in a house-to-house poll. The committee, headed

[1] "Philo-Veritas" in *Pa. Gaz.*, July 19, 1770; "Talionis" in *Pa. Chron.*, Aug. 8.
[2] *Pa. Gaz.*, Aug. 2, 1770.
[3] *Ibid.*, July 26, 1770.
[4] "True Philadelphian" and "Pennsylvanian" in *ibid.*, Aug. 23, 1770.

by Charles Thomson and William Fisher, replied that the agreement itself provided the only method of its amendment,—through a general meeting of subscribers after three days' notice.[1] Without consulting the committee further, the fourteen sent notices around to the subscribers to meet at Davenport's Tavern on Thursday, September 20.[2] Only one hundred and thirty-five persons attended, and the importers had, through assiduous effort, succeeded in collecting a majority favorable to their design. The committee appeared, made a fervent appeal to the meeting to be loyal to the liberties of America, and presented a list of three carefully worded questions to be voted on, with the purpose of preventing any alteration except in concert with the other provinces and of patterning the alteration, should any be made, on the Maryland or Virginia association. The importers submitted a counter-list of questions, which put squarely before the gathering the expediency of restricting non-importation to tea and other dutied articles, as the New Yorkers had done. The meeting voted to consider the last list of questions first and passed them in the affirmative. A trial vote on one of the committee's questions showed an adverse vote of 89 to 45. The committee then contended that the inhabitants in general should have a vote in the matter and that, in any case, the subscribers not present should be consulted. But they could make no headway against the majority; and Charles Thomson, speaking for the eleven members of the committee, declared that they deemed that the agreement had been broken and announced their resignation.

The people of Philadelphia did not accept the decision

[1] *Pa. Gaz.*, Sept. 20, 1770.
[2] For accounts of this meeting, *vide ibid.*, Sept. 27, Oct. 11, 1770; and especially the circular letter of the "late Committee" in *Pa. Chron.*, Oct. 1.

without loud protest. A grand jury, of which John Gibson, one of the resigned committeemen, was foreman, declared that they would unite with their fellow-citizens to discountenance the use of British goods until the parliamentary claim to colonial taxation was relinquished, the tea duty repealed, the jurisdiction and power of the vice-admiralty courts restricted, the Customs Board dissolved, and the standing army removed or placed under direction of the civil authority.[1] A mass meeting of inhabitants voted, with only one dissenting voice, to adopt the resolutions which the committee had submitted in vain to the merchants' meeting; and a formal request was made that the merchants should re-consider their action.[2] Meantime, the merchants had chosen a new committee to supervise enforcement of the altered agreement; and on Saturday, the twenty-ninth, the *London Packet* sailed with the orders of the merchants for British merchandise.[3]

It was scarcely to be expected that the merchants at Boston should continue their non-importation when all about them yielded to the stern call of necessity. " Some who have been leaders would have been glad to hold out longer," wrote Dr. Andrew Eliot, " but persons in trade were weary, and, as interest is generally their god, began to be furious."[4] After all, their purpose of bringing pressure to bear upon British merchants and manufacturers was already defeated by the defection of New York and Philadelphia. The first indication of weakening came when the merchants, notwithstanding their intense indignation, failed to pass resolutions of boycott when New York departed the agreement.[5]

[1] September 24; *Pa. Gas.*, Sept. 27, 1770.
[2] September 27; *ibid.*, Oct. 4, 1770.
[3] *Pa. Chron.*, Sept. 24, 1770; *N. Y. Journ.*, Oct. 11.
[4] *4 M. H. S. Colls.*, vol. iv, p. 458.
[5] *Vide* sarcastic comment in *Newport Merc.*, Aug. 6, 1770; also

On September 11, a few days before the final steps to dissolve the Philadelphia agreement had been taken, a great meeting of the Boston trade was held, at which it was estimated that not less than one thousand were present, including " a very great Number of the principal and most wealthy Merchants, as well as the most respectable Tradesmen of the Town." The assemblage voted to propose to Philadelphia an interprovincial congress of merchants to plan ways and means of strengthening the union of the provinces.[1] The letter reached Philadelphia after the committee of that city had become non-existent. The news of the desertion of Philadelphia brought the Boston merchants to a decision after a few weeks of irresolution; on October 12, they met at the British Coffee House and unanimously voted to open the importation of all British goods, except tea and such other articles as were or might be subject to revenue duties.[2] A week later, the goods which had been placed in store were delivered up to their owners.[3]

The downfall of non-importation in the commercial provinces meant that the associations to the southward must soon crumble also. The merchants of Baltimore lost little time in sending forth a call for a meeting of the General Committee of Maryland at Annapolis when they learned that the Philadelphia merchants had forsaken their agreement. They resolved, furthermore, that if the provincial meeting

Mass. Spy, Aug. 14. The *Mass. Spy* on November 5 quoted from a London paper that "at a late Meeting of the American Merchants, it was agreed to give unlimited Credit to such of the Colonies as should follow the Example of New York, by a general Importation." Such rumors, whether true or not, served no doubt to increase the sentiment for renewing importation.

[1] *Bos. Gaz.*, Sept. 17, 1770; *Pa. Chron.*, Oct. 1.
[2] *Mass. Spy*, Oct. 13, 1770; also *Mass Gaz. & Post-Boy*, Oct. 15.
[3] *Mass. Spy*, Oct. 20, 1770.

should not be held, they would consider the association dissolved and open the importation of all goods save tea and other dutied articles.[1] A provincial meeting was duly held on October 25, but it proved a rather heterogeneous gathering, consisting of a majority of the Assembly, several Annapolis merchants, some members of the Council, a number of planters, and of properly chosen deputations from only three counties. Jonathan Hudson, representing the Baltimore merchants, defiantly informed the meeting that his constituents were determined to depart the association notwithstanding any resolutions they might adopt, and that he had been instructed to agree to no terms short of a dissolution of the association. The meeting answered by voting that the association should be strictly adhered to and that all trade should be stopped with the Baltimore merchants or any other violators.[2] The Annapolis incident proved to be only a piece of theatricalism so far as the merchants of the province were concerned. "A Merchant of Maryland" ridiculed the gathering as "a fortuitous Collection, not of Merchants, but of Counsellors, Representatives, Lawyers, and others, who had been convened at Annapolis on other public Business;" and he remarked "how absurd, not to say indecent, it is for Men whose Occupations and Employments lie altogether in a different Walk, to attempt giving Law to the mercantile Part of the Community."[3] The subsequent months showed that he spoke with entire truthfulness when he said that the merchants did not intend to pay "the least Regard to those flaming and ridiculous Resolutions which were lately flashed off," but that they would confine their non-importation only to tea and other dutied articles.

[1] October 5, *Md. Gaz.*, Oct. 11, 1770; also *Pa. Gaz.*, Oct. 18.
[2] *Md. Gaz.*, Nov. 1, 1770; also *Pa. Gaz.*, Nov. 8.
[3] *Ibid.*, Dec. 13, 1770.

In the latter part of October the South Carolina General Committee addressed a circular letter to the northern provinces with the purpose of learning whether the body of the people acquiesced in the decision of the mercantile portion in altering the non-importation.[1] While the liberal terms of the South Carolina Association and its comparatively recent adoption had prevented the growth of the intense dissatisfaction which had disrupted the northern agreements, yet the defection of the commercial provinces, joined with a widespread belief that the declining price of rice was due to the non-importation,[2] resulted in seriously weakening the sentiment in South Carolina. On November 20, the General Committee announced that a meeting of the subscribers of the association would be held on December 13 to decide as to their future course.[3] The merchant, Henry Laurens, presided at the meeting. The non-importing faction were led by Thomas Lynch, planter and radical, who came fifty miles for the purpose and "exerted all his eloquence & even the trope of rhetorical tears for the expiring liberty of his dear country which the merchants would sell like any other merchandize."[4] It was quickly evident that the importers controlled a majority; a motion to delay action until the General Assembly met, and an effort to continue the association with an open importation from Holland, met with defeat. The assemblage thereupon voted to limit

[1] *S. C. Gaz.*, Nov. 1, 1770; also *Mass. Spy*, Jan. 3, 1771.

[2] "A Planter" in *S. C. Gaz.*, Dec. 27, 1770. Current newspapers show that rice averaged 70s. per hundredweight in 1768 (before the non-importation); 60s. during 1769; 45s. during 1770.

[3] *S. C. Gaz.*, Nov. 22, 1770. For an account of the meeting, *vide ibid.*, Dec. 13.

[4] Bull to Hillsborough, quoted in McCrady, *S. C. under Royal Govt.*, pp. 682-683.

non-importation and non-consumption to tea and other articles subject to duty.[1]

In Virginia, the non-importation spirit, which had been feeble throughout, gradually subsided. A meeting of associators was called for December 14, 1770, at Williamsburg; but so few attended that they did nothing but adjourn until the following summer.[2] In February Thomas Jefferson sent an order for goods to an English merchant with instructions to send immediately only such goods as were admissible by the association; by June he felt so confident that the approaching meeting would repeal the association, except for dutied articles, that he took time by the forelock and ordered the shoes and other debarred articles to be shipped at once.[3] Early in July the Virginia meeting took the action that Jefferson had anticipated.[4] In North Carolina, no record apparently remains of the passing of the non-importation.

Before leaving the subject of the second non-importation movement, it would appear desirable to determine the effects of the colonial plan of commercial coercion on Great Britain. Statistics of trade show that the English merchants and manufacturers dependent upon American commerce suf-

---

[1] A committee was appointed to send a protest in behalf of South Carolina against the conduct of the northern provinces. There appeared to be a strong sentiment in favor of stopping trade with those parts, especially since it was held that that commerce drained specie from South Carolina "mostly for mere Trash." But this action was not taken, apparently because "the defection not having been among the *Landholders, Farmers and Mechanicks* . . . it would be unjust to retaliate upon *them*, for the Injuries received from *some* of the *Merchants* in those Colonies." *S. C. Gaz.*, Dec. 27, 1770.

[2] *Brit. Papers* ("*Sparks Mss.*"), vol. ii, p. 70.

[3] *Writings* (Ford), vol. i, pp. 387-389, 394-395.

[4] Washington, *Writings* (Ford), vol. ii, pp. 334-338.

fered a great loss of trade.¹ Friends of parliamentary taxation in England were quick to claim that the colonies were being partially supplied by means of a clandestine trade by way of Quebec and Halifax; but there was little basis for this charge in fact.² Yet, notwithstanding the decline of American trade, very little actual distress was experienced in England during the period of the non-importation. This was the result of several fortuitous circumstances unconnected with the American situation. Crops in England were better than they had been in years, and the material condition of the workingmen was much improved by the general reduction of the price of provisions.³ Further than this, the Russo-Turkish war, which broke out in 1768, and the increased demand for woolens in Germany, as well as other unusual circumstances, served to neutralize the effects which the American non-importation agreements would otherwise have produced.⁴

" Not a manufacturing village in this kingdom complains

---

[1] Exports to the thirteen colonies fell from £2,157,218 in 1768 to £1,336,122 in 1769; imports from the colonies, from £1,251,454 to £1,060,206. *Vide* Macpherson, *Annals of Com.*, vol. iii, under the appropriate dates, for these and the other figures cited hereafter.

[2] *Pa. Gaz.*, June 21, Sept. 6, 1770; *N. Y. Journ.*, Aug. 30, Sept. 6. There was probably some evasion of non-importation by way of Canada, for the purpose, it would appear, of providing Albany traders with merchandise for the Indian trade. English importations at Quebec increased from £110,598 in 1768 to £174,435 in 1769; at Newfoundland, from £46,761 to £64,080; at Nova Scotia, there was a small decrease. A suspicious increase of imports occurred at Jamaica, from £473,146 in 1768 to £570,468 in the following year; but contemporary writers failed to prefer any charges on this score.

[3] *Bos. Chron.*, Nov. 16, 1769; also *N. Y. Gaz. & Merc.*, Nov. 27.

[4] This was repeatedly averred. *E. g., vide* 5 *M. H. S. Colls.*, vol. ix, pp. 384-385; *Pa. Gaz.*, Jan. 4, Sept. 6, 1770; *Bos. Chron.*, June 11; *N. Y. Gaz. & Post-Boy*, May 21; *N. Y. Journ.*, Sept. 27; *Mass. Spy*, Sept. 15; Adams, John, *Works*, vol. ii, p. 352; *N. Y. Gaz. & Merc.*, Nov. 27, 1769.

of a slack trade," declared a London newspaper of November 27, 1768, " nay, what is more, when some of them were applied to, at the close of last session to sign a petition setting forth their distresses arising from the suspension of the American orders, they said that they were then so fully employed that they could not, with any colour of truth, sign such a petition." [1] An American travelling in England wrote back to Philadelphia friends in May, 1770, that goods were scarce and prices advanced at Birmingham, Halifax and Leeds, and only at Sheffield were prices lower than formerly.[2] Even the merchant, Barlow Trecothick, while arguing before the House of Commons for a total repeal of the Townshend duties in April, 1770, admitted that " at present all our manufacturers were employed and all our manufactures vended," pointing out, however, that the woolens trade with Germany and northern Europe was only transitory, " a passing cloud." [3]

" The merchants here," wrote Dr. Franklin from London in March, 1770, " were at length prevailed on to present a petition, but they moved slowly, and some of them, I thought, reluctantly." [4] Some of the merchants in American trade were buoyed up by the rumors from Boston that the agreements were collapsing;[5] others declared impatiently that non-importation " is now a stale device and will not do a second time;" [6] still others had gotten their share of

[1] *N. Y. Journ.*, Feb. 22, 1770.

[2] *Pa. Gaz.*, Aug. 16, 1770; also *N. Y. Journ.*, Aug. 30.

[3] *Bos. Chron.*, June 11, 1770; 5 *M. H. S. Colls.*, vol. ix, pp. 430-431. In face of this universally accepted evidence, however, it should be noted that the statistics in Macpherson's *Annals of Commerce* do not disclose any abnormal increase in English exportations to Russia, Holland or Germany.

[4] *Writings* (Smyth), vol. v, p. 252.

[5] *Bos. Chron.*, Jan. 8, 1770; also *N. Y. Journ.*, Jan. 18.

[6] *N. Y. Gaz. & Merc.*, Sept. 3, 1770.

the new trade with northern Europe. At the instigation of the colonial agents, the merchants in American trade at Bristol and London finally petitioned Parliament in January and February, 1770, for a total repeal of the Townshend duties.[1] The manufacturing towns absolutely refused to move; and thus the memorials lacked the solid business support which had been given to the demand for the repeal of the Stamp Act. The petition of the London merchants furnished merely the occasion, not the cause, for Lord North's motion to repeal all the Townshend duties save the tea tax. The ministry had announced its intention as early as 1769 so to proceed; and Lord North's motion was based on the claim that the Townshend law, the product of a former ministry, was "preposterous" in so far as it imposed taxes on British manufactures.[2] He did not deny that "dangerous combinations" had been formed beyond the Atlantic and that the British merchants with American connections were discontented; but it was clear that the former consideration made him reluctant to make any concessions at all, while the force of the latter was minimized by the practical certainty that the non-importation agreements could not continue much longer. In conclusion, then, it would appear that the effects of American trade coercion were off-set by a fortuitous expansion of British commerce; and that the partial repeal was produced by a desire to correct a law, passed by a former ministry and based upon a principle injurious to British commercial interests.

[1] *Va. Mag.*, vol. xii, p. 164; *Pa. Gaz.*, Apr. 26, 1770.
[2] *Parliamentary History*, vol. xvi, pp. 853-855; *5 M. H. S. Colls.*, vol. ix, pp. 421-422.

CHAPTER VI

COLONIAL PROSPERITY AND A NEW PERIL (1770-1773)

THE three years that followed the breakdown of the great mercantile combination were, for the most part, years of material prosperity and political calm. In the earlier years the merchants of the commercial provinces had been the backbone of the demand for a restricted parliamentary control; but in the period following the autumn of 1770 the alliance of the commercial interests and the radicals was broken. The merchants were dominated by a desire to prevent any further strengthening of non-mercantile power in provincial politics and by a substantial satisfaction in the concessions that Parliament had made. The influence of the moderates generally was thrown in favor of "letting well enough alone;" and the return of better times seemed an irrefutable argument in favor of this position. Happy it would have been for the merchant class and for the stability of the British empire if the merchants had not been induced to depart from this position during a few critical weeks in the fall of 1773!

Colden at New York observed: "All Men of property are so sensible of their danger, from Riots and tumults, that they will not rashly be induced to enter into combinations, which may promote disorder for the future, but will endeavour to promote due subordination to legal authority." [1] Even Thomas Cushing, who as speaker of the Massachusetts House of Representatives had been a leading spokesman for

---

[1] *N. Y. Col. Docs.*, vol. viii, p. 217.

radical colonial demands and who as a merchant continued somewhat restive under the existing trade regulations, preferred that "high points about the supreme authority of Parliament" should "fall asleep" lest there be "great danger of bringing on a rupture fatal to both countries."[1] John Adams wrote in his diary at this time that he had learned wisdom from his experience in fighting in behalf of the people's rights: "I shall certainly become more retired and cautious. I shall certainly mind my own farm and my own office."[2] As "Chronus" expressed it, the public had become impatient with the "group of gloomy mortals" who prated unceasingly of tyranny. He noted that justice was duly administered by "learned and judicious men who have estates and property of their own and who are therefore likely to be as tenacious of the public rights and liberties as any other person can be;" that shops were filled with merchandise, business thriving; that ships were plying a brisk trade abroad and farmers were busily cultivating their own lands. Were such men slaves groaning from lack of liberty? he queried; and he reminded his readers of the evils resulting in the past from following "officious Patriots," men who "have nothing to lose, but when public rule and order are broken in upon and all things are thrown into confusion, they may be gainers."[3]

After six years of almost continuous agitation and bad business conditions, the merchants turned, with a sense of profound relief, to the pleasant task of wooing the profits of commerce. Conditions generally were favorable to the pursuit of this beguiling occupation. The non-importation had caused a net balance of trade in favor of the com-

[1] 4 *M. H. S. Colls.*, vol. iv, p. 360.
[2] *Works* (Adams, C. F.), vol. ii, p. 260.
[3] *Mass. Gaz. & Post-Boy*, Jan. 6, 1772.

mercial provinces; and for the first time in memory, gold was imported from England in the course of commerce. The great demand for corn in France, Spain and Italy, caused by devastating floods, had enabled the American merchants to pay off their standing debts in England; and, due to the non-importation, they had ordered their balance to be transmitted to them in bullion instead of in the form of merchandise.[1] It was with great elation that a Philadelphia newspaper announced that the brig *Dolphin* had brought to Philadelphia £6000 sterling in specie from London, and a little later, that two vessels had arrived with £10,000 more, " this being some of the golden fruits of the Non-Importation. . ."[2] The same thing went on at other ports.[3]

With so much inactive capital on hand, the re-opening of trade in the last months of 1770 caused the colonial merchants to invest in great quantities of British wares. English houses met them more than half way with liberal extensions of credit in order to regain the American market. In such centres as New England and Pennsylvania, British importations increased three- to fivefold. "Commerce never was in a more flourishing state."[4] In fact, business was experiencing too rapid a recovery from depression; the merchants became greatly overstocked, and in the course of the next year or so, competition at times caused goods to sell lower than the first cost and charges.[5] Meantime, however,

[1] *Mass. Gaz. & Post-Boy*, Sept. 24, 1770; *Mass. Spy*, Oct. 30; *London Chron.*, Nov. 8; *Parliamentary History*, vol. xvi, p. 861.

[2] *Pa. Journ.*, Aug. 30, Nov. 1, 1770.

[3] *S. C. Gaz.*, Nov. 22, 1771; *Am. Hist. Rev.*, vol. viii, p. 320.

[4] Hutchinson, *Mass. Bay*, vol. iii, p. 350.

[5] Collins, *Letter-Book 1761-1773*, Dec. 6, 1771; Feb. 28, Oct. 8, 1772; Mch. 23, Apr. 28, Aug. 3, 1773; Brown, *John Hancock His Book*, p. 175; "A Merchant" in *Mass. Spy*, Jan. 9, 1772.

the merchants felt they were enjoying a deserved feast after a long and trying fast.

The newspaper advertising indicated that colonial agricultural products and certain varieties of domestic manufactures were enjoying a wider sale than ever before. The Bostonian and New Yorker could expect to find in the local shops Pennsylvania flour and iron, " Choice Philadelphia Beer," potash kettles cast at Salisbury, Conn., Rhode Island cheese, Virginia tobacco, and Carolina pitch, indigo and rice. The first volume of Blackstone was reprinted at Boston for two dollars although the price of the British edition was three times as great. Lynn shoes for women, New England cod-fish hooks, Milton paper and Boston-made sails had an established clientele. Philadelphia newspapers advertised locally-made watches, bar steel, pot and pearlashes. Governor Franklin of New Jersey transmitted to the home government the report that, during the non-importation struggle, a new slitting mill had been erected in Morris County, so contrived as to be an appendage to a grist mill and in such a manner as to evade the parliamentary prohibition.[1]

The general satisfaction of the merchants was not disturbed by the vestiges of the old restrictive and revenue measures which still remained on the statute book. Even complaints against the absence of a circulating medium ceased, until the resumption of commercial relations with Great Britain again drained off the gold supply; and in May, 1773, Parliament took steps to ameliorate the condition of currency stringency that had been potentially present since the prohibition of legal tender in 1764. This act provided that paper, issued by the colonies as security to their public

---

[1] *1 N. J. Arch.*, vol. x, p. 444.

creditors, might be made, by the colonial assemblies, a legal tender for the payment of provincial duties and taxes.[1]

The conduct of the merchants and their customers toward the importation and use of duty-laden tea during this period throws considerable light upon their philosophical attitude toward those " high points about the supremacy of Parliament" which, according to Cushing, should best " fall asleep." Outside of the ports of New York and Philadelphia, the tea duty was universally acquiesced in, notwithstanding the widespread resolutions of boycott that had been adopted against customed articles in 1770. No efforts whatsoever were made to enforce the non-importation in these provinces, so far as the newspapers recorded;[2] and the popular apathy failed to provoke criticism or protest. Even the arch-radical, John Adams, could confide to his diary, on February 14, 1771, that he had " dined at Mr. Hancock's with the members, Warren, Church, Cooper, &c. and Mr. Harrison, and spent the whole afternoon, and drank green tea, from Holland, I hope, but don't know."[3]

When in the autumn months of 1773 public sentiment underwent an abrupt and radical change for reasons that will be discussed later, further light was thrown on the state of public mind that had existed prior to that time. Thus, in August, 1774, Robert Findlay was adjudged by the Charles County, Md., Committee to have " fully and satisfactorily exculpated himself of any intention to counteract the resolutions of America " because he showed that his

[1] 13 George III, c. 57. *Vide* also Macpherson, *Annals of Com.*, vol. iii, p. 538.

[2] The single recorded instance in *any* of the thirteen provinces was the case of John Turner, a New York shopkeeper, who was detected in the act of selling some dutied tea about six weeks after the New York agreement had been adopted. *N. Y. Gaz. & Merc.*, Aug. 20, 1770.

[3] *Works* (Adams, C. F.), vol. ii, p. 255.

orders for duted tea had been sent in the fall of 1773.¹ Likewise T. C. Williams & Company of Annapolis issued a statement in October, 1774, with reference to the tea consigned to them in the *Peggy Stewart*, in which they declared:

When we ordered this tea [in May, 1774], we did nothing more than our neighbours; for it is well known that most merchants, both here and in Baltimore, that ordered fall goods, ordered tea as usual; and to our certain knowledge, in the months of April, May and June last, near thirty chests were imported into this city by different merchants, and the duties paid without the least opposition. . . . We therefore think it hard, nay cruel usage, that our characters should be thus blasted for only doing what most people in this province that are concerned in trade, have likewise done.²

At Charleston, S. C., the importation of dutied tea had also been carried on during the years 1771-1773 with absolutely no attempt at concealment.³ At the public meeting, held in December, 1773, upon the arrival of the East India Company's ship, it was strongly argued that "Tea had ever been spontaneously imported and the Duty paid; that every subject had an equal right to send that article from the Mother Country into their Province, and therefore it was unreasonable to exclude the Hon. East India Company from the same privilege."⁴ Indeed, while the people were still in session, some dutied teas on board the tea-ship, not owned by the East India Company, were landed and carted past the meeting-place to the stores of private merchants!⁵

[1] *Md. Gaz.*, Aug. 11, 1774; also 4 *Am. Arch.*, vol. i, pp. 703-704.
[2] *Md. Gaz.*, Oct. 27, 1774.
[3] *S. C. Gaz.*, Nov. 29, Dec. 6, 20, 1773.
[4] *N. Y. Gazetteer*, Dec. 23, 1773.
[5] Drayton, J., *Memoirs of the American Revolution* (Charleston, 1821), vol. i, p. 98.

This contemporary evidence [1] is abundantly supported by the official figures of the British government on the tea importations into the colonies.[2] At Boston, a total of 373,077 pounds of dutied tea was imported from December 1, 1770 to January 5, 1773 without articulate protest from the radicals.[3] "Three hundred whole and fifty-five half Chests came in Vessels belonging to Mr. John Hancock the Patriot," stated the comptroller of customs at Boston in a letter of September 29, 1773, to John Pownall, under-secretary of state in the colonial department.[4] In the other importing provinces, the amount of dutied tea received from December 1, 1770 to January 5, 1773 was less in quantity but probably about equal in proportion to their normal volume of trade. At Rhode Island, the quantity of dutied tea entered was 20,833 pounds; at Patuxent, Md., 33,304 pounds; at the several Virginia ports, 79,527 pounds; at Charleston, S. C., 48,540 pounds; and at Savannah, 12,931 pounds. The total for all provinces, always excepting New York and Pennsylvania, was 580,831 pounds, on which the duty was paid without arousing comment.

New York and Philadelphia were the only parts of British America where the people faithfully observed the

[1] For further confirmatory evidence, vide, in the case of Massachusetts, Mass. Gaz. & Post-Boy, Dec. 6, 1773; for Maryland, Md. Gaz., Aug. 18, 1774; for Georgia, Ga. Gaz., July 27, 1774. Cf. Meredith's statement in House of Commons, 4 Am. Arch., vol. i, pp. 1624-1625.

[2] Abstract prepared in the office of the inspector of imports and exports; quoted by Channing, History of U. S., vol. iii, p. 128 n.

[3] "Q" in the Bos. Eve. Post, Nov. 15, 1773, declared that 173 different merchants were concerned in this importation; but a letter from Boston in the Pa. Packet, Dec. 13, 1773, claimed that the number of importers had been confounded with the number of importations.

[4] Letter of Benjamin Hallowell; Stevens, Facsimiles, vol. xxiv, no. 2029, p. 5. A chest contained 340 pounds. Vide also John Adams's Works, vol. ii, p. 381.

boycott against dutied tea.[1] These places were the chief centers for tea-smuggling in America. Unembarrassed by the presence of the Customs Board, the enterprising merchants of these ports drove a brisk trade with Holland, Sweden and Germany and with the Dutch island of St. Eustatius for contraband tea, powder and other supplies but particularly for the forbidden tea.[2] Lieutenant Governor Colden and Lord Dartmouth exchanged views on the subject, agreeing in the sentiment that the illicit trade between New York and Holland prevailed " to an enormous degree."[3] " It is well known," wrote Samuel Seabury in 1774, " that little or no tea has been entered at the Customs House for several years. All that is imported is smuggled from Holland, and the Dutch Islands in the West Indies."[4] Gilbert Barkly, a Philadelphia merchant of sixteen years' standing, wrote in May, 1773, of the extensive smuggling of tea " from Holland, France, Sweden, Lisbon &c, St. Eustatia, in the West Indies &c."[5] Smuggling " has amazingly encreased within these twenty years past," asserted "A Tradesman of Philadelphia."[6] Hutchinson informed the home government that " in New York they import scarce any other than Dutch teas. In Rhode Island and Pennsylvania, it is little better."[7] Since smuggled tea was

[1] Contemporaries realized this. E. g., vide "A Tradesman of Philadelphia" in *Pa. Journ.*, Aug. 17, 1774.

[2] Letters of Hutchinson in *Mass. Arch.*, vol. xxvii, p. 317; *Bos. Gaz.*, Nov. 27, Dec. 4, 1775; *N. Engl. Chron.*, July 29.

[3] *N. Y. Col. Docs.*, vol. viii, pp. 487, 510-512.

[4] *Free Thoughts on the Proceedings of the Continental Congress ... By a Farmer* (1774). Also vide Becker, *N. Y. Parties, 1760-1776*, p. 84, n. 158.

[5] Drake, F. S., *Tea Leaves* (Boston, 1884), p. 201.

[6] *Pa. Journ.*, Aug. 17, 1774.

[7] Letter of Sept. 10, 1771; *Bos. Gaz.*, Nov. 27, 1775. Newport probably ranked next in importance to New York and Philadelphia as a centre for tea-smuggling. Vide Drake, *op. cit.*, pp. 194-197.

cheaper for the consumer to drink than dutied tea and the profits of the tea dealer greater, the systematic neglect of the dutied article in New York and Philadelphia corresponded as much to self-interest as devotion to principle, and gave fair occasion for the coining of the epigram that " a smuggler and a whig are cousin Germans . . ." [1]

The smuggling merchants experienced little difficulty in getting their teas into America. Notwithstanding all the regulations of recent years, there were still many secluded landing places on the extensive coast line and all the tricks which the mind of a resourceful skipper could invent to deceive the customs officials.[2] There were, furthermore, customs officials who, from lack of reward from the government, did not care to risk " the rage of the people," [3] or who, because of the freehandedness of the smugglers, found rich reward in conniving at the traffic. Colden cited the case of his grandson, recently appointed surveyor and searcher of the port of New York, who was given to understand by interested parties that " if he would not be officious in his Duty, he might depend upon receiving £1500 a year." [4]

The views of contemporary observers throw some light on the proportion of imported tea which failed to pay the parliamentary duty. Governor Hutchinson, who seems to have furnished the brains for the tea business carried on

[1] " Massachusettensis " in *Mass. Gaz. & Post-Boy*, Jan. 2, 1775.

[2] *E. g.*, filling the interstices of a lumber cargo with tea, carrying false bills of lading, and the like; private letters in *Pub. Rec. Off.*: C. O. 5, no. 138 (*L. C. Transcripts*), pp. 151-152, 175. *Vide* the sailing orders of Captain Hammond for obtaining a tea cargo at Göteborg or Hamburg and for running it past the customs officials at Newport. *R. I. Commerce*, vol. i, pp. 332-333.

[3] Letters of Hutchinson to Hillsborough, Aug. 25, Sept. 10, 1771, in *Bos. Gaz.*, Nov. 27, 1775.

[4] *Letter Books*, vol. ii, pp. 370-372.

by his sons at Boston, estimated that the total annual consumption of teas in America was 19,200 chests or 6,528,000 pounds.[1] For approximately the same period, the amount of tea that paid the duty was about 320,000 pounds.[2] Hutchinson's estimate was evidently wide of the mark, for even Samuel Wharton, who gravely averred that the frontiersmen and many Indians shared the popular habit of imbibing tea twice a day, placed the total consumption at a million and a half pounds less.[3] The London tea merchant, William Palmer, judged more dispassionately when he hazarded a figure about half of that named by Hutchinson, remarking that Hutchinson's estimate of " 19,200 chests is more than has been hitherto annually imported from China by all foreign companies." [4] Assuming Palmer's conservative figure to be approximately correct, the conclusion would seem valid that in a year, like 1771, marked by unusually large importations of customed tea, more than nine-tenths of the tea consumed was illicitly imported.[5]

The incentive to smuggling existed in spite of the well-intentioned efforts of the British government. The Townshend act of 1767, although imposing a small import duty of threepence a pound in America, had removed all British im-

[1] *Bos. Gaz.*, Nov. 27, 1775.

[2] The amount of dutied tea imported from Dec. 1, 1770 to Jan. 5, 1772 was 344,771 pounds, according to an abstract prepared in the office of the inspector of imports and exports; quoted by Channing, *op. cit.*, vol. iii, p. 128 n.

[3] " Observations," *Pa. Mag.*, vol. xxv, p. 140.

[4] Drake, *op. cit.*, p. 197.

[5] Hutchinson in 1771 set the figure at nine-tenths for New York and Philadelphia and five-sixths for Massachusetts. *Bos. Gaz.*, Nov. 27, 1775. He said elsewhere that the contraband tea consumed at Boston came there by way of New York and Philadelphia. *Mass. Arch.*, vol. xxvii, p. 317.

port duties from tea exported to America,[1] and had thus, for a time at least, reduced the cost of English tea to the American consumer below that of the contraband article. This advantageous situation of English tea could, in the nature of things, continue only so long as the wholesale price of the tea in the English market did not go up, or the price of smuggled fell. The former occurred. The East India Company, although not permitted to sell at retail, were permitted to name an upset price at their public auction sales. Treading the edge of a quicksand of bankruptcy and obliged by the act of 1767 to make good any deficiency in the revenues resulting from the discontinuance of certain tea duties, the company sought to recoup its losses by advancing the upset price of tea. Governor Hutchinson wrote to Lord Hillsborough on August 25, 1771: " If the India company had continued the sale of their teas at 2s. 2d. to 2s. 4d. as they sold two years ago, the Dutch trade would have been over by this time; but now that the teas are at 3s. the illicit traders can afford to lose one chest in three . . ."[2] Meantime, Dutch teas were selling in Holland from 18d. to 2s. per pound and paid no import duty into America.[3] Hutchinson urged constantly in his business and political correspondence that " by some means or other the price of Teas in England to the Exporter ought to be kept nearer to the price in Holland."[4]

The next act of Parliament dealing with the East India

[1] 7 George III, c. 56. *Vide* Farrand's article already referred to, in *Am. Hist. Rev.* vol. iii, pp. 266-269.

[2] *Bos. Gaz.*, Nov. 27, 1775.

[3] Drake, *op. cit.*, pp. 191, 192, 194-197. Hutchinson calculated the cost of landing smuggled tea at five per cent.

[4] Letters to William Palmer and Lord Hillsborough, in *Mass. Arch.*, vol. xxvii, pp. 206-207; *Bos. Gaz.*, Nov. 27, Dec. 4, 1775. *Vide* also memorial of Barkly, the Philadelphia merchant, to the same purpose. Drake, *op. cit.*, pp. 199-202.

Company, enacted in June, 1772, relieved the company from future liability for deficiency in the tea revenues but granted a drawback of only three-fifths of the English import duties on tea exported to America instead of a complete reimbursement as formerly.[1] This act failed to alter the situation materially, so far as the American dealer in dutied teas was concerned.[2] The tea smuggler continued to control the situation, particularly at New York and Philadelphia; and in the period from December 1, 1770 to the termination of the customs service in 1775, only 874 pounds of customed tea were imported at New York and 128 pounds at Philadelphia.[3]

Illicit traffic in other commodities was also carried on, although probably in lesser volume than ever before. The total duties collected on wines and molasses in all the colonies increased steadily until 1773.[4] During the year 1772, ships-of-war all along the coast displayed greater activity and more than doubled the amount of their seizures.[5] Exces-

[1] 12 George III, c. 60. The East India Company were obliged to pay the British government more than £115,000 as a result of the falling off of the tea revenues during the first four years under the act of 1767.

[2] It would appear that certain other trading conditions discouraged the merchants of the Middle Colonies from undertaking the importation of English teas. English ports, unlike those of Holland and certain other foreign countries, were seldom open for the importation of American corn and flour; and even when they were, the sales of the East India Company occurred at such irregular intervals that colonial merchants did not know when to direct their proceeds to be invested in teas as homeward freight. Moreover, American merchants received preferential treatment at the foreign ports,—a moderate price and "Advantageous Terms of Discount, Difference of Weight &c, amounting in the whole, to near 20 per Centum." *Pa. Mag.*, vol. xxv, p. 140.

[3] Channing, *op. cit.*, vol. iii, p. 128 n.

[4] *Vide* table compiled from accounts of cashier of the American customs; quoted by Channing, *op. cit.*, vol. iii, p. 90 n.

[5] Seizures by ships-of-war amounted to £719 in 1771; £2017 in 1772.

sive zeal on the part of the customs officials still had a tendency to excite popular fury; and indeed it was an incident growing out of this situation that produced the first serious clash between the British government and the colonists during this period. Already in November, 1771, the comptroller of the customs at Falmouth had been aroused from his slumbers by disguised men and, at the point of a pistol, forced to divulge the name of the person who had lodged an information with him.[1] In the same month, a mob of thirty disguised men had overcome, with some brutality, the crew of a revenue schooner anchored near Philadelphia, and had rescued a captive vessel that was laden with contraband tea, claret and gin.[2]

Resistance to customs authority reached its climax in the destruction of the revenue vessel *Gaspee* on the night of June 9, 1772. The commander of the vessel, Lieutenant Dudingston, had, in patrolling Narragansett Bay and the connecting waters, displayed " an intemperate, if not a reprehensible zeal to aid the revenue service." [3] He had made himself obnoxious to legitimate traders as well as to smugglers, and was believed to have contributed, through his officiousness, " not a little to enhance the price of fuel and provisions " in Rhode Island.[4] One day while pursuing a

However, seizures by land officers fell from £607 to £378. *Vide* Channing, *op. cit.*, vol. iii, p. 89 n. Notices of the Vice-Admiralty Court in the Boston newspapers showed that large quantities of goods were being condemned for illegal importation, especially molasses, sugars and wines. For an example of increased activity at New York, *vide R. I. Commerce*, vol. i, p. 383.

[1] *4 Am. Arch.*, vol. i, pp. 26-27.
[2] *Pa. Col. Recs.*, vol. x, pp. 8-15.
[3] Report of the royal Commission of Inquiry; Bartlett, J. R., *A History of the Destruction of His Britannic Majesty's Schooner Gaspee* . . . (Providence, 1861), p. 128.
[4] Governor Wanton to Hillsborough; *ibid.*, p. 39.

colonial vessel, the *Gaspee* ran aground on a narrow spit of land about six miles from Providence. Led by John Brown, the most opulent merchant of that town, and by Abraham Whipple, a ship captain in the West Indian trade, a band of citizens boarded the vessel in the night, seized the crew and set the vessel on fire.[1] A commission of inquiry was appointed by the king to sift the matter and to convey the perpetrators out of the colony for trial. Although the names of those who had taken part in the affair were known to at least a thousand persons, no one could be found to inform the commissioners against them. Moreover, Stephen Hopkins, chief justice of Rhode Island and a shipbuilder and ex-smuggler himself, declared that not a person should be removed for trial outside of the colony's limits. The commissioners abandoned the inquiry and reported their failure to the home government. The latter did not appear anxious to make an issue of the *Gaspee* incident. Lieutenant Dudingston was sued by some Rhode Island merchants for alleged unlawful conversion of sundry casks of rum and sugar. After three trials in local courts, he acknowledged himself beaten, and the Customs Board at Boston made good his losses to the extent of £363.[2] In general, revenue vessels relaxed their vigilance during the year 1773; and their seizures fell off almost three-fifths.[3]

The keener minds among the radicals were not blind to the change that had come over the merchant class and to the resulting paralysis which had seized on the public mind.

---

[1] Based on statement of a participant many years later; *ibid.*, pp. 19-20. "Many of them appeared like men of credit and tradesmen; and but few like common men," declared the deposition of Midshipman Dickinson. *Ibid.*, p. 31.
[2] Channing, *op. cit.*, vol. iii, p. 126.
[3] *Ibid.*, p. 89 n.; Stevens, *Facsimiles*, vol. xxiv, no. 2029, p. 5.

Sam Adams's comment when the Boston merchants decided to abandon their general suspension of trade for tea non-importation alone showed keen appreciation of the economic basis of mercantile discontent. Admitting freely that the merchants had held out longer than he had expected and that his connection with them had been " but as an Auxiliary in their Nonimportation Agreement," he wrote to a brother radical in South Carolina in this strain:

Let the Colonies still convince their implacable Enemies that they are united in constitutional Principles, and are resolved they *will not* be Slaves; that their Dependance is not upon Merchants or any particular Class of Men, nor is their dernier resort a resolution *barely* to withhold Commerce with a nation that would subject them to despotic Power.[1]

In effect, he was saying that the merchant class had been utilized to the utmost as fertilizers of discontent; that their spirit for trade redress had sustained them surprisingly well in their opposition to England but that henceforth the struggle of the colonies must be divorced from the self-interest of the merchant class and rest on a broader popular basis.

Adams labored hard to keep alive radical sentiment in Boston. James Otis, in his intervals of sanity, was pursuing a strongly reactionary course.[2] John Adams withdrew himself from public life, devoting himself to his profession; and for a time he ceased even to use his pen in defense of popular rights. Sam Adams's chief care was to keep hot the coals of Hancock's resentment against Parliament, for Hancock was the local Croesus,[3] and some of his funds and all

[1] To Peter Timothy, Nov. 21, 1770; Adams, *Writings* (Cushing), vol. ii, p. 65. *Vide* also *ibid.*, p. 58.

[2] Adams, J., *Works* (Adams), vol. ii, p. 266.

[3] John Adams credited the statement that "not less than one thousand families were, every day in the year, dependent on Mr. Hancock for their daily bread." *Ibid.*, vol. x, p. 260.

of his influence had been employed to promote the antiparliamentary movement in the preceding years. But, as was the case with many another merchant, Hancock's business affairs had gone awry while he was playing the politician;[1] and he was averse to any further agitation by the radicals while the golden fruits of commerce invited picking. "All friendship between them was suddenly at an end," wrote Hutchinson in his history, "and Mr. Hancock expressed his dissatisfaction with the party, and with their extending their designs further than appeared to him warrantable."[2] For the next couple of years, Hancock, although resisting all efforts of Governor Hutchinson to commit him to the other side, pursued the course of the typical merchant, and at several critical times threw his influence and vote in favor of conciliation and against the disturbing schemes of Adams.[3]

What the radical cause lacked was, first, a compelling issue, and, second, an organization divorced from the control of the merchant class. The home government supplied promising material for the first when the report reached Boston in late September, 1772, that the salaries of the judges would thereafter be paid out of the customs revenue. No propagandist ever utilized an opportunity more dexterously than did Sam Adams on this occasion. Masquerading under the signature "Valerius Poplicola," he appeared in the *Boston Gazette* of October 5, 1772 in an eloquent protest against the innovation. "The Merchants of this Continent," he declared,

have passively submitted to the Indignity of a Tribute; and

[1] Brown, *John Hancock His Book*, pp. 158, 163, 168.
[2] *Mass. Bay*, vol. iii, p. 346. See also Wells, *Samuel Adams*, vol. i, pp. 458, 459.
[3] Hutchinson, *op. cit.*, vol. iii, pp. 348, 356, 361; Wells, *op. cit.*, vol. i, pp. 465-475.

the Landholders, tho' Sharers in the Indignity, have been perhaps too unconcern'd Spectators of the humiliating Scene. . . . Had *the Body of this People* shown a proper Resentment, at the time when the proud Taskmasters first made their appearance, we should never have seen *Pensioners* multiplying like the Locusts in Egypt. . . . Is it not High Time for the People of this Country explicitly to declare, whether they will be Freemen or Slaves? . . . Let us . . . calmly look around us and consider what is best to be done. . . . Let it be the topic of conversation in every social Club. Let every Town assemble. Let Associations & Combinations be everywhere set up to consult and recover our just Rights.[1]

With the radical program so outlined, Adams decided to work out the plan through the agency of the town meeting. Of these town meetings, Hutchinson had already written several months earlier: they are "constituted of the lowest class of the people under the influence of a few of a higher class, but of intemperate and furious dispositions and of desperate fortunes. Men of property and of the best character have deserted these meetings, where they are sure of being affronted."[2] According to Adams' plan, a petition for a town meeting was at once presented to the selectmen. Hancock was a selectman and, with three or four others, he unhesitatingly rejected the petition, disapproving of what seemed to him precipitate measures. Other petitions were then set on foot, and finally, after more than three weeks' delay, the selectmen yielded to the pressure.[3] The meeting

[1] Adams, S., *Writings* (Cushing), vol. ii, pp. 332-337.
[2] This letter of Mch. 29, 1772 to Hillsborough continued: "By the constitution £40 stg., which they say may be in cloaths, household furniture or any sort of property, is a qualification; and even with that there is scarce ever any inquiry, and anything with the appearance of a man is admitted without scrutiny." Hosmer, *Hutchinson*, p. 231.
[3] Hutchinson, *op. cit.*, vol. iii, pp. 361-362; Wells, *op. cit.*, vol. i, pp. 490-491.

occurred on Wednesday, October 28, and two adjourned sessions were needed to carry on an animated colloquy with Governor Hutchinson over the question of the judges' salaries.[1] At the last meeting, on November 2, the temper of the citizens had reached the proper pitch; Adams seized the moment to introduce a motion for a standing committee of correspondence with the purpose

> to state the Rights of the Colonists and of this Province in particular . . . , to communicate and publish the same to the several Towns in this Province and to the World as the sense of this Town, with the Infringements and violations thereof that have been or from time to time may be made; also requesting of each Town a free Communication of their Sentiments.[2]

The motion was carried unanimously.

Adams had succeeded in arousing the town meeting; he had yet to convince the men who had been leaders in the late agitation against the Townshend duties of the propriety of his course. A number of these men, although asked to serve on the committee, declined their appointments. Three of the Boston representatives in the Assembly, Speaker Cushing, Hancock and William Phillips, and three selectmen, Samuel Austin, John Scollay and Thomas Marshall, all merchants, excused themselves, each alleging " his private Business would not then admit of it." At least three others took a like step.[3] James Otis was induced to accept the chairmanship. The twenty-one men who composed the committee were the best who could be obtained under the circumstances, and probably served Adams' purposes better

---

[1] *Mass. Gaz. & Post-Boy*, Nov. 2, 9, 1772.

[2] *Bos. Com. Cor. Mss.*, vol. i, p. 1; also *Bos. Town Recs. (1770-1777)*, pp. 92-93.

[3] Benjamin Austin, Benjamin Kent and Samuel Swift. " Q. E. D." in *Mass. Gaz. & News-Letter*, Nov. 12, 1772.

than if the more weighty citizens had been persuaded to sacrifice their private interests. Otis soon retired to the madhouse; and the "Grand Incendiary of the Province"[1] himself assumed the chairmanship, a substitution which, to Hutchinson's view, was probably little better than a change from Philip drunk to Philip sober. In the committee as completed, the merchant element was in the minority; and the effective activity of the committee was largely directed by the chairman. Hutchinson had as yet no suspicion that "the foulest, subtlest and most venomous serpent that ever issued from the eggs of sedition"[2] was growing before his eyes. "The restless faction," he wrote jeeringly to England, were unable "to revive the old plan of mobbing; and the only dependence left is to keep up a correspondence through the Province by committees of the several towns, which is such a foolish scheme that they must necessarily make themselves ridiculous."[3]

The plan began to yield fruit when the committee reported to the town meeting on November 20 a cogently reasoned paper, written by Adams, which was unanimously accepted by the three hundred men present. This document revealed the consummate ability of the master agitator. Frankly designed to arouse the public from their lethargic sleep, the paper bristled with allusions to past irritations and future perils; it gave to current abstractions a practical application; it made bold appeals to the self-interest of smuggling merchants and to the self-esteem of home-manufacturing farmers; it pictured the dwindling sphere

[1] Hutchinson's characterization of Adams; Wells, *op. cit.*, vol. i, p. 488.

[2] The well known phrase of "Massachusettensis," in *Mass. Gaz. & Post-Boy*, Jan. 2, 1775.

[3] Letter of Nov. 13, 1772 to Secretary Pownall; Hosmer, *op. cit.*, p. 235.

of provincial self-government, and dangled the bogey of an American episcopate. The lengthy " List of Infringements & Violations of Rights " was presented in terms which could be understood by the least imaginative. The revenue duty on tea was represented as an entering wedge for other taxes which might affect lands; the arbitrary powers of the customs officials with respect to searching vessels or houses for smuggled goods were fully dilated upon; the presence of " Fleets and Armies " for supporting " these unconstitutional Officers in collecting and managing this unconstitutional Revenue " was noted; the extension of the power of the vice-admiralty courts was once more condemned; the laws against slitting mills and the transportation of hats and wool were cited as " an infringement of that right with which God and nature have invested us." Regarding the payment of the governor's and judges' salaries, *i. e.* of " the men on whose opinions and decisions our properties liberties and lives, in a great measure, depend," the divorcing of these branches from popular control was deplored as fatal to free government. References were also made to interferences in provincial home rule through the agency of royal instructions, and to minor matters.[1]

This document, which, according to Hutchinson, " was calculated to strike the colonists with a sense of their just claim to independence, and to stimulate them to assert it," [2] was sent to all the towns in the province, with a circular letter urging that they freely communicate their own sentiments and give appropriate instructions to their representatives in the Assembly. The maneuver of Boston met with immediate success. Groups of extremists in the various

[1] *Bos. Town Recs.* (*1770-1777*), pp. 94-108; also Adams, S., *Writings* (Cushing), vol. ii, pp. 350-374.

[2] *Mass. Bay*, vol. iii, p. 366.

localities engineered town meetings, which approved the Boston resolutions or adopted others more radical, and appointed standing committees of correspondence composed of radicals. In all, seventy-eight such meetings, mostly of inland towns but including the ports of Plymouth, Marblehead and Newburyport, were noted in the journals of the Boston Committee of Correspondence or in the newspapers.

Thus, all on a sudden, from a state of peace, order, and general contentment, as some expressed themselves, the province, more or less from one end to the other, was brought into a state of contention, disorder and general dissatisfaction; or, as others would have it, were aroused from stupor and inaction, to sensibility and activity.[1]

The merchants as a class continued to hold aloof from the organized popular clamor.[2] When the Assembly met in January, 1773, Governor Hutchinson, now keenly alive to the danger, denounced the committee of correspondence system as unwarrantable and of dangerous tendency, and asked the body to join him in discountenancing such innovations.[3] This unwise action produced a storm of messages and replies that, for the time, fanned higher the flame which was already beginning to die for lack of fuel.

Indeed the weakness of Adams' plan was that the manifesto of the Boston town meeting was largely a recitation of old grievances, and the leading new issue could scarcely

[1] Hutchinson, *op. cit.*, vol. iii, p. 370 n. Note some of the extravagant protests against "these mighty grievances and intolerable wrongs," so freshly discovered! *Ibid.*, pp. 369-370 n.

[2] It is significant that Salem failed to take action, and that twenty-nine of substance and character at Marblehead expressed their "entire disapprobation." *Mass. Gaz. & Post-Boy*, Dec. 28, 1772; Adams, S., *Writings* (Cushing), vol. ii, p. 350. The little town of Weston refused to appoint a committee by a large vote.

[3] Hutchinson, *op. cit.*, vol. iii, pp. 370-390; Hosmer, *op. cit.*, pp. 396 *et seq.*

be an enduring one to a people who had been complaining for generations against the burden of paying high salaries to governors and judges. Moreover, the radical propaganda had not yet advanced to a stage where it could be sustained without the support of the merchant class. Adams, however, had an abiding faith in the efficacy of a campaign of education and agitation, and in the establishment of a popular organization which would be ready for action when the time should arrive.

The matter of salaries was in form a local issue, and was not likely to stir the people of other provinces to the point of organization. However, the radicals of the Virginia House of Burgesses, in March, 1773, seized the opportunity to establish a single committee of correspondence for the whole province, when news reached them that a royal commission of inquiry of large powers had been appointed to investigate the *Gaspee* affair. This committee composed almost entirely of radical planters, was empowered "to obtain the most early and authentic intelligence of all such acts and resolutions of the British parliament, or proceedings of administration, as may relate to or affect the British colonies in America," and to carry on a correspondence with the sister provinces respecting these matters.[1] On April 10, 1773, Adams wrote to a member of the Virginia committee, urging the establishment of municipal committees of correspondence in every province;[2] but he did not understand, as they did, that political leadership in Virginia was held by the planting class and that the few urban centres were dominated by the narrow views of merchants and factors. The Virginia type of committee became at

[1] Frothingham, *Rise of Republic*, pp. 279-281. Collins, E. D., "Committees of Correspondence of the American Revolution," *Am. Hist. Assn. Rep.* (*1901*), vol. i, pp. 243-271, is important in this connection.

[2] To R. H. Lee; *Writings* (Cushing), vol. iii, p. 26.

once the popular plan of organization among the radicals; and by July, 1773, five assemblies had followed the lead of that province.[1] It was not until Great Britain adopted measures which affected all provinces alike and which aroused the powerful merchant class once more to protest that the organization of committees in local subdivisions throughout the continent was made possible. After July, 1773, the flurry of discontent stirred up by the radicals of Massachusetts and Virginia quickly subsided.[2] The mercantile and conservative classes had made their influence felt once more. General apathy again reigned.

As destiny would have it, Lord North, not Sam Adams, was responsible for the abrupt determination of the merchant class to take up cudgels again in a struggle for commercial rights in the fall of 1773. It was the enactment of a new tea act by Parliament in May, 1773, that caused the merchants to throw discretion to the winds and to seek again popular support for commercial reform. Like the earlier tea legislation, this act was designed to accomplish a double purpose: to help the East India Company to sell their surplus tea stock, amounting to seventeen million pounds; and to enforce the collection of the parliamentary tax in America.[3]

[1] R. I., Conn., N. H., Mass., S. C. A second group of assemblies acted from September, 1773, to February, 1774: Ga., Md., Del., N. Y., N. J. *Vide* Collins's article, *loc. cit.* There seemed to be little or no connection between the later movement and the agitation against the East India Company which was developing concurrently.

[2] For one thing, the commission to investigate the *Gaspee* affair had failed to exercise any of their extraordinary powers.

[3] With reference to the second purpose, the revenue arising from all the various duties in America during 1772 had yielded a balance of less than £85 above the expenses of collection, not counting the cost of maintaining ships-of-war for the suppression of smuggling. Franklin, *Writings* (Smyth), vol. v, p. 460; vol. vi, pp. 2-3. Under the circumstances, it was cheaper for the home government to adopt some expedient for

The act of 1773 involved no new infringement of the constitutional or natural rights of the Americans, so far as the taxation principle was concerned. Continuing the three-penny import duty in America, the act provided that, in place of a partial refund, a full drawback of English import duties should be given on all teas re-shipped to America, thus restoring the arrangement which had existed under the Townshend Act save that the company were not to be liable for deficiencies in the revenue. The radical innovation was introduced in the provision which empowered the East India Company, if they so chose, to export tea to America or to " foreign parts " from their warehouses and on their own account, upon obtaining a license from the commissioners of the treasury.[1]

In other words, the East India Company, which hitherto had been required by law to sell their teas at public auction to merchants for exportation, were now authorized to become their own exporters and to establish branch houses in America. This arrangement swept away, by one stroke, the English merchant who purchased the tea at the company's auction and the American merchant who bought it of the English merchant; for the East India Company, by dealing directly with the American retailer, eliminated all the profits which ordinarily accumulated in the passage of the tea through the hands of the middlemen. From another point of view, as Joseph Galloway has pointed out,

the consumer of tea in America was obliged to pay only one

carrying out Hutchinson's oft-repeated suggestion of sinking the selling price of tea. The particular method adopted had already been suggested by Samuel Wharton in London and Gilbert Barkly, the Philadelphia merchant, and by others. *Pa. Mag.*, vol. xxv, pp. 139-141; Drake, *op. cit.*, pp. 199-202.

[1] 13 George III, c. 44. Such exportation was to be permitted only when the supp'y of tea in the company's warehouses amounted to at least 10,000,000 pounds.

profit to the Company, another to the shopkeeper. But before the act, they usually paid a profit to the Company, to the London merchant, who bought it of the Company and sold it to the American merchant, and also to the American merchant, besides the profit of the retailer. So that, by this act, the consumer of this necessary and common article of subsistence was enabled to purchase it at one-half of its usual price . . .[1]

The colonial merchant class saw at once that the new act, if permitted to go into effect, would enable the American consumer to buy dutied teas, imported directly by the East India Company, at a cheaper rate than dutied teas imported in the customary manner by private merchants or than Dutch teas introduced by the illicit traders. Therefore, when the colonial press announced in September, 1773, that the East India Company had been licensed to export more than half a million pounds of tea to the four leading ports of America, an alliance of powerful interests at once appeared in opposition to the company's shipments.

As Governor Hutchinson at Boston put it in a letter of January 2, 1774:

Our liberty men had lost their reputation with Philadelphia and New York, having been importers of Teas from England for three or four Years past notwithstanding the engagement they had entrd into to the contrary. As soon as the news came of the intended exportation of Teas [by the] E. I. Company which must of course put an end to all Trade in Teas by private Merchants, proposals were made both to Philadelphia and York for a new Union, and they were readily accepted, for although no Teas had been imported from England at either of those places, yet an immense profit had been made by the Importation from Holland, which wou'd entirely cease if the Teas

---

[1] Galloway, *Historical and Political Reflections on the Rise and Progress of the American Rebellion* (London, 1780), pp. 17-18. For similar statements, *vide* also "Z" in *Boston Eve. Post*, Oct. 25, 1773, and "Massachusettensis" in *Mass. Gazette and Post-Boy*, Jan. 2, 1775.

from the E. I. Company should be admitted. This was the consideration which engaged all the merchants.[1]

An extended controversy began in newspaper and broadside, which not only revealed the fundamental antagonism between the undertaking of the British trading corporation and the interest of the colonial tea merchants, but also pointed out the far-reaching menace which the new act held for American merchants in general. To broaden the basis of the popular protest, the old theoretical arguments against the taxing authority of Parliament were exhumed; and new and bizarre arguments were invented.

An examination of the propagandist literature and of a few private letters will bear out this preliminary analysis. Most of the writings against the tea shipments issued from the presses of Boston, New York and Philadelphia and, with varying emphasis, covered substantially the same ground. The Charleston newspapers reprinted many of the northern arguments, and the events there may therefore be said to have been determined in large part by the same sentiments.

At Boston, the newspaper writers laid great stress on the fact that the legitimate traffic in English teas was assailed with destructive competition. "A Consistent Patriot" declared that the new statute would displace the men in the American tea trade and force them to seek their living elsewhere "in order to make room for an East India factor, probably from North-Britain, to thrive upon what are now the honest gains of *our own* Merchants."[2] "Surely all the

---

[1] *Mass. Archives*, vol. xxvii, p. 610. Such also was the view of the *Annual Register* (1774), p. 48: "All the dealers, both legal and clandestine, . . . saw their trade taken at once out of their hands. They supposed it would fall into the hands of the company's consignees, to whom they must become in a great measure dependent, if they could hope to trade at all." *Vide* also Ramsay, *History of the American Revolution* (Philadelphia, 1789), vol. i, p. 96.

[2] *Mass. Spy*, Oct. 14, 1773.

London Merchants trading to America and all the American Merchants trading with Britain," said " Reclusus," " must highly resent such a Monopoly, considered only as it effects their private Interest " and without regard to the fact that everyone who buys the tea will be paying tribute to the " harpy Commissioners " and to Parliament; the newly-appointed tea consignees " can't seriously imagine that the Merchants will quietly see themselves excluded from a considerable branch of Trade . . . that they and the odious Commissioners may riot in luxury." [1] "A Merchant " expressed surprise that the merchants and traders had not met to take action in the crisis, noting, among other commercial ills, that " those gentlemen that have dealt in that article will altogether be deprived of the benefit arising from such business." [2] The loyalist town of Hinsdale, N. H., resolved unanimously that the tumult against the tea was not due to objections against a revenue tax, " but because the intended Method of Sale in this Country by the East India Company probably would hurt the private Interest of many Persons who deal largely in Tea." [3]

At New York and Philadelphia, the chief smuggling ports, greater emphasis was placed on the threatened ruin awaiting the illicit tea traffic. The Philadelphia merchant, Thomas Wharton, pointed out that " it is impossible always to form a true judgment from what real motives an opposition springs, as the smugglers and London importers may both declare that this duty is stamping the Americans with the badge of slavery." [4] A tea commissioner at Boston believed

---

[1] *Boston Eve. Post*, Oct. 18, 1773.

[2] *Mass. Spy*, Oct. 28, 1773.

[3] *N. H. Gazette*, June 17, 1774. Other acts of Parliament, added the town meeting, infringe our rights more than that law—thus, the molasses duty and the late act establishing custom-house fees—and yet no complaint is made against them.

[4] Drake, *op. cit.*, p. 273.

that the agitation against the act was " fomented, if not originated, principally by those persons concerned in the Holland trade," a trade " much more practised in the Southern Governments than this way."[1] "A Citizen" conceded cautiously in the *New York Journal* of November 11, 1773, that " we have not been hitherto altogether at the mercy of those monopolists [the East India Company], because it has been worth the while for others to supply us with tea at a more reasonable price," but that hereafter " if tea should be brought us from any foreign market, the East India Company might occasionally undersell those concerned in it, so as to ruin or deter them from making many experiments of the kind." A loyalist writer expressed the same thought from a different point of view when he affirmed to the people of New York that every measure of the radical cabal

is an undoubted proof that not your liberties but their private interest is the object. To create an odium against the British company is the main point at which they have laboured. They have too richly experienced the fruits which may be reaped from a contraband trade ... to relinquish them to others without a struggle.[2]

One of the tea commissioners at New York declared that " the introduction of the East India Company's tea is violently opposed here by a set of men who shamefully live by monopolizing tea in the smuggling way."[3] Governor Tryon and others entertained a similar opinion.[4]

[1] Drake, *op. cit.*, pp. 261-262.
[2] *N. Y. Gazetteer*, Nov. 18, 1773.
[3] Abram Lott to W. Kelly, Nov. 5, 1773; Drake, *op. cit.*, p. 269.
[4] *N. Y. Col. Docs.*, vol. viii, pp. 400, 408. A similar opinion was shared by Haldimand, at New York, *Brit. Papers* ("*Sparks Mss.*"), vol. iii, p. 175; and by the anonymous authors of letters in *4 Am. Arch.*, vol. i, p. 302 n., and of an address in *ibid.*, p. 642.

To rob the new law of the appeal it held for the pocketbooks of the tea purchasers, the writers impeached the good faith of the company in undercutting prices. " Reclusus " predicted confidently that " tho' the first Teas may be sold at a low Rate to make a popular Entry, yet when this mode of receiving Tea is well established, they, as all other Monopolists do, will meditate a greater profit on their Goods, and set them up at what Price they please." [1] " Hampden " wrote:

Nor let it be said, to cajole the poor, that this importation of tea will lower the price of it. Is any temporary abatement of that to be weighed in the balance with the permanent loss that will attend the sole monopoly of it in future, which will enable them abundantly to reimburse themselves by raising the price as high as their known avarice may dictate?[2]

In the words of " Mucius,"

Every puchaser must be at their mercy . . . The India Company would not undertake to pay the duty in England or America—pay enormous fees to Commissioners &c &c unless they were well assured *that the Americans would in the end reimburse them for every expence their unreasonable project should bring along with it.*[3]

The writers sought to show that the present project of the East India Company was the entering wedge for larger and more ambitious undertakings calculated to undermine the colonial mercantile world. Their opinion was based on the fact that, in addition to the article of tea, the East India Company imported into England vast quantities of silks,

[1] *Boston Eve. Post*, Oct. 18, 1773. *Vide* also *Bos. Com. Cor. Mss.*, vol. vi, p. 452.

[2] *N. Y. Journal*, Oct. 28, 1773.

[3] *Pa. Packet*, Nov. 1, 1773.

calicoes and other fabrics, spices, drugs and chinaware, all commodities of staple demand; and on their fear that the success of the present venture would result in an extension of the same principle to the sale of the other articles. Perhaps no argument had greater weight than this; nor, indeed, was such a development beyond the range of possibility.[1]

If they succeed in their present experiment with tea, argued "A Mechanic,"

they will send their own Factors and Creatures, establish Houses among US, Ship US all other East-India Goods; and, in order to full freight their Ships, take in other Kind of Goods at under Freight, or (more probably) ship them on their own Accounts to their own Factors, and undersell our Merchants, till they monopolize the whole Trade. Thus our Merchants are ruined, Ship Building ceases. They will then sell Goods at any exorbitant Price. Our Artificers will be unemployed, and every Tradesman will groan under dire Oppression.[2]

"Hampden" warned the New Yorkers:

If you receive the portion [of tea] designed for this city, you will in future have an India warehouse here; and the trade of all the commodities of that country will be lost to your mer-

[1] In a letter of Oct. 5, 1773 to Thomas Walpole, Thomas Wharton proposed the extension of the East India Company's trade, under the new regulations, to include pepper, spices and silks. Drake, *op. cit.*, pp. 274-275. Dickinson, in an essay in July 1774, quoted a contemporary writer in England as proposing "that the Government, through the means of a few merchants acquainted with the American trade . . . , should establish factors at Boston, New-York, and a few other ports, for the sale of such cargoes of British manufactures as should be consigned to them; and to consist of such particularly as were most manufactured in the Province, with directions immediately and continually to undersell all such Colony manufactures." *4 Am. Archives*, vol. i, p. 575 n. The probability of some such scheme was also contemplated by "An American Watchman" in Pinkney's *Va. Gazette*, Jan. 26, 1775.

[2] *Pa. Gazette*, Dec. 8, 1773. *Vide* also a letter in *Pa. Chron.*, Nov. 15, 1773, and "A Countryman" in *Pa. Packet*, Oct. 18, 1773.

chants and be carried on by the company, which will be an immense loss to the colony.¹

A customs commissioner writing to the home government from Boston noted that it was pretended that " when once the East India Company has established Warehouses for the Sale of Tea, all other articles commonly imported from the East Indies and Saleable in America, will be sent there by the Company." ²

That the fear of monopoly was the mainspring of American opposition is further evidenced by the trend of discussion in the early weeks before it was known definitely that the new law provided for the retention of the threepenny import duty. The report gained currency that the tea shipped by the East India Company was to be introduced free of the American import duty. This understanding was based upon a misreading of that portion of the statute which empowered the company " to export such tea to any of the British colonies or plantations in America, or to foreign parts, discharged from the payment of any customs or duties whatsoever, anything in the said recited act, or any other act, to the contrary notwithstanding." ³ Had this been a correct interpretation of the law, there is every reason to believe that the course of American opposition would have developed unchanged and the tea would then have been dumped into the Atlantic as an undisguised and unmixed protest against a grasping trading monopoly.

¹ *N. Y. Journal*, Oct. 28, 1773.

² Stevens, *Facsimiles*, vol. xxiv, no. 2029, p. 4. *Vide* also Hancock's view, expressed in the annual oration of Mar. 5, 1774. *1 M. H. S. Procs.*, vol. xiii, p. 187.

³ Unsigned article in *N. Y. Gazetteer*, Oct. 28, 1773. *Vide* also " Poplicola," *ibid.*, Nov. 18, 1773. "A construction strongly implied by the liberty granted to export the same Commodity to foreign Countries free of Duties," wrote Tryon to Dartmouth, Nov. 3, 1773. *N. Y. Col. Docs.*, vol. viii, pp. 400-401.

Governor Tryon, of New York, in a letter to the home government made reference to the animated discussion over the question; and added:

If the Tea comes free of every duty, I understand it is then to be considered as a Monopoly of the East India Company in America; a monopoly of dangerous tendency, it is said, to American liberties . . . So that let the Tea appear free or not free of Duty those who carry on the illicit Trade will raise objections, if possible, to its being brought on shore and sold.[1]

Tryon's analysis of the situation is confirmed by the tone of newspaper discussion during the weeks of uncertainty.

Even if the tea bears no duty, wrote a New Yorker to his friend in Philadelphia, " would not the opening of an East-India House in America encourage all the great Companies in Great Britain to do the same? If so, have we a single chance of being any Thing but *Hewers of Wood and Drawers of Waters* to them? The East Indians are a proof of this."[2] In like spirit, "A Mechanic" declared scornfully that it made no difference whether the tea was dutied or not. "Is it not a gross and daring insult, to pilfer the trade from the Americans, and lodge it in the hands of the East India Company?" he queried. "It will first most sensibly affect the Merchants; but it will also very materially affect . . . every Member of the Community."[3]

In the vigorous words of "A Citizen," " Whether the duty on tea is taken off or not, the East India Company's scheme has too dangerous an aspect for us to permit an experiment to be made of it." In the same letter he said:

The scheme appears too big with mischievous consequences

[1] *N. Y. Col. Docs.*, vol. viii, p. 400.
[2] *Pa. Chron.*, Nov. 15, 1773.
[3] *Pa. Gazette*, Dec. 8, 1773.

and dangers to America, [even if we consider it only] . . . as it may create a monopoly; or, as it may introduce a monster, too powerful for us to control, or contend with, and too rapacious and destructive, to be trusted, or even seen without horror, that may be able to devour every branch of our commerce, drain us of all our property and substance, and wantonly leave us to perish by thousands . . .[1]

All ambiguity as to the true meaning of the statute was removed by the lucid pen of John Dickinson and others and finally by a reported opinion of His Majesty's attorney and solicitor general. It was shown, by careful analysis of the act, that the East India Company were merely exempted from the payment of all duties and customs chargeable in England and that the American import duty remained as before.[2] Even after this time, the New Yorkers were afraid that Parliament might heed the American protest against taxation and proceed to repeal the threepenny duty without rescinding the monopoly rights granted to the East India Company. In a remarkable letter written more than two months after the Boston Tea Party, the New York Committee of Correspondence asserted frankly:

Should the Revenue Act be repealed this Session of Parliament, as the East India Company by the Act passed the last Session have liberty to export their own Tea, which is an advantage they never had before and which their distress will certainly induce them to embrace, we consider such an event as dangerous to our Commerce, as the execution of the Revenue Act would be to our Liberties. For as no Merchant who is acquainted with the certain opperation of a Monopoly on that

---

[1] *N. Y. Journal*, Nov. 4, 1773.

[2] "Y. Z." (Dickinson) in *Pa. Journal*, Nov. 3, 1773, also in Dickinson's *Writings* (Ford, P. L., ed.), vol. i, pp. 457-458; "'Cato" and "A Tradesman" in *N. Y. Gazetteer*, Nov. 4, 18, 1773; "A Citizen" in *N. Y. Journal*, Nov. 4, 1773; letter in *Pa. Journal*, Nov. 10, 1773.

or this side the Water will send out or order Tea to America when those who have it at first hand send to the same market, the Company will have the whole supply in their hands. Hence it will necessarily follow that we shall ultimately be at their Mercy to extort from us what price they please for their Tea. And when they find their success in this Article, they will obtain liberty to export their Spices, Silk etc. . . . And therefore we have had it long in contemplation to endeavor to get an Agreement signed not to purchase any English tea till so much of the Act passed the last session of Parliament enabling the Company to ship their Tea to America be repealed. Nothing short of this will prevent its being sent on their account.[1]

In view of the subordinate place which the argument of violated rights held in the minds of the propagandists, protests against "taxation without representation" were made chiefly for rhetorical effect.[2] This may be shown by a few examples. In a letter written by a committee of the Massachusetts Assembly after the Boston Tea Party, the new act was characterized as "introductive of monopolies which, besides the train of evils that attend them in a commercial view, are forever dangerous to public liberty," also as " pregnant with new grievances, paving the way to further impositions, and in its consequences threatening the final destruction of liberties."[3] "A Consistent Patriot"

[1] Letter to Boston Committee of Correspondence, Feb. 28, 1774; *Bos. Com. Cor. Mss.*, vol. ix, pp. 742-746. The letter added that the committee would "feel the pulse" of the Philadelphia Committee and the other committees to the southward and requested the Boston Committee to urge the matter on the committees at Rhode Island, Philadelphia and Charleston, S. C. I have found no replies to the New York proposal.

[2] The smugglers and dissatisfied merchants "made a notable stalking horse of the word LIBERTY," declared "A Tradesman of Philadelphia," "and many well meaning persons were duped by the specious colouring of their sinister zeal." *Pa. Journal*, Aug. 17, 1774.

[3] Letter of Dec. 21, 1773, to Arthur Lee, signed by Thomas Cushing, Samuel Adams, John Hancock and William Phillips; *4 M. H. S. Colls.*, vol. iv, p. 377.

stigmatized the act as " a plan not only destructive to trade, in which we are all so deeply interested but . . . designed to promote and encrease a revenue extorted from us against our consent." [1] The new statute, declared " Causidicus," was a case of

taxation without consent and monopoly of trade establishing itself together. . . . Let the trade be monopolized in particular hands or companies, and the privileges of these companies lye totally at the mercy of a British ministry and how soon will that ministry command all the power and property of the empire? [2]

Even the members of the First Continental Congress treated the matter from an unchanged viewpoint when they declared, on October 21, 1774, in their *Memorial to the Inhabitants of the British Colonies* that "Administration . . . entered into a monopolizing combination with the East India Company, to send to this Continent vast quantities of Tea, an article on which a Duty was laid. . . ." [3]

Protests against the tea act as a violation of a theoretical right caused a tea commissioner at Boston to remark skeptically:

But while there is such a vast quantity [of tea] imported every Year, by so considerable a number of persons who all pay the duty thereof on its arrival, I do not see why every importer, nay every consumer thereof, do not as much contribute to enforce the Tea act as the India Company themselves, or the persons to whom they may think proper to consign their Tea for sale.[4]

[1] *Mass. Spy*, Oct. 14, 1773.
[2] *Ibid.*, Nov. 4, 1773. *Vide* also "Joshua, the son of Nun," *ibid.*, Oct. 14, 1773, and "Scaevola" in *Pa. Chron.*, Oct. 11, 1773.
[3] *Journals of the Continental Congress* (L. C. edn.), vol. i, p. 98.
[4] Drake, *op. cit.*, pp. 261-262.

The people of New York and Philadelphia might, with clearer conscience, discuss the tea tax as an invasion of American liberties; but, as " Z " pointed out, all Americans were guilty of a glaring inconsistency in denouncing that trifling duty whilst silently passing over " the Articles of Sugar, Molasses, and Wine, from which more than three quarter parts of the American Revenue has and always will arise, and when the Acts of Parliament imposing Duties on these Articles stand on the same Footing as that respecting Tea and the Moneys collected from them are applied to the same Purposes." [1]

Of the other arguments used to stir up opposition, the most interesting was the attempt to discredit the present undertaking of the East India Company by reason of the company's notoriously bad record in India. John Dickinson was the most forceful exponent of this view in a broadside which had wide popularity in both Philadelphia and New York. Writing under the signature of " Rusticus," he declared:

Their conduct in Asia, for some Years past, has given ample Proof, how little they regard the Laws of Nations, the Rights, Liberties, or Lives of Men. They have levied War, excited Rebellions, dethroned Princes, and sacrificed Millions for the Sake of Gain. The Revenues of mighty Kingdoms have centered in their Coffers. And these not being sufficient to glut their Avarice, they have, by the most unparalleled Barbarities, Extortions and Monopolies, stripped the miserable Inhabitants of their Property, and reduced whole Provinces to Indigence and Ruin. Fifteen hundred Thousand, it is said, perished by Famine in one Year, not because the Earth denied its Fruits, but this Company and its Servants engrossed all the Necessaries of Life, and set them at so high a Rate, that the Poor could not purchase them. Thus having drained the Sources of that

[1] *Bos. Eve. Post*, Oct. 25, 1773.

immense Wealth . . . , they now, it seems, cast their Eyes on America, as a new Theatre, whereon to exercise their Talents of Rapine, Oppression and Cruelty. The Monopoly of Tea, is, I dare say, but a small Part of the Plan they have formed to strip us of our Property. But thank God, we are not Sea Poys, nor Marrattas, but *British Subjects,* who are born to Liberty, who know its Worth, and who prize it high.[1]

The hygienic objections to tea drinking, much agitated at the time of the colonial opposition to the Townshend duties, were again called up. It was not altogether without significance that one of the leading men to urge this view was Dr. Thomas Young, a physician who spent more time in the Boston Committee of Correspondence meditating a rigorous physic for the body politic than in prescribing for private patients.[2] Dr. Young cited Dr. Tissot, professor of physic at Berne, and other eminent authorities, to prove that the introduction of tea into Europe had caused the whole face of disease to change, the prevailing disorders now being "spasms, vapors, hypochondrias, apoplexies of the serous kind, palsies, dropsies, rheumatisms, consumptions, low nervous, miliary and petechial fevers."[3] "Philo-Alethias"

---

[1] *Writings*, vol. i, pp. 459-463. According to "A Mechanic," "The East-India Company, if once they get Footing . . . , will leave no Stone unturned to become your Masters. . . . They themselves are well versed in Tyranny, Plunder, Oppression and Bloodshed" and so on. *Pa. Gazette*, Dec. 8, 1773. A town meeting at Windham, Conn., on June 23, 1774, denounced the East India Company, declaring: "Let the Spanish barbarities in Mexico and the name of a Cortez be sunk in everlasting oblivion, while such more recent, superior cruelties bear away the palm, in the history of their rapine and cruelty." *Mass. Spy*, July 7, 1774. *Vide* also "A. Z." in *Pa. Journal*, Oct. 20, 1773, and "Hampden" in *N. Y. Journal*, Oct. 28, 1773.

[2] Edes, H. H., "Dr. Thomas Young," *Col. Soc. Mass. Pubs.*, vol. xi, pp. 2-54.

[3] *Bos. Eve. Post*, Oct. 25, 1773. *Vide* also his article in the *Mass. Spy*, Dec. 30, 1773.

added "the great Boerhaave" and Dr. Cullen, professor of medicine at Edinburgh, to the authorities already noted, and suggested seventeen possible substitutes, beneficial in their effects, that could be brewed from plants of American growth.[1] "An old Mechanic" recalled with a sigh

the time when Tea was not used, nor scarcely known amongst us, and yet people seemed at that time of day to be happier, and to enjoy more health in general than they do now. [Since those days, a sad change has occurred] . . . we must be every day bringing in some new-fangled thing or other from abroad, till we are really become a luxurious people. No matter how ugly and deformed a garment is; nor how insipid or tasteless, or prejudicial to our healths an eatable or drinkable is, we must have it, if it is the *fashion*.[2]

"A Woman's" intuition suggested the fitting retort to these alarmist writings when she remarked scornfully that no one had heard of these "scarecrow stories" until tea had become a political issue.[3] The little town of Hinsdale, N. H., undertook to expose the hypocrisy of the health advocates in a different way. Assembled in town meeting, the inhabitants resolved unanimously that "the Consequences attending the use of New England Rum are much more pernicious to Society than the Consequences attending the use of Tea," destroying "the Lives and Liberties of Thousands where Tea hath or ever will One," and that Hinsdale would banish the use of tea when those towns and persons who declaimed so loudly against tea should abstain from the use of rum.[4]

[1] *Pa. Journal*, Dec. 22, 1773; also *Mass. Spy*, Jan. 27, 1774.
[2] *Pa. Journ.*, Oct. 20, 1773.
[3] *Mass. Spy*, Dec. 23, 1773.
[4] *N. H. Gazette*, June 17, 1774.

If the colonists stood ready to back their words with resolute measures, it began to appear that tea would soon be added to molasses and wine as among those essential ingredients which the historian of later days, in imitation of John Adams, might record as entering into American independence.

CHAPTER VII

THE STRUGGLE WITH THE EAST INDIA COMPANY
(1773-1774)

DUE to the animated discussion, public opinion was well fertilized by the time that news reached America that the shipments of the East India Company were on their way across the Atlantic. The thought of the newspaper writers was quickly translated into action by mass meetings in the great trading towns. These meetings spoke the crisp vernacular of popular rights rather than the colorless phrases of mercantile profit and loss; but their activities were directed by merchants who believed that their business existence was jeopardized. In the great trading towns, the chief object was to form combinations to prevent the landing of the tea, it being well understood that the only way to prevent consumers from partaking of the forbidden herb was to remove the temptation.[1]

The first public meeting of protest was held at Philadelphia, partly because the merchant-aristocracy was exceptionally strong there, partly because the workingmen had recently developed a sense of their collective importance, and, perhaps, partly also because the city had a direct acquaintance with the unscrupulous methods of the East India Company. It was none other than Charles Thomson who declared afterward that " the merchants led the people into an opposition to the importation of the East India

[1] *Annual Register* (1774), p. 48; Galloway, *Reflections*, p. 58.

Company's tea."[1] The workingmen had emerged from the struggle against the Townshend duties conscious for the first time of their power in the community. At the first election after the termination of the non-importation, an article, signed by "A Brother Chip," called upon the mechanics and tradesmen to unite in support of one or two mechanics as members of the assembly.[2] This plan apparently met with success in this and the succeeding annual election; and the workingmen then effected a formal secret organization, under the significant name of "Patriotic Society," for the purpose of voting *en bloc* at elections.[3] As for the local bitterness toward the East India Company, only as recently as two years before, the first manufacture of chinaware had been begun in Pennsylvania; immediately the price of imported china fell five shillings in the pound, through the reputed manipulation of that company; and the new manufacture survived only through appeals for popular support.[4]

[1] Stillé, *Life of Dickinson*, p. 345. *Vide* also Reed, W. B., *Life and Correspondence of Joseph Reed* (Philadelphia, 1847), vol. i, pp. 54-55.

[2] The writer pointed out that the usual custom was for a coterie of leading men to nominate a ticket of candidates without consulting the mechanics, who formed the great mass of the population of the city, and that "the Assembly of late Years has been chiefly composed of Merchants, Lawyers and Millers (or Farmers) . . ." The mechanics were held up as a class with interests which should have representation; and it was declared "the greatest Imprudence to elect Men of enormous Estates," who thus added political power to the influence of their wealth. *Pa. Gaz.*, Sept. 27, 1770.

[3] *Ibid.*, Aug. 19, 1772.

[4] "The East-India Company would avail themselves of these Foibles of Humanity," said this appeal; "if they could demolish one noted Manufacture, they would certainly clip twenty Years from the Growth of American Improvements; and what they lost in the present and following Year by lowering their Prices, they would gain in succeeding Years, with sufficient Interest." *Ibid.*, Aug. 1, 1771.

Shortly after news of the new tea statute reached Philadelphia, the inhabitants met at the State House and adopted a set of eight resolutions which became the model for similar votes in other cities. The tea duty was branded as taxation without representation, and the shipment of teas by the East India Company was denominated an open attempt to enforce the ministerial plan. Anyone in any wise countenancing this plan was denounced as " an enemy to his country." Finally, a committee was appointed to wait on the tea consignees and request them to resign.[1] With some natural reluctance, these latter acquiesced. A second public meeting was then held, which gave their undivided voice against the entry of the tea ship upon its arrival at the custom house and against the landing of the tea.[2] Sometime later, dire threats in the form of broadsides issued forth to the Delaware pilots, asking them to prevent the arrival of the tea ship or, if that were impossible, to give the merchants timely notice of the event.[3] In this posture affairs remained for the time.

At Boston the course of opposition assumed a somewhat different aspect because of the peculiar situation of things at that port. As the seat of the Customs Board and the apex of the revenue system of the continent, there were, from the outset, grave possibilities of friction and violence at Boston, although an executive bent upon conciliation might have avoided disaster. Governor Hutchinson was not now such a man, notwithstanding his moderation during non-importation times and his yielding to the popular demand in withdrawing the troops after the Massacre. No doubt he was led to overestimate the influence of the

[1] October 16, 1773. *Pa. Packet*, Oct. 18, 1773.
[2] *Pa. Chron.*, Jan. 3, 1774.
[3] *Pa. Mag.*, vol. xv, pp. 390-391; *Mass. Gaz. & Post-Boy*, Dec. 13, 1773.

conservative elements in the community by reason of the tranquillity of recent years;[1] but he had other reasons for firmness. Among the beneficiaries of the new law at Boston were his sons, Thomas and Elisha, and his nephew, Richard Clarke. He himself, as his correspondence shows, acted as business mentor to his sons; and it is probable that he was also financially interested in the firm. At any rate, he was in the habit of writing long letters to William Palmer, the great tea merchant, inquiring about the tea market at London, ordering shipments of the herb for the firm, and dickering about the prices and quality of the teas sent.[2] His personal interest in the treatment of the tea, the landing of which some people in Boston were determined to prevent, could not have been without effect on the bold unyielding course he adopted toward the opposition.

It is not necessary here to recount the oft-repeated tale of the tea destruction at Boston. The story need not be retold until some skilled detective of historical research has brought to light such elusive facts as the transactions of the radicals at the home of Edes, publisher of the *Boston Gazette;* the whispered conferences of the more radical mer-

[1] Thus, Hutchinson wrote to the Directors of the East India Company, Dec. 19, 1773: "As double the quantity of Tea proposed to be ship'd by Company had been imported in a year and the duty paid without any disturbance, I flattered myself for several months after I first heard of the intentions to ship on account of that Company that I should find no more difficulties than upon Teas [which] have been ship'd by private merchants." *Mass. Arch.*, vol. xxvii, pp. 597-598.

[2] *Mass. Arch.*, vol. xxv, pp. 200, 528, 542; vol. xxvii, pp. 203, 206-207, 234, 274, 317, 413, 460, 483. Bancroft was aware of Hutchinson's personal interest in the sale of the teas: *History of U. S.* ('1876), vol. vi, pp. 173, 174, 175, 183, 271. *Vide* also Barry, J. S., *History of Massachusetts* (Boston, 1855-1857), vol. ii, p. 467. Governor Hutchinson was criticised by a speaker in Parliament in 1774 for having permitted his sons to be appointed consignees. *Parliamentary History*, vol. xvii, p. 1209. Besides those named, the Boston consignees were Benjamin Faneuil, Jr., and Joshua Winslow.

chants in their counting-rooms; the infinite craft and resourcefulness of the *deus ex machina*, Sam Adams. Adams had his long awaited opportunity. His effort to foster a continuous discontent throughout the province had failed of success because it lacked a substantial issue and the backing of the business classes. The opposition to the East India Company received a wide support from the merchants; the clear inference from his course of action is that he designed to utilize this discontent to drive the populace to extreme measures, thereby to commit the province irrevocably to the cause of revolution and independence.[1]

Several features of the Boston transactions need to be noted.[2] From the beginning, the merchants as a class joined in the popular demand for the resignation of the consignees and against the landing of the tea. Their vehicle of action was a legal gathering of the town; further than that the majority of them, at the beginning, had no desire to go: popular tumult and the destruction of life and property were not normally in their program to secure relief from a commercial grievance.[3] The effort, therefore, of the bulk of the merchant class was, on the one hand, to give effective expression to the popular will through the town meeting; on the other hand, to restrain or prevent mob outrages. They were outmaneuvered by the strategy of Adams and the obstinacy of Hutchinson.

Almost a month before the arrival of the first of the tea-

[1] *Cf.* Hutchinson, *op. cit.*, vol. iii, pp. 439-440.

[2] The principal documents relative to the tea episode may be found in: *Bos. Town Recs.* (*1770-1777*); *1 M. H. S. Procs.*, vol. xiii, pp. 155-183; vol. xx, pp. 10-17; *Col. Soc. Mass. Pubs.*, vol. viii, pp. 78-89; Boston newspapers, Nov. and Dec.; *Bos. Com. Cor. Mss.*, vol. vi, pp. 452-459.

[3] Referring to "the greater part of the merchants," Hutchinson wrote on Nov. 15, 1773: "though in general they declare against mobs and violence, yet they as generally wish the teas may not be imported." *1 M. H. S. Procs.*, vol. xiii, p. 165.

ships, a mob gathered under Liberty Tree to witness the consignees resign their commissions; and when they found they were to be cheated out of their performance, they stormed the store of Richard Clarke & Sons and were driven off only with great difficulty by the consignees and their friends. It was this exhibition of violence which apparently convinced the more substantial classes that further developments should be under the visible authority of the town meeting. Accordingly, two days later, on November 5 and 6, a town meeting assembled over which John Hancock presided as moderator. The four hundred tradesmen among those present took occasion to disavow unanimously their authorship of a handbill, thrown about Faneuil Hall, which accused the merchants of fomenting discontent for purposes of self-aggrandizement. The meeting adopted the Philadelphia resolutions and further voted their expectation that no merchant should thereafter import any dutied tea. A committee of the body was appointed to secure the resignation of the consignees; but those gentlemen declined to comply, upon the ground that they did not yet know what obligations, moral or pecuniary, they were under to fulfil their trust. On the seventeenth, the mob once more took matters into its own hands and attacked the home of Richard Clarke with bricks and stones. Again the town meeting was quickly summoned, with Hancock in the chair; but demands upon the consignees only brought the response that advices from England now informed them that their friends there had entered into engagements in their behalf which put it out of their power to resign.

Adams now called into being a new agency of the popular will, which was destined to supplant the merchant-controlled town meeting and which was the natural fruitage of the committee of correspondence system. This was a joint meeting of the committees of Boston, Dorchester,

Roxbury, Brookline and Cambridge, representing a largely rural and therefore less conservative constituency than the Boston committee alone. This new body, meeting on November 22, resolved unanimously " to use their Joint influence to prevent the Landing and Sale of the Teas . . . ," and the Boston committee was instructed to arouse all the towns to an " immediate and effectual opposition."

The first tea ship, the *Dartmouth*, made its appearance in the harbor on Saturday, November 27, the other two arriving some days later. This was the signal for the next progressive step in the development of the radical organization — a meeting of all the inhabitants of the towns represented in the joint committee. It was this irresponsible mass-gathering of inhabitants of Boston and the nearby towns that now assumed direction of events, the town meeting being entirely superseded.[1] The mass meeting sat through Monday and Tuesday and, because of great numbers, adjourned from Faneuil Hall to Old South Meeting House.[2] One of the very first votes was a unanimous resolution that the tea shipped by the East India Company " shall not only be sent back but that no duty shall be paid thereon," and this was later supplemented by a vote apply-

---

[1] " Massachusettensis," writing in the *Mass. Gaz. & Post-Boy*, Jan. 2, 1775, remarked on this supplanting of the town meeting, observing that: " A body meeting has great advantages over a town-meeting, as no law has yet ascertained the qualification of the voters; each person present, of whatever age, estate or country, may . . . speak or vote at such an assembly; and that might serve as a skreen to the town where it originated, in case of any disastrous consequence."

[2] " A more determined spirit was conspicuous in this body than in any of the former assemblies of the people. It was composed of the lowest as well, and probably in as great proportions, as of the superior ranks and orders, and all had an equal voice. No eccentric or irregular motions, however, were suffered to take place. All seemed to have been the plan of but few, it may be, of a single person." Hutchinson, *Mass. Bay*, vol. iii, p. 433.

ing the same principles to private shipments of tea. These resolves constituted the ultimatum of the radicals, who were now clearly in the ascendant: the town meeting had never gone beyond the demand that the tea should be returned unladen. Henceforth the destruction of the tea was inevitable, unless Hutchinson should weaken. The governor gave no indications of a faltering resolution, for the sheriff in his name confronted the assemblage with a proclamation commanding them " to disperse and to surcease all further unlawful proceedings;" but the only effect was to arouse " a loud and very general hiss." The meeting carried on negotiations with the consignees, and with Rotch, owner of the *Dartmouth*, but failed to secure satisfactory concessions. The meeting adjourned after establishing watches for the *Dartmouth* and the other tea ships as they should arrive. Copies of the transactions were sent to Philadelphia and New York.

The excitement at Boston prompted the committees of correspondence in other towns of the province to secure the passage of resolutions, pledging their support to Boston and decreeing the non-importation of dutied teas.[1]

Monday, December 13, arrived — the seventeenth day after the arrival of the *Dartmouth*; and Rotch still lingered in his preparations to send the vessel to sea. The situation had become somewhat complicated through the fact that the vessel had been entered at the custom house in order to unload drygoods and other merchandise belonging to the merchants.[2] Under a statute of William III, this entry made the vessel liable to seizure at the end of twenty

[1] From Nov. 26 to Dec. 16, the following towns acted, in the order named: Cambridge, Brookline, Roxbury, Charlestown, Marblehead, Plymouth, Malden, Gloucester, Lexington, Groton, Newburyport, Lynn and Medford. *Bos. Com. Cor. Mss.*, vols. vi and vii, *passim*.

[2] Hutchinson, *op. cit.*, vol. iii, p. 430 n.; *Pa. Mag.*, vol. xiv, p. 78.

days by the customs officers for the non-payment of duties. Affairs had reached a critical stage. On Tuesday afternoon the mass meeting again assembled and "enjoined" Rotch to demand a clearance for his ship at the custom house. The plan was that, in case of refusal, he should enter a protest, and then, securing a permit from the governor, proceed to sea. Accompanied by a committee of ten, Rotch made the demand, but the customs collector refused an answer until he had had time to consult with his colleagues. Thursday was the last of the twenty-day period; and early in the morning the country people began to pour into town by the fifties and the hundreds. Almost eight thousand people attended the meeting which was to hear the outcome of the conference. Greatest impatience was manifested when they were told that a clearance had been refused while the dutiable articles remained on board. Rotch was ordered upon his peril to enter a protest and to demand of the governor a permit for his ship to pass the Castle.

Hutchinson, meantime, had not been idle.[1] He had renewed in writing the orders which used to be given to the commander of the Castle to allow no vessel to pass the fortress without a permit; and a number of guns were loaded in anticipation of trouble. Fearing that the vessel might try to escape through a different channel, two warships, which had been laid up for the winter, were, at his request, sent to guard the passages out of the harbor. Was it a portent that, on the very day the storm broke, the armed brig *Gaspee* should arrive from Rhode Island for action? When Rotch made his request of Hutchinson, the governor, feeling his mastery of the situation, replied that he "could not give a pass till the ship was cleared by the

---

[1] Hutchinson's own account to Hillsborough; *Mass. Arch.*, vol. xxvii, pp. 586-587.

Custom-House." ¹   The waiting assemblage learned the news with greatest exasperation. There were angry speeches in the flickering candle-light. Then Sam Adams arose to his feet and pronounced clearly the talismanic words: "This meeting can do nothing more to save the country." There was an answering war-whoop out of doors; and a disciplined mob, disguised as Mohawk Indians, hastened to the wharf, and with great expedition dumped into the harbor not only the tea on board the *Dartmouth* but also that on board the other two ships. No other property was injured; no person was harmed; no tea was allowed to be carried away; and a great crowd on the shore looked quietly on.

The mob that worked silently and systematically that night was evidently no ordinary one. Exhaustive research many years later brought forth a list of participants; but, as very few of the men ever cared to avow their connection with the lawless undertaking, the identity of the persons will never definitely be known.² However, it is evident that

---

¹ " His granting a pass to a vessel which had not been cleared at the custom-house, would have been a direct violation of his oath, by making himself an accessary in the breach of those laws which he had sworn to observe." Hutchinson, *op. cit.*, vol. iii, pp. 436-437. This is the best defense of Hutchinson's action. *Vide* also Hutchinson, *Diary and Letters of Thomas Hutchinson*, vol. i, pp. 103-104; *Mass. Arch.*, vol. xxvii, p. 611. Nevertheless, in the preliminary weeks Hutchinson had every opportunity, through his personal relations with the tea consignees, to prevent the situation from reaching such an acute stage. Had the public mind been less inflamed, the merchants as a class would never have lent their support to the act of destruction. In view of the dire consequences, which Hutchinson might very well have foreseen, it would appear that he should have stretched his discretionary powers to the point of permitting Rotch to depart without clearance. In this connection it is worth noting that Lord Mahon in his *History of England* (Boston, 1853-1854), vol. vi, p. 2, thought that Hutchinson was "perhaps unwise" in refusing the permit.

² *Vide* Drake, *Tea Leaves*. *Cf.* Pierce, E. L., " Recollections as a

STRUGGLE WITH THE EAST INDIA COMPANY 289

the better class of citizens toiled side by side with carpenters, masons, farmers, blacksmiths and barbers. The names of fifteen merchants of the more radical stamp, including William Molineux and Henry Bass, have been included in the list; and it is known that Lendall Pitts, brother to John Pitts, the selectman, had charge of one portion of the mob. John Hancock was probably speaking the truth when he disclaimed all knowledge of any detail of the tea destruction.[1] But it is clear that many merchants, who went into the movement against the East India Company with the intention of resorting only to peaceful opposition, were swept by the surge of popular feeling into measures of which their best judgment disapproved.[2] Two days after the tea affair, Governor Hutchinson described in some amazement the apparent callousness of the public toward the destruction of £15,000 of property belonging to the English company. The Stamp Act riots had excited horror and pity, he declared, because the great loss fell upon two or three individuals; but now no pity was expressed for " so great

Source of History," *2 M. H. S. Procs.*, vol. x, pp. 473-480. Drake's list includes 111 names. Contemporary accounts fixed the number of participants variously from 50 to 200. Hutchinson said: "So many of the actors and abettors were universally known, that a proclamation, with a reward for discovery, would have been ridiculed." *Mass. Bay*, vol. iii, p. 439. Edes, at whose house the "Indians" rested in waiting, was, according to his son, the only person who had a complete list of participants; and after his death the list was taken, it would appear, by the merchant, Benjamin Austin, as a paper whose contents he wished not to be publicly known. Thereafter it disappeared. *1 M. H. S. Procs.*, vol. xii, pp. 174-176.

[1] Brown, *John Hancock His Book*, p. 178. Loyalist contemporaries claimed insistently that he was one of the mob.

[2] Hutchinson wrote shortly after the tea destruction: "All this time nobody suspected they would suffer the tea to be destroyed, there being so many men of property active at their meetings, as Hancock, Phillips, Rowe, Dennie, and others, besides the selectmen and the town clerk who was clerk of all the meetings." *1 M. H. S. Procs.*, vol. xiii, p. 170.

a body as the East India Company; it is said to be a loss which will never be felt." [1]

At Philadelphia, the eventful day arrived some days later than at Boston. In the weeks following the public resolutions of October 16 there had seemed for a time serious danger that the workingmen of Philadelphia would separate themselves from the opposition to the East India Company because of the unreasonably high prices which shopkeepers were demanding for the smuggled tea. Early in December, however, a committee of investigation was appointed by the inhabitants; and, after some difficulty, they succeeded in forcing the price of tea down to a level of six shillings a pound.[2] This allayed the mutterings. On Saturday evening, December 25, it was learned that the tea ship, commanded by Captain Ayres, had arrived at Chester; and armed by this forewarning, the vessel was stopped the next day at Gloucester Point, about four miles from the city.[3] Captain Ayres, being brought ashore, was made acquainted with the feeling of the townsmen; and he promised that he would go to sea when the people had so expressed themselves in public meeting. Upon Monday, eight thousand people of all ranks assembled in the Square, and in spirited resolutions directed Captain Ayres not to enter the vessel at the custom house but to depart immediately for England. So it came about that, within six days after the tea ship entered the Capes, she was on her way out again with her cargo undisturbed. By preventing entry

[1] *Mass. Arch.*, vol. xxvii, p. 594. A fourth tea-ship, not yet arrived, was cast ashore on the back of Cape Cod by a storm about this time. *Ibid.*, p. 587.

[2] *Pa. Gaz.*, Dec. 8, 1773; also *Pa. Chron.*, Dec. 13.

[3] The principal documents relative to the tea episode in Philadelphia may be found in *Pa. Mag.*, vol. xv, pp. 385-303.

at the custom house, the Philadelphians succeeded in avoiding the difficulties which the Bostonians had faced, although thereby Thomas Wharton found himself deprived temporarily of the use of a fine chariot which was consigned to him, and other merchants had to go without their winter stocks.[1]

The public meeting, after voting instructions for Ayres's guidance, resolved their hearty approval of the destruction of the tea at Boston. The passage of this resolve awoke the only discord at the meeting, for the committee, which had prepared the other resolutions in advance, had rejected this one by a vote of ten to two. The tenor of the resolution was contrary to the sentiments of "the substantial thinking part," and had been carried in open meeting only through the eloquence of the two advocates and the unthinking enthusiasm of the crowd.[2]

At New York, as elsewhere, the merchants were active in stirring up opposition to the East India Company's shipments; but the development of events revealed, more clearly than elsewhere, the fundamental conflict between merchants and radicals as to the proper mode of procedure.[3] Preparations for the arrival began on November 10, when a printed notice, signed by "Legion," directed the pilots to refuse to guide the tea ship into the harbor. As the vessel was expected sometime in December, a committee of citizens exerted pressure upon the consignees to resign their

[1] *Pa. Mag.*, vol. xiv, pp. 78-79.

[2] Wharton to Walpole; Wharton, *Letter-Book* (Hist. Soc. of Pa.), pp. 33-34.

[3] The best accounts of these events are: the narrative by "Brutus" in *N. Y. Gazetteer*, May 12, 1774, reprinted in *4 Am. Arch.*, vol. i, pp. 251-258 n.; and the modern treatment of Becker, *N. Y. Parties, 1760-1776*, pp. 102-111. *Vide* also the New York newspapers during this period.

commissions; and this they cheerfully did on December 1, although meantime an open threat of violence had been made against them in a broadside issued by the "Mohawks." It was clearly necessary to reach an agreement as to the nature of the opposition which should be directed against the expected tea ship; and for this purpose a document, entitled the "Association of the Sons of Liberty," was prepared as a common platform for all classes. This paper denounced all persons who should aid in the introduction of dutied teas as enemies to their country and declared a boycott against them. As an onlooker of the event put it, this document embodied "the strongest terms of opposition, without actual violence . . . , leaving [by implication] the use of force . . . to be resolved in some future time in case any emergency might thereafter render the measure necessary."[1] The association was general enough in its terms to be signed by a great number of inhabitants, including "most of the principal lawyers, merchants, landholders, masters of ships, and mechanics."

The radicals were content with the association as a beginning; and one of the ultra-radicals, Alexander McDougall, assured Sam Adams in a letter of December 13 that: "The worst that can or will happen here is the landing of the Tea and storing it in the Fort."[2] The boldness of the people grew with the news of the early transactions at Boston; and in order to capitalize the excitement, the Sons of Liberty and "every other Friend to the Liberties and Trade of America" were summoned to a mass meeting on December 16. Two thousand were present notwithstanding the inclement weather, and they readily agreed to the suggestion of the radical, John Lamb, that a committee of

[1] "Brutus," *loc. cit.*
[2] *Bos. Com. Cor. Mss.*, vol. vi, pp. 472-473.

correspondence be appointed to communicate with the other provinces. The assemblage formally ratified the association; and when the mayor appeared with a proposition from the governor that the tea upon its arrival should be stored in the Fort and not be removed except at noonday, the offer was greeted with a thrice-repeated negative and indications of intense indignation. The radicals had advanced beyond the stage of halfway measures.

This meeting alarmed the more conservative merchants, who saw plainly that affairs were drifting in the direction of mob control. Four days later, a few persons, among whom Isaac Low and Jacob Walton were most active, circulated a paper, the avowed purpose of which was to pledge the signers not to resort to force in opposing the introduction of the tea. The project made some headway, but was abandoned on the next day because of the excitement aroused by the receipt of news of the Boston Tea Party. From that moment, as Governor Tryon informed Dartmouth, all hope of a temperate opposition was gone.[1] The consignees felt no uncertainty as to the peril, and on December 27 wrote to Captain Lockyer, of the tea-ship, a letter to be delivered upon his arrival at Sandy Hook, notifying him of their resignation and advising him to return to sea " for the safety of your cargo, your vessel, and your person . . ."[2] But the master of the tea ship had already heard echoes of the clamor at Boston and elsewhere in far-off Antigua, whither adverse winds had driven him while making for New York.[3] When he arrived at Sandy

[1] " The landing, storing and safe keeping of the Tea when stored could be accomplished, but only under the protection of the Point of the Bayonet and Muzle of the Cannon . . . ," wrote Tryon. *N. Y. Col. Docs.*, vol. viii, pp. 407-408.

[2] Drake, *op. cit.*, p. 358.

[3] *Mass. Spy*, Apr. 7, 1774.

Hook on Monday, April 18, 1774, he pursued a most circumspect course, refusing to betake himself personally to the city without permission of the committee of correspondence, and promising not to make entry at the custom house and to continue speedily on his way.

Capain Lockyer saved the property of the East India Company by his caution; for the populace were alert and ready for violent measures. This was shown by an incident which occurred before Lockyer returned to sea. On Friday of this week Captain Chambers arrived in the *London* with a personal consignment of eighteen chests of tea, whose presence on board he attempted in vain to conceal. The facts were laid before a meeting of citizens and the " Mohawks " were prepared for action at a concerted signal, when some impatient souls thronged on board the vessel, stove in the chests, and cast the tea into the waters.[1] The New Yorkers had now surpassed the Bostonians in their radicalism, for the latter had exhausted all other expedients before employing force. The New Yorkers acted in resentment of the glaring duplicity of Captain Chambers, who only six months before had received the gratitude of a New York meeting for having been one of the first captains to refuse a tea consignment of the East India Company.

The course of opposition in the commercial centers of the North thus took the form of an uncompromising refusal to permit the tea to be landed. In every instance, the movement was crowned with success, because it was engineered by an alliance of radicals and the generality of the merchants. The fourth port to which the tea was consigned

---

[1] "Several persons of reputation were placed below to keep tally and about the companion to prevent ill-disposed persons from going below the deck." " Brutus," *loc. cit.*

presented a situation in which such a union of forces was difficult to accomplish; and therefore the resistance to the East India Company yielded results only partially successful.

When news of the new commercial advantages granted to the East India Company reached Charleston, the newspapers hardly did more than to reprint some of the more trenchant pieces from the northern newspapers. The Charlestonians in general experienced considerable difficulty in discovering why they should be alarmed at receiving dutied tea directly from the East India Company when they had complaisantly accepted it from merchants who had themselves bought it of the company. It was some of the more radical planters who began to propagate the doctrine of an active resistance to the East India Company and invented the pleasant fiction that the private orders of customed tea had been imported in the belief that the duty would soon be repealed by Parliament.[1] The merchants were loath to take any part in the movement, many of them being factors and thus bearing a relationship to their English firms not unlike that of the tea consignees to the East India Company. Furthermore, a non-importation of dutied teas would inure to the benefit of a very small smuggling class, and the merchants had no reason to prefer their welfare to that of a legitimate trading company. The merchants also had large quantities of dutied teas in their stores and, in any event, desired to dispose of this stock before opposing the East India Company. The problem of the radicals was to secure the backing of the mercantile element, and to accomplish this end by making as few concessions as possible.

On Thursday morning, December 2, the tea ship *London*

---

[1] "Junius Brutus" in *S. C. Gaz.*, Nov. 29, 1773.

came to anchor before the town, containing the consignment of the East India Company as well as several tea consignments to private merchants. At once handbills were distributed about the streets inviting all inhabitants and particularly the landholders to assemble at the Exchange the next day.[1] The people responded in such numbers as to cause the main beams of the structure to give way. In the heated debates, it was urged that the East India Company had the same right to import dutied teas as the private merchants had been enjoying; but the greater number held otherwise. They prevailed upon the tea consignees to resign their commissions, and framed an agreement, pledging the merchants who should sign it to a non-importation of dutied teas. Captain Curling, of the tea ship, being present, was instructed to return to England with the tea; but no action was taken with reference to the private tea orders on board, which were publicly landed by their owners.

The committee entrusted with the circulation of the agreement, headed by Chris Gadsden and composed mostly of planters, met with little success. Even the appearance of a new agreement, signed by the " principal planters and landholders " and threatening boycott against dealers in dutied teas, had no visible effect on the merchants. Their objection was that the proposed agreement was aimed against dutied teas only and would directly enrich and enlarge the smuggling class.[2] The cause of the merchants was suffering from lack of organization; and in order to secure a greater solidarity, they established, on December 9, the " Charles-Town Chamber of Commerce," which thereafter devoted itself to promoting mercantile interests, polit-

[1] For the events of Dec. 2 and 3, *vide S. C. Gaz.*, Dec. 6, 1773; *N. Y. Gazetteer*, Dec. 23; Drayton, *Memoirs*, vol. i, pp. 97-98.

[2] Two letters of the Charleston consignees; *Pub. Rec. Off., C. O. 5,* no. 133 (*L. C. Transcripts*), f. 40d.

ical as well as economic.¹ The planters met at Mrs. Swallow's tavern on Wednesday, the fifteenth, in preparation for a general meeting which had been called for Friday; and it was probably more than a coincidence that their natural allies, the mechanics, held a meeting there at the same time. The merchants took occasion to hold a secret meeting of preparation on the following day. Under these circumstances, the crowd assembled at the Exchange on Friday, December 17. The chairman, George Gabriel Powell, opened the meeting by strongly recommending moderation.

Both radicals and merchants were represented by able speakers; the former appeared at first to have the upper hand, and a vote was passed for the non-importation of dutied teas. The moderates now rallied their forces, and succeeded in amending the motion to include all teas " from any Place whatsoever." By this amendment, legitimate traders and smugglers were placed on an equal footing. The merchants gained a further point in that six months were allowed for the consumption of the teas on hand. The radicals made a final attempt to commit the meeting to the fundamental principle of " no taxation without representation;" a motion was made to prohibit from the province wine, molasses and everything else subject to a revenue duty imposed by Parliament. On the plea that the hour was late, the meeting adjourned with a resolution to take up the matter for consideration at a meeting early in January.² This, as the sequel showed, proved to be a final disposition of the matter.³

Meantime the period for the payment of the tea duty expired on Tuesday night, December 21. As in the case of

¹ *S. C. Gaz.*, Dec. 13, 1773; *S. C. Gaz. & Coun. Journ.*, Dec. 28.
² Drayton, *op. cit.*, vol. i, pp. 97-98; *S. C. Gaz.*, Dec. 20, 1773; *Pub. Rec. Off.*, C. O. 5, no. 133 (*L. C. Transcripts*), f. 40d.
³ Drayton, *op. cit.*, vol. i, p. 100.

the Boston tea ship, Captain Curling had entered at the custom house and landed a part of his cargo. The resolutions of the two public meetings foreboded a spirited resistance to the seizure of the tea by the customs officials, but the lukewarm support given by the merchants was a cold douche to the hopes of the radicals.[1] The customs officers began to land the tea about seven o'clock Wednesday morning, and by noon all of it was placed on shore and about half of it in the warehouse. "There was not the least disturbance," wrote the comptroller of the customs; "the gentlemen that came on the wharf behaved with their usual complaisance and good nature to me . . ."[2] The tea remained undisturbed in the government warehouse for three years, when it was auctioned off for the benefit of the new revolutionary government.

It is apparent from this recital of events that the British government and its reluctant ally, the East India Company, had been foiled in their attempt to effect the sale of dutied tea, owned by the company, in the colonies. The results of this politico-business venture were to be far reaching. Meantime the radicals and merchants of America, having beheld the fruits of their coalition, found time to reflect on the situation in which they found themselves. Of the four instances of opposition to the East India Company, the Boston Tea Party was best calculated to enkindle the public mind; but, to the surprise of the radicals, there was no bursting forth of the flame that had swept over the country at the time of the Stamp Act and again during the Townshend

---

[1] Governor Bull believed that, if the merchants had been a little more aggressive in showing disapprobation of the public meetings and the consignees had shown a little more backbone, the plan of the East India Company would have been put peaceably into operation. Drake, *op. cit.*, pp. 339-341.

[2] *Ibid.*, p. 342.

Acts, save in Massachusetts where the fuse had been carefully laid by the committees of correspondence. The merchant class generally was shocked into remorseful silence by the anarchy that had laid profane hands upon property belonging to a private trading company; and many other people, more liberally inclined, were of their cast of mind.

As a conservative Boston journal quoted with approval:

Whenever a factious set of People rise to such a Pitch of Insolence, as to prevent the Execution of the Laws, or destroy the Property of Individuals, just as their Caprice or Humour leads them; there is an end of all Order and Government, Riot and Confusion must be the natural Consequence of such Measures. It is impossible for Trade to flourish where Property is insecure: Whether this has not been the Case at Boston for some time past, you are the best Judge. There is a strange Spirit of Licentiousness gone forth into the World, which shelters itself under the venerable and endearing Name of LIBERTY, but is as different from it as Folly is from Wisdom.[1]

Furthermore, what right did the Bostonians have to pose as the jealous guardians of the principle of local taxation, it was asked in many parts of British America, when Bostonians had been the most notorious importers of dutied teas during the last two or three years? Even Dr. Franklin, who from his official position at London represented all America more nearly than any other one man, called the tea destruction " an Act of violent Injustice on our part." He wrote at length to the Massachusetts Committee of Correspondence:

I am truly concern'd as I believe all considerate Men are with you, that there should seem to any a Necessity for carrying Matters to such Extremity, as, in a Dispute about Publick

[1] Words of an Englishman writing to an American friend; *Mass. Gaz. & News-Letter*, Nov. 17, 1774.

Rights, to destroy private Property. . . . I cannot but wish & hope that before any compulsive Measures are thought of here, our General Court will have shewn a Disposition to repair the Damage and make Compensation to the Company.[1]

As has been suggested, Sam Adams's committee system taught the inhabitants of Massachusetts and the nearby provinces to react differently, although even here the maritime town of Bristol, R. I., saw fit to qualify its resolutions against the East India Company by declaring:

Some may apprehend there is danger from another quarter, generally unforeseen and unsuspected; that anarchy and confusion, which may prevail, will as naturally establish tyranny and arbitrary power, as one extreme leads to another; many on the side of liberty, when they see it degenerating into anarchy, fearing their persons are not safe, nor their property secure, will be likely to verge to the other extreme. . . .[2]

From the moment of the sinking of the tea at Boston, public sentiment in Massachusetts entirely escaped any bounds that the mercantile element could have set for it. It has been shown how, in the earlier months, the popular demands, originally directed against the dutied shipments of the British trading monopoly alone, were extended to include consignments to private merchants as well. Immediately after the tea destruction, the radicals proceeded to take the logical next step—the boycott of all teas, whether dutied or smuggled. This may have been done to propitiate the dealers in legal teas; but it also had the effect of preventing the selling of customed teas to unsuspecting persons who believed they were buying the contraband article.[3]

[1] Letter of Feb. 2, 1774; *Writings* (Smyth), vol. vi, pp. 178-180. *Vide* also *ibid.*, p. 223.

[2] *R. I. Col. Recs.*, vol. vii, pp. 274-275.

[3] "Concordia" and "Deborah Doubtful" in *Mass. Spy*, Jan. 13, 27, 1774.

Many believed this step to be "chimerical;"[1] certainly the smugglers were robbed of their pecuniary interest in the struggle, but they were too deeply involved to withdraw their support now. Within a week after the tea destruction, the tea dealers of Boston agreed to suspend the sales of all teas, dutied or otherwise, after January 20, 1774. When that day arrived, two barrels of Bohea still unsold were publicly burned in front of the custom house.[2]

The nearby town of Charlestown co-operated with the Boston measures; and the Boston plan was also adopted by Worcester, Acton, Lunenburgh, and perhaps by other towns.[3] Most Massachusetts towns, however, were content to decree merely the abstention from dutied teas. Up until the first of April, 1774, forty towns had passed resolutions;[4] most of them affixed a boycott as the sanction of the resolves; and several towns appointed belated committees of correspondence. The height of radical fervor was reached in a resolution of the town of Windham, which declared: "That neither the Parliament of Britain nor the Parliament of France nor any other Parliament but that which sits supreme in our Province has a Right to lay any Taxes

[1] *Mass. Spy*, Jan. 13, 20, 1774.

[2] Seventy-nine dealers agreed to the resolutions; nine would oppose dutied tea only; and four refused even a qualified assent. *Mass. Spy*, Dec. 30, 1773, Jan. 20, 1774; *Bos. Eve. Post*, Jan. 24, Feb. 7, 1774.

[3] *Mass. Spy*, Dec. 30, 1773, Jan. 6, Feb. 10, 1774; *Bos. Com. Cor. Mss.*, vol. viii, pp. 644-649, 681-683.

[4] *Abington*, Bedford, Berwick, *Beverly, Bolton, Boxford, Braintree, Cape Elizabeth, Colerain, Concord, Dedham, Dorchester,* Eastham, *Falmouth, Framingham,* Gorham, *Grafton,* Harvard, *Hull, Ipswich, Lincoln, Medfield,* Medway, *Newton, Newbury,* Pembrooke, Salem, Sandwich, Scarborough, Shirley, *Shrewsbury, Sudbury, Topsfield,* Townshend, *Truro, Watertown, Wellfleet, Wells, Westford,* Windham. For these resolutions, *vide* the current newspapers and *Bos. Com. Cor. Mss.*, vols. vi, vii and viii, *passim*. The towns italicized included the boycott.

on us for the purpose of Raising a Revenue." Only a few towns took unfavorable action, Marshfield hoping to see the perpetrators of the Boston violence brought to justice, and Littleton discharging its committee of correspondence.[1] At Sandwich the radicals defeated unfriendly action by refusing to hold a meeting; and at Eastham they succeeded in rescinding the condemnatory resolves of an earlier meeting.[2]

The excitement over the tea was utilized by the Boston radicals, though with only partial success, in an attempt to stir up the nearby provinces to protest and action. According to Governor Wentworth, of New Hampshire, " the unwearied applications from Boston communicated the flame here."[3] A town meeting met at Portsmouth on December 16, 1773, and passed strong resolutions against the importation of duties teas similar to the Philadelphia resolutions of October 16.[4] Shortly after, several other towns followed the example of the capital.[5] It was not until the end

[1] In both cases the radicals signed their names to published protests. *Mass. Spy*, Feb. 10, 24, 1774.

[2] *Mass. Spy*, Apr. 7, 1774; *Bos. Com. Cor. Papers*, vol. iii, pp. 307-310. The sincerity of the widespread resolutions was quickly evidenced by a number of instances of enforcement. E. g., vide *Mass. Spy*, Jan. 13, Feb. 17, Mch. 17, 31, Apr. 7, July 21, 1774. The country peddler proved to be the most persistent offender. At Boston the determination to prevent the shipment of customed teas to private merchants led to a second Tea Party on March 8, 1774, when 28½ chests of tea on board the brig *Fortune* were cast into the harbor by the omnipresent "Indians." The Boston Committee declared in a letter that "this event must convince the Merchants in England that the extorted duty on that Article is as disagreeable to the good People of this Province as the intended monopoly of the East India Company." *Bos. Com. Cor. Mss.*, vol. ix, pp. 726-729; *Mass. Spy*, Mch. 10, 17, 1774.

[3] *Brit. Papers* ("*Sparks Mss.*"), vol. i, p. 21.

[4] *N. H. Gaz.*, Dec. 24, 1773.

[5] Barrington, Exeter, Hampton, Haverhill, Newcastle. *Mass. Spy*, Jan. 13, 1774; *Mass. Gaz. & Post-Boy*, Jan. 10; *N. H. Gaz.*, Feb. 25, Mch. 4.

of June, 1774, that the flame, whereof Wentworth had spoken, showed how defective were its incendiary properties. On the twenty-fifth, a vessel arrived at Portsmouth with a consignment of twenty-seven chests of dutied tea for a private merchant. The tea was landed; the town meeting which assembled to consider the situation was temperate beyond the hope of the governor. A committee, composed chiefly of "discreet men who . . . detested every idea of violating property," was appointed to treat with the consignee, while the town meeting chose "a guard of freeholders to protect and defend the Custom House and the tea from any attempt or interruption." The merchant readily accepted the committee's offer to export the tea to any market he chose at the town's expense; and thereupon the duty was openly paid and the tea publicly carted back to the vessel. The whole episode passed off without disturbance, an incipient attempt being quelled by the townsmen themselves.[1]

The people at Newport, R. I., were even more belated in adopting resolutions, although urged to do so by a letter from the Boston Committee of Correspondence. Finally, on Saturday, January 1, 1774, a notice was mysteriously posted at the Brick Market, signed by "Legion," and threatening that the town officials would surely be opposed in any office in town or colony to which they might aspire, unless a town meeting were called to adopt resolutions like Boston and the other towns. The notice had its effect: a town meeting was held on the following Tuesday, and at an adjournment on January 12 the town adopted the Philadelphia resolutions *verbatim* and appointed a committee of correspondence.[2] This prompted the smaller towns to pass

[1] *N. H. Gaz.*, July 1, 8, 1774; 4 *Am. Arch.*, vol. i, pp. 512-513.
[2] *Mass. Gaz. & Post-Boy*, Jan. 17, 1774; *Bos. Eve. Post*, Jan. 24.

similar resolutions and became a signal for the establishment of the committee of correspondence system throughout Rhode Island.¹ Only one New England province remained silent; and no amount of urging from Boston was sufficient to arouse the people of Connecticut to a sense of danger.²

At New York we have seen that news of the Boston vandalism had, for the moment, turned the tide in favor of the radicals, and that at Philadelphia resolutions of approval had been impulsively adopted contrary to the judgment of the " substantial thinking part." Nevertheless, the sober judgment of both towns and of the remaining provinces was against the action of the Bostonians. Several meetings of the people of Charleston, S. C., prompted by the radicals in January and March, 1774, proved futile in their outcome.³ The ebbing of the radical movement seemed apparent on almost every hand.

¹ By the end of March, Providence, Bristol, Richmond, New Shoreham, Cumberland and Barrington had acted. *R. I. Col. Recs.*, vol. vii, pp. 272-280, 283. The town of Scituate chose a committee in September.

² *Bos. Com. Cor. Mss.*, vol. ix, pp. 717-718.

³ *S. C. Gaz.*, Jan. 24, Mch. 7, 21, 28, 1774; Drayton, *Memoirs*, vol. i, p. 100. At the Charleston meeting of Mch. 16, a standing committee of forty-five was appointed with power to act as executive body and to call the inhabitants together upon occasion.

CHAPTER VIII

CONTEST OF MERCHANTS AND RADICALS FOR DOMINANCE IN THE COMMERCIAL PROVINCES (MARCH–AUGUST, 1774)

THE enactment of the coercive acts by Parliament called forth the union of interests and action in America, which the opposition to the East India Company in the leading seaports had failed to evoke. The chief of these laws were intended to deal with the lawless conditions which had arisen in the province of Massachusetts Bay out of the tea commotions. The first of the series, the Boston Port Act, received the royal assent on the last day of March, 1774.[1] This act provided for the closing of the harbor of Boston to commerce from and after June 1 and the transfer of the custom house to Marblehead and the capital to Salem. The port of Boston was to be re-opened when the East India Company and the customs officers and others had been reimbursed for the losses sustained by them during the riots, and when the king in privy council was satisfied that trade might be safely carried on there and the customs duly collected.

After an interval of two months, two other acts were passed which provided for thorough-going alterations of the constitution of the province.[2] The governor's council, which, being elective by the Assembly, had hitherto ob-

[1] 14 George III, c. 19. For the parliamentary debates on this and the following acts, *vide Parliamentary History*, vol. xvii, pp. 1159-1325.
[2] 14 George III, c. 45, c. 39.

structed all efforts to suppress rioting, was now made appointive by the king, as in all other royal provinces. A direct blow was aimed at the system of committees of correspondence by the provision placing town meetings under the immediate control of the governor from and after August 1, and permitting only the annual meeting for the election of officers to be held without his express authorization. The way was prepared for a rigorous execution of the customs laws by providing that a person might be tried in another province or in Great Britain, who was charged with a capital crime committed " either in the execution of his duty as a magistrate, for the suppression of riots or in the support of the laws of revenue, or in acting in his duty as an officer of revenue," or as acting in a subordinate capacity in either case. The three acts passed with great majorities.[1] A motion to rescind the tea duty called forth a remarkable speech in favor of repeal by Edmund Burke; but the motion was lost by a large vote.

The receipt of the news of the Boston Port Act put a new face on public affairs in America. It changed completely the nature of the contest with Parliament which had been going on intermittently since 1764. It created the basis for a realignment of forces and strength, the importance of which was to be a fundamental factor in the later development of events. Hitherto the struggle with Parliament had been, in large part, inspired and guided by the demand of the mercantile class for trade reforms. Each new act of Parliament had accentuated or ameliorated business distress in the colonies; and in proportion to the remedial character of the legislation, the barometer of American discontent had risen or fallen. To carry on their propa-

[1] In June, the Quebec Act and the Quartering Act were added to the trilogy of measures already enacted. These acts merely added fuel to the blaze that had already started in the colonies.

ganda successfully, the merchants had found it necessary to form alliances with their natural enemies in society—with the intelligent, hopeful radicals who dreamed of a semi-independent American nation or something better, and with the innumerable and nameless individuals whose brains were in their biceps, men who were useful as long as they could be held in leash. The passage of the Boston Port Act and the other laws brought things to an issue between these two elements, already grown suspicious of each other. The question in controversy between Parliament and the colonies was changed in an instant from a difference over trade reforms to a political dispute, pure and simple, over the right of Parliament to punish and prevent mob violence through blockading Boston and expurgating the Massachusetts constitution.[1]

[1] Gouverneur Morris flippantly described the development of events in New York in these terms: "It is needless to premise, that the lower orders of mankind are more easily led by specious appearances than those of a more exalted station. . . . The troubles in America, during Grenville's administration, put our gentry upon this finesse. They stimulated some daring coxcombs to rouse the mob into an attack upon the bounds of order and decency. These fellows became the Jack Cades of the day, the leaders in all the riots, the belwethers of the flock. The reason of the manoeuvre in those who wished to keep fair with the Government, and at the same time to receive the incense of popular applause, you will readily perceive. On the whole, the shepherds were not much to blame in a politic point of view. The belwethers jingled merrily, and roared out liberty, and property, and religion, and a multitude of cant terms, which every one thought he understood, and was egregiously mistaken. For you must know the shepherds kept the dictionary of the day; and, like the mysteries of the ancient mythology, it was not for profane eyes or ears. This answered many purposes; the simple flock put themselves entirely under the protection of these most excellent shepherds. By and bye behold a great metamorphosis, without the help of Ovid or his divinities but entirely effectuated by two modern Genii, the god of Ambition and the goddess of Faction. The first of these prompted the shepherds to shear some of their flock, and then, in conjunction with the other, converted the belwethers into shepherds. That we have been in hot water with

In this new aspect of the controversy the merchants found themselves instinctively siding with the home government. No commercial principle was at stake in the coercive acts; and the Boston violence was a manifestation of mob rule which every self-respecting merchant abhorred from his very soul. Nor could he see any commercial advantage which might accrue from pursuing the will-o'-the-wisp ideas of the radicals. The uncertain prospect which the radical plans held forth was not comparable with the tangible benefits which came from membership in the British empire under existing conditions; even absolute freedom of trade meant little in view of the restrictive trade systems of the leading nations of the world, the comparative ease with which the most objectionable parliamentary regulations continued to be evaded, and the insecure, if not dangerous, character of any independent government which the radicals might establish. When all was said and done, the merchants knew that their welfare depended upon their connection with Great Britain—upon the protection afforded by the British navy, upon the acquisition of new markets by

the British Parliament since every body knows. Consequently these new shepherds had their hands full of employment. The old ones kept themselves least in sight, and a want of confidence in each other was not the least evil which followed. The port of Boston has been shut up. These sheep, simple as they are, cannot be gulled as heretofore. In short, there is no ruling them; and now, to change the metaphor, the heads of the mobility grow dangerous to the gentry, and how to keep them down is the question." Letter to Penn, May 20, 1774; Sparks, J., *Life of Gouverneur Morris* (Boston, 1832), vol. i, pp. 23-26; also *4 Am. Arch.*, vol. i, pp. 342-343. *Vide* also an unsigned letter in *ibid.*, 302 n., and Governor Martin's letter in *N. C. Col. Recs.*, vol. ix, pp. 1083-1087. In the case of Massachusetts, *vide* the statement of "A Converted Whig" who, although a member of the Boston Committee of Correspondence, began to desert the radical cause after the Boston Tea Party. *4 Am. Arch.*, vol. ii, pp. 103-106. For a similar view in the case of Pennsylvania, *vide* Charles Thomson's letter to Drayton, Stillé, *Life of Dickinson*, p. 345.

British arms, upon legislation which fostered their shipping, subsidized certain industries and protected the merchants from foreign competition in British markets.[1] Many details of this legislation had proved defective, but Parliament had shown a disposition to correct the worst features; and this disposition would, in all probability, continue, since British capital invested in American trade had a powerful representation in Parliament.

From the time of the passage of the coercive acts by Parliament, thus, there became evident a strong drift on the part of the colonial mercantile class to the British viewpoint of the questions at issue. Many merchants at once took their stand with the forces of government and law and order; these men may properly be classed as conservatives, or loyalists, in the same sense that the royal official class were. Others believed that all was not yet lost and that, by remaining in the movement, they could restrain its excesses and give it a distinctly conservative cast. Such men were, for the time being at least, moderates, being willing, though for partisan reasons, to indulge in extra-legal activities.

But the coercive acts were equally important in making converts to the radical position. Whereas the mob destruction of the tea had antagonized many people, the enactment of the severe punitive acts served, in the judgment of many of them, to place the greater guilt on the other side. A significant instance was the case of Dr. Franklin, who in February, 1774, had denounced the Boston Tea Party as an unjustifiable act of violence. Writing after the passage of the acts, he declared to his loyalist son:

[1] For contemporary expositions of this view, *vide The Interest of the Merchants and Manufacturers of Great Britain in the Present Contest with the Colonies Stated and Considered* (London, 1774); broadside, "To the Inhabitants of New-York," 4 *Am. Arch.*, vol. i, pp. 886-888; "Mercurius" in *Ga. Gaz.*, Sept. 28, 1774.

I do not so much as you do wonder that the Massachusetts [Assembly] have not offered Payment for the Tea . . . [Parliament and the ministry] have extorted many Thousand Pounds from America unconstitutionally, under Colour of Acts of Parliament, and with an armed Force. Of this Money they ought to make Restitution. They might first have taken out Payment for the Tea, &c. and returned the rest.[1]

Another conspicuous and important instance of conversion was that of William Henry Drayton, the wealthy young South Carolinian who, with fiery zeal, had excoriated Chris Gadsden and the non-importers in 1769. A nephew of Governor Bull and favored by appointment to various offices in the gift of the king, he now turned definitely to the side of the popular party. To use his own words:

The same spirit of indignation which animated me to condemn popular measures in the year 1769, because although avowedly in defence of liberty, they absolutely violated the freedom of society, by demanding men, under pain of being stigmatized, and of sustaining detriment in property, to accede to resolutions, which, however well meant, could not . . . but be . . . very grating to a freeman, so, the *same spirit* of indignation . . . actuates me in like manner, *now to assert* my freedom *against the malignant* nature of the late five Acts of Parliament.

His course was consistent, he asserted: "I opposed succeeding violations of my rights, then, by a temporary democracy, now, by an established monarchy."[2]

Governor Penn described the transformation of opinion at Philadelphia. "They look upon the chastisement of

[1] Letter of Sept. 7, 1774; *Writings* (Smyth), vol. vi, p. 241.
[2] "Letter from Freeman," Aug. 10, 1774; Gibbes, *Documentary History*, vol. ii, pp. 12-13. Drayton felt it necessary to deny the aspersion of his enemies that his change of faith was occasioned by disappointment at failing to receive a permanent appointment as assistant judge. Indeed, this charge will not bear serious analysis.

Boston to be purposely rigorous, and held up by way of intimidation to all America . . . ," he wrote. " Their delinquency in destroying the East India Company's tea is lost in the attention given to what is here called the too severe punishment of shutting up the port, altering the Constitution, and making an Act, as they term it, screening the officers and soldiers shedding American blood." [1] In Virginia a similar change of opinion was revealed in the resolutions adopted by county meetings. Patrick Henry's own county of Hanover acknowledged in its resolutions:

Whether the people there [at Boston] were warranted by justice when they destroyed the tea, we know not; but this we know, that the Parliament by their proceedings have made us and all North America parties in the present dispute . . . insomuch that, if our sister Colony of Massachusetts Bay is enslaved, we cannot long remain free.[2]

The counties of Middlesex and Dinwiddie condemned without qualification the Boston Tea Party as an " outrage," and added their determined protest and opposition to the force acts of Parliament.[3]

The Boston Port Act reached Boston on May 10, 1774. The people realized at once that the prosperity of the great port hung in the balance, and two groups were quickly

[1] Letter to Dartmouth, July 5, 1774; *4 Am. Arch.*, vol. i, p. 514.

[2] *Ibid.*, vol. i, p. 616. *Vide* the similar resolutions of a mass meeting of Granville County, N. C. *N. C. Col. Recs.*, vol. ix, pp. 1034-1036.

[3] *4 Am. Arch.*, vol. i, pp. 551-553. Equally significant is the fact that the passage of the coercive acts served as a signal for the people of the tobacco provinces to manifest their first opposition to private shipments of dutied tea. *Vide* the affair of the *Mary and Jane* in Maryland and Virginia; *Md. Gaz.*, Aug. 11, 18, 1774, and Rind's *Va. Gaz.*, Aug. 25; also *4 Am. Arch.*, vol. i, pp. 703-705, 727-728.

formed as to the course which should be pursued.[1] The extremists, including the more radical merchants, opposed any restitution to the East India Company and insisted on an immediate commercial opposition, which should go to lengths hitherto unattempted, including not only non-importation but also non-exportation, and affecting not only Great Britain but also every part of the West Indies, British and foreign.[2] This party believed that the salvation of Boston and the province depended upon swift and effective coercion of Great Britain, and they were entirely willing to sacrifice temporary business benefits for what they esteemed a larger political good. The other party, composed of merchants and of conservatives generally, held that the Tea Party had been an unjustifiable act of mob violence, and that the best good of port and province would be served by paying for the tea and conforming to the conditions imposed by the act. A member of this group analyzed the division in public affairs in this manner: "the merchants who either will not or cannot make remittances, the smugglers, the mechanicks, and those who are facinated with the extravagant notion of independency, all join to counteract the majority of the merchants, and the lovers of peace and good order." [3]

[1] "The present dispute," wrote one of the radicals, "seems confined to these two sentiments: either to pay, or not to pay for the tea." *Ibid.*, vol. i, pp. 487-489.

[2] They wished to include the British West Indies in the boycott because an important group in Parliament owned sugar plantations there; and they demanded that the foreign islands should likewise be placed beyond the pale in order to make the boycott easier to administer and also to cause the French, Danish and Dutch governments to protest to Great Britain. Thomas Young to John Lamb, May 13, 1774; Leake, I. Q., *Memoir of the Life and Times of General John Lamb* (Albany, 1850), p. 85.

[3] 4 *Am. Arch.*, vol. i, pp. 506-508.

On Friday, May 13, 1774, the town meeting of Boston adopted a resolution which was designed to arouse the united opposition of the continent to the act threatening Boston. The resolution was worded to attract the support of moderate folk throughout the commercial provinces, but in general, though not absolutely, it advocated the measures desired by the Boston radicals. It was resolved that "if the other colonies come into a joint resolution to stop all importations from Great Britain, and exportations to Great Britain, and every part of the West Indies, till the Act for blocking up this harbour be repealed, the same will prove the salvation of North America and her Liberties;" otherwise "there is high reason to fear that fraud, power and the most odious oppression will rise triumphant over right, justice, social happiness and freedom." [1] A committee was appointed to carry the resolutions in person to Salem and Marblehead, both towns being beneficiaries of the odious law; and the committee of correspondence was ordered to dispatch messengers with the vote to the other towns of Massachusetts and to the other provinces.

The resolution of May 13, soon to become famous throughout British America, was seconded by a circular letter sent forth the same day by the Boston Committee of Correspondence with the concurrence of the committees of eight adjoining towns.[2] The single question, according to this letter, was: do you consider Boston as now suffering in the common cause of America? if so, may we not "rely on your suspending Trade with Great Britain at least . . ." A few days later the town meeting resolved:

[1] *Mass. Gaz. & Post-Boy*, May 16, 1774; also *Bos. Town Recs.* (*1770-1777*), pp. 172-174.

[2] Charlestown, Cambridge, Brookline, Dorchester, Lexington, Lynn, Newton and Roxbury. *Bos. Com. Cor. Mss.*, vol. x, pp. 810-811.

That the trade of the town of Boston has been one essential link in that vast chain of commerce, which, in the course of a few ages, has raised New England to be what it is, the Southern provinces to be what they are, the West Indies to their wealth, and, in one word, the British Empire to that heighth of oppulence, power, pride and splendor, at which it now stands.[1]

The radicals waited to hear the response to the Boston appeal before pushing for more extreme measures.

Town meetings at Salem and Marblehead rose splendidly to the occasion in spite of their privileged position under the act, and endorsed the Boston resolutions.[2] Their benefits from the act were indeed more imaginary than actual, " Boston being the grand engine that gives motion to all the wheels of commerce " in the province and supplying in particular an entrepôt for the West Indian imports of those ports.[3] Twenty-eight merchants of Marblehead invited the merchants of Boston to use their storerooms and wharves free of charge.[4] Without at present considering the attitude of the seaports in other provinces, other towns in Massachusetts responded favorably to the appeal of Boston.[5]

The town of Boston faced a difficult problem, that of

[1] May 18. *Mass. Spy*, May 19, 1774; also *Bos. Town Recs.* (*1770-1777*), pp. 174-175.

[2] *Essex Gaz.*, May 24, 1774; *Bos. Gaz.*, May 30. The Marblehead resolutions omitted mention of non-intercourse but expressed willingness to enter any "rational" agreement that might be generally adopted.

[3] Letter of John Scollay, 4 *Am. Arch.*, vol. i, pp. 369-370; address of Salem merchants, *Mass. Spy*, June 23, 1774.

[4] *Ibid.*

[5] E. g., the towns of Gloucester, Lunenburgh, Salisbury and Glassenburg and the merchants of Newburyport acted before the end of June. *Ibid.*, May 19, 1774; *Bos. Com. Cor. Papers*, vol. ii, pp. 155, 233; *Bos. Com. Cor. Mss.*, vol. viii, p. 713; vol. x, p. 802.

providing labor and sustenance for the hundreds of workingmen thrown out of employment by the closing of the port. The task of feeding the poor was somewhat simplified by the generous donations of food and money which poured in from neighboring towns and from provinces as far away as South Carolina.[1] But this outside aid entailed a responsibility for administering the donations equitably; and the inevitable, though ill-founded, charges of corruption appeared.[2] The committee appointed to deal with the unemployment question resorted to all sorts of expedients (such as, for instance, the building of a wharf with capital furnished by the wealthier citizens); but the best results were gotten from the employing of men to repair pavements, clean public docks, dig public wells, *etc.*, from the establishment of a brickyard on town land, and the subsidizing of cotton and flax spinning.[3]

While the first anger aroused by the receipt of the Boston Port Act was still high, the merchants of the town were prevailed upon by the committee of correspondence to sign an agreement for severing all trade relations with Great Britain upon condition that their brethren in the other commercial provinces should embrace the same measure.[4] But of what they did in haste they soon repented at leisure. At a town meeting on May 30, the merchants and trades-

[1] For the correspondence of the Boston committee with the contributors of the donations, *vide* 4 *M. H. S. Colls.*, vol. iv, pp. 1-278.

[2] "A Friend to Boston" in *N. Y. Journ.*, Sept. 15, 1774; refutation of the committee, 4 *M. H. S. Colls.*, vol. iv, pp. 277-278.

[3] *Bos. Town Recs.* (*1770-1777*), pp. 174-175, 181, 185-189; 4 *M. H. S. Colls.*, vol. iv, pp. 275-277.

[4] May 21, 1774. *Bos. Com. Cor. Papers*, vol. iii, p. 187. This action was pressed through in face of the zealous opposition of merchants whom the committee of correspondence characterized as "the tools of Hutchinson and of the Commissioners." *Bos. Com. Cor. Mss.*, vol. x, pp. 808-810.

men attended two or three hundred strong, most of them determined to use their endeavors to secure payment for the tea.

But [if a contemporary may be believed] so artful and industrious were the *principal heads* of the opposition to *government,* that they placed themselves at the doors of the *hall* and told the tradesmen as they entered that now was the time to save our *country.* That if they gave their voice in favor of paying for the tea, we should be undone, and the chains of slavery rivitted upon us! which so terrified many honest well meaning persons, that they thought it prudent not to act at all in the affair . . .[1]

The meeting succeeded in adopting a mild non-consumption agreement, the signers whereof agreed not to purchase any British manufactures that could be obtained in the province and to boycott those who conspired against the measures of the town.[2]

The impending departure of Governor Hutchinson for England and the arrival of the new governor, Thomas Gage, gave the merchants and conservatives an opportunity to make a quasi-official statement of their principles in public form. An address from "the Merchants and Traders of the town of Boston and others" was presented to Hutchinson on May 30. This document, shrewdly enough, contained a well-reasoned criticism of the Boston Port Act at the same time that it pledged the signers in opposition to the plans of the radicals. It praised the "wise, zealous, and faithful Administration" of Hutchinson, expressed a belief that the Boston Port Act would have been more just

---

[1] Gray, H., *A Few Remarks upon Some of the Votes and Resolutions of the Continental Congress* . . . (Boston, 1775), pp. 6-7. Reprinted in *Mag. N. Engl. Hist.*, vol. ii, pp. 42-58.

[2] *Bos. Town Recs.* (1770-1777), pp. 175-176.

if Boston had been given the alternative of conforming to its conditions within a specified period or of suffering the harsh consequences, bore solemn testimony against popular tumults, and asked Hutchinson to inform the king that the signers of the address would gladly pay their share of the damages suffered by the East India Company.[1] The paper was signed by one hundred and twenty-four men, of whom sixty-three were merchants and shopkeepers by admission of the radicals themselves and four others were employees of merchants.[2] According to the lawyer, Daniel Leonard, the signers consisted "principally of men of property, large family connections, and several were independant in their circumstances and lived wholly upon the income of their estates. . . . A very considerable proportion were persons that had of choice kept themselves from the political vortex . . . while the community remained safe" but now rallied to the cause of law and order.[3] When five gentlemen went to Governor Gage and inquired what the value of the tea destroyed was, he intimated that they would

[1] *Mass. Spy*, June 2, 1774; also *1 M. H. S. Procs.*, vol. xii, pp. 43-44. The address of welcome of the merchants, traders and others to the new governor expressed substantially the same sentiments, condemning "lawless violences" and promising support in reimbursing the East India Company. *Bos. Eve. Post*, June 13, 1774. One hundred and twenty-seven signatures were attached. Loyal addresses, purporting to come from the merchants, traders and other inhabitants of Marblehead and of Salem, were likewise sent to the two gentlemen. Curwen, *Journal*, pp. 426-427, 431-432.

[2] A complete tabulation shows 37 merchants and factors, 4 employees, 26 shopkeepers, 7 distillers, 12 royal officials, 6 retired or professional men, 20 artisans or mechanics, 5 farmers, 7 uncertain. *1 M. H. S. Procs.*, vol. xi, pp. 392-394. A number of the merchants had made themselves unpopular in the earlier non-importation movement, such as William Jackson, Benjamin Greene & Son, Colburn Barrell, Theophilus Lillie, James Selkrig, and J. & P. McMasters.

[3] "Massachusettensis" in *Mass. Gaz. & Post-Boy*, Jan. 2, 1775.

learn when either the town of Boston in its corporate capacity or the General Court applied to him.[1]

Fortunately for the merchants, an opportunity came to them to retrace the step they had taken in proposing a joint agreement of non-intercourse to the other merchants of the commercial provinces. In the early days of June, word arrived that the merchants in the leading ports outside of Massachusetts were not willing to join in this measure.[2] The members of the trading body at Boston considered themselves absolved from their conditional pact, and refused absolutely to accept the repeated suggestions of Sam Adams and the radicals to go ahead independently in the matter. The Reverend Charles Chauncy, of Boston, voiced radical opinion, when he wrote on May 30, 1774, with reference to the merchants:

> so many of them are so mercenary as to find within themselves a readiness to become slaves themselves, as well as to be accessory to the slavery of others, if they imagine they may by this means serve their own private separate interest. Our dependence, under God, is upon the *landed interest,* upon our freeholders and yeomonry. By not buying of the merchants what they may as well do without, they may keep in their own pockets two or three millions sterling a year, which would otherwise be exported to Great-Brittain. I have reasons to think the effect of this barbarous Port-act will be [such] an agreement . . .[3]

Such indeed was the strategy of which the radicals now availed themselves. Convinced that the merchants could

---

[1] Letter to Philadelphia friend; *4 Am. Arch.*, vol. i, p. 380. The merchant, George Erving, for instance, was willing to subscribe £2000 sterling toward a reimbursement fund for the East India Company. *1 M. H. S. Procs.*, vol. viii, p. 329.

[2] "Y. Z." in *Mass. Gaz. & Post-Boy,* June 27, 1774; "Candidus" (Sam Adams) in *Bos. Gaz.*, June 27, and *Mass. Spy*, July 7.

[3] *2 M. H. S. Procs.*, vol. xvii, pp. 266-268.

not be relied upon to adopt the policy of non-intercourse, they decided to appeal to the people directly over their heads. On June 5, 1774, the Boston Committee of Correspondence adopted a form of agreement for country circulation and adoption, which, in the fulness of their political sagacity, they named the "Solemn League and Covenant."[1] It was hoped, no doubt, that the country people would be inspired by recollections of the doughty pact which their Cromwellian progenitors had made against King Charles more than a century before. The object of the agreement was not the reform of commercial legislation but the repeal of punitive laws "tending to the entire subversion of our natural and charter rights." For this purpose, the subscribers, who might be of either sex, covenanted with each other "in the presence of God, solemnly and in good faith" to suspend all commercial intercourse with Great Britain thenceforth, and neither to purchase nor use any British imports whatsoever after October 1. All persons who refused to sign this or a similar covenant were to be boycotted forever, and their names made public to the world.

In fathering the Covenant, the Boston Committee of Correspondence acted secretly, without authorization of the town, and without intending to circulate the Covenant among the people of Boston. In truth, it was the purpose of the committee to have the Covenant appear to be the spontaneous action of the non-mercantile population of the

[1] On June 2 a sub-committee, consisting of Dr. Joseph Warren, Dr. Benjamin Church and Mr. Greenleaf, had been instructed "to draw up a Solemn League and Covenant." *Bos. Com. Cor. Mss.*, vol. ix, pp. 763-764. According to Sam Adams, the committee bestowed "care, pains, repeated and continued consideration upon a subject confessedly the most difficult that ever came before them." "Candidus" in *Mass. Spy*, July 7, 1774. For text of the Covenant, *vide Mass. Gaz. & Post-Boy*, June 27; also 4 *Am. Arch.*, vol. i, pp. 397-398.

province. Thus the radical organ, the *Boston Gazette*, declared on June 13:

We learn from divers Parts of the Country that the People in general, having become quite impatient by not hearing a Non-Importation Agreement has yet been come into by the Merchants, are now taking the good Work into their own Hands, and have and are solemnly engaging not to purchase any Goods imported from Great-Britain, or to trade with those who do import or purchase such Goods. . . .

A few days later, the committee felt no qualms in declaring unequivocally in their correspondence: "this Effectual Plan has been origanated and been thus far carried thro' by the two venerable orders of men stiled Mechanicks & husbandmen, the strength of every community." [1]

The merchants importing goods from England were, almost without exception, totally opposed to the Covenant when they learned of its circulation in the country towns.[2] A formal protest, signed by many merchants, declared that the Covenant was "a base, wicked and illegal measure, calculated to distress and ruin many merchants, shopkeepers and others in this metropolis, and affect the whole commercial interest of this Province." [3] The argument was taken

[1] Letter to N. Y. Committee, June 18, 1774; *Bos. Com. Cor. Mss.*, vol. x, pp. 819-820. *Vide* also *Mass. Spy*, June 30, 1774; "Candidus" in *ibid.*, July 7, and in *Bos. Gaz.*, June 27. When concealment of the truth was no longer possible, the committee simply claimed that the plan had been "intimated to them by their brethren in the country." *Bos. Com. Cor. Mss.*, vol. x, pp. 822-824.

[2] Adams, S., *Writings* (Cushing), vol. iii, p. 145; letters of John Andrews in *1 M. H. S. Procs.*, vol. viii, pp. 329-332; "An Old Man" in *Mass. Spy*, July 21, 1774.

[3] They declared that the staple articles of trade would cease, such as oil, pot and pearlash, flax seed, naval stores and lumber, and that shipbuilding would be seriously affected. *Mass. Gaz. & Post-Boy*, July 4, 1774; also *4 Am. Arch.*, vol. i, pp. 490-491.

up by many newspaper writers in the mercantile interest, who declaimed against the harebrained scheme and underhanded methods of the committee of correspondence.[1] The very legality of the existence of the committee of correspondence was questioned in view of the fact that it had been appointed in November, 1772, to perform a particular task and its tenure could not continue longer than the end of that year at the furthest.[2]

In anticipation of the gathering storm, the radicals hastened to call a town meeting on June 17, which furnished the committee of correspondence with the formal legal sanction which its existence had lacked. The committee were thanked for the faithful discharge of their trust and desired to continue their vigilance and activity.[3] Though taken by surprise, the merchants and conservatives determined to bring about the discharge of the committee of correspondence. After a number of secret conferences, they decided that the effort should be made at a town meeting on Monday, June 27.[4] Great numbers of both parties

[1] The whale fishery and the cod fishery, which employed so many, would be ruined, declared some, and without these profits merchants would be unable to pay debts owing to entirely blameless persons in England. *Mass. Gaz. & Post-Boy*, June 23, July 4, 1774. How could two-thirds of the traders in the seaports, live? queried "Zach Freeman." *Ibid.*, July 18. "Y. Z." spoke tearfully of his "sweet little prattling Innocents" who were now being threatened with "all the Horrors of Poverty, Beggary and Misery." *Ibid.*, June 27. Others pointed out that the boycott feature made the Covenant "as tyrannical as the Spanish inquisition." *Ibid.*, July 4, 18.

[2] *Vide* particularly the protest signed by John Andrews, Thomas Amory, John Amory, Caleb Blanchard, Samuel Eliot and four others. *Ibid.*, July 4, 1774.

[3] *Ibid.*, June 20, 1774; also *Bos. Town Recs.* (*1770-1777*), pp. 176-177.

[4] The official account of this meeting is in *ibid.*, pp. 177-178; also *Mass. Spy*, June 30, 1774. For other contemporary accounts, *vide* "Candidus" in *Mass. Spy*, July 7; Gage's account, *4 Am. Arch.*, vol. i, pp. 514-515; letter of William Barrell, *M. H. S. Mss.*, 41 F 66; anonymous account in *Mass. Spy*, June 30.

attended, and Sam Adams was chosen moderator. A motion was passed for the reading of all letters sent by the committee of correspondence since the receipt of the Boston Port Act; and when this performance promised to be too lengthy, another motion was carried for confining the reading to the Covenant and letters particularly called for. This done, Mr. [Harrison?] Gray offered the momentous motion that the committee of correspondence be censured and dismissed from further service. Adams now voluntarily vacated the chair until the subject of the committee, whereof he was chairman, should be disposed of; and a moderate radical, Thomas Cushing, was chosen in his stead. The debates which ensued lasted far into dusk; and the meeting was adjourned to the following morning to continue the discussion. The speakers on the mercantile side marshaled forth all the arguments which had been ventilated in the newspapers; and even some of the more radical merchants complained against the shortness of time allowed for receiving goods from England before the Covenant went into effect. Ardent enthusiasm and a well-knitted organization now served well the purposes of the radicals; the motion for censure was lost by a large majority, not more than fifty or sixty hands being in favor. The town then voted their approval of " the upright Intentions and . . . honest Zeal of the Committee of Correspondence . . ." To Governor Gage the whole affair appeared to be clearly a case of " the better sort of people " being " out voted by a great majority of the lower class."

Defeated in their main purpose, the merchants now used such means as were yet at hand to discredit the Covenant. One hundred and twenty-nine inhabitants of the town signed a protest against the doings of the town meeting, and a second protest, differing but slightly, appeared with eight signatures.¹ Governor Gage also issued a proclamation which denounced "certain persons calling themselves a Committee of Correspondence for the town of Boston," for attempting to excite the people of the province " to enter into an unwarrantable, hostile and traitorous combination," and which commanded all magistrates to arrest all persons who circulated the so-called Covenant.²

The disapproval of the Boston merchants and of the government served only to increase the popularity of the Covenant in the rural districts. At Hardwicke, a magistrate, brave old Brigadier Ruggles, announced that he would conform to Gage's proclamation and jail any man who signed the paper; whereupon almost one hundred men signed and left him powerless.³ Worcester adopted a modified form of the Covenant, inserting the date August 1 in place of October 1 as the time after which all British imports should be boycotted.⁴ The Worcester alteration soon superseded the Boston plan in popular favor. Exclusive of the places already named, the Covenant in one form or other was adopted by at least thirteen towns, before the meeting of the Continental Congress in September, 1774.⁵ Many other towns sympathized with the intent of the Covenant but postponed action because of the certainty that an

¹ *Mass. Gaz. & Post-Boy*, July 4, 1774; also *1 M. H. S. Procs.*, vol. xi, pp. 394-395.

² *Mass. Spy*, June 30, 1774; also *4 Am. Arch.*, vol. i, pp. 491-492. The justices of the County of Plymouth also adopted an address, in which they promised to maintain order and justice in face of all illegal combinations. *Mass. Gaz. & Post-Boy*, July 18, 1774; also *Am. Arch.*, vol. i, pp. 515-516.

³ *Bos. Gaz.*, July 4, 1774.

⁴ *Pickering Papers*, vol. xxxix, p. 54.

⁵ Athol, Bernardston, Billerica, Braintree, Brimfield, Cape Elizabeth, Charlton, Colerain, Gloucester, Gorham, Hopkinton, Lincoln, Shrewsbury. Vide correspondence of *Bos. Com. Cor.* and current newspapers.

interprovincial congress would assemble to deal with the whole question.[1] Of serious opposition, there was little or none.[2]

The covenant movement gained further impetus by reason of the fact that various county conventions took an interest in the matter; and when the provincial convention of Massachusetts met in October, that body resolved, on the twenty-eighth of the month, that whereas no explicit directions had yet arrived from the Continental Congress (which had adjourned but two days before), and as the great majority of the people of the province had entered into agreements of non-importation and non-consumption, they earnestly recommended to all the inhabitants of Massachusetts to conform to these regulations until the Continental Congress or the provincial convention should direct otherwise. The convention recommended that all recalcitrant importers be boycotted, and declared the non-consumption of " all kinds of East India teas," urging the local committees to post the names of violators.[3] The action of the pro-

[1] The committees of the maritime towns of Marblehead and Salem named this as the cause of their inactivity, and entered the further objection that Boston herself had not adopted the Covenant. *Bos. Com. Cor. Papers*, vol. iii, pp. 475-477, 491-492; *Pickering Papers*, vol. xxxiii, p. 96. At least six other towns announced themselves in favor of the principles of the Covenant, but declared they would await the outcome of the Continental Congress: Acton, Charlemont, Charlestown, Falmouth, Palmer, Springfield. *Bos. Com. Cor. Papers*, vol. iii, *passim; Pickering Papers*, vol. xxxiii, *passim.*

[2] Forty-six traders and freeholders of Easton announced to Governor Gage, under their signatures, that they were opposed to the Covenant and to riots and routs. *4 Am. Arch.*, vol. i, pp. 613-614; also *Mass. Gaz. & Post-Boy*, July 25, 1774. At Worcester, the conservatives made an abortive attempt to unseat the local committee of correspondence. *Ibid.*, July 4. *Vide* also *Mass. Spy*, Dec. 8.

[3] *4 Am. Arch.*, vol. i, pp. 840, 848; also *Mass. Spy*, Oct. 27, Nov. 3, 1774. County conventions in Berkshire, Suffolk, Plymouth and Bristol had gone furthest in their resolutions of non-importation and non-consumption. *Ibid.*, July 28, Sept. 15, Oct. 6, 13.

vincial convention capped the movement that had begun in a small way through locally adapted covenants. Because of the lateness of the occurrence, however, the event had no practical importance.

Outside of Massachusetts the Solemn League and Covenant failed to make headway, although the Boston Committee urged it on all the New England provinces. The Portsmouth, N. H., Committee sent out a covenant for adoption closely modeled on the Worcester plan, but it was apparently adopted nowhere.[1] The towns of Rhode Island and Connecticut objected to the measure as inexpedient. As Silas Deane wrote to the Boston Committee in behalf of the Connecticut General Assembly, it was the general opinion that:

A congress is absolutely necessary previous to almost every other measure . . . The resolves of merchants of any individual town or province, however generously designed, must be partial when considered in respect to the whole Colonies in one general view; while, on the other hand, every measure recommended, every resolve come into by the whole united colonies must carry weight and influence with it on the mind of the people and tend effectually to silence those base insinuations . . . of interested motives, sinister views, unfair practices and the like, for the vile purposes of sowing seeds of jealousy between the Colonies . . .[2]

In Rhode Island the towns of Providence, Newport and Westerly expressed their willingness to enter into a plan of

[1] *2 M. H. S. Procs.*, vol. ii, pp. 481-486. *Vide* also *4 Am. Arch.*, vol. i, pp. 745-746.
[2] Letter of June 3, 1774; *N. Y. Journ.*, Mch. 9, 1775; also *4 Am. Arch.*, vol. i, pp. 303-304. *Vide* also *Bos. Com. Cor. Papers*, vol. ii, pp. 111-112, 251-253; *Conn. Hist. Soc. Colls.*, vol. ii, pp. 129-130; Adams, S., *Writings* (Cushing), vol. iii, pp. 114-116, 125-126.

joint non-intercourse, as proposed in the Boston circular letter of May 13; and Providence instructed her deputies in the General Assembly to propose a continental congress as the best means of devising an effective plan.[1] In Connecticut New Haven responded favorably to the Boston circular letter on May 23; and in June, town meetings in at least fourteen towns pledged their support to any reasonable plan of non-intercourse drawn up by a general congress.[2] In almost every case committees of correspondence were appointed; and thus this occasion marks the extension to Connecticut of the plan of municipal committees for radical propaganda.

The truth was that the Covenant was a device that was particularly well adapted to the purposes of the radicals of Massachusetts, where there had been imminent danger that the conservative merchants would stem the tide of opposition. But there was no very good reason why other New England provinces should join in the measure; the Boston

[1] These instructions, adopted May 17, were the first instance of agitation for a continental congress by a public body. *R. I. Col. Recs.*, vol. vii, pp. 280-281, 289-290; *4 Am. Arch.*, vol. i, pp. 343-344.

[2] Canterbury, Farmington, Glastenbury, Groton, Hartford, Lyme, Middletown, New Haven, New London, Norfolk, Norwich, Preston, Wethersfield, Windham. Five towns adopted similar resolves later: Bolton, Enfield, Goshen, Greenwich, Windsor. *Vide* files of *Conn. Gaz.*, *Conn. Cour.* and *Conn. Journ.* in this period. Only two communities, Brooklyn parish in Pomfret and the town of Stonington, entered an immediate agreement of non-consumption along the lines of the Covenant. *Bos. Com. Cor. Papers*, vol. ii, 199-200, 215-218, 237-239. As late as September an effort was made by the Hartford Committee, while Silas Deane was absent at the Continental Congress, to call a provincial convention in order to adopt a general non-consumption agreement for the province. On September 15, delegates from four counties gathered to consider the matter, but concluded upon vigorous resolutions in support of the anticipated measures of the Continental Congress. *Conn. Cour.*, Sept. 19, 1774; *Conn. Hist. Soc. Colls.*, vol. ii, pp. 151-152.

invitation of May 13 for co-operative measures among the provinces commended itself as a more feasible mode of procedure. As the movement for a continental congress gained ground in other provinces, the New England provinces did not lag in taking effective action in that direction. The radicals used the instruments which came readiest to hand. On June 15 the General Assembly of Rhode Island chose delegates to the Continental Congress.[1] In Connecticut the House of Representatives delegated the function to the legislative committee of correspondence, which designated delegates to the congress on July 13.[2] The path of the radicals in New Hampshire was beset with greater difficulties. Early in July the legislative committee of correspondence called a meeting of the late members of the House of Representatives at Portsmouth for the selection of delegates to Congress; but when the gentlemen convened, Governor Wentworth confronted them with doughty speech and deterrent proclamation, and they betook themselves to the tavern where, over the warming victuals, they agreed to call a provincial convention to accomplish what they had failed to do. This convention, composed of representatives from many towns, met on July 21 and duly chose delegates to the congress.[3]

The Boston circular letter of May 13 was carried to the main ports throughout the commercial provinces by Paul Revere. Before the swift rider had started for New York, however, a copy of the Port Act had arrived there; and Isaac Sears and Alexander McDougall, acting, it would appear, for the ultra-radical committee of correspondence appointed during the anti-tea commotions, transmitted to

[1] *Mass. Spy*, June 23, 1774; also *4 Am. Arch.*, vol. i, pp. 416-417.
[2] *Conn. Hist. Soc. Colls.*, vol. ii, p. 138 n.
[3] Letters of Wentworth, *4 Am. Arch.*, vol. i, pp. 516, 536, 745-746.

the Boston Committee a promise of ardent support. The writers stated that they had " stimulated " the merchants to meet on the next evening in order to agree upon non-intercourse with England and a limited non-exportation to the West Indies.[1] Apparently they had no suspicion that they would not be able to carry things their own way; but they had strangely misapprehended the situation. For their task, the radicals, confronted with heavy odds, needed a leader of the caliber of Sam Adams. Could their forces have been directed by a man of dominant personality, with a mind skilled in political artifice and a single-minded devotion to a great idea, the story of the subsequent two months might have been different. Instead, these qualities were possessed by the moderate party; and the fate of the radical cause was in the hands of men of second-rate ability, who sought to promote their ends by a species of indirection and who were, in the disappointing sense of the word, opportunists.

McDougall was regarded by the moderates as "the Wilkes of New York,"[2] Sears as "a political cracker" and a "*quidnunc* in politics;"[3] and they experienced "great pain . . . to see a number of persons [such as John Morin Scott and John Lamb, no doubt] who have not a shilling to lose in the contest, taking advantage of the present dispute and forcing themselves into public notice."[4] As for the committee of correspondence, it was composed " of eight or ten flaming patriots without property or anything else but impudence."[5] Colden correctly pictured the reaction

[1] *Bos. Com. Cor. Papers*, vol. ii, pp. 343-346. Letter of May 15.
[2] Colden to Dartmouth, *Letter Books*, vol. ii, pp. 346-347.
[3] "A Merchant of New York" in *N. Y. Gazetteer*, Aug. 18, 1774.
[4] "Mercator" in *ibid.*, Aug. 11, 1774.
[5] Letter from New York in *London Morning Post*, reprinted in *N. Y. Journ.*, Aug. 25, 1774; also 4 *Am. Arch.*, vol. i, pp. 299-302 n. *Vide* also Colden's characterization, *Letter Books*, vol. ii, pp. 339-340.

which had set in since the destruction of the tea at New York, when he wrote on September 7, 1774: "the Gentlemen of Property and principal Merchants attended the meetings of the populace, when called together by their former Demagogues, who thereby have lost their Influence and are neglected. The Populace are now directed by Men of different Principles & who have much at stake." [1]

The merchants' meeting was duly held on Monday evening, May 16, and the radicals who attended found that, instead of having their own way, the existing committee was discharged, their slate for a new committee of twenty-five was rejected, and a new committee of fifty, proposed by the men of property, was nominated.[2] The committee thus nominated included in its membership such men as Sears and McDougall as a concession to the radicals, but the majority of the members were "the most considerable Merchts and Men of cool Tempers who would endeavour to avoid all extravagant and dangerous Measures." [3] Some of them had never before "join'd in the public proceedings of the Opposition and were induced to appear in what they are sensible is an illegal Character, from a Consideration that if they did not the business would be left in the same rash Hands as before." [4] Others, such as the chairman, Isaac Low, had been the prime movers in the earlier contests for remedial trade legislation, and were now determined to master the whirlwind which they had then so recklessly sown. At least twenty-five of the fifty committee-

[1] Letter to Dartmouth; *Letter Books,* vol. ii, pp. 359-360.

[2] *4 Am. Arch.,* vol. i, pp. 393-394. In this and all later accounts of New York politics, the author has frequently and gratefully consulted Professor Becker's *History of Political Parties in the Province of New York, 1760-1776.*

[3] Colden, *Letter Books,* vol. ii, pp. 346-347.

[4] *Ibid.,* vol. ii, pp. 339-341. *Vide* also unsigned letter, *4 Am. Arch.,* vol. i, p. 302 n.

men had been among those merchants and traders who had " exerted themselves in a most extraordinary manner " to cause New York to break through the non-importation agreement in July, 1770.[1]

A mass meeting of the city and county was called for Thursday, May 19, to confirm the nominations made at the merchants' meeting.[2] When the citizens assembled, Gouverneur Morris stood watching them from the balcony of the Coffee House. "On my right hand," he wrote later, "were ranged all the people of property, with some poor dependants, and on the other all the tradesmen, &c., who thought it worth their while to leave daily labour for the good of the country."[3] The merchants quickly showed their superior strength by the selection of Isaac Low as chairman of the meeting. The merchants' slate was confirmed with little difficulty; as an eleventh-hour and unimportant concession to the radicals, the name of Francis Lewis was added to the committee by unanimous consent, making the membership fifty-one.[4] At the very first meeting of the Fifty-One, the Committee of Mechanics, which had now superseded the Sons of Liberty as the radical organization, sent in a letter, according their concurrence in the election of the new committee.[5]

[1] *Vide* list of the latter in *Bos. Gaz.*, July 23, 1770. Nineteen members of the committee later became avowed loyalists. Becker, *op. cit.*, p. 116, n. 16.

[2] The notice of the meeting declared, by way of reassurance, that "the gentlemen appointed are of the body of merchants; men of property, probity, and understanding, whose zeal for the public good cannot be doubted, their own several private interests being so intimately connected with that of the whole community . . ." *4 Am. Arch.*, vol. i, p. 293 n.

[3] Sparks, *Gouverneur Morris*, vol. i, pp. 23-26.

[4] *4 Am. Arch.*, vol. i, pp. 294-295. For names of the original fifty, *vide ibid.*, p. 293.

[5] *Ibid.*, vol. i, p. 295.

Gouverneur Morris, who himself possessed strong moderate sympathies, reflected upon the election of the Fifty-One in this wise:

The spirit of the English Constitution has yet a little influence left, and but a little. . . . The mob begin to think and to reason. Poor reptiles! it is with them a vernal morning; they are struggling to cast off their winter's slough, they bask in the sunshine, and ere noon they will bite, depend upon it. The gentry begin to fear this. Their Committee will . . . deceive the people, and again forfeit a share of their confidence. And if these instances of what with one side is policy, and with the other perfidy, shall continue to increase, and become more frequent, farewell aristocracy.[1]

At their very first meeting on May 23, the Committee of Fifty-One, thus constituted and controlled, drew up a reply to the Boston circular letter of May 13. Phrased with excessive caution, this answer expressed deep concern at the dilemma of Boston, but declared in favor of postponing all active measures until an interprovincial congress should be held.[2] On June 3, they sent a letter to the supervisors of all the counties, proposing the appointment of committees of

---

[1] Sparks, *op. cit.*, vol. i, pp. 23-26.

[2] *4 Am. Arch.*, vol. i, pp. 297-298. No course could have been more unsatisfactory to the leaders of the popular party at Boston, as they at once made clear. The Boston Committee responded that, even if the congress assembled with the greatest possible expedition, it would be many months before a non-intercourse could become effective, whereas an immediate suspension of trade would have "a speedy and irresistable operation" upon the British government. *Bos. Com. Cor. Papers*, vol. x, pp. 807-808. Furthermore, the Bostonians were aware, even if they were silent on the point, that the postponement opened a wide door for the importation of British goods at New York in anticipation of a possible non-intercourse later. The New York Committee remained unmoved. *4 Am. Arch.*, vol. i, pp. 303-304; *N. Y. Journ.*, June 2, 1774

correspondence in the various towns.[1] The motive of the Fifty-One seems to have been to adapt the Massachusetts plan of radical agitation to the sterling purposes of conservative indoctrination. They took this step with the greater assurance, because the rural towns, except Albany, had been notoriously apathetic, if not unsympathetic, during the troubles over the Stamp Act and the Townshend duties. The instinctive conservatism of the great landowners, and the natural intellectual torpidity of the small farmers, undisturbed by the yeast of a constant exercise in local government or by the machinations of a group of city politicians (as in Massachusetts), seemed in this instance to make the rural population the natural allies of the great merchants. The latter failed to perceive, however, that the mass of inland people, engaged in the pressing task of making a livelihood, would be inclined to be unresponsive to any approaches from outside, whether from the one side or the other; either that, or, as the canny Colden feared, "the Business in the Counties will be left to a few forward intemperate Men, who will undertake to speak for the whole . . ."[2]

Both eventualities seem to have occurred. The invitation of the Fifty-One met with little response, only four towns, it would appear, appointing committees of correspondence in the subsequent two months; and three of these towns belonged to Suffolk County at the eastern end of Long Island, which had been founded by natives of Connecticut. The resolutions of these towns were more extreme than the Fifty-One wished, all of them favoring some form of non-intercourse along the lines proposed by

[1] 4 *Am. Arch.*, vol. i, pp. 300-301.

[2] "Could their sentiments be fairly known I make no doubt a large Majority would be for the most Moderate & Prudent Measures." Colden to Tryon, June 2, 1774; *Letter Books*, vol. ii, p. 345.

Boston.¹ In Cumberland County, the supervisors deliberately withheld the letters from the towns; but when in September the existence of the letters became known, delegations from two towns insisted that the instructions of the Fifty-One be carried out, and in October a county convention was held at Westminster, which adopted vigorous resolutions of a radical character.²

Defeated in their original fight for a friendly committee of correspondence, the radical leaders at New York City now undertook to turn the tables on the moderates by devising a method of selecting delegates to the impending congress, who would go pledged to carry out radical ideas. Realizing their inability to attain their ends through the aid of the moderate majority of the Fifty-One, the radicals now began to claim for the Committee of Mechanics a coordinate authority in nominating a ticket of delegates to the congress.³ On June 29, McDougall made a motion that a ticket of five names should be proposed by the Fifty-One, sent to the Committee of Mechanics for their concurrence, and then submitted to the freeholders and freemen of city and county for their ratification. When the discussion became protracted, a vote on the question was postponed until the next meeting on July 4, when the radical plan was swamped by a vote of 24 to 13.⁴ A motion providing for

¹ Southhaven, Easthampton and Huntington in Suffolk County; Orange Town in Orange County. Becker, *op. cit.*, pp. 136-138 and references. Other towns may have acted.

² 4 *Am. Arch.*, vol. ii, pp. 218-219, 1064-1066.

³ It will be recalled that the election of the Fifty-One had been formally assented to by the Committee of Mechanics, though this action came without any solicitation from the moderates.

⁴ This vote reveals the personnel of the radical minority, as follows: Abraham Brasher, John Broome, Peter T. Curtenius, Joseph Hallett, Francis Lewis, Leonard Lispenard, P. V. B. Livingston, Abraham P. Lott, Alexander McDougall, John Moore, Thomas Randall, Isaac Sears, Jacobus Van Zandt. However, on later votes Moore sided with the majority. *Ibid.*, vol. i, pp. 307-308.

exclusive nomination by the Fifty-One and later ratification by the freeholders and freemen was at once adopted by nearly the same numbers. Sears immediately placed in nomination the names of Isaac Low, James Duane, Philip Livingston, John Morin Scott and Alexander McDougall for the coveted positions. This list was offered by the radicals with a genuine hope of its adoption, for it was composed of two confirmed moderates, Low and Duane, merchant and lawyer; the merchant, Livingston, who possessed inclinations both ways;[1] and the two out-and-out radicals. But the majority failed to see any occasion for compromise; and they substituted the moderates, John Jay and John Alsop, lawyer and merchant, for the two radical nominees. They then passed a motion calling a public meeting for Thursday, July 7, to concur in their nominations or to choose others in their stead.[2]

The radicals had an interval of two days before the meeting of the seventh in which to retrieve the disaster which had again been visited upon them, and they set to work to accomplish this through the agency of the Committee of Mechanics. On Tuesday, July 5, that body took under consideration the nominations made by the " Committee of Merchants," as they preferred to style the Fifty-One, and placed a negative on Duane and Alsop, substituting McDougall and Lispenard in their stead. They issued an appeal to the public, explaining that " the Committee of Merchants did refuse the Mechanics a representation on their body, or to consult with their committee, or offer the names of the persons nominated to them for their concurrence," and they exhorted " the mechanics . . . and every other friend to the liberty of his country " to rally to the support

---

[1] *Vide* Becker's note on Livingston, *op. cit.*, p. 122, n. 29.
[2] *4 Am. Arch.*, vol. i, pp. 308-309.

of the new ticket at the Thursday's meeting.[1] The radicals next arranged a public demonstration in the Fields on the following evening, July 6, the night before the meeting called by the Fifty-One. Naturally no moderates attended; and the " numerous meeting " under the chairmanship of the energetic McDougall adopted unanimous resolutions in support of Boston, and forthwith " instructed, empowered and directed " the New York delegates to the congress to agree for the city to a non-importation and to " all such other measures " as Congress should deem necessary for a redress of American grievances.[2] The radicals expected to accomplish a *coup d'état;* obviously the giving of instructions properly belonged to the public meeting regularly called by the Fifty-One.

The labors of the radicals were not without effect, although the results fell short of what they desired to accomplish. When the public meeting assembled Thursday noon, it was unanimously voted that a canvass of the freeholders, freemen and taxpayers of the city should be made on the two tickets, under the joint supervision of the Fifty-One and the Committee of Mechanics.[3] The moderate majority had thus been forced to recognize the Committee of Mechanics and to extend the franchise beyond the freeholders and freemen; indeed, all later canvasses of the city, with a single unimportant exception, were on the basis of this ex-

[1] Advertisement of July 6; *Broadsides* (N. Y. Hist. Soc.), vol. i.

[2] *N. Y. Gaz.*, July 11, 1774; also *4 Am. Arch.*, vol. i, pp. 312-313.

[3] *Ibid.*, vol. i, pp. 309-310. Freemen were those who had purchased the privilege of engaging in certain occupations within the corporations of New York and Albany. The electoral freeholders were those who possessed, free of incumbrance, an estate in fee, for life, or by courtesy, of the value of £40. The proportion of electors to the total population was about 12 per cent in 1790, and no doubt smaller in the earlier years. Becker, *op. cit.*, pp. 10-11.

tended suffrage. But in a session the same evening, the Fifty-One formally disavowed, by the usual majority, the proceedings of the irregular meeting of the night before on the ground that they were intended to reflect on the Fifty-One and create divisions among the citizens; and they appointed a committee of their own to draw up proper instructions.[1] While a motion was being made to depart from the usual custom of secrecy maintained by the Fifty-One and to publish this vote of disavowal, a number of the radicals withdrew in a rage, ordering their names to be struck from the committee roster and shouting along the streets, " The Committee is dissolved, the Committee is dissolved." [2]

On the next day matters between the radicals and the moderates came to a head. The conference between the sub-committees of the Fifty-One and the Committee of Mechanics reached an absolute deadlock over the manner of conducting the canvass of the city;[3] arrangements for a vote thus came to a halt. Later in the day eleven radical m mbers of the Fifty-One announced their resignation in a public statement, alleging as their chief reason the vote of

[1] 4 *Am. Arch.*, vol. i, pp. 310-312.

[2] " One of the Committee" in *ibid.*, vol. i, pp. 314-315; also *N. Y. Gazetteer*, July 14, 1774.

[3] The former insisted that the voters must make a blanket choice between the two lists. The latter held that the voters should select any five of the seven candidates. (It will be recalled that, although the two tickets contained ten names, the names of Low, Livingston and Jay appeared on both tickets.) As the real contest lay between Duane and Alsop of the moderate slate and McDougall and Lispenard of the radical slate, the voting of a split ticket, it was believed, would work to the benefit of McDougall, who was a man of considerable popularity; while it was not thought that many voters would be willing to sacrifice both Duane and Alsop in order to vote for him. McDougall withdrew his candidacy, alleging the unfairness of the plan of the Fifty-One. McDougall to the Freeholders, July 9, 1774; *Broadsides*, vol. i.

disavowal and censure passed by the committee on the previous evening.[1] Until July 13, matters remained at a deadlock, each side apparently awaiting some move of the other. On the evening of July 13, the "Fifty-One" adopted a set of resolutions, which defined their platform of public policy in sharp contrast with that of the radicals. They called a public meeting at the Coffee House for Tuesday, July 19, in order to act on these resolutions and to ratify the committee's nominations for Congress. As a matter of fact, these resolutions marked little or no advance beyond the non-committal letter written by the Fifty-One on May 23 in answer to the Boston circular letter. On the issues of primary concern, they asserted that, while all delegates ought to go to Congress empowered to bind the provinces they represented, it would be premature for any one province to anticipate Congress's conduct by giving instructions; that only dire necessity would justify commercial opposition; and that a non-importation, only partially observed like the last one, would be worse than none at all.[2]

Of the public meeting of July 19 no satisfactory account remains; but it is clear that the generalship of the moderates proved temporarily inadequate. The resolutions proposed by the "Fifty-One" were rejected as "void of vigour, sense and integrity;" and the meeting, determined to decentralize the power of the "Fifty-One," entrusted the formulation of new resolutions to a specially-created committee, consisting of ten radicals and five moderates. As for the ticket of delegates submitted to the meeting, it would appear that three of the nominations (Low, Alsop and Jay) were ratified and two "unexceptionable friends

[1] Brasher, Broome, Hallett, Lewis, Lispenard, P. V. B. Livingston, Lott, McDougall, Randall, Sears and Van Zandt. *4 Am. Arch.*, vol. i, pp. 313-314.
[2] *Ibid.*, vol. i, p. 315; *Broadsides*, vol. i.

of liberty" were added.¹ The moderates at once bent every energy to discredit completely the doings of the public gathering. At a session in the evening the "Fifty-One" wrote into their minutes their opinion that "as only a small proportion of the citizens attended the meeting" at noon and "the sentiments of the majority" continued "uncertain," a canvass of the town should be made to ascertain the opinion of the people on this matter and also on the ticket of delegates nominated by the Fifty-One.² In other words, they repudiated entirely the public meeting which they themselves had called. Their action gained moral weight the next day when Low, Alsop and Jay declared that they could not deem themselves or any others as properly nominated as delegates until the sentiments of the town had been ascertained with greater precision. Likewise, four of the five moderates, appointed on the new committee of fifteen for drawing up resolutions, resigned their appointments.³ This committee, however, with depleted membership, went ahead with its work and prepared resolutions for public ratification which, in substance if not in spirit, resembled the radical platform of July 6.⁴ But the moderates were again in control of the situation; and when the

¹ *N. Y. Gaz.*, July 25, 1774; 4 *Am. Arch.*, vol. i, pp. 315, 317-318.

² *Ibid.*, vol. i, pp. 315-317. For this purpose the resolutions of the "Fifty-One" were slightly modified but in no important respect. *Vide* summary in Becker, *op. cit.*, p. 133, n. 57.

³ Duane, the fifth moderate, was not in town. 4 *Am. Arch.*, vol. i, pp. 317-318.

⁴ The tenth resolution promised obedience to the conclusions of the Continental Congress, and the twelfth declared that it was "highly necessary" that Congress should adopt a non-importation with Great Britain. An innovation was the eleventh resolution, which proposed a provincial convention as the proper mode of electing delegates. *N. Y. Gaz.*, July 25, 1774.

meeting, called to endorse the radical resolutions, assembled on July 25, " nothing decisive was resolved upon." [1]

The subsequent events leading to the election of delegates can be explained only on the theory that the radicals realized that the moderates were the dominant factor in molding public opinion, and that therefore they felt, in order to save any part of their platform, they must resort to opportunism.[2] The "Fifty-One" at their meeting of July 25 voted that a poll be opened on Thursday, July 28, at the usual places of election in each ward to elect delegates to Congress; and the Committee of Mechanics were invited to co-operate with them in helping to superintend the election.[3]

On the following day a group of radicals sent a communication to the delegates nominated by the Fifty-One, promising their support in case the candidates pledged their "utmost endeavours" at the congress in support of a non-importation agreement; that otherwise a rival ticket would be nominated. The candidates responded that they would use their "utmost endeavours" to promote every measure at the congress that might "then" be thought conducive to the general welfare, and that "at present" they believed that a "general non-importation faithfully observed" would prove the best means of procuring redress.[4] This reply clearly failed to make the concession which the interrogators had demanded and which had been the *sine qua non* of the radical position all along. Indeed the only detail in which the reply differed from the resolutions proposed by

[1] *N. Y. Gaz.*, Aug. 1, 1774.

[2] As late as Oct. 5 Colden believed that "in the City a large Majority of the People" were against a non-importation agreement. *Letter Books*, vol. ii, pp. 366-368.

[3] *4 Am. Arch.*, vol. i, p. 318.

[4] Only four of the candidates replied, as Duane was still absent from the city. *Ibid.*, vol. i, pp. 319-320; also *N. Y. Gazetteer*, Aug. 4, 1774.

the "Fifty-One" was that the delegates entertained a *present* opinion that a non-importation faithfully observed would prove the most effective measure. This slight concession was apparently sufficient to save the self-respect of the radicals, and they acquiesced in the moderate ticket. Accordingly, at the Thursday's poll, Low, Jay, Livingston, Alsop and Duane were unanimously chosen for the city and county of New York.

The "Fifty-One" lost no time in informing the rural counties of the action of New York and requested them either to appoint delegates of their own or to give express authorization to the New York delegates to act for them.[1] This appeal brought somewhat better results than the earlier request for the formation of committees of correspondence, although it is clear that, as before, affairs were carried through "by a very few Persons, who took upon themselves to act for the Freeholders."[2] Nevertheless, the proposal went to the counties with the seal of approval of the wholly moderate committee at New York and thus elicited interest from the large landholders as well as the more volatile elements in the population. Only three counties elected delegates of their own—the New-England-infected county of Suffolk and the nearby counties of Kings and Orange. Colden was informed by a person present at the Orange County meeting that not twenty men were present for the election, though the county contained more than one thousand freeholders.[3] In Kings, it would appear that two congenial souls gathered; one was chosen chairman, the other clerk; and the latter certified to Congress that the former, Simon Boerum, was unanimously elected to repre-

[1] July 29, 1774. *4 Am. Arch.*, vol. i, p. 322. For the action of the counties, *vide* Becker, *op. cit.*, pp. 139-141, and references.
[2] Colden, *Letter Books*, vol. ii, pp. 366-368.
[3] *Ibid.*

sent the county.[1] Four counties—Albany, Dutchess, Ulster and Westchester—adopted the alternative plan proposed by the "Fifty-One," and in a more or less regular fashion authorized the city delegates to act for them. Thus, including New York County, eight counties in all, "representing a great majority of this Colony, whether this is determined by Counties, inhabitants, wealth or the number of members they send to the General Assembly," took action favorable to the congress, of a more or less representative character.[2] Six counties remained unresponsive to the appeal of the "Fifty-One."

The progress of events at Philadelphia, when news of the Boston Port Act arrived there, resembled that which had occurred at New York. The moderate element, which had always had a strong hold on the city and province, was composed chiefly of the great importers of British goods and the generality of the Quaker sect to which most of them belonged. This party, heartily condemning the destruction of the tea at Boston and likewise disapproving of the punitive measures of Parliament, believed that the only proper method of opposition was a memorial or remonstrance drawn up by the Assembly; a few of them were willing to favor an interprovincial congress if its activities were limited to the single function of presenting a petition of grievances. The radicals, on the other hand, led by the resourceful Charles Thomson, were determined to make immediate common cause with Boston, and, through popular meetings, to force Philadelphia as far in that direction as they could. John Dickinson, by his earlier leadership of

[1] Joseph Galloway repeated this tale on the authority of "almost all the Delegates of New York." *The Examination of Joseph Galloway, . . . before the House of Commons . . .* (London, 1780), pp. 11, 66.
[2] "To the Publick," Jan. 18, 1775; *4 Am. Arch.*, vol. i, pp. 1188-1189.

the trade-reform movement and his more recent abstention from public affairs, possessed the confidence of both sides. Being the most influential man then in the province, his presence at a meeting of protest was deemed highly desirable by the radicals, his support of their measures infinitely more so.

When Paul Revere arrived on May 19 with the Boston circular letter, Thomson and two fellow-spirits, Joseph Reed and Thomas Mifflin, proceeded at once to get in touch with Dickinson.[1] A public meeting having been called for the next evening (May 20), the three men took dinner with Dickinson at his country home earlier in the same day, a politico-gastronomic device which has always been found to be of great utility by politicians. As they sat over their cups and conversed afterward, the men urged Dickinson to attend the meeting and take an active part in behalf of oppressed Boston, reminding him that the present hostility to parliamentary encroachment had been largely created by his own earlier efforts. Dickinson offered sundry excuses, having himself disapproved of the Boston Tea Party and appearing to feel uncertain as to what lengths they wished to carry opposition. At last he seemed to consent to attend, provided that he would be allowed to carry through moderate measures. Thomson, suspecting that Dickinson was reluctant to play only "a second part," proposed that Reed, more conservatively inclined than the others, should open the meeting, Mifflin and he would follow with fervid

[1] This account is based chiefly on Thomson's letter to Drayton, written many years later, which purported to reveal "the secret springs and reality of actions" at this time. Stillé, *Life of Dickinson*, pp. 340-344. However, the lapse of years before the letter was written has made it necessary to utilize other narratives to correct errors of view and fact, particularly: Reed, W. B., *Life and Correspondence of Joseph Reed* (Philadelphia, 1847), vol. i, pp. 65-67; 4 *Am. Arch.*, vol. i, pp. 340-341; *Pa. Mag.*, vol. xxxiii, pp. 336-339; Stillé, *op. cit.*, pp. 107-108.

speeches advocating co-operation with Boston, and Dickinson should close with a plea for temperate measures. Whether indeed vanity was the cause of Dickinson's hesitation, or a suspicion of the good faith of the intriguers, is not clear. At any rate, this plan being agreed upon, Dickinson accompanied Thomson that evening, the other men having gone ahead in order to avoid the appearance of collusion.

A relatively small number, not more than two or three hundred inhabitants, were in attendance at the meeting; and the prearranged program was carried through as planned. After reading the Boston circular letter, Reed addressed the body with "moderation but in pathetic terms," proposing that the governor be asked to call the Assembly to petition for a redress of grievances; Mifflin spoke next with "warmth & fire;" Thomson followed with an ardent plea "for an immediate declaration in favour of Boston & making common cause with her."[1] "Great clamour was raised against the violence of the measures proposed." Dickinson now rose and lent his efforts in support of Reed's motion, speaking with "great coolness, calmness, moderation and good sense." Dickinson's motives are not clear; but Governor Penn was probably right when he averred that: "the movers of this extraordinary measure had not the most distant expectation of succeeding in it [because of the certainty of the governor's refusal], but that their real scheme was to gain time by it to see what part the other Colonies will take in so critical a conjuncture."[2]

A number of persons were present who had never before attended public meetings, among them the importer, Thomas Wharton, and Dr. Smith, provost of the College of Phila-

[1] Thomson fainted in the midst of his speech, "for he had scarce slept an hour two nights past."
[2] 4 *Am. Arch.*, vol. i, pp. 367-368.

delphia; and these men helped to carry the day for the Reed-Dickinson motion. If Thomson was surprised at the outcome of his scheme, he at least tried to recover such ground as he could by moving that a committee be appointed to answer the Boston letter; and when that carried, a slate of radicals was handed to the chair for submission to the meeting. A list representing the other party was submitted at the same time; and great confusion ensued as to which list should be voted on first. At length it was proposed that the two lists be combined to compose the committee; and this was accordingly done, with the understanding that the committee should be altered at a later meeting of inhabitants.

The committee of nineteen, thus selected, was dominated by the moderates, and fairly represented the sentiment of the city.[1] The letter sent to Boston on May 21 frankly reflected this cautious spirit. With circumspect phrase, the committee conceded that Boston was suffering in the common cause but hesitated to venture further expressions inasmuch as " the sense of this large city " had not yet been ascertained, and even when this were done, the " populous province " had yet to express itself. They took occasion to express their distaste for the Boston Tea Party by declaring that if compensating the East India Company " would put an end to this unhappy controversy, and leave us on the footing of constitutional liberty for the future, it is presumed that neither you nor we could continue a moment in doubt what part to act." Finally, they had " reason to think " that it would be most agreeable to the people of Pennsylvania to summon a general congress to send a petition of rights to the king, and that the Boston plan of non-intercourse should be reserved as " the last resource." [2]

[1] *Vide* letter of George Clymer; *4 Am. Arch.*, vol. i, pp. 406-407.
[2] *Ibid.*, vol. i, pp. 341-342; also *Pa. Gaz.*, June 8, 1774. The letter was

The radical leaders backed the petition for calling the Assembly in apparent good faith, in order " to convince the pacific [Thomson confessed afterward] that it was not the intention of the warm spirits to involve the province in the dispute without the consent of the representatives of the people." As they expected, the governor refused the petition, though it was signed by almost nine hundred people.[1] They now urged a large meeting of the Philadelphia public to choose a new committee and to take further action. As the Nineteen showed no disposition to proceed to that step, notices were posted for a meeting of the mechanics of the city and suburbs on the evening of June 9 in order to organize themselves and to appoint a committee of their own. This maneuver had the desired effect. When the twelve hundred workingmen assembled on Thursday night, the chairman was able to inform them that the Nineteen had sent word that a mass meeting of the city and county would be called in the near future to choose " one Grand Joint Committee." Whereupon, the gathering decided to take no action " at present." [2]

The moderates determined to control the action of the mass meeting; and in order to do this it was necessary to

---

written by Dr. Smith. The Boston Committee of Correspondence responded in much the same spirit they did to the New York epistle, which had been written about the same time. *Bos. Com. Cor. Papers*, vol. ii, pp. 417-420. Sam Adams wrote privately to Thomson: " The Trade will forever be divided when a Sacrifice of their Interest is called for. . . . Is it not necessary to push for a Suspension of Trade with Great Britain as far as it will go, and let the yeomanry . . . resolve to desert those altogether who will not come into the Measure?" *Writings* (Cushing), vol. iii, p. 124. Note the approving attitude of the N. Y. Committee with reference to the Philadelphia letter. *4 Am. Arch.*, vol. i, p. 298.

[1] Stillé, *op. cit.*, pp. 344-345; *4 Am. Arch.*, vol. i, pp. 391-392.

[2] *Pa. Gaz.*, June 15, 1774; also *4 Am. Arch.*, vol. i, pp. 405-406.

gain the support of the body of the Quakers who "had an aversion to town meetings & always opposed them." Therefore the Nineteen called into an informal caucus six representatives of each religious society in the city; and this body agreed upon the presidents of the meeting, the speakers "who were obliged to write down what they intended to say & submit their several speeches to the revision of the presidents," the nature of the resolutions to be adopted, and, finally, the personnel of the new committee.[1] Upon their ticket they thoughtfully placed seventeen members of the existing committee,[2] including Dickinson as chairman, and chose twenty-seven others from their respective religious organizations. From another point of view, the list contained a clear majority of moderate merchants and professional men, but the radical leaders still held membership and at least six mechanics were included. The spirit controlling the proposed membership was well expressed by Thomas Wharton when he explained that the reason he permitted his name to be used was "a sincere desire in myself to keep the transactions of our city within the limits of moderation and not indecent or offensive to our parent state."[3]

In view of these preparations, the meeting of the city and county on June 18 was hardly more than a formality, although probably only a handful of the great throng real-

[1] Thomson's account in Stillé, *op. cit.*, p. 344; Thomas Wharton's account, *Pa. Mag.*, vol. xxxiii, pp. 436-437; Dr. Smith's *Notes and Papers* (Hist. Soc. Pa. Mss.), pp. 9-11.

[2] Joseph Fox and John Cox were left out.

[3] *Pa. Mag.*, vol. xxxiii, pp. 436, 439. Likewise, Dr. Smith declared, on a later occasion, that he would remain on the committee as long as he could be "of any Use in advising Measures consistent with the Principles I profess and that Allegiance and subordination which we owe to the Crown and Empire of Great Britain." *Notes and Papers*, pp. 17-18.

ized it. Two resolutions were adopted, declaring that Boston was suffering in the common cause and that a congress of deputies from the colonies was the proper way of obtaining redress of grievances. No mention was made of the Boston proposal for non-intercourse. The ticket of forty-four names, prepared by the caucus, was elected with little difficulty, although it would appear that James Pemberton, a pillar of the Society of Friends, withdrew his name at once, thus leaving forty-three.[1] This committee was instructed to correspond with the rural counties and with the sister provinces, and to devise a means of choosing delegates to the Continental Congress. The next few weeks saw the establishment of committees of correspondence in most of the counties and the adoption of resolutions for an interprovincial congress as proposed by the Forty-Three at Philadelphia.[2]

The Forty-Three were as moderate in temper as the Fifty-One of New York and strove for the same objects. But under the gracious leadership of the chairman, John Dickinson, a sharp clash was avoided between the radical minority of the committee and the dominant element; and indeed the two factions found it to their interest to unite forces, upon most occasions, against a common enemy. This common foe, of which there was no exact counterpart in New York, was the strongly consolidated conservative group entrenched in the lower house of the Assembly under the leadership of Joseph Galloway, the speaker. Galloway

[1] His name is included in *4 Am. Arch.*, vol. i, pp. 426-428, but not in the newspaper accounts: *Pa. Gaz.*, June 22, 1774; *Pa. Journ.*, June 22; *Pa. Packet*, June 27. For Pemberton's sentiments, *vide* statement of Quakers, May 30, 1774; *4 Am. Arch.*, vol. i, pp. 365-366, and his letter in Sharpless, *Quakers in Revolution*, pp. 107-109.

[2] From June 18 to July 13 committees were appointed in the counties of Chester, Northampton, Berks, York, Bucks, Lancaster, Bedford, Cumberland and Chester. *Vide* files of *Pa. Gaz.*, and *Pa. Journ.*

had long been an opponent of Dickinson in provincial politics over the issue of proprietary *vs.* royal government for Pennsylvania; he had upon one occasion declined a challenge from Dickinson, but the two men fought many a wordy duel in broadside and newspaper.[1] Like many another gentleman of wealth and prestige who chose the British side when the war broke out, Galloway believed in the justice of many of the American demands. He was a constructive critic of the colonial policy of the home government and believed that alleviation could, and should properly, come only through the traditional and legal channel of legislative memorials to Parliament. Efforts at popular control through extra-legal action were to him a species of anarchy, and he held himself aloof from all popular movements whatever their purpose.[2] Confronted with a popular movement of continental proportions and alarmed by the vigorous and unusual measures of Parliament against

[1] Baldwin, E. H., "Joseph Galloway, the Loyalist Politician," *Pa. Mag.*, vol. xxvi, particularly pp. 161-191.

[2] Says Galloway's biographer: "With a conservatism natural to wealth, and with inherited aristocratic tendencies, Mr. Galloway observed with no small concern the growth of republican ideas. That there could be any true liberty, or any safety even, under a democracy, or what he considered was nearly, if not quite, the same thing, mob rule, he believed impossible. It was with no small degree of apprehension, therefore, that he viewed the growing differences between Great Britain and her Colonies. With a property-holder's natural aversion to taxation, and with a realization of the injustice which might result from measures of taxation by Parliament, he aided in all ways that he considered proper to remove the causes of complaint. The very suggestion that the remedy for the troubles lay in independence was repugnant to him. The remedy lay rather in a closer union with the mother country. The political experiences of Mr. Galloway in Pennsylvania made him naturally suspicious of the intentions of the noisy elements among the people, and he soon came to the conclusion that ultimate independence was their aim; at least their conduct could lead to nothing else. Hence he determined to exert his best efforts to prevent such a deplorable occurrence." *Ibid.*, p. 440.

Boston, Galloway was now willing to favor an interprovincial congress if it should be composed of delegates chosen by the members composing the popular branches of the several provincial legislatures. Such a congress, he believed, might formulate a plan of " political union between the two countries, with the assent of both, which would effectually secure to Americans their future rights and privileges." [1]

The policy of the Forty-Three was to conciliate and unite all factions in the province in support of the approaching congress. Therefore, although the mere existence of an extra-legal committee represented a principle hateful to the Galloway party, the Forty-Three adopted a plan of action which enlisted the co-operation of Galloway almost in spite of himself. The Forty-Three had been instructed by the public meeting to devise a means of ascertaining the sense of the province and of electing delegates to the Continental Congress. At a meeting on June 27, they decided that they would ask Speaker Galloway to call the members of the House together for an unofficial session to consider the alarming situation, and that they would summon, for the same time, a convention of county committees " to consult and advise on the most expedient mode of appointing delegates for the general congress and to give their weight to such as may be adopted." [2] This latter body, the radical leaders had already learned " under colour of an excursion of pleasure," [3] would be definitely radical in its composition, for in it the western counties would have a much larger voice than under the unfair system of representation main-

[1] *Vide* letter signed by Galloway and three others as members of the committee of correspondence of the Assembly. *Pa. Gaz.*, July 13, 1774; also 4 *Am. Arch.*, vol. i, pp. 485-486. *Cf.* the scathing comment of a New York newspaper writer. *Ibid.*, vol. i, p. 486 n.

[2] *Pa. Gaz.*, June 29, July 6, 1774; Lincoln, *Revolutionary Movement in Pa.*, pp. 173-175.

[3] 4 *Am. Arch.*, vol. i, p. 434. *Vide* also *ibid.*, p. 726.

tained by the House of Representatives.¹ Thus, their object was to leave the actual appointment of the delegates to the members of the House, as the Galloway party wished, but, through the popular convention, to dictate the terms upon which the delegates should be chosen.

The governor made unnecessary the informal assembling of the House by summoning a legislative session for Monday, July 18, on the pretext of some Indian disturbances. When, therefore, the Forty-Three sent their circular letter to the counties, they noted this fact, and asked the provincial convention to assemble on July 15 " in order to assist in framing instructions, and preparing such matters, as may be proper to recommend" to the members of the House." ² For the next several weeks, newspaper articles served to keep alive the public interest and to indicate the trend of public opinion. "A Philadelphian" argued against non-importation as a mode of opposition because the burden would fall wholly on the drygoods importers whereas the interests of all were involved.³ " Brutus " believed that the plan, proposed by the Boston circular letter, was dictated more by " heated zeal than by approved reason and moderation," and maintained that the proper course would be for Congress to petition the British government for redress.⁴ But, according to " Sidney," those who espoused the method of petition were " men who prefer one cargo of British goods to the salvation of America," and he demanded an immediate non-importation.⁵ "Anglus Americanus " would also include a non-exportation, particularly

---

¹ For the "rotten borough" system in Pennsylvania, *vide* Adams, J., *Works*, vol. x, pp. 74-75; Lincoln, *op. cit.*, pp. 40-52.

² *Pa. Gaz.*, July 6, 1774.   ³ *Ibid.*, Aug. 17, 1774.

⁴ *Ibid.*, July 20, 1774.   ⁵ *Pa. Journ.*, Aug. 31, 1774.

to the West Indies.¹ Rural opinion was well expressed by Edward Shippen when he advocated a total non-importation and non-exportation, insisting that the Boston Port Act contained the names of all the provinces, " only they are written in lime juice and want the heat of fire to make them legible." ² On July 11 the mechanics and small tradesmen of Philadelphia held a meeting to urge another mass meeting of the city and county, at which the Pennsylvania delegates should be given unrestricted power to agree to a trade suspension by the congress. But the Forty-Three saw in this gathering a design to undermine their authority, and nothing came of the matter.³

The provincial convention assembled at Carpenters' Hall on Friday, July 15, with one or more deputies from every county in the province.⁴ Thomas Willing was chosen chairman, Charles Thomson, clerk. The dominant voice of the rural members was at once insured by an agreement that the voting should be by counties. The work of the first day consisted in the adoption of a platform, or set of resolutions, which voiced the opinion of the convention in a significant way. " Unanimously " the convention resolved that it was their " earnest desire that the Congress should first try the gentler mode " of petitioning for redress before resorting to " a suspension of the commerce of this large trading province." " By a great majority " it was voted that, notwithstanding, if Congress should deem a

¹ *Pa. Journ.*, June 29, 1774.

² Balch, T., *Letters and Papers Relating Chiefly to the Provincial History of Pennsylvania* (Philadelphia, 1855), pp. 238-239.

³ " Russel " in *Pa. Gaz.*, July 20, 1774. "An Artisan" in *ibid.*, Aug. 31, and " A Mechanic " in *Pa. Packet*, Sept. 5, argued boldly for a new committee.

⁴ For the proceedings of the convention, *vide Pa. Gaz.*, July 27, 1774; also *4 Am. Arch.*, vol. i, pp. 555-593.

non-importation and non-exportation against Great Britain expedient, the people of the province would join the other leading provinces in that measure. "By a majority" it was resolved that, if any further proceedings of Parliament should cause Congress to take more drastic steps than a suspension of trade with Great Britain, the inhabitants would do all in their power to support the action of Congress. The convention agreed unanimously upon resolves for the maintenance of the customary prices during a non-importation, and for a boycott of any province, town or individual failing to adopt the plan agreed upon by Congress.

Most of the next four days was consumed in considering and amending a draft of instructions for the delegates, which had been prepared in advance by a sub-committee of the Forty-Three, of which Dickinson was the leading spirit. Finally, on Wednesday, the twentieth, a set of resolutions was agreed upon, which displayed many internal evidences of a conflict of interest among the members. The lengthy document was addressed to the House of Representatives, and commenced with a Dickinsonian essay on the rights of the colonies and a request that the House should appoint delegates to the impending congress.[1] The draft of instructions was transmitted "in pursuance of the trust imposed" on them by the inhabitants of the several counties qualified to vote—a delicate intimation of the common source of authority of the two bodies. The instructions themselves bear comparison with the resolutions adopted on the first day of the convention. After naming a comprehensive list of grievances extending back into the years, it was de-

[1] According to Thomson's account, the convention resolved "at the same time, in case the Assembly refused, to take upon themselves to appoint deputies." Stillé, *op. cit.*, p. 346. This does not appear in the extract of the proceedings accessible; but in any case it undoubtedly represented the temper of the convention.

clared that the minimum demands of Congress should include the repeal of British measures "relating to [the quartering of] the troops; internal legislation; imposition of taxes or duties hereafter; the thirty-fifth of Henry the Eighth, chapter the second; the extension of Admiralty Courts; the port of Boston and Province of Massachusetts Bay." In return for these concessions, the Americans should agree to settle a certain annual revenue on the king and "to satisfy all damages done to the East India Company."

With regard to the best method of obtaining redress, the delegates were advised to advocate a petition to the British government; but if Congress should decide upon an immediate severance of all trade, "we have determined, in the present situation of publick affairs, to consent to a stoppage of our commerce with Great Britain only." Should a partial redress be granted, the boycott should be modified in proportion to the degree of relief afforded; on the other hand, should Parliament pass further oppressive acts, the inhabitants of the province would support such action as Congress might adopt more drastic than a suspension of trade. Finally, the convention informed the House of Representatives that, " though we have, for the satisfaction of the good people of this Province, who have chosen us for this express purpose, offered to you such instructions as have appeared expedient to us, yet it is not our meaning that, by these or by any you may think proper to give them, the Deputies appointed by you should be restrained from agreeing to any measures that shall be approved by the Congress." It was this last clause which, no doubt, reconciled the radicals in the convention to a pseudo-endorsement of half-way expedients, which the experience of former years had, in their judgment, decisively discredited. As for the personnel of the delegates, the convention contented itself with proposing the names of three of its members, Dickinson, Willing and James Wilson, with the suggestion that the House should select these three together with four of its own members.[1]

On the next day, Thursday the twenty first, the convention went in a body to the chamber of the House of Representatives and presented their resolutions and instructions.[2] Without according any further formal recognition to the doings of the convention, the House resolved to take under consideration on the following day the letters received in behalf of a general congress from the committees of correspondence of the assemblies of Massachusetts, Rhode Island and Virginia. On the eve of the morrow's session, a broadside emanating from the Galloway party was handed to the members of the House. The paper drew its inspiration from the quotation of Hume's with which it opened: "All numerous Assemblies, however composed, are mere mobs, and swayed in their debates by the least motive . . . An absurdity strikes a member, he conveys it to his neighbours and the whole is infected. . . . The only way of making people wise, is to keep them from uniting into large Assemblies." By what legal authority, it was asked, has the convention assembled? "We know not where such precedents may terminate; setting up a power to controul you, is setting up anarchy above order—IT IS THE BEGINNING OF REPUBLICANISM."[3]

---

[1] This transaction does not appear in the familiar extract of the proceedings, but it is sufficiently well authenticated; *4 Am. Arch.*, vol. i, p. 607 n.; "Censor" in *Pa. Eve. Post*, Mch. 5, 1776; Thomson's narrative, Stillé, *op. cit.*, p. 346.

[2] *4 Am. Arch.*, vol. i, pp. 557, 606.

[3] The writer, who signed himself "A Freeman," also denounced the rule of voting in the convention, by which the vote of a frontier county was equal to that of "this opulent and populous city and county." *Ibid.*, vol. i, pp. 607-608 n.

On the next day, the House resolved, in words very similar to the vote of the convention, that a congress was "an absolute necessity." They did not follow the cue given them by the convention as to the personnel of the delegates, and selected seven members out of their own body, including Galloway himself. A day later, instructions were voted to "the Committee of Assembly appointed to attend the General Congress." These instructions, composed by Galloway, were drawn with a frank disregard of the elaborate directions submitted by the convention. In brief form, they stated that the trust reposed in the delegates was of such a nature and the modes of performance might be so diversified in the course of the deliberations of Congress that detailed instructions were impossible; that the delegates should strive their utmost to adopt measures for redress and the establishment of union and harmony with Great Britain while avoiding "every thing indecent or disrespectful to the mother state."[1]

Had the personnel of the delegates been different, the radicals would have been well pleased with this blanket delegation of authority. But under the circumstances, Galloway expected to control the action of the delegates; and his own judgment called for the sending of commissioners to England to adjust differences and for the scrupulous abstention from measures of non-intercourse.[2] Governor Penn could well assure the Earl of Dartmouth that "the steps taken by the Assembly are rather a check than an encouragement to the proceedings of the Committee [convention]."[3] The radicals improved their situation somewhat by securing the addition of Dickinson to the delegates by

[1] *4 Am. Arch.*, vol. i, pp. 606-609; also *Pa. Gaz.*, July 27, 1774.
[2] Letter to William Franklin; *1 N. J. Arch.*, vol. x, pp. 475-477.
[3] *4 Am. Arch.*, vol. i, p. 661.

the roundabout process of electing him to the House on October 15, and he took his seat in Congress after it had been in session six weeks. From a broader point of view, the victory lay with the radicals; for, although the House had professed to act of their own independent will throughout, there had been, in a real sense of the term, a " setting up [of] a power to controul " them, a " setting up [of] anarchy above order." Galloway himself had decided, as a lesser of evils, to take part in a great continental assemblage elected in most irregular and informal ways.[1]

The trend of sentiment in New Jersey was dominated, it would appear, by the course of the two great trading towns that controlled her commercial destinies.[2] On May 21 and 23 the Philadelphia and New York committees had informed the Boston Committee of Correspondence of their unwillingness for positive action until the meeting of a general congress; and news of their position became known at once in New Jersey. On the last day of the month, the committee of correspondence of the New Jersey Assembly transmitted to the Boston committee their endorsement of a congress, as proposed by the neighboring provinces, to draw up " a Non-Importation and perhaps a Non-Exporta-

[1] The resolution of the House appointing Galloway and his colleagues described the congress as composed of committees or delegates appointed by provincial " Houses of Representatives, or by Convention, or by the Provincial or Colony Committees." Galloway justified his conduct upon the ground that the assemblies had not been permitted to meet in some provinces. *Pa. Mag.*, vol. xxvi, p. 309.

[2] This was hinted at in the first set of resolutions issued by a public body in New Jersey—a meeting of the inhabitants of Lower Freehold township in Monmouth County. *4 Am. Arch.*, vol. i, p. 390; also *N. Y. Journ.*, June 7, 1774. The radicalism which characterized the rural population in most provinces was in New Jersey subdued by the presence of large numbers of Quakers, particularly in the western portion.

tion Agreement."[1] This was the signal for a series of county meetings throughout the province, which adopted resolutions expressing the same view.[2] They also appointed committees of correspondence, who were instructed to meet with the other committees in a provincial convention for the purpose of choosing delegates to the general congress. This convention of committees gathered at New Brunswick on July 21, and seventy-two delegates took part in the three days' deliberations. Their resolutions denied the right of Parliament to impose revenue taxes and denounced the coercive acts recently passed. A continental congress was endorsed as the best means of uniting opposition; and a general non-importation and non-consumption agreement was recommended as the best course for the congress to adopt. Delegates were appointed to the congress; but an effort to procure an instruction that the East India Company should not be reimbursed met with failure.[3]

The action of the Delaware counties was, on the whole, less restrained than that taken at Philadelphia. Published appeals for arousing public resentment raked over the embers of past disputes with Parliament in a bitterly partisan way.[4] The first mass meeting, held in Newcastle

[1] *Bos. Com. Cor. Mss.*, vol. viii, pp. 709-710.

[2] From June 8 to July 20, it is recorded that eleven of the thirteen counties acted; in chronological order: Essex, Bergen, Morris, Somerset, Hunterdon, Salem, Middlesex, Sussex, Gloucester, Monmouth and Burlington. *4 Am. Arch.*, vol. i, 403-404, 450, 524-525, 553-554, 594, 610-613; *Pa. Journ.*, July 20, 1774. These meetings endorsed a suspension of trade contingent upon the approval of the congress, most of them preferring non-importation and non-consumption alone. Salem County showed some individuality in introducing the act of Parliament against slitting and plating mills as a grievance and denouncing it as "an absolute infringement of the natural rights of the subject."

[3] *Pa. Gaz.*, July 27, 1774; also *4 Am. Arch.*, vol. i, pp. 624-625. *Vide* also Adams, J., *Works* (Adams), vol. ii, p. 356.

[4] *4 Am. Arch.*, vol. i, pp. 419-420, 658-661.

County on June 29, recommended a continental congress as the proper agency for securing redress, and appointed a committee to correspond with the other counties and provinces with reference to the matter. One resolve requested the speaker of the House of Assembly to convene the members of that body not later than August 1, in order to appoint delegates to the congress, no request being made of the governor because of his refusal in the case of the Philadelphia petition.[1] A few weeks later county meetings in Kent and Sussex took similar action.[2] The convention assembled at Newcastle on August 1. Its resolutions arraigned the British Parliament for restricting manufactures in the colonies, for taking away the property of the colonists without their consent, for introducing the arbitrary powers of the excise into the customs in America, for making all revenue causes tryable without a jury and under a single dependent judge, and for passing the coercive acts. Delegates were chosen to the approaching congress.[3]

[1] *4 Am. Arch.*, vol. i, p. 664; also *Pa. Gaz.* July 6, 1774.
[2] *Ibid.*, Aug. 3, 1774; also *4 Am. Arch.*, vol. i, pp. 664-666.
[3] *Ibid.*, vol. i, pp. 666-667.

CHAPTER IX

Contest of Merchants and Radicals for Dominance in the Plantation Provinces (May–October, 1774)

It is apparent that a revolution of sentiment had occurred among the merchants of the northern seaports. Those who had promoted movements of protest against earlier acts of Parliament now sought to stop or restrain the present popular uprising. By this reversal of front, they occupied the same position of obstruction in 1774 that the merchants and factors of the plantation provinces had maintained on all occasions since the beginning of the commotions ten years before. For this reason, the course of the plantation provinces in response to the circular letter of the Boston town meeting of May 13, 1774, does not show the marked contrast to the events in the commercial provinces that had characterized the earlier occasions.

The nature of the contest in 1774 struck closer home to the Southern planters than the earlier quarrels over trade reforms, for the issue was more clearly one of personal liberty and constitutional right, and in the school of dialectic the plantation provinces acknowledged no superiors. The long-standing indebtedness of the planters to the British merchants was a source of irritation that undoubtedly induced radical action, in the tobacco provinces and in North Carolina in particular. The demand for a suspension of debt collections played a part in the popular movement in these provinces, and, at a later time, in South Carolina as well. On the present occasion, the merchants of Charleston and Savannah were able to command support from the rural districts of their provinces, due to peculiar local conditions; but in Virginia and North Carolina, where the merchants were forced to stand alone, the planters adopted the most radical measures of commercial opposition that were to be found anywhere in British America. Maryland was only less extreme in the measures adopted.

The movement to take action in response to the Boston circular letter received its initial impulse in Maryland at a meeting of the inhabitants of Annapolis on May 25, 1774. The resolutions were an advance beyond anything that had been adopted elsewhere up to this time. The meeting declared that all provinces should unite in effectual measures to obtain the repeal of the Boston Port Act and that the inhabitants of Annapolis would join in an oath-bound association in conjunction with the other Maryland counties and the other principal provinces for an immediate non-importation with Great Britain and a suspended non-exportation. The inhabitants would immediately boycott any province that refused to enter similar resolutions with a majority of the provinces. The meeting further resolved that no lawyer should bring suit for the recovery of any debt due from a Marylander to any inhabitant of Great Britain until the Port Act should be repealed. A committee of correspondence was appointed, with instructions to join with similar committees to be appointed elsewhere in the province to form one grand committee.[1] The dec-

[1] *Md. Gaz.*, May 26, 1774; also *4 Am. Arch.*, vol. i, pp. 352-353.

laration about the payment of debts at once aroused protest in the city; and two days later a second meeting was held to re-consider the question, and the resolution was carried again, forty-seven to thirty-one.[1] Daniel Dulany, Jr., was one of those opposed to the resolution but later he admitted: "I would have agreed to it if it had extended to merchants in this country as well as foreign merchants."[2]

All the subsequent meetings in Maryland were county assemblages, thus reducing the opportunities for mercantile influence. Within three weeks eight of the sixteen counties were recorded as following the example of the town of Annapolis.[3] Six of these meetings favored a non-exportation and non-importation, simultaneous or successive; Caroline preferred a modified non-importation only; and Kent was silent on the subject. A suspension of debt collections, foreign and domestic, was advocated by four counties, in case of complete non-intercourse.[4] Six counties declared that all provinces failing to adopt the general plan should be boycotted. All the meetings organized committees of correspondence and appointed delegates to the forthcoming province convention.

The convention of committees assembled at Annapolis on Wednesday, June 22, for a four days' sitting, with ninety-two members representing every county in the

[1] *Md. Gaz.*, June 2, 1774; also *4 Am. Arch.*, vol. i, p. 353.

[2] *Ibid.*, vol. i, pp. 354-355. A formal protest against the resolution, signed by one hundred sixty-three names, mostly of stay-at-home citizens, appeared a few days later. *Ibid.*, pp. 353-354.

[3] In chronological order: Queen Anne's, Baltimore, Kent, Anne Arundel, Harford, lower part of Frederick, Charles, Caroline, Frederick. *Ibid.*, vol. i, pp. 366-367, 379, 384-386, 402-403, 409, 425-426, 433-434; also *Md. Gaz.*, June 9, 16, 30, 1774.

[4] Anne Arundel, Caroline, Frederick, Harford.

province. It was agreed that every county should cast one vote. The resolutions denounced the punitive acts of Parliament and declared the willingness of the province to join in a retaliatory association, in company with the principal provinces of the continent, to stop all, or almost all, commercial intercourse with the mother country, at a date to be fixed by the general congress. This latter resolve occasioned long debates on Friday, lasting from ten in the morning until nine at night. The division, it would appear, was on the question whether the non-intercourse should be absolute, as proposed by the preliminary county meetings, or qualified. The moderates forced a compromise by which it was agreed that the non-exportation of tobacco should not take place without a similar restraint in force in Virginia and North Carolina, and that articles should be excepted from the non-importation in case a majority of the provinces should so decide. Further resolutions declared that merchants must not raise prices, on pain of boycott; and that the province would sever all relations with any province or town which declined the plan recommended by the congress.[1] Apparently there was little thought of adopting an association which should go into effect independently of Congress; the resolutions were in the nature of instructions to the delegates to Congress, who were forthwith chosen.

The Virginia House of Burgesses was in session when news was received at Williamsburg of the passage of the Boston Port Act. Richard Henry Lee, one of the members, urged that an immediate declaration be made in behalf of Boston, but was dissuaded by some "worthy

[1] *Md. Gaz.*, June 30, 1774; also *4 Am. Arch.*, vol. i, pp. 439–440. *Vide* a letter from Annapolis in *Pa. Journ.*, June 29.

members" who desired first to dispose of necessary provincial business.[1] "Whatever resolves or measures are intended for the preservation of our rights and liberties," wrote George Mason, who was a spectator of these events, "will be reserved for the conclusion of the session. Matters of that sort here are conducted and prepared with a great deal of privacy, and by very few members; of whom Patrick Henry is the principal."

Finally, on Tuesday, May 24, the House resolved that the first of June, the day on which the harbor of Boston was to be closed, should be set aside as a "day of fasting, humiliation and prayer." Governor Dunmore, suspecting rightly that the fast was intended to prepare the minds of the people to receive other and more inflammatory resolutions, dissolved the House two days later. Not to be foiled, eighty-nine burgesses met in their private capacities in the Long Room of the Raleigh Tavern on Friday morning, with Peyton Randolph as chairman, and adopted an association in which they declared war on the East India Company by recommending the disuse of dutied tea and of all East India commodities, save saltpetre and spices. It was further recommended to the legislative committee of correspondence to invite the various provinces to meet in annual congress for the sake of deliberating on measures of common concern. In point of time, this was the first pronouncement by a meeting representing a whole province in favor of an interprovincial congress; but, as we have seen, the proposal had already been made by many town gatherings in various other provinces.

[1] This account is based chiefly on: *4 Am. Arch.*, vol. i, pp. 350-352, 387-388, 445-446; Washington, *Writings* (Ford), vol. ii, pp. 412-415, n. 2; letter of a burgess in Rind's *Va. Gaz.*, Sept. 22, 1774; Rowland, *George Mason*, vol. i, pp. 168-171.

These measures, which Richard Henry Lee denominated as "much too feeble," were entered into independently of any knowledge of what had been done elsewhere. When the Boston circular letter arrived, with other letters from the north, on Sunday, May 29, most of the ex-burgesses had departed for their homes; but Peyton Randolph succeeded in collecting twenty five of them for a meeting on Monday morning. Most of those present believed it absolutely necessary to enlarge the association to include a general non-importation, but they were badly divided as to the expediency of stopping exportation. Furthermore, they felt that, in any case, their number was too small to permit them to alter the association. Therefore they addressed a circular letter to the absent gentlemen, explaining the situation, asking them to collect the sense of their constituents, and to assemble in Williamsburg on August 1 to take final action.

This referendum to the people, occupying a space of two months, showed conclusively that the temper of the rural constituencies was far more radical than the action of their representatives at the Williamsburg meeting indicated. The chief source of opposition to the popular measures was disclosed by James Madison, when he wrote that "the Europeans, especially the Scotch, and some interested merchants among the natives, discountenance such proceedings as far as they dare; alledging the injustice aud perfidy of refusing to pay our debts to our generous creditors at home. This consideration induces some honest, moderate folks to prefer a partial prohibition, extending only to the importation, of goods."[1] It was reported in London newspapers that

[1] Madison, *Writings* (Hunt), vol. i, p. 26.

when a meeting of merchants at Norfolk, the chief trading centre, had the Boston circular letter under consideration, a wag present observed that "the request put him in mind of the old fable of the fox that had lost his tail and who would have persuaded his brethren to cut off theirs." He believed that "as amputation is a dangerous operation . . . it will be better to take time to consider of it." The meeting accordingly adjourned without action.[1]

The first county meeting was held at Dumfries in Prince William County on June 6. One resolution declared boldly: "that as our late Representatives have not fallen upon means sufficiently efficacious to secure to us the enjoyment of our civil rights and liberties, it is the undoubted privilege of each respective county (as the fountain of power from whence their delegation arises) to take such proper and salutary measures as will essentially conduce to a repeal" of the coercive acts.[2] This resolve marked the tempo with which all the counties acted. In the period up to the time of the provincial convention on August 1, thirty-one, perhaps more, counties gave expression to their sentiments as to a proper mode of opposition to the mother country.[3]

[1] *Mass. Gaz. & Post-Boy*, Sept. 12, 1774. *Vide* also *Pa. Gaz.*, Aug. 24. This no doubt expressed the views of the merchants; but the inhabitants of the borough in general were ready to adopt measures of protest. *4 Am. Arch.*, vol. i, pp. 370-372.

[2] Rind's *Va. Gaz.*, June 9, 1774; also *4 Am. Arch.*, vol. i, p. 388. *Vide* also the Stafford resolutions, *ibid.*, p. 617.

[3] In chronological order: Prince William, Frederick, Dunmore, Westmoreland, Spotsylvania, Richmond, Prince George's, James City, Norfolk, Culpepper, Essex, Fauquier, Nansemond, New Kent, Chesterfield, Caroline, Gloucester, Henrico, Middlesex, Dinwiddie, Surry, York, Fairfax, Hanover, Stafford, Isle of Wight, Elizabeth City, Albemarle, Accomack, Princess Anne, Buckingham. *Ibid.*, vol. i, pp. 388-644 *passim*. The resolutions of Isle of Wight County appeared in Rind's *Va. Gaz.*, July 28, 1774.

All meetings agreed that Parliament lacked power to impose taxes collectable in America, and denounced the Boston Port Act. Twenty counties announced themselves in favor of the extreme measure of commercial non-intercourse with Great Britain, in conjunction with the other provinces, although eight of these preferred to have non-exportation go into effect at a stated interval after non-importation. Three other counties recommended merely the adoption of an unqualified non-importation;[1] and five others proposed a non-importation with certain articles excepted, as in former associations.[2] The remaining three counties indicated their willingness to accept any conclusions reached at the provincial convention.[3] A declaration in favor of the suspension of judicial processes for the collection of debts during non-exportation was made by eight counties, on the ground that the people, under such circumstances, had not the means of paying.[4] Gloucester County resolved that, if Maryland and North Carolina withheld the exportation of tobacco to Great Britain, Virginia should adopt the same measure.

Ten counties scrupulously said that they would follow the advice of the former burgesses and boycott goods handled by the East India Company, with certain exceptions. Six counties denounced the importation of slaves as an economic fallacy, saying, in the words of Nansemond, "the African trade is injurious to this Colony, obstructs the population of it by freemen, prevents manufacturers and other useful emigrants from

---

[1] Buckingham, Caroline, Nansemond.

[2] Chesterfield, Culpepper, Middlesex, Prince George's, York.

[3] Accomack, Dinwiddie, Isle of Wight.

[4] Essex, Fairfax, Fauquier, Gloucester, Prince William, Stafford, Richmond, Westmoreland.

Europe from settling among us, and occasions an annual increase of the balance of trade against this Colony."[1] The resolutions of three counties contained a declaration against the advancing of prices by merchants. Several counties recommended the abandonment of extravagance and display. Albemarle favored the repeal, not only of the Boston Port Act, but also of all laws levying duties in America, restricting American trade and restraining colonial manufacturing. It was proposed by Fairfax that, after an interprovincial association had been drawn up, its enforcement should be left to committees in every county on the continent, with instructions to publish all violators as traitors. Norfolk County thought it necessary to suggest, with a view perhaps of discrediting the moral of the fable about the fox, that the Virginia committees be composed "of respectable men, fixed and settled inhabitants of their respective counties." Nine counties announced the boycott as the proper penalty for individuals who failed to adopt the agreed plan of opposition; and seven counties urged a boycott of delinquent provinces.

The meeting of the provincial convention was preceded by several spirited appeals, the most important being the series, published by the planter, Thomson Mason, under the pseudonym, "British American," in six issues of Rind's *Virginia Gazette*, beginning June 16.[2] These articles were particularly aimed to stimulate to radical action those "countrymen whose own industry, or the frugality of their ancestors, have blessed . . . [them]

---

[1] Caroline, Culpepper, Nansemond, Prince George's, Princess Anne, Surry. Slavery was condemned by Fairfax and Hanover as a moral evil.

[2] Reprinted in *4 Am. Arch.*, vol. i, pp. 418-419, 495-498, 519-522, 541-544, 620-624, 648-654. *Vide* also *ibid.*, p. 647.

with immense wealth;" and to this end, great stress was laid on the danger of submitting "to a double taxation and to two supreme Legislatures," in one of which the legislative power was wielded by men who, "from their situation, will reap the advantages but cannot share in the inconveniences" of their oppressive laws. With much ingenuity, the writer argued that Parliament lacked power to legislate for the colonies, and then turned to consider the possible methods of opposition. Rejecting non-intercourse as a temporizing measure and impracticable, he urged that the delegates to the Continental Congress be instructed to refuse flatly to obey all laws, including the acts of navigation and trade, made by Parliament since the first settlements, and in defense of this position, to resort to armed resistance and secession, if necessary. After the convention had gotten under way, another article appeared in favor of the policy of non-intercouse, contending that "we need not on the present occasion shed our blood to secure our rights . . ."[1] This latter article and the series of county resolutions preliminary to the convention struck the true keynote of the convention's deliberations.

The Virginia convention began its work promptly on August 1 and completed its deliberations on the sixth.[2] Of the debates that occurred we know nothing; but delegates were chosen to the Continental Congress, and the association adopted marked the crest of the radical wave set in motion by the late acts of Parliament. In view of the striking similarity between the Virginia Association and the later Continental Association, there can be no doubt that the former paper was the model

[1] *4 Am. Arch.*, vol. i, pp. 685-686.
[2] *Ibid.*, vol. i, pp. 686-690; also *Md. Gaz.*, Aug. 18, 1774.

for the latter. The action of the delegates faithfully reflected the sentiments of their constituents. The delegates boldly set the dates at which the various parts of the association were to go into effect, subject to such changes as might be assented to by the Virginia delegates in the Continental Congress; and the association was to be religiously adhered to "before God and the world" until the redress of all grievances which might be named by Congress.[1] The immediate non-importation and disuse of tea "of any kind whatever" was agreed upon,[2] with the understanding that if Boston were compelled to reimburse the East India Company, the boycott should be extended to all articles handled by the company till the money was returned. On November 1, 1774, an absolute boycott of all goods (except medicines) imported thereafter, directly or indirectly, from Great Britain was to become effective;[3] and the agreement was to extend likewise to negroes imported from Africa, the West Indies or elsewhere.[4] If colonial grievances were not redressed by August 10, 1775, an absolute non-exportation was to be declared, of all articles intended to be sent, directly or indirectly, to Great Britain.[5] This postponement was granted in order to enable as quick and full payment of debts to Britain as possible and in order to get the profits on the present tobacco crop. As non-exportation would be a blow to tobacco culture, planters were advised thereafter to de-

[1] Or until the association should be amended or abrogated by a later provincial convention.

[2] *Cf.* Continental Association, Arts. i and iii. Appendix, present volume.

[3] *Cf. ibid.*, Art. i.

[4] *Cf. ibid.*, Art. ii.

[5] *Cf. ibid.*, Art. iv.

vote their fields to the growing of raw materials for manufacturing; and a pledge was given to improve the breed of sheep and to increase their number.[1] Merchants were warned to maintain the prices usual during the past year on pain of boycott.[2] In order to supervise the execution of the association and to correspond with the general committee of correspondence at Williamsburg, it was recommended that a committee be chosen in each county.[3] Merchants and traders were required, on threat of boycott, to obtain certificates from the committee that they had signed the association. If any merchant or other person received forbidden importations, the goods should be forthwith re-shipped or stored under supervision of the committee;[4] otherwise "the truth of the case" should be published in the gazettes and all dealings severed with the offender. A similar treatment should await the violator of non-exportation.[5]

North Carolina followed in the train of the Virginia movement, and thus won the distinction of being the second most radical province in the measures adopted. Under stimulus of the succession of county meetings in Virginia, a meeting of six counties in the district of Wilmington was held on July 21 under the chairmanship of William Hooper, a transplanted Bostonian who had studied law under James Otis at the zenith of his radicalism. A committee was appointed to send a circular

[1] *Cf.* Continental Association, Art. vii.
[2] *Cf. ibid.*, Art. ix.
[3] *Cf. ibid.*, Art. xi.
[4] *Cf. ibid.*, Art. x.
[5] *Cf. ibid.*, Art. xi.

to all the counties, proposing a general meeting in the latter part of August to adopt measures in concert with the other provinces; and it was voted that a general congress was the best way to effect a uniform plan for all America.[1] Before the date of the provincial meeting, most of the counties and two of the towns had responded by adopting resolutions and choosing delegates.[2] The resolutions still extant varied in tone. Only Anson County went so far as to counsel the stoppage of all trade with Great Britain (save in a few necessary articles), Granville declaring that it was a "measure not to be entered into with precipitation." Rowan County and Halifax expressed a preference for a modified non-importation; Chowan favored economy and the promotion of manufactures; while Johnston simply indicated a willingness to abide by the findings of the Continental Congress. The necessity of suspending debt collections on some equitable principle, in case of non-intercourse, was noted by Anson; but Granville County and Halifax showed a distinct repugnance to the policy which had attained considerable local popularity in Virginia and Maryland, and declared themselves explicitly in favor of keeping all courts open. Anson and Rowan announced themselves in favor of a boycott of such provinces as declined to enter the general measures, the latter county also inveighing against the slave trade as an obstacle to a free immigration and the development of manufacturing.

[1] *S. C. Gaz.*, Sept. 12, 1774; also *N. C. Col. Recs.*, vol. ix, pp. 1016-1017.

[2] Only six sets of resolutions have been examined; in chronological order: Rowan, Johnston, Granville, Anson and Chowan counties, and the town of Halifax. *Ibid.*, vol. ix, pp. 1024-1026, 1029-1038.

When Governor Martin got wind of these proceedings, he issued a proclamation on August 13, forbidding such "illegal Meetings" and particularly the provincial meeting, which was soon to occur.[1] The pronunciamento had the same effect as the executive interdicts, in other provinces, of the right of the people to organize and act. The provincial convention of August 25 assembled at Newbern with a representation from thirty-two of the thirty-eight counties and two of the six towns, while the governor and his council sat futilely by. Governor Martin noted the readiness with which the "intemperate resolutions" of the Virginia convention were "re-echoed;"[2] but it is possible that a complete collection of county resolutions would show that the Newbern meeting merely reflected the views of the county gatherings.[3] The convention chose delegates to the Continental Congress and adopted a modified form of the Virginia Association.[4] In one respect the association exceeded the Virginia plan, for a threat of boycott was held up over any province, or any town or individual within the

[1] *S. C. Gaz.*, Sept. 12, 1774; also *N. C. Col. Recs.*, vol. ix, pp. 1029–1030.

[2] *4 Am. Arch.*, vol. i, pp. 761–762.

[3] However, it is impossible to know what weight to give, at this time, to the old Regulator antipathy to the personnel of the tidewater radicals. *Vide* Bassett, J. S., "The Regulators of North Carolina," *Am. Hist. Assn. Rep.* (*1894*), pp. 209–210.

[4] No "East India tea" was to be used after September 10, 1774. Beginning with January 1, 1775, there should be a total stoppage of all East Indian and all British importations, by way of Great Britain or the West Indies, except medicines; after November 1, 1774, no slaves should be imported from any part of the world. Unless American grievances were redressed before October 1, 1775, a non-exportation to Great Britain was to become effective. Merchants were warned to continue their customary prices. Committees were to be chosen to supervise the execution of the association and to correspond with the provincial committee of correspondence. *Pa. Gaz.*, Sept. 16, 1774; also *N. C. Col. Recs.*, vol. ix, pp. 1041–1049.

province, which failed to adopt the plan formulated by the Continental Congress.

The first news of the Boston Port Act reached Charleston on May 31 in a letter from the Philadelphia committee transmitting the Boston circular letter.[1] Peter Timothy's newspaper took the lead in declaring that America had never faced a more critical time, that South Carolina, like Boston, had obstructed the tea act, and that the time had come to sacrifice private interest, to abolish all parties and distinctions and combine in a general non-importation and, if necessary, non-exportation.[2] But in spite of the best efforts of Timothy and Chris Gadsden,[3] private interest continued to assert itself and economic groups and distinctions became more clearly defined than on any earlier occasion.

The opposition to a total suspension of trade centered very largely in the merchants and factors, on the one hand, and the rice planters, on the other. The Norfolk story of the Boston fox that had lost his tail gained currency with

[1] *S. C. Gaz.*, June 6, 1774; also *4 Am. Arch.*, vol. i, p. 370.

[2] *S. C. Gaz.*, June 13, 1774; also *4 Am. Arch.*, vol. i, pp. 382-384.

[3] As has already been pointed out, Gadsden himself, though possessing important mercantile interests as well as planting connections, acted politically with an entire disregard of self-interest. This is shown strikingly in a letter he wrote to Samuel Adams on June 5, 1774: "I have been above Seven Years at hard Labour and the Utmost Risk of my Constitution about One of the most extensive Quays in America . . . at which thirty of the Largest Ships that can come over our Barr can be Loading at the Same time . . . and have exceeding good and Convenient Stores already Erected thereon Sufficient to Contain 16000 Teirces of Rice; in Short in this Affair, all my Fortune is embarked . . no motives whatever will make me neglect or Slacken in the Common Cause, as I hope I would sooner see every inch of my Quay (my whole Fortune) totally destroyed Rather than be even Silent . . . let the ministry change our Ports of Entrey to what distance from Charleston and as Often as the Devil shall put it in their heads." *Bos. Com. Cor. Papers*, vol. ii, pp. 509-511.

the trading body.¹ The merchants faced losses in case either importation or exportation should be stopped; they preferred the former measure to the latter, if necessity pressed, but were determined to delay a decision on either as long as possible. As for the rice planters, they were opposed to a stoppage of exports, at least until November 1 when the rice from the present crop had been shipped off and the time for a new planting had arrived.² The mercantile and planting interests found it easy to develop a public opinion in favor of a postponement of all positive measures until a general congress, because the people in general were inclined to look askance at a northern invitation to enter a non-intercourse regulation when they remembered "the Overhasty breaking through and forsaking the first Resolution [four years earlier] without previously Consulting or so much as Acquainting our Committee," and when they observed that no commercial province had entered the measure which the South Carolinians were asked to adopt by Boston.³

On June 13 the General Committee at Charleston summoned a "General Meeting of the inhabitants of this Colony" for Wednesday, July 6, at Charleston, and dispatched circular letters to leading men throughout the province urging them to send representatives.⁴ Timothy's

¹ "Non Quis sed Quid" in *S. C. Gaz.*, July 4, 1774.

² Letter of Gadsden to Hancock and others, *Bos. Com. Cor. Papers*, vol. ii, pp. 517-518. The planters had another motive for temporizing in that Parliament had under advisement a renewal of the act authorizing the shipment of rice from South Carolina to the West Indies and the southern parts of Europe. The renewal was granted for seven years on June 2 (14 George III, c. 67), but the fact was certainly not known in South Carolina until some weeks later.

³ Letters of Gadsden and Timothy to S. Adams, *Bos. Com. Cor. Papers*, vol. ii, pp. 509-511, 529-532.

⁴ *4 Am. Arch.*, vol. i, p. 408; also *S. C. Gaz.*, June 13, 1774.

Gazette contained articles arguing for decisive measures at the coming meeting. "A Carolinian" insisted on specific instructions to the delegates to the Continental Congress for a very general suspension of trade with Great Britain, the West Indies and Africa, and exhorted that "one common Soul animate the Merchant, the Planter and the Tradesman."[1] "Non Quis sed Quid" gave his pen to the advocacy of a modified non-importation, and told the planters and merchants that this expedient would give them a chance to extricate themselves from debt.[2] Meantime, the newly-formed Chamber of Commerce had become the center of discussion as to what should be the proper course for the body of merchants to take. On July 6, before the meeting assembled in the Exchange, the Chamber of Commerce decided not to accede to any measure of non-importation or non-exportation, and, in order to contribute to the defeat of the same proposition in the Continental Congress, they drew up a slate of candidates who held the same view and pledged their support to them.[3]

The Charleston meeting, comprising one hundred and four members, was the largest public assemblage that had ever been held in that town. From the standpoint of the representative principle, it was defective in many respects, for some counties elected ten delegates, others less, two counties and one parish sent no representation, and the General Committee of forty-five represented Charleston. But the leaders of all factions were well pleased with the mis-

[1] *S. C. Gaz.*, June 20, 27, 1774.

[2] *Ibid.*, July 4, 1774; also *4 Am. Arch.*, vol. i, pp. 508–512.

[3] This account of the general meeting is based chiefly on: Drayton, *Memoirs*, vol. 1, pp. 112–132; official record in *S. C. Gaz.*, July 11, 1774, also *4 Am. Arch.* vol. i, pp, 525–527; three epistolary accounts, *ibid.*, pp. 525, 531–534; Edward Rutledge's account, Izard, R., *Correspondence*, vol. i, pp. 2–5.

cellaneous gathering, for it afforded an excellent opportunity for political manipulation. Indeed, one of the very first resolutions adopted provided that votes should be given by each person present and not by parishes, and that " whoever came there might give his vote." After the adoption of resolutions for asserting American rights, the debates of the first two days turned upon a consideration of a practical application of the declaration of the meeting: " to leave no justifiable means untried to procure a repeal " of the oppressive acts of Parliament. The one party favored the sending of delegates to Congress with unconditional instructions, and the adoption in the meantime of the Boston proposal of a non-importation and non-exportation. The other party favored restricted instructions and the postponement of all measures until the Congress.

In favor of the Boston circular letter, the radical speakers resorted to sensational delineations of the fate awaiting South Carolina from British tyranny, and repeated the telling arguments which had become hackneyed in similar controversies in other provinces. By the opposing party, it was maintained that non-intercourse would ruin thousands in the province; that if South Carolina entered into it, there was no assurance that other provinces would follow, and indeed much evidence to the contrary. It was further argued that the formulation of a uniform plan was the proper function of a general congress, and that even that body ought not adopt the measure until after petitions and remonstrances had failed of effect. When the vote was taken on the second day, it was found that the proposal for an immediate non-intercourse was rejected.

The fight was warmly renewed, in altered form, over the question of what instructions the delegates to the Congress should be given, the radicals contending that the powers of the delegates should be unrestricted. By a close vote it was decided that the delegates should be granted "full power and authority" to agree to "legal measures" for obtaining a redress of grievances, and the moderates found solace in the clause declaring that the South Carolina delegates must concur in any measure of the Congress before it became binding on the province. Victory now lay clearly with the party that could control the personnel of the delegation.

It was provided that a vote for this purpose should be taken that very day from two o'clock to six, and that every free white in the whole province should be entitled to vote— an arrangement that was a thin covering for a strategem concocted in the Chamber of Commerce. The merchants had in mind to elect Henry Middleton, John Rutledge, Charles Pinckney, Miles Brewton and Rawlins Lowndes, men who stood for moderate measures and opposed non-intercourse except as an ultimate resort.[1] The radicals concentrated their strength on Gadsden, Thomas Lynch and Edward Rutledge, and concurred, it would appear, in the nominations of Middleton and John Rutledge. Just what the object of the radicals was it is difficult to comprehend now, as Edward Rutledge, one of their nominees, had clearly identified himself with the moderate element in the debates of the meeting. However, he was Gadsden's son-in-law. The merchants went to the poll in a body, and also sent for their clerks to come and vote. But they had overreached themselves; the radicals took alarm at such mobilizing of voters, "ran to all parts of the town to collect people and bring them to the poll." In consequence, the slate of the Chamber of Commerce suffered defeat, save the

[1] For the opinions held by John and Edward Rutledge, *vide* Izard, *Correspondence*, vol. i, pp. 2-5; by Miles Brewton, *4 Am. Arch.*, vol. i, p. 534. The South Carolina delegates shifted their position somewhat when they reached the Continental Congress, but their new position, as we shall see, served the purposes of their friends at home as well as their original one.

two candidates upon whom both factions had joined; and Gadsden, Lynch and Edward Rutledge were chosen in addition, by a majority of almost four hundred. Notwithstanding, Edward Rutledge's presence on the delegation assured the moderates a safe majority.

On the third and last day, the meeting resolved to appoint a general committee for the province in place of the existing committee of forty-five. The new committee was authorized to correspond with the other provinces and to "do all matters and things necessary" to carry the resolutions into execution, a phraseology which virtually vested the committee with unlimited power during its existence. The committee was then carefully constituted to exercise this power in an approved manner. The membership was fixed at ninety-nine; fifteen merchants and fifteen mechanics represented Charleston, and sixty-nine planters, chosen forthwith by the meeting and not by the rural districts, were designated to represent the rest of the province.[1]

The moderates had cause for rejoicing; but the radicals were not dismayed. They could claim excellent salvage from the wreckage: the "Sam Adams of South Carolina" was one of the delegates to the Continental Congress; the delegates had powers to agree to the measures supported by the great and magnetic personages of the sister provinces; and, finally, the merchants by their active participation in the meeting were pledged to support such action as Congress might take. Indeed, some of the people were so "uneasy" over the obstructive tactics of the merchants that several of the latter felt it was expedient to declare that the merchants in general would countermand their orders until the results of the Congress were known.

[1] Charles Pinckney and Miles Brewton were given places on the committee, and Peter Timothy was chosen as one of the mechanic members. Pinckney was chosen chairman, and Timothy secretary. For list of the Charleston members, *vide 4 Am. Arch.*, vol. i, pp. 526–527.

Greater semblance of legality was given to the election of delegates when the Commons House of Assembly met on August 2. All but five of the members had participated in the Charleston meeting; and by assembling privately at the unusual hour of eight in the morning, while the governor still reclined in the arms of Morpheus, they succeeded in ratifying the election and voting money for the delegates' expenses.[1] In the succeeding weeks, the General Committee found little else to do than to guard against tea importations. Two incidents occurring in late July and early August showed that the committee believed in only the most moderate methods of resistance. Two vessels arrived with private consignments of tea for Charleston merchants. In each instance, the committee assured themselves that the tea would not be received in Charleston, and then quietly waited for its seizure by the customs officials at the termination of the twenty-day period.[2]

If the radicals of South Carolina had a difficult time in maneuvering their province into line, the small group of radicals in Georgia may be said to have had a practically insurmountable task. The sparse population of that infant province had every reason to be pleased with the home government and none to be displeased. Not yet self-supporting as a colony, Georgia received an annual subsidy from Parliament, besides money and presents intended for the Indians.[3] This condition served to give Georgia "as many

[1] *4 Am. Arch.*, vol. i, pp. 532, 671-672; Drayton, *Memoirs*, vol. i, pp. 137-141. Governor Bull wrote to Dartmouth the next day: "Your Lordship will see by this instance with what perseverance, secrecy and unanimity, they form and conduct their designs; how obedient the body is to the heads, and how faithful in their secrets." *4 Am. Arch.*, vol. i, p. 672.

[2] The *Magna Charta* and the *Briton*. *S. C. Gaz.*, June 27, July 4 25, Sept. 19, 1774.

[3] Letter from a Georgian, *4 Am. Arch.*, vol. i, p. 733.

place-men and publick officers with their connections, as the largest and most populous Government on the Continent, and those with independent salaries from Government." [1] Furthermore, the inhabitants were in constant peril of an attack from the Creeks, who threatened to wipe out the back-country settlements. "We have an enemy at our backs, who but very lately put us into the utmost consternation," wrote a Georgian. "We fled at their approach; we left our property at their mercy; and we have implored the assistance of Great-Britain to humble these haughty Creeks. . . . Our entering into resolutions against the Government, in the present case, can answer no end but to injure our infant province, by provoking the Mother Country to desert us." [2] It is not surprising that the frontier parishes were unsympathetic to the propaganda against Parliament.

In view of these facts, the radicals were unsuccessful in arousing indignation by references to past injustices, especially as they had failed signally in the earlier years in obtaining effective action from Georgia. There was only a handful of radicals in the province—a few active ones in Christ Church Parish, wherein lay the coast town of Savannah, and a compact group, of New England nativity, in St. John's Parish, immediately to the south.[3] Late in July, at the instance of the South Carolina radicals,[4] appeals began

[1] Letter from Savannah correspondent in *Pa. Gaz.*, Dec. 28, 1774; also *4 Am. Arch.*, vol. i, pp. 1033-1034.

[2] "Mercurius" in *Ga. Gaz.*, Aug. 10, 1774.

[3] St. John's Parish was appropriately named "Liberty County" at a later time. Medway, the chief settlement, was founded by people from Dorchester, Mass., after they had failed in a similar enterprise in South Carolina. These folks "still retain a strong tincture of Republican or Oliverian principles," wrote Governor Wright to Dartmouth. White, *Ga. Hist. Colls.*, p. 523.

[4] Letter of Wright to Dartmouth, *4 Am. Arch.*, vol. i, pp. 633-634.

to appear in the *Georgia Gazette* exhorting the inhabitants to make common cause with Boston.[1] In "The Case stated," it was declared that the single question was: had Parliament a right to levy what sums of money on the Americans they pleased and in what manner they pleased; for "they that have a right or power to put a duty on my tea have an equal right to put a duty on my bread, and why not on my breath, why not on my daylight and smoak, why not on everything?" The answer of the moderates rang clear and true: the real issue was not one of taxation but "whether Americans have a right to destroy private property with impunity." "That the India Company did send tea to Boston on their own account is undeniable," declared the writer. "That they had a *right* so to do and to undersell the Merchants there (or rather the Smugglers) is equally undeniable," and the destructive act of the Bostonians "must, in the judgment of sober reason, be highly criminal and worthy of exemplary punishment."[2]

On July 20 the *Gazette* contained an unsigned call for a provincial meeting of delegates at Savannah. A meeting was accordingly held at the Watch-House on Wednesday, July 27.[3] It is impossible to ascertain how many persons were present, but a radical account claimed that "upwards of an hundred from one Parish [St. John's] came resolved on an agreement not to import or use British manufactures till America shall be restored to her constitutional rights." It is clear that the great body of the province was unrepresented. After several had declined the doubtful honor,

[1] "The Case stated" and "A Georgian" in issue of July 27, 1774.

[2] "Mercurius" in *ibid.*, Aug. 10, 1774.

[3] This narrative is based chiefly on the radical accounts in *4 Am. Arch.*, vol. i, pp. 638–639; the moderate version in a protest of Savannah inhabitants, *Ga. Gaz.*, Sept. 7, 1774; and the radical rejoinder in *ibid.*, Sept. 21.

John Glenn was chosen chairman. A motion was made to appoint a committee to draft resolutions "nearly similar to those of the Northern Provinces," but it was lost by "a large majority of the respectable inhabitants." Letters were then read from the General Committee of South Carolina and other northern committees; and while the reading was going on, many moderates, believing that the main issue had been settled, withdrew from the meeting. The radicals quietly swelled their own numbers by gathering in " several transients and other inconsiderable people;" and a motion for a committee was put a second time and announced as carried, in face of the protest of several gentlemen that, if the names of the persons on both sides were put down, it would appear that a majority of the freeholders present opposed the motion. A committee of thirty-one was forthwith chosen; but it was deemed wiser, in view of the irregular composition of the convention and the high indignation of the moderate party, to postpone the adoption of resolutions until a convention of regularly-appointed delegates should meet at Savannah on August 10. It was voted, however, that the resolutions agreed upon at the forthcoming meeting by a majority of those present "should be deemed the sense of the inhabitants of this Province."

When Governor Wright learned that the committee was summoning the several parishes and districts to a provincial convention, he adopted the usual course of royal executives, and on August 5 interposed a proclamation denouncing the action as "unconstitutional, illegal and punishable by law." [1] More indicative of public opinion was a protest against the coming meeting, signed by forty-six inhabitants of St. Paul, one of the most populous parishes of the province. The paper declared that since the Georgians were not involved

---

[1] *S. C. Gaz.*, Sept. 12, 1774; also *4 Am. Arch.*, vol. i, pp. 699-700.

in the same guilt as the Bostonians, they could have no business in making themselves partakers of the ill-consequences of that guilt; and particular stress was laid on the fact that " the persons who are most active on this occasion are chiefly those whose property lies in or near Savannah; and therefore are not so immediately exposed to the bad effects of an Indian war; whereas the back settlements of this province, and our parish in particular, would most certainly be laid waste and depopulated, unless we receive such powerful aid and assistance as none but Great-Britain can give." [1]

The tenth of August arrived, and, according to the authorized account published in the *Gazette*, a " General Meeting of the Inhabitants of the Province " assembled at Savannah and " *nemine contradicente* " adopted resolutions condemning the coercive acts as illegal and pledging the concurrence of Georgia " in every constitutional measure " for redress adopted by the sister provinces.[2] The deputies present were added to the existing committee of thirty-one to act as a General Committee for the province. This meager and colorless account intentionally failed to disclose the tense excitement and unscrupulous methods that prevailed at the meeting, or even the fact, admitted later by a radical, that a motion to send delegates to the Continental Congress failed of adoption.[3] But the facts, suppressed in the official version were voluntarily supplied by indignation meetings in various parts of the province. A protest, signed by James Habersham, councillor and merchant, and one hundred and one other inhabitants of Savannah and Christ

---

[1] Now McDuffie County. *Ga. Gaz.*, Oct. 12, 1774; incorrectly printed in *Ga. Rev. Recs.*, vol. i, pp. 24-26.

[2] *Ga. Gaz.*, Aug. 17, 1774; also *4 Am. Arch.*, vol. i, pp. 700-701.

[3] Letter from St. John's Parish; *Pa. Journ.*, Oct. 5, 1774; also *4 Am. Arch.*, vol. i, pp 766-767.

Church Parish, recounted the devious practices of the radicals at the meeting of July 27, and charged that the important parish of St. Paul was not represented at the meeting of August 10 and that several other parishes had been induced to send deputies through a misrepresentation of the purpose of the gathering. It was further alleged that, in absence of notification to the contrary, all but the select few in the secret supposed that the second meeting would be held at the same place as the earlier one, but in fact it " was held in a tavern, with the door shut for a considerable time, and it is said twenty-six persons answered for the whole province and undertook to bind them by Resolution; and when several gentlemen attempted to go in, the tavern-keeper, who stood at the door with a list in his hand, refused them admittance, because their names were not mentioned in that list." [1]

These charges were elaborated and confirmed by protests emanating from three other parishes. The burden of three different protests from St. Paul Parish, signed in all by two hundred and eighty-seven names, was that the meeting had been secret, small, unrepresentative, and even, according to the belief of the Augusta signers, illegal.[2] From one portion of St. George Parish came the plaint that, though many of the subscribers had voted to send deputies to the Savannah meeting, " it was because we were told that unless we did send some persons there, we would have the Stamp Act put in force," while the western district of the same parish announced that they had known nothing of the

[1] *Ga. Gaz.*, Sept. 7, 1774; reprinted in incomplete form in *Ga. Rev. Recs.*, vol. i, pp. 18-21.

[2] Protests from 126 inhabitants of the Kyoka and Broad River Settlements, 123 inhabitants of the township of Wrightsborough and places adjacent, and from 38 inhabitants of the town and district of Augusta; *Ga. Gaz.*, Oct. 12, 1774; also *Ga. Rev. Recs.*, vol. i, pp. 22-24, 27-30, where the Augusta resolves are given inaccurately.

appointment of deputies.[1] In similar strain, a protest from St. Mathew Parish declared that the signers there had been told that the meeting would petition the king for mercy for Boston " as a child begs a father when he expects correction," and that unless they signed, the Stamp Act would be imposed on them.[2]

The radicals made no effective answer to these apocryphal accounts.[3] A publication of the committee in the *Gazette* of September 21 called attention to the fact that only about one-fifth of the effective men in the parish had signed the Savannah protest; it justified the presence of " transient and inconsiderable persons " at public meetings, and denied that the doors of the tavern had been closed, although acknowledging that several persons had been denied admittance without the knowledge of the committee. These facts were, in any case, non-essential, it was declared, for the great issue was whether Parliament had the right to tax America and whether or not Boston was suffering in the common cause.

The undaunted radicals of St. John's Parish made one

[1] Protests from 123 inhabitants of St. George Parish and from 53 inhabitants of Queensborough and the western district of the parish; *Ga. Gaz.*, Sept. 28, 1774; also *S. C. & Am. Gen. Gaz.*, Oct. 7.

[2] The protest bore 35 signatures to the body of it and 12 others to an addendum; *Ga. Gaz.*, Sept. 2, 1774; also *Ga. Rev. Recs.*, vol. i, pp. 32-34.

[3] Apparently it was left for the patriotic historians writing in after years to discover that the papers of protest had been "placed in the hands of the governors' influential friends and sent in different directions over the country to obtain subscribers, allowing a sum of money to each of those persons proportioned to the number of subscribers they obtained," and that in some instances the number of signers exceeded the population of the parishes or were, in part, recruited from those who had long since passed away. McCall, H., *History of Ga.* (1816) vol. ii, pp. 24 25. For Governor Wright's letters to Dartmouth, stating that the papers of protest had been written by the people themselves, *vide Parliamentary History*, vol. xviii, pp. 141-142.

more effort to secure the election of delegates to the Continental Congress, and passed resolutions that they would join with a majority of the parishes for that purpose. A meeting was held in St. John's Parish on August 30, at which appeared deputies from the parishes of St. George and St. David; and this meager gathering went so far as to nominate a delegate (Dr. Lyman Hall in all probability) to go to the Congress, if the other parishes assented.[1] But that assent was never forthcoming. Georgia was the only one of the thirteen provinces that failed to be represented at the First Continental Congress.

In the period intervening between the appointment of delegates to the Continental Congress in the various provinces and the day of the adjournment of that body, sundry incidents indicated that the activity and influence of the radicals was increasing with the passage of the weeks. In the commercial provinces, the most striking development was the combination of workingmen of two of the chief cities to withhold their labor from the British authorities at Boston. Early in September, 1774, Governor Gage sought to hire Boston workingmen for fortifying Boston Neck, but was met with refusals wherever he turned. The Committee of Mechanics of Boston, learning that the governor would now apply at New York, warned their New York brethren of this fact.[2] Independently of the Boston transactions, the radicals at New York had already begun to bring pressure to bear on labor contractors to prevent the exportation of carpenters to Boston, and upon the merchants to prevent the use of their vessels for the transportation of troops and military stores.[3] The Boston warning

[1] *Pa. Journ.*, Oct. 5, 1774; also *4 Am. Arch.*, vol. i, pp. 766-767.
[2] *N. Y. Journ.*, Sept. 29, 1774; also *4 Am. Arch.*, vol. i, pp. 803-804.
[3] *Ibid.*, vol. i, p. 782; also *N. Y. Journ.*, Sept. 15, 1774.

had the desired effect; and on September 24 the New York Committee of Mechanics gave a unanimous vote of thanks to "those worthy Mechanicks of this city who have declined to aid or assist in the erecting of fortifications on Boston Neck . . ."[1]

Aided by the pressure of the widespread unemployment, Gage was successful, a little later, in getting Boston carpenters and masons to work on barracks for the soldiers for a few days.[2] The apparent change of front caused a joint committee of the selectmen and members of the committee of correspondence on September 24 to vote their opinion that the probable result of such disloyal conduct would be the withholding of contributions from Boston by other provinces.[3] Two days later the workingmen deserted their jobs.[4] In order to seal the labor market of the surrounding country to the British commander, a meeting, composed of the committees of thirteen towns, resolved that, should any inhabitants of Massachusetts or the neighboring provinces supply the troops at Boston " with labour, lumber, joists, spars, pickets, straw, bricks, or any materials whatsoever which may furnish them with requisites to annoy or in any way distress " the citizens, they should be deemed " most inveterate enemies " and ought to be prevented and defeated. The leading towns represented at the meeting appointed " Committees of Observation and Prevention " to enforce the resolves, and the resolves were communicated to every town in the province.[5] The rural towns took heed;

[1] *N. Y. Journ.*, Sept. 29, 1774; also *4 Am. Arch.*, vol. i, pp. 803–804.
[2] *Ibid.*, vol. i, p. 804.
[3] *Ibid.*, vol. i, p. 802; also *Mass. Gaz. & Post-Boy*, Sept. 26, 1774.
[4] *Ibid.*, Oct. 3, 1774; *4 Am. Arch.*, vol. i, pp. 814–815, 820.
[5] The committees in attendance were from Boston, Braintree, Cambridge, Charlestown, Dedham, Dorchester, Malden, Milton, Mystic, Roxbury, Stow, Watertown and Woburn. *Ibid.*, vol. i, pp. 807–808; also *N. Y. Journ.*, Oct. 20, 1774.

and the labor boycott was made effective.¹ The troops did not get into barracks until November, after Gage had sent to Nova Scotia for fifty carpenters and bricklayers and had succeeded in obtaining a few additional ones from New Hampshire through Governor Wentworth's aid.²

Gage was more successful in dealing with merchants. Although the merchants at Philadelphia refused contracts for blankets and other supplies for the troops at Boston, those at New York lent a willing ear. When a mass meeting, called without authority of the " Fifty-One," appointed a committee to intimidate the merchants in question, the transactions were repudiated and denounced by the " Fifty-One," and the merchants completed their orders.³ In the early months of 1775 the same problem arose in slightly different form. Certain persons had been induced to supply the troops at Boston with wagons, entrenching tools and other equipage for field operations. At the request of the committees of Boston and numerous other towns, the provincial congress, then in session, " strongly recommended " that all such persons should be deemed " inveterate enemies to America " and opposed by all reasonable means.⁴

Equally significant during these months was the trend toward violent opposition to the tea duty, noticeable in cer-

---

[1] *E. g.*, the committee of the little town of Rochester, N. H., found Nicholas Austin guilty of acting as a labor contractor for the Boston military. On his knees the culprit was made to pray forgiveness and to pledge for the future that he would never act " contrary to the Constitution of the country." *N. H. Gaz.*, Nov. 11, 1774; also *4 Am. Arch.*, vol. i, p. 974.

[2] *Ibid.*, vol. i, pp. 981, 991–992; *Mass. Gaz. & News-Letter*, Nov. 10, 1774; *N. Y. Gaz.*, Nov. 21.

[3] *Ibid.*, Oct. 3, 1774, also *4 Am. Arch.*, vol. i, pp. 326–327, 809; Colden, *Letter Books*, vol. ii, pp. 366–368.

[4] *Mass. Spy*, Feb. 9, 1775; also *4 Am. Arch.*, vol. i, pp. 1329–1330.

tain portions of the plantation provinces. Although the people had quietly paid the duty since the partial repeal in 1770, the passage of the coercive acts and the attendant excitement in America had wrought a change of opinion; and with the passage of months the lawless element in the community was more and more getting the upper hand. This is best shown in the episode of the brig *Peggy Stewart*.[1] This vessel arrived at Annapolis, Maryland, on Friday, October 14, 1774, laden with more than a ton of dutied tea, consigned to the local firm of T. C. Williams & Company. The *Peggy Stewart* was chiefly owned by Anthony Stewart, of Annapolis, but his father-in-law, James Dick, had a financial interest in the venture. These two gentlemen had achieved unpopularity on a former occasion when, as importers in the *Good Intent*, they had sought to introduce British goods contrary to the will of the people of Annapolis.[2] The orders for the tea had been sent by Williams & Company in May, 1774, at a time when other Maryland merchants were doing the same thing without arousing disfavor.[3] Immediately upon the arrival of the brig, Stewart hastened to pay the duty on the tea. When news of the affair came to the Anne Arundel County Committee a few hours later, they convened a public meeting in the evening to consider what measures should be taken. The consignees and others concerned in the importation were called before the meeting; and it was unanimously

[1] Mr. Richard D. Fisher, of Baltimore, collected the chief source accounts of this episode and published them, with editorial comment, in the *Baltimore News* during the years 1905-1907. A scrapbook of these clippings, entitled *The Arson of the Peggy Stewart*, is in the Library of Congress. Some of the less accessible of these papers have been republished in the *Md. Hist. Mag.*, vol. v, pp. 235-245.

[2] *Vide supra*, pp. 200-201.

[3] *Vide* statement of Joseph and James Williams in *Md. Gaz.*, Oct. 27, 1774; also *supra*, p. 245.

resolved that the tea should not be landed in America. The meeting adjourned to Wednesday, the nineteenth, and for the interim a special committee was appointed to attend the unloading of the other merchandise on board the brig and to prevent the landing of the tea. Thus far the incident did not differ from many similar occurrences. Apparently a concession from the importers to the effect that the tea should be re-shipped at once or, at most, that the tea should be cast into the sea would close the incident. Stewart sought to explain his action in paying the duty, in a broadside on Monday, in which he told of the leaky condition of the vessel, the need of the fifty-three souls on board to land after a three months' voyage, and the impossibility of entering the vessel without the tea. He expressed his sorrow for his unintentional transgression.

From the viewpoint of the orderly elements in the community, the postponement of final action until the public meeting of Wednesday proved to be a tactical blunder. During the interval handbills were dispersed through the nearby counties containing notice of the meeting, and popular feeling was aroused to a high pitch. To the meeting on Wednesday came parties of extremists from various parts of the province determined upon violence: one group from Prince George's County, headed by Walter Bowie (or Buior), a planter; one from Baltimore County, led by Charles Ridgely, Jr., member of the Assembly; one from the town of Baltimore, led by Mordecai Gist and John Deavor; one from the head of Severn River, led by Rezen Hammond; and two from Elk Ridge in Anne Arundel County, headed respectively by Dr. Ephraim Howard and Dr. Warfield.[1] When the great assemblage were ready

[1] Affidavit of R. Caldeleugh, manager of Stewart's rope factory; *Md. Hist. Mag.*, vol. v, pp. 241-244. *Cf.* Galloway's account; *Pa. Mag.*, vol. xxv, pp. 248-253.

for business, Stewart and the Williamses appeared before them with an offer to destroy the tea and to make such other amends as might be desired. The Anne Arundel Committee advised the meeting that this offer should be deemed sufficient; but the boisterous minority in attendance would not have it that way. "Matters now began to run very high and the people to get warm," declared a participant later; "some of the Gentlemen from Elk Ridge and Baltimore Town insisted on burning the Vessel" as well as the tea.[1] Charles Carroll, the barrister, and Matthias Hammond proposed, as a compromise, that the tea should be unloaded and burnt under the gallows; but the extremists were beyond halfway measures. "Old Mr. Dick," one of the owners of the brig and the father of Stewart's wife, now gave his consent to the destruction of the vessel, for fear that the rage of the mob would be directed against the Stewart home where Mrs. Stewart lay in a critical condition. "Mr. Quyn then stood forth," averred the observer already quoted, "and said it was not the sense of the majority of the people that the Vessell should be destroyed, and made a motion which was seconded that there should be a vote on the Question. We had a Vote on it and a Majority of ⅞ of the people; still the few that was for destroying the Brigg was Clamorous and insinuated that if it was not done they would prejudice Mr. Stewart more than if the vessel was burnt; the Committee then with the Consent of Mr. Dick declared that the Vessell and Tea

[1] Galloway's account. "Americanus" declared in the London *Public Ledger*, Jan. 4, 1775, that the bitter feeling against the principals in the affair was caused by Stewart's earlier activity in opposing the resolution for the suspension of debt collections, and by the jealousy of other merchants because Williams & Co. had a splendid assortment of merchandise on board. These charges do not bear close examination. The Anne Arundel County Committee stigmatized them as "false, scandalous and malicious." *Md. Gaz.* (Annapolis), Apr. 13, 1775.

should be burnt."[1] Stewart and the consignees made a written acknowledgment of their "most daring insult."

While preparations were being made for burning the vessel, many of the substantial inhabitants began to believe that undue weight had been given to the threats of the violent minority, and determined to prevent the injustice; but as they were going to the waterfront, they were met by "poor Mr. Dick," who entreated them "for God sake not to meddle in the matter" or Mr. Stewart's house would be burnt, which would be a greater loss. The other program was therefore duly carried out; and the *Peggy Stewart*, with sails and colors flying, was consumed in the presence of a great crowd of spectators. "This most infamous and rascally affair . . . ," commented the observer quoted before, "makes all men of property reflect with horror on their present situation to have their lives and propertys at the disposal & mercy of a Mob . . ."

Such an incident could scarcely have occurred six months, or even three months, earlier in a plantation province. The truth was that the leaders of an orderly opposition to British measures were losing their mastery of the situation. The destruction of the *Peggy Stewart* involved a monetary loss of £1896 to owners and consignees. The public meeting had, in effect, refused to accept as adequate an act of destruction similar to that which had served to make the Boston Tea Party heinous in the eyes of the British home government. That the act was forced by an ungovernable minority subtracts in no degree from the seriousness or significance of the incident. In a word, Annapolis had out-Bostoned Boston.

[1] That this decision was forced by an aggressive minority is also apparent from other contemporary accounts, *e. g.*: Eddis, *Letters from America*, no. xviii; Ringgold's account in *Pa. Mag.*, vol. xxv, pp. 253-254; letter from Annapolis in *London Chronicle*, Dec. 31, 1774. The ingeniously-worded official account does not deny it. *4 Am. Arch.*, vol. i, pp. 885-886.

CHAPTER X

THE ADOPTION OF THE CONTINENTAL ASSOCIATION
(SEPTEMBER–OCTOBER, 1774)

THE First Continental Congress was the product of many minds. More than any other occurrence of the eventful decade, the movement for an interprovincial congress was of spontaneous origin. When the time was ripe, the thought seemed to leap from the minds of men with the thrill of an irresistible conclusion. It would be misleading to give Providence, Rhode Island, the credit of originating the idea, simply because the town meeting there proposed a continental congress four days before the Philadelphia Committee, six days before the New York Committee, and ten days before the dissolved burgesses of Virginia. All these proposals were antedated by suggestions in private letters and by a newspaper propaganda to the same end;[1] and all advocates drew their inspiration from a common source—the logic of the times.

In its inception the project of a general congress was favored — and feared — by all shades of opinion, governmental and non-governmental, conservative, moderate and radical, mercantile and non-mercantile. Governor Franklin and "many of the Friends of Government" in New Jersey approved of such a congress if it should be authorized by the Crown and be composed of governors and selected members of the provincial legislatures.[2] Joseph Galloway

[1] For a summary of newspaper writings in support of a general congress, vide Frothingham, *Rise of Republic*, pp. 314, 329, 331-333 n.
[2] *1 N. J. Arch.*, vol. x, pp. 464-465.

wanted a congress consisting preferably of delegates " chosen either by the Representatives in Assembly or by them in Convention." [1] Both men desired to forestall a resort to lawless action and to have the relations of the mother country and the colonies defined in enlightened terms. Many conservatives of Massachusetts believed that a general congress would be " eminently serviceable " in prevailing upon the Bostonians to make restitution to the East India Company and in formulating a plan of permanent conciliation; " Tories as well as whigs bade the delegates God speed." [2] The Rhode Island legislators and the Virginians meeting at Raleigh Tavern appeared to have in mind a permanent union of the provinces in annual congresses, chosen by the several legislatures, for the sake of the common concerns. The merchants of New York and Philadelphia wanted a congress, constituted upon almost any principle, in order to postpone or prevent the adoption of a plan of non-intercourse, and in order to effect a uniform and lenient plan in case non-intercourse could not be prevented. Dickinson advocated a congress, elected by assemblies wherever possible, for the purpose of formulating a uniform boycott against England and avoiding the dreadful necessity of war.[3] Sam Adams rendered lip-service to the cause of a congress, but strained every energy to committing the continent to a radical program before the body could assemble.[4] Silas Deane criticized the premature activity of Adams and favored a congress as a preventive of " narrow partial and indigested " plans of action.[5]

On the other hand, Governor Franklin in June feared

[1] 4 *Am. Arch.*, vol. i, pp. 485-486.
[2] " Massachusettensis " in *Mass. Gaz. & Post-Boy*, Mch. 27, 1775.
[3] *Pa. Journ.*, June 15, 1774; also *Writings* (Ford), vol. i, pp. 499-500.
[4] *Writings* (Cushing), vol. iii, pp. 114-116, 125-127.
[5] *Conn. Hist. Soc. Colls.*, vol. ii, pp. 129-130.

"the Consequences which may result from such a Congress as is now intended in America, chosen by the Assemblies, or by Committees from all the several Counties, in each of the Provinces;"[1] while, conversely, the radical, Josiah Quincy, warned Dickinson two months later that: "Corruption (which delay gives time to operate) is the destroying angel we have most to fear. . . . I fear much that timid or lukewarm counsels will be considered by our Congress as prudent and politic."[2] And Governor Gage, of Massachusetts, writing at almost the same moment as Governor Franklin, inclined to the opinion of Quincy when he said: "I believe a Congress, of some sort, may be obtained; but when or how it will be composed is yet at a distance, and after all, Boston may get little more than fair words."[3]

The original idea of the New England radicals seems to have been for "a congress of the Merchants, by deputies from among them in every seaport town, . . . with power to establish a plan for the whole . . ."[4] Paul Revere, after a fortnight's trip through the commercial provinces, reported a sentiment in favor of a congress, so constituted, in order to place a restriction on the trade to the West Indies.[5] When the widespread demand seemed to call for an assemblage of a more general character, the Boston Committee of Correspondence suggested that: "There must be both a political and commercial congress."[6]

[1] *1 N. J. Arch.*, vol. x, pp. 464-465.
[2] *4 Am. Arch.*, vol. i, p. 725.
[3] *Ibid.*, vol. i, p. 451.
[4] Letter of Boston Committee of Correspondence to Providence Committee of Correspondence, May 21, 1774; *Bos. Com. Cor. Mss.*, vol. x, pp. 796-798.
[5] *Mass. Spy*, June 2, 1774.
[6] *Bos. Com. Cor. Mss.*, vol. x, pp. 796-798.

This quickly proved to be unfeasible; and the *Massachusetts Spy* declared on June 16, 1774: "A POLITICO-MERCANTILE CONGRESS seems now to be the voice of all the Colonies from Nova-Scotia to Georgia; and New York the place of meeting proposed by private letters: However, our generous brethren of that metropolis are pleased to complement Boston with the appointment both of time and place; which invitation will undoubtedly be accepted with grateful alacrity." On the very next day, the Massachusetts House of Representatives acted with the promised "alacrity." While the secretary of the province read the governor's proclamation of dissolution to a curious audience on the wrong side of the locked door, the house chose delegates to the Congress and announced the place of meeting to be Philadelphia on September 1.[1] Already on June 15 the Rhode Island Assembly had appointed delegates; and in the subsequent weeks every province of the thirteen designated representatives, in one fashion or other, except Georgia.[2]

What was to be the program of the Congress when it met? The answer to the question depended upon a proper evaluation of a number of factors, principally the following: the instructions given to the members-elect of the Congress; the crystallization of public opinion in the period prior to the assembling of that body; the character and temper of the members and of the interests functioning through them; the steeplechase of ultimatum and concession which was certain to occur after the Congress had assembled.

Although the instructions of the delegates obviously had a bearing on the action of Congress, it would be misleading to ascribe to these papers any commanding importance;

[1] *Mass. Spy*, June 23, 1774; also *4 Am. Arch.*, vol. i, pp. 421-423.
[2] *Vide supra*, chapters viii and ix, *passim*.

for the instructions represented not so much what the dominant elements in a community really wanted, as what they dared to say that they wanted. These instructions had originated in divers ways, although in almost every instance they had been issued by the body which had chosen the delegates.[1] The keynote of all instructions was the injunction that the delegates should adopt proper measures to extricate the colonies from their difficulties with the mother nation, and that they should establish American rights and liberties upon a just and permanent basis and so restore harmony and union. Some difference of opinion was apparent concerning the nature and extent of the colonial grievances which should be redressed. About half the provinces deemed these too patent, or the occasion premature, for a particular definition of them in the instructions.

The other provinces were unanimous in naming parliamentary taxation of the colonies as a grievance, and almost without exception they included the punitive acts of 1774, particularly the Boston Port Act.[2] The Pennsylvania convention had gone so far as to suggest the maximum con-

[1] In Massachusetts, Rhode Island and Connecticut, the lower house of the legislatures gave the instructions. In New Hampshire, New Jersey, Delaware, Maryland, Virginia and North Carolina, provincial conventions were responsible for the instructions. Both kinds of bodies participated in South Carolina and Pennsylvania. In the province of New York, the delegates were uninstructed in the technical sense of the term, but a majority of them had been forced to announce their platform in response to popular pressure. All the instructions may be found in *4 Am. Arch.*, vol. i. Consult index under name of the province desired.

[2] Virginia, Delaware and the Pennsylvania convention added the revived statute of Henry VIII and the extension of the powers of the admiralty courts. South Carolina included the "unnecessary restraints and burthens on trade" and the statutes and royal instructions which made invidious distinctions between subjects in Great Britain and in America; Delaware, the curtailing of manufacturing; and the Pennsylvania convention, the quartering of troops.

cessions which Congress should make in return for the favors desired, *i. e.*, the settlement of an annual revenue on the king and the reimbursement of the East India Company.

The widest divergence of opinion appeared on the important point of the nature of the opposition which should be directed against Great Britain. Most of the commercial provinces instructed their delegates to adopt " proper " or " prudent " or " lawful " measures without specifying further details.[1] New Jersey and Delaware, provinces largely agricultural in their economy, were the only ones of the group to recommend a plan of non-importation and non-exportation to Congress. In contrast to the commercial provinces, three of the four planting provinces that took action instructed their delegates for a non-importation and non-exportation with Great Britain.[2]

If the absence of such instructions in the northern provinces suggested the dominance of the business motive in that section, the form of the boycott plan proposed in various parts of the South revealed the presence of powerful agricultural interests there. The instructions to the Maryland delegates carefully specified that that province would not withhold the exportation of tobacco unless Virginia and North Carolina did so at the same time. By the Virginia instructions, the delegates were told unconditionally that non-exportation must not become operative be-

[1] There were unimportant exceptions. The New York delegates had been maneuvered into avowing a present inclination toward a non-importation regulation. The Pennsylvania Assembly had refused to give detailed instructions; but the provincial convention had recommended the sending of petitions as a first resort, and had intimated that Pennsylvania would, under no circumstances, go further than a non-importation and non-exportation with Great Britain, unless Parliament should adopt further measures of aggression.

[2] Md., Va., N. C. South Carolina was silent on this point.

fore August 10, 1775, because that date would "avoid the heavy injury that would arise to this country from an earlier adoption of the non-exportation plan after the people have already applied so much of their labour to the perfecting of the present [tobacco] crop . . ."[1] Probably from a similar motive, the North Carolina delegates were instructed to delay the operation of non-exportation until October 1, 1775, if possible. Virginia wished the non-importation to become effective on November 1, 1774; North Carolina preferred January 1, 1775. The instructions of the South Carolina delegates observed a discreet silence as to the adoption of a boycott plan; but the rice planters had safeguarded their interests by inserting a provision pledging the province only to such measures of the Congress as commanded the support of the South Carolina delegates as well as the majority of Congress.

A closer scrutiny of the several sets of instructions would only serve to enforce the conclusion that, although the plantation provinces stood rather clearly for a two-edged plan of commercial opposition, the instructions of no province contemplated a comprehensive and skilfully articulated plan such as the Continental Association turned out to be. Every province, touching on the matter, specifically limited the proposed suspension of trade to Great Britain, except Maryland and New Jersey. Only Maryland authorized her delegates to agree to "any restrictions upon exports to the West Indies which may be deemed necessary by a majority of the Colonies at the general Congress."

[1] This instruction provoked a writer in the commercial provinces to query whether this restraint did not tend to render Congress totally ineffective, inasmuch as every province had an equal right to safeguard its material interests; thus Pennsylvania, the importation of cloth, New York, the importation of hats and tea, New England, the importation of flannels, calicoes, *etc.* *Pa. Journ.*, Sept. 28, 1774; also 4 *Am. Arch.*, vol. i, pp. 755-756.

The scope, the symmetry, the enforcement provisions of the Continental Association clearly did not proceed from the instructions of the delegates.

The development of public opinion in the interval between the giving of instructions and the assembling of Congress marked a long stride in advance of the views embodied in the instructions. The direction of the gathering opinion was influenced, to some degree, by correspondents in London, both of native and colonial birth, many of whose letters appeared in the colonial press and all of whom argued that the hard times then prevailing in England made some form of trade suspension the logical mode of opposition.[1] To a larger degree, the public mind was influenced by the trenchant articles with which the propagandists filled the newspapers. As one newspaper writer phrased it: " The Delegates must certainly desire to know the mind of the country in general. No rational man will think himself so well acquainted with our affairs as that he cannot have a more full and better view of them." The questions which would confront Congress, the same writer declared, were chiefly the following: In what manner and in what spirit shall we make our application to Great Britain? " Shall we stop importation only, or shall we cease exportation also? Shall this extend only to Great Britain and Ireland, or shall it comprehend the West India Islands? At what time shall this cessation begin? Shall we stop trade till we obtain what we think reasonable and which shall secure us for time to come; or shall it be only till we obtain relief in those particulars which now oppress us? Shall we first apply for relief and wait for an answer be-

---

[1] *E. g., vide* letters in *Pa. Gaz.*, May 18, June 1, Aug. 10, 1774; *N. H. Gaz.*, May 26, 1775; *Mass. Spy*, May 12, 1774. *Vide* also Dr. Franklin's letters to Cushing, Thomson, Timothy and others in his *Writings* (Smyth), vol. vi, pp. 238-244, 249-251, 303-311; vol. x, pp. 274-275.

fore we stop trade, or shall we stop trade while we are making application?" In what manner ought we to offer to bear our proper share of the public expenses? Shall we offer to pay for the tea that was destroyed?[1]

Press discussion occupied itself very largely with the problems of commercial warfare here presented. "A Distressed Bostonian" noted a general disposition to oppose the oppressive measures of the home government; but, he added acutely: "We are variously affected, and as each feels himself more or less distres'd he is proportionately warm or cool in the opposition."[2] A few typical extracts will indicate the trend of newspaper discussion. "A Letter from a Virginian to the Members of the Congress" entreated the delegates to avoid all forms of the boycott, reminding them that the resources of the mother country were infinite, and asking: "Shall we punish ourselves, like froward Children, who refuse to eat when they are hungry, that they may vex their indulgent Mothers? . . . We may teize the Mother Country, we cannot ruin her."[3] "A Citizen of Philadelphia" took a slightly more advanced view.

---

[1] *N. Y. Journ.*, Aug. 4, 1774; also *4 Am. Arch.*, vol. i, pp. 634-637.

[2] *Bos. Eve. Post*, Sept. 5, 1774. A writer in the *Pa. Journ.*, Sept. 28, 1774, expanded the same thought in these words: "The farmer, who insists that the dry goods merchant shall cease to import, though the measure should even deprive him of bread; and yet, through fear of some frivolous loss to himself, very wisely protests against non-exportation, certainly merits the utmost contempt. Nor does the farmer, in this case, stand alone. The miller lays claim to public spirit; talks loudly for liberty; and also insists upon a non-importation; and in order to enforce the scheme upon the merchant, will readily agree to a general non-consumption; but no sooner is non-exportation sounded in his ear, than his mighty public spirit, like Milton's devils at their Pandemonium consultation is instantly dwarfed. 'My interest, sir! I cannot part with that! Alas! if a general non-exportation takes place, what shall I do with my mill?'"

[3] *N. Y. Gaz.*, Aug. 22, 1774.

He proclaimed himself in favor of a general non-importation with England; but he roundly condemned a non-exportation as a weapon which would inflict "a more deadly wound" on America than on England, and he opposed a suspension of trade with the West Indies as a punishment to a people who were innocent of wrong-doing.[1] "Juba" addressed himself to "The honourable Delegates," who were soon to convene in Congress, and advocated a non-importation and non-exportation agreement which included Great Britain, Ireland and the West Indies in its operation. "I know many objections to a plan of this kind will be started by self-interested men," he declared, "but is this a time for us to think of accumulating fortunes, or even adding to our estates?"[2]

A comprehensive plan of trade suspension, such as was advocated by "Juba," was urged on the colonists by many American sympathizers in Great Britain,[3] and received the widest newspaper support in the colonies, although it had received no sanction in any of the instructions to members-elect of Congress. The realization dawned upon the radical writers that the coercive operation of the measures adopted should be speedy and far-reaching, notwithstanding the severe blow to colonial trading interests and the personal guiltlessness of the populations affected. By withdrawing American exports from Great Britain, it was estimated that the public revenue would be reduced nearly one million pounds sterling per annum, about half of which sum arose from the single article of tobacco.[4] Indeed, "the

[1] *Pa. Packet*, June 20, 27, 1774; also *N. Y. Gaz.*, June 27, July 4.

[2] *N. Y. Gazetteer*, Sept. 2, 1774; also 4 *Am. Arch.*, vol. i, pp. 754-755.

[3] E. g., vide anonymous letters printed in *Pa. Journ.*, Sept. 14, 21, 1774; *Pa. Gaz.*, Sept. 21; *Mass. Spy*, June 2; *Md. Gaz.*, May 26.

[4] "To the People of America" (Boston, Sept., 1774), in 4 *Am. Arch.*, vol. i, pp. 756-759. *Vide* also *Mass. Spy*, Mch. 23, 1775.

shipping, manufactures and revenue [of England] depend so much on the Tobacco and Carolina Colonies that they alone, by stopping their exports, would force redress." [1] The want of American naval stores, particularly pitch, tar and turpentine, would also be felt in England immediately.[2] By stopping the exportation of colonial flaxseed to Ireland, the linen manufacturers of England would be deprived of their raw material and more than three hundred thousand employees thrown out of work.[3]

The design of stopping all trade with the West Indies was even a bolder conception, because of the basic importance of that branch of commerce to American business prosperity. The plan derived its inspiration from the fact that more than seventy members of Parliament owned plantations in the West Indies and they thus exposed an Achilles-heel to the darts of the Americans. " Suspending our trade with the West Indies," declared one writer, " will ruin every plantation there. They can neither feed their negroes without our corn nor save their crops without our lumber. A stoppage of North American supplies will bring on a famine and scarcity too ruinous to be risked without the most stupid madness." [4] " If the West India Planters, who have great influence in Parliament," said another, " are content to see their estates ruined, and their slaves perish, if they will quietly resign these their possessions, *let it be*, and let the crime be added to the enormous account

[1] *4 Am. Arch.*, vol. i, pp. 237-238.

[2] Unsigned letter (probably of Dr. Franklin) in *Mass. Gaz. & Post-Boy*, Oct. 24, 1774; also *4 Am. Arch.*, vol. i, pp. 701-702.

[3] *Ibid.*, vol. i, pp. 756-759.

[4] " To the People of America," *ibid.*, vol. i, pp. 756-759. *Vide* also letter to Bos. Com. Cor., *ibid.*, p. 347; "Queries," *ibid.*, p. 755; "Camillus" in *N. H. Gaz.*, Aug. 5, 1774; " Plain Dealer " in *N. Y. Journ.*, July 21; "A Country Man" in *ibid.*, Dec. 15.

of the British Parliament." [1] "There will be opposers to this scheme even among our friends (*self-interest is strong*)," he added. " I know it requires a great sacrifice to stop trade to the West Indies. . . . But *I see no justice that the merchant trading to Great Britain should be the only sufferer, the West-India merchant ought to suffer also*, and especially when his sufferings will absolutely work the most forceably." A third writer recalled a long-rankling grievance of the Americans against the West India planting element. No less than seventy-four members of Parliament " are West India planters and proprietors," he declared. "And I am also credibly informed that they were the means of fomenting these difficulties by first getting [in 1764] a duty laid on all sugars, molasses, coffee, &c., not imported from the English West-India Islands; it will therefore be necessary to shew them of how much importance we are, by distressing them for want of our trade." [2]

An animated discussion occurred over the question whether remittances should be withheld from the British merchants as well as trade connections. If we liquidate our annual indebtedness of £3,000,000 sterling as usual, queried "A Plain Dealer," will the British merchants not be enabled thereby to employ the manufacturers for one whole year after importation has ceased, a period during which our measures will be felt only by ourselves? [3] While conceding the theoretical injustice involved in a refusal to pay debts, a Philadelphia writer contended that the case under consideration was an exception to the rule; for, if two neighbors shared a lifelong friendship and one of them took it into his head to kidnap and enslave the child of the

---

[1] "A Distressed Bostonian," *Bos. Eve. Post*, Sept. 5, 1774.
[2] *Mass. Spy*, Aug. 25, 1774, quoting from *Conn. Gaz.*
[3] *N. Y. Journ.*, July 21, 1774.

other at a time when the other owed him money, would it be unjust for the debtor to withhold payment until the child was returned? He concluded that, though Britain had a demand of debt against the colonists, the Americans had a demand of a different nature, but superior in value. against her; and that when Britain granted "liberty, peace and a free trade," the colonists should repay their debts."[1] The opponents of non-remittance held that it was a dishonorable expedient and not necessary under the circumstances. Indeed, a "Citizen of Philadelphia" believed that, if the colonists should suspend the payment of their debts, the British merchants would retaliate and influence Parliament to stop all trade connections between American ports and Europe in order to prevent trade with foreign nations from being carried on on capital properly theirs.[2]

As John Adams and his brother delegates of Massachusetts traveled the irksome distance from Boston to the meeting-place of the Continental Congress at Philadelphia in the latter weeks of August, they received first-hand evidence of the accelerated progress of popular sentiment toward extreme measures of boycott, and learned better than through correspondence the character of the opposition elements in other provinces. Upon his arrival at Hartford, Adams had a talk with Silas Deane and his step-sons who had come over from Wethersfield to greet the Massachusetts delegates; and though these men were "largely in trade," they announced that they were "willing to renounce all their trade," Deane declaring that the resolutions of Congress would be regarded in Connecticut as "the laws of the Medes and Persians."[3] Stopping at

---

[1] *Pa. Journ.*, Sept. 28, 1774; also *4 Am. Arch.*, vol. i, pp. 811-814.

[2] "A Few Political Reflections," *Pa. Packet*, June 27, 1774; also *N. Y. Gaz.*, July 4.

[3] Adams, J., *Works* (Adams), vol. ii, p. 341.

Middletown, the members of the local committee of correspondence and many other persons assured the delegates that "they would abide by whatever should be determined on, even to a total stoppage of trade to Europe and the West Indies."[1] Reaching New Haven, a chief trading town of Connecticut, the chorus of approval was marred by a false note or two. In one discussion some serious doubts were cast upon the coercive effect of a total non-exportation to the West Indies, even if well executed; while from another source Adams was informed that a boycott agreement would serve no good purpose because Congress would lack power to enforce it. He learned from the tavern keeper that the fine parade which had greeted the delegates seven miles from the city on their arrival had been contrived at the last moment by the moderates " in order to divert the populace from erecting a liberty pole, &c."[2]

Arriving in due time in New York city, the delegates lingered nearly a week, sightseeing and "breakfasting, dining, drinking coffee, &c.," amidst "all the opulence and splendor" of that city. Much of this time was spent in the company of McDougall, John Morin Scott, Isaac Sears and other radicals, from whom Adams gained much intimate knowledge of the local political situation. McDougall warned the Massachusetts delegates to moderate their language in order not to frighten the timorous elements there that had combined, from various motives, in support of the Congress.[3] While the visiting delegates were yet in

[1] Adams, J., *Works* (Adams), vol. ii, p. 342.

[2] *Ibid.*, vol. ii, p. 344.

[3] These groups, McDougall reported, were chiefly the following: those men who had been induced to join the movement by assurances that commercial coercion would secure relief without any danger of civil commotions; those who were fearful "lest the levelling spirit of the

the city, the "Fifty-One" held a session to discuss the business of the approaching Congress for the benefit of the New York delegates. Three of the latter attended; and a very clear intimation was given that the best course would be for Congress to recommend to the Bostonians to reimburse the East India Company and that America should then return to a non-importation of dutied goods; but should they be reduced to the "last sad alternative of entering into a non-importation agreement," then it should not be a partial one as before, but should include every European commodity from all parts of the world.[1] Whether or not this measured advice reached the ears of John Adams he does not record in his diary; and he probably lost his best opportunity of hearing of it a few nights later when the "Fifty-One" dined the Massachusetts delegates with "a profusion of rich dishes, &c., &c.," and Adams spent the evening talking shop with James Duane, the lawyer of the "sly, surveying eye."

When the Massachusetts delegation rode into Philadelphia on Monday, August 29, "dirty, dusty, and fatigued," they found a score or more of the delegates already gathered in the city. The few days intervening before the opening of Congress were spent by the waiting delegates in meeting and appraising each other and in comparing notes as to recent political developments in various parts of America.[2] Of the fifty-six delegates who eventually ap-

New England Colonies should propagate itself into New York;" those who entertained "Episcopalian prejudices" against New England; "merchants largely concerned in navigation, and therefore afraid of non-importation, non-consumption, and non-exportation agreements;" and those who looked to the government for favors. Adams, J., *Works* (Adams), vol. ii, pp. 345-355.

[1] *N. Y. Gazetteer*, Sept. 2, 1774; also *4 Am. Arch.*, vol. i, p. 324 n.

[2] Adams, J., *Works* (Adams), vol. ii, pp. 357-364; *N. Y. Hist. Soc. Colls.*, vol. xix, pp. 12-19.

peared from the twelve provinces, most of the men met for the first time.[1] A large proportion of them had taken active part in the popular house of the provincial legislatures;[2] six of them had served in the Stamp Act Congress; practically all of them were members of committees of correspondence. All of them were of American nativity; and they must have felt a responsibility almost personal for the critical situation in which America found herself. As leaders of local movements for larger colonial rights and exemptions in the preceding years, their names were, for the most part, well known to each other. Their present intentions, however, were a matter for conjecture and apprehension.

Friends and foes of the Congress alike appreciated the difficulties of the situation. "An assembly like this," wrote the Connecticut delegates, " though it consists of less than sixty members, yet, coming from remote Colonies, each of which has some modes of transacting public business peculiar to itself,—some particular Provincial rights and interests to guard and secure, must take some time to become

---

[1] John Dickinson, who had earlier been excluded from election through the efforts of Galloway, took his seat on October 17. Prior to this time, however, Dickinson was in close touch with the delegates in small dinner-groups and in other informal ways; *e. g., vide* Adams, J., *Works* (Adams), vol. ii, pp. 360, 363, 379, 381, 382, 386, 397. James Bowdoin, of Massachusetts, had refused his election at the hands of the Assembly, because his relatives thought his great fortune ought not to be hazarded. Hazelton, *Decl. of Inde.*, p. 9; *Hibernian Chronicle* (London), October 27, 1774. William Samuel Johnson, of Connecticut, had declined his appointment on the ground of an important law case which required his attendance at Albany, an excuse which produced no end of skeptical comment. *4 Am. Arch.*, vol. i, p. 895; *Conn. Cour.*, Aug. 2, 1774; *Journals Cont. Cong.* (L. C. Edition), vol. i, p. 18 n. Wolcott and Law, of the same province, had also declined, pleading poor health.

[2] Forty of them had served in provincial legislatures, ten or more of them in the speakership.

so acquainted with each one's situations and connections, as to be able to give an united assent to the ways and means proposed for effecting what all are ardently desirous of . . . Every one must be heard even on those points or subjects which in themselves are not of the last importance; and indeed, it often happens that what is of little or no consequence to one Colony is of the last to another." [1] In this Congress, affirmed John Adams, " is a diversity of religions, educations, manners, interests, such as it would seem impossible to unite in one plan of conduct." [2]

The delegates from the plantation provinces were, as we have seen, for the most part instructed to push for a limited non-importation and non-exportation agreement; and the rising tide of radical feeling in the North, as indicated in the newspapers, gave promise that many delegates from that section would also join in the movement. Indeed, considering that only eleven delegates in the whole Congress were merchants and these, for the most part, men more addicted to politics than to trade, some plan of non-importation and non-exportation was the inevitable outcome of the Congress. The agricultural interests clearly possessed the controlling influence; but it is impossible to give precise figures, for one-half of the membership were content to

[1] *4 Am. Arch.*, vol. i, pp. 854-855.
[2] Adams, J., *Works* (Adams), vol. ix, pp. 346-348. *Vide* also Ward's view, in Staples, *R. I. in Cont. Cong.*, pp. 16-17. A comment of an unfriendly observer (probably William Kelly, the New York merchant) is not without significance in this connection. After predicting that the Congress would end in confusion, he wrote: " My Reasons for thinking so are, that Men, 1500 Miles asunder, have very different Interests; that there will be near a Hundred Deputies assembled, most of which being Merchants, Shopkeepers, and Attornies, the latter of them will certainly rule, for no Men are so true to their own Interest as Lawyers, for they will not stick at any Thing in prosecuting their Interest." He proposed that the ministry should bribe some of the leading lawyers! *London Gazetteer*, Sept. 28, 1774; also *S. C. Gaz.*, Dec. 5.

classify themselves as lawyers although frequently their incomes were derived in large part, if not chiefly, from agricultural holdings.[1] The ultimate conscious object of the boycotters in Congress was not merely the repeal of the punitive acts of 1774 but the goal that had formerly been so dear to the merchant class—a return to the conditions of the years before 1763. Within the ranks of this group there was a clear understanding of the economic interests endangered by a suspension of trade and a willingness, on the part of many of them, to shift the anticipated losses on their brethren in the other provinces.

The chief danger to the adoption of a plan of continental non-intercourse came from a determined and plausible group of moderates, led by Joseph Galloway, who insisted that the only permanent relief was to be found in an enlightened definition of imperial relations and colonial liberties in the form of a plan of union. This group saw in commercial coercion only a source of irritation to Great Britain, and wagered their faith on memorializing and petitioning. Galloway averred, somewhat unjustly, that the men who favored his plan of union " were men of loyal principles, and possessed of the greatest fortunes in America; the other were congregational and presbyterian republicans, or men of bankrupt fortunes, overwhelmed in debt to the British merchants." [2]

The first three weeks of the meeting of the Continental Congress might furnish an object-lesson for the skilled parliamentarian of any age.[3] " We [Massachusetts delegates]

[1] *E. g.*, Sullivan of N. H., Dickinson of Pa., Henry of Va. and the Rutledges of S. C.

[2] *Historical and Political Reflections on the Rise and Progress of the American Rebellion* (London, 1780), pp. 66-67.

[3] The sources of information for the proceedings of the First Continental Congress are meager, however. They are contained in: *Journals of the Continental Congress* (L. C. Edition), vol. i; John Adams's notes,

have had numberless prejudices to remove here," wrote John Adams on September 27. " We have been obliged to act with great delicacy and caution. We have been obliged to keep ourselves out of sight, and to feel pulses and sound the depths; to insinuate our sentiments, designs, and desires, by means of other persons; sometimes of one Province, and sometimes of another." [1] Sam Adams found himself in his element. " He eats little, drinks little, sleeps little, thinks much and is most decisive and indefatigable in the pursuit of his objects," declared the organizing spirit of the opposite party.[2]

The first test of strength between the groups came on the very first day of meeting, Monday, September 5, when Congress refused the invitation, tendered by Galloway, to meet in the State House and, in face of negative votes from Pennsylvania and New York, resolved to hold their sessions in Carpenters' Hall, a decision naturally " highly agreeable to the mechanics and citizens in general." [3] Congress then proceeded to the unanimous election of Charles Thomson as secretary, much to the surprise of Galloway who deemed him " one of the most violent Sons of Liberty (so called) in America," and contrary to the expressed desires of Jay and Duane.[4] Both measures, according to Galloway, had

Works (Adams), vol. ii, pp. 365-402; Samuel Ward's diary, in *Mag. Am. Hist.*, vol. i, 438-442, 503-506, 549-561; certain pamphlets of Joseph Galloway; the correspondence of the members; and a few contemporary pamphlets and newspaper articles. On the whole, the pledge of secrecy was excellently observed.

[1] *Works* (Adams), vol. ii, p. 382 n. *Vide* also *ibid.*, vol. ii, p. 391 n.; vol. ix, pp. 342-346.

[2] Galloway, *Reflections*, pp. 66-67.

[3] *Conn. Hist. Soc. Colls.*, vol. ii, p. 172; Adams, J., *Works* (Adams), vol. ii, p. 365.

[4] *1 N. J. Arch.*, vol. x, pp. 477-478; Adams, *Works* (Adams), vol. ii, p. 365. Adams dubbed Thomson "the Sam Adams of Philadelphia." *Ibid.*, p. 358.

been "privately settled by an Interest made out of Doors." Peyton Randolph, of Virginia, late Speaker of the House of Burgesses, was chosen president without opposition.

For the next few weeks the proceedings assumed an appearance of "flattering tranquillity," as Galloway put it. The radicals were biding their time;[1] and meanwhile the members established a rule of secrecy (except upon occasion when Congress should direct otherwise), and agreed that the delegates of each province should cast one vote collectively. Both regulations later served the purposes of the radicals by giving to the proceedings a false appearance of unanimity. The unit rule made it possible to publish resolutions as having passed unanimously, even when large minorities in various delegations, amounting sometimes to one-third of the total membership of Congress, were in the negative.[2]

The first committee appointed by the Continental Congress was one to state the rights and grievances of the colonies and propose the best means of obtaining redress; and on the same day another committee was named "to examine and report the several Statutes which affect the Trade and Manufactures of the Colonies." The second committee submitted its report ten days later, when it was thought proper that the report should be referred to the former committee for further consideration and action.[3] But before the committee on rights and redress had submitted its report, Congress had already taken the definite steps which established the policy of trade coercion.

The radicals threw off their mask on September 17, when they carried through a vote endorsing a set of resolutions

[1] Galloway, *Reflections*, pp. 66-67; Cooper, *What Think Ye of Congress Now?* (New York, 1775), p. 13.

[2] Galloway, *Examination* (London, 1780), p. 61.

[3] *Journals Cont. Cong.* (L. C. Edition), vol. i, pp. 25-29, 40-41, 63-73. All later references to the *Journals* are to this edition.

adopted by a convention of Suffolk County in Massachusetts. This step was, according to Galloway, a "complete declaration of war" on the part of the "republicans."[1] The "Suffolk Resolves" rejected the recent legislation against Massachusetts as unconstitutional and void, and called for a civil government to be organized by the people and for the establishment of a militia for defensive purposes. Furthermore, the fourteenth resolve declared that, as a measure for obtaining redress, the people of Suffolk County (and the same action was recommended to the other counties) would "withhold all commercial intercourse with Great Britain, Ireland and the West Indies" and enter into a non-consumption of British and East India wares, subject to such alterations as Congress might make.[2] By endorsing these resolutions, Congress, among other things, committed itself to the principle of an extensive plan of commercial opposition.

As a matter of practical strategy, however, it was deemed safer to induce the members to agree to several separate propositions regarding trade suspension before uniting the parts into a single comprehensive whole. First was brought up the proposal of a non-importation with Great Britain and Ireland, the mildest kind of commercial warfare and therefore the most widely acceptable of any. On Thursday, September 22, Congress paved the way for its own action by ordering the publication throughout the continent of an official request that the merchants should send no more orders to Great Britain and should suspend the execution of orders already given, until the further sense of Congress should be signified.[3]

[1] Galloway, *Reflections*, pp. 66-67.
[2] *Journals*, vol. i, pp. 31-39.
[3] *Ibid.*, vol. i, p. 41. Among other newspapers, this resolution appeared in the *Pa. Packet*, Sept. 26, 1774; *Md. Gaz.*, Sept. 29; Rind's (Pinkney) *Va. Gaz.*, Sept. 29; *S. C. Gaz.*, Oct. 10; *Mass. Spy*, Oct. 13.

Parts of three days were given over by Congress to a consideration of the exact form of the non-importation.[1] The original motion for a non-importation with the British Isles was made by Richard Henry Lee. Chase of Maryland, an impetuous radical during these years of his life, spoke in opposition to non-importation as an insufficient measure, and proposed instead the cessation of exportation and the withholding of remittances. But Chase's plan apparently had a single supporter, Lynch of South Carolina. The chief question at issue was as to the time at which Lee's motion would become operative. Cushing, a merchant from the blockaded port of Boston, favored an immediate non-importation and non-consumption. Most speakers thought otherwise. Mifflin of Pennsylvania believed that the first of November would be sufficiently late to allow for the arrival of orders already sent to Great Britain in April and May, and he held that orders given after that date had been dishonestly given to defeat the anticipated non-importation. Gadsden of South Carolina likewise argued for the first of November. It would appear that there were a number who strenuously favored a much longer postponement; and Patrick Henry therefore moved, by way of compromise, that December be inserted instead of November, remarking: "We don't mean to hurt even our rascals, if we have any." The non-importation resolution, as adopted by Congress on September 27, thus fixed December 1 as the date after which no goods should be imported, directly or indirectly, from Great Britain and Ireland; and as a warning to stubborn importers, it was resolved that goods imported contrary to this resolution should not be purchased or used.

On the next day, Galloway formally presented to Con-

[1] Sept. 24, 26, 27; *Journals*, vol. i, pp. 42-43. Notes on the discussion are in Adams, J., *Works*, vol. ii, pp. 382-386.

gress the plan of union, which constituted the platform of the moderates; and he solemnly warned the body against non-exportation, as an illegal measure which would bring British warships and troops down upon American ports. Galloway's extremely reasonable proposal received warm support—from Jay and Duane of New York, from Edward Rutledge of South Carolina, and in general from the members of fortune and property.[1] In spite of all the efforts of the radicals, the plan was entered in the minutes by a vote of six provinces to five; but, notwithstanding this temporary success, the moderates were never thereafter able to secure consideration for the plan. The zeal of the radicals in later expunging from the record all traces of this proceeding throws an interesting sidelight on their methods.

The time of Congress was now devoted, for a considerable part of three days, to debates over the adoption of a non-exportation resolution.[2] No good account remains of the protracted discussion at this stage; but the nature of the remarks and the attitude of leading members may be reconstructed from John Adams's notes on an earlier occasion and from some scattered comments to be found elsewhere.[3] Cushing adopted as his slogan: " a non-importation, non-exportation, and non-consumption, and immediately," and was joined in this by Dyer of Connecticut. Lynch and the Rutledges of South Carolina favored Cush-

[1] *Journals*, vol. i, pp. 43-51; Adams, J., *Works*, vol. ii, pp. 387-391; *1 N. J. Arch.*, vol. x, pp. 503-507; Galloway, *Reflections*, pp. 72, 81; his *Examination*, pp. 48, 52 n.; his *A Reply to an Address to the Author of a Pamphlet, entitled "A Candid Examination . . . "* (London, 1780), p. 109.

[2] Sept. 28, 29, 30; *Journals*, vol. i, pp. 51-52.

[3] *Works*, vol. ii, pp. 382-386, 391 n., 394, 476-478; Drayton, *Memoirs*, vol. i, p. 168.

ing's proposal if the suspension of trade were made absolute with the whole world, not merely with British territory. John Adams asked Congress to accept the logical implication of endorsing the "Suffolk Resolves," and to resolve that, should further hostilities be pursued against Massachusetts, or any persons seized under the revived statute of Henry VIII, the several provinces " ought *immediately* to cease all exportation of goods, wares and merchandise to Great Britain, Ireland, and the West Indies."

Chase, who had sniffed at a non-importation, argued for an immediate non-exportation and a withholding of debts, which, he believed, would represent a total loss to British merchants and manufacturers of £7,000,000 for the year. He also urged an immediate non-exportation of lumber to the West Indies, for the lumber-vessels exchanged their cargoes for sugar and carried the latter to England, to the great gain of the merchants there and of the British revenue. In this latter position he was supported by Mifflin of Pennsylvania and Sullivan of New Hampshire; but Isaac Low of New York warned against a total prohibition of all exports to the West Indies, as a measure which would "annihilate the fishery" by wiping out the West Indian market. Dyer proposed the withholding of flaxseed from Ireland.

These and other suggestions were made by various delegates; but it quickly became clear that, although opinion was rapidly converging upon a plan of non-exportation, the Virginia tobacco planters, and the South Carolina delegates representing powerful rice and indigo interests, were determined to protect the industries of their respective provinces, in case such a plan were adopted. For a time, attention was centered upon the question of suspending tobacco exportation. The Maryland delegates had instructions not to enter into any arrangement for the non-exportation of tobacco without the concurrence of Virginia and North Carolina; and the Virginia delegates were explicitly instructed not to consent to a non-exportation before August 10, 1775, in order to allow time for the marketing of the growing crop. This situation caused the exasperated Chase to declare: "A non-exportation at a future day cannot avail us. What is the situation of Boston and the Massachusetts? A non-exportation at the Virginia day will not operate before the fall of 1776." It was urged by Gadsden and others that the other provinces should, in this measure, act independently of Virginia; but for taking this step the Marylanders pleaded their lack of power and claimed that, even were a different course possible, it would be undesirable, for Maryland and North Carolina tobacco would be carried to Virginia ports and the latter would run away with their trade. Fortunately for the Virginians, other provinces were also willing to postpone the operation of the non-exportation; and the date agreed upon in the resolution eventually adopted was September 10, 1775, one month later than the Virginia instructions required.

The South Carolina delegates, from the narrow nature of their demands, were not equally successful in enlisting the support of other provinces in their cause. What they desired (Gadsden excepted) was nothing less than that rice and indigo, the staples of the province, should be exempted from the operation of the non-exportation to Great Britain.[1] They held that, out of due regard to the interests of their constituents, it was necessary either that the non-exportation should be made operative against the whole world, or that, in case exportation were suspended with Great Britain alone, rice and indigo should be made exceptions to the regulation, being products which could (except under cer-

[1] Drayton, *Memoirs*, vol. i, pp. 169-170; Izard, *Correspondence*, vol. i, pp. 21-25; statement of S. C. delegates, *N. Y. Journ.*, Dec. 8, 1774.

tain limited circumstances) be exported to Great Britain only, whereas the markets of the world were open to the wheat, flour, fish and oil of the commercial provinces.[1]

The South Carolina delegates were able to show that but a small part of the export trade of the commercial provinces was with Great Britain, while on the contrary nearly all of the indigo and two thirds of the rice of South Carolina went to the ports of Great Britain. Edward Rutledge felt justified in remarking that: " People who are affected but in speculation [*i. e.* in theory] and submit to all the hardships attending it will not shut up their ports, while their neighbors, who are objects of ministerial vengeance, enjoy, in a great degree, the benefits of commerce." Furthermore, they maintained that the commercial provinces would be enabled to pay off their British debts by the returns of their foreign trade and thus greatly ameliorate the rigor of the trade suspension. In explaining the position of the South Carolina delegation before the South Carolina convention a few months later, John Rutledge declared that: " Upon the whole, . . . the affair seemed rather like a commercial scheme among the flour Colonies to find a better vent for their Flour through the British Channel, by preventing, if possible, any Rice from being sent to those markets; and that, for his part, he could never consent to our becoming the dupes to the people of the North or in the least to yield to their unreasonable expectations."

Much bitter feeling was generated in the Congress. Edward Rutledge declared: "A gentleman from the other end of the room talked of generosity. True equality is the

[1] It will be recalled that only enumerated commodities of the colonies were required to be exported to Great Britain and that many American products were not on the enumerated list. Rice and indigo were enumerated, but under temporary acts a way was opened by which rice could be exported to Southern Europe and to regions in America south of Georgia.

only public generosity." But it quickly became apparent that the vast majority were opposed to adopting the drastic expedient of blotting out American export relations with the entire world; and that they were equally disinclined to cater to the self-interest of the rice and indigo planters of South Carolina. Richard Henry Lee pleaded earnestly that: "All considerations of interest, and of equality of sacrifice, should be laid aside." In face of the vehement protests of the South Carolinians, the resolution for non-exportation was carried on September 30. According to its terms, *all* exportation to the British Isles and the West Indies should cease on September 20, 1775, unless American grievances were redressed before that time. The South Carolina delegates had thus lost their first battle. But they did not accept defeat, and they laid plans to make a final stand before Congress adjourned.

The principal features of the plan of commercial resistance had now been adopted by Congress. The work of drawing up a complete plan " for carrying into effect the non-importation, non-consumption and non-exportation " was now confided to a special committee, consisting of Cushing of Massachusetts, Low of New York, Mifflin of Pennsylvania, Lee of Virginia, and Johnson of Maryland.[1] It is worth noting that the committee on rights and redress, composed of two members from each province, was ignored in this connection, although it still had its report under consideration; and that, of the committee of five, all but Low had the reputation of favoring radical measures. Low had been included probably because, as a conservative merchant of great wealth, his name would lend prestige to the work of the committee.

Meantime, Congress did not give the special committee

[1] Sept. 30; *Journals*, vol. i, p. 53.

an absolutely free hand, for portions of three days were occupied in formulating an additional resolution for their guidance.[1] This discussion was very largely confined to the advisability of extending the non-importation regulation to apply to commodities upon which an import duty had been imposed by the revenue acts of 1764 and 1766. The Southern members wished to phrase the resolution so as to avoid the confusion arising from the importation of smuggled articles of the same kind as the dutied articles. " How is the purchaser to know whether the molasses, sugar, or coffee has paid the duty or not?" asked Pendleton of Virginia. " It can't be known." " Many gentlemen in this room know how to bring in goods, sugars and others, without paying duties," declared Lynch significantly. Chase urged the same practical objection as Pendleton, and objected further because of the principle involved. " Our enemies will think," he said, " that we mean to strike at the right of Parliament to lay duties for the regulation of trade." This caused Lynch to reply: " In my idea, Parliament has no power to regulate trade. But these duties are all for revenue, not for regulation of trade." Low felt himself called upon to defend the merchant class, of which he was so respectable a member. " Gentlemen have been transported, by their zeal, into reflections upon an order of men, who deserve it least of any men in the community." He argued against the exclusion of West India rum, sugar and molasses from the provinces as a measure ruinous to American business; and he proposed that, as the importation of East India Company tea had been suspended by the resolution of September 27, smuggled Dutch tea should likewise be placed under the ban.[2]

[1] Oct. 1, 5, 6; *Journals*, vol. i, pp. 53, 55n., 57. Notes on the discussion are in Adams, J., *Works*, vol. ii, pp. 393-394.

[2] Low gained his point later in Art. i of the completed Association.

The outcome of the discussion was a resolution of October 6, which declared against the importation of the most important dutied articles after December 1 next, *i. e.* molasses, coffee and pimento from the British plantations, or from Dominica, formerly a French possession; wines from Madeira and the Western Islands; and foreign indigo. The special committee of five were instructed to include this new regulation in their report. Pendleton might well exclaim: " Shan't we by this hang out to all the world our intentions to smuggle?" As finally phrased in the completed Association, the importation of syrups and paneles (*i. e.*, brown unpurified sugar) was also forbidden from the British plantations and Dominica.

On Wednesday, October 12, the committee of five reported the results of their deliberations in the form of an "Association," which was ordered to lie on the table for the perusal of the delegates. Time was spent on the subject on the following Saturday, and again on Monday; finally, on Tuesday, October 18, the form of association was adopted after sundry amendments, and was ordered to be transcribed that it might be signed by the members.[1] The vote of passage was not recorded as unanimous, and this makes it extremely probable that the South Carolina delegation delivered their ultimatum at this juncture.[2] Lynch, Middleton and the Rutledges, speaking for their province, demanded the exclusion of rice and indigo from the nonexportation regulation as the price of their signatures. Their proposition met with an angry dissent. Forty-eight

---

[1] Oct. 12, 15, 17, 18; *Journals*, vol. i, pp. 62, 74, 75. No record of the debates remains.

[2] For this episode, *vide* Drayton, *Memoirs*, vol. i, pp. 169-170; *N. Y. Journ.*, Dec. 8, 1774; Izard, *Correspondence*, vol. i, pp. 21-25; Cooper, *What Think Ye of Congress Now?*, p. 40; Stevens, *Facsimiles*, vol. xxiv, no. 2034.

hours were allowed to pass, during which all parties had an opportunity to digest the situation. Without the accession of the South Carolina delegates to the Association, the province of South Carolina would not be bound thereby, for such were the terms of the instructions which had been granted the delegates.[1] On the other hand, the South Carolina delegates were too earnest in their opposition to parliamentary encroachment to be willing to be detached from co-operation with the sister provinces, if their demands could be partially met. On Thursday, October 20, the final trial of strength came. The Association was read to the assembled Congress, and the delegates advanced to the table to attach their signatures. Thereupon the four delegates of South Carolina departed from the hall, leaving only the stout-hearted Gadsden, who offered to sign his name alone and to trust to the generosity of his constituents for vindication. But wiser counsels prevailed. For the sake of preserving the union of the provinces, the departed delegates were recalled; they agreed to abandon their point regarding indigo, and, in return, Congress conceded the advantage they demanded for the article of rice.

According to Galloway, the majority were forced to resort to some further strategy before they succeeded in obtaining his signature and those of the other delegates who had voted against many parts of the Association. At the end of the document were placed the words: " The fore-

[1] Before the Congress met, Dr. Franklin had addressed these words to a friend in Pennsylvania: "Your province will surely be wise enough not to enter into violent measures without the strictest concert with the other Colonies, particularly Maryland, Virginia, and the Carolinas, because on them depend the whole effect of the American non-exportation. The Northern Colonies have all the European markets almost for their chief exports, but those Colonies have hardly any but the English markets for their chief exports of tobacco and naval stores . . . " *Mass. Gaz. & Post-Boy*, Oct. 24, 1774.

going Association being determined upon by the Congress, *was ordered* to be subscribed by the *several* Members thereof; and thereupon, we have hereunto set our *respective* names *accordingly*." [1] The recalcitrant delegates were told that they were in the position of a Speaker of Assembly, who signed, by order, a bill that was contrary to his personal judgment, a proceeding which could not be considered as his private act but that of the majority who made the order. This story bears the earmarks of truth, though it is clear that Galloway also felt impelled to sign " on the ground of preventing the Congress from proceeding to more violent measures." [2] Galloway remarked afterward that he would rather have cut off his hand than sign.[3] Congress directed that one hundred and twenty copies of the Association should be struck off; but the document was not made public until the close of the session.

The Association was the most remarkable document put forth by the Congress. Of its authorship nothing is known definitely, perhaps for the reason that the instrument was the outgrowth of the experience of all the delegates through a decade of trade-suspension agreements and thus did not embody the views of any one man or any single committee. In part, the Association was the standardization and nationalization of the systems of commercial opposition which had hitherto been employed upon a local scale; the earlier experiments in non-importation, non-consumption, and various forms of the secondary boycott bore fruit in a number of

---

[1] Galloway, *A Reply to an Address, etc.*, pp. 114-115. The italics are Galloway's. *Vide* also Colden, *Letter-Book*, vol. ii, p. 374.

[2] Galloway, *Examination*, p. 56. *Vide* also *Pa. Mag.*, vol. xxvi, pp. 320-321.

[3] *Conn. Hist. Soc. Colls.*, vol. ii, p. 201. Several delegates were absent on Oct. 20 and affixed their signatures later. *Journals*, vol. i, p. 81 n. The Association was published in the *Pa. Packet*, Oct. 31, 1774, and *Mass. Spy*, Nov. 10.

carefully drawn provisions of the Association. The influence of the southern delegates was plainly discernible in many portions of the paper. The very name, "Association," was of southern origin, and had been used in that section in earlier years in preference to the northern term, "Agreement." Most of the basic features of the Association were, in substance, identical with the Virginia Association of August, 1774.[1] Furthermore, one important purpose of the Association made it natural that the plantation delegates should lead in its formulation. The Association, though framed with the primary object of bringing industrial pressure to bear upon England, was a worthless fabric unless the colonial merchants could be compelled to observe its provisions. This was a problem with which the planters in the South had had to deal in the earlier periods of non-importation, whereas the northern delegates, with the exception of Massachusetts, knew nothing of the difficulty, because their non-importation agreements had been made and enforced by the merchants themselves.

The Association was a document of more than two thousand words divided into a preamble and fourteen articles.[2] The introductory paragraphs avowed allegiance to the king, and declared that commercial coercion was adopted as " the most speedy, effectual, and peaceable " method of obtaining redress from the " ruinous system of colony administration," inaugurated by Great Britain about the year 1763 and modified and elaborated in the subsequent years. Therefore, continued the paper, "we do, for ourselves and

[1] *Vide supra,* pp. 368-370. By this avenue of reasoning, it might appear that Richard Henry Lee, a member of the committee of five, should have major credit for the content of the Association. On the other hand, it is known that he held much narrower views at the opening of Congress. Adams, J., *Works,* vol. ii, p. 362.

[2] Text in *Journals,* vol. i, pp. 75-81; also in appendix, present volume.

the inhabitants of the several colonies, whom we represent, firmly agree and associate, under the sacred ties of virtue, honour and love of our country . . ." The demand for a return to the conditions prevailing before 1763 was, in a later portion, made specific and unmistakable by an enumeration of the acts that must be repealed. These were named as of three groups: (1) the duties on tea, wine, molasses, syrups, paneles, coffee, sugar, pimento, indigo, foreign paper, glass, and painters' colors, and the act extending the powers of the admiralty courts beyond their ancient limits; (2) that part of the act for better securing the royal dockyards, ships, *etc.* (12 George III, c. 24) by which any person in America, charged with an offense therein described, might be transported to England for trial; and (3) the three acts of 1774 against Boston and Massachusetts and the Quebec Act.[1]

Of the fourteen articles which made up the directive portion of the Association, ten were devoted to establishing rules of conduct with reference to non-importation and the cognate subject, non-consumption, and with reference to the adjustment of the American standard of living to the situation. Three articles applied to both non-importation and non-exportation and contained the most important executory provisions.

Non-importation was to become effective on December 1, 1774. Beginning with that date, no goods whatever were to be imported from the British Isles, directly or indirectly; new conditions created by a suspension of trade. One article dealt solely with the establishment of non-export; no East India tea was to be imported from any part of the world (thus affecting the smuggled as well as the legal article); the importation of molasses, syrups, paneles, coffee

[1] Art. xiv.

or pimento from the British plantations and Dominica was forbidden, of wines from Madeira and the Western Islands, of indigo from foreign parts.[1] It was further declared specifically that no slaves were to be imported after that date.[2]

Next, as " an effectual security for the observation of the non-importation," a non-consumption regulation was devised. No goods should be purchased or used which there was cause to suspect had been imported after December 1, 1774, except under special conditions described in Article x; likewise in the case of slaves.[3] Venders of imported goods were warned not to take advantage of the scarcity of goods but were required to sell at their customary rates during the preceding year.[4] An immediate non-consumption of dutied tea was announced, with the provision that after March 1, 1775, the use of smuggled tea should also be abandoned.[5]

Article x provided for the disposal of merchandise imported contrary to the Association. If any such imports arrived during the first two months of the non-importation (*i. e.*, before February 1, 1775), the owner should have the option of re-shipping the goods immediately, or of storing the goods at his own risk with the local committee during the duration of the non-importation, or of authorizing the committee to sell the goods. In the last case, the owner was to receive from the proceeds of the sale the first cost and charges; the profit, if any, was to be applied toward employing the victims of the Boston Port Act. Should any goods arrive after February 1, 1775, they " ought forthwith to be sent back again, without breaking any of the packages thereof."

Sumptuary regulations were made in preparation for the

[1] Art. i.
[2] Art. ii.
[3] Arts. iii and ii.
[4] Art. ix.
[5] Art. iii.

radical change which the absence of imported goods was certain to produce in the life of the average American. "Utmost endeavours" were to be made to improve the breed of sheep and to increase their number.[1] "Agriculture, arts and the manufactures of this country, especially that of wool," were to be promoted.[2] All American manufactures were required to be sold at reasonable prices, so that no undue advantage might be taken of a future scarcity of goods.[3] Rigid economy was to be practised: we "will discountenance and discourage every species of extravagance and dissipation, especially all horseracing, and all kinds of gaming, cock-fighting, exhibitions of shews, plays, and other expensive diversions and entertainments." Economy in mourning was revived from the days of 1765-1766, detailed directions being given.[4]

The non-exportation regulation was announced to become operative on September 10, 1775, if Parliament had not made amends by that time. Beginning with that date, no goods whatsoever should be exported, directly or indirectly, to the British Isles or the West Indies, except rice to Europe.[5] Another part provided that no sheep should be exported to the West Indies or elsewhere; and this regulation was to become effective immediately.[6]

In some respects, the most important portions of the Association related to the means of enforcement. Lacking legal sanction, the Continental Congress were compelled to create their own administrative and judicial machinery and to impose their own penalties. This machinery was to consist of a committee in every county, city and town, chosen by those qualified to vote for representatives in the legislature. These committees were "attentively to observe the

[1] Art. vii.
[2] Art. viii.
[3] Art. xiii.
[4] Art. viii.
[5] Art. iv.
[6] Art. vii.

conduct of all persons touching this association," and, in case of a violation, to publish " the truth of the case " in the newspapers, to the end that all such " enemies of American liberty " might be universally contemned and boycotted.[1]

At this point the Association exposed its real character as a quasi-law, inasmuch as its binding force was not limited to those who accepted its provisions but was made applicable to " all persons." It was one thing for two or more men to agree with each other not to buy goods from British merchants; quite another to agree that, if a man not a party to the compact, bought goods, they would restrain him and ruin his business. For fear that this regulation would not reach non-residents, it was provided that any British or Irish merchant guilty of transgressing the non-importation should likewise be published and boycotted;[2] that captains of American vessels should be forbidden to receive on board prohibited imports on pain of immediate dismissal;[3] and that no vessels should be hired or commodities sold to those engaged in the slave trade after December 1, 1774.[4] The principle of the boycott was invoked against whole provinces in the provision that " no trade, commerce, dealings or intercourse whatsoever " should be sustained with any province in North America which did not accede to or hereafter violated the Association.[5] The committees of correspondence of the various provinces were instructed to inspect the custom-house entries frequently and to inform each other of " every material circumstance that may occur relative to this association."[6] Finally, great elasticity was given to the enforcement provisions by the blanket recommendation that the provincial conventions and the committees in the various provinces should " estab-

[1] Art. xi.
[2] Art. v.
[3] Art. vi.
[4] Art. ii.
[5] Art. xiv.
[6] Art. xii.

THE CONTINENTAL ASSOCIATION 429

lish such farther regulations as they may think proper, for carrying into execution this association." [1]

A few days after Congress had completed the Association, a resolution was passed for calling another continental congress to meet on May 10, 1775, if American grievances should not then be redressed.[2] Thus, a second congress was to be held four months before the time at which the non-exportation regulation was scheduled to go into effect, —which obviously meant that an opportunity would be afforded for further modifications of that measure, if any should prove desirable. The balance of the time of Congress was spent in drawing up a declaration of rights and grievances, and in formulating addresses to the people of Great Britain, to the inhabitants of the British colonies, to the inhabitants of Quebec, and to the king.[3] These papers varied widely in form and phraseology and intent, but all joined in endorsing the sentiment: " Place us in the same situation that we were at the close of the last war, and our former harmony will be restored.' [4] The declaration of rights and grievances undertook to define the colonial theory of the power of Parliament. This matter had caused considerable difficulty in Congress. Five provinces maintained that Parliament had the right to regulate trade; five provinces denied this view; and Massachusetts and Rhode Island were divided within themselves.[5] A statement was finally agreed upon to the effect that the colonial legisla-

[1] Art. xiv.
[2] Oct. 22; *Journals*, vol. i, p. 102.
[3] John Adams wrote to Jefferson in 1813: "I never bestowed much attention on any of those addresses, which were all but repetitions of the same things, the same facts and arguments . . . I was in a great error, no doubt, . . . for those things were necessary to give popularity to our cause, both at home and abroad." *Works*, vol. x, p. 80.
[4] *Journals*, vol. i, p. 89.
[5] Adams, J., *Works*, vol. ii, p. 397.

tures had exclusive powers of law-making in all cases of taxation and internal polity, subject only to the royal negative; and that from the necessity of the case the colonists did "cheerfully consent" to the *bona fide* regulation of their external commerce by Parliament when it was done for the good of the whole empire and contained no "idea of taxation, internal or external, for raising a revenue on the subjects in America, without their consent." [1] The list of acts, whose repeal was held by the declaration of rights and grievances to be "essentially necessary," was somewhat more comprehensive than the group of laws named as the object of the Association, and included the Currency Act of 1764, the act establishing the board of customs commissioners and reorganizing the customs service, and the quartering act of 1774. [2]

The Boston Tea Party—the episode that had precipitated the present crisis—received scant notice. In the address to the colonists, it was noted that the British administration had entered into a "monopolizing combination" with the East India Company to send a dutied commodity to America, and that the tea sent to Boston was destroyed because Governor Hutchinson would not suffer it to be returned.[3] A longer discussion of the affair appeared in the address to the people of Great Britain; some slight effort was made to justify the destruction, but most emphasis was placed on the thought that: "even supposing a trespass was thereby committed and the proprietors of the Tea entitled to damages, the Courts of Law were open" for the prosecution of suits, instead of which thirty thousand souls had been reduced to poverty and distress upon unauthenticated *ex parte*

[1] *Journals*, vol. i, pp. 68–69.
[2] *Ibid.*, vol. i, pp. 71–73.
[3] *Ibid.*, vol. i, p. 98.

THE CONTINENTAL ASSOCIATION 431

evidence, for the act of thirty or forty.¹ No mention whatever was made of the matter in the other documents.

Congress adjourned on Wednesday, October 26, and the great majority of the delegates departed for their homes with the feeling that effective measures for a reconciliation had been taken. But there were some dissenting minds.² Furthermore, the supreme test was yet to come: what would the country think of the work of Congress? how would the people receive the Association? would the Association prove workable?

¹ *Journals*, vol. i, pp. 85-87.
² Adams, J., *Works*, vol. x, pp. 278-279; letter of Dickinson, 4 *Am. Arch.*, vol. i, p. 947.

CHAPTER XI

Ratification of the Continental Association
(November, 1774–June, 1775)

Enough has been said to make clear that the action of the First Continental Congress involved a defeat for the moderates and the mercantile interests. The radicals had achieved several important ends. They had reproduced on a national scale a type of organization and a species of tactics that in many parts of British America had enabled a determined minority to seize control of affairs. It is not too fantastic to say that they had snatched from the merchant class the weapons which the latter had fashioned to advance their own selfish interests in former years, and had now reversed the weapons on them in an attempt to secure ends desired solely by the radicals. Finally, they had defined—nationalized—the issue at stake in such a manner as to afford prestige to radical groups, wherever they were to be found, and to weaken the hold of the moderate elements, on the ground that the latter were at variance with the Continental Congress.

An ultra-radical interpretation of the radical victory was made at the time in these words: " The American Congress derives all its power, wisdom and justice, not from scrolls of parchment signed by Kings, but from the *People*. A more august, and a more equitable Legislative body never existed in any quarter of the globe . . . The Congress, like other Legislative bodies, have annexed penalties to their laws. They do not consist of the gallows, the rack, and the stake . . . but INFAMY, a species of infamy . . . more dreadful to a freeman than the gallows, the rack, or the stake. It is this, he shall be declared in the publick papers to be *an enemy to his country*. . . . The least deviation from the Resolves of the Congress will be treason:—such treason as few villains have ever had an opportunity of committing. It will be treason against the present inhabitants of the Colonies: Against the millions of unborn generations who are to exist hereafter in America: Against the only liberty and happiness which remain to mankind: Against the last hopes of the wretched in every corner of the world.—In a word, it will be treason against God." [1]

Such sentiments stiffened the radical party in all parts of the continent, and it hardly occasions wonder that a reverend divine of Charleston, S. C., should have been dismissed from his congregation "for his audacity in standing up in his pulpit, and impudently saying that *mechanics* and country *clowns* had no right to dispute about politics, or what kings, lords and commons had done!" Nor was it necessary for the *Newport Mercury* to add that: "All *such* divines should be taught to know that mechanics and country clowns (infamously so called) are the real and absolute masters of king, lords, commons and priests . . ." [2]

The moderates began to realize that they had committed an error in lending countenance to the movement for an extra-legal congress. In the eyes of many of them, any direct connection with this congress and its committees became equivalent to rebellion; typical of this group, Joseph Galloway now withdrew from the extra-legal activities altogether. Others, like Isaac Low, lingered in the movement.

---

[1] "Political Observations, without Order; Addressed to the People of America," *Pa. Packet*, Nov. 14, 1774; also *4 Am. Arch.*, vol. i, pp. 976-977. This article created wide interest. Two replies appeared in the *N. Y. Gazetteer*, Dec. 1, 1774.

[2] *Newport Merc.*, Sept. 26, 1774; also Pinkney's *Va. Gaz.*, Oct. 13.

persuaded that they could salvage in their local politics what had seemed shipwrecked in the Continental Congress, or because, like John Andrews of Boston, they were swayed by the impalpable influences of environment, temperament, habit, education or social connections.[1] As the months

[1] John Andrews was a well-to-do merchant of Boston, who sat complacently at home drinking tea while the mob made their descent upon the East India Company's shipments at the wharf. He wrote a witty letter about it a few days later, and did not discover his indignation over the destruction until it became apparent to him that, between the Scylla of the Boston Port Act and the Charybdis of the radicals' Solemn League and Covenant, his business would surely be wrecked. At this time he had stock on his shelves amounting to about £2000 sterling and almost as much more out in debts. He could say with feeling that he opposed "Tyranny exerciz'd either in England or America." He was disposed to favor the opening of the port of Boston through reimbursing the East India Company for their losses. Later, he entertained hopes that the Continental Congress would afford relief that would be "lasting and permanent." About this time it would appear that he began to be affected by the excited state of public opinion and was himself much irritated by the rudeness and immorality of the soldiers. He wrote on August 20, 1774: "When I seriously reflect on the unhappy situation we are in, I cant but be uneasy least ye trade of the town should never be reinstated again: but on the other hand, when I consider that our future welfare depends altogether upon a steady and firm adherence to the common cause, I console myself with the thoughts that if, after using every effort in our power, we are finally oblig'd to submit, we shall leave this testimony behind us, that, not being able to stem the stream, we were of necessity borne down by the torrent." However, his mood became less exalted in October, and he wrote, with reference to mob violence: "every day's experience tells me that not only good policy, but our own quiet, absolutely depends upon a bare acquiescence at least. Therefore I esteem them very blameable who have persisted in opposition to them, as *vox populi, vox Dei*—and their resentment is so great in return, that it's a chance whether (if their struggles should produce better times) they will ever admit of *such* passing their future days uninterrupted among 'em." Andrews became more closely identified with the radical side as time passed and was a patriot at the time of the Declaration of Independence. *1 M. H. S. Procs.*, vol. viii, pp. 326-331, 339, 343-344, 377.

passed, there was presented to every merchant, with increasing sharpness, the alternative of adhering to Congress, even if it meant rebellion and independence, to which his class had always been opposed, or of adhering to Great Britain, even if that meant submission to those parliamentary measures to which his class were also opposed. The increasing tendency of the moderates was to follow the counsel offered by one who himself had once been zealous in meetings and organizations of the people: "As we have already done what we ought not to have done, and left undone what we ought to have done, let us . . . in time return to our Constitution, and by our Representatives, like honest men, state our grievances, and ask relief of the mother state; let us do this with that plainness and decency of language that will . . . remove every suspicion that we have the least intention or desire to be independent." [1]

The publication of the Continental Association was greeted with a storm of protest from the moderate press in the leading commercial provinces. These tracts were reminiscent of the controversial literature produced under somewhat similar circumstances by Drayton at Charleston and by the writers in Mein's *Boston Chronicle* in the years 1769-1770.[2] The chief plaint was directed against those

[1] "Z" in *N. Y. Gazetteer*, Dec. 1, 1774; also *4 Am. Arch.*, vol. i, pp. 987-989. (For identity of "Z," vide ibid., pp. 1096-1097.) Vide also Seabury, *Free Thoughts on the Proceedings of the Continental Congress* . . . (New York, 1774), p. 29: "Renounce all dependence on Congress and committees. . . . Turn your eyes to your constitutional representatives . . ."

[2] The principal writings were: the articles by "Massachusettensis" (Daniel Leonard) in *Mass. Gaz. & Post-Boy*, at intervals from Dec. 12, 1774, to April 3, 1775, afterwards published as a pamphlet; a series, addressed "To the Honourable Peyton Randolph, Esq., late President of the American Continental Congress," by "Grotius" in the same newspaper; the anonymous pamphlets, *What Think Ye of Congress Now?*, *Free Thoughts on the Proceedings of the Continental Congress*

provisions which seemed to establish the Continental Congress as a sort of *de facto* government. "Massachusettensis" claimed that the Association contained all the constituent parts of a law, including an enacting clause, the establishment of rules of conduct, and the affixing of pains and penalties. Although the terms "request" and "recommend" were sometimes used, the usual style was that used by an authoritative assemblage—that such and such a thing "be" done. "By their assuming the powers of legislation, the Congress have not only superseded our provincial legislatures, but have excluded every idea of monarchy; and not content with the havock already made in our constitution, in the plenitude of their power have appointed another Congress to be held in May."[1] The Association, according to another writer, "is calculated for the meridian of a Spanish Inquisition; it is subversive of, inconsistent with, the wholesome laws of our happy Constitution; it abrogates or suspends many of them essential to the peace and order of Government; it takes the Government out of the hands of the Governour, Council, and General Assembly; and the execution of the laws out of the hands of the Civil Magistrates and Juries."[2]

A third writer agreed that the committees appointed to enforce the Association were "a court established upon the same principles with the *papish Inquisition*. No proofs, no evidence are called for. . . . No jury is to be impannelled.

. . . by a Farmer, and *The Congress Canvassed* . . . by *A. W. Farmer*, probably written by Samuel Seabury; a pamphlet, *Alarm to the Legislature of New York* . . ., by Isaac Wilkins; articles in the *N. Y. Gazetteer* by "Z," "A Freeholder of Essex," and others.

[1] *Mass. Gaz. & Post-Boy*, Mch. 27, 1775. *Vide* also *Congress Canvassed*, p. 14.

[2] *N. Y. Gazetteer*, Feb. 16, 1775; also *4 Am. Arch.*, vol. i, pp. 1211-1213. *Vide* also *Congress Canvassed*, p. 20; *Alarm to Legislature*, pp. 7, 9.

No check is appointed upon this court; no appeal from its determination." [1] The means prescribed for carrying out the Association, affirmed "Grotius" in an open letter to the recent president of Congress, " would shock the soul of a savage; your tenth, eleventh and fourteenth articles contain such a system of lawless tyranny as a Turk would startle at; it is a barbarous inroad upon the first rights of men in a social state; it is a violent attack upon the *lawfully acquired property* of honest, industrious individuals." [2]

One unworldly Connecticut parson furnished another ground for objection: " The Saviour of the world, whose servant I am, hath commanded me to feed the hungry, to give drink to the thirsty, to clothe the naked . . . Here it will be to no purpose to say that such and such persons are mine ENEMIES; because our Lord hath expressly . . . commanded me to extend my good offices to mine *enemies* as such. And I beg the Committee to remember that Ministers of the gospel are, in a particular manner, commanded to keep *hospitality*." [3] " Had an Act of Parliament formed such an inquisition . . . ," declared another writer, " how should we have heard of the liberty of the subject, his right to trial by his peers, &c., &c. Yet these men, at the same time they arraign the highest authority on earth, insolently trample on the liberties of their fellow-subjects; and, without the shadow of a trial, take from them their property, grant it to others, and not content with all this, hold them up to contempt, and expose them to the vilest injuries." [4]

---

[1] *Congress Canvassed*, p. 14.

[2] *Mass. Gaz. & Post-Boy*, Feb. 6, 1775.

[3] " I am no politician, am not connected with politicians as such; and never will be either," he added. Rev. John Sayre, Fairfield, Conn., in *N. Y. Journ.*, Sept. 28, 1775. For a scriptural answer, *vide ibid.*, Oct. 26.

[4] " Z " in *N. Y. Gazetteer*, Dec. 1, 1774; also *4 Am. Arch.*, vol. i, pp. 987-989.

The opinion of the average moderate was well expressed by the sentiment: "If I must be enslaved, let it be by a KING at least, and not by a parcel of upstart lawless Committee-men. If I must be devoured, let me be devoured by the jaws of a lion, and not gnawed to death by rats and vermin."[1]

A great deal was said about the impracticability of the Association as a means of redress. The pamphlet, *Free Thoughts on the Proceedings of the Continental Congress*, went extensively into the matter. It was predicted that there would be twenty times as much confusion and distress in America as in Great Britain; that prices would soar; that the American merchants would lose their trade permanently, for Great Britain would look elsewhere for raw materials; that Parliament would block up all American ports; that legal processes would be suspended; that the farmers would be the chief sufferers; and all this calamity in a fruitless effort to obtain results which should be sought only through the usual legal channels.

The moderate members of Congress were frankly accused of having been outwitted and outmaneuvered by the radicals. "You had all the honors,—you had all the leading cards in every sute in your own hands," one writer told the moderates, "and yet, astonishing as it may appear to by-standers, you suffered *sharpers* to get the odd trick."[2] A New York writer stated that he had reason to believe that the New York delegates had opposed the headlong measures of Congress and still disapproved of them; and he called upon

---

[1] *Free Thoughts*, p. 23. *Vide* also "A Freeholder of Essex" in *N. Y. Gazetteer*, Jan. 5, 1775; also 4 *Am. Arch.*, vol. i, pp. 1094-1096.

[2] "Grotius" in *Mass. Gaz. & Post-Boy*, Feb. 6, 1775. "Adams, with his crew, and the haughty Sultans of the South juggled the whole conclave of the Delegates," was the way a Maryland merchant phrased it in a published letter. 4 *Am. Arch.*, vol. i, p. 1194.

them to assert themselves despite the obligations of perpetual secrecy.¹

The special concession granted to South Carolina in the Association caused much comment, even in radical circles. The writer just mentioned called upon the New York delegates to state why the South Carolina delegates had succeeded better than they in securing special indulgences for their constituents.² A Virginia scribbler protested that the tobacco interests had been sacrificed to the rice planters and wheat exporters.³ One distracted fellow burst into verse, eighty-two stanzas in length, in the following manner:

LIX

Suppose all truth the Congress say,
No doubt they make the worst;
Can we, my Friends, for many a day,
Be so completely curst,

LX

As have no cloaths, no grog, no tea,
To cheer our drooping spirits;
And snug in clover smugglers see,
Who have not half our merits.

LXI

Isn't it now a pretty story,
One smells it in a trice,
If I send wheat, I am a Tory,
But Charles-town may send RICE.⁴

Even the Albany Committee of Correspondence, upon a plea of the necessity for harmony, took occasion to inquire of the New York delegates upon what principle a discrimination had been allowed in favor of South Carolina.⁵

¹ *What Think Ye of Congress Now?*, pp. 23-24. *Vide* also *Alarm to Legislature*, p. 9 n.
² *What Think Ye of Congress Now?*, p. 40.
³ *N. Y. Gazetteer*, Apr. 13, 1775; also 4 *Am. Arch.*, vol. ii, p. 163.
⁴ *Poor Man's Advice to his Poor Neighbours* (New York, 1774).
⁵ *N. Y. Journ.*, Feb. 16, 1775; also 4 *Am. Arch.*, vol. i, pp. 1097-1098.

Notwithstanding the polemics of the opposition, the work of establishing the administrative machinery for the Association had gotten irresistibly under way. The fact of the matter was that the moderate elements lacked an organization through which to express their opposition at this critical juncture.[1] Indeed, the logic of their own position inclined them to avoid all extra-legal organization even for purposes of self-defense.[2] Furthermore, the *coup* of the radicals in nationalizing the committee system shook to the center such control as the moderates had already established in various localities. The energies of the friends of the Association were first directed to the appointment of committees of observation and inspection in the local subdivisions of the several provinces, and to obtaining formal sanction for the Association from the provincial assembly or other provincial meeting. It was not specified in the Association that endorsement by a provincial body was necessary—though perhaps it was hinted at in Article xiv—but in any case it was good politics. The remainder of this chapter will be devoted to the progress that was made along these lines.

Massachusetts, being the storm centre of the contest with Great Britain, was one of the earliest provinces to move. The leading ports (Boston harbor being closed) led the way: Marblehead and Newburyport appointed committees

[1] *Cf.* Gage's view; *4 Am. Arch.*, vol. i, p. 981.

[2] "Pray examine the Province law throughout, and all other law authorities that ever were held in repute by the English nation," declared "Spectator" to the signers of a loyalist association, "and you will not find one instance wherein they justify a number of men in combining together in any league whatsoever to support the law, but quite the reverse; for the law is supported in another manner; it is maintained by Magistrates and Officers . . . and not by a number of men combining together." *N. H. Gaz.*, Mch. 31, 1775; also *4 Am. Arch.*, vol. ii, p. 252.

early in November, and Salem about a month later. Governor Gage had deemed it unsafe to permit the Assembly to meet; and the radical leadership of the province had therefore devolved upon the provincial congress, which was, to a large extent, the rejected Assembly under a different name. When the provincial congress met on November 23, 1774, in their first session after the adjournment of the Continental Congress, they lost no time in taking under consideration the proceedings of the Continental Congress; and on December 5 they voted their endorsement, recommending that committees of inspection be chosen in every town and district not already having such committees.[1]

The town of Boston now acted. After unanimously voting to continue the committee of correspondence—that grain of mustard that had now become a great tree—the town meeting on December 7 appointed a committee of sixty-three, headed by Cushing, Hancock and Sam Adams, to enforce the Association. It is significant of the trend of events that a goodly majority of the Sixty-Three were small shopkeepers, mechanics and other men of non-mercantile employment; and that among the members appeared such names as Thomas Chase and John Avery, the distillers, Paul Revere, the silversmith, and Henry Bass, the radical merchant,—men who had been " Sons of Liberty " in the earlier times and had hitherto been nameless for the purposes of the public press and committee rosters.[2] The

[1] *Mass. Spy*, Dec. 8, 1774; also 4 *Am. Arch.*, vol. i, pp. 993-998.

[2] An unfriendly characterization of the Sixty-Three supplies interesting facts concerning certain obscure members of this committee. John Pulling was "Bully of the Mohawk tribe;" John Winthrop, Jr., was "Alias Joyce Jr., Chairman of the Committee for tarring and feathering;" Captain Ruddock, "supposed to be one Abiel Ruddock, formerly head of the Mob on the fifth of November;" Joseph Eayres, "carpenter, eminent for erecting Liberty poles." 2 *M. H. S. Procs.*, vol. xii, pp. 139-142.

meeting recommended that the towns of the province should follow the example of Weymouth and facilitate enforcement by publishing copies of the Association in sufficient number to supply every head of family.[1]

Most of the towns followed the advice of the provincial congress, and did not go to the trouble of appointing special committees of observation and inspection; for they had already established committees for the enforcement of the Solemn League and Covenant, now superseded by the Association. Marshfield presented the only instance of a determination to defeat the Association by town action. The citizens of that town had won for themselves the privilege of drinking tea and killing sheep by obtaining the presence of a detachment of British troops; and on February 20, 1775, a town meeting, duly licensed by Governor Gage under the Massachusetts Government Act, rejected the resolves of the Continental and Provincial Congresses and all other illegal assemblages. A minority protest, signed later by sixty-four names, made the most of a bad situation by charging trickery and misrepresentation.[2] In summing up, it would appear that Massachusetts was well equipped with machinery to prevent any systematic infringements of the Association.

New Hampshire had always been laggard in entering into extra-legal organization. While the Continental Congress was yet in session, organized opposition to the outcome of the Congress was begun in Hillsborough County.[3]

[1] *Mass. Spy*, Dec. 8, 1774; also *Bos. Town Recs.* (*1770-1777*), pp. 205-207.
[2] *Bos. Eve. Post*, Mch. 6, 13, 1775; also *4 Am. Arch.*, vol. i, pp. 1177-1178, 1249-1251.
[3] Twenty-three inhabitants of Frances-Town and fifty-four inhabitants of New Boston signed agreements pledging their opposition to the unlawful proceedings of men who pretended to maintain the very liberties that they were trampling under foot. On Nov. 7, the town

However, in October, the fifty-two voters in attendance at a town meeting at Portsmouth rescinded the action of fifty-six voters at a previous meeting against furnishing donations to stricken Boston, and proceeded to appoint a "Committee of Ways and Means" of forty-five members. One-half of the number refused to act, according to Governor Wentworth; but when news of the proceedings of the Continental Congress reached Portsmouth, the remainder of the committee at once assumed the duties of supervising the execution of the Association. Governor Wentworth reported on December 2 that the measures of the Continental Congress were "received implicitly" by the province.[1] On the same day as his letter, the provincial committee, which had been appointed by the first New Hampshire convention, called upon the inhabitants of the province for a general submission to the Association. In the subsequent weeks, the various towns began to establish committees of inspection.[2]

Since the Assembly had not met for ten months past and was not likely to sit again soon, a convention of the province was held at Exeter on January 25, 1775, which unanimously endorsed the Association. In an address to the province, the inhabitants were exhorted to adhere to it strictly and to support their committees of inspection.[3] Just how many

of Hollis in the same county adopted similar resolutions. *N. H. Gaz.*, Nov. 18, 1774, Feb. 10, 1775. While the Continental Congress was still sitting, a mob at Portsmouth prevented the landing of a shipment of tea but permitted the payment of the duty on it. *Ibid.*, Sept. 16, 23, 1774; *4 Am. Arch.*, vol. i, pp. 786-787.

[1] *4 Am. Arch.*, vol. i, pp. 981-982, 1013.

[2] The organization of the following committees was noted in the newspapers: in December, Exeter, New Market; in January, Parish of Hawke, Temple, Kingstown, Epsom, Greenland. At Brentwood, the committee of correspondence took over the duties of the committee of inspection in February.

[3] *4 Am. Arch.*, vol. i, pp. 1180-1182.

New Hampshire towns finally organized committees of inspection, it is impossible to say. It is important to note, on the one hand, that much had been done to develop a public opinion favorable to the Association; and on the other, that the chief avenues of trade with the world were well guarded by the presence of the "Forty-Five" at Portsmouth, and by a network of committees along the overland routes through Massachusetts.

In Rhode Island, the first official action appears to have been taken on December 5, 1774, when the General Assembly voted its thanks to the Continental Congress and recommended the selection of committees of inspection to the towns of the provinces.[1] Within two weeks Newport and Providence, the leading ports, had acted on the recommendation.[2] It would appear that similar action was taken by the smaller towns.

The course of Connecticut was not unlike that of Rhode Island, in many respects. Early in November, 1774, the Connecticut General Assembly unanimously approved the proceedings of Congress and sent orders into the several towns for a strict compliance therewith.[3] The action of the legislature gained immediate attention; and by the end of the year the establishment of twenty-eight committees had been noted in the newspapers.[4] Other towns acted later.

[1] *R. I. Col. Recs.*, vol. vii, p. 263.
[2] *Ibid.*, vol. vii, pp. 284-285.
[3] *Mass. Gaz. & Post-Boy*, Nov. 14, 1774; Hollister, G. H., *History of Connecticut* (Hartford, 1857), vol. ii, p. 159.
[4] In November, the ten parishes of New Haven County; Woodbury, Pomfret, Waterbury, Derby, Milford, Wallingford; in December, Windham, Saybrook, Danbury, Lebanon, Guilford, Simsbury, New London, Stratford, Hartford, Norwich, Sharon, Fairfield.

RATIFICATION OF THE ASSOCIATION

One section of Connecticut, represented by a group of the smaller towns of Fairfield County in the western part of the province, sought to prevent the acceptance of the Association. The animus appears to have been sectarian, being one phase of the long-standing antagonism of the strong Episcopalian element in these towns to Congregationalist undertakings.[1] The two largest towns of the county, Stratford and Fairfield, chose committees of inspection in December, and the town of Redding took similar action a little later. But on January 30, 1775, a town meeting at Ridgefield rejected the Association with only three dissenting votes out of a total present of nearly two hundred, and denounced the Congress as unconstitutional.[2] A large meeting of the town of Newtown rejected the Association with but one dissenting vote a week later.[3] These defiant resolutions emboldened one hundred and forty-one inhabitants of Redding and the vicinity to denounce and forswear all committees in a written statement;[4] and caused the town of Danbury to revoke the appointment of a committee of inspection, made at an earlier meeting, and to refuse to send delegates to a projected county convention.[5] But Danbury underwent another change of heart, for when the convention of Fairfield County assembled on February 14,

---

[1] *N. Y. Gazetteer*, Feb. 16, 1775. *Vide* also Gilbert, G. A., " The Connecticut Loyalists," *Am. Hist. Rev.*, vol. iv, pp. 273-281. One-third of the people of Fairfield County were Episcopalians. Beardsley, *History of the Episcopal Church in Conn.* (Boston, 1865), vol. i, p. 289.

[2] *N. Y. Gazetteer*, Feb. 2, 1775; also *4 Am. Arch.*, vol. i, pp. 1202-1203.

[3] *Ibid.*, vol. i, p. 1215; also *N. Y. Gazetteer*, Feb. 23, 1775.

[4] *Ibid.*, Feb. 23, 1775; also *4 Am. Arch.*, vol. i, pp. 1258-1260. One hundred and twenty men signed similar resolves at New Milford, a town in Litchfield County across the Housatonic from Fairfield County. *Ibid.*, vol. i, p. 1270; also *N. Y. Gazetteer*, Mch. 16.

[5] *Ibid.*, Feb. 23, 1775; also *4 Am. Arch.*, vol. i, pp. 1038-1039, 1215-1216.

Ridgefield and Newtown were the only towns not represented.

Now began a series of efforts on the part of the radicals to discredit and defeat these opponents of the Association. The county convention denounced a selectman of Newtown who had sold some copies of the Association for a pint of flip, and called upon those citizens of Ridgefield and Newtown, who were attached to their country, to stand forth and affix their signatures to the measures of Congress, so that all commerce and connection might be withdrawn from the other inhabitants of the towns.[1] In view of the approaching session of the Assembly at New Haven, the town meeting at the capital resolved unanimously that no person should entertain the deputies who were expected from the delinquent towns.[2] The Connecticut Assembly, when it met in March, appointed a committee to investigate conditions in the two towns and to determine how far any persons holding provincial commissions were concerned in promoting resolutions in direct opposition of the repeated resolves of the legislature.[3] The dissentients at Redding were held up for public neglect by the committee of observation of that town.[4]

These tactics of the radicals brought only partial results.[5] On March 20, fifty-five inhabitants of Ridgefield accepted the invitation of the county convention and pledged themselves to the Continental Association. By April 12, seventy inhabitants of Newtown had signed a statement disowning the action of the town meeting. Finally, in December, 1775, Ridgefield appointed a committee of inspection and

[1] *4 Am. Arch.*, vol. i, pp. 1236-1238; also *N. Y. Journ.*, Feb. 23, 1775.
[2] *Conn. Cour.*, Mch. 6, 1775; *Mass. Gaz. & Post-Boy*, Mch. 13.
[3] *4 Am. Arch.*, vol. ii, p. 107.
[4] *Ibid.*, vol. i, pp. 1259-1260; also *N. Y. Journ.*, Apr. 20, 1775.
[5] *4 Am. Arch.*, vol. i, pp. 1238-1239; vol. ii, p. 1135.

fell heartily into line. The town of Newtown remained obdurate with respect to the Association, although the selectmen and principal inhabitants were prevailed upon to give bond not to take up arms against the colonies. An active loyalist sympathizer was able to write as late as October, 1781, that "Newtown and the Church-of-England part of Redding were, he believed, the only parts of New England that had refused to comply with the doings of Congress."[1] But so far as Connecticut as a whole was concerned, the province was exceedingly well organized to supervise the enforcement of the Association. Ridgefield and Newtown were, after all, small inland towns and of no importance commercially.

In New York the movement for establishing committees of observation and inspection displayed many of the earmarks of the earlier contests between moderate and radical. But there were some significant differences. Thus, the measures adopted by the Continental Congress contained, by implication, a sanction of the radical party in New York city, hitherto discredited and outgeneraled by the moderates.[2] It remained to be proved whether the radicals could realize on this asset. The leading radical organization, the Committee of Mechanics, took an early occasion to transmit their thanks to the New York delegates for the "wise, prudent and spirited measures" of the Congress—measures which they well knew had been adopted against the best judgment of these very delegates.[3]

[1] *Am. Hist. Rev.*, vol. iv, p. 279 and n.

[2] "Behold the wretched state to which we are reduced," wrote Wilkins in *Alarm to the Legislature*, "A *foreign power* is brought in to *govern this province*. Laws made at Philadelphia, by factious men from New-England, New Jersey, Pennsylvania, Maryland, Virginia and the Carolinas, are imposed upon us by the most imperious menaces."

[3] *N. Y. Gazetteer*, Nov. 24, 1774; also 4 *Am. Arch.*, vol. i, p. 987.

The moderates found themselves in something of a dilemma: either they must oppose the united voice of the continent as embodied in the Congress and thus list themselves with the office-holding gentry, or they must perpetuate their ascendancy in the extra-legal movement and thus keep a controlling hand in the enforcement of the Association. The academic minds of the party chose the logical course; and important members of the community, like the Reverend Samuel Seabury, the Reverend Miles Cooper, the Reverend Charles Inglis and the Reverend Thomas Chandler, denounced the Congress and all its doings, and became " loyalists," or " Tories." But the men of practical affairs, of large business connections and of political experience, did not dare to follow their lead, for they had too much at stake. " The Merchants," wrote Colden on November 2, 1774, " are at present endeavouring to sift out each others Sentiments upon the Association proposed by the Congress. A certain sign, I take it, that they wish to avoid it." [1] Eventually they accepted the necessities of their situation and determined to make a fight for the control of affairs, reserving for a future contingency their exit from the movement.[2] Thus, Isaac Low continued to exert his influence as head of the " Fifty-One," and served as chairman of the later committees of Sixty and One Hundred; but, aware that his influence was waning, he refused to participate in the provincial convention in the latter part of April, and likewise eliminated himself as a candidate for the Second Continental Congress.

The old committee of " Fifty-One," the bulwark of the mercantile interests, made the first move with reference to the Association. Expressing no intention of dissolving

[1] Colden, *Letter Books*, vol. ii, pp. 369-370.
[2] *Vide ibid.*, vol. ii, p. 372.

their present organization, they issued a call for ward meetings of the freemen and freeholders for the purpose of electing a committee of inspection for each ward.[1] It is clear that the " Fifty-One " intended to supervise the ward committees and to keep a close rein on affairs generally. This plan met with the resolute disapproval of the Committee of Mechanics, and, fearing to brook their opposition in the changed face of public affairs, the " Fifty-One " requested a conference with them on the subject. The outcome of the conference was a virtual defeat for the merchants and the adoption of a plan that was in entire harmony with the spirit of the Association. The "Fifty-One" were to be dissolved; instead of ward committees, there should be one general committee of inspection; the " Fifty-One " and the Committee of Mechanics should exchange one hundred names, out of which the new committee should be nominated.[2] Furthermore, the election was to be held at the city hall, where, because of the crowd, it would be difficult to restrict the vote to freemen and freeholders. On November 22 this plan was duly carried out, and a committee of sixty was chosen, although, according to Colden's account, only thirty or forty citizens were present.[3]

The outcome of the election was a victory for the radicals. The Committee of Sixty was essentially radical in character although all varieties of opinion were represented and the merchant, Isaac Low, continued as chairman.[4]

[1] *4 Am. Arch.*, vol. i, pp. 328-329, 967.

[2] *Ibid.*, vol. i, p. 330. The Committee of Mechanics continued in existence.

[3] *Letter Books*, vol. ii, p. 372.

[4] Professor Becker's analysis of the Sixty is as follows: 29 members of the original Fifty-One found places on the Sixty, and of these 21 gave active or passive support to the War for Independence. Of the rejected members of the Fifty-One, 17 of the 22 became loyalists or neutrals with loyalist sympathies. The 31 members of the Sixty who

With such zealots in the saddle as Sears and McDougall, no merchant of insight could longer hope that the enforcement of the Association would be merely nominal. "Anti-Tyrannicus" might well lament after four months of the rule of the Sixty: " While the late Committee of Fifty-One acted as a Committee of Correspondence for this City, the generality of its inhabitants, particularly the most sensible and judicious part of them, were happy in reposing the trust with so respectable a body, composed as it was of the principal citizens; but when the present Committee was formed out of the ruins, as I may say, of the old Committee, was there a cool considerate man among us, who did not forbode evil?"[1]

Early in November the "Fifty-One" had sent a circular letter to the rural counties recommending the appointment of committees of inspection pursuant to the Association.[2] Enthusiastic response could hardly be expected in view of the lassitude exhibited at the time of the election of delegates to Congress; and there was even a possibility that the moderate elements would become active and defeat the plans of aggressive radical minorities. Actually the results were much the same as on the earlier occasion. Only three of the thirteen rural counties gave the Association a favorable reception at this early time—Suffolk, comprising central and eastern Long Island; and on the mainland, the adjoining counties of Ulster and Albany. The most radical action was taken by Suffolk County. On November 15, the county committee of correspondence voted a full approval

were not members of the Fifty-One included about ten who became active radicals and not more than five or six loyalists. *N. Y. Parties, 1760-1776*, pp. 167-168.

[1] *N. Y. Gazetteer*, Mch. 23, 1775.

[2] *4 Am. Arch.*, vol. i, p. 329. Professor Becker has assembled all the facts in the discussion that follows in *op. cit.*, pp. 169-173, 187.

of the Association and recommended it to the several towns to see that its provisions were executed. Within two months most of the towns and districts of the county had taken favorable action.[1] Next to Suffolk, the Association gained widest support in Ulster County, where a joint meeting of the freeholders of five towns recommended the appointment of committees on January 6, 1775. In the subsequent months such action was taken by five or more towns.[2] In Albany County, the county committee of correspondence endorsed the Association, with some misgivings, on December 10, 1774, and effected a reorganization of the committee, by which the three city wards and the rural precincts were given representation. The action of endorsement met with no public expostulation, except from a meeting in King's district under the leadership of five of the king's justices.

The contest over the acceptance of the Association was sharp in Queens and Tryon Counties and the outcome was a partial and barren victory for the radicals. Committees of inspection were appointed in the former county at Jamaica and Newtown, but the action was quickly repudiated by numbers of inhabitants. At Flushing in the same county, it would appear that about one-seventh of the freeholders, having come together at a funeral, appointed the committee. At Oyster Bay, a meeting called for that particular purpose adjourned without action. In Tryon County the radicals succeeded in appointing committees in only four districts.[3] In the eight remaining counties the Association was either disowned, ignored, or combated by

[1] Among them were Huntington, Smithtown, Islip and Southhaven. Because of opposition, Brookhaven did not appoint a committee of inspection until June 8, 1775.
[2] Shawangunk, Hanover, Wallkill, New Windsor and Kingston.
[3] Palatine, Canajoharie, German Flatts and Mohawk.

means of loyalist associations which asserted the "undoubted right to liberty in eating, drinking, buying, selling" etc.[1]

The rather general disapprobation which the Association met outside of the city and county of New York made some form of provincial endorsement extremely important; and a determined effort was put forth to secure the sanction of the Assembly. This Assembly, which came together on January 10, 1775, had been in existence since 1769; and although it had passed a vote in the earlier year approving the non-importation regulations which the merchants themselves had established, the body was not likely to prove responsive to the altered condition of public affairs in 1775.[2] Nevertheless the game was sufficiently uncertain to warrant a trial by the radicals.[3] On January 26 an initial attempt was made to get the Assembly to pass judgment on the Continental Congress, but through a resort to the previous question the matter was stopped by a vote of eleven to ten. The loyalist speakers pointed out that Congress was seeking to wield powers properly belonging to a legislature, and charged openly that the New York delegates in Congress had opposed the proceedings.[4] In the subsequent

[1] Quoted from the Dutchess County Association; *N. Y. Gazetteer*, Feb. 9, 1775. A committee, appointed at White Plains in Westchester County, was repudiated by 45 freeholders.

[2] *Mass. Spy*, Feb. 16, 1775; also *4 Am. Arch.*, vol. i, p. 1191.

[3] Colden himself entertained doubts as to the course that the Assembly would take. *Letter Books*, vol. ii, p. 378.

[4] *4 Am. Arch.*, vol. i, pp. 1189-1191, 1286-1287; *Conn. Hist. Soc. Colls.*, vol. ii, pp. 193-194; Brush's speech in *N. Y. Gazetteer*, Mch. 2, 1775. "Worthy old Silver Locks," when he learned of the vote of the Assembly, "cried out—Lord, now lettest thou thy servant depart in peace." A moderate's letter in *Mass. Gaz. & Post-Boy*, Feb. 6, 1775. It is to be noted that Colden was in charge of the New York government at the three most trying times during the revolutionary movement: the Stamp Act, the tea episode, and the period of the First Continental Congress.

RATIFICATION OF THE ASSOCIATION 453

four weeks, as tardy members made their appearance, three more attempts were made to commit the Assembly in the matter, but all to no purpose.[1] These defeats convinced the radicals that they could hope for nothing from the Assembly, and they proceeded to do all in their power to undo the damage which the course of the Assembly had wrought the cause.

One spirited article, circulated in the newspapers, analyzed the personnel of the New York government, and purported to show that most of the members of the Council and Assembly either themselves had access to the public crib through lucrative contracts or well-paid positions, or else were related to those who did.[2] A report, originating in London, was given publicity, to the effect that several members of the majority in the Assembly had received bribes of £1000 for their votes, and that large land grants, pensions and high offices were to be rewards for the leaders of the majority.[3] It is possible that the radicals would now have followed the example of Massachusetts, New Hampshire and other provinces and sought an endorsement of the Association at the hands of a provincial convention.[4] But much valuable time had been lost in the futile efforts with the Assembly; and, furthermore, means had been found of rendering the Association effectual without such

[1] On Feb. 17, a motion to thank the New York delegates for their services was lost, 15 to 9. On Feb. 21, a motion to thank the merchants and inhabitants of the province for their adherence to the Association was defeated, 15 to 10. On Feb. 23, a motion to appoint delegates to the next Continental Congress was rejected, 17 to 9. 4 Am. Arch., vol. i, pp. 1289-1297.

[2] Pa. Journ., Feb. 22, 1775; also Conn. Cour., Apr. 10.

[3] The identity of the members was but thinly disguised in most instances. Pa. Journ., May 17, 1775.

[4] A letter from the South Carolina General Committee, dated Mch. 1, 1775, urged this course on New York. N. Y. Journ., Apr. 6, 1775; also 4 Am. Arch., vol. ii, pp. 1-3.

sanction.¹ When, therefore, the radicals reached the decision of calling a provincial convention, it was only with a view to the election of delegates to the impending Second Continental Congress.

Fortunately for the administration of the Association, the negative attitude of the Assembly and the absence of committees of inspection in most of the rural parts were matters of no essential importance. New York city was the entrepôt of commerce for the entire province, as well as for portions of Connecticut and New Jersey; and as long as this portal was well guarded, no serious violations of the Association could occur. The Committee of Sixty, stationed there, was clearly of radical complexion; and its successor, the Committee of One Hundred, elected upon the receipt of the news of Lexington and Concord, was even more largely so. On its roll were many members of the old Sixty; and among the new members were such unmitigated radicals as John Morin Scott, John Lamb, and Daniel Dunscomb, long chairman of the Committee of Mechanics.²

¹ Colden wrote to Dartmouth on May 3, 1775 that, from the time the Assembly deviated from the general association of the colonies, " a Design was evidently form'd in the other Colonies to drive the People Here from acquiescing in the Measures of the Assembly, & to force them into the General Plan of Association & Resistance. This Design was heartily seconded by many among ourselves. Every species of public and private Resentment was threatened to terrify the Inhabitants of this Province if they continued Disunited from the others. The certainty of looseing all the Debts due from the other Colonies, which are very considerable, and every other Argument of private Interest that could Influence the Merchants, or any one, was industriously circulated." *Letter Books*, vol. ii, p. 401.

² After making a careful analysis of the new committee and its most active members, Professor Becker concludes: " it is clear that the committee of One Hundred . . . was largely dominated by those who had directed the Sixty, assisted by newly elected radicals; whatever it represented ostensibly, it was in fact the organ of that conservative-radical combination which was destined to inaugurate the revolution and achieve independence." *Op. cit.*, pp. 197-199.

RATIFICATION OF THE ASSOCIATION

Unless some nearby harbors in New Jersey should furnish opportunity for evasion, the province was pretty effectually sealed. The people of Jersey, however, as we shall see, were definitely committed to the Continental Association.

The movement for ratifying the Association in New Jersey got under way early in December, 1774, when the three precincts of Essex County observed the directions of Article xi and appointed committees of observation.[1] The movement spread rapidly, and the example of Essex County in establishing committees of inspection in the local subdivisions was widely copied. By February 1, 1775, committees of observation and inspection had been appointed in eight of the thirteen counties;[2] and at least two other counties acted shortly after.[3] Every populous county, with the possible exception of Salem, was now organized for the enforcement of the Association. No public opposition of any importance appeared against the establishment of committees.[4] With such a broad basis of popular support, it was not surprising that the Assembly of the province voted approval of the proceedings of Congress on January 24, 1775.[5]

---

[1] Elizabeth, Newark and Acquackanonck. *4 Am. Arch.*, vol. i. 1009-1010, 1012-1013, 1028; *N. Y. Gaz.*, Dec. 26, 1774.

[2] Other than Essex, these counties were in chronological order: *Monmouth*, Gloucester, *Somerset*, Cumberland, *Middlesex*, *Hunterdon*, and *Morris*. The italicization indicates the counties in which township committees of inspection were organized. *4 Am. Arch.*, vol. ii, p. 35; *Pa. Gaz.*, Dec. 21, 1774; *N. Y. Gaz.*, Dec. 26; *Pa. Packet*, Jan. 19, 1775; *4 Am. Arch.*, vol. i, pp. 1083-1084, 1163-1164, 1106.

[3] Burlington and Bergen; *ibid.*, vol. i, pp. 1235-1236; vol. ii, p. 579.

[4] For two instances, however, *vide ibid.*, vol. i. p. 1165; vol. ii, pp. 130-131.

[5] An appearance of unanimity was given to this vote through the skilful manipulation of "the Junto at Elizabeth Town," *i. e.*, William Livingston, John DeHart and Elias Boudinot. *1 N. J. Arch.*, vol. x,

The fact that Philadelphia had been the scene of the transactions of the Continental Congress gave decided impetus to the movement for ratification of the Association throughout Pennsylvania. In the city the chief source of opposition was the group of wealthy Quaker merchants, who controlled the policy of the sect to which they belonged. Galloway, outwitted in his first attempt to play politics on a continental scale, was seeking balm for his wounded sensibilities in the company of congenial spirits in the city and in New York; and he did not appear in public denunciation of Congress until after the radicals had firmly established their organization in Pennsylvania.

The existing Committee of Forty-Three at Philadelphia, representing city and county, had never been entirely satisfactory to the ultra-radicals; it had been accepted by them simply as the best committee that could be obtained under the circumstances then prevailing. Even before the Continental Congress had begun its sessions, appeals had appeared in the press, emanating avowedly from the laboring class, demanding the appointment of a new committee.[1] As the Continental Association pointed to the selection of a new committee, the radicals at once made known their opinion that separate committees should be chosen for the city and for the county. Their purpose evidently was to preclude the possibility of the city moderates dominating the action of the county, as they had done to a certain de-

---

pp. 537, 575-577. The Quaker members of the Assembly made an exception to "such parts [of the proceedings of Congress] as seem to wear an appearance, or may have a tendency to force (if any such there be) as inconsistent with their religious principles." *4 Am. Arch.*, vol. i, p. 1124. It would appear, however, that this saving clause was removed on Jan. 25. *Vide ibid.*, vol. i, p. 1287; *1 N. J. Arch.*, vol. x, p. 546.

[1] "An Artisan" in *Pa. Gaz.*, Aug. 31, 1774; "A Mechanic" in *Pa. Packet*, Sept. 5.

gree in the election of the Forty-Three; but they tactfully based their objections on the ground of convenience and greater effectiveness of action.[1] They also demanded, in curious contrast to their New York brethren, that the election be held by ballot, for the reason, it would appear, that the voters could thus be best protected from the " undue influence " and " electioneering attempts " of the citizens of wealth and position.[2]

The Forty-Three had already sent out a call for a public meeting on Saturday, November 12, 1774, to elect a joint committee for city and county.[3] On Monday of that week. a mass meeting, summoned without authority of the Forty-Three, came together at the state house, and resolved by unanimous vote that the election should be held in the several wards by ballot of those who could vote for representatives in the Assembly, and that the city and its suburbs should elect a committee of sixty separate from the county.[4] The plan adopted by this meeting, unauthorized though it was, prevailed. Separate tickets of names for membership in the city committee were made out by the two parties, and these were printed and distributed for electioneering purposes. On election day the list of sixty names submitted by the radicals won by a great majority.[5] At the particular request of the freeholders of two suburban districts, addi-

[1] *Pa. Gaz.*, Nov. 2, 1774; also *4 Am. Arch.*, vol. i, pp. 956-957.

[2] " Cassandra," a radical, in *Pa. Gaz.*, Mch. 20, 1776.

[3] *Ibid.*, Nov. 2, 1774; also *4 Am. Arch.*, vol. i, p. 956.

[4] *Ibid.*, vol. i, pp. 965-967; also *Pa. Gaz.*, Nov. 9, 1774.

[5] It is evident that only a small minority of all the citizens participated in the voting. 517 votes in all were cast in the city and the Northern Liberties; and of these, 499 were for the radical ticket, with very few exceptions to any one name. " Tiberius " in *Pa. Ledger*, Mch. 16, 1776. Not one-sixth of the people voted, according to a Philadelphia writer in the *N. Y. Gazetteer*, Feb. 23, 1775.

tional members were included in the committee, making the total number sixty-six.[1]

The radical character of the Sixty-Six is indicated by the fact that, in the election of the two committees that in turn succeeded to the functions of this committee, few alterations were made in the personnel. The Sixty-Six included only seventeen members of the old Forty-Three; and these were, for the most part, men of the more radical stamp, like Dickinson, Thomas Mifflin, Joseph Reed and Charles Thomson. Thomas Wharton and the Reverend Dr. Smith were dropped permanently from committee rolls. Of the new men on the Sixty-Six, William Bradford, editor of the radical *Pennsylvania Journal*, was the best known. The others were, for the greater part, small tradesmen, mechanics, and nobodies who had been active in popular demonstrations in earlier years. It is not necessary to accept literally the scornful comment of a contemporary that "there are many of this Committee who could not get credit for 20s.;" and it would be difficult, if not impossible, to verify his further statement that one of the Sixty-Six, "an avowed Republican, had lately met with some disappointments . . . ; another had acquired his fortune partly by an illicit trade last war, and partly by taking advantage of a Resolve of the people here, not to deal with the Rhode-Islanders, after they had broke through the Non-Importation Agreement, by supplying them with Goods, when no other Merchant would do it; another was an illiterate Merchant; another too insignificant to notice, &c."[2]

The counties of the province quickly emulated the ex-

---

[1] The names of the original sixty and of the four members from Southwark are in *Pa. Gaz.*, Nov. 16, 1774; the names of the two from Kensington are in *ibid.*, Nov. 23. Lincoln states that the committee was composed of sixty-seven. *Rev'y Movement in Pa.*, p. 185.

[2] *N. Y. Gazetteer*, Feb. 23, 1775; also *4 Am. Arch.*, vol. i, p. 1232.

ample of Philadelphia in preparing for the enforcement of the Association. In Philadelphia County, committees were first selected for each township; and at a meeting of these committees on November 26 a general committee of forty was named.[1] By the middle of February seven other counties had chosen committees of inspection;[2] and the committee of correspondence of another county had assumed the function of executing the Association.[3] There is no record of action in the case of the two sparsely settled frontier counties of Northumberland and Westmoreland.

Ratification of the Continental Association was easily carried in the Pennsylvania Assembly. That body had held its first session while the Continental Congress was still in session; and its first act had been to elect a successor to Joseph Galloway, who had been speaker for so many years. The second session began on December 5, and on the tenth the proceedings of Congress were approved by a unanimous vote.[4] Three days later, Galloway made his first appearance in this Assembly. During the remainder of the session and in the February session he proceeded quietly and indefatigably to work up sentiment among the members in opposition to the measures of Congress, and he gained an increasingly large following. But he was laboring against heavy odds; and the excitement, produced by the acceleration of public events, contributed in defeat-

[1] This committee contained three members of the old Committee of Forty-Three. *Pa. Gaz.*, Nov. 16, 30, 1774.

[2] In chronological order: Berks, Bucks, York, Chester, Northampton, Cumberland and Lancaster. *Vide 4 Am. Arch.*, vol. i, *passim*, and contemporary newspapers. Galloway wrote from his country seat in Bucks County: "A Committee has been appointed for this County by a few warm People of neither Property or significance among us." *Pa. Mag.*, vol. xxi, p. 478.

[3] Bedford; *4 Am. Arch.*, vol. i, pp. 1226-1227, 1229-1230.

[4] *Ibid.*, vol. i, pp. 869, 1023; Lincoln, *op. cit.*, p. 185.

ing his efforts.¹ Meanwhile the Sixty-Six at Philadelphia, feeling that the time had come for frankly discarding the leadership of the Assembly, had called into being a second provincial convention. When that body assembled on January 23, 1775, it immediately adopted a unanimous resolution endorsing the Continental Association and pledging obedience to its provisions.²

In general, the situation in Pennsylvania was extremely favorable for a close observance of the Association. With the only port of entry well guarded, the chief source of danger lay in the course which the Quaker merchants might choose to pursue.

There was nothing distinctive about the movement to ratify the Association in the Delaware Counties. On November 28, 1774, a committee of inspection was chosen in Newcastle County. Kent County followed this example on December 7. Apparently no committee was chosen at this early stage in Sussex County, where the preponderance of Episcopalians made it more difficult for the radicals to carry their objects.³ At the first session of the House of Assembly following the dissolution of the Continental Congress, several unanimous resolves were passed on March 15, 1775, expressing high approval of the proceedings of Congress.⁴

Of the plantation group, the earliest action was taken by

¹ For Galloway's account of the sharp politics of this unavailing struggle, *vide* his letters to Governor Franklin, *1 N. J. Arch.*, vol. x, pp. 572-575, 579-586; his *A Reply to the Observations of Lieutenant General Sir William Howe*, etc., pp. 127-128; and his letters to Verplanck, *Pa. Mag.*, vol. xxi, pp. 477-484.
² *Pa. Gaz.*, Dec. 28, 1774, Feb. 1, 1775; also *4 Am. Arch.*, vol. i, p. 1169.
³ Adams, J., *Works* (Adams), vol. x, pp. 81-82.
⁴ *N. Y. Gaz.*, Mch. 27, 1775; also *4 Am. Arch.*, vol. ii, pp. 126-127.

Maryland. The counties in which Annapolis and Baltimore were located took the lead; and by the end of November committees had been chosen in six of the sixteen counties.[1] On the twenty-first of the month a provincial convention had assembled at Annapolis, but because of the shortness of the notice several counties were not represented. Before adjourning, the convention voted unanimous approval of the proceedings of Congress and recommended to the people of Maryland an inviolable obedience to the Association. The convention renewed its vote at a full meeting on December 8-12.[2] Under stimulus of these provincial meetings, a committee of observation was chosen in St. Mary's County, and several of the old committees were enlarged so as to afford a broader representation.[3] In the counties that failed to appoint committees, it would appear that the existing committees of correspondence took over the new functions. The province proved to be adequately organized to execute the Association.

In the neighboring province of Virginia, committees of observation were chosen with almost clocklike precision. Five counties acted in November; eleven counties and the town of Williamsburg in December; five counties in January; and at least four others in the subsequent months.[4]

[1] In chronological order: Anne Arundel, Baltimore, Calvert, Charles, Frederick, Prince George's. Consult *4 Am. Arch.*, vol. i, index.

[2] *Ibid.*, vol. i, pp. 991, 1031; also *Md. Gaz.*, Dec. 1, 15, 1774.

[3] The size of committees was increased in Baltimore, Anne Arundel, Frederick, Charles and Prince George's. Consult *4 Am. Arch.*, vol. i, index.

[4] In November, Henrico, Elizabeth City, Warwick, Chesterfield and James City; in December, Richmond, Essex, Isle of Wight, Princess Anne, Caroline, Prince William, King and Queen, Northampton, Charles City, Orange, Williamsburg, Accomack; in January, Charlotte, Prince George's, Fincastle, Pittsylvania and Westmoreland; in February, Lancaster; in April, Bedford; in May, Mecklenburgh and Augusta. *Vide ibid.*, vols. i, ii, *passim*, and Pinkney's *Va. Gaz.*, *passim*.

In the provincial convention, which began to meet on March 20, every one of the sixty-two counties was represented; which makes it probable that a great many more counties than those noted here appointed committees of observation. On March 22 the members of the provincial convention voted their unanimous approval of the measures of the Continental Congress.[1] The new House of Burgesses, the first since the dramatic dissolution of May, 1774, was not called into session until the first of June, 1775; and on the fifth of the month they also resolved, without a dissenting voice, their entire approval of the proceedings of Congress.[2]

Thus, excellent machinery of enforcement was established in all parts of the province. A source of weakness was the small but powerful body of merchants and factors, who could not be expected to relinquish without a struggle their prospects of recovering the great sums which the planters owed them; but even these professed an allegiance to the Association.

The movement in North Carolina for the appointment of committees proceeded sluggishly, except at the principal port, Wilmington, where a city committee of observation was chosen on November 23, 1774, and a county committee some weeks later.[3] Pitt County appointed a committee on December 9, and other tidewater counties probably followed this example.[4] A pronounced and effective opposition to the Association was made in the populous backcountry counties, where the Regulators had risen up several years before in opposition to the oppressive practices of the very tidewater leaders who now sought their support

[1] *Va. Gaz.*, Mch. 30, 1775; also *4 Am. Arch.*, vol. ii, p. 167.
[2] *Ibid.*, vol. ii, p. 1193.
[3] *N. C. Col. Recs.*, vol. ix, pp. 1088-1089, 1107-1108, 1154.
[4] *Ibid.*, vol. ix, p. 1095; vol. x, pp. 37-38.

against England.¹ Addresses were sent to Governor Martin, signed by many inhabitants of Anson, Rowan, Surry and Guilford Counties, condemning the "lawless combinations and unwarrantable practices" introduced into North Carolina from other provinces.²

When a provincial convention assembled at Newbern on Monday, April 3, 1775, nine county and two town constituencies, most of them in the back country, failed to send representatives; and Governor Martin averred that: "in many others the Committees consisting of 10 or 12 Men took upon themselves to name them and [in] the rest they were not chosen according to the best of my information by 1-20 part of the people."³ The convention met one day before the time fixed for the sitting of the Assembly. This was of considerable convenience, physically and politically, since every member of the Assembly who appeared was, with a single exception, also a member of the convention.⁴ Sturdy John Harvey acted as "Mr. Moderator" of the one body and "Mr. Speaker" of the other; and indeed the two bodies met in the same room, changing character with chameleonlike suddenness when occasion demanded. Governor Martin issued a proclamation for dispersing the convention; and on Tuesday he sent a message to the Assembly denouncing the convention and all committees of observation.⁵ While the House on the following day set about preparing an answer to the governor, the convention took occasion to ratify the Continental Association in a formal vote, and all the members of the convention, with a few ex-

[1] Bassett, "Regulators of North Carolina," *Am. Hist. Assn. Rep.* (*1894*), pp. 209-210.
[2] *N. C. Col. Recs.*, vol. ix, pp. 1157, 1160-1164.
[3] *Ibid.*, vol. ix, p. 1228.
[4] There were more delegates, however, than Assemblymen.
[5] *Ibid.*, vol. ix, pp. 1187, 1190-1196.

ceptions, signed their names to it.[1] The situation became intolerable to Governor Martin when, on Friday, the seventh, the House presented an address in defense of the convention and the committees and voted approval of the Association.[2] On the following day he dissolved the Assembly. Although not as thoroughly organized as many other provinces, North Carolina was in position to carry through the Association, since the burden of enforcement rested with the tidewater communities where committees were in existence.

In South Carolina the General Committee at Charleston took the initiative in bringing about a ratification of the Association. The situation presented some peculiar difficulties because of the partiality shown to the rice planters in the non-exportation regulation of the Association. Ultra-radicals like Gadsden did not like the appearance of a sales-price attached to South Carolina patriotism, and they resolved to ratify the Association with the proviso that the rice exemption be stricken out. On the other hand, the indigo interests saw no reason why the welfare of the rice planters should be safeguarded by the Association and their own, equally meritorious, ignored.

The General Committee sought to disarm both elements of opposition by the course it adopted. On November 9, 1774, a call was sent out for a provincial congress to meet at Charleston on Wednesday, January 11, for the purpose of acting on the Continental Association and choosing a new committee.[3] The committee then proceeded to have copies of the Association (of which they signified their high

---

[1] *N. C. Col. Recs.*, vol. ix, pp. 1180-1182, 1184-1185.

[2] *Ibid.*, vol. ix, pp. 1198-1205. The North Carolina provincial congress, which assembled on Aug. 20, 1775, voted a formal acceptance of the Association on the twenty-third. *Ibid.*, vol. x, p. 171.

[3] *S. C. Gaz.*, Nov. 21, 1774.

approval) distributed to the members in the various parts of the province; and with this document they also sent copies of a justification which the South Carolina delegates in the Continental Congress had drawn up to explain their course there.[1] This latter paper was a shrewd piece of writing. It endeavored to show, on the one hand, that the apparent discrimination in the Association in favor of South Carolina served, in fact, only to place the province on a basis of equality with the other provinces, and that therefore any charge of commercialized patriotism was ill-founded.[2] The larger part of the document was spent in an effort to convince the indigo growers that the rice planters had no desire to take unfair advantage of them. Three reasons were offered why rice had been permitted to be exported by Congress instead of indigo: rice was a perishable commodity; it did not serve the people of Great Britain as provision, nor, as in the case of indigo, as an aid in manufacturing; furthermore, lands which produced rice could be devoted to no other use whereas most of the indigo lands might be advantageously planted with wheat, barley and hemp. In conclusion, the delegates proposed that the superior advantage of the rice planters should be counterbalanced by a compensatory arrangement with the indigo growers; that is, " that a reasonable proportion of all rice made after the present crop be appropriated to the purchase of indigo made by such planters as are so situated as to be unable to turn their lands to the production of articles

[1] A copy of this justification may be found in *N. Y. Journ.*, Dec. 8, 1774.

[2] Thus it was declared: " That while the other colonies had the exportation of wheat, flour, oil, fish and other commodities open, Carolina would (without the exception of rice) have had no sort of article to export at all;" and further, " That Carolina, having no manufactures, was under a more immediate necessity of some means to purchase the necessaries of life, particularly negro clothing."

which may be exported; and that the indigo so purchased become the property of those for whose rice it was exchanged."

The appeal of the delegates was well calculated to accomplish their purpose; and it proved particularly effective in healing the breach that had appeared between the rice planters and the indigo growers. A strong note of dissent was still to be heard, however, in certain quarters. A letter written at Charleston on the last day of the year claimed that: "Most of the inhabitants of this province are displeased that their Delegates asked an exception of rice from the Non-Exportation agreement."[1] In the *South Carolina Gazette* of January 2, 1775, "A Country Rice Planter" asked if the South Carolina delegates were "ever instructed by the People to hold out in that Article and to refuse their Vote if not complied with?"; and suggested that: "Even supposing we were not upon a Level as to the Privilege of Exportation with some other Colonies, is it the grand struggle now, Whether we shall be upon a *Level?* or is it, Whether we shall be *free*, and who shall *do* most and *suffer* most to establish this Freedom?" The rice planters were advised to repudiate their exemption outright rather than agree to "the *Scheme of Barter* proposed, which it will not only be as difficult to obtain the Assent of the Colony to as the above—but be infinitely more difficult to accomplish to Satisfaction." As late as the opening day of the provincial congress, an onlooker at Charleston predicted that positive instructions would be given the delegates to the Second Continental Congress to put a stop to the exportation of rice when the non-exportation regulation should take effect.[2] But these writers, as the result showed, undervalued the persuasive appeal of self-interest to the planting element.

[1] *N. Y. Journ.*, Jan. 26, 1775.
[2] *Mass. Spy*, Feb. 16, 1775.

The provincial congress, which began its sessions on Wednesday, January 11, had a membership almost four times as large as that of the House of Assembly, and all parishes and districts of the province were represented according to a predetermined ratio. Colonel Charles Pinckney, chairman of the General Committee, was chosen as chairman of the congress, and the omnipresent Peter Timothy served as secretary.[1] On the first day, the delegates to the Continental Congress being in attendance, the Association was taken under consideration. The last four words of Article iv—" except rice to Europe "—gave rise to a long and violent debate. Gadsden spoke for the motion, recounted the critical situation precipitated by his four colleagues in the Continental Congress, and declared that the reluctant concession granted by the other provinces had created a jealousy of the rice provinces which ought to be removed at the earliest possible time. John Rutledge now undertook to defend the action of the majority of the South Carolina delegation. He contended that the northern provinces " were less intent to annoy the mother country in the article of trade than to preserve their own trade;" which made it seem only " justice to his constituents to preserve to them their trade as entire as possible." In vigorous language he emphasized the point that, since rice and indigo were enumerated products, non-exportation in those articles meant entire ruin for those staples of South Carolina, whereas the northern provinces, having export connections chiefly with foreign countries, were little affected by a non-exportation to British countries. For one, he could not consent to the Carolinians becoming "dupes to the people

[1] Journal of the congress in *4 Am. Arch.*, vol. i, pp. 1109-1118; Drayton's detailed account of the debates in Drayton, *Memoirs*, vol. i, pp. 168-176; brief accounts in *S. C. Gaz.*, Jan. 23, 1775; *N. Y. Gaz.*, Feb. 6; and *N. Y. Journ.*, Feb. 9.

of the North." He even charged "a commercial scheme among the Flour Colonies" to seize for themselves the markets which had hitherto been supplied by South Carolina rice *via* Great Britain. Turning to the indigo group, he expatiated on the justice and practicability of a scheme of compensation as a method of equalizing burdens.

The subject was thus complicated by the question of compensation, and the debate became more general. Among the principal speakers in opposition to the compensation plan were Gadsden, Rawlins Lowndes, and the Rev. William Tennent. If the rice exemption must needs be retained, yet, they asked, why should the benefits of compensation be monopolized by the indigo growers alone?; "it should afford in justice also relief to the Hemp Grower, the Lumber Cutter, the Corn Planter, the Makers of Pork and Butter, &c." It was said that "this odious distinction has cruelly convulsed the Colony." On the other side the chief speakers were William Henry Drayton, the Rutledges, and the Lynches, father and son. In this manner the whole day was consumed, and at sunset a committee was appointed to formulate a plan of compensation. The report was made late next morning to an assemblage that had been waiting impatiently for two hours. All parties united in voting through the first part of the report, which authorized the committees of the several parishes and districts to sit as judges and juries in all matters affecting the collection of debts. But the details of the plan for compensation proved unsatisfactory and were rejected.

The debate reverted to the original question of expunging the words, "except rice to Europe," and continued until dark. "Great heats prevailed and the members were on the point of falling into downright uproar and confusion." When the question was at length put by candle-light, a demand was made that the vote be taken by roll-call instead of *viva voce;* and " by this mode [says Drayton] some were overawed, either by their diffidence, circumstances, or connexions; and to the surprise of the nays, they themselves carried the point by a majority of twelve voices—eighty-seven to seventy-five." A formal endorsement of the Continental Association was then voted. A day or so later the members succeeded in agreeing upon a plan of compensation and exchange, in which the benefits of the arrangement were extended far beyond the original intention of relief for the indigo growers exclusively. After the tenth of September the rice planters were to deliver to designated committees one-third of their crop and receive, at a stated rate of exchange, not more than one-third of certain other commodities produced in the province, such as indigo, hemp, lumber, corn and pork.

Before adjourning, the provincial congress took the precaution of appointing committees in each parish and district to carry into effect the Continental Association; and in every case members of congress composed a majority of the committee.[1] In this way, according to Drayton, no time was lost " in giving a complete appearance to the body politic and the greatest energy to their operations." Future vacancies in the committees were to be filled by the inhabitants of the parishes and districts. South Carolina was thus equipped with a well-solidified extra-legal organization, invigorated by an interested public opinion.

The province of Georgia had been unrepresented in the Continental Congress, although the zealous radicals of St. John's Parish, assisted by some congenial spirits at Savannah in Christ Church Parish, had employed their utmost endeavors to bring the province into line. From some points of view, prospects for radical action were brighter

[1] For the names of the members of these committees, *vide 4 Am. Arch.*, vol. i, pp. 1113-1114.

in the months following the Continental Congress, inasmuch as the threatened Indian war had failed to materialize and as rice, one of the staples of the province, had been given a favored position in the Continental Association. In other respects, the situation was more complicated because of a division among the radicals themselves as to the question of tactics. Some of them insisted that the province should be induced to accept the Continental Association in the form in which it was issued by Congress; others believed that a bid should be made for mercantile support by further postponing the time at which the non-importation and non-exportation regulations were to become effective. The extremists of St. John's Parish were uncompromising advocates of the former course and they hastened to adopt the Association *in toto* on December 1.[1] The radicals at Savannah and the radical members of the Assembly were inclined to the more conciliatory course.

" Since the Carolina Deputies have returned from the Continental Congress . . . , every means possible have been used to raise a flame again in this Province," wrote Governor Wright on December 13, 1774.[2] The first step in the direction of provincial action was taken by the Savannah radicals on December 3, when a call was issued for a provincial congress to assemble on January 18, 1775.[3] At the time appointed, delegates appeared from only five of the twelve parishes and districts to which the radicals had particularly written, and some of these were under injunctions as to the form of the Association which should be adopted.[4] It would appear, also, that, with the exception

[1] A convention of the District of Darien did the same on Jan. 12, 1775. *4 Am. Arch.*, vol. i, pp. 1135-1136.

[2] *Ibid.*, vol. i, p. 1040.

[3] *Ga. Gaz.*, Dec. 7, 1774; also *Pa. Gaz.*, Dec. 28.

[4] This account of the Georgia congress and the meeting of the

of St. John's Parish, small radical minorities had carried through the election of delegates.[1] Furthermore, the delegation from St. John's Parish, headed by Dr. Lyman Hall, although present in Savannah, refused to take part in the congress because of the known intention of that body to deviate from the Continental Association, which the men of St. John's had adopted *verbatim*.

Under these circumstances the members of the congress found themselves in a dilemma. Representing a small and amorphous minority of the people and estranged for the time being from the ultra-radicals of St. John's, they did not dare to represent their action as the voice of the province; on the other hand, they did not wish the endorsement of the Continental Congress to fail by default. They decided therefore to take advantage of an opportunity afforded by the presence of the Assembly in town. That body had already given indications of its friendliness when it had laid on the table without comment two petitions signed by a number of "principal people," condemning the measures of the northern provinces, and when it had adopted the declaration of rights and grievances of the Continental Congress. The plan was that the provincial congress should formulate a course of action with reference to the Association and then present its conclusions to the House of Assembly, which would adopt them in a few minutes before the governor could interfere by means of dissolution.

Upon this understanding, the members of the congress

Assembly is based on various contemporary narratives, friendly and unfriendly, in *4 Am. Arch.*, vol. i, pp. 1156-1163; vol. ii, pp. 279-281; and *Pa. Journ.*, Mch. 8, 1775.

[1] Thus, it was alleged that 36 men had acted in St. Andrew's Parish, which contained at least 800 men of military age; and that eighty men had done the work in St. Paul's, a parish of equal size.

now proceeded. Ignoring the insistent messages transmitted from time to time by the St. John's delegation that the Association be ratified *verbatim*, they adopted it with modifications, the most important of which postponed the beginning of non-importation from December 1, 1774, to March 15, 1775, and exempted goods necessary for the Indian trade from its operation, and provided that non-exportation should start on December 1, 1775, instead of September 10, 1775. These changes were made on the plea of allowing the Georgia merchants approximately the same time for arranging their business for the suspension of trade that the merchants of other provinces had enjoyed. The congress also chose three inhabitants of Savannah as delegates to the Second Continental Congress. These matters were now ready to be presented to the House of Assembly for ratification " when the Governour, either treacherously informed, or shrewdly suspecting the step, put an end to the session." The members of the provincial congress made the most of a bad situation by issuing their Association on January 23, with their signatures attached, and pledging their constituents to its execution.

Thus the effort to unite the province in radical measures with the other provinces proved a failure. The delegates chosen to the Second Continental Congress refused to serve in that capacity on the ground that they were not in position to pledge the people of Georgia to the execution of any measure whatsoever. The radicals in general awaited the action which the Second Congress would take in the circumstances. The committee of St. John's Parish, unbending in their self-sufficiency, began to cast about for some way of escaping the boycott, which threatened them, as well as the rest of the province, under Article xiv of the Continental Association.

CHAPTER XII

FIVE MONTHS OF THE ASSOCIATION IN THE COMMERCIAL
PROVINCES (DECEMBER, 1774–APRIL, 1775)

IN studying the actual workings of the Association two important considerations should be borne in mind. Warned by the trend of public discussion in the months preceding the adoption of the Association, and allowed several weeks of open importation by the provisions of the Association, the merchants had an opportunity to provide against future scarcity by importing much greater quantities of merchandise than customary. Richard Oswald quoted a British exporter as saying that in July, 1774, an extraordinarily brisk export trade set up, which swept the warehouses for American goods clean and advanced the price of many articles from ten to fifteen per cent.[1] Other evidences of the inflated conditions of exportation to America are abundant. Wrote a London merchant to his New York correspondent on July 29, 1774: "The peqple of Philadelphia have encreased their orders triply this fall; from whence I am persuaded they mean to have a Non-Importation Agreement."[2] "I hear the merchants are sending for double the quantity of goods they usually import," wrote Governor Gage in August, "and in order to get credit for them, are sending home all the money they can collect, insomuch that bills have risen at New-York above five per cent."[3] "So

---

[1] Stevens, *Facsimiles*, vol. xxiv, no. 2037, p. 14.
[2] *N. Y. Gazetteer*, Sept. 22, 1774. *Vide* also *Pa. Journ.*, Aug. 24.
[3] *4 Am. Arch.*, vol. i, pp. 742-743.

great has been the exportation to America, particularly to New-England, for these six weeks past," wrote a London correspondent in the same month, " that it is the opinion of some Merchants conversant with American Trade that, if the Colonies do agree in a non-importation scheme, it will hardly be felt by our Manufacturers for six months or a year." [1] The Boston Committee of Correspondence entertained the same general view of the situation. " We learn by private papers from England," they wrote on September 7, " that prodigious quantities of goods are now shipping for the Colony of Rhode Island, New York and Philadelphia." [2]

As a result of the augmented importation into America prior to the time that the Association went into effect, the conditions of life under the non-importation regulation were greatly ameliorated for the colonists. It was generally estimated that the stock of goods on hand on December 1, 1774, would suffice without replenishment for two years.[3]

[1] *N. Y. Gaz.*, Sept. 26, 1774.

[2] *4 Am. Arch.*, vol. i, p. 784. Dr. Samuel Cooper wrote to John Adams in similar strain in October. *Ibid.*, p. 878. *Vide* also *N. Y. Journ.*, Sept. 29, 1774; *N. C. Col. Recs.*, vol. ix, p. 1093. A convention of several Connecticut counties and a meeting of the town of Pomfret protested against the flood of goods which was pouring into Connecticut from New York. *Conn. Cour.*, Sept. 19, 1774; *Bos. Com. Cor. Papers*, vol. ii, pp. 217-218, 307-310. A comparison of the imports from England during the years 1773 and 1774 confirms these statements, although it is only fair to note that the former year was an off year, due to the excessive importations of 1771 and 1772 following the breakdown of the earlier non-importation agreement. English importations into New York increased from £289,214 in 1773 to £437,937 in 1774; into Pennsylvania from £426,448 to £625,652; into Maryland and Virginia from £328,904 to £528,738. There was a slighter increase in the case of New England and the Carolinas—from £527,055 to £562,476 in case of the former, and from £344,859 to £378,116 in case of the latter. Georgia showed a decrease. Macpherson, *Annals of Commerce*, vol. iii, pp. 549-550, 564.

[3] *E. g., vide 4 Am. Arch.*, vol. i, p. 1740. "A Friend of Liberty"

This was something of an overestimate, however. This supply of merchandise rendered the enforcement of the non-importation during the first twelvemonth easier than it would otherwise have been, for the merchants who had laid in goods were not easily tempted to defy the regulations of Congress and the committees. On the other hand, the utility of the Association as an instrument of coercion was not materially lessened by the advance importations. The great consignments of British wares had to reach America before December 1, 1774, or, at the most, not later than February 1, 1775; and thereafter British mercantile houses and manufactories became idle so far as American business was concerned. They were threatened with dull times and industrial depression at a time when their capital was more largely than usual tied up in American ventures.

The second consideration to be kept in mind in examining the Association in operation is that, after the non-importation regulation had been in force for four and a half months, events occurred which changed the whole face of public affairs and rapidly converted the Association from a mode of peaceful pressure into a war measure. The action of the " embattled farmers " at Lexington and Concord and the military operations that followed showed the radicals that the Association as a method of redress had suddenly become antiquated and that it must be altered, if not altogether abandoned, to meet the greatly changed conditions. This realization was at once acted upon by local committees and by Congress; and by the middle of

averred that this was the understanding upon which the colonists had associated. Pinkney's *Va. Gaz.*, Feb. 2, 1775. Alexander Hamilton believed that the merchants' stocks would be exhausted in eighteen months, but that with the clothes which the people already possessed imported articles would be in use for three years. "The Farmer Refuted," Hamilton, *Works* (Lodge), vol. i, p. 151.

1775 the Continental Association was rapidly losing its original character. The military purposes to which the machinery of the Association was turned became increasingly important, so that by September 10, 1775, when the non-exportation was to begin, the character of that measure had also to be changed. Thus, the bold experiment, inaugurated by the First Congress — to establish the several self-denying regulations of the Association through the mobilizing of public opinion—was brought to a premature close by the call to arms.

Certain generalizations may be made with reference to the workings of the Association before taking up the practice of the provinces separately. In Massachusetts, where the war fever was high, and, to a lesser extent, in the neighboring provinces, the committees and conventions felt called upon to concern themselves with military preparations even before the outbreak of war. Every province without exception availed itself of the suggestion made in the Association that such further regulations should be established by the provincial conventions and committees as might be deemed proper to enforce the Association. Non-importation and sumptuary regulations occupied the entire attention in the period before the opening of hostilities, save for the non-exportation of sheep, inasmuch as the general non-exportation was not to become effective until September 10, 1775. For the present, the period of enforcement prior to the outbreak of war will be considered.

Almost the first collective action taken in Massachusetts to strengthen the Continental Association locally was an agreement, signed by forty-one blacksmiths of Worcester County on November 8, 1774, that they would refuse their work to all persons who did not strictly conform to the Association. They agreed further that they would not perform any kind of work, after December 1, for persons of Tory leanings, particularly Timothy Ruggles of Hardwick, John Murray of Rutland, James Putnam of Worcester, their employees and dependents.[1] By this latter resolve hung a tale, for Timothy Ruggles and his friends, with the active co-operation of Governor Gage, were seeking to promote a loyalist association for the purpose of defeating the Continental Association. By the terms of this association the subscribers pledged themselves to defend, with lives and fortune, their "life, liberty and property" and their "undoubted right to liberty in eating, drinking, buying, selling, communing, and acting . . . consistent with the laws of God and the King." "When the person or property of any of us shall be invaded or threatened by Committees, mobs, or unlawful assemblies," said one portion of the paper, "the others of us will, upon notice received, forthwith repair, properly armed, to the person on whom . . . such invasion or threatening shall be, and will to the utmost of our power, defend such person and his property, and, if need be, will oppose and repel force with force."[2]

This brave pledge of opposition failed to win signers, for the reason that every signer of the paper at once exposed himself to the swift wrath of the radicals. The provincial congress on December 9 recommended to the committees of correspondence to give "the earliest notice to the publick of all such combinations, and of the persons signing the same, . . . that their names may be published to the world, their persons treated with that neglect, and their memories transmitted to posterity with that ignominy which such un-

[1] *Bos. Gaz.*, Nov. 28, 1774.
[2] *Mass. Gaz. & Post-Boy*, Dec. 26, 1774; also *4 Am. Arch.*, vol. i, pp. 1057-1058.

natural conduct must deserve." ¹ It was under influence of this resolution that, a few weeks later, a mob of people at Wrentham coerced five loyalists to plead, with heads uncovered, the forgiveness of Heaven, and to pledge undeviating adherence to the Continental Association.² Marshfield was the only town where as many as one hundred and fifty men signed the loyalist association, and the associators discreetly sent a hurry-call to Gage for troops for their protection.³ Gage complained that the "considerable people" of Boston were "more shy of making open declarations," notwithstanding that they were in a fortified town, than the people in the country.⁴ The failure of the loyalist association was due to the superior organization of the radicals rather than to lack of support for it.

The provincial congress, meeting in late November and early December, 1774, passed a number of resolutions to supplement and strengthen several portions of the Continental Association. They also recommended that the ministers of the gospel throughout the province instruct their congregations to cleave to the Association; and in a fervent address directly to the inhabitants of the province they urged the organization of minute-men as a protection against Gage's troops who would certainly be employed to defeat the Association.⁵

There was unmistakable evidence that the non-importation regulation was strictly enforced. In accordance with Article x, importers of merchandise which arrived between December 1, 1774, and February 1, 1775, were given the

¹ *Bos. Gaz.*, Dec. 19, 1774; also *4 Am. Arch.*, vol. i, p. 1004. *Vide* also the resolution of April 12, 1775; *ibid.*, pp. 1360-1361.

² *N. Y. Gaz.*, Jan. 23, 1775.

³ *4 Am. Arch.*, vol. i, pp. 1177-1178, 1249-1251.

⁴ *Ibid.*, vol. i, p. 1634; *vide* also *ibid*, pp. 1046-1047.

⁵ *Ibid.*, vol. i, pp. 1000, 1005-1006.

choice of immediately re-shipping the goods, storing the goods with the local committee, or having them auctioned off under direction of the committee. In the last case, the owner was reimbursed to the extent of his actual investment and the profits were devoted to the uses of the Boston needy. The provincial congress provided that such sales must be advertised in the Boston and Salem papers at least ten days in advance, and that the goods should be sold to the highest bidder.[1] The newspapers related many instances of each course of procedure; and even the loyalist writings did not seek to represent otherwise. The chief centers of activity were Marblehead, Salem and Plymouth. Many, perhaps most, importers preferred to offer their goods at committee auction than to tie up their capital for an indefinite period by storing the goods—a choice which, by the way, afforded them an opportunity to buy back their own goods.

As an example of such sales, the committee of inspection at Marblehead offered at auction on December 26 such part of the cargo of the London ship *Champion* as had then been delivered to the committee, consisting of Russia duck, osnaburgs, ticklinburgs, baizes, hemp, linens, hats, books, women's hose, nails, needles, calicoes, velvets and medicines to the value of £2410 sterling; and also the entire cargo of the Falmouth brigantine *Polly*, consisting of lemons, wines, raisins and figs. The rest of the goods imported in the *Champion* were disposed of in January.[2] The complete cargoes of the schooners *Lynn, Britannia* and *Adventure*, all from Falmouth, were sold a few weeks later.[3] As the result of their enterprise, the Marblehead

[1] *Mass. Spy*, Dec. 16, 1774.
[2] *Salem Gaz.*, Dec. 23, 1774; *Essex Gaz.*, Jan. 3, 1775: *Bos. Gaz.*, Jan. 23.
[3] *Mass. Spy*, Feb. 9, 1775.

committee of inspection derived profits amounting to £120, which they turned over to Boston.¹ Meantime, the Salem Committee were disposing of importations from Bristol, London, Falmouth, Jamaica and Dominica. Their method of sale was indicated by their advertisement that: " Each invoice will be put up at the sterling cost and charges, one per cent advance, and half per cent each bidder." ² Their contribution to Boston, as a result of the sales, amounted to £109 9s. 5d.³ In the same period the Plymouth committee of inspection made profits for Boston amounting to £31 5s. 6½.⁴

After February 1 few vessels arrived in Massachusetts ports as compared with former and better days. When they did come, the cargoes were almost invariably re-shipped without breaking bulk.⁵ One instance of defiance occurred at Falmouth in March, when a small sloop arrived from Bristol with rigging, sails and stores for a vessel which Thomas Coulson was in the process of building. The committee of inspection resolved that the materials should be returned by the same vessel; but Coulson would conform to their demands only in part. He brought on his head the condemnation of the Cumberland County convention, which shortly after assembled at Falmouth; and as Coulson continued obdurate, the committee of inspection published him as a violator of the Association.⁶

Few efforts were made to violate the regulation for the non-exportation of sheep. In December, Captain Hamilton

¹ *Bos. Gaz.*, Mch. 13, 1775.
² *Mass. Spy*, Jan. 5, 1775.
³ *Essex Gaz.*, Apr. 11, 1775.
⁴ *Bos. Gaz.*, Mch. 27, 1775.
⁵ *E. g.*, a cargo of molasses arriving at Marblehead from Dominica on March 2; *Essex Journ.*, Mch. 15, 1775.
⁶ *4 Am. Arch.*, vol. ii, pp. 311-313; *Bos. Eve. Post*, Apr. 3, 1775.

at Salem planned to send thirty sheep to Jamaica; but when the committee of inspection explained that he would be violating the Association, he readily desisted.[1] The committee later stopped another consignment. The regulations concerning non-consumption were harder to administer, because of the practical difficulty of distinguishing between goods which might properly be bought and those which could not. The committee at Newburyport met this difficulty by requiring shopkeepers to produce a certificate from some committee of inspection, testifying that the wares offered for sale had been imported before December 1 or, if later, that they had been disposed of according to Article x.[2] The provincial congress simplified the situation for the future by passing a sweeping resolution forbidding the sale, after October 10, 1775, of goods which fell under the ban of the non-importation regulation, even if the goods were unsold stock remaining from the period prior to December 1.[3]

The most frequent infractions of the non-consumption regulation occurred with reference to the article of tea. An example of the vigilance of the committees of inspection was afforded by the prompt apprehension of Thomas Lilly, of Marblehead, for the purchase of a pound and a quarter of tea from Simon Tufts, a Boston dealer, after March 1, 1775. When Lilly had burnt the tea in the presence of a large crowd, and had signed a confession, which read in part: " I do now in this publick manner ask their pardon, and do solemnly promise I will not in future be guilty of a like offence," the Marblehead committee announced that he might " be justly entitled to the esteem and employ of all

[1] *Essex Gaz.*, Dec. 13, 1774.
[2] *Essex Journ.*, Dec. 28, 1774.
[3] *4 Am. Arch.*, vol. i, pp. 998-999. This resolution was repealed on Sept. 30, 1775, however, before it became effective. *Ibid.*, vol. iii, p. 1445.

persons as heretofore." The Boston committee examined into Tufts' action and secured from him a statement, made under oath before a justice of the peace, that the tea had been sold to Lilly by the clerk without the knowledge or consent of himself and that in the future his conduct should not be open to misconstruction.[1] Some difficulty arose from the practice of peddlers and petty chapmen going through the country towns and selling teas and other East India goods which, there was reason to suspect, had been imported after December 1. On February 15, 1775, the provincial congress urged the committees of inspection to prevent such sales, and recommended to the inhabitants not to trade with peddlers for any article whatever.[2]

Some effort was made by the provincial congress to stimulate local industry, although it hardly went beyond an exhortation to the people to form societies for the purpose of promoting manufacturing and agriculture. A number of articles were named, whose production should be encouraged — such as nails, steel, tin-plates, buttons, paper, glass and hosiery, gunlocks, saltpetre and gunpowder. A few months later, the provincial congress asked every family in the province to save rags in order that a paper mill erected at Milton might have a sufficient supply. The people were also asked to refrain from killing sheep except in cases of dire necessity.[3] Local manufacturers made some progress if one may judge from the advertising columns of the *Massachusetts Spy* in January, 1775. Fish-hooks, made at Cornish, were offered for sale by Lee & Jones. Enoch Brown advertised sagathies, duroys, camblets, calamancoes and shalloons of Massachusetts-make, and decanters, cruets

[1] *Essex Gaz.*, Mch. 28, 1775, and *Bos. Gaz.*, Apr. 3; also 4 *Am. Arch.*, vol. ii, p. 234.
[2] *Ibid.*, vol. i, pp. 1339-1340.
[3] *Ibid.*, vol. i, pp. 1001-1002, 1334; vol. ii, p. 1514; vol. iii, p. 329.

and other glassware imported from Philadelphia. Boston-made buttons could be purchased from John Clarke.

Tendencies toward a greater frugality were to be found in other respects as well. The Marblehead committee of inspection voted unanimously that " the meeting of the inhabitants of this town in parties at houses of entertainment, for the purposes of dancing, feasting, &c., is expressly against the Association," and that future offenders should be held up to public notice.[1] The regulation with reference to simplicity in mourning seems to have been well observed,[2] although the committee of inspection at Newburyport felt it necessary to declare that: " If any should . . . go into a contrary practice, they may well expect that their friends and neighbours will manifest their disapprobation . . . by declining to attend the funeral." [3]

In New Hampshire the enforcement of the Association depended in large degree on the faithfulness and energy of the Committee of " Forty-Five " at Portsmouth, the only port of entry. This committee proved equal to its responsibilities. Before news of the adoption of the Association reached Portsmouth, Captain Pearne, a merchant, had commissioned a brig to proceed to Madeira for a cargo of wine; but before the vessel sailed the provisions of the Association were learned and the merchant agreed to send her to the West Indies instead.[4] The committee also stopped Captain Chivers who was on the point of exporting fifty sheep to the West Indies; and he was forced to dispose of them otherwise at some loss to himself.[5] On December 2 Governor Wentworth wrote that most people

[1] *Essex Gaz.*, Jan. 17, 1775; also *Salem Gaz.*, Jan. 20.
[2] *Mass. Spy*, Nov. 24, 1774.
[3] *Essex Journ.*, Dec. 28, 1774.
[4] *N. H. Gaz.*, Nov. 18, 1774.
[5] *4 Am. Arch.*, vol. i, p. 1013; *N. H. Gaz.*, Nov. 18, 1774.

accepted the regulations of Congress "as matters of obedience, not of considerate examination, whereon they may exercise their own judgment."[1] When sixty pounds of dutied tea was found in possession of a shopkeeper on January 18, the culprit exhibited the better part of valor by burning it in the presence of a large crowd.[2] On February 10 the committee recommended that all who furnished accommodations for cards and billiards should discontinue their unjustifiable proceedings at once.[3] So energetic was the committee that the conservatives endeavored to set on foot an association in opposition to the Continental Association; but the movement came to nought.[4]

In the towns outside of Portsmouth, the greatest difficulty was experienced in dealing with country peddlers and chapmen. These men were accused of contravening the non-importation and non-consumption regulations and also of "tempting women, girls and boys with their unnecessary fineries." The town of Exeter voted to permit no itinerant traders to sell wares there.[5] A town meeting at Epsom established the same regulation "upon no less penalty than receiving a new suit agreeable to the modern mode and a forfeiture of their goods."[6] The committees at Kingstown, New Market and Brentwood announced that the provincial law prohibiting peddling would now be rigidly enforced.[7] When a provincial convention met on January 25, they endorsed this last method as the most effective way of coping with the difficulty.[8] The conven-

[1] 4 *Am. Arch.*, vol. i, p. 1013.
[2] *N. H. Gaz.*, Jan. 27, 1775.
[3] *Ibid.*, Feb. 10, 1775; also 4 *Am. Arch.*, vol. i, p. 1223.
[4] *Ibid.*, vol. ii, p. 251; also *N. H. Gaz.*, Mch. 31, 1775.
[5] *Ibid.*, Jan. 6, 1775; also 4 *Am. Arch.*, vol. i, pp. 1105-1106.
[6] *Ibid.*, vol. i, p. 1105; also *N. H. Gaz.*, Jan. 20, 1775.
[7] *Ibid.*, Jan. 13, 1775.
[8] *Ibid.*, Feb. 3, 1775; also 4 *Am. Arch.*, vol. i, p. 1182.

tion also issued an address to the inhabitants in behalf of the Association and, among other things, recommended the immediate and total disuse of tea whether dutied or smuggled. The people were also urged to promote home manufactures and shun all forms of extravagance. It was not until the provincial congress met in May that the subject of local production received further attention. Then linen and woolen manufactures were mentioned as being particularly worthy of encouragement, and farmers were enjoined to kill no lambs before the first of August following.[1]

The non-importation regulation appears to have been well enforced in Rhode Island. Several vessels intending for the African coast were actually laid up at Newport because they could not be gotten ready to depart by December 1.[2] The Newport committee remitted to Boston the sum of £5 15s. 3d. sterling as the profits of sales of importations prior to February 1, 1775.[3] Late in January, the committee at Providence auctioned off a quantity of merchandise, valued at £1200 sterling, imported from Liverpool by way of New York, and derived a profit of £16 6s. 1d. for the relief of Boston.[4] Particular attention was given in Rhode Island to the regulations for the non-exportation of sheep. In November, 1774, the Providence committee exhorted obedience to these regulations; a few days later they sent to Boston, as a gift, one hundred and thirty-six sheep that had originally been intended for exportation to the West Indies but which the town had bought instead.[5] Until late in February, Newport would not even

[1] 4 *Am. Arch.*, vol. ii, p. 651.
[2] *Pa. Journ.*, Feb. 8, 1775; also 4 *Am. Arch.*, vol. i, pp. 1098-1099.
[3] 4 *M. H. S. Colls.*, vol. iv, p. 265.
[4] *Bos. Eve. Post*, Feb. 20, 1775; *Essex Gaz.*, Mch. 7.
[5] 4 *M. H. S. Colls.*, vol. iv, p. 154.

permit the shipment of sheep to associated provinces; then, the Salem committee succeeded in pointing out the error of this interpretation of the Association.[1]

Providence facilitated the enforcement of the non-consumption regulation by requiring all dealers to show a certificate that the goods offered for sale conformed in every way to the specifications of the Association.[2] On March 2, 1775, the day after the total disuse of tea became effective, the event was celebrated at Providence by a bonfire of three hundred pounds of tea that had been collected from the inhabitants.[3] The situation in Rhode Island may be summarized in the language of the Newport committee to their Philadelphia brethren: " so far as we can learn, the Association hath been strictly adhered to by the merchants in this colony . . ."[4] Apparently little was done to encourage manufacturing or to foster the simple life. However, the graduating class at Rhode Island College induced the college authorities to abandon the public commencement exercises as out of harmony with Article viii.[5]

The chief problem in Connecticut was not that of non-importation (for her imports came largely by way of Massachusetts and New York), but that of non-consumption. The Norwich committee required all dealers to comply with the regulation, which was rapidly becoming popular, of vouching for the character of new stock by displaying certificates from whence the merchandise came.[6] An early tendency was observable for prices to rise, due to the fact

---

[1] *Pickering Papers* (M. H. S. Mss.), vol. xxxiii, p. 122; vol. xxxix, p. 100.

[2] *R. I. Col. Recs.*, vol. vii, pp. 285-287.

[3] *4 Am. Arch.*, vol. ii, p. 15.

[4] *Pa. Journ.*, Feb. 8, 1775; also *4 Am. Arch.*, vol. i, p. 1099.

[5] *Ibid.*, vol. ii, pp. 935-936.

[6] *Conn. Gaz.*, Dec. 30, 1774.

that the importers had sold to the Connecticut retailers at an advance and the former could not easily be reached because of their residence in other provinces. On January 25, 1775, a joint meeting of committees of inspection of Hartford County resolved that, even if the importers violated the Association, the retailers should not be excused, and that no better rule could be fixed regarding prices than Article ix of the Association.[1] A few days later the committee of inspection at Farmington in the same county obtained from James Percival, a local dealer, a written confession of his guilt in violating this regulation and a promise to deposit his surplus profit with the committee for use of the Boston unfortunate.[2] The same action with respect to prices was taken by the counties of New Haven, Fairfield and Litchfield. All these counties also directed attention to the importance of improving sheep, raising flax and encouraging manufactures.[3]

As Connecticut possessed no commercial metropolis, special effort was made in that province to standardize the practice of trying persons accused of transgressing the Association in the several small river and coast towns. The movement was set on foot, it would appear, at the meeting of the committees of inspection of Hartford County on January 25. In executing the Association, it was there agreed that proceedings against an accused should be conducted in an "open, candid and deliberate manner;" that formal summons should be served upon him, containing the nature of the charge, with an invitation to defend himself before the committee at some time not sooner than six days later; that witnesses and other evidence should be "openly, fairly and fully heard;" and that no conviction should be

[1] *Conn. Cour.*, Jan. 30, 1775.
[2] *Ibid.*, Feb. 13, 1775.
[3] *Ibid.*, Feb. 27, 1775; *Conn. Journ.*, Mch. 8.

made " but upon the fullest, clearest and most convincing proof." [1] The same mode of procedure was adopted by the counties of New Haven, Fairfield and Litchfield.[2]

Trials of offenders by the committees of inspection bore every evidence of being fair and impartial hearings, although mistakes were occasionally made. In March three men failed to appear before the Fairfield committee who had been summoned to answer charges; and upon an *ex parte* examination the committee held unanimously that the accused were guilty of a breach of the Association and should forfeit all commercial connections with the community. Five weeks later, two of the men came before the committee, proved their innocence and were restored to public favor.[3] At Guilford Captain Griffin appeared before the committee and demanded that his character be cleared of the aspersions cast upon it by a letter from Martinique, which had been printed in the *Journal* and which accused him of having violated Article vii by taking fourteen sheep to Martinique. After investigation the committee decided that Griffin was not guilty and recommended him to the favorable consideration of the public.[4] In general, the view expressed by Thomas Mumford of Groton to Silas Deane in October, 1775, may be accepted as correct: " This Colony universally adheres to all the Resolves of Congress." [5] Even in Fairfield County, where, it will be recalled, the greatest disaffection existed, the principal towns were actively engaged in executing the Association.

[1] *Conn. Cour.*, Jan. 30, 1775.
[2] *Ibid.*, Feb. 27, 1775; *Conn. Journ.*, Mch. 8.
[3] *Conn. Gaz.*, Apr. 4, May 12, 1775.
[4] *N. Y. Gaz.*, Apr. 3, 1775; also *4 Am. Arch.*, vol. ii, p. 222.
[5] *Conn. Hist. Soc. Colls.*, vol. ii, p. 310. *Vide* also *4 Am. Arch.*, vol. ii, pp. 252-253.

In New York province the responsibility of enforcing the non-importation regulation rested with the Committee of Sixty at the port of entry. However, the first occasion for enforcement of the Association was the attempt of an inconsiderate citizen to ship some sheep to the West Indies. The shipment was prevented through the energy of a group of inhabitants who acted without consulting the Committee of "Fifty-One," then still in office.[1] A few days later the distillers of the city signified their hearty approval of the pending non-importation by resolving to distill no molasses imported from the British West Indies or Dominica nor to sell any rum for the purpose of carrying on the slave traffic.[2] In the two months prior to February 1, 1775, the Committee of Sixty showed a record of astonishing activity. Their official report testifies that they conducted auctions for the sale of goods imported in twenty-one vessels, as well as for the sale of a trunk of calicoes imported from London by way of Philadelphia.[3] These cargoes were made up of a variety of articles representing many quarters of the globe and evidencing the colorful romance of colonial commerce. A great deal of space was taken up in the newspapers by announcements of sales. The greatest profit arose from the sale of merchandise brought in the large London ship *Lady Gage*, from which £182 18s. was cleared for Boston. In a number of cases the selling price covered merely the first cost and charges. The total profits from all sales amounted to £347 4s. 1d.

After February 1 the Sixty displayed equal diligence in returning cargoes without breaking bulk. For the purpose of facilitating this work a sub-committee was appointed to supervise the arrival of all vessels.[4] The most difficult case

[1] *4 Am. Arch.*, vol. i, p. 963; also *N. Y. Journ.*, Nov. 10, 1774.
[2] *Ibid.*, Nov. 10, 1774.
[3] *Ibid.*, Apr. 27, 1775; also *4 Am. Arch.*, vol. ii, pp. 342-343.
[4] *N. Y. Journ.*, Feb. 2, 1775.

of enforcement proved to be that of a vessel that arrived on the second day of the new dispensation. This was the ship *James*, commanded by Captain Watson and bringing a cargo of coal and drygoods from Glasgow. The captain was promptly warned by the sub-committee not to enter at the custom house and not to delay in departing with his cargo unbroken. But the loyalists were determined to make this a trial of strength; and although the consignees refused to appeal to the authorities for aid, they obtained the not unwilling ear of Captain Watson and employed men to go aboard and bring the colors ashore with a view to raising a posse to assist in landing the goods. A great mob assembled on the shore; and the captain, much alarmed, dropped down about four miles below the city, where he remained several days attended by a boat containing representatives of the committee. On Thursday evening, the ninth, the ship reappeared in the harbor escorted by an officer and some men belonging to the royal vessel *Kingfisher*, which had just come on the scene. The people again assembled in great numbers, seized the captain who was lodging in town, and paraded him about the streets until he was glad to flee to the man-of-war. After two days of sober reflection he prepared to depart with his ship, but was now ordered to desist by an overzealous lieutenant from the *Kingfisher*. Again the people collected; and the captain of the *Kingfisher*, hearing of the unauthorized act of the lieutenant, permitted the departure of the *James*. That vessel was watched far beyond Sandy Hook, as she swept out to sea, by the committee's boat.[1]

The vigilance of the Sixty was again tested later in the month upon the arrival of the *Beulah* from London. After lying at anchor for almost three weeks in an effort to elude

[1] *N. Y. Journ.*, Feb. 9, 16, 1775; *Pa. Journ.*, Feb. 8; Colden, *Letter Books*, vol. ii, p. 389.

the watchfulness of the committee's boat, the vessel fell down to Sandy Hook to await a favorable wind for the return voyage. After two days' delay, she put to sea. Word quickly reached the Sixty that, under shelter of darkness, a boat from Elizabethtown, New Jersey, had taken off some goods while the ship lingered at the Hook. Investigation was at once undertaken by the Elizabethtown committee, and the truth of the case was being ferreted out when Robert and John Murray, merchants of New York, appeared before the Sixty and confessed that they were the principals in the affair. The return of the *Beulah* with an unbroken cargo meant great financial loss to them, but it is evident that they feared the blast of the boycott even more greatly. They made a sworn statement of the goods that had been landed and promised to re-ship them in seven days' time. Finally, to propitiate public feeling, they subscribed £200 for the repair of the hospital, recently damaged by fire. The Sixty published these facts without comment; and the Elizabethtown committee proscribed John Murray, and his son-in-law of that town—the actual participants in the affair—as violators of the Association.[1]

The Sixty exhibited less concern about the advancing of prices. While the First Continental Congress was yet in session, the old "Fifty-One" had taken cognizance of the discontent arising from "the exorbitant price to which sundry articles of goods, particularly some of the necessaries of life," had advanced in anticipation of non-importation; and they had induced a meeting of importers at the Exchange to agree to maintain prices at the usual level, discourage engrossing, and to boycott retailers who acted con-

[1] *N. Y. Journ.*, Feb. 23, Mch. 9, 23, Apr. 6, 1775. The son-in-law was restored to public favor, after public contrition, by act of the New Jersey provincial congress, Oct. 24, 1775. *4 Am. Arch.*, vol. iii, p. 1232. For the later history of the Murrays, *vide infra*, p. 565 and n. 1.

trariwise.¹ Nevertheless, by January, claims were made in the leading loyalist organ that prices had actually risen. Thus, coarse osnaburgs were said to have advanced a full third in the hands of the wholesaler; the price of coarse linens and Russia sheetings had increased also.² These allegations may not have fairly represented the situation, or else the committee may have thought it unwise to supervise the merchants too closely on this point. In any case the Sixty paid no attention to the charges.

An obvious effort was made to simplify the standard of living. When Mrs. Margaret Duane died early in January, her remains were interred in accordance with the directions of Article viii.³ The London ship *Lady Gage* brought two puppet shows to New York; and in the midst of their first performances, a committee of citizens stopped the proceedings and, while the audiences dispersed in much confusion, secured the promise of the managers not to show again.⁴

The project of establishing local manufacturers on some systematic plan attracted little interest at first. When, however, some enterprising Philadelphians established a manufacturing company a few months later, the Sixty decided to make use of the same plan, under the name " The New York Society for employing the Industrious Poor and Promoting Manufactory." The object was to manufacture woolens, linens, cottons and nails; but subscriptions for stock failed to materialize, and it was not until January, 1776, that a partial trial of the scheme was made possible by a subsidy granted by the committee of safety at New York city.⁵ This was too late to be of any practical use because of the British occupancy of the city soon after.

¹ *N. Y. Gaz.*, Oct. 10, 1774; also 4 *Am. Arch.*, vol. i, p. 328.
² *N. Y. Gazetteer*, Jan. 19, 26, Apr. 6, 1775.
³ *N. Y. Gaz.*, Jan. 16, 1775.   ⁴ *N. Y. Journ.*, Dec. 15, 1774.
⁵ 4 *Am. Arch.*, vol. iii, pp. 1263-1264, 1424-1426; *Constitutional Gaz.*, Jan. 27, 1776.

Apart from the three rural counties of Albany, Ulster and Suffolk, the outlying districts were not at this time sufficiently organized to enforce the non-consumption regulations. It should be noted, however, that the energy and intelligence of the Sixty at the metropolis reduced the importance of such enforcement, inasmuch as foreign wares seldom, if ever, penetrated that far. Probably the worst infractions occurred in the matter of tea drinking after March 1, when no tea either duty or smuggled was to be consumed. On April 7, Jacobus Low of Kingston in Ulster County was proscribed by the Kingston committee as the only dealer in town who would not refuse to sell tea. A long and somewhat abusive controversy ensued; but at the end of two months Low appeared before the committee and made all the concessions they required.[1]

Since the mercantile houses of New York city were the feeders for the country stores of Connecticut and New Jersey, the inviolability of the non-importation in the metropolis was trebly important. That it was well kept the foregoing incidents testify. A group of conservatives in Dutchess and Westchester Counties sought to promote a loyalist association for personal liberty, modeled on Brigadier Ruggles's association in Massachusetts; but it made no headway.[2] Lieutenant Governor Colden, who had originally been skeptical of the success of the Continental Association, uttered a dependable judgment when he wrote on March 1: "the non importation association of the Congress is ever rigidly maintained in this Place."[3]

The spirit of the New Jersey associators has already been suggested by the conduct of the Elizabethtown committee

[1] *4 Am. Arch.*, vol. ii, pp. 298, 448, 548, 917.
[2] *Ibid.*, vol. i, p. 1164; *N. Y. Gaz.*, Mch. 20, 1775.
[3] *Letter Books*, vol. ii, p. 389. *Vide* also *ibid.*, pp. 369-370, 373.

in the Murray affair. On December 6, 1774, Governor Franklin informed the home government that: "Altho' the Proceedings of the Congress are not altogether satisfactory to many of the Inhabitants of the Colonies, yet there seems at present little Reason to doubt but that the Terms of Association will be generally carried into Execution, even by those who dislike Parts of it. But few have the Courage to declare their Disapprobation publickly, as they all know, if they do not conform, they are in Danger of becoming Objects of popular Resentment, from which it is not in the Power of Government here to protect them." [1] The public meetings of Gloucester County and of Woodbridge Township in Middlesex County expressly instructed their committees of observation that they should " as carefully attend to and pursue the rules and directions for their government . . . set forth in the said association, as they would if the same had been enacted into a law by the legislature of this province." [2]

The committees had to devote very little time to the prevention of importation because of the absence of any good ports. However, a consignment of merchandise, which had come by way of New York in the *Lady Gage*, was sold at auction at New Brunswick; and another importation from Bristol in the *Fair Lady* via the same port was sold at Elizabethtown.[3] An effort was made to land secretly a quantity of dutied tea at Greenwich in Cumberland County. The consignment was seized by some inhabitants; and while the committee of observation was gravely deliberating as to its disposition, Indians *à la* Boston made a bonfire of it.[4]

[1] *1 N. J. Arch.*, vol. x, p. 503.
[2] *Pa. Gaz.*, Dec. 21, 1774; *4 Am. Arch.*, vol. i, pp. 1102-1103.
[3] *N. Y. Journ.*, Jan. 19, 26, 1775.
[4] *Pa. Packet*, Jan. 19, 1775; Andrews, F. D., *Tea-Burners of Cumberland County* (Vineland, N. J., 1908).

In February the committees of observation of Elizabethtown and Woodbridge suspended commercial intercourse with the obdurate inhabitants of nearby Staten Island, who had neglected to join the Association.[1]

Of the various committees that passed resolutions in behalf of economy and home production, the Hanover committee in Morris County established the most comprehensive regulations. They promised to take note of all horse-racing, cock-fighting and gambling and to prosecute the offenders in accordance with the law. To Article vii of the Association they added the requirements that no sheep should be taken from the county without the committee's permission and that no sheep should be killed until it was four years old. They recommended the wide cultivation of flax and hemp, and inveighed against any dealers who should advance prices.[2]

An illustration of the effectiveness of the boycott was accorded by the action of Silas Newcomb, a member of the Cumberland County committee, in announcing voluntarily on March 6 that he had been drinking tea in his family since March 1 and that he proposed to continue the practice. All dealings were thereupon broken off with him; and on May 11 he appeared before the committee and made an abject apology for his offense; that body accepted his "recantation."[3]

In Pennsylvania the chief obstacle to a perfect execution of the Association was the hostility of the Quaker merchant aristocracy at Philadelphia, the only port of entry. These men were too shrewd to expose themselves to the rigors of

[1] *N. Y. Journ.*, Feb. 16, Mch. 9, 1775; also *4 Am. Arch.*, vol. i, pp. 1234-1235, 1249.
[2] *Ibid.*, vol. i, pp. 1240-1241; also *N. Y. Journ.*, Feb. 23, 1775.
[3] *4 Am. Arch.*, vol. ii, pp. 34-35.

the boycott through personal infractions of the Association; but, being wealthy and influential members of the Society of Friends, they were able to conduct a campaign against the Association by controlling the official utterances of that organization.

As early as May 30, 1774, the day before the Boston Port Act became effective, the several meetings of the society in Philadelphia joined in declaring that, if any Quakers had countenanced the plan of suspending all business on June 1, " they have manifested great inattention to our religious principles and profession, and acted contrary to the rules of Christian discipline established for the preservation of order and good government among us." [1] In the following months the constant effort of the Quaker leaders, in striking contrast with earlier years, was to keep the members of the society clear of radical activities. " This has occasioned no small care and labor," wrote James Pemberton on November 6, " but has been so far of service that I hope it may be said we are generally clear; tho' there have been instances of some few who claim a right of membership with us that have not kept within such limits and bounds as we could wish." [2] Joseph Reed, fixed in his singleness of purpose, seriously impugned their sincerity. They " act their usual part," he wrote on the same day as Pemberton's letter. " They have directed their members not to serve on the Committee, and mean to continue the same undecisive, neutral conduct until they see how the scale is like to preponderate. . . . But American Liberty in the mean time must take her chance with them." [3]

Finally, on December 15, a meeting for sufferings at Philadelphia appointed a committee to wait on the Quaker

[1] *4 Am. Arch.*, vol. i, pp. 365-366.
[2] Sharpless, *Quakers in Revolution*, p. 108.
[3] *4 Am. Arch.*, vol. i, pp. 963-964.

members of the provincial assembly and reprimand them for having given their votes to a resolution ratifying the doings of the Continental Congress five days earlier.[1] This was preliminary to the action taken by the meeting for sufferings for Pennsylvania and New Jersey, held at Philadelphia on January 5, 1775. At this meeting disapproval was expressed of the measures which were being prosecuted against Great Britain, and all members of the society were earnestly requested to avoid joining in such measures as inconsistent with their religious principles.[2] A gathering of Quaker representatives from the two provinces later in the month was even more explicit in their "testimony" against "every usurpation of power and authority in opposition to the Laws and Government, and against all Combinations, Insurrections, Conspiracies and Illegal Assemblages."[3]

Many members differed with the official utterances of the society, some perhaps because they had increased their stocks in anticipation of the non-importation, many others because they could not see why they should abstain from extra-legal activities at this juncture inasmuch as Quakers had been leaders in commercial combinations against Great Britain during Stamp Act times. A contemporary noted that the Quakers were divided; that many of them disapproved of the Testimony, just alluded to, and indeed that the Testimony had been adopted by a gathering of only twenty-six people.[4] "B. L.," writing in the *Pennsylvania Journal* of February 1, 1775, reasoned blandly that the Testimony could not have been directed against extra-legal

[1] Sharpless, *op. cit.*, p. 107.
[2] *N. Y. Gaz.*, Jan. 30, 1775; also *4 Am. Arch.*, vol. i, pp. 1093-1094.
[3] *Ibid.*, vol. i, pp. 1176-1177; also *Pa. Journ.*, Feb. 8, 1775.
[4] *4 Am. Arch.*, vol. i, p. 1270.

measures, since that supposition would condemn the very meeting which had issued the paper, and since James Pemberton, the secretary of the meeting, was well known as an active participant in the selection of the committee last summer. The upshot was that the Society of Friends was not able to fasten an official stigma on the radical measures nor to control the actions of all of its members, although it continued to seek to do so.

The Committee of Sixty-Six at Philadelphia made careful arrangements for the enforcement of the non-importation regulation. The membership of the committee was divided into six districts, and one person from each district was required to attend every morning at the London Coffee House to inspect the arrival of vessels.[1] All importers after December 1 were warned to consult with this sub-committee as to whether new merchandise should be stored, auctioned off, or re-shipped. Detailed regulations were laid down for public sales, such as, for instance, that in ordinary cases no lots worth more than £15 sterling nor less than £3 sterling should be offered for sale.[2]

Unfortunately no record has been found in the newspapers or elsewhere of the performance of the committee in the first two months of the non-importation; but that the committee was faithful to its trust there can be no doubt. " There seems to be too general a disposition every where to adhere strictly to the Resolutions of the Congress," wrote Deputy Governor Penn on December 31.[3] The Sixty-Six declared on February 16, 1775, that they had " not met with the least impediment or obstruction in carrying into execution any one Resolution of the Continental Congress,"

---

[1] *Pa. Gas.*, Dec. 7, 1774; also *N. Y. Journ.*, Dec. 15.
[2] *Pa. Gas.*, Dec. 14, 1774; also *Essex Journ.*, Dec. 28.
[3] *4 Am. Arch.*, vol. i, p. 1081.

although, like in every community, there were persons who, placing private interest against public good, had a malignant pleasure in stirring up dissension.[1] " The Non Importation is Strictly adheard to . . . ," wrote Eliza Farmar on February 17; " all ships that came in after the first of Decr, the goods were deliverd to the Commities to be sold by Auction agreeable to the order of the Congress." [2]

After February 1 the newspapers from time to time published instances of the return of cargoes without breaking bulk. So, with some pipes of Madeira wine that arrived early in February; and so, also, with a large consignment of Irish beef which arrived in April.[3] " All Ships with goods after the 1st of this month are not Sufferd to unload," reported Eliza Farmar in the letter noted above; " several have been obliged to go to the West Indies."

It would appear likely that the Sixty-Six showed some laxity in the regulation of prices; and this may have been done to appease the merchants in order to accomplish the larger purposes of the non-importation. While the First Continental Congress was still sitting, it was charged that pins had advanced to 15s. a pack, pepper to 3s. 6d. a pound, *etc.*, in anticipation of a suspension of trade.[4] On November 30, the Sixty-Six took official notice of advances made by " a few persons " and recommended to the public that the boycott, prescribed by Article ix in such cases, should be promptly carried out.[5] The provincial convention in January added the weight of its influence to this timely

---

[1] *N. Y. Gaz.*, Mch. 31, 1775; also *4 Am. Arch.*, vol. i, p. 1243. An abusive reply to the committee's assertion did not deny that the non-importation had been faithfully observed. *Ibid.*, vol. ii, pp. 238-242.

[2] *Pa. Mag.*, vol. xl, pp. 202-203.

[3] *Pa. Packet*, Feb. 13, 1775; *Pa. Eve. Post*, Apr. 20.

[4] Letter in *N. Y. Gazetteer*, Oct. 6, 1774.

[5] *Pa. Gaz.*, Nov. 30, 1774; also *4 Am. Arch.*, vol. i, p. 1010.

advice.[1] However, in March, 1775, it was freely charged that the drygoods merchants were, without the least opposition, asking prices for goods representing an increase of twenty-five to one hundred per cent over former prices;[2] and as late as September of the same year Chase declared publicly in the Second Congress that prices had been advanced fifty per cent in Philadelphia.[3]

The spirit of the enforcement outside of the city was indicated by the resolution of the provincial convention that, if opposition should be offered to any committee of observation, the committees of the other counties should render all the assistance in their power to keep the Association inviolate.[4]

The distinctive feature of the working of the Association in Pennsylvania was the importance that was given to the development of home production and to the introduction of simpler modes of living. Community sentiment was well fertilized for such an undertaking by the religious teachings of the Friends as well as by the homely maxims of "Poor Richard" through a long period of years. The funeral regulations, recommended by Congress, were well observed, even such a prominent man as Thomas Lawrence, ex-mayor of Philadelphia, being buried in accordance with these directions.[5] The Sixty-Six on November 30 recommended that no ewe-mutton be purchased or eaten in the country until May 1, 1775, and none after that day until October 1, and that thereafter none at all should be used. Notices in English and German were published throughout the prov-

---

[1] 4 *Am. Arch.*, vol. i, p. 1172; also *Pa. Journ.*, Feb. 1, 1775.
[2] "An Englishman," 4 *Am. Arch.*, vol. ii, p. 239.
[3] Adams, J., *Works* (Adams), vol. ii, p. 447.
[4] *Pa. Journ.*, Feb. 1, 1775; also 4 *Am. Arch.*, vol. i, pp. 1170.
[5] *Pa. Journ.*, Jan. 25, 1775.

ince to warn the country people against selling sheep to butchers contrary to the regulation.[1] Sixty-six butchers of Philadelphia agreed to be bound by the recommendation of the committee, and the butchers of Reading signed a similar agreement.[2] In January the provincial convention resolved unanimously that after the first of March no sheep under four years of age should be killed or sold, except in cases of extreme necessity.[3]

The provincial convention made many recommendations respecting the commodities and wares which the province seemed best fitted to produce. Raw wool should be utilized in the making of coatings, flannels, blankets, hosiery and coarse cloths; and dyes should be obtained from the cultivation of madder, woad and other dye stuffs. Of the farther-reaching proposals were the recommendations that fulling-mills should be erected, and mills should be established for the manufacture of woolcombs and cards, of steel, nails and wire, of paper, of gunpowder, of copper kettles and tinplates. As the demand for Pennsylvania-made glass exceeded the supply, it was recommended that more glass factories be established. To carry these proposals more speedily into effect, local societies should be established, and premiums awarded in the various counties.[4] The Bedford County Committee, among others, acted on these recommendations a few weeks later, and offered five pounds to the person who erected the first fulling-mill in the county,

---

[1] Because several city butchers had a stock of sheep on hand, the regulation was not to become operative until January 1 in Philadelphia. *Pa. Gaz.*, Nov. 30, Dec. 21, 1774; also 4 *Am. Arch.*, vol. i, p. 1010.

[2] *Ibid.*, vol. i, pp. 1050-1051, 1144; also *Pa. Gaz.*, Dec. 21, 1774, and *Pa. Journ.*, Jan. 25, 1775.

[3] *Ibid.*, Feb. 1, 1775; also 4 *Am. Arch.*, vol. i, p. 1171.

[4] *Ibid.*, vol. i, pp. 1171-1172; also *Pa. Journ.*, Feb. 1, 1775.

and four smaller money prizes to the persons making the best pieces of linen cloth within a given period.¹

The most ambitious venture of this character was the United Company of Philadelphia for Promoting American Manufactures, established in March, 1775. The company was financed through the sale of stock at ten pounds a share; and the efforts of the company were devoted to the manufacture of woolen, cotton and linen textiles. Daniel Roberdeau was chosen first president. At the start, some mistakes were made, owing to the inexperience of the managers; but soon nearly four hundred spinners were employed, and at the end of six months the board of managers announced that the enterprise was not only practicable but promised to be profitable for the stockholders. More stock was then sold to enlarge the scope of the company's operations.²

In the light of this array of facts, the announcement, made on February 27, 1775, by the Sixty-Six testifying to "the uniform spirit and conduct of the people in the faithful execution" of the Association, and a private statement, made on the same day, that the "City Committee have subdued all opposition to their Measures," bear the stamp of truth.³ As President Roberdeau of the United Company of Philadelphia put it, "The Resolves of the Congress have been executed with a fidelity hardly known to laws in any Country . . ."⁴

Possessing no important commercial connections, it

¹ *Pa. Journ.*, Mch. 8, 1775; also *4 Am. Arch.*, vol. i, pp. 1226-1227.

² *Ibid.*, vol. i, pp. 1256-1257; vol. ii, pp. 140-144; vol. iii, pp. 73, 820-821; also *Pa. Gaz.*, Feb. 22, Aug. 9, 1775, and *Pa. Journ.*, Mch. 22, Sept. 27.

³ *4 Am. Arch.*, vol. i, pp. 1269, 1270.

⁴ *Ibid.*, vol. ii, p. 141; also *Pa. Ledger*, Apr. 15, 1775.

would appear that the Association went quietly into force in the Lower Counties on the Delaware. If any decided opposition developed in Sussex County, where no committee was yet appointed, no record of it remains. In Newcastle and Kent, the chief attention was given to carrying out the popular Pennsylvania regulation regarding the conservation of sheep and to the elimination of extravagance and dissipation.[1] Letters written to Philadelphia in February declared that " the greatest unanimity subsists in putting into force the Resolves of the Continental Congress." [2]

[1] *E. g., vide* 4 *Am. Arch.*, vol. i, p. 1022; Niles, *Prins. & Acts*, p. 239.
[2] *Pa. Journ.*, Feb. 15, 1775.

CHAPTER XIII

FIVE MONTHS OF THE ASSOCIATION IN THE PLANTATION PROVINCES. GENERAL CONCLUSIONS

THE problem of enforcing the Continental Association in the plantation provinces differed in one respect markedly from that in the commercial provinces. The old antagonism between merchant and planter — between creditor and debtor — that had raised its forbidding head at various times during the previous years, had now become more acute. The conditions, imposed by a non-intercourse, increased the difficulties of the planters to repay their obligations; and the economic dominance of the merchants and factors made it necessary that their power be broken before the Association could be successfully administered. The plantation provinces thus, without exception, resorted to extreme measures against the merchant-creditors.

The execution of the non-importation and non-consumption regulations in Maryland was somewhat complicated by the fact that there were more than twenty rivers in the province navigable by large ships. However, commerce centered naturally at Baltimore and Annapolis; and the zeal and watchfulness of the radicals probably reduced evasions of the Association to a minimum in all parts of the province.

It was well understood that the merchant and factor class were likely to be the most pertinacious offenders against the Association, and therefore the Maryland convention, meeting in December, 1774, resolved that lawyers should prosecute no suits for violators of the Association, and that, if the violator were a factor, lawyers should not conduct debt prosecutions for the store of which he was manager.[1] Influenced in the interval by the example of Virginia, where the mercantile interests were even more deeply intrenched, the Maryland convention went to greater lengths in August, 1775. They resolved that no civil actions (with a few specified exceptions) should be commenced or renewed in any court of law, save by permission of the committee of observation of the county in which the debtors and defendants resided. These committees were instructed to permit the trial of cases where debtors refused to renew their obligations, or to give reasonable security, or to refer their disputes to one or more disinterested parties, or when the debtors were justly suspected of an intention to leave the province or to defraud their creditors.[2]

In the first two months of the non-importation, public sales of merchandise imported in contravention of the Association were reported at Annapolis, Chestertown, Piscataway and Calvert County. For example, James Dick and Anthony Stewart, who were in bad odor for past indiscretions, were concerned in an importation of Madeira wines at Annapolis; and the consignment was sold, at their request, at a profit of £1 11s. 1d. for the Boston poor.[3] In the months following February 1, 1775, many instances of effective execution were noted in the newspapers. Thus, to cite one case that required more than usual skill in its management, the captain of the brig *Sally* from Bristol appeared before the Baltimore committee and attested under oath that his cargo consisted of twenty-four indentured

[1] *Md. Gaz.*, Dec. 15, 1774; also 4 *Am. Arch.*, vol. i, p. 1032.
[2] *Ibid.*, vol. iii, pp. 117-118.
[3] *Md. Gaz.*, Dec. 15, 1774. For other instances, *vide ibid.*, Feb. 23, Mch. 2, June 29, 1775.

servants and one hundred tons of British salt. Clearly the bringing in of servants did not violate the Association, and Dr. John Stevenson, the consignee, maintained to the committee that the salt ought to be considered merely as ballast and thus not contrary to the Association. But the committee voted unanimously that the salt should not be landed.

A week later the captain and the consignee were called before the committee again and charged with having unladen a portion of the salt in defiance of the decision of the committee. Stevenson replied that he had understood the resolution to apply to Baltimore County only and that he had shipped a quantity on board four bay-craft to various parts of Maryland and Virginia. Inasmuch as there was a colorable pretext for this interpretation, the committee decided not to boycott him upon his pledge to give the proceeds of the sales to the relief of Boston and not to land the remainder of the salt anywhere between Nova Scotia and Georgia. Word was sent out to various parts of the province to stop the sale of the salt and to punish all persons guiltily involved. In Prince George's County Thomas Bailey was discovered to be implicated and, after a hearing, declared to have wilfully violated the Association.[1]

The more usual procedure in cases of forbidden importation was for the captain to take his vessel away at the command of the local committee without disturbing the cargo.[2] A little out of the ordinary was the arrival of a tomb-stone in Charles County, which had been brought there from a vessel that had stopped in the Potomac. The committee ordered that the stone should be broken to pieces.[3] With regard to non-consumption regulations, some

---

[1] *Md. Gaz.*, Mch. 30, June 15, 1775; also *4 Am. Arch.*, vol. ii, pp. 34, 308.

[2] *E. g., vide ibid.*, vol. ii, pp. 123, 175-176, 659-660, 1122-1123.

[3] *N. Y. Gaz.*, July 24, 1775.

difficulty was experienced in preventing the use of tea. In the instance of one obdurate tea dealer, the committee for the Upper Part of Frederick County sentenced the offender, one John Parks, to set fire to his tea with head uncovered and then to suffer the rigors of the boycott. Not content with these measures, the populace derived some satisfaction from breaking in his door and windows.[1] Usually, however, offenders acquiesced without trouble.

The supervision of prices received careful attention. In December, 1774, the Maryland convention noted the wide range of prices in different parts of the province during the preceding twelve months, and resolved that all merchants must observe a uniform rule which the convention announced: that wholesale prices should not be more than 112½ per cent, retail prices cash not more than 130 per cent, and retail prices on credit not more than 150 per cent, advance on the prime cost.[2] Alexander Ogg, a merchant of Huntington, was found guilty of infringing this rule by the Calvert County Committee and published as an enemy to his country. He offered to give store credit for every farthing he had charged beyond the limit fixed, but his plea fell on deaf ears.[3]

The rigorous observance of the boycott was attested by the petitions of John Baillie, Patrick Graham and Alexander Ogg to the provincial convention.[4] The first two had been proscribed for knowingly importing goods forbidden by the Association, at a public meeting called by the Charles County committee. Baillie declared that he had suffered " the extremity of a heavy, though just, sentence " which

[1] *4 Am. Arch.*, vol. i, p. 1009; also *Md. Journ.*, Nov. 16, 1774, and *Md. Gaz.*, Dec. 22.
[2] *Ibid.*, Dec. 15, 1774; also *4 Am. Arch.*, vol. i, pp. 1031-1032.
[3] *Ibid.*, vol. ii, p. 281; also *Md. Gaz.*, Apr. 13, 1775.
[4] *4 Am. Arch.*, vol. ii, p. 727; vol. iii, pp. 101, 102, 106, 119-121.

had been " executed with such rigour that it has been with the most extreme and hazardous difficulty he could obtain the necessary food to support a life rendered miserable by his conduct and the abovementioned sentence;" and he promised exemplary conduct if his offense were forgiven. Graham testified that he had " already suffered greatly, not only in his own person, property and reputation, but should he continue much longer in the present situation, his offence must reduce an innocent wife and four children to beggary and ruin." Ogg, who had advanced prices unduly, declared that he had not been able to carry on his business or to collect the debts due to him. The convention squarely rejected Baillie's petition; but Graham and Ogg, because of mitigating circumstances, were allowed to resume their earlier occupations, the former under some restrictions.

A resolution of the Maryland convention in December 1774, sought to prevent the killing of any lamb under four years of age. Because the terms of this resolution were much more severe than the recommendation in the Continental Association, considerable confusion arose from the representations of violators that they were entirely in harmony with the Continental Association and therefore ought not to be proscribed. To relieve the situation the resolution was withdrawn by the Maryland convention in August, 1775.[1] The provincial convention of November, 1774, recommended that balls be discontinued in this time of public calamity.[2] The Jockey Club at Annapolis called off the races which had been arranged to conclude the club subscription.[3] In April, 1775, the Baltimore committee unanimously recommended to the people of the county not to en-

[1] *4 Am. Arch.*, vol. i, p. 1031; vol. ii, pp. 308-309, 903-904; vol. iii, pp. 104, 117.
[2] *Ibid.*, vol. i, p. 991; also *Md. Gaz.*, Dec. 1, 1774.
[3] *Ibid.*, Nov. 3, 1774.

courage or attend the approaching fair because of its tendency to encourage horse-racing, gaming, drunkenness and other dissipation.[1]

In view of the abundant evidence, it is scarcely necessary to quote Governor Eden's words of December 30, 1774, to the effect that he firmly believed that the Marylanders would " persevere in their nonimportation and nonexportation experiments, in spite of every inconvenience that they must consequently be exposed to, and the total ruin of their trade."[2]

In Virginia the chief dissent to the Association came from the merchant and factor element, largely Scotch by nativity. The fact that a majority of the faculty of William and Mary College were non-associators elicited unfavorable comment from the radical press;[3] but their opposition was no more important than that of the small Quaker element in the population, which Madison noted,[4] or of the royal office holding class, since none of these groups was in position to enforce their views even if they wanted to.

The opposition of the Scotch was clandestine but none the less pertinacious. The body of the trade at Williamsburg, numbering more than four hundred, professed support of the Association in a written pledge early in November, 1774, and received the thanks of Peyton Randolph and other delegates of the province for disregarding the influence of their commercial interest in the great struggle for liberty.[5] And the Norfolk committee affirmed on Decem-

[1] *Md. Gaz.*, May 4, 1775; also *4 Am. Arch.*, vol. ii, p. 337.
[2] *Ibid.*, vol. i, p. 1076; also *Pa. Eve. Post*, June 6, 1775.
[3] Pinkney's *Va. Gaz.*, Dec. 22, 1774; Jan. 5, 26, 1775.
[4] *Writings* (Hunt), vol. i, pp. 28-29.
[5] *Pa. Gaz.*, Nov. 30, 1774; also *4 Am. Arch.*, vol. i, pp. 972-973.

ber 6 that the whole trading body of the province had cheerfully subscribed to the Association.[1] Whether or not the motive of the merchants at this early time was to gain the good will of the radical planters who owned them large sums of money, the facts are clear that they had to regulate their conduct ultimately by the instructions of the English houses they represented or, in any case, be tempted almost beyond endurance by the prospect of obtaining monopoly prices during the suspension of importation.

Suspicion of the good faith of the Scotch merchants had too deep a hold on many radicals to permit acceptance of their protestations at face value. "It is generally believed, by this time, that the Scotch have all signed the association," declared one newspaper writer. "If they have, I would ask if it is not through compulsion?" He urged that, while there was still time, the province should be purged of such filth by withdrawing all trade from them.[2] Another writer deplored "that antipathy to the Scotch, which appears to be so general amongst us," and showed that despite their personal predilections they must as a matter of duty defer to their British employers with respect to the Association.[3] When the period for enforcing the non-importation arrived, the Scotch as a class proved to be the most numerous offenders. The climax came when Purdie's *Virginia Gazette* of December 22 and 29, 1775, published a number of intercepted letters, which showed that the leading Scotch merchants were as unprincipled as the most skeptical radicals had believed them to be. A letter was printed, written by Andrew Sprowle, chairman of the Williamsburg trade, who had headed the merchants

[1] 4 *M. H. S. Colls.*, vol. iv, pp. 160-161.
[2] Charles M'Carty, of Richmond County, in Pinkney's *Va. Gaz.*, Jan. 19, 1775.
[3] "A Citizen of the World" in *ibid.*, Jan. 26, 1775.

when they signed the Association in November, 1774. In this letter Sprowle ordered some invoices of goods from Greenock, Scotland, and declared further: "I would have no fear in bringing in a vessel with Osnabrugs, Irish linen, and other sortable goods, [as they] would be protected by a man of war." Robert Shedden of Portsmouth had written to his Glasgow correspondent: "Depend upon it you will never have such another opportunity to make money by dry goods in this country. Osnabrugs, canvass, &c and every necessary article; a large and full assortment of goods, nails, &c; bring as many as you can get credit for. . . . If you bring 20,000 l. in goods, they will sell to advantage." Wrote the Norfork merchant, John Brown, to London: "You are hereby ordered to ship, by the first opportunity, £1000 sterling value in linen goods, &c."

Meantime, the merchants and factors had been taking advantage of their position in another way—they had been hastening to press their debtors for the payment of long-outstanding obligations before the latter became entirely bankrupt from the suspension of trade. This prudent business transaction worked a grievous hardship on many planters, and estates were sold for debt in divers places.[1] A demand arose for a boycott against merchants who used excessive caution in extending credit; and Peyton Randolph felt impelled to declare in a public statement that the Association furnished no remedy, that it did not empower committees to dictate to merchants to whom they should sell on credit or for what time they should give credit.[2]

Unless the radicals could devise effective countermeasures, the merchants seemed about to cut the ground from under them. The radicals had foreseen this situation, to some extent, and their course of action was designed to

[1] "A Scotchman" in Pinkney's *Va. Gaz.*, Mch. 23, 1775.
[2] *Ibid.*, Feb. 2, 9, 1775.

cripple, if not to destroy, the economic power of the merchants. The provincial convention of August, 1774, closed up the county courts of justice on the ground that the last session of the Assembly had not renewed the Fee Act; and " the men of fortune and pre-eminence joined equally with the lowest and meanest " in bringing this to pass, averred Governor Dunmore.[1] They also recommended that lawyers and witnesses stay away from the approaching General Court of Judicature, except in criminal cases; and they succeeded in carrying their point. On March 25, 1775, a later provincial convention gave their sanction to the suspension of judicial proceedings. They declared that, on account of the unsettled state of public affairs, the lawyers, suitors and witnesses ought not to take part in civil cases at the next General Court; that county courts ought not to hear any suits on their dockets, except attachments, nor give judgment, save in the case of sheriffs or other collectors for money or tobacco received by them, or in cases where judgment should be voluntarily confessed or in amicable proceedings for the settlement of estates.[2] Though exhorted by Governor Dunmore, the House of Burgesses in June refused " to interpose legislative authority in order to compel the Magistrates to open the courts of civil jurisdiction, and thereby expose the people to cruel exactions." They justified their refusal as an answer to the act of Parliament, recently passed, restraining their trade, and declared it was best for the courts to remain closed until wisdom had returned to the British administration.[3]

These measures afforded an effective shield against the merchant-creditors and saved the situation for the radicals.

[1] *4 Am. Arch.*, vol. i, pp. 775, 1062.
[2] *Ibid.*, vol. ii, pp. 168-169; also Pinkney's *Va. Gaz.*, Mch. 30, 1775.
[3] *4 Am. Arch.*, vol. ii, pp. 1188, 1190-1191.

Indeed, on August 25, a petition was presented to the Virginia convention by sundry factors and mercantile agents, complaining of the ill-grounded prejudices which had been aroused against them as natives of Great Britain and pledging their aid in the civil contest with the parent country in every respect except that of taking up arms against the people among whom they had been born. The convention resolved unanimously that the petition was reasonable and instructed the local committees "to treat all natives of Great Britain resident here, as do not show themselves enemies to the common cause of America, with lenity and friendship. . . ."[1]

In carrying out the Association in Virginia, the plan was adopted of requiring all the inhabitants to attach their signatures to the document. Other provinces had been willing and anxious to let sleeping dogs lie; the Virginia radicals were so confident of the power of public opinion behind them that they carried this challenge to every inhabitant, so far as it proved practicable.[2] Thus, the Northampton committee divided the county into seven districts with sub-committees appointed to present the Association to all the inhabitants.[3] The committee for Princess Anne County delivered a list of non-associators to every merchant in the county and posted other copies at various public places and at Norfolk, with the recommendation that all commercial intercourse with the delinquents be stopped. When Benjamin Gray, one of the proscribed, was reported to have called the committee " a pack of damn'd rascals," his additional offense was also given publicity.[4] In Nansemond

[1] 4 *Am. Arch.* vol. iii, pp. 391-392; also Pinkney's *Va. Gaz.*, Aug. 31, 1775.
[2] Madison, *Writings* (Hunt), vol. i, pp. 28-29.
[3] 4 *Am. Arch.*, vol. i, p. 1045.
[4] *Ibid.*, vol. ii, pp. 76-77; also Pinkney's *Va. Gaz.*, Mch. 23, 1775.

County, the Reverend John Agnew was held up to public censure for roundly condemning the Association in his sermons and private conversations; and a man who rented a "flatt" from the parson was obliged to give it up.[1] Examples like this abounded. The Virginia plan forced every inhabitant into a position of either active friendship or open hostility; and since it was entirely possible for a man to disapprove of the Association without ever violating its provisions, the number of those subject to neglect and boycott was vastly greater than in other provinces. The Virginia radicals thus took an advanced stand—a stage which the other provinces did not reach until the bloodshed of April, 1775, had occurred.

In early November, 1774, a mob at Yorktown went on board the *Virginia* and dumped into the river two half-chests of tea, with the entire approval of the county committee. The London shippers and the consignees at Williamsburg were both held up for neglect by the York committee and the adjoining Gloucester County committee.[2] This little "tea party" exceeded the provisions of the Association, but marked the enthusiasm which characterized the execution of the non-importation regulation. Public sales of cargoes that arrived between December 1, 1774, and February 1, 1775, were reported at Norfolk and Williamsburg and in fourteen counties.[3] Many of these sales showed small profits or none at all; but occasionally a shipment brought a substantial advance, like Andrew Wodrow's in King George County, which yielded a profit of

[1] *4 Am. Arch.*, vol. ii, pp. 226-228; *N. C. Col. Recs.*, vol. ix, p. 1164.

[2] Pinkney's *Va. Gaz.*, Nov. 24, 1774; also *4 Am. Arch.*, vol. i, pp. 964-965.

[3] Charles City, Dinwiddie, Elizabeth City, Essex, Fairfax, Goochland, Henrico, Isle of Wight, King George, Nansemond, New Kent, Princess Anne, Spotsylvania and Surry. *Vide* files of the three *Virginia Gazettes*, edited by Pinkney, by Purdie, and by Dixon & Hunter.

£19 14s. for the Boston needy.[1] For this reason, it is improbable that the Scotch merchants felt tempted to withhold importations from committee auction.

One interesting case of defiance occurred. Late in January an importation of medicines worth £200 sterling arrived for Dr. Alexander Gordon, a well-known physician of Norfolk; and he requested that he might be allowed to receive the goods agreeable to the terms of the provincial association of August, 1774. The committee informed him that their rule of conduct now was the Continental Association, and advised him to submit the medicines for sale in accordance with Article x, as had been done by other physicians. He expressed a preference for storing the goods under charge of the committee; but while arrangements were being made for this purpose, he quietly landed the medicines and took possession of them himself. It proved impossible for the committee to get the merchandise away from him, and with very evident reluctance they held him up for public censure.[2]

The regulation against the importation of slaves had caused very little difficulty in the northern provinces; but the Norfolk committee found it necessary to proscribe John Brown, a Scotch merchant who had been in Virginia since 1762, for being concerned in the importation of twenty slaves in the brig *Fanny* from Jamaica. He stoutly protested his innocence, but his letter-books proved the contrary.[3]

[1] Dixon & Hunter's *Va. Gaz.*, Jan. 28, 1775.

[2] Pinkney's *Va. Gaz.*, Feb. 16, 1775; also *4 Am. Arch.*, vol. i, pp. 1217-1278.

[3] *Ibid.*, vol. ii, pp. 33-34; also Pinkney's *Va. Gaz.*, Mch. 23, 1775. *Vide* also memorial of the Browns in A. O. no. 55: *N. Y. Loyalist Claims Transcripts*, vol. xxvii, pp. 459, 467-471. The Chesterfield County committee also took occasion to voice their indignation and to declare the suspension of all dealings with him. Purdie's *Va. Gaz.*, May 5, 1775.

After February 1 the number of incoming vessels fell off, and when goods were brought contrary to the Association they were almost invariably re-shipped. In one case, that of the brigantine *Muir* from Antigua, the captain had sold some merchandise before he learned of the Association; and the Essex County committee absolved him from public censure when he signed the Association and re-shipped the goods, including the portion sold.[1] On the other hand, the Norfolk committee declared Captain Sampson, of the snow *Elizabeth* from Bristol, an enemy to his country for practising deception in landing a cargo of salt and then seeking protection of a man-of-war.[2] The non-consumption regulations required little attention from the committees, except the prohibition of tea drinking, which was effectively administered.[3]

The upward trend of prices gave more trouble. According to the Continental Association prices were not to advance beyond the customary charge for articles during the twelve months preceding. A disgusted radical of Northumberland County averred that, when it came to the investigation of prices, one Scotch merchant would swear to another's lies—they were "determined to be clannish, even at the expence of their souls!"[4] This practice was probably not restricted entirely to the Scotch traders. At any rate, it quickly caused the committees to adopt the practice of examining the daybooks and invoices of any merchant under suspicion. Should he refuse access to his accounts, he was deemed to be guilty by the very fact. For example, in December, 1774, the committee of Caroline County in-

---

[1] Pinkney's *Va. Gaz.*, Mch. 16, 1775.

[2] *Ibid.*, Apr. 6, 1775; also 4 *Am. Arch.*, vol. ii, pp. 174-175.

[3] *E. g.*, Pinkney's *Va. Gaz.*, Dec. 1, 1774, June 1, 1775; Dixon & Hunter's *Gaz.*, Feb. 4; Purdie's *Gaz.*, July 7.

[4] Charles M'Carty in Pinkney's *Va. Gaz.*, Jan. 19, 1775.

spected the books of four merchants, declaring them innocent, and pronounced six others subject to boycott because they had withheld their books. Within less than a month the six permitted their accounts to be examined; and the committee declared that they also had adhered to the Association.[1] In Gloucester County, Captain Charles Marshall, who had been acting consistently with his avowal that "every man has a right to sell his goods for as much as he could get," was disciplined by the committee; whereupon he signed the Association, and issued a confession in which he said: "These are offenses I am (as have been some other North Britains) taught to know, at this time, deserve severe punishment."[2] Great activity in the regulation of prices was also recorded in other counties, especially Prince William, Charlotte, Spotsylvania, Hanover, Richmond and Fairfax.[3]

The promotion of local manufacturing met with ready response, partly no doubt because it contributed to the weakening of the economic position of the factors and merchants. Interest centered in the production of cotton and woolen textiles, and of gunpowder. The Northampton County committee in January, 1775, offered a bonus of £40 sterling to the first person who in the next eighteen months should make one thousand pairs of wool-cards in the province and agreed to buy them at the rate of 2s. a pair. A premium of £40 was also offered to the first person who should manufacture five thousand pounds of gunpowder in the province in the next eighteen months. The committee appealed to other counties to add to these premiums, so that

[1] Pinkney's *Va. Gaz.*, Jan. 12, 1775; and Dixon & Hunter's *Va. Gaz.*, Feb. 4.
[2] Pinkney's *Va. Gaz.*, Jan. 19, 1775.
[3] 4 *Am. Arch.*, vol. i, pp. 1034, 1138-1139; Pinkney's *Va. Gaz.*, Jan. 19, Feb. 2, May 18, 1775; Purdie's *Gaz.*, Feb. 17, Apr. 21.

the total sum would foster a widespread interest in manufacturing.[1] Other counties quickly acted on the suggestion;[2] and on March 27 the provincial convention outlined a comprehensive program of industrial development by adopting bodily the main resolutions passed by the Pennsylvania convention in January. After May 1 no sheep were to be killed under four years of age, except in cases of necessity. Woolen, cotton and linen manufactures should be established; steel, woolcombs, paper, gunpowder, *etc.*, should be manufactured. These various undertakings should be promoted by the formation of local societies for that purpose and by the offering of premiums.[3] In September, James Stewart returned to Virginia after eighteen months' stay in England where he had been studying the culture and preparation of dyes and machines for manufacturing cotton. He brought with him a large quantity of seeds and roots of the standard dyes, for planting in various parts of the province, and planned to instruct persons in the construction of cotton machines.[4] What success he met with we do not know.

In no province was the practice of gambling more deeply rooted than in Virginia; and determined efforts were made to discourage this wasteful manner of living. Thus, information was received by the Northumberland County committee that William Lewis had violated the Association by gaming with Anthony McKenley of Maryland. Witnesses were called, sworn and examined; and the evidence showed

[1] Dixon & Hunter's *Va. Gaz.*, Feb. 4, 1775; also *4 Am. Arch.*, vol. i, pp. 1045-1046.

[2] *E. g.*, Isle of Wight, Cumberland, Essex, Gloucester and Bedford; *ibid.*, vol. i, p. 1247; vol. ii, pp. 13-14, 387-388; Pinkney's *Va. Gaz.*, Feb. 13, 1775.

[3] *Ibid.*, Mch. 30, 1775; also *4 Am. Arch.*, vol. ii, pp. 170-171.

[4] *Ibid.*, vol. iii, p. 716; also Purdie's *Va. Gaz.*, Sept. 15, 1775.

that Lewis had won "a Silver Watch, two pair of Leather Breeches, and two men's fine Hats." Both men were adjudged guilty and were publicly advertised as violators of the Association.[1] The Southampton County committee recommended four men, who had been gaming, to the mercy of the public, upon their offer to refund all they had won and to observe the Association strictly in the future.[2] In another instance, the Hanover County committee "honourably acquitted" Samuel Overton of the charge of encouraging horse-racing.[3]

The degree of efficiency attained by the committees in executing the Association aroused Governor Dunmore to righteous indignation in his well-known letter of December 24, 1774, to Lord Dartmouth. His conclusions in that epistle were that the Association was being enforced "with the greatest rigour" and that "the Laws of Congress" received from the Virginians "marks of reverence which they never bestowed on their legal Government, or the Laws proceeding from it." By way of pathetic afterthought he added: "I have discovered no instance where the interposition of Government, in the feeble state to which it is reduced, could serve any other purpose than to suffer the disgrace of a disappointment, and thereby afford matter of great exultation to its enemies and increase their influence over the minds of the people."[4]

In North Carolina the development of events was influenced by the example of nearby Virginia. The old Regu-

[1] Pinkney's *Va. Gaz.*, Mch. 2, 1775; also *4 Am. Arch.*, vol. i, pp. 1178-1179.

[2] *Ibid.*, vol. ii, pp. 299-300.

[3] Pinkney's *Va. Gaz.*, Jan. 19, 1775.

[4] *Ibid.*, Apr. 28, 1775; also *4 Am. Arch.*, vol. i, pp. 1061-1063. For radical answers to Dunmore's assertions, *vide ibid.*, vol. ii, pp. 502-504, 525, 1204, 1210-1215, 1222-1225.

lator class held aloof from the Continental Association, although it made some progress among them;[1] being segregated in the interior counties, they were not in position to impair the operation of the Association in its more important aspects. There was, however, a small, compact group of Scotch merchants at Wilmington, the chief trading town;[2] and, as in Virginia, they obeyed the Association only so far as it served their interests so to do. In the first two months of the non-importation they co-operated with the Wilmington committee in permitting their importations to be sold under the terms of the Association. The records show that at least thirteen merchants received goods between December 1, 1774, and February 1, 1775, which were offered for public sale by the Wilmington committee, and that at the smaller town of Edenton two merchants observed the same regulation.[3] For example, at a meeting of the Wilmington committee on December 30, Hogg & Campbell submitted an invoice of salt imported in the *North Star* from Lymington, and four other firms submitted invoices of anchors, cables, canvass, osnaburgs and other merchandise imported in the *Thetis* from Glasgow. The goods were sold at public vendue the next day.[4] In general, it may be said that the sales yielded little or no profit; from all the sales conducted by the Wilmington committee, the profits for Boston amounted to only £25 2s. 5d.[5]

In six or seven instances the committee at Wilmington secured the re-shipment of slaves that had been imported

---

[1] Note the means used to convert three pertinacious inhabitants of Anson County to the Association. *N. C. Col. Recs.*, vol. x, pp. 125-129, 161, 182.

[2] *Ibid.*, vol. x, p. 48.

[3] *Ibid.*, vol. ix, pp. 1095-1154 *passim*.

[4] *Ibid.*, vol. ix, pp. 1103-1104.

[5] *Ibid.*, vol. ix, pp. 1153-1154.

IN THE PLANTATION PROVINCES 521

contrary to the Association.¹ After February 1, when the new period of non-importation began, fewer vessels arrived at Wilmington, and the cargoes were re-shipped without trouble. Two interesting exceptions were made—once for paper intended for use of the press, and another time for household goods intended for personal use.²

Through their possession of large stocks, the Wilmington merchants were in position to demand high prices and thus discredit the Association, unless the radicals resorted to drastic measures. Therefore every effort was made to supervise prices carefully. On December 17, 1774, the Pitt County committee fixed a maximum price for salt with the penalty of boycott for violation.³ About the same time the Wilmington committee conducted an investigation into the prices of rum and gunpowder, and in January they called a meeting of merchants and traders in order to agree on prices and prevent advantage being taken of the suspension of importation. On January 27 the committee decided upon maximum prices for salt and drygoods; and about two weeks later they compelled Jonathan Dunbilrie to return to a purchaser the excess profit he had received for a bushel of salt.⁴ The Rowan County committee also displayed great activity in this direction.⁵

As a still further check upon the merchants, the Wilmington committee in March, 1775, adopted the Virginia device of requiring all friends of the Association to attach their signatures to the document. On the following day all the housekeepers in town were given the opportunity, and

---
[1] *N. C. Col. Recs.*, vol. ix, pp. 1098-1099, 1112-1113, 1168, 1171, 1222, 1266; vol. x, p. 24.
[2] *Ibid.*, vol. ix, pp. 1185-1186; vol. x, pp. 50, 279.
[3] *Ibid.*, vol. ix, p. 1100.
[4] *Ibid.*, vol. ix, pp. 1099-1100, 1113, 1126.
[5] *Ibid.*, vol. x, pp. 9-10.

only eleven persons refused. Seven of these were Scotch merchants; five of them had formerly submitted their importations for committee auction. The committee resolved that unless the eleven revised their decision within six days they would have no dealings or intercourse whatsoever with them. Eight promptly gave their signatures; and when the six day period expired, only three — two tailors and one merchant, by name McKenzie, McNight and McDonnel — remained obdurate.[1]

The way was easy for the radicals to hamper the collection of debts, for, owing to a quarrel between the governor and the Assembly, the law for the establishment of courts, which had expired in February, 1773, had never been renewed. At the brief session of the Assembly in April, 1775, Governor Martin urged the importance of a law for the permanent establishment of courts. But the radical leaders would have nothing to do with it, openly avowing, according to Governor Martin, that courts "would be injurious at this time unless their operation could be suspended, since they would furnish the merchants with opportunity to harrass their Debtors while the people at large, having bound themselves by the Resolves of Congress, could not convert their commodities into money to pay their Debts." Furthermore, the governor declared that it was well known that among the radical leaders there were "some whose desperate circumstances make them dread the long arms of Courts of unlimited jurisdiction which would extend to their own cases . . ."[2] Not content with merely negative action, the North Carolina congress in September, 1775, went the full length, as had the neighboring provinces, and resolved that no actions should be begun or

[1] *N. C. Col. Recs.*, vol. ix, pp. 1149-1150, 1152-1153, 1166.
[2] *Ibid.*, vol. ix, pp. 1225-1226.

continued in the courts except by consent of the committee of the county in which the debtor resided.[1]

Perhaps the most interesting case of boycott, because of the prominence and wealth of the gentleman concerned, was that of Thomas Macknight, of Currituck, a county in the extreme northeastern part of the province. As a member of the provincial convention of April, 1775, Macknight spoke against a motion, which expressed high approval of the Association, on the ground that a great many colonists, like himself, owed money in Great Britain which the non-exportation regulation would render them unable to pay. Notwithstanding his opposition, the convention proceeded to adopt the motion, and then voted that every member should sign the Association. Macknight protested; he said that he would "conform" to the Association but that he could not endorse it by the attaching of his signature. The sense of the convention was taken on his statement of adherence, and the body divided fourteen counties against fourteen. Macknight continued to withhold his signature, but offered to change the word "conform" to "accede."

This was voted as acceptable by a majority, but an uncompromising minority declared they would withdraw from the convention if any subscription different from theirs was accepted from him. To restore harmony, Macknight himself now voluntarily withdrew; and the convention thereupon passed a resolution holding him up "as a proper object of contempt to this Continent" to be subjected to a rigorous boycott. The other members from Currituck also withdrew as well as two members of the Pasquotank delegation. It would appear that Macknight did not at once suffer any serious consequences from this resolution inasmuch as the more substantial leaders among the radicals

[1] *4 Am. Arch.*, vol. iii, p. 208. Some changes in detail were made in this resolution by the provincial council in October. *Ibid.*, p. 1093.

realized that he had not asserted his right to act contrary to the community but merely to think as he pleased. However, with the development of events in the next twelvemonth, Macknight's offense began to appear more heinous, and he was forced to abandon his estate and flee to the British for protection.[1]

Interest in the promotion of domestic manufacturing developed later in North Carolina than in most other provinces, but assumed a more practicable form. A beginning was made in March, 1775, by the Chowan County committee, who offered premiums to the first persons in the province who should make a stated quantity of wool cards and cotton cards, with the added inducement that the articles should be purchased by the committee at a higher price than the same articles made in England commanded. Other awards were announced for the making of steel, bleached linen and fulled woolen cloth.[2] The provincial convention in April, 1775, recommended that the other counties follow out the same plan.[3] Most counties proving apathetic, the provincial congress in September set an example for the continent by offering twenty premiums, amounting in all to £2965, for the encouragement of local manufacturing. Among the manufactures named for subsidies were nails, pins, needles, steel and pig iron, cotton and wool cards, linens and woolens, salt, powder and saltpetre.[4]

As in other provinces, the foibles of the people were subjected to the pitiless surveillance of the committees. This was strikingly true in the case of Wilmington, where the

---

[1] *N. C. Col. Recs.*, vol. ix, p. 1227; vol. x, pp. 31-37; *Pub. Rec. Off.*, C. O. 5, no. 147, pp. 447-457 (*L. C. Transcripts*) ; *4 Am. Arch.*, vol. ii, pp. 269-272.

[2] *N. C. Col. Recs.*, vol. ix, pp. 1133-1134; *4 Am. Arch.*, vol. ii, pp. 30-31.

[3] *Ibid.*, vol. ii, p. 270.

[4] *Ibid.*, vol. iii, pp. 209-212; also *N. C. Col. Recs.*, vol. x, pp. 216-219.

IN THE PLANTATION PROVINCES 525

subscription races in November and January were stopped, billiard tables were abolished, and dances, private as well as public, were prevented.[1]

In conclusion, it is a safe generalization that the essential features of the Association were well executed. The inhabitants of Anson, Rowan, Surry and Guilford, the old Regulator counties, remained quiet and no doubt violated the non-consumption regulations whenever opportunity afforded — which was seldom. Governor Martin paid his respects to the efficiency of the radical organization when, in his proclamation of March 1, 1775, he referred to the "Tyrannical and arbitrary Committees which have already in many instances proceeded to the Extravagance of forcing his Majesty's subjects contrary to their consciences to submit to their unreasonable, seditious and chimerical Resolves . . ."[2]

The temper of the radicals at Charleston, South Carolina, was made manifest by the measures they pursued while the First Continental Congress was still in session.[3] The General Committee prevented a merchant from filling an order for the exportation of arms and ammunition. They warned the merchants against the mercenary practice of engrossing and recommended that the merchants should receive only their customary profits. They actively promoted an association for the non-consumption of India teas, dutied or otherwise, to be effective on November 1; and at their instigation the schoolboys of the city collected from private houses the tea that remained on that day and burned it publicly on Gunpowder Plot Day, November 5. Twenty-four chests of tea were discovered in the cargo of

[1] *N. C. Col. Recs.*, vol. ix, pp. 1090-1150 *passim*.
[2] *Ibid.*, vol. ix, pp. 1145-1146.
[3] *S. C. Gaz.*, Oct. 17, 31, Nov. 21, 1774.

the ship *Britannia* which arrived from London in the first few days of November, and the merchants to whom they were consigned were induced by the committee to go on board and throw the tea into the river. On the same day six chests of smuggled tea were re-shipped to the port whence they had come, with a caution to the shipper not to venture any more.

The non-importation regulations of the Association were enforced with as great impartiality and enthusiasm. Although the details of the transactions have not come down to us, Timothy's *Gazette* makes it evident that importations arriving between December 1, 1774, and February 1, 1775, were sold at committee auction almost as quickly as the vessels arrived.[1] After February 1, the committee displayed great diligence in effecting the return of cargoes without landing any part of them. Three vessels arrived in February: one was turned away; and in the case of the other two, the consignees preferred to cast into the sea their merchandise, consisting of 3844 bushels of salt, 35 caldrons of coal, 45,500 tiles and two tons of potatoes, rather than return it.[2] In March, four more vessels were turned away.[3] Of the brigantine *Industry*, Timothy's *Gazette* remarked laconically: "Nothing was landed but a Man, his Wife, and six fine Children."

The affair of Robert Smyth brought the zeal of the populace into play. Smyth had returned to Charleston in the snow *Proteus*, bringing with him from London his household furniture and two horses that belonged to him. Upon an appeal to the General Committee it was decided by a bare majority of the thirty-three members present that this

[1] *E. g., vide S. C. Gaz.*, Dec. 19, 26, 1774.
[2] *Ibid.*, Feb. 27, Mch. 6, 1775. *Vide* also letter in *Mass. Gaz. & Post-Boy*, Apr. 3.
[3] *S. C. Gaz.*, Mch. 6, 13, 27, Apr. 3, 1775.

importation did not violate the spirit of the Association. This decision caused mutterings and threats among the people, and a couple of days later a petition, signed by more than two hundred and fifty people, was presented to the General Committee, asking for a reconsideration of the decision in a full meeting. In consequence, another meeting was held at which seventy members were present as well as a great crowd of the tumultuous townsmen. Gadsden moved to rescind the part of the former vote that had authorized the landing of the horses. He urged that it was contrary to the Association; that it would alarm the northern provinces; that, in any case, the committee as servants of the people, were bound to yield to their constituents. On the other side, Thomas Lynch, the Rutledges and Rawlins Lowndes were the chief speakers. They contended that to reverse the vote would be to cast contempt upon the committee; and that the spirit, not the letter, of the Association should be observed. William H. Drayton arose in reply. He argued that if the committee refused to change for fear of contempt, the king of England might reasonably use the same justification for his course; and, furthermore, that it was always safer to follow the letter than to explore the spirit of a law. When the vote was put, Gadsden's motion prevailed by a vote of thirty-five to thirty-four.[1] "It is worthy of remark," Drayton records, "that this is the first instance of a point of importance and controversy being carried against those by whose opinion the people had been long governed."

Like the other plantation provinces, the radicals sought to safeguard the operation of the Association by endeavoring to paralyze the pecuniary power of the mercantile class. The provincial congress of January, 1775, passed a unani-

---

[1] Drayton, *Memoirs*, vol. i, pp. 182-187; *S. C. Gaz.*, Mch. 27, 1775.

mous resolution vesting the local committees of observation with complete control over prosecutions for debt. No action for debt should be commenced in the court of common pleas, nor any such action begun there since the September return should be proceeded in, without the consent of the parish or district committee. In certain cases the committees were instructed to permit prosecution: whenever debtors refused to renew their obligations or to give reasonable security; when they were justly suspected of an intention to depart the province or defraud their creditors; or whenever there should appear any other reasonable cause for granting permission.[1]

The only action in behalf of domestic production emanated from the provincial congress in January. The inhabitants were asked to give a preference to their own manufactures, to cultivate cotton, hemp, wheat, barley and hops, and to kill no sheep for sale after March 1 following. A resolution was passed to employ storekeepers at Charleston, Georgetown and Beaufort to buy all the wool that might be brought to them, at stated rates, and to sell the wool to weavers at cost price; and also to market domestic linens, woolens and cottons without charge to the manufacturers.[2] Apparently not so much attention was paid to the sumptuary regulations as in Virginia and Maryland. However, the mourning regulations were widely observed. Also, at Charleston the concerts of the St. Coecilia Society were suspended; and the races at Georgetown were called off.[3]

All things considered, the statement of the General Committee in a letter to the Committee of Sixty at New York

[1] 4 *Am. Arch.*, vol. i, p. 1113.
[2] *Ibid.*, vol. i, pp. 1112-1113, 1116.
[3] *S. C. Gaz.*, Nov. 21, Dec. 19, 1774.

on March 1, 1775, seems well substantiated so far as the essential features of the Association were concerned. "We have the pleasure to inform you," the letter said, "that in this colony the Association takes place as effectually as law itself. . . . We may assure you of our fixed determination to adhere to the resolutions at all hazards; and that ministerial opposition is here obliged to be silent."[1]

While the Continental Association was being put into operation in the twelve Associated Provinces, certain other parts of continental British America, of lesser importance, held sternly aloof from the movement. This brought into operation the comprehensive boycott recommended by Article xiv against dissentient provinces. South Carolina was most intimately concerned in the failure of Georgia to join the league of provinces, as the staples of the two provinces were the same. Therefore, on February 8, 1775, the General Committee at Charleston decreed that thereafter all "Trade, Commerce, Dealings or Intercourse" should cease with the inhabitants of that province.[2]

A few weeks later delegates from St. John's Parish in Georgia arrived in Charleston and sought to show reason to the General Committee why St. John's Parish should be exempted from the boycott. They contended that Article xiv should " be considered as a general rule only, and as respects this Province [Georgia] considered in a mixed or promiscuous sense; but, as we of this Parish are a body detached from the rest by our Resolutions and Association, and sufficiently distinct by local situation, large enough for particular notice . . . , adjoining a sea-port . . . , there-

---

[1] *N. Y. Journ.*, Apr. 6, 1775; also *4 Am. Arch.*, vol. ii, p. 2.

[2] *Ibid.*, vol. i, p. 1163; also *S. C. Gaz.*, Mch. 6, 1775. South Carolinians, owning plantations in Georgia or having debts due from there, were specifically exempted from the terms of the resolution.

fore we must be considered as comprehended within the spirit and equitable meaning of the Continental Association." But the General Committee felt constrained to adhere to a literal interpretation of the Association, and advised the people of St. John's to present their case before the ensuing Continental Congress.[1] This course the St. John's committee perforce determined to adopt. Meantime, being denied trade with South Carolina, the parish found it impossible to subsist without some limited trading connections with the merchants at Savannah; and so they were forced to forego an absolute boycott for a carefully regulated trade under the supervision of a committee especially appointed for the purpose.[2]

Georgia was not the only British province on the continent to be delinquent on this important occasion, although it was the only one of the old thirteen in which the Continental Association was not being effectively executed. The First Continental Congress had invited Quebec, St. John's Isle,[3] Nova Scotia, and East and West Florida to accede to the Association;[4] and the threat of boycott in Article xiv applied, by its terms, to " any colony or province in North-America." Not one of these places was of importance commercially; but it was deemed desirable by the radical party that British America should offer a united front to the mother country. Early in February, 1775, it developed that there was an inclination among the British merchants in the city of Quebec to adopt the Association; but no

---

[1] *S. C. Gaz.*, Mch. 6, 1775; also 4 *Am. Arch.*, vol. i, pp. 1161-1163.

[2] *Journals Cont. Cong.* (L. C. Edn.), vol. ii, pp. 45-48. For Governor Wright's view of this arrangement, *vide* White, *Ga. Hist. Colls.*, p. 523.

[3] The early name for Prince Edward Island.

[4] *Journals Cont. Cong.*, vol. i, pp. 101, 103, 105-113.

action was taken because, according to one merchant there, "it would only serve to throw the trade out of our own hands into those of the French, who would never listen to any proposals of that kind but rejoice in such an opportunity to wrest the trade from us."[1] It was true of all these regions that, due to a preponderance of aliens in the population, a sympathetic understanding of the constitutional and governmental principles at stake was lacking. Furthermore, the inhabitants relished the prospect of diverting to themselves the rich trade which had been monopolized by the older and more populous communities.[2]

After a lull of several weeks following the action of South Carolina with reference to Georgia, the northern provinces began to pass resolutions of boycott which affected all the dissentient provinces. On April 17, the Philadelphia committee served warning on the local merchants that such a measure impended; and ten days later a resolution was adopted for suspending all exportation to Georgia, Quebec, Nova Scotia, Newfoundland and all parts of the fishing coasts and fishing islands until the Continental Congress should direct otherwise.[3] The fisheries were included in the boycott because of the news, recently received, of the act of Parliament restraining New England from the fisheries. On May 1, the Maryland provincial convention passed a similar resolution, and in turn extended the boycott to include the town of Boston, which was now occupied by the British forces as an armed camp after the fighting at Lexington and Concord.[4] On the same day the

[1] Letter of Dec. 24, 1774, *Pa. Packet*, Feb. 13, 1775; also *Mass. Gaz. & Post-Boy*, Feb. 27.
[2] *E. g., vide Pub. Rec. Off., C. O. 5*, no. 138 (*L. C. Transcripts*), p. 404; *4 Am. Arch.*, vol. i, pp. 1164-1165.
[3] *Ibid.*, vol. ii, pp. 338, 421; also *Pa. Eve. Post*, Apr. 18, 29, 1775.
[4] *Md. Gaz.*, May 4, 1775; also *4 Am. Arch.*, vol. ii, p. 380.

New York committee took like action;[1] and the committees of Cumberland County, Va., and Newark, N. J., followed later in the month.[2]

When the Second Continental Congress assembled on the tenth of May, one of the first questions that had to be settled concerned the status of St. John's Parish under the Association. Dr. Lyman Hall presented himself as the delegate of the parish, and his admission to the membership was voted unanimously.[3] On the seventeenth when a resolution was passed suspending exportation to all the recalcitrant provinces, St. John's Parish was expressly exempted from its terms. The resolution applied to the rest of Georgia, to Quebec, Nova Scotia, Newfoundland, St. John's Isle, East and West Florida, and the British fisheries on the American coasts.[4] Thus, so far as action of Congress could effect it, the export trade of the twelve Associated Provinces was withheld from these parts. The provincial congress of New Jersey took occasion on May 26 to recommend to the people of that province to adhere " religiously " to the resolution,[5] and the Virginia House of Burgesses took a similar step on June 19.[6] On June 7, the Wilmington, N. C., committee voted to withhold all exportations destined for the British army and navy, for Newfoundland, and for the northern provinces from whence provisions could be had for these purposes.[7]

---

[1] *4 Am. Arch.*, vol. ii, p. 469; also *N. Y. Journ.*, May 4, 1775.

[2] Purdie's *Va. Gaz.*, July 7, 1775, and *N. Y. Journ.*, June 1; also *4 Am. Arch.*, vol. ii, pp. 622, 634.

[3] He was not permitted to vote in cases where the ballot was taken by provinces. *Journals*, vol. ii, pp. 44-45, 49-50.

[4] *Ibid.*, vol. ii, p. 54.

[5] *N. Y. Gaz.*, May 29, 1775; also *1 N. J. Arch.*, vol. x, pp. 597-598.

[6] *4 Am. Arch.*, vol. ii, p. 1221.

[7] *N. C. Col. Recs.*, vol. x, p. 12.

IN THE PLANTATION PROVINCES

These resolutions, it would appear, were excellently kept. For example, the Philadelphia committee in May prevented the departure of two cargoes intended for Newfoundland;[1] and in September the New York committee held up for public neglect the owners of two vessels that had been trading with Nova Scotia and Newfoundland.[2] The effect of the boycott was not what had been expected. Deep distress was experienced at Newfoundland and the various fishing settlements because of their reliance on New England for food; but after a time the British government succeeded in affording them some relief, and they were also surreptitiously aided by the enterprise of Nantucket fishermen.[3] The people of East Florida also found themselves temporarily in want of provisions.[4] Quebec and Nova Scotia, as has been already noted, probably felt no serious inconvenience and were, on the other hand, receiving enhanced prices in the West Indies for their grain, flour and flax-seed.[5] Only Georgia found herself in distress, without prospect of relief, and torn by civil discord. But Georgia's adhesion to the Continental Association was to come only through the shock caused by the outbreak of hostilities.

[1] *Journals*, vol. ii, p. 52.

[2] *N. Y. Gaz.*, Sept. 4, 1775; also *4 Am. Arch.*, vol. iii, pp. 622-624.

[3] Letters from Newfoundland in *N. Y. Journ.*, June 29, Aug. 24, 1775. English exports to Newfoundland increased from £77,263 in 1774 to £130,280 in 1775. Macpherson, *Annals of Com.*, vol. iii, pp. 564, 585. The act of 16 George III, c. 37, permitted the exportation of peas and biscuit to Newfoundland, Nova Scotia and Labrador.

[4] *4 Am. Arch.*, vol. iii, pp. 703-707. English exports to Florida increased from £52,149 in 1774 to £85,254 in 1775. Macpherson, *op. cit.*, vol. iii, pp. 564, 585.

[5] *4 Am. Arch.*, vol. i, pp. 1164-1165; *Pub. Rec. Off., C. O.* 5, no. 138 (*L. C. Transcripts*), p. 404. At Quebec English imports increased from £307,635 in 1774 to £472,368 in 1775; at Nova Scotia, from £47,148 to £56,308. Macpherson, *op. cit.*, vol. iii, pp. 564, 585.

Before the Continental Association had been in effect many weeks it had become perfectly evident not only that provinces and towns that held aloof from the Association must be boycotted but that a close degree of co-operation must be maintained among the Associated Provinces in order to prevent evasions of the compact by means of the coastwise trade. About the middle of November, 1774, a Salem merchant engaged in coastwise trade with Virginia requested of the Salem Committee of Correspondence a certificate vouching for his firmness in the cause of Americal liberty, so that he might carry it with him. This being an innovation, the Salem committee consulted with the Boston Committee of Correspondence; and the reply was a whole-hearted endorsement of the plan and the suggestion that the device be regularly employed.[1] The committees of the other provinces fell in with the plan sooner or later, Providence, Rhode Island,[2] and the Virginia counties being among the first.[3] The best form of certificate was that prescribed by the Philadelphia committee in June, 1775. The importer of merchandise into that metropolis was required either to produce a certificate from the committee from whence the goods had come signifying that they had been imported into America in accordance with the Association, or to produce a qualification, taken before a magistrate, testifying to the identity of the goods, the time of importation into America, and the name of the vessel in which they had been brought.[4] A few months later, when the object was not only to safeguard the Association but also to prevent provisions and merchandise from reaching

[1] *Bos. Com. Cor. Papers*, vol. iii, pp. 651, 653.
[2] *R. I. Col. Recs.*, vol. vii, pp. 285-287.
[3] Richmond, Westmoreland, Prince William, Prince George and Accomack. *Vide* the Virginia newspapers, Feb.-June, 1775, *passim*.
[4] *Pa. Eve. Post*, June 8, 1775; also 4 *Am. Arch.*, vol. ii, pp. 909-910.

IN THE PLANTATION PROVINCES 535

the British army, the provincial bodies of Massachusetts and New York required that coastwise traders should give bond that the goods they took away would be landed at the destination named.[1] These precautions aided greatly in simplifying the enforcement of the Association for individual provinces.

It is now possible to reach some conclusions with reference to the workings of the Continental Association in the twelve Associated Provinces during the first four and a half months. In general, the situation bore a very hopeful aspect for those Americans who believed that the salvation of British America depended upon an effective administration of the Association. The administrative machinery of the Association had been established in the twelve provinces; and all features of the document, which were intended to have a coercive effect upon the mother country, were being vigorously enforced. Indeed, the Association was receiving a more faithful obedience than the provincial laws ordinarily did, as many a royal governor mournfully testified. While it has not been possible to obtain statistics confined to the period of non-importation which is now being particularly examined, yet the comparative figures of importations during the years 1774 and 1775 are a suggestive index to the true condition of affairs. English imports fell off from £562,476 in 1774 to £71,625 in 1775 in the New England provinces; from £437,937 to £1,228 at New York; from £625,652 to £1,366 at Philadelphia; from £528,738 to £1,921 in Maryland and Virginia; and from £378,116 to £6,245 in the Carolinas.[2] The total decline in the import trade from England in 1775 as compared with

[1] 4 *Am. Arch.*, vol. iii, pp. 1468, 1625.
[2] Macpherson, *op. cit.*, vol. iii, pp. 564, 585.

the preceding year was almost ninety-seven per cent. Making due allowance for such part of this disparity as came from the abnormal importations in the latter part of 1774, the contrast still remains an eloquent testimonial to the activity and efficiency of the radical organization. In the same period imports into Georgia only increased from £57,518 to £133,377.

Further evidence of the effective enforcement of the Association was afforded by the course pursued, in the early months of 1775, by the business men in Great Britain who possessed American connections and investments. Although they had watched indifferently while Parliament passed the coercive acts of 1774,[1] they were now galvanized into sudden activity by the realization that the American Association was closing their chief markets to them.[2] Beginning in January and continuing for almost three months, the merchants and manufacturers concerned in the American trade carried on a systematic propaganda for the purpose of convincing the ministry and Parliament that the acts of 1774 should be repealed. The movement was inaugurated by a series of meetings of the London merchants in the North American trade at King's Arms Tavern at Cornhill,[3] and by joint meetings of the West India merchants and the absentee proprietors of West Indian plantations at London Tavern.[4] Petitions were addressed to Parliament, and word was sent to the manufacturing towns to

---

[1] *Mass. Gaz. & Post-Boy*, May 16, 1774; *Mass. Spy*, July 15.

[2] *E. g.*, a commercial correspondent declared in a London newspaper that from January 1 to April 27, 1775, the following ships cleared from Bristol carrying nothing but ballast: seven for New York, three for Maryland, three for Philadelphia, three for Virginia, one for North Carolina, and three for South Carolina. *N. Y. Gazetteer*, Aug. 24, 1775; also *4 Am. Arch.*, vol. ii, pp. 921-922.

[3] *Ibid.*, vol. i, pp. 1086-1091, 1107-1110, 1513-1515, 1525-1526.

[4] *Ibid.*, vol. i, pp. 1082-1083, 1147-1152, 1540.

join in the agitation.¹ The latter responded with alacrity. When Parliament reassembled on January 19, 1775, the House of Commons was deluged with petitions in the ensuing weeks. The merchants, traders and manufacturers of Bristol, Glasgow, Birmingham, Manchester, Liverpool, Leeds, Belfast, and many other places joined in the chorus of lamentation, complaining that business conditions were already poor and foretelling the suspension of debt collections, bankruptcy and widespread unemployment.²

But the ministry were as adamant. They believed that England was reaping the whirlwind that had been sown when indulgent ministries had granted concessions to the colonists on the occasion of the two earlier non-importation leagues. As one man friendly to the ministry wrote: "there will be no end of it, if the Americans may rebel at their pleasure, and then slip behind their creditors for security."³ Solicitor General Wedderburn presented the issue with unmistakable clearness to the House of Commons. "He gave every allowance for, and paid all deference to, the interests of Commerce and Manufactures; but contended that in the present case interests were concerned of yet greater consequence; that all the world must acknowledge that when the clearest rights of the Legislative power of a country are invaded and denied, and when in consequence the people so denying are in actual and open

[1] *Mass. Gaz. & News-Letter*, Mch. 23, 1775.

[2] Petitions also came from Norwich, Dudley, Wolverhampton, Newcastle, Burslem, Tunstall, Colridge, Shelton, Hanly, Stoke Lane, Delf Lane End, Nottingham, Bridgport, Wakefield, Halifax, Bradford, Huddersfield, Whitehaven, and Waterford, Ireland. *4 Am. Arch.*, vol. i, pp. 1513-1540, 1567, 1627-1638, 1698-1703; Franklin, *Writings* (Smyth), vol. vi, pp. 303-308, 315-317. There were a few petitions praying the government to stand firm—from Birmingham, Leeds, Wakefield, Halifax, Bradford, Nottingham and Huddersfield, usually from the aldermen, sheriffs, gentlemen and principal manufacturers.

[3] *Mass. Gaz. & Post-Boy*, May 23, 1774.

rebellion, that then there are points of greater importance to be settled and decided than points of Commerce and Manufacture. An enemy in the bowels of a Kingdom is surely to be resisted, opposed and conquered; notwithstanding the trade that may suffer, and the fabrics that may be ruined. That descriptions of the immense consequence of our American trade were arguments against the opposing Members than for them; for the greater the consequence of the Commerce, the greater the care ought to be, and the firmer the policy that is to preserve it; that the question is not now the importance of the American Colonies, but the possession of the Colonies at all."[1]

For a decade colonial governors had been urging that Parliament should declare non-importation agreements illegal as combinations in restraint of trade. Lord North's plan was more penetrating: "as the Americans had refused to trade with this Kingdom," he was reported to have said, "it was but just that we should not suffer them to trade with any other Nation."[2] His first bill was directed against the New Englanders, whom he believed to be at the bottom of the American troubles. This bill became a law on March 30, 1775, and provided that, until peaceful conditions of business had been restored, no New England province should, after July 1, trade with any part of the world, save the British Isles and the British West Indies, nor after July 20 should be permitted to use the fisheries.[3]

[1] *Pa. Gaz.*, Apr. 12, 1775; also *4 Am. Arch.*, vol. i, p. 1547. *Vide* also *ibid.*, pp. 1526-1527, 1624-1625.

[2] *Ibid.*, vol. i, p. 1622; also *N. Y. Journ.*, Apr. 20. 1775. North had this plan in mind as early as September 21, 1774—before the Continental Association had been adopted. Hutchinson, *Diary and Letters*, vol. i, p. 245.

[3] 15 George III, c. 10. The inhabitants of Nantucket were exempted from the provisions of the act so far as the whale fisheries were concerned, and the inhabitants of Marshfield and Scituate so far as the mackerel, shad and alewife fisheries were concerned.

Meantime it had become evident that most of the other colonies had ratified the Continental Association;[1] and so, by Lord North's second bill, enacted April 13, the terms of the first act were extended to New Jersey and Pennsylvania, Maryland, Virginia and South Carolina after July 20.[2] The commerce of New York, the Delaware Counties, North Carolina and Georgia was left unmolested for the time being, upon the belief that with such encouragement these colonies would hold off from union with the Associated Colonies—an illusory hope.

The indignation of the merchants and manufacturers in Britain, who had thus been ignored and chastised by the government, was at first unbounded. But several events soon transpired which reconciled them to the situation. Undoubtedly the affair at Lexington and Concord in April sharpened the understanding of many of them as to the nature of the issues at stake. Equally important was the amelioration of business conditions in Great Britain which began to be felt about the middle of the year 1775. This was in no sense due to any relaxation of the enforcement of the Association in America, but to increased orders for manufactures which began to pour in from various parts of Europe — particularly from the Baltic countries and Germany, owing to the establishment of peace between Russia and the Porte and the pacification of Poland, and from Spain in consequence of warlike preparations against Algiers. At the same time great wheat exportations from America and the advanced prices paid for American tobacco and oil enabled the colonial merchants to discharge their debts better than usual, and thus increased the amount of capital which the British merchants and manufacturers

---

[1] *4 Am. Arch.*, vol. i, p. 1701.

[2] Exclusion from the fisheries was not included, however. 15 George III, c. 18.

might use in developing this new business.¹ This analysis of the revival of business confidence, made by a gentleman of American sympathies in England, was borne out by abundant and indubitable testimony of a varied character.²

Fortuitous occurrences thus robbed the Continental Association of its coercive consequences and enabled the British administration to develop its policy without uncomfortable pressure from the commercial and manufacturing interests. When Parliament assembled in the fall of 1775, scores of votes of confidence were presented from towns all over Great Britain, and the few mercantile petitions that were sent in behalf of the Americans did not plead the cause of the colonists on the ground of commercial distress.³ Under these auspicious circumstances Parliament, on December 23, enacted as a war measure the law that provided for entirely closing up the thirteen colonies to trade with any part of the world after March 1, 1776.⁴

---

¹ *4 Am. Arch.*, vol. iii, p. 818.
² Macpherson, *op. cit.*, vol. iii, pp. 589-591; Izard, *Corresp.*, vol. i, pp. 116-117; *Pub. Rec. Off., C. O. 5*, no. 154 (*L. C. Transcripts*), pp. 281-283; letter in *N. Y. Gaz.*, Nov. 6, 1775; *4 Am. Arch.*, vol. iii, pp. 1010-1011, 1111-1112, 1115-1116, 1261-1262, 1381-1382, 1520, 1641.
³ *Ibid.*, vol. iii, pp. 802-1704 *passim*.
⁴ 16 George III, c. 5.

CHAPTER XIV

Transformation of the Association (April, 1775–July, 1776)

THE tocsin of war, sounded on the historic April day at Lexington and Concord, wrought a radical change in the nature of the opposition directed by the Americans against the British measures. This did not mean that a struggle for independence had begun, but it did mean that armed rebellion had superseded commercial coercion as the dependence of the radicals in their struggle for larger liberties. Thereafter the Continental Association lost its distinctive character as a method of peaceful coercion; it became subordinated to the military necessities of the times.

The transformation which the Association was undergoing revealed itself in five ways: in the widespread adoption of defense associations; in the determination of the Georgia moderates to adopt the Continental Association as a deterrent to the more violent methods advocated by the radicals there; in the spontaneous action of the extra-legal bodies in the several provinces in taking on disciplinary and military functions; in the adoption, by provinces exposed to the perils of war, of non-exportation regulations prior to the time fixed in the Association; and in the important alterations made in the text of the original Association by the Second Continental Congress.

News of the gallant stand made by the Massachusetts minutemen was carried down the coast and through the country by swift couriers. The radical organizations of the

Associated Colonies were faced with the decision whether they should follow the Massachusetts extremists into armed resistance just as they had followed them a little earlier into commercial opposition. The air was electric with excitement. As individuals, some radicals hesitated or deserted the cause; as organizations, they were too deeply committed to do anything but give loyal support to their brethren of Massachusetts. The New England group of provinces, quickened by the hazardous proximity of the British forces, responded in April and May by reorganizing their militia and putting it on a war footing.[1] Their action hardly more than consolidated the military companies that had been drilled and equipped in the towns and counties during the several preceding months.

In the remaining provinces the almost invariable form of action was the adoption of defense associations; and indeed the same device was also utilized by Connecticut where the loyalists were thick in Fairfield County. This plan of procedure was fashioned frankly on the principle of the old associations for commercial coercion; and acting through the same machinery, it gained prestige by reason of the fact. In phraseology the associations appeared to vary according to the character of the population. In the more moderate provinces, like New York and New Jersey, the subscribers agreed solemnly to " carry into execution *whatever measures* may be recommended by the Continental Congress or resolved upon by our Provincial Convention;"[2]

---

[1] The Massachusetts provincial congress had taken its measures earlier. *Vide* particularly the votes of Oct. 26, 1774 and April 5, 1775. *4 Am. Arch.*, vol. i, pp. 843-845, 1350-1355. For the acts of the other provinces, *vide* New Hampshire provincial congress, May 20, in *ibid.*, vol. ii, pp. 652-653; Rhode Island Assembly, Apr. 25, in *ibid.*, vol. ii, p. 390; Connecticut Assembly, Apr. 26, in *ibid.*, vol. ii, pp. 411-418.

[2] The italics are Governor Franklin's. *1 N. J. Arch.*, vol. x, p. 592.

in ultra-radical communities, like Maryland, South Carolina and certain North Carolina counties, the subscribers pledged their "lives and fortunes" in defense of the American cause. But whatever the form, the underlying meaning of all associations was the same. The defense associations appeared spontaneously in the various provinces, and were afterwards usually adopted formally by the provincial congress or convention with the provision that the male adult inhabitants be given an opportunity to sign, and the further provision frequently that the names of dissentients be listed. The act of signing the defense association was a more rigid test of loyalty to the radical cause than acceptance of the Continental Association and largely superseded it in public attention and importance.[1] These associations spread southward through the Associated Provinces in the spring and early summer of 1775.[2]

The course of New York exemplified, in its main outlines, the progress of the defense association in every prov-

---

[1] Connecticut, New York, New Jersey, Maryland and South Carolina provided that lists of non-signers should be drawn up.

[2] The central radical organizations of the several provinces adopted defense associations as follows: the New York provincial congress on May 26, *4 Am. Arch.*, vol. i,, p. 1256; the New Jersey provincial congress on May 31, *ibid.*, vol. ii, p. 690; the Pennsylvania Assembly on June 30, *ibid.*, vol. ii, p. 1172; the Maryland provincial convention on Aug. 12, *ibid.*, vol. iii, pp. 107-108; the North Carolina provincial congress on Aug. 23, *ibid.*, vol. iii, p. 187; the South Carolina provincial congress on June 3, *ibid.*, vol. ii, pp. 896-897; the Connecticut Assembly in October, *ibid.*, vol. iii, p. 1026. In the Delaware Counties, no record of action has been found; however, an out-and-out military association was signed in Kent County on May 25; *ibid.*, vol. ii, p. 704. In Virginia, it would appear that this method was not tried; but the militia was reorganized by resolution of the provincial convention of Mch. 25, 1775; *ibid.*, vol. ii, pp. 169-170. Some of the county associations in North Carolina were more plainspoken than the association adopted by the provincial congress, being modeled on the South Carolina association; *e. g., ibid.*, vol. ii, p. 1030.

ince.[1] We have Lieutenant Governor Colden's word that "the first accounts of the action between the King's Troops and People near Boston was spread with horrid and aggravating circumstances. The Moment of Consternation and anxiety was seized, the People were assembled, and that Scene of Violence and Disorder was begun which has entirely prostrated the Powers of Government and produced an Association by which this Province has solemnly united with the others in resisting the Acts of Parliament."[2] For nearly a week after the receipt of the fateful news the city was ruled by the mob. Under the leadership of ultra-radicals like Sears and Lamb, the arsenal was raided and the muskets distributed; the custom house was shut up; business was at a standstill; and armed citizens paraded about the streets.

Out of this "State of anarchy" issued three things of great import. An association was set on foot in New York city on April 29 by which the subscribers, professing alarm at the revenue plans of the ministry and at "the bloody scene now acting in the Massachusetts-Bay," resolved never to become slaves, and associated, under all the ties of religion, honor and love of country, to carry into execution whatever measures were determined upon by the Continental Congress or the provincial congress for the purpose of preserving the constitution and opposing the arbitrary and oppressive acts of Parliament.[3] A new committee of one hundred, of more radical complexion even than the Sixty, was chosen on May 1 with power to act in "the present unhappy exigency of affairs as well as to observe

---

[1] In the following account, Professor Becker's discussion, with his references, has been relied upon where no other authority is cited. *N. Y. Parties, 1760-1776*, pp. 193-227.

[2] *Letter Books*, vol. ii, p. 402. Vide also *ibid.*, p. 404.

[3] *N. Y. Journ.*, May 4, 1775; also 4 *Am. Arch.*, vol. ii, p. 471.

the conduct of all persons touching the Association." A call was sent out for a provincial congress "at the present alarming juncture" to meet on May 22. The defense association was taken up by the two latter bodies, when they met, and applied to the inhabitants of the province as a touchstone of their allegiance to the radical organization.

At the first meeting of the One Hundred on May 1, it was resolved to offer the association of April 29 to every inhabitant in the county, save Colden only, the names of those refusing to subscribe to be recorded. In the high excitement of the hour the association was quickly signed by more than a thousand persons; and within a month eighteen hundred had subscribed in the city alone.[1] On May 26 a resolution was passed by the provincial congress that all members be desired to sign the association of April 29; and arrangements were made for county committees to tender the association to every inhabitant of the province and return to the congress a list of signers and non-signers not later than July 15. No penalty for dissentients was imposed. By the time fixed, the defense association had been subscribed by one hundred members of the provincial congress, fourteen failing to do so. "The official returns show in five districts of Orange County approximately 1,550 signers and 250 non-signers; in seven districts of Ulster County, approximately 1,770 and 80 non-signers; in seven or eight districts of Suffolk County, 2,060 signers and 200 non-signers; in six precincts of Dutchess County, 1,680 signers and 882 non-signers; in one district of Charlotte County, 110 signers; in three districts of Cumberland County, 123 signers and 10 non-signers; in Queens County, 17 signers and 209 non-signers."

[1] Colden, *Letter Books*, vol. ii, p. 424. Colden added, however: "there must be at least three Times that number who have an equal Right to Sign."

By September the policy of the provincial congress toward non-signers began to be defined. "Although this Congress have a tender regard for freedom of speech, the rights of conscience, and personal liberty," declared the resolution of September 1, yet, for the public safety, any person denying the authority of the provincial or continental congress or any county or district committee should be disarmed, and, for a second offense, should be confined at his own expense. This vote did not apply in terms to non-signers; and two weeks later the provincial committee of safety voted to disarm all of the latter by force if necessary. This was disapproved by the provincial congress in October; and there the matter rested until March, 1776, when the committee of safety again ordered the disarming of non-associators. This time the provincial congress gave its support.

The net outcome of the circulation of the defense association was that the Continental Association was elbowed into the background; for the new association by its spirit not only exacted obedience to the old regulations of commercial opposition, but in explicit terms demanded allegiance to unnamed radical measures yet to be formulated. Incidentally the propaganda attendant upon the promotion of the defense association had served the purpose of extending radical organization into rural parts of New York that had been untouched on the several earlier occasions.

Of the old British provinces, Georgia had succeeded thus far in holding off from any union in measures against Great Britain. The widespread resolutions of censure and boycott had not been without a chastening influence on her; but it was the news of the beginning of hostilities that, by a curious indirection, now brought Georgia over to the side of the Continental Association.[1] In June, 1775, a defense

[1] Wright to Gage, June 27, 1775; Gibbes, *Doc'y History*, vol. ii, pp. 98-99.

association, copied *verbatim* from the New York association of April 29, was circulated in various parts of the province.[1] The Georgia moderates perceived that, in spite of the success of their obstructive tactics hitherto, the floodtide of insurrection surging high in other provinces threatened to sweep the malcontents of Georgia into extreme measures unless discreet concessions were made. Whereas the moderates had opposed the adoption of the Continental Association when the alternative was peaceful opposition to Great Britain or no opposition, many of them were now willing to join in pacific measures of opposition when the choice seemed to lie between that alternative and the imminence of violent resistance.[2] This at once made possible a coalition of the more progressive moderates with the more conservative radicals of the Savannah stamp.[3] It was this union of factions that sought to control the movement for a provincial congress, called for July 4, 1775.

At a caucus held at Savannah on June 13 and attended by thirty-four citizens, many of whom later joined the British side, the program of the coalition was formulated as follows: (1) "we will use our utmost endeavours to preserve the peace and good order of this Province; . . . no person behaving himself peaceably and inoffensively shall be molested in his person or property" notwithstanding his

[1] *4 Am. Arch.*, vol. i, pp. 1136-1137; vol. ii, pp. 1551-1552. *Vide* also *ibid.*, vol. ii, p. 471.

[2] *Vide* Wright's letter to Dartmouth; *Ga. Hist. Soc. Colls.*, vol. iii, p. 183. Read Dr. Zubly's sermon at the opening of the provincial congress in the light of this interpretation. *4 Am. Arch.*, vol. ii, pp. 1557-1567. Zubly became a loyalist eventually.

[3] "From Georgia we learn that a Coalition of Parties is likely to take place," said the *S. C. & Am. Gen. Gaz.*, July 7, 1775. "The Tories in Georgia are now no more; the Province is almost universally on the right side, and are about to choose Delegates to send to the Congress," wrote a Charlestonian on June 29; *Pa. Gaz.*, July 19, also *4 Am. Arch.*, vol. ii, p. 1129.

private sentiments; (2) in the absence of the General Assembly, the provincial congress should adopt a petition to the king for redress of grievances, expressive of the sense of all who choose to sign it; (3) the interest of Georgia is inseparable from that of the mother country and all the sister provinces, and to act apart from the latter would be a just cause for their resentment; (4) Georgia ought forthwith to " join the other Provinces in every just and legal measure to secure and restore the liberties of all America and for healing the unhappy divisions now subsisting between Great Britain and her Colonies." [1] On June 22 a meeting of the inhabitants of the town and district of Savannah at Liberty Pole chose a committee for the purpose of carrying out the Continental Association.[2]

The moderates were playing with fire, but they were left with no alternative. The provincial congress of July contained delegates from every part of the province except the two small parishes of St. James and St. Patrick. Some parishes which had hitherto been apathetic or else actively opposed to extra-legal measures " manifested a very Laudable Zeal upon this Occasion." [3] On the second day of the meeting, the resolutions adopted by the Savannah caucus were presented, and the congress voted that the paper should " lie upon the table for the perusal of the members." A few days later the congress voted its opinion that the paper " ought not to have been entitled or dressed in the form of Resolves, but rather as recommendations, or in the

---

[1] 4 *Am. Arch.*, vol. ii, p. 1544.

[2] For names of the members, *vide* McCall, *Hist. Ga.*, vol. ii, pp. 44-45. For a slightly different list, *vide Ga. Rev. Recs.*, vol. i, p. 72.

[3] Official communication of the Georgia congress to the Second Continental Congress; *Journals Cont. Cong.*, vol. ii, p. 193 n. The journal of the provincial congress may be found in *Ga. Rev. Recs.*, vol. i, pp. 229-280; also 4 *Am. Arch.*, vol. ii, pp. 1543-1568.

nature of a Petition or Address to this Congress." This was fair warning that the radicals of the St. John's stamp were making themselves felt in the congress.

The Savannah coalition were permitted to carry things pretty largely their own way during the first few days. The congress resolved unanimously on July 6 to "carry into execution all and singular the measures and recommendations of the late Continental Congress," particularly the Declaration of Rights and the Continental Association. The provisions of the latter were re-stated and explicitly adopted, with no alterations of importance.[1] A concession was even made to the opinion prevalent in the plantation provinces in favor of a suspension of prosecutions for debt: no summons was to be issued or civil warrant granted unless, in the opinion of the magistrate concerned, there were good grounds to believe that the defendant intended to abscond. This was a moderate version of the popular regulation which gave the supervision of actions for debt to radical committees rather than to provincial officials. A petition for redress was sent to the king; and five delegates, one of whom was loyalist in sympathies, were chosen to represent the province in the Second Continental Congress, then in session.

At this point the radical elements began to assert their control. Strengthened by the sentiment aroused by the Lexington affair, they were able to carry through resolu-

[1] Such changes of date were introduced as were made necessary by the fact that the non-importation regulation was going into effect at a later date than that fixed in the original Association. The provision in Article x as to the disposition of goods imported before February 1 was omitted as no longer applicable. The provision in Article xiv authorizing provincial bodies to establish further regulations did not appear. To the list of parliamentary acts which must be repealed were added the two laws, lately passed, for restraining the trade of most of the colonies.

tions asserting the right of the provincial congress to levy taxes and issue paper money, and pledging Georgia to her share of the " expenses which have or may accrue in the defence of the violated rights of America." They endorsed the defense association which had been circulated about Georgia in June and appointed a committee to present a copy for the signature of all the inhabitants of the town and district of Savannah. Finally, they recommended that in the election of delegates to the next provincial congress the inhabitants should pledge their lives and fortunes to support the measures which they might adopt. A general committee, composed of the Savannah delegates and such other delegates as might be in town, was appointed to supervise the execution of the resolutions of the continental and provincial congresses and to advise with all the parochial and district committees.

The radicals were in the saddle, although their seat was by no means secure. The work of establishing committees to enforce the Association went forward. Governor Wright wrote to the home government that there " are very few Men of real Abilities, Gentlemen, or Men of Property in their Tribunals. The Parochial Committee are a Parcel of the Lowest People, Chiefly Carpenters, Shoemakers, Blacksmiths &c. with a Few at their Head; in the General Committee and Council of Safety there are Some better Sort of Men and Some Merchants and Planters, but Many of the Inferior Class; and it is really Terrible, my Lord, that Such People Should be Suffered to Overturn the Civil Government and most arbitrarily determine upon, and Sport with Other Mens Lives Libertys and Propertys." [1] The accession of Georgia to the Continental Association relieved the province of the ban placed on it by the Conti-

[1] Letter of Dec. 19, 1775; *Ga. Hist. Soc. Colls.*, vol. iii, p. 228.

nental Congress, although it does not appear that Congress took any formal step to that effect beyond admitting the Georgia delegates to their seats.[1]

The non-importation regulations of the Association were well enforced in Georgia thereafter.[2] On August 1, Governor Wright informed the home government that: "The Committee here take upon themselves to Order Ships and Vessells that arrive to Depart again without suffering them to come up to Town and unload. Some they admit, some they Order away just as they please, and exactly copy after Carolina, and are making a very Rapid Progress in the execution of their Assumed Powers."[3] A few days later he added with reference to the defense association that: "Every Method has been used to *Compell* the People to Sign the Association; and those who Decline, they threaten to Proscribe, and for fear of that, and losing their Property, or having it Destroyed, Great Numbers have been Intimidated to Sign, and I suppose by far the greater Part of the Province have signed it; indeed it is said there are few in the Country who have not."[4] On September 23, he described the situation in Georgia as: "Government totally Annihilated, and Assumed by Congresses, Councils and Committees, and the greatest Acts of Tyranny, Oppression, Gross Insults &c &c &c commited, and not the least means of Protection, Support, or even Personal Safety . . ."[5] On October 14 he closed his case by stating: "The Poison has Infected the whole Province, and

[1] The General Committee at Charleston revived trading connections on August 1, 1775. *S. C. Gaz.*, Sept. 7, 1775.

[2] *E. g., Ga. Rev. Recs.*, vol. i, pp. 81, 90; *Ga. Hist. Soc. Colls.*, vol. iii, pp. 210, 215; *Journs. Cont. Cong.*, vol. ii, pp. 251-252.

[3] *Ga. Hist. Soc. Colls.*, vol. iii, p. 205.

[4] *Ibid.*

[5] *Ibid.*, vol. iii, p. 213.

neither Law, Government, or Regular Authority have any Weight or are at all attended to." [1]

The April events had meanwhile been leaving their impress on the character and functions of the committees of observation and inspection in the several provinces. By swift, though natural, stages, these committees appointed to enforce the Continental Association became the nuclei of military organization and the engines for crushing loyalist opinion. In the chief commercial provinces, where political activity radiated from the centers of population, the new functions devolving upon the committees were frankly recognized by the selection of new city committees.[2] Where the population was diffused and urban communities unimportant, the central radical organization usually decreed a new establishment of committees for the whole province, with the dual purpose of standardizing their method of selection and of entrusting them with the additional powers necessitated by the imminence of war.[3] In all cases provincial conventions and congresses were assembled to guide and supplement the committees in the discharge of their new functions.

These committees were of great practical assistance to the patriot military. The wide scope of their services may

[1] *Ga. Hist. Soc. Colls.*, vol. iii, p. 215.

[2] Thus, the Boston Committee of Correspondence, Safety and Inspection, appointed May 1; the New York Committee of One Hundred, on May 1; the Philadelphia Committee of One Hundred, on Aug. 16. *Bos. Town Recs.* (*1770-1777*), p. 233; *4 Am. Arch.*, vol. ii, p. 459; vol. iii, pp. 145-146.

[3] Thus, the South Carolina provincial congress on June 17; the New Jersey provincial congress on Aug. 12; the Maryland convention on Aug. 14; the Virginia convention on Aug. 25; the North Carolina provincial congress on Sept. 9. *Ibid.*, vol. ii, p. 1016; vol. iii, pp. 42, 114-116, 420-424, 207-208.

be indicated by some illustrative instances in various provinces.[1] The Kensington, N. H., committee exacted obedience from a man who had refused to equip himself with arms and ammunition as directed by a resolution of the provincial congress. The New York committee declared a boycott against any person who should dispose of arms and ammunition to any person inimical to American liberty. The New York provincial congress instructed the local committees to purchase and rent weapons, and to organize their jurisdiction into " beats " for the formation of military companies. The Morris County, N. J., committee collected arms and ammunition and promoted the enlistment of men. All committees of the province were instructed by the New Jersey congress in October to apprehend deserters from the American army. The Maryland committees played an important part in organizing and training the militia of the province. The Virginia committees undertook to supervise enlistments and to examine all strangers and suspects for correspondence and the like. In North Carolina four committees raised money for the purchase of gunpowder; and the Newbern committee intercepted some letters written by the governor.

Efforts that had hitherto been turned to the promotion of manufacturing in general were now frankly devoted to the production and increased output of weapons and gunpowder, saltpetre and sulphur. Some of the money inducements offered for the carrying on of such manufactures have already been noted. Every province joined in the movement with zest and determination, through action of its central organization or its local committees or both. The Philadelphia committee erected its own saltpetre works.

[1] These examples and many others like them may be found in *4 Am. Arch.*, vols. ii and iii, *passim*.

The Virginia convention established a factory at Fredericksburg for the manufacture of arms.

The most characteristic, if not most important, aspect of the new work of the committees and conventions was their activity in drawing a sharp line between friends and enemies of the American cause and in converting and silencing all opponents. The phrase, "enemies of American liberty," had been used in the Continental Association to stigmatize persons who had actually violated the commercial regulations of that document; now its meaning was rapidly extended to comprehend any persons who expressed verbal disapproval of *any* phase of radical activities, or who acted in an unfriendly manner with respect to them. Under the Continental Association the only punishment visited on offenders was the suspension of all dealings with them; with the new developments the boycott gave place, in an increasing number of cases, to such penalties as fine, imprisonment and banishment.

The radicals in Massachusetts had already employed the boycott in pointing out persons who supported the Massachusetts Charter Act of 1774, especially in designating for discipline the detested "mandamus councillors."[1] In January, 1775, the town of Marblehead had even deemed it necessary to appoint a committee "to attend to the Conduct of ministerial Tools and Jacobites in this Town, and to report their Names to the Town from Time to Time, that it may take effectual Measures for either silencing or expelling them from this Community."[2] With the outbreak of rebellion, committees in the other provinces assumed inquisitorial powers and began a systematic campaign to suppress freedom of speech on the part of the loyalists.

[1] *4 Am. Arch.*, vol. i, pp. 984, 1000, 1335, 1346.
[2] *Mass. Gaz. & Post-Boy*, Jan. 16, 1775.

Regarding the radicals, "A Converted Whig" bemoaned: " In contending for liberty, they seem inclinable to engross it all themselves; . . . they are arbitrary and even tyrannical in the whole tenour of their conduct; they allow not to others who differ from them the same liberty of thinking and acting that they claim themselves, but shamefully abuse them, and treat them with spite, malice, and revenge." [1] The justification of the radicals was neatly put in a resolution of the Philadelphia committee in September, 1775: " That, in the opinion of the Committee, no person has a right to the protection of a community or society he wishes to destroy; and that if any inhabitant, by speeches or writing, evidences a disposition to aid and assist our enemies, or endeavours to persuade others to break the Association, or by force or fraud to oppose the friends of liberty and the Constitution, . . . such person, being duly convicted thereof before the Committee, ought to be deemed a foe to the rights of British America, and unworthy of those blessings which it is hoped will yet be secured to this and succeeding generations by the strenuous and noble efforts of the United Colonies." [2]

The nature and scope of this new function of the committees may be suggested by a few typical examples. Abiel Wood was deprived of the benefits of society by the committee of inspection of the East Precinct of Pownalborough, Mass., because, among other offenses, he had declared that " Hancock, Adams and others acted out of selfish views in destroying the tea " and offered his oath that Hancock was the first man on board, and because he had stated that the members of the Continental Congress had drunk thirty bumpers of wine apiece before passing their resolutions and that the provincial congress consisted of "dam'd vil-

---

[1] 4 *Am. Arch.*, vol. ii, p. 106.
[2] *Ibid.*, vol. iii, p. 731; also *Pa. Eve. Post*, Sept. 23, 1775.

lains."[1] Abijah Brown was found guilty by the Waltham selectmen of having belittled the general of the Massachusetts army and the committeemen as "a set of idiots and lunaticks;" but he was restored to public favor by the provincial committee of safety on the ground that he had temporarily fallen under the influence of "disaffected antagonists."[2] The committee of Sheffield, Mass., subjected Job Westover to boycott for holding the sentiment that Parliament had a right to tax the Americans and that an American victory in the impending war would be prejudicial to the best interests of the colonies.[3] The extra-legal "General Court" recommended to the Corporation and Overseers of Harvard College to dismiss from the faculty all those who by their present or past conduct appeared to be unfriendly to the liberties of the colonies.[4] On May 19 the New Hampshire congress recommended to the committees to have a watchful eye over all "persons who, through inadvertence, wilful malice, or immoderate heat, have thrown out many opprobrious expressions respecting the several Congresses, and the methods of security they have thought proper to adopt . . ."[5]

The committee at New Milford, Conn., published the names of seven for having declared their opposition to the Continental Congress and announced the recantation of forty others.[6] Amos Knapp was found guilty by the Greenwich committee of "cursing the honourable Continental

[1] *Bos. Gaz.*, Sept. 11, 1775. For later proceedings with reference to Wood, *vide 4 Am. Arch.*, vol. iii, pp. 151-156, 941.

[2] *Ibid.*, vol. ii, pp. 720-721.

[3] *Ibid.*, vol. ii, p. 545.

[4] *Ibid.*, vol. iii, p. 1451.

[5] *Ibid.*, vol. ii, p. 652. For examples of enforcement, *vide ibid.*, pp. 552, 701, 1652, 1659.

[6] *Conn. Cour.*, July 3, 1775.

TRANSFORMATION OF THE ASSOCIATION 557

Congress, with all the leading men of the Country, and threatening to join the enemy, in case the King's standard was erected."[1] On August 4, the New York committee held one Archer up as an enemy because he had spread the report that the Continental Congress had passed a resolution for independence if American grievances were not redressed by March 1.[2] In February, 1776, J. Thorn of Dutchess County was proscribed for refusing to accept continental paper money.[3] A boycott was declared against Ezekiel Beach of Mendham, N. J., for failing to appear before the committee of observation to defend himself against the charge of "unfriendly conversation and conduct towards the Continental Association."[4] The committee of Bucks County, Pa., accepted as satisfactory the contrition expressed by Thomas Smith " for having uttered expressions derogatory to the Continental Congress, invidious to a particular denomination of Christians, and tending to impede the opposition of my countrymen to ministerial oppression."[5]

The Dover committee in the Delaware Counties found Daniel Varnum guilty of using such expressions as "he had as lief be under a tyrannical King as a tyrannical Commonwealth, especially if the d——d Presbyterians had the rule of it," and then accepted his recantation.[6] George Munro's unfriendliness was discovered by the committee of Bladensburgh, Md., through an intercepted letter, and his protestations of contrition availed him nothing.[7] Thomas

[1] 4 *Am. Arch.*, vol. iii, p. 941.
[2] *Ibid.*, vol. iii, p. 21.
[3] *N. Y. Gaz.*, Mch. 11, 1776.
[4] 4 *Am. Arch.*, vol. ii, p. 1610.
[5] *Ibid.*, vol. iii, p. 690.
[6] *Ibid.*, vol. iii, p. 1072.
[7] *Ibid.*, vol. iii, pp. 51-56.

Anderson of Hanover County, Va., was exempted by the committee from further prosecution when he expressed his deep sorrow for "declaring that this Country was in a state of rebellion, and aimed at a state of independence more than opposition to parliamentary taxation." [1] The committee of Pitt County, N. C., advertised John Tison in May for speaking disrespectfully of the committee and Congress, and in October he confessed his offense and promised under oath never to do the like again.[2]

In the instances here cited, the boycott was the punishment prescribed. But the boycott was essentially a weapon to be resorted to by a minority in a community; as the government of one community after the other fell under control of the rebels, methods of punishment more immediately efficacious were adopted. Thus, in May, 1775, the Massachusetts provincial congress recommended to the committees of correspondence and selectmen of the various towns to confiscate the arms of those persons who were unfriendly to the American cause, and forbade any inhabitants to remove from the province with their effects, except by leave of the local committee of correspondence or the provincial congress. In June the provincial congress directed the selectmen and committees of correspondence of the several towns to take charge of the effects and estates of those persons who had fled within the British lines at Boston or elsewhere, to improve the same to the best advantage, and to render a true account of the profits arising therefrom to the congress.[3] The New Hampshire provincial congress on June 30 sentenced Colonel John Fenton to an indefinite confinement in jail for being "an enemy to the liberties of

---

[1] *4 Am. Arch.*, vol. iii, p. 644.
[2] *N. C. Col. Recs.*, vol. ix, pp. 1240, 1266; vol. x, pp. 243, 261.
[3] *4 Am. Arch.*, vol. ii, pp. 793, 1804, 1431 n.

America." [1]   The Rhode Island General Assembly in November passed a law punishing, with death and forfeiture of property, any persons assisting the British enemy with information, provisions or munitions.[2]   In September the New York provincial congress established a series of penalties for persons inimical to America; and these penalties included imprisonment, disarming, fines, and banishment from the province, according to the enormity of the offence.[3] Several persons were sent to jail in October by the Pennsylvania committee of safety for unfriendly correspondence with the enemy, and one of them was later released under bond of £500 for good behavior.[4]   The committee of Newbern, N. C., ordered the disarming of all those who had not signed the defense association.[5]   In June, 1775, the secret committee of the General Committee at Charleston sentenced two men, who had declined the defense association, to tar and feathers.[6]

The radical committees and organizations in many of the provinces also found it necessary to limit or prohibit exportations, although the non-exportation regulation of the Continental Association was not to become effective until September 10.   The prime purpose of such regulations was to distress the British troops; a subsidiary object was to facilitate the provisioning of the American forces.   The Connecticut Assembly was the first to act, in April, 1775, by placing an embargo upon the exportation by water of cereals,

[1] *4 Am. Arch.*, vol. ii, pp. 698, 1180, 1181.
[2] *Ibid.*, vol. iii, pp. 1376-1377.
[3] *Ibid.*, vol. iii, pp. 573-574.
[4] *Ibid.*, vol. iii, pp. 1815, 1822-1823.
[5] *Ibid.*, vol. iii, p. 100.
[6] *Ibid.*, vol. ii, pp. 922-923.

meats and live cattle, except necessary ship supplies.[1] In May the Rhode Island Assembly passed a similar act.[2] The Massachusetts provincial congress in June resolved that no fish or other provision should be shipped from the province unless the committee having jurisdiction should decide that the victuals were intended for the use of the inhabitants of some New England province.[3]

Even before the fateful day at Lexington, the populace at New York had become alarmed at the exportation of nails, spades and other implements to the British troops at Boston, and at a mass meeting on April 6 they adopted resolutions demanding that the practice stop. Two merchants, William and Henry Ustick, who were active in this traffic, were held up as "inveterate foes to American freedom," although, as these gentlemen maintained, they had not violated any part of the Continental Association.[4] In May the One Hundred forbade the exportation of provisions from New York city, and in August the provincial congress applied the same principle to shipments from the entire province.[5] The Virginia convention resolved, on July 24, to withhold the exportation of cereals and other provisions after August 5 and to prevent even the collection of them in large quantities in towns or near navigable streams. The merchants and inhabitants of Norfolk and Northampton entered vigorous protests; and when word arrived, on August 8, that the Maryland convention would not join in

[1] *4 Am. Arch.*, vol. ii, pp. 410, 562; vol. iii, pp. 269, 1018.

[2] *Ibid.*, vol. ii, p. 1151.

[3] *Ibid.*, vol. ii, p. 1404. For subsequent modifications of this resolution, *vide ibid.*, vol. ii, pp. 1435, 1440, 1462; vol. iii, pp. 320, 362, 1440-1441.

[4] *Ibid.*, vol. ii, pp. 242-243, 282-283; *N. Y. Gaz.*, Apr. 17, 24, 1775.

[5] *4 Am. Arch.*, vol. ii, pp. 636-637; vol. iii, pp. 445-447, 536-537. More stringent regulations were adopted later in the month. *Ibid.*, vol. iii, pp. 558-559, 560, 561, 565.

similar resolutions, the convention rescinded its action.[1] However, the various county committees endeavored to keep supplies away from British warships in Virginia waters.[2] The General Committee at Charleston resolved on May 26, that no rice or Indian corn should thereafter be exported from the province; and on June 9 the provincial congress declared that this embargo should continue for three months.[3]

The conduct of the fishermen of Nantucket furnished a knotty problem for the radicals to solve and involved again the use of non-exportation prior to the time set by the Continental Association. The islanders had no scruples about profiting by their exemption from the New England Restraining Act in respect to the whale fisheries. Furthermore, they were suspected of furnishing the British ships and troops in Massachusetts with food, and of carrying provisions to Newfoundland and the fishing settlements. In order to check this traffic, the Second Continental Congress voted on May 29, 1775, that no provisions or necessities of life should be exported to Nantucket, except from Massachusetts, and then only in sufficient quantities for domestic consumption.[4] This proved to be an impracticable arrangement because of the difficulty of providing an adequate supervision. The Massachusetts provincial congress placed the regulation of exportation under charge of the provincial committee of safety; but it soon became evident that, notwithstanding their precautions, the islanders were preparing a large quantity of provisions with the intention of availing themselves of their exclusive privilege to engage in

[1] *4 Am. Arch.*, vol. iii, pp. 102, 103, 122, 369, 372, 373, 376.
[2] *Ibid.*, vol. iii, pp. 218, 655-656.
[3] *Ibid.*, vol. ii, pp. 710, 938.
[4] *Journals*, vol. ii, pp. 70-71.

the whale fisheries. On July 7, therefore, the provincial congress decided to withhold all provisions and necessities from the island until the inhabitants showed proof that the food they had on hand would be used in domestic consumption.[1]

The islanders apparently gave little heed to this resolution. They managed to get a little food from other provinces;[2] but by September they found themselves in severe straits. The Massachusetts "House of Representatives," successor of the provincial congress, being made cognizant of this situation, took steps on September 28 to re-open exportation, and they instructed the committee of correspondence of the town of Falmouth to supply the island with enough food for sustenance of the inhabitants.[3] This method of regulation likewise failed;[4] and on December 11, 1775, the Continental Congress took the matter in hand. The selectmen of the town of Sherburne in Nantucket were instructed to prepare an estimate of the provisions and fuel necessary for the use of the island and to lay it, under their oath or affirmation, before three or more justices of the peace of Barnstable County, Mass. The justices were then empowered to grant licenses to any master or owner of vessels in the island to import supplies up to the amount specified.[5] This resolution of Congress appears to have afforded a reasonably satisfactory solution for the difficulty while the British troops remained at Boston.

The Second Continental Congress convened on May 10, 1775, three weeks after the beginning of war at Lexington.

[1] *Journals*, vol. iii, pp. 420-422.
[2] *E. g., ibid.*, vol. iii, pp. 15, 21-22, 60.
[3] *Ibid.*, vol. iii, p. 1444.
[4] *Ibid.*, vol. iv, p. 1331.
[5] *Journals*, vol. iii, pp. 420-422.

Similar to the First Continental Congress in the irregularity of its election, the problem that it had to face was a more complicated one. The Congress had to solve on a national scale the problem that the provincial and local organizations had been trying to solve within their smaller jurisdictions. As Robert R. Livingston told his fellow-members in a speech on the floor of Congress, "We are between hawk and buzzard; we puzzle ourselves between the commercial and warlike opposition."[1] This was indeed the most serious dilemma; but, in addition, it was necessary to settle certain questions of interpretation and omission arising from the Continental Association and to adapt the document frankly to the new war conditions.

Accepting the Lexington affray as a declaration of war, the Congress began to assume direction of the rebellion and to exercise the powers of a *de facto* government. In June Washington was appointed commander-in-chief of the army of the United Colonies, and rules for regulating the army and navy were promulgated. Many other plans for military operations were adopted in the subsequent months. On July 6 a declaration was issued, which said, in effect, that the attempt of the British government to accomplish by force of arms what by law or right they could never effect had made it necessary for the colonists to change the ground of opposition and to close with the British appeal from reason to arms.[2]

As the interprovincial organization of the radicals, the Congress undertook to standardize and supplement some of the new functions which the committees of observation in the several provinces had assumed of their own accord. In June it was resolved that no provisions should be furnished the British army and navy in America and that no bills of

[1] Adams, J., *Works* (Adams), vol. ii, p. 461.
[2] *Journals*, vol. ii, pp. 140-153.

exchange of army or navy officers should be honored.[1] In December vessels employed in transporting British troops or carrying supplies for them were declared liable to confiscation.[2] In October it was recommended to the provincial organizations to arrest every person whose going at large might endanger the liberties of America;[3] and on January 2, 1776, these bodies were authorized to invoke the aid of the continental troops in order to disarm all who spoke or acted against America, and to arrest or place under bond the more dangerous among them.[4] Later in January it was resolved that any person who refused continental currency should be published by the local committee or provincial body as " an enemy of his country " and be subjected to boycott.[5] In March the radical organizations were instructed to disarm all who had refused to sign defense associations or who were notoriously disaffected.[6]

Congress also sought to encourage widespread activity in manufacturing, particularly the production of saltpetre, sulphur and gunpowder.[7] Further than this, it was recommended, in March, 1776, that the manufacturing of duck and sail-cloth and of steel should be introduced into those provinces where the processes were understood, and that a society for the improvement of agriculture, arts, manufactures and commerce should be established in every province.[8]

[1] *Journals*, vol. ii, p. 78.   [2] *Ibid.*, vol. iii, p. 437.
[3] *Ibid.*, vol. iii, p. 280.
[4] *Ibid.*, vol. iv, pp. 18-20. On January 3, Congress itself enforced this resolution against the loyalist inhabitants of Queen's County, N. Y. *Ibid.*, pp. 25-27, 34, 114.
[5] *Ibid.*, vol. iii, pp. 367-368; vol. iv, p. 49. *Vide* also *ibid.*, vol. iv, p. 383; vol. v, pp. 475-476.
[6] *Ibid.*, vol. iv, p. 205.
[7] *Ibid.*, vol. iii, pp. 345-348, 349; vol. iv, pp. 170-171.
[8] *Ibid.*, vol. iv, p. 224.

TRANSFORMATION OF THE ASSOCIATION 565

Certain questions which had arisen from the omissions and ambiguities of the Continental Association also received careful consideration at the hands of Congress. One of these grew out of the failure of the Association to provide a means by which a contrite offender, adjudged guilty in the usual manner, might be restored to public favor. Many committees had not waited to ask the opinion of Congress in this matter, but had devised their own measures. But the question was presented to Congress through a petition of Robert and John Murray, of New York, asking that they might be restored " to their former situation with respect to their commercial privileges." In response to this petition, Congress in May, 1775, established a general regulation to the effect that the convention of the province, in which the offence was committed, should settle the terms upon which a repentant offender might receive the forgiveness of the public.[1]

On July 4 Congress added the New England Restraining Act and the General Restraining Act to the list of those laws whose repeal was aimed at by the Continental Association.[2] To settle all doubts as to the meaning of the words, " Great Britain " and " West Indies," as used in the Association, it was declared in August that the former term included all exportation to and importation from the islands of Jersey, Guernsey, Sark, Alderney and Man, and every European island and settlement within the British dominions; and that the latter term comprehended exportation to all the West India islands, British and foreign, and to the Summer Islands, Bahamas, Berbicia, Surinam, and every

---

[1] *Journals*, vol. ii, pp. 49, 53, 67. The boycott against the Murrays was removed by action of the New Jersey congress on May 31 and of the New York congress on June 10. *4 Am. Arch.*, vol. ii, pp. 689-690, 1284, 1291.

[2] *Journals*, vol. ii, p. 125.

island and settlement between the latitude of southern Georgia and the equator.[1] Congress was called upon for a further interpretation of the non-importation regulation when a vessel arrived from London with the books and household furniture of Dr. Franklin. A resolution was adopted that such an importation was not comprehended within the meaning of Article i and should be landed.[2]

The most important action taken by Congress with reference to the Association was the series of resolutions pertaining to the non-exportation regulation. One of these resolutions terminated the painful controversy which had grown out of the privileged position enjoyed by the rice planters in the Association. The method of solution had been foreshadowed by the embargo placed upon rice by the General Committee at Charleston in May and by the South Carolina congress in June.[3] Congress took no action in the matter until November 1, although the general non-exportation regulation had been in effect since the tenth of September; and then it was resolved: "That no Rice be exported under the exception contained in the fourth article of the Association, from any of the United Colonies to Great Britain, Ireland or the Islands of Jersey, Guernsey, Sark, Alderney or Man, or any other European island or settlement within the British Dominions."[4]

On July 15, 1775, Congress authorized for a period of nine months the clandestine importation of munitions in return for American produce, "the non-exportation agreement notwithstanding."[5] This resolution, which was with-

---

[1] *Journals*, vol. ii, pp. 238-239.
[2] *Ibid.*, vol. ii, p. 247.
[3] *4 Am. Arch.*, vol. ii, pp. 710, 938.
[4] *Journals*, vol. iii, pp. 314-315.
[5] *Ibid.*, vol. ii, pp. 184-185; vol. iii, p. 306. The regulation of this traffic was left to the committees in the several provinces. On Sept. 19,

TRANSFORMATION OF THE ASSOCIATION 567

held from the newspapers until October 26, was not altogether clear in its meaning. But whether or not a relaxing of the non-importation regulation was intended, it clearly permitted a limited exportation to Great Britain and the West Indies, even after the date September 10,[1] and sanctioned a smuggling traffic in munitions with foreign countries. Incidentally it afforded some relief to the merchants, shipowners and sailors, who were beginning to suffer from the straitening effects of the non-importation.[2] Without withdrawing the resolution of July 15, which applied primarily to shipments undertaken upon private initiative, Congress, on October 26, recommended to the provincial organizations to export to the foreign West Indies, at the expense of the province, provisions and other produce in return for munitions. The secret committee of Congress was empowered to do the same on the continental account, on November 8.[3] These later resolutions also contravened the non-exportation provisions of the Association. On January 3, 1776, the breach in the Association was made larger by a blanket instruction of Congress to the secret committee to "pursue the most effectual measures for importing" drygoods and certain other merchandise into America.[4]

Congress established a secret committee to look after the importation of munitions for continental military purposes. *Ibid.*, vol. ii, p. 253; vol. iii, p. 280; Adams, J., *Works*, vol. ii, pp. 460-461.

[1] *E. g., vide Journals*, vol. iv, pp. 172-173, 183.

[2] Dyer, of Connecticut, complained in September that there were not ten men in Connecticut who were worth as much money as the Philadelphia firm of Willing & Morris would make out of a contract with Congress for the importation of powder. Adams, J., *Works*, vol. ii, pp. 448-449.

[3] *Journals*, vol. iii, pp. 308, 315, 336; vol. iv, p. 414. Certain classes of live stock were excepted in each instance. For the practice of Congress in special cases, *vide ibid.*, vol. iii, pp. 408-409, 438-439; vol. iv, pp. 95-96, 108, 120, 176, 193.

[4] *Ibid.*, vol. iv, pp. 24-25.

This resolution practically annulled both the non-importation and non-exportation regulations of the Association, so far as the powers of the secret committee were concerned.

Meantime, Congress had taken some steps for re-opening trade with the British West Indies, contrary to the spirit and wording of the Continental Association. Depending upon the continental provinces for their food supply, the British residents in those islands feared a servile insurrection when the non-exportation regulation should become effective. In July, 1775, the Bermuda Assembly passed a law placing an embargo upon the shipping of provisions from the island.[1] Leading inhabitants dispatched a vessel to Philadelphia to lay their case before the Continental Congress. When that body took the matter under consideration, in November, 1775, the continent was already beginning to feel the lack of salt and was in bad need of war munitions; and therefore Congress decided that, as "the inhabitants of the island of Bermuda appear friendly to the cause of America," enough food should be sent them from time to time as might be necessary for their subsistence and home consumption, upon condition that payment should be made in salt and munitions.[2] The distress of the people of the island of New Providence was alleviated temporarily when Congress permitted the exportation of one hundred bushels of flour, on November 29, in return for muskets.[3]

[1] *N. Y. Journ.*, July 27, 1775.

[2] *Journals*, vol. iii, pp. 362-364. The annual exportation to Bermuda was fixed at 72,000 bushels of Indian corn, 2,000 barrels of bread or flour, 1,000 barrels of beef or pork, 2,100 bushels of peas or beans, and 300 tierces of rice.

[3] *Ibid.*, vol. iii, pp. 389-390. The *Connecticut Gazette*, Feb. 16, 1776, reported that the non-exportation was beginning to be severely felt in the West Indies, where the most ordinary beef sold for seven or eight pounds per barrel, common flour at six pounds currency per barrel,

Congress was confronted with a practical problem of serious import by the action of Parliament, in April, 1775, in exempting four colonies from the provisions of the General Restraining Act. The radical organizations in these colonies had taken active steps to prevent any advantage being taken of the parliamentary exemption. But as the need for war supplies became greater, Congress began to consider the practicability of making the United Colonies the beneficiaries of these privileged trade-channels. Throughout October the matter was under active consideration by Congress.[1] Willing of Pennsylvania argued: "Shall we act like the dog in the manger—not suffer New York and the lower counties and North Carolina to export because we can't? We may get salt and ammunition by those ports." Johnson of Maryland and Jay of New York spoke to the same purpose. Lee of Virginia believed that for the exempted colonies to trade would be exactly answering the purpose of the British administration, for "jealousies and dissensions will arise, and disunion and division. We shall become a rope of sand." Gadsden of South Carolina, Wythe of Virginia and Chase of Maryland agreed, Chase adding: "A few weeks will put us all on a footing; New York &c are now all in rebellion, as the ministry call it, as much as Massachusetts Bay." John Rutledge of South Carolina chided the opposition for wanting to break the

and that little was to be had at any price. The islanders were "under terrible Apprehensions" of the effect of reduced rations upon the negro slaves. On October 4, this sheet reported further that an insurrection had broken out among the Jamaica negroes and that some merchant vessels, just arrived in Connecticut, had been detained because of a food embargo there and had sailed finally with a short allowance of provisions.

[1] Adams, J., *Works*, vol. ii, pp. 452-457, 469-484; *Journals*, vol. iii, pp. 276, 280, 283, 286, 287, 291-292, 301-302, 307, 312. The exempted provinces were New York, Delaware, North Carolina and Georgia.

Association so soon and reminded the members, with some bitterness, that " if we had abided by a former non-importation, we should have had redress." Finally, on November 1, Congress came to a decision. It was resolved that no persons in the four privileged provinces should apply at the custom houses for clearance papers; and the thanks of Congress was voted for their self-denial in the past.[1]

The tenth of September, 1775, was the date set by the Continental Association for the prohibition of exportation to Great Britain, Ireland and the West Indies; and for months the merchants had been looking forward with dread to the event. The non-importation had continued to be effectively enforced — the British warships proving of unintentional service after July in their efforts to prevent the smuggling of tea, trade with the foreign West Indies, *etc.*, under the provisions of the General Restraining Act—and there was every reason to believe that the non-exportation regulation would be equally well executed, except of course in such cases as Congress had chosen to make exceptions. Throughout the spring and summer of 1775 the merchants of the North and the planters of the South had increased their shipments to Great Britain and the West Indies in order to provide against the approaching abstention. Comparative figures for the years 1774 and 1775 show that at New York the value of exports to England increased from £80,008 to £187,018; at Philadelphia, from £69,611 to £175,962; in Maryland and Virginia, from £612,030 to £758,356; in the Carolinas, from £432,302 to £579,549; and in Georgia, from £67,647 to £103,477; and that even in New England there was a slight increase from £112,248 to £116,588.[2] For the colonies as a whole there was an increase of nearly forty per cent.

[1] *Journals*, vol. iii, p. 314.
[2] Macpherson, *Annals of Com.*, vol. iii, pp. 564, 585.

When news of the Lexington affair electrified the continent, it was widely rumored that Congress would move forward the date of the non-exportation. In the early days of May, 1775, owners of vessels at Philadelphia got them out of the harbor as fast as they could; the millers hurried their flour to market, some of them near the city selling wheat out of their mills without grinding. Vessels were not to be had at any price; flour advanced from 13s. to 14s. 6d.[1] Thomas Mumford, an exporter of horses at Groton, Conn., wrote to his brother-in-law, Silas Deane, a member of Congress, for definite information as to the possibility of an earlier non-exportation, pointing out that he had several vessels which he was thinking of fitting out. Deane informed his wife in a letter a few weeks later that it was still uncertain what action Congress would take, but he added: " Tell my brother to get his vessel away as quick as possible, somewhere or other, if he sends her at all; this is what the merchts are doing here."[2]

Such precautions proved unnecessary, as Congress did not tamper with the date originally set for non-exportation. Considerable public sentiment, however, was aroused by the enterprise of merchants, in several parts of the continent, in collecting great quantities of flaxseed in the last weeks of open commerce for exportation to Ireland. While such exportation did not contravene the terms of the Association, it was felt that it was nevertheless injurious to the American cause and thus contrary to the spirit of the Association. When New York merchants sent agents into Connecticut to buy up flaxseed for this purpose, the committees at New Haven, Milford, Fairfield and other places sternly warned the inhabitants against dealing with them.[3] On August 12,

[1] Clifford, *Correspondence* (L. C. Mss.), vol. xxix, letters of May 2, 6, 30, 1775.
[2] *Conn. Hist. Soc. Colls.*, vol. ii, pp. 263, 276.
[3] *Conn. Journ.*, Aug. 16, 23, 1775; *N. Y. Journ.*, Aug. 24.

fourteen business houses of New York city applied to the New York provincial congress for a definition of their rights in shipping flaxseed; and that body responded that, since the Continental Congress had left the provision unchanged, exportation might continue until September 10.[1] Nevertheless the *New York Journal* announced, five days after this action, that " some Merchants of this City, who had chartered a Vessel to load her with Flax Seed for Ireland, have altered her Voyage, rather than give Dissatisfaction to our Fellow Citizens." When a town meeting at Providence, R. I., learned on September 7 that a large quantity of flaxseed was about to be exported from the town, they at once placed a ban on its shipment.[2]

There was a great bustle at Philadelphia in the last week of open trade; and no doubt the scene there was paralleled in many other ports of the continent. Produce of all sorts was brought to town and in such quantities that not enough vessels could be found to carry it off. On the very last day, fifty-two ships sailed from port, leaving hardly a vessel behind. Several of these ships had arrived and taken a cargo in forty-eight hours.[3]

With the advent of non-exportation, conditions were far different from those anticipated by the framers of the Continental Association. Military necessity, as we have seen, had taken away from the non-exportation regulation its primary *raison d'être, i. e.* a self-denying ordinance for purposes of commercial coercion, and had converted it very largely into a mechanism for procuring military supplies. The work of enforcing the non-exportation regulation in cases where it applied was zealously undertaken by the rad-

[1] *4 Am. Arch.*, vol. iii, pp. 96, 529.
[2] *Ibid.*, vol. iii, pp. 661-662.
[3] *Pa. Journ.*, Sept. 13, 1775; Clifford, *Corresp.*, vol. xxix, Sept. 8; *Conn. Hist. Soc. Colls.*, vol. ii, p. 305.

ical committees, notwithstanding that they were occupied with a multitude of other duties. The presence of British warships in American waters, pursuant to the General Restraining Act, was a mild deterrent to American ventures to the foreign West Indies no doubt, and thus assisted the observance of the non-exportation. The absolute prohibition of American trade, enacted by Parliament in December, 1775, imposed a heavier burden on the British navy, and, when the prohibition became effective in March, 1776, served further to discourage American exportations. However, smuggling past the British vessels off the coast presented no insurmountable difficulties; and the real burden of enforcing the regulation fell upon the local committees.

One of the first questions that arose was whether vessels that had, for some legitimate reason, been delayed in their departure should be permitted to sail after September 10 to any of the forbidden places. The committee of safety at Wilmington, N. C., had warned the merchants there in advance that their vessels could not depart after the tenth on the excuse that their cargoes were not yet completely laden.[1] The Continental Congress permitted a vessel to sail that had been much damaged in a storm on her outward voyage and had been forced to return to Norfolk for refitting. But when a mercantile house asked permission to charter a vessel to export a cargo of wheat after the tenth, upon the plea that the one that they had engaged had foundered in a storm, the petition was tabled.[3]

The various privileged exportations, under license of the Continental Congress or of provincial organizations, com-

---

[1] *N. C. Col. Recs.*, vol. x, p. 151. The provincial convention confirmed this action. *Ibid.*, p. 183.

[2] *Journals*, vol. ii, p. 246. Similar action was taken in some other cases. *Ibid.*, vol. iii, pp. 354-355.

[3] *Ibid.*, vol. iii, p. 264.

plicated the problem of enforcement for the committees. Thus, in February, 1776, a representation was made to Congress by the Philadelphia committee that vessels were loading with produce for Great Britain, Ireland and the British West Indies. Congress appointed a committee to examine into the circumstances and then permitted them to sail as being within the terms of the congressional resolution of July 15.[1]

Recorded instances of enforcement are not many. The Newcastle, Del., committee compelled the *Peace and Plenty*, which had arrived from Belfast on September 8, to make her return voyage in ballast.[2] Arthur Upshur, of Accomack County, Va., was held up to the public by the county committee for having sent a cargo of grain to the West Indies after the tenth.[3] The Georgians came under the criticism of the South Carolina council of safety for their apparent laxness in enforcing non-exportation;[4] nevertheless, it is a matter of record that more than five thousand barrels of rice, which Governor Wright had prepared for exportation in 1775, were withheld from shipment through their zeal.[5]

Very illuminating was the statement, made by Robert Haliday, customs collector at Charleston, S. C., that by the non-importation regulation the emoluments of his office had been greatly reduced, and by the non-exportation regulation "entirely annihilated."[6] Thomas Clifford, the Philadelphia merchant, wrote on October 25, 1775, that he was laying up his ships as fast as they came in, "there being no

[1] *Journals*, vol. iv, pp. 172-173, 183.
[2] *Pa. Journ.*, Sept. 27, 1775; also 4 *Am. Arch.*, vol. iii, p. 726.
[3] *Ibid.*, vol. iii, p. 935; Jefferson, *Writings* (Ford), vol. ii, pp. 118-119.
[4] White, *Ga. Hist. Colls.*, pp. 86-87; *Ga. Rev. Recs.*, vol. i, pp. 89, 108, 111-112.
[5] *Loyalist Claims Transcripts*, vol. xxxiv, p. 91.
[6] *Ibid.*, vol. lv, pp. 359-360.

Prospect of Employ abroad worth sending them to seek in ballast," that most people were doing the same thing, and that " this Port and we believe all the others along the Continent have been strictly kept shut from the Exportation of Produce agreeable to the Congress Resolves." [1] Indeed, there is no reason to believe that the non-exportation regulation was otherwise than well kept.

For a period of four months, beginning November 1, 1775, the partial non-exportation established by the Continental Association, was converted into a total non-exportation by resolution of the Continental Congress. This decision was the outcome of warm debates in Congress and was determined upon in face of a determined effort to secure the exemption of tobacco and lumber from its terms and in spite of Robert R. Livingston's insistence that the non-exportation policy be abandoned instead of extended.[2] Edward Rutledge of South Carolina advocated the resolution that passed as the only absolutely certain way of keeping exports from British ports and as the most effective way to promote domestic manufacturing. The purpose animating the majority was probably the desire to prevent food supplies from reaching the enemy through capture by the British warships off the coast.[3] The resolution of November 1 provided that no produce of the United Colonies should be exported until March 1, excepting only licensed shipments for military supplies or for any other purpose designated by Congress.[4]

[1] *Correspondence*, vol. xxix, Oct. 25, 1775.
[2] Adams, J., *Works*, vol. ii, pp. 453-456, 483-484.
[3] *Cf. Journals*, vol. ii, p. 201.
[4] *Ibid.*, vol. iii, p. 314.

CHAPTER XV

TRANSFORMATION OF THE ASSOCIATION (*Continued*)

THE early months of 1776 witnessed further notable modifications of the Continental Association. The four months of total non-exportation had the effect of aggravating the distresses of the mercantile and agrarian interests dependent upon the export trade for profit; it also gave momentum and direction to the sentiment, that had long been entertained by radicals of the doctrinaire school, for an entire freedom of trade with the nations of the world. As early as July 21, 1775, the committee of the Continental Congress appointed to devise ways and means of protecting colonial commerce had submitted a report to the effect that all ports in the United Colonies should on January 20, 1776, be declared thenceforth " open to the ships of every state in Europe that will admit our commerce and protect it." [1] The series of resolutions, the first of which was passed on July 15, had sanctioned smuggling with foreign countries for the purpose of procuring munitions; the committee's proposition was far more comprehensive and revolutionary, nothing less than that the acts of trade and the famous navigation act should be repudiated and that trade should be opened with foreign nations in foreign or domestic vessels. The committee's report was postponed from time to time for further consideration; but in every debate on trade

[1] *Journals Cont. Cong.*, vol. ii, pp. 200-201. It would appear that resolutions covering this matter were submitted by both Dr. Franklin and Richard Henry Lee.

conditions from that time forward, allusion was almost invariably made to the proposal as a desirable or unacceptable or desperate alternative.

On August 26, 1775, a member of the Continental Congress hazarded the opinion in a private letter that in the course of the coming winter Congress would adopt the measure, adding: "Whether that will not be one means of dissolving our connections entirely with Great Britain, I shall leave to wiser heads to determine." [1] During the month of October the matter came up again for active discussion in Congress; but when a decision was reached to establish a general non-exportation until March 1, 1776, interest again waned, and it was not until it became necessary to determine what the status of trade should be after that date that the discussion was renewed, in the weeks after Christmas Day, 1775.

The chief opposition to opening trade with the world came from the members who wished to safeguard such American shipping as still remained and from those members who saw in the measure a virtual declaration of independence.[2] Willing of Philadelphia, shipowner as well as exporter, emphasized the fact that the profits of carrying would go to foreigners. "Carriage is an amazing revenue," he declared. "Holland and England have derived their maritime power from their carriage." Likewise, Johnson of Maryland pointed out shrewdly that the measure, while injuring the merchant and shipbuilder, would leave the farmer unscathed. "The grower, the farmer, gets the same, let who will be the exporter," he declared, "but the community does not. The shipwright, rope-maker, hemp-grower, all shipbuilders, the profits of the merchant, are all

[1] *4 Am. Arch.*, vol. iii, pp. 435-436.
[2] The October debates are summarized in Adams, J., *Works* (Adams), vol. ii, pp. 452-457, 469-483.

lost, if foreigners are our sole carriers, as well as seamen." Chase of Maryland asserted that he had not absolutely abandoned all hope of reconciliation, and until that time came he would oppose a free trade with foreign nations. Zubly of Georgia declared that there was no assurance that the world would trade with the Americans and the measure gave the appearance of a design to separate from England.

The chief speakers on the other side were Lee and Wythe of Virginia, Gadsden of South Carolina, and the Adamses of Massachusetts. The point that they stressed in the early stages of the discussion was that, lacking a navy, the colonists were in danger of being cut off from the world by the British warships, whereas foreign nations would come in and protect their own vessels engaged in American trade.[1] On January 20, 1776, the Virginia delegates were instructed by the Virginia provincial convention to use their endeavors to have such a measure adopted.[2] It soon became apparent in Congress that the whole matter was intimately related to the question of political independence. As Sherman of Connecticut asserted on February 16: "A treaty with a foreign power is necessary, before we open our trade, to protect it;" and Wythe completed the thought when he said that, to accomplish this, "we must declare ourselves a free people."[3] John Adams wrote later in his autobiography: "This measure of opening the ports, &c, labored exceedingly because it was considered a bold step to independence. Indeed, I urged it expressly with that view, and as connected with the institution of government in all the States, and a declaration of national independence. The party against me had an art and influence as yet to evade,

---

[1] Adams, J., *Works*, vol. ii, pp. 453, 454, 456, 485-486.
[2] Dixon & Hunter's *Va. Gaz.*, Apr. 13, 1776.
[3] Adams, J., *Works*, vol. ii, pp. 485-486.

retard, and delay every motion that we made. Many motions were made and argued at great length, and with great spirit on both sides, which are not to be found in the Journals." [1]

On March 1 the period of total non-exportation expired, and the partial non-exportation that had subsisted prior to November, 1775, became effective again. In the weeks immediately following, it became evident that the merchants' stocks, acquired in the days before the non-importation regulation, were approaching depletion. There was a growing scarcity of goods, which exceedingly distressed the poor and, in view of the inadequate supply of domestic manufactures, made imperative the opening of trade with foreign nations. It was argued also that such a freedom of commerce would attract specie to the colonies and serve to check the depreciation of the continental currency. On April 2 the Philadelphia committee of inspection was asked to bring these facts to the attention of the Continental Congress, in an address from the Committee of Privates of the local Military Association, signed by the retailer, William Adcock, as president.[2]

An added incentive to the adoption of drastic measures of relief was the news, that had arrived at Philadelphia on February 26, that Parliament had enacted that after January 1, 1776, all American vessels found on the coast of the British Isles were to be seized and confiscated; all American vessels sailing into and out of American ports after March 1 were to be seized and confiscated; and all foreign vessels trading to America after June 1 were to be seized. The colonies were to be isolated from the world, save such districts as would make submission.[3] On the day following

[1] Adams, J., *Works*, vol. iii, p. 29.
[2] *Pa. Eve. Post*, Apr. 4, 1776.
[3] 16 George III, c. 5.

the arrival of the news a Maryland member of Congress, who had often reprobated the idea of independence both in public and private, wrote: " What measures Congress may pursue in consequence of this act, I know not. With me, every idea of reconciliation is precluded by the conduct of Great Britain; and the only alternative, absolute slavery or independency." [1]

The public prints were meantime urging the opening of commerce as a measure conditioned by a declaration of independence.[2] But Congress, fearing the potency of an ill-timed phrase, preferred to do the seemingly illogical thing. On April 6, without allusion to political independence, the fateful step was taken. It was then provided that any goods and wares, except staves and empty casks under certain conditions, might be exported from the United Colonies, in colonial or foreign vessels, to any parts of the world not under dominion of Great Britain; and that any goods and merchandise might be imported into the United Colonies in like fashion, except articles produced in or shipped from British possessions, East India tea, and slaves. It was further provided that all merchandise and wares imported into the United Colonies directly or indirectly from Great Britain or Ireland contrary to the regulations of Congress should be forfeited and disposed of under rules made by the several assemblies.[3]

After this event a declaration of political independence, however great its sentimental importance, was a mere formality. The Adamses, for example, appreciated this fully and it gave them good occasion for exultation. Not only has Congress raised armies and a navy, fought battles and

[1] Robert Alexander; *4 Am. Arch.*, vol. iv, pp. 1507-1508.

[2] *Ibid.*, vol. iv, pp. 470-473, 527-530, 920-922, 1141-1144; vol. v, pp. 225-227, 860-862, 918-919, 921-926.

[3] *Journals*, vol. iv, pp. 257-259.

commissioned privateers against the British, wrote Sam Adams to a congenial spirit, but now we have " torn into Shivers their Acts of Trade, by allowing Commerce subject to Regulations to be made by *our selves* with the People of all Countries but such as are Subjects of the British King." [1]

The nullification of the acts of trade and navigation was followed by the introduction of two other important changes in the Continental Association, one relating to the provision for the non-consumption of tea, the other dealing with the regulation of prices. Both changes represented concessions to the merchants who had not yet detached themselves from the radical cause. With reference to the first, it should be recalled that Article iii had provided for the total disuse of tea, smuggled as well as dutied, after March 1, 1775. This prohibition expressed a real protest against tea drinking on hygienic grounds, but it had obtained its widest support because of the impracticability of distinguishing between English dutied tea and Dutch undutied tea and because of the desire to refute the charge that the tea smugglers had instigated the uprising against British measures.

In the spring months of 1775 little difficulty had been experienced by the committees of observation in enforcing the prohibition; but by midsummer, cases of violation began to become numerous. Thus, the committee at Providence, R. I., forced the recantation of the tea dealer, Nathan Angell, in October and seized such of his stock as remained unsold; but they admitted that they had reason to suspect, from the frequent complaints of country people, that some dealers in Providence still continued the practice.[2] It was openly asserted in Congress in September that ninety-nine

[1] To Joseph Hawley, Apr. 15, 1776; Adams, S., *Writings* (Cushing), vol. iii, pp. 279-280.
[2] *4 Am. Arch.*, vol. iii, pp. 975-976.

out of one hundred in New York drank tea, although this was obviously an exaggeration.[1] A persistent tea seller at Reading, Pa., was tarred and feathered and ridden on a horse with his face to the tail, " to the great diversion of the inhabitants who, I believe, hardly ever beheld a more ridiculous figure." [2]

The truth was, as the Continental Congress was at length forced to admit, that the period allowed by the Continental Association for the consumption of tea, which was then in stock, was too short, " whereby many zealous friends to the American cause, who had imported large quantities of that commodity, with design not merely to advance their fortunes, but to counteract the plan then pursued by the ministry and India company to introduce and sell in these colonies tea subject to duty, are likely to become great sufferers; the greater part of the estates of many of them being vested in that article, and they, by that means, rendered incapable not only of paying their debts and maintaining their families, but also of vigorously exerting themselves in the service of their country." [3]

Great pressure was brought to bear upon Congress to permit the sale of such teas as had been imported before Article iii of the Association became effective. Alexander McDougall of New York urged the matter on the attention of Richard Henry Lee, a member of Congress, in a letter of June 5, 1775; but the latter replied that, although such suffering was to be found in all the provinces, " Should Congress determine to admit the sale and the use of what

---

[1] Adams, J., *Works*, vol. ii, p. 447.

[2] *Pa. Merc.*, Oct. 20, 1775. For other examples, *vide 4 Am. Arch.*, vol. ii, pp. 920, 1678; vol. iii, pp. 729, 937-938; *Pa. Journ.*, May 17, 1775; *Conn. Cour.*, Apr. 8, 1776.

[3] Preamble to the congressional resolution of Apr. 13, 1776; *Journals*, vol. iv, pp. 277-278.

tea is on hand, may not bad men take the advantage of the impossibility of distinguishing this from newly imported Tea . . . ?"[1] The New York provincial congress, in a letter to the New York delegates at the Continental Congress on July 28, declared that the smuggling merchants had so much capital tied up in unsalable Dutch teas that they were deprived of the means of introducing into the province Dutch textiles and munitions, which were badly needed. The delegates were therefore instructed to urge Congress to authorize the sale of teas in stock, at a fixed price, with a tax of one shilling imposed as a penalty on " the obstinate consumers."[2]

On July 31, 1775, the question of renewing the sale of teas was formally presented to Congress in the form of two petitions, one from sundry New York merchants and the other from sundry merchants of Philadelphia. Due to the pressure of other business, the matter did not receive consideration for some months. Finally, on November 28, the petitions were rejected.[3] The matter did not rest here, the Maryland delegates receiving instructions from their provincial convention to press Congress to permit the consumption of all teas imported before February 1, 1775. The subject was debated for two days in mid-January, 1776, with Dr. Franklin and Thomas Lynch as the chief opposition speakers, and was finally lost by a vote of seven provinces to five.[4]

Meantime it became increasingly evident that the prohibi-

[1] Lee, R. H., *Letters* (Ballagh), vol. i, pp. 143-144.

[2] *4 Am. Arch.*, vol. ii, p. 1805. For the reply of the delegates *vide ibid.*, vol. iii, p. 750.

[3] *Journals*, vol. ii, p. 235; vol. iii, pp. 294, 298, 388-389.

[4] The negative provinces were New York, New Jersey, Pennsylvania, Delaware and Maryland. *4 Am. Arch.*, vol. iv, p. 887; *Am. Hist. Rev.*, vol. i, pp. 308, 309.

tion of tea drinking was serving no useful purpose and was, on the other hand, fomenting divisions within radical ranks. " Whenever the reason of any law ceases," declared "Aesculapius," " the law ceases . . . whether the law is in a formal manner repealed or not;" and he added: " If we should drink tea three times a day, we shall not be taxed for it to Great-Britain—no one can import it from there while we remain in our present situation." [1] Congress yielded to the increasing pressure finally on April 13, one week after trade had been opened with foreign nations. They voted that all teas imported before December 1, 1774, should be placed on sale, except such as had been imported by the East India Company. To guard against excessive prices, it was provided that Bohea tea should not retail at more than three-fourths of a dollar a pound and that the prices of other teas should be fixed by the local committees.[2]

In somewhat similar fashion, the provisions of the Association for maintaining the customary level of prices had, after the first year of the non-importation, become increasingly difficult to administer. In the plantation provinces the chief trouble was found in regulating the price of salt. That commodity was of essential importance as being practically the only preservative of meat and fish; and the supply in the South had nearly reached the point of exhaustion by the autumn following the cessation of importation. Beginning in the spring of 1775, the provincial conventions of Virginia, Maryland and the Carolinas offered pecuniary inducements to private individuals who would undertake the manufacture of salt.[3] The people in the uplands of Vir-

[1] *Conn. Cour.*, Apr. 8, 1776.

[2] Teas found in the cargo of prizes were also permitted to be sold. *Journals*, vol. iv, pp. 277-278.

[3] Virginia, Mch. 27; Maryland, Aug. 14; North Carolina, Sept. 10; and South Carolina, Nov. 28; Smith, C. S., " Scarcity of Salt in the Revolutionary War," *1 M. H. S. Procs.*, vol. xv, pp. 221-227.

ginia, suffering from the great scarcity, did not hesitate on several occasions to descend upon some of the tidewater merchants and seize such salt as they could lay hands on.[1]

The local committees in these provinces did what they could to prevent the inevitable rise in prices. For example, in August, 1775, the Surry County committee in Virginia published Robert Kennon, a factor, for advancing the price from 2s. 6d. per bushel to 3s.[2] In November the Baltimore County, Md., committee established a maximum price for salt, and authorized past purchasers of salt to collect from dealers any money charged beyond that amount.[3] Such treatment, however, did not penetrate to the source of the trouble; so, on December 29, 1775, the Continental Congress took measures to afford relief. Virginia, Maryland and North Carolina, where the need was greatest, were authorized to import as much salt from any foreign country as their conventions or committees of safety might think necessary and to export produce therefor.[4] The conventions of all the continental provinces were urged to offer bounties for salt making. Most of the provinces acted upon this advice in the following year.[5]

At the leading northern ports and in the rural districts which were their markets, the regulation of prices had created more or less trouble from the beginning of non-importation.[6] The cause of high prices in the early months had been the greed of forestallers and monopolists; nor did the city committees always take prompt action in such cases, especially if the articles in question were not widely used or

[1] Pinkney's *Va. Gaz.*, Dec. 6, 1775.
[2] *Ibid.*, Aug. 22, 1775.
[3] *Md. Journ.*, Nov. 22, 1775; also *4 Am. Arch.*, vol. iii, p. 1541.
[4] *Journals*, vol. iii, pp. 464-465; *Am. Hist. Rev.*, vol. i, p. 299.
[5] Smith, *loc. cit.*
[6] *Vide supra*, chapter xii.

the advance in price moderate. By the winter of 1775-1776, after the non-importation had been effective for about a year, the upward trend of prices indicated the approaching depletion of mercantile stocks;[1] but the radicals in general still preferred to believe that private avarice was the sole animating cause. The chief centers of trouble were the ports of Philadelphia and New York and the markets tributary to them. The dearth and high price of West India commodities created greatest uneasiness because of their former cheapness and wide household use.

At Philadelphia the committee reported in September, 1775, after a careful investigation of the rising price of salt, that there was a sufficient supply of the article in the city; and they warned the dealers to charge prices that would not call for the interference of the committee.[2] In December the committee fixed wholesale and retail prices for oil.[3] On March 5, 1776, the district committees of Philadelphia made a careful examination into the prices of certain West India commodities and others, and reached the conclusion that the exorbitant prices were the result of engrossing. Therefore, on March 6, the committee established a schedule of prices, with the warning that violators of the regulation would be published "as sordid vultures who are preying on the vitals of their country in a time of general distress." The commodities regulated were molasses, common West India rum, country rum, coffee, cocoa, chocolate, pepper, several varieties of sugar, Lisbon and Liverpool salt, and Jamaica spirits.[4] Before the month was past

---

[1] *Vide* a clear analysis of this situation in a circular letter of the Pennsylvania Committee of Safety, May 22, 1776; *Pa. Journ.*, June 19, 1776.

[2] *Pa. Eve. Post*, Sept. 7, 1775.

[3] *Pa. Journ.*, Dec. 20, 1775.

[4] *Pa. Ledger*, Mch. 9, 1776; also *4 Am. Arch.*, vol. v, pp. 74, 85-86.

two inhabitants had violated the resolution: William Sitgreaves had sold coffee at a penny more than the committee's rate, and Peter Ozeas had bought and sold two barrels of coffee at a price higher than the limit. Both offenses were published, and the men quickly sued for pardon.[1]

At New York the extravagant price of pins aroused feeling in September, 1775; and the city committee appointed a sub-committee to inform the offending merchants that their conduct would be published unless they reformed their ways.[2] In November it was proven to the committee that Robinson & Price had overcharged for pins and other articles, and the firm was duly published.[3] In March, 1776, the merchant Archibald M'Vicker was held up for a similar offence.[4] The extraordinary enhancement in the price of West India products caused the New York committee, on March 9, to establish a scale of wholesale prices after the fashion of Philadelphia. The committee, however, declared that they intended, from time to time, to examine into the circumstances of newly-imported commodities from the West Indies and to regulate the prices accordingly.[5] Five days later, six or seven hundred mechanics held a meeting with the Committee of Mechanics and "delivered a very pathetic address of thanks to the general committee of inspection for their kind attention to the public good, in particular for their resolve of the ninth instant limiting the prices of West-India produce."[6] The committee at New-

---

[1] *Pa. Ledger*, Apr. 6, 1776.

[2] *4 Am. Arch.*, vol. iii, p. 702.

[3] *Ibid.*, vol. iii, pp. 1625-1627. They were restored to public favor by the New York provincial congress in March, 1776, after an expression of contrition. *N. Y. Journ.*, Mch. 14, 1776.

[4] *N. Y. Gaz.*, Mch. 4, 1776.

[5] *Ibid.*, Mch. 11, 1776; also *N. Y. Journ.*, Mch. 14.

[6] *N. Y. Gaz.*, Mch. 18, 1776.

ark, N. J., followed the example of the New York committee with reference to West India commodities on March 15, advancing the scale of prices sufficiently to allow for transportation, waste and retailers' profits. Violators were not only to be boycotted but were to lose the protection of the committee for their person and property.[1]

The people of Connecticut had been complaining since the early months of trade suspension against the high prices which the New York merchants charged the Connecticut merchants and retailers and which the latter had sought to shift on to the consumers. Various expedients had been tried to eradicate this evil; but by the early months of 1776 these efforts had definitely failed of their purpose. Many protests appeared in the local newspapers. The New York merchants were said to have raised their rates thirty to forty per cent; the local dealers were accused of " making merchandize of their country and its liberties;" the " poor consumer " and the " poor mechanic and labourer " were shown to be the victims of this situation.[2] Other writers charged that the farmers were equally guilty of extortion.[3]

At length the leading towns adopted the device, which had become popular elsewhere, of establishing prices for the chief West India commodities. The committees of inspection of the towns in New London County resolved upon this measure at a joint meeting on March 14, 1776, and the committees of the fifteen towns of Hartford County took like action on the twenty-seventh.[4]

The same upward climb of prices was to be found in the

[1] *N. Y. Gaz.*, Apr. 22, 1776; also *2 N. J. Arch.*, vol. i, pp. 86-87.

[2] " R " in *Conn. Cour.*, Jan. 29, 1776; "Fabius" in *ibid.*, Mch. 25; "Philo Patriae" in *Conn. Gaz.*, Mch. 8.

[3] "Fabius" in *Conn. Cour.*, Mch. 25, 1776; "A Small Merchant" in *ibid.*, Apr. 8.

[4] *Conn. Gaz.*, Mch. 8, 1776; *Conn. Cour.*, Apr. 8.

other New England provinces. Abigail Adams wrote to her husband at Philadelphia on December 10, 1775, that at Braintree English goods of all kinds had doubled in price, West India molasses had advanced from 1s. 8d., l. m., to 2s. 8d., cotton-wool from 1s. per bag to 3s.; linens were to be had at no price.[1] The Providence, R. I., committee reported numerous complaints and issued warnings from time to time against advanced prices "on any pretence whatever."[2] The New Hampshire provincial congress, in a resolution of September 1, 1775, acknowledged gross violations of the price regulation of the Association and attributed them to the fact that many members of the committees of inspection were themselves engaged in trade. The congress therefore resolved that such violators might be cited before any committee within a radius of ten miles of the scene of the offense.[3]

The unavailing efforts of the committees to prevent the rise of prices furnished a strong argument in favor of a frank abandonment of the plan by the Continental Congress. The depletion of the colonial warehouses and the opening of trade with the world convinced Congress that the time for taking the step had arrived. Asserting that merchant adventurers should be encouraged to import from foreign countries by the prospect of profits proportionate to the danger and expense incurred, they resolved on April 30, 1776, that "the power of committees of inspection and observation to regulate the prices of goods (in other instances than the article of green Tea) ought to cease."[4]

---

[1] Adams, John, and Abigail, *Familiar Letters* (Adams, C. F., ed., Boston, 1875), p. 130. *Vide* also 4 *Am. Arch.*, vol. iv, p. 159 n.

[2] *Ibid.*, vol. iii, pp. 662, 975.

[3] *Ibid.*, vol. iii, p. 521.

[4] *Journals*, vol. iv, p. 320.

Like the resolution of a few weeks earlier for re-opening the sale of teas, this resolution was a *douceur* to the merchants within radical ranks and to those wavering in their allegiance. The merchants availed themselves of these new opportunities without delay. Teas were everywhere displayed for sale, little regard being paid in most cases to the rates prescribed by the Continental Congress or by the local committees.[1] The prices of other commodities, freed of all restrictions by Congress, soared beyond anything dreamed of before. The " enormous rise of the article of rum " caused Connecticut innkeepers to agree to buy no more until the price was somewhat reduced.[2] In the middle of May it was reported that at Boston pins had advanced from 8d. to 6s., cards from 2s. 6d. to 6s. 6d., handkerchiefs from 4s. to 12s., steel from 9d. to 3s.[3] The worthy spouse of John Adams declared that the cost of living had doubled within the space of a year.[4] In various parts of New Jersey mobs were formed to intimidate merchants into lowering prices; and the provincial committee of safety were forced to warn the people that the enforced reduction of prices would discourage smugglers from undertaking trade with foreign countries and would thus work a hardship on the poorer people in the long run.[5]

The greatest distress was everywhere caused by the exorbitant charge made for the necessary article of salt; and Congress intervened on May 30 to advise the committees

---

[1] *E. g., Mass. Spy*, July 5, 1776; *Conn. Cour.*, Aug. 5; *N. Y. Gaz.*, May 6, June 10; *Pa. Gaz.*, Aug. 28; Adamses, *Familiar Letters*, pp. 182-183.

[2] At Windham and in Hartford County; *Conn. Gaz.*, May 24, 1776; *Conn. Cour.*, June 10.

[3] *Conn. Gaz.*, May 17, 1776.

[4] Adamses, *Familiar Letters*, pp. 182-183.

[5] *N. Y. Gaz.*, May 27, 1776.

of observation and inspection " so to regulate the price of salt, as to prevent unreasonable exactions on the part of the seller, having due regard to the difficulty and risque of importation; subject however to such regulations as have been, or shall hereafter be made, by the legislatures of the respective colonies."[1] Provincial authorities and committees of observation acted upon the recommendation, not only regulating the price of salt but offering bounties for its production.[2] In all other respects prices were left undisturbed by Congress until the latter part of the year 1777, upon the hope that the influx of goods from foreign countries under the resolution of April 6, 1776, would bring down prices.[3]

Before considering the critical decision which confronted the merchants when independence was declared, it seems desirable to re-state, by way of summary, the part which the merchant class had played in the development of the revolutionary movement prior to that event. Threatened with bankruptcy by the parliamentary legislation of 1764-1765, the merchants of the commercial provinces were the instigators of the first discontents in the colonies. The small factor class in the plantation provinces, by reason of the limited nature of their trade, had no interest in the adverse effects of this legislation, and because of their close connection with their British employers were not at this or any other time inclined, as a group, to lend support to the

[1] *Journals*, vol. iv, pp. 397-398, 404.
[2] Contemporary newspapers; Smith, *loc. cit.*
[3] Before this could occur, however, the excessive issues of paper money served to keep prices in an inflated condition. For a lucid discussion of the troubles over prices in the later period with special reference to Massachusetts, *vide* Davis, A. McF., "The Limitation of Prices in Massachusetts, 1776-1779," *Col. Soc. Mass. Pubs.*, vol. x, pp. 119-134.

projects of the northern merchants. Their attitude therefore need not be considered in the present summary.

The merchants of the great northern ports were startled by the mob excesses and destruction of property which their agitation had caused; but only the official class and the social class with which it was allied were moved to place themselves squarely on the side of parliamentary authority thereafter. The developments of the years 1767-1770, fomented by the mercantile interests in large part, brought the merchants to a serious realization of the growing power of the irresponsible elements and of the drift of events toward lawlessness. But for the ill-advised attempt of the British ministry to assist the East India Company to monopolize the tea market at the expense of the colonial merchants, it is probable that the great influence of the trading class would have been thrown on the side of law and order at this time, and the separation of the colonies from the mother country postponed or prevented. Some merchants did indeed abstain from further activity against parliamentary measures; but a majority joined with the radicals to defeat the dangerous purposes of the British trading company.

The disastrous outcome of this unnatural alliance convinced the merchants as a class that their future welfare rested with the maintenance of British authority. As a matter of tactics, many individuals lingered in the radical movement for the purpose of controlling it; others were there because persuaded in spite of their self-interest. With the advent of the First Continental Congress and its brood of committees, other merchants withdrew from radical affiliations, some of them becoming active loyalists. The outbreak of hostilities at Lexington and Concord furnished another opportunity for decision. Finally, in the spring and summer months of 1776, when the dismemberment of the British empire was impending, came the time for the supreme choice. The position of the merchants in these last months needs to be examined in some detail.

Their natural disrelish for the idea of separation was increased by the character of the arguments which the radicals were using at this time to inform and consolidate the mechanic and agrarian classes in support of independence.[1] Thus, Tom Paine's pamphlet, *Common Sense*, which appeared on January 9, 1776, repelled the typical merchant while it carried ready conviction to the man of ordinary "common sense," who, impatient of the fine-spun political disquisitions and cautious policies of past years, was eager for a political philosophy of plain, unqualified phrases and for a definite program of action in which he could take aggressive part. That this great piece of propagandist writing, with its crudities and bad taste, proved entirely satisfactory to men of this type is shown by the fact that one hundred thousand copies were quickly needed to spread the gospel of *Common Sense* to the uttermost portions of the United Colonies,[2] and that Paine's pamphlet became the progenitor of a brood of lesser tracts and articles.

[1] The radical writers made it clear that merchants were no longer to be regarded as the directors of public policy. "Remember the influence of wealth upon the morals and principles of mankind," admonished "A Watchman" in the *Pa. Packet*, June 24, 1776. "Recollect how often you have heard the first principles of government subverted by the calls of Cato and other Catalines [loyalist writers], to make way for men of fortune to declare their sentiments upon the subject of Independence, as if a minority of rich men were to govern the majority of freeholders in the province."

[2] *Vide* Tyler, M. C., *Literary History of the American Revolution* (New York, 1897), vol. i, pp. 469-474. "The temper and wishes of the people supplied every thing at that time," says John Adams in his Autobiography, "and the phrases, suitable for an emigrant from Newgate, or one who had chiefly associated with such company, such as, 'The Royal Brute of England,' 'The blood upon his soul,' and a few others of equal delicacy, had as much weight with the people as his arguments." *Works*, vol. ii, p. 509.

But such appeals to passion produced a very different effect on the wavering merchants, who regarded themselves still as the only true conservators of colonial rights. Well might a writer familiar with the long cherished aspirations of the merchant class and of the moderates generally, indignantly deny that "all men who oppose the scheme of Independence are advocates for absolute tyranny. Were this once proved, as it had been often asserted, the contest would be at an end, and we should all unite in hand and heart for their beloved Utopian plan; but it never has been, it never can be proved. The opposers of Independence in every publick body, from the Congress downwards, and in the mass of the people, are the true Whigs, who are for preserving the Constitution, as well against the secret machinations of ambitious innovators as against the open attacks of the British Parliament; they are the men who first set on foot the present opposition, and who, I trust, will, if they are permitted to go on, bring it to a happy conclusion." And he added, by way of warning to his fellow-citizens, that "a set of men whom nobody knows . . . are attempting to hurry you into a scene of anarchy; their scheme of Independence is visionary; they know not themselves what they mean by it."[1]

On the other hand, the three resolutions of Congress, passed in April, 1776, for annulling the acts of navigation and trade, reviving the sale of teas, and removing all price restrictions, made strong appeal to mercantile self-interest. This advantage was followed up by radical writers who de-

---

[1] "Civis," Philadelphia, Apr. 30, 1776; 4 *Am. Arch.*, vol. v, pp. 1141-1142. Some months earlier "Phileirene" at Boston had remarked of independence that "in whatever light we consider this truly Utopian project, the more attentively we view it, and the more thoroughly we scan it, the more impracticable, absurd, and ridiculous it appears." *Ibid.*, vol. i, p. 1188.

picted the presumed materialistic benefits of independence. They painted a Golden Age of commerce in the future more glorious than that which had existed before 1763.[1] They even restrained their impatience when cautious members of the trading class called for a bill of particulars.

Thus, a writer at Philadelphia voiced the opinion of a good many merchants in the commercial provinces when, in an open letter to the writers on both sides of the question, he urged that the whole question of separation be entered into " fairly, fully and freely." To explain what he meant, he continued: " with respect to Independence, some people will be satisfied with nothing short of such clear and demonstrative evidence; you must tell them, also, of the particular new trades, which will be opened to us; the prices our goods will bear at home to the farmer, and what they will bring at such and such ports, and how much those prices exceed what we have been used to get for them at the markets we were allow'd to trade to; in this you must name the articles, the prices, and the places; you must then tell us, the advantages of buying linens, woolens, cottons, silks and hard ware in France, Spain and Portugal, and other countries in Europe, and how much cheaper they are than in England and Ireland; . . . and whether those places will take in exchange, our lumber, our naval stores, our tobacco, our flax seed, &c &c and what prices they will give; what credit it is customary for those several places to allow to foreigners on what we commonly call dry goods . . . Next you must shew, that the charge of supporting government will be less, in a state of Independence, than it hath been heretofore . . . Lastly you are to consider, after all things are candidly stated, whether the sums annually raised on the one hand to protect ourselves, and the absolute gain in

[1] Articles were also written to belittle the advantages of the period before 1763; *e. g.*, "An American," *ibid.*, vol. v, pp. 225-227.

trade (over and above what we used to make) on the other hand, do or do not render it most for our interest to separate from Britain."

In like manner this writer demanded that the opponents of independence should make a ledger account of their side of the question: "they must shew . . . what were the customary expences of government in America, before the present rupture; what are the exclusive privileges, we derive from exporting goods to Great-Britain; whether there are acts of Parliament in favour of the Colonies, to the prejudice of other nations, . . . and whether these are equivalent to any loss we may sustain, by having our trade confined to them; . . . you are to particularize the ports we may trade to under the old regulations; and the different articles of America, which we may carry directly to foreign ports; you must also shew that the principal part of the goods we import from England and Ireland could not be supplied us upon as good terms, from any other country, and that those nations, with whom we might incline to trade, would not grant us bounties upon naval stores, and sundry other articles, in the same manner as England does, the amount of which, annually paid to the Colonists, you should sum up. You should also shew cause (if you can) why America ought not to take credit to herself, for all the taxes paid by the English manufacturers, before they send their goods to the Colonies, it being generally granted that the consumer ultimately pays all charges; you must also shew, whether taxes on goods imported into America from Holland, France or Spain (where imposts are very heavy) are or are not added to the cost of the said goods, in the same manner as we reckon them on English goods. Also whether the long established credit, our American merchants have obtained in England in the interior part of the kingdom, with the original manufacturers, cannot be as well accomplished in the new countries we may go to; or whether we must take their goods from merchants at the out-ports, with all the middle men's or intervening dealer's profits added to them . . .

"Whether it is not a general established custom with all trading nations, to trust foreigners with whom they have no legal or political constitutional connexion as freely as their own subjects in distant parts of the world; if this is not generally the case, you should shew why America can't make treaties with such powers, in order to obtain credit . . . You should also shew . . . whether if France, Spain and Holland should refuse to give credit to every young merchant going out for a cargo, with a tolerable recommendation, as the traders in England have been accustomed to do, I say, if this should be the case, and the importations should fall wholly into the hands of a few rich merchants, why might not some mode of restriction be entered into, for preventing the exorbitant exactions they might be guilty of, to the great injury of the consumers? . . .

"You must also prove that England, on a reunion, would grant us such protection as would secure our property in any part of the world . . . ; or if a reunion should not take place, you are to point out sufficient reasons to justify you in the supposition that America has not, or may not, have a naval power competent to the task, of doing herself justice. . . . And you must lastly shew, that by a reconciliation on constitutional principles, we shall return to the free money-getting trade we formerly enjoyed, and that we shall have it enlarged to us upon a grand national scale, without any regard to the private emolument of this or that party; but upon principles of the general interest of the whole empire, without our paying any taxes for the support of government more than what we have been used to (the debt arising from the present dispute only excepted). That the administration of justice, and security of property, will be as upright and safe as heretofore; and that the present happiness and future liberty of America would be as well maintained in a reunion as by a separation. I shall read your controversy with great attention, and so will thousands beside me; and if, upon an impartial hearing, it shall appear to be the real interest of America to cut the Gordian Knot and establish Independence—I declare with the utmost sincerity and solemnity, that I will give it my hearty concurrence." [1]

While the controversial writers never achieved the particularity which this writer demanded, the radicals labored hard to portray the economic advantages which a state of independence promised for merchants and for men of means generally. "Some think they say everything against a state of independence by crying out that in a state of dependance we enjoyed the protection of Great-Britain . . . ," wrote "Salus Populi." "But do we not pay dearly for this protection? The restriction of our trade alone is worth ten times the protection, besides the sums we pay in customs and other duties to the amount of more than a million annually. The customs of the port of London alone are worth £2,000,000 sterling per annum. . . . Let us for once suppose an independency, that we may observe the consequence. We should then trade with every nation that would trade with us, i. e. with every nation in Europe at least. Suppose we were attacked by some foreign power in this state of independency, for this is the bugbear; what then? The nation that would be fool enough to do it would raise a hornet's nest about its ears . . . Every nation which enjoyed a share of our trade would be guarantee for the peaceable behaviour and good conduct of its neighbours . . . To ask

---

[1] "A Common Man" in the *Pa. Ledger*, Mch. 30, 1776.

what we should do for fleets to protect our trade, is as absurd as to ask if timber grows in America. . . . But the war once over, fleets to protect our trade will be nearly unnecessary. Our trade will protect itself. It never will be the interest of any nation to disturb our trade while we trade freely with it, and it will ever be our interest to trade freely with all nations. As long as the wide Atlantic ocean rolls between us and Europe, so long will we be free from foreign subjection were we once clear of Great-Britain: And as long as we remain free from foreign subjection, so long will our trade protect itself."[1]

"What will be the probable benefits of independence?" queried another writer. "A free and unlimited trade; a great accession of wealth, and a proportionable rise in the value of land; the establishment, gradual improvement, and perfection of manufactures and science; a vast influx of foreigners . . . ; an astonishing increase of our people from the present stock. Where encouragement is given to industry; where liberty and property are well secured; where the poor may easily find subsistence, and the middling rank comfortably support their farms by labour, there the inhabitants must increase rapidly."[2] In a similar strain, "A. B." argued the advantages of independence: "Let us try what improvements we may be drawn into by a general correspondence with the whole world, with people who will require from us every different article our lands, our different climates, can produce; and from whom may be had directly, at first hand, every thing requisite for us. Let us have access to the lowest and best markets for every commodity. Let this be the case, but for half the time the

---

[1] *Pa. Journ.*, Feb. 14, 1776; also 4 *Am. Arch.*, vol. iv, pp. 1142-1143.
[2] "Questions and Answers," Feb. 17, 1776; *ibid.*, vol. iv, pp. 1168-1171.

Colonies have already existed, and the doubts and struggles too, concerning independence, will be at an end."[1]

On the other hand, in the plantation provinces, where from the outset the factor class had consistently sacrificed the interest of the community at large to that of themselves and their British employers, no effort was made to win mercantile support. Due to their British nativity and the pecuniary indebtedness of the planters to them, the factors had come to be regarded as a parasitic excrescence on the community. Chief emphasis was placed by the radical writers on the fact that political independence would also mean emancipation from the power of factors and British mercantile houses. "A Planter" cited Virginia as an example of the conditions prevailing in the provinces from Maryland to Georgia. " You are without merchants, ships, seamen, or ship-builders . . . ," he declared to the Virginians in a newspaper article. "Your trade is confined to a single spot on the globe, in the hands of the natives of a distant Island, who fix the market of all commodities at their pleasure, and we may be very sure will rate yours at the lowest, and their own at the highest prices, they will in any conscience bear. Every article of merchandise, that is not the produce of Britain, must first pay its duties to the Crown, perhaps must be increased in the price a very large advance per cent there, and then be re-exported to Virginia, and undergo an additional advance of seventy-five, and sometimes near one hundred and fifty per cent here." In the northern colonies, he pointed out, linens and broadcloth were sold by the retail merchants at the same price that the Virginia factors claimed they paid as prime cost in Britain. "By this means you fairly lose seventy-five pounds currency on every one hundred pounds sterling worth of

[1] "Plain Hints on the Condition of the Colonies," Feb. 28, 1776; 4 *Am. Arch.*, vol. iv, p. 1524.

merchandise you import from Great Britain that is not native to that country;" a loss amounting annually to probably £200,000, which might be saved by the opening up of a free and independent trade with the world.

Furthermore, he continued, there were probably fifty foreign houses or companies and two thousand factors, who had charge of the trade of Virginia. "It is not unreasonable to say, that every house or company makes fifteen thousand pounds a year, net gain, by the trade of this Colony; and, consequently, fifty houses will annually export seven hundred and fifty thousand pounds sterling to Scotland and England; which will be just so much saved to the Colony, whenever its own natives shall become its merchants." Supposing the factors to lay aside £60 on the average, here was to be found £120,000 more, which was expended abroad. The total loss from these two sources alone amounted to £870,000 sterling, or £1,087,500 currency.

Another instance of exploitation was to be seen, he declared, in the marketing of the Virginia staple, tobacco, "upon which the Government of England and the merchants of Scotland, have it in their power to put what price they please." The present rate of about 20s. per hundredweight was considered a very good average price. This tobacco was exported to Britain, paid a duty almost four times the price it bore in Virginia, and their merchants made their fortunes out of it afterwards.[1] By exporting the tobacco directly to the countries that consumed it, the Virginia planter would receive five pounds per hundredweight instead of 20s. Making large allowance for losses, if the colonies separated from Great Britain which now consumed

---

[1] A reply by "A Virginian" pointed out that this duty was remitted when tobacco was re-exported from Great Britain. Dixon & Hunter's *Va. Gaz.*, Apr. 27, 1776.

a large proportion of the tobacco, its common price would still be £3, or 40s. more than the planters received at present. Figuring on an average exportation of 110,000 hogsheads per year, the gain to Virginia in a state of independence would be £2,200,000.

In summary, this writer estimated the commercial losses due to dependence on Great Britain, so far as Virginia was affected, substantially as follows:

1. On imports, as above	£200,000 currency
2. Merchants' net profits	1,087,500
3. Tobacco planters' gross profits	2,200,000
4. On wheat, flour, hemp, flax, &c., at least half as much; but say	1,000,000
5. That part of the gross profits of the merchants that would go to the artisans, seamen, sail-makers, dealers in cordage, anchors, etc.	1,500,000
Sum total	£5,987,500 currency

"That is, it [independence] will increase the real property among us annually to near six millions. . . . Here is a fund sufficient for defraying all the expenses . . . for the preservation of our liberties against the avarice of a nation much more powerful than the English, and not a farthing of our present property touched. . . . If we aim *only* at *interest* in the present contest, it appears plainly what part we ought at once to resolve upon." [1]

Turning again to the situation in the commercial provinces, it should be recognized that, when the moment for the crucial decision came, the choice which every merchant had to make was not, and could not be, a mere mechanical one, premised upon strict considerations of an informed class interest. Like other human beings, his mind was affected or controlled by the powerful influences of temperament,

[1] *Va. Gaz.*, Apr. 13, 1776; also *4 Am. Arch.*, vol. v, pp. 914-917.

environment and tradition. Furthermore, the degree to which his wealth was removable was an important factor in his decision, for his business and the good will of his customers were not commodities to be packed up and carried bodily over into British lines. These facts caused many a merchant to follow the line of least resistance when independence was promulgated.

Henry Laurens of South Carolina has left on record that he wept when he first heard the Declaration of Independence read; but he aligned himself with the revolutionists.[1] John Ross of Philadelphia, who "loved ease and Madeira much better than liberty and strife," was one type of a large group who claimed the right to be neutral.[2] The Quakers, whose membership embraced the principal merchants of Philadelphia, took an official stand against independence at a meeting of representatives of Pennsylvania and New Jersey Quakers on January 20, 1776. They resolved that: "The benefits, advantages and favours we have experienced by our dependence on, and connection with, the kings and government . . . appear to demand from us the greatest circumspection, care and constant endeavours, to guard against every attempt to alter, or subvert that dependence and connection;" and they urged Friends to unite firmly "in the abhorrence of all such writings and

[1] Wallace, *Laurens*, pp. 224-225, 377.

[2] Graydon, *Memoirs of His Own Times*, p. 118. Another interesting example is Peter Van Schaack, a New York lawyer, who had favored the Continental Association. In May, 1775, he removed to Kinderhook where he studied Vattel, Pufendorf, Grotius and other writers in the hope of finding precedents to support colonial resistance. Having made up his mind to remain neutral, he declined to sign the defense association, and in 1777 refused to take the oath of allegiance to the state of New York. The following year he was banished and went to England where he remained until 1785. Then he returned to America and resumed the practice of law. Van Schaack, H. C., *Life of Peter Van Schaack* (New York, 1842), *passim*.

measures as evidence a desire and design to break off the happy connection we have heretofore enjoyed with the kingdom of Great-Britain, and our just and necessary subordination to the king and those who are lawfully placed in authority under him . . ." [1] They attempted, during the war for independence, to steer a middle course, although many of the younger members, in defiance of their elders, joined heartily in the American cause.[2]

Many merchants, on the other hand, actuated by a broader understanding of class interest, frankly cast their lot with the mother country. In Massachusetts, where the conversion of the merchants to the loyalist side had occurred earlier than in the other provinces, more than two hundred members of the trade accompanied the British troops upon the evacuation of Boston in March, 1776. The elder Thomas Wharton, a foremost member of the merchant-aristocracy of Philadelphia and a "non-importer" of earlier days, had forsaken extra-legal activities when the results of the First Continental Congress showed that his efforts to guide events in approved channels had proven futile. A year or so later he was exiled to Virginia because his presence in Philadelphia was deemed dangerous to the patriot cause in view of the proximity of the British army after the battle of Brandywine. In South Carolina Miles Brewton, a wealthy merchant who had been a candidate of the Charleston Chamber of Commerce for nomination to the First Continental Congress, departed for England with most of his movable property when independence was declared, a destination he was not fated to reach.[4]

[1] *Pa. Ledger*, Jan. 27, 1776; also Sharpless, *Quakers in the Revolution*, pp. 125-128.
[2] *Ibid.*, pp. 130-137.
[3] Sabine, L., *Biographical Sketches of Loyalists of the American Revolution* (Boston, 1864), vol. i, p. 25.
[4] McCrady, *S. C. under Royal Gov't*, p. 406.

In New York the great leader of the mercantile reformers, Isaac Low, had fought a noble battle against the engulfing tide of radicalism, and did not begin seriously to doubt his ability to control events until the bloody occurrences in mid-April, 1775. Dismayed for the moment, he declined membership in the provincial convention of April 20-22 and thus deliberately rendered himself ineligible for election to the Second Continental Congress. But on sober second thought he accepted the chairmanship of the new city committee of One Hundred, and sought to guide the action of the provincial congress which began its sessions in May. He would probably have accepted election to the second provincial congress in November, but the radical party would have none of him. He welcomed the British troops when they occupied the city in August, 1776. When at a later period Low petitioned the British government for compensation, it is no wonder that his prominence in the revolutionary movement was misunderstood and that his application was not at first favorably received. Many other New Yorkers had followed the same course as Low. There had been nineteen men of this stripe on the committee of Fifty-One, thirteen or fourteen on the committee of Sixty, and perhaps eighteen on the committee of One Hundred.[1]

Of the merchants who remained in America after the Declaration of Independence, many retained the convictions that had animated their class throughout the ten years' struggle for commercial reform; and they made the most of a difficult situation by becoming passive spectators or secret abettors of the British in the struggle. They had the mournful satisfaction, when the war closed, of finding their worst fears confirmed in the inefficient government which the radicals established and in the enfeebled state of Amer-

[1] Becker, *N. Y. Parties, 1760-1776*, pp. 116 n., 168 n., 197-198. Some of these men served on all three committees, of course.

ican commerce and business at home and abroad. In the troubled years that followed, the merchants of the country regardless of their antecedents drew together in an effort to found a government which would safeguard the interests of their class. Thus, once more united, the mercantile interests became a potent factor in the conservative counter-revolution that led to the establishment of the United States Constitution.[1]

[1] Marshall, J., *Life of Washington* (1850), vol. ii, p. 99; Beard, C. A., *An Economic Interpretation of the Constitution of the United States* (New York, 1913), pp. 40-49, 56-57, 149-151, 175, and *passim*.

APPENDIX

THE CONTINENTAL ASSOCIATION [1]

[The footnotes refer to pages of the *Journals of the Continental Congress* on which subsequent alterations of the Association may be found.]

WE, his majesty's most loyal subjects, the delegates of the several colonies of New-Hampshire, Massachusetts-Bay, Rhode-Island, Connecticut, New-York, New-Jersey, Pennsylvania, the three lower counties of New-Castle, Kent, and Sussex, on Delaware, Maryland, Virginia, North-Carolina, and South-Carolina, deputed to represent them in a continental Congress, held in the city of Philadelphia, on the 5th day of September, 1774, avowing our allegiance to his majesty, our affection and regard for our fellow-subjects in Great-Britain and elsewhere, affected with the deepest anxiety, and most alarming apprehensions, at those grievances and distresses, with which his Majesty's American subjects are oppressed; and having taken under our most serious deliberation, the state of the whole continent, find, that the present unhappy situation of our affairs is occasioned by a ruinous system of colony administration, adopted by the British ministry about the year 1763, evidently calculated for inslaving these colonies, and, with them, the British empire. In prosecution of which system, various acts of parliament have been passed, for raising a revenue in America, for depriving the American subjects, in many instances, of the constitutional trial by jury, exposing their lives to danger, by directing a new and illegal trial beyond

---

[1] The text is taken from the *Journals of the Continental Congress* (Library of Congress Edition, Ford, W. C., and Hunt, G., eds.), vol. i, pp. 75-81.

the seas, for crimes alleged to have been committed in America: and in prosecution of the same system, several late, cruel, and oppressive acts have been passed, respecting the town of Boston and the Massachusetts-Bay, and also an act for extending the province of Quebec, so as to border on the western frontiers of these colonies, establishing an arbitrary government therein, and discouraging the settlement of British subjects in that wide extended country; thus, by the influence of civil principles and ancient prejudices, to dispose the inhabitants to act with hostility against the free Protestant colonies, whenever a wicked ministry shall chuse so to direct them.

To obtain redress of these grievances, which threaten destruction to the lives, liberty, and property of his majesty's subjects, in North America, we are of opinion, that a non-importation, non-consumption, and non-exportation agreement, faithfully adhered to, will prove the most speedy, effectual, and peaceable measures: and, therefore, we do, for ourselves, and the inhabitants of the several colonies whom we represent,, firmly agree and associate, under the sacred ties of virtue, honour and love of our country, as follows:

1. That from and after the first day of December next, we will not import, into British America, from Great-Britain or Ireland, any goods, wares, or merchandise whatsoever, or from any other place, any such goods, wares, or merchandise, as shall have been exported from Great-Britain or Ireland;[1] nor will we, after that day, import any East-India tea from any part of the world; nor any molasses, syrups, paneles, coffee, or pimento, from the British plantations or from Dominica; nor wines from Madeira, or the Western Islands; nor foreign indigo.[2]

2. We will neither import nor purchase, any slave imported after the first day of December next; after which time, we

---

[1] *Journals*, vol. ii, pp. 238-239, 247.
[2] *Ibid.*, vol. iv, pp. 257-259.

will wholly discontinue the slave trade, and will neither be concerned in it ourselves, nor will we hire our vessels, nor sell our commodities or manufactures to those who are concerned in it.

3. As a non-consumption agreement, strictly adhered to, will be an effectual security for the observation of the non-importation, we, as above, solemnly agree and associate, that, from this day, we will not purchase or use any tea, imported on account of the East-India company, or any on which a duty hath been or shall be paid; and from and after the first day of March next, we will not purchase or use any East-India tea whatever;[1] nor will we, nor shall any person for or under us, purchase or use any of those goods, wares, or merchandise, we have agreed not to import, which we shall know, or have cause to suspect, were imported after the first day of December, except such as come under the rules and directions of the tenth article hereafter mentioned.

4. The earnest desire we have, not to injure our fellow-subjects in Great-Britain, Ireland, or the West-Indies, induces us to suspend a non-exportation until the tenth day of September, 1775; at which time, if the said acts and parts of acts of the British parliament herein after mentioned are not repealed, we will not, directly or indirectly, export any merchandise or commodity whatsoever to Great-Britain, Ireland, or the West-Indies, except rice to Europe.[2]

5. Such as are merchants, and use the British and Irish trade, will give orders, as soon as possible, to their factors, agents, and correspondents, in Great-Britain and Ireland, not to ship any goods to them, on any pretence whatsoever, as they cannot be received in America; and if any merchant residing in Great-Britain or Ireland, shall directly or indirectly ship any goods, wares, or merchandise, for America, in order to break the said non-importation agreement, or in any manner contravene the same, on such unworthy conduct being well

---

[1] *Journals*, vol. iv, pp. 277-278.

[2] *Ibid.*, vol. ii, pp. 184-185, 238-239; vol. iii, pp. 308, 314, 315, 336, 362-364, 389-390, 464-465; vol. iv, pp. 257-259.

attested, it ought to be made public; and, on the same being so done, we will not, from thenceforth, have any commercial connexion with such merchant.

6. That such as are owners of vessels will give positive orders to their captains, or masters, not to receive on board their vessels any goods prohibited by the said non-importation agreement, on pain of immediate dismission from their service.

7. We will use our utmost endeavours to improve the breed of sheep, and increase their number to the greatest extent; and to that end, we will kill them as seldom as may be, especially those of the most profitable kind; nor will we export any to the West-Indies or elsewhere; and those of us, who are or may become overstocked with, or can conveniently spare any sheep, will dispose of them to our neighbours, especially to the poorer sort, on moderate terms.

8. We will, in our several stations, encourage frugality, economy, and industry, and promote agriculture, arts, and the manufactures of this country, especially that of wool; and will discountenance and discourage every species of extravagance and dissipation, especially all horse-racing, and all kinds of gaming, cock-fighting, exhibitions of shews, plays, and other expensive diversions and entertainments; and on the death of any relation or friend, none of us, or any of our families, will go into any further mourning-dress, than a black crape or ribbon on the arm or hat, for gentlemen, and a black ribbon and necklace for ladies, and we will discontinue the giving of scarves at funerals.[1]

9. Such as are venders of goods or merchandise will not take advantage of the scarcity of goods, that may be occasioned by this association, but will sell the same at the rates we have been respectively accustomed to do, for twelve months last past.—And if any vender of goods or merchandise shall sell any such goods on higher terms, or shall, in any manner, or by any device whatsoever violate or depart from this agreement, no person ought, nor will any of us deal with any such person,

---

[1] *Journals*, vol. iv, p. 224.

or his or her factor or agent, at any time thereafter, for any commodity whatever.[1]

10. In case any merchant, trader, or other person, shall import any goods or merchandise, after the first day of December, and before the first day of February next, the same ought forthwith, at the election of the owner, to be either re-shipped or delivered up to the committee of the county or town, wherein they shall be imported, to be stored at the risque of the importer, until the non-importation agreement shall cease, or be sold under the direction of the committee aforesaid; and in the last-mentioned case, the owner or owners of such goods shall be reimbursed out of the sales, the first cost and charges, the profit, if any, to be applied towards relieving and employing such poor inhabitants of the town of Boston as are immediate sufferers by the Boston port-bill; and a particular account of all goods so returned, stored, or sold, to be inserted in the public papers; and if any goods or merchandises shall be imported after the said first day of February, the same ought forthwith to be sent back again, without breaking any of the packages thereof.

11. That a committee be chosen in every county, city, and town, by those who are qualified to vote for representatives in the legislature, whose business it shall be attentively to observe the conduct of all persons touching this association; and when it shall be made to appear, to the satisfaction of a majority of any such committee, that any person within the limits of their appointment has violated this association, that such majority do forthwith cause the truth of the case to be published in the gazette; to the end, that all such foes to the rights of British-America may be publicly known, and universally contemned as the enemies of American liberty; and thenceforth we respectively will break off all dealings with him or her.[2]

[1] *Journals*, vol. iv, pp. 320, 404.
[2] *Ibid.*, vol. ii, p. 67.

12. That the committee of correspondence, in the respective colonies, do frequently inspect the entries of their custom-houses, and inform each other, from time to time, of the true state thereof, and of every other material circumstance that may occur relative to this association.

13. That all manufactures of this country be sold at reasonable prices, so that no undue advantage be taken of a future scarcity of goods.

14. And we do further agree and resolve, that we will have no trade, commerce, dealings, or intercourse whatsoever, with any colony or province, in North-America, which shall not accede to, or which shall hereafter violate this association, but will hold them as unworthy of the rights of freemen, and as inimical to the liberties of their country.

And we do solemnly bind ourselves and our constituents, under the ties aforesaid, to adhere to this association, until such parts of the several acts of parliament passed since the close of the last war, as impose or continue duties on tea, wine, molasses, syrups, paneles, coffee, sugar, pimento, indigo, foreign paper, glass, and painters' colours, imported into America, and extend the powers of the admiralty courts beyond their ancient limits, deprive the American subjects of trial by jury, authorize the judge's certificate to indemnify the prosecutor from damages, that he might otherwise be liable to from a trial by his peers, require oppressive security from a claimant of ships or goods seized, before he shall be allowed to defend his property, are repealed.—And until that part of the Act of the 12 G. 3. ch. 24, entitled "An act for the better securing his majesty's dock-yards, magazines, ships, ammunition, and stores," by which any persons charged with committing any of the offences therein described, in America, may be tried in any shire or county within the realm, is repealed—and until the four acts passed in the last session of parliament, viz. that for stopping the port and blocking up the harbour of Boston—that for altering the charter and government of the Massachusetts-Bay—and that which is entitled "An act for the better administration of justice, &c."—and

that "for extending the limits of Quebec, &c." are repealed.[1] And we recommend it to the provincial conventions, and to the committees in the respective colonies, to establish such farther regulations as they make think proper, for carrying into execution this association.

The foregoing association being determined upon by the Congress, was ordered to be subscribed by the several members thereof; and thereupon, we have hereunto set our respective names accordingly.

In Congress, Philadelphia, October 20, 1774.

[1] *Journals*, vol. ii, p. 125.

BIBLIOGRAPHY

PRIMARY SOURCES

1. Unprinted Sources

Barrell Correspondence. Letters of the brothers William, of Boston, and Joseph, of Philadelphia, merchants of their respective cities, covering the period June 16, 1773, to Aug. 12, 1776. In Mass. Hist. Soc. Library. For other Barrell letters *vide Mercantile Papers of Stephen Collins & Son,* below.

Boston. *Minutes of the Committee of Correspondence, November, 1772-December, 1774.* 13 v. Mostly in handwriting of William Cooper. Part of the George Bancroft collection in the New York Public Library. Referred to in this work as: *Bos. Com. Cor. Mss.*

Boston. *Papers of the Committee of Correspondence.* 3 v., covering the years 1772-1775. Intraprovincial and interprovincial correspondence, about 650 items in all, in the handwriting of Samuel Adams, Joseph Warren, Benjamin Church, Thomas Young and others. Part of the George Bancroft collection in the New York Public Library.

Boston. *Papers of the Boston Merchants, 1763-1774.* In Mass. Hist. Soc. Library.

British Papers relating to the American Revolution. 3 v. Transcripts of the correspondence of colonial governors and answers of the colonial office during the years 1763-1775, forming vol. xliii of the "Sparks Mss." in Harvard Library.

Chalmers, George, *Letter to Lord Mansfield on the History of the American Colonies 1780.* Transcript in "Sparks Mss.," vol. vii, in Harvard Library.

Charlestown, Mass. *Papers of the Charlestown Committee of Correspondence.* Cover the period 1774-1775. In Mass. Hist. Soc. Library.

Clifford Correspondence 1722-1832. 29 v. Vols. v, xxviii, and xxix contain important letters of Thomas Clifford, a Philadelphia merchant, bearing on colonial economic conditions, 1763-1775. In Historical Society of Pa. Library.

Collinses, *Mercantile Papers of Stephen Collins & Son.* 90 v., covering the period 1754-1813. Consists of the journals, ledgers, letter books and miscellaneous correspondence of this Philadelphia firm. In Library of Congress.

BIBLIOGRAPHY

Hutchinson, Thomas, *Hutchinson's Correspondence.* 3 v., covering the periods 1743-1773, 1761-1770 and 1770-1774 respectively. They form vols. xxv, xxvi and xxvii of the *Mass. Archives* in the State House in Boston.

Library of Congress Transcripts. They are listed in Andrews, C. M., and Davenport, F. G., *Guide to the Manuscript Materials for the History of the United States to 1783, in the British Museum, in Minor London Archives, and in the Libraries of Oxford and Cambridge* (Washington, 1908), pp. 431-445; and in Andrews, C. M., *Guide to the Materials for American History to 1783, in the Public Record Office of Great Britain* (Washington, 1912-1914), vol. i, pp. 308-309; vol. ii, p. 368.

Loyalists. *Transcripts of the Manuscript Books and Papers of the Commission of Enquiry into the Losses and Services of the American Loyalists held under Acts of Parliament of 23, 25, 26, 28 and 29 of George III, preserved amongst the Audit Office Records in the Public Record Office of England, 1783-1790.* 59 v. Includes applications, memorials and petitions to the British Government for aid and is rich in biographical material. In the New York Public Library.

Philadelphia. *Papers of the Committee of Merchants of Philadelphia, Feb. 6, 1769-Dec. 19, 1769.* Transcripts selected from Charles Thomson's papers in 1828, forming sub-vol. vii of vol. lxii of the " Sparks Mss." in Harvard Library.

Salem, Mass. The papers of the Salem Committee of Correspondence, July 12, 1772-Oct. 30, 1776, form a part of the *Pickering Papers,* vols. xxxiii and xxxix, in the Mass. Hist. Soc. Library.

Smith, William, *Notes and Papers on the Commencement of the American Revolution.* Dr. Smith was provost of the College of Philadelphia. In Historical Society of Pa. Library.

Stevens, B. F., ed., *Facsimiles of Manuscripts in European Archives Relating to America, 1773-1783; with Descriptions, Editorial Notes, Collations, References and Translations.* 25 v. London, 1889-1898.

Wharton, Thomas, *Wharton Letter Book 1773-1784.* In Historical Society of Pa. Library. Selections from the letter book of this prominent Philadelphia merchant have been reprinted in the *Pa. Mag. of Hist. and Biog.,* vol. xxxiii, pp. 319-339, 432-453; vol. xxxiv, pp. 41-61.

2. Printed Sources

A. Contemporary Histories and Descriptions

Burnaby, A., *Travels through the Middle Settlements in North America, in the Years 1759 and 1760.* London, 1775.

BIBLIOGRAPHY

Chalmers, G., *An Introduction to the History of the Revolt of the American Colonies.* 2 v. Boston, 1845.

Cluny, A., *The American Traveller: Containing Observations on the present State, Culture and Commerce of the British Colonies in America . . . By an Old and Experienced Trader.* Philadelphia, 1770.

Drayton, J., *Memoirs of the American Revolution, from its Commencement to the Year 1776, inclusive; as relating to the State of South Carolina,* etc. 2 v. Charleston, 1821.

Eddis, W., *Letters from America, 1769-1777.* London, 1792.

Gordon, W., *History of the Rise, Progress, and Establishment of the Independence of the United States of America.* 4 v. London, 1788.

Hewatt, A., *Historical Account of the Rise and Progress of the Colonies of South Carolina and Georgia.* 2 v. London, 1779.

History of the Origin, Rise and Progress of the War in America between Great Britain and the Colonies, 1764-1774. Boston, 1780.

Hutchinson, T., *History of the Colony [and Province] of Massachusetts Bay.* 3 v. Boston and London, 1795-1828.

Jones, T., *History of New York during the Revolutionary War and of the Leading Events in the Other Colonies at that Period.* E. F. de Lancey, ed. 2 v. New York, 1879.

Macpherson, D., *Annals of Commerce, Manufactures, Fisheries, and Navigation,* etc. 4 v. 1805.

Minot, G. R., *Continuation of the History of Massachusetts, 1748-1765.* 2 v. Boston, 1798-1803.

Moultrie, W., *Memoirs of the American Revolution, so far as it related to the States of North and South Carolina and Georgia.* 2 v. New York, 1802.

Postlethwayt, M., *Great Britain's Commercial Interest Explained and Improved,* etc. 2 v. London, 1759.

——, *The Universal Dictionary of Trade and Commerce, Translated from the French of the Celebrated M. Savary . . . with large Additions and Improvements,* etc. 2 v. London, 1751.

Pownall, T., *The Administration of the British Colonies.* 2 v. London, 1777.

Ramsay, D., *The History of the American Revolution.* 2 v. Philadelphia, 1789.

——, *The History of the Revolution of South Carolina.* 2 v. Trenton, 1785.

Sheffield, Lord (John Baker Holroyd), *Observations on the Commerce of the American States.* London, 1783.

Thacher, B. B., *Traits of the Tea Party.* New York, 1835.

Young[?], Arthur, *American Husbandry.* 2 v. London, 1775.

BIBLIOGRAPHY

B. CORRESPONDENCE, DOCUMENTS, MEMOIRS

Adams, John, *The Works of John Adams, with a Life of the Author, Notes and Illustrations.* C. F. Adams, ed. 10 v. Boston, 1850-1856.

Adams, John and Abigail, *Familiar Letters of John Adams and his Wife Abigail Adams,* etc. C. F. Adams, ed. Boston, 1875.

Adams, Samuel, *The Writings of Samuel Adams.* H. A. Cushing, ed. 4 v. New York, 1904-1908.

Andrews, John, "Correspondence of John Andrews, 1772-1776," *1 Mass. Hist. Soc. Procs.,* vol. viii, pp. 322-412.

Aspinwall Papers (4 Mass. Hist. Soc. Colls., vols. ix and x). 2 v. Boston, 1871.

Balch, T., ed., *Letters and Papers Relating Chiefly to the Provincial History of Pennsylvania.* Philadelphia, 1855.

Barrington, W. W. B., and Bernard, F., *The Barrington-Bernard Correspondence . . . 1760-1770 (Harvard Hist. Studies).* E. Channing and A. Coolidge, eds. Cambridge, 1912.

Bartlett, J. R., ed., *A History of the Destruction of His Britannic Majesty's Schooner Gaspee,* etc. Providence, 1861.

Bernard, F., *Letters of Governor Bernard, 1763-1768.* Boston, 1769.

——, *Letters to The Right Honourable The Earl of Hillsborough, 1768-1769.* Boston, 1769.

Bland, Theodorick, Jr., *The Bland Papers.* C. Campbell, ed. Petersburg, 1840.

Bogart, E. L., and Thompson, C. M., eds., *Readings in the Economic History of the United States.* New York, 1916.

Boston. *Reports of the Record Commissioners of the City of Boston.* 38 v. Boston, 1876-1908. Vol. xvi: *Boston Town Records 1758-1769.* Vol. xviii: *Boston Town Records 1770-1777.* Vol. xx: *Selectmen's Minutes 1764-1769.* Vol. xxiii: *Selectmen's Minutes 1769-1775.*

Boudinot, Elias, *The Life, Public Services, Addresses and Letters of Elias Boudinot, LL.D.* J. J. Boudinot, ed. 2 v. Boston, 1896.

Byrd, William, *The Writings of Colonel William Byrd.* J. S. Bassett, ed. New York, 1901.

Callender, G. S., ed., *Selections from the Economic History of the United States, 1765-1860.* Boston, 1909.

Cobbett, W., ed., *Parliamentary History of England from the Norman Conquest in 1066 to the Year 1803,* etc. 36 v. London, 1806-1820.

Colden, Cadwallader, *The Colden Letter Books, 1760-1775 (N. Y. Hist. Soc. Colls.,* vols. ix and x). 2 v. New York, 1876-1877.

Commerce of Rhode Island, 1726-1800 (7 Mass. Hist. Soc. Colls., vols. ix and x). 2 v. Boston, 1914-1915.

Cooper, Samuel, "Letters of Samuel Cooper to Thomas Pownall, 1769-1777," *Am. Hist. Rev.,* vol. viii, pp. 301-330.

BIBLIOGRAPHY

Curwen, Samuel, *Journal and Letters of the Late Samuel Curwen*, etc. G. A. Ward, ed. New York, 1842.

Cushing, Thomas, "Letters of Thomas Cushing from 1767 to 1775," *4 Mass. Hist. Soc. Colls.*, vol. iv, pp. 347-366.

Deane, Silas, "Correspondence of Silas Deane, Delegate to the First and Second Congress at Philadelphia, 1774-1776," *Conn. Hist. Soc. Colls.*, vol. ii, pp. 129-377.

De Berdt, Dennys, "Letters of Dennys de Berdt, 1757-1770," *Colon. Soc. Mass. Pubs.*, vol. xiii, pp. 293-461.

Dickinson, John, *The Writings of John Dickinson, 1764-1774* (*Mems. Hist. Soc. of Pa.*, vol. xiv). P. L. Ford, ed. Philadelphia, 1895.

Drake, F. S., ed., *Tea Leaves: being a Collection of Letters and Documents relating to the Shipment of Tea to the American Colonies in the Year 1773 by the East India Company*. Boston, 1884.

Drinker, Henry, "Effects of the Non-Importation Agreement in Philadelphia, 1769-1770," *Pa. Mag. Hist. and Biog.*, vol. xiv, pp. 41-45.

Eliot, Andrew, "Letters from Andrew Eliot to Thomas Hollis," *4 Mass. Hist. Soc. Colls.*, vol. iv, pp. 398-461.

Fisher, R. D., ed., *The Arson of the Peggy Stewart and the Annapolis, Md., Mob of October 19, 1774*. A scrapbook in the Library of Congress, containing important documents printed by Mr. Fisher in the *Baltimore News* during 1905-1907.

Force, P., comp., *American Archives: Consisting of a Collection of Authentick Records, State Papers, Debates and Letters and Other Notices of Publick Affairs*, etc. Fourth series. 6 v. Washington, 1837-1846.

Ford, W. C., and Hunt, G., eds., *Journals of the Continental Congress* (*Library of Congress Edition*). Washington, 1904-. In progress.

Franklin, Benjamin, *The Writings of Benjamin Franklin*. A. H. Smyth, ed. 10 v. New York, 1907.

Frothingham, R., Jr., ed., "Correspondence in 1774 and 1775 between a Committee of the Town of Boston and Contributors of Donations for the Relief of the Sufferers by the Boston Port Bill," *4 Mass. Hist. Soc. Colls.*, vol. iv, pp. 1-278.

Galloway, Joseph, "Some Letters of Joseph Galloway, 1774-1775," *Pa. Mag. Biog. and Hist.*, vol. xxi, pp. 477-484.

Gibbes, R. W., ed., *Documentary History of the American Revolution*, etc. 3 v. New York, 1853-1857.

Graydon, Alexander, *Memoirs of his Own Time*. J. S. Littell, ed. Philadelphia, 1846.

Habersham, James, *The Letters of Honorable James Habersham, 1756-1775* (*Ga. Hist. Soc. Colls.*, vol. vi). Savannah.

Hamilton, Alexander, *The Works of Alexander Hamilton*. H. C. Lodge, ed. 8 v. New York, 1885-1886.

Hancock, John, *John Hancock His Book*. A. E. Brown, ed. Boston, 1898.
Hays, I. M., ed., *The Record of the Celebration of the Two Hundredth Anniversary of the Birth of Benjamin Franklin*, etc. 6 v. Philadelphia, 1906-1908. Vols. ii-vi contain a calendar of Franklin papers in the libraries of American Philosophical Society and University of Pennsylvania.
Henry, Patrick, *Patrick Henry, Life, Correspondence and Speeches*. 3 v. W. W. Henry, ed. New York, 1891.
Hutchinson, Thomas, *The Diary and Letters of His Excellency Thomas Hutchinson, Esq.* P. O. Hutchinson, ed. 2 v. London, 1883-1886.
Izard, Ralph, *Correspondence of Mr. Ralph Izard, of South Carolina*. A. I. Deas, ed. 2 v. New York, 1844.
Jay, John, *The Correspondence and Public Papers of John Jay*. H. P. Johnston, ed. 4 v. New York, 1890-1893.
Jefferson, Thomas, *The Writings of Thomas Jefferson*. P. L. Ford, ed. 10 v. New York, 1892-1899.
——, *The Writings of Thomas Jefferson*. A. A. Lipscomb and A. E. Bergh, eds. 20 v. Washington, 1903.
Johnson, Joseph, *Traditions and Reminiscences, chiefly of the American Revolution in the South, particularly of the Upper Country*. Charleston, 1851.
Johnson, William Samuel, "Letters of William Samuel Johnson," *5 Mass. Hist. Soc. Colls.*, vol. ix, pp. 211-490.
Kimball, G. S., ed., *Correspondence of the Colonial Governors of Rhode Island*, etc. 2 v. Boston, 1902-1903.
Lee, Richard Henry, *The Letters of Richard Henry Lee*. J. C. Ballagh, ed. 2 v. New York, 1911-1914.
Madison, James, *The Writings of James Madison*. G. Hunt, ed. 9 v. New York, 1900-1910.
Marshall, Benjamin, "Extracts from the Letter-Book of Benjamin Marshall, 1763-1766," *Pa. Mag. Hist. and Biog.*, vol. xx, pp. 204-212.
Marshall, Christopher, *Passages from the Diary of Christopher Marshall*. W. Duane, Jr., ed. Philadelphia, 1839.
Maury, Ann, *Memoirs of a Huguenot Family*, etc. New York, 1872.
Moore, F., ed., *Diary of the American Revolution*. 2 v. New York, 1855.
Morris, Gouverneur, *The Diary and Letters of Gouverneur Morris*. A. C. Morris, ed. 2 v. New York, 1888.
Murray, James, *Letters of James Murray, Loyalist*. N. M. Tiffany and S. I. Lisley, eds. Boston, 1901.
Nelson, W., ed., *Extracts from American Newspapers, relating to New Jersey* (*1 N. J. Archives*, vols. xi-xii, xix-xx, xxiv-xxvii). 8 v. [1704-1771]. Paterson, 1894-1905.
Niles, H., ed., *Principles and Acts of the Revolution in America*. New York, 1876.

Quincy, Josiah, Jr., *Memoir of the Life of Josiah Quincy, Jr., of Massachusetts Bay, 1744-1775.* Boston, 1874.

——, *Reports of Cases Argued and Adjudged in the Superior Court of Judicature of the Province of Massachusetts Bay, between 1761 and 1772, by Josiah Quincy, Jr.* S. L. Quincy, ed. Boston, 1865.

Reed, Joseph, *Life and Correspondence of Joseph Reed.* W. B. Reed, ed. 2 v. Philadelphia, 1847.

Rhoads, Samuel, Jr., "Extracts from the Letter-Book of Samuel Rhoads, Jr., of Philadelphia," *Pa. Mag. Hist. and Biog.*, vol. xiv, pp. 421-426.

Rowe, John, *Letters and Diary of John Rowe, Boston Merchant, 1759-1762, 1764-1779.* A. E. Cunningham, ed. Boston, 1903.

Sharpe, Horatio, *Correspondence of Governor Horatio Sharpe (Archives of Md.*, vols. vi, ix, xiv, xxxi). W. H. Browne, ed. 4 v. Baltimore, 1888-1911.

Smith, Richard, "Diary of Richard Smith in the Continental Congress, 1775-1776," *Am. Hist. Rev.*, vol. i, pp. 288-310, 493-516.

Thomson, Charles, "Account of Mr. Dickinson's Attitude during the Revolution, furnished to Honorable W. H. Drayton for his Proposed History of that Period," in C. J. Stillé's *The Life and Times of John Dickinson* (Philadelphia, 1891), pp. 340-351.

——, "The Papers of Charles Thomson," *N. Y. Hist. Soc. Colls.*, vol. xi, pp. 1-286.

Virginia Committee of Correspondence, "Proceedings of the Virginia Committee of Correspondence, 1759-1770," *Va. Mag. Hist. and Biog.*, vol. x, pp. 337-356; vol. xi, pp. 1-25, 131-143, 345-354; vol. xii, pp. 157-169, 225-240, 353-364.

Ward, Samuel, "Diary of Governor Samuel Ward," *Mag. Am. Hist.*, vol. i, pp. 438-442, 503-506, 549-561.

Washington, George, *The Writings of George Washington.* W. C. Ford, ed. 14 v. New York, 1889-1892.

White, G., ed., *Historical Collections of Georgia.* New York, 1855.

Wilkes, John, "John Wilkes and Boston," *Mass. Hist. Soc. Procs.*, vol. 47, pp. 190-214.

Wright, James, "Letters from Governor Sir James Wright to the Earl of Dartmouth and Lord George Germain . . .," *Ga. Hist. Soc. Colls.*, vol. iii, pp. 157-375.

C. NEWSPAPERS AND PERIODICALS, 1763-1776

The Annual Register, 1763-1776. London, 1764-1777.

Connecticut. *The Connecticut Courant*, 1764-1774. Title varies: *The Connecticut Courant and Hartford Weekly Intelligencer*, 1774-1776. Published at Hartford.

——. *The Connecticut Gazette*, 1763-1767. Published at New Haven.
——. *The Connecticut Journal and New-Haven Post-Boy*, 1767-1775. Title varies: *The Connecticut Journal*, 1775-1776. Published at New Haven.
——. *The New-London Gazette*, 1764-1773. Title varies: *Connecticut Gazette and the Universal Intelligencer*, 1774-1776. Published at New London.
——. *Norwich Packet, and the Connecticut, Massachusetts, New-Hampshire, and Rhode-Island Weekly Advertiser*, 1773-1776. Published at Norwich.
Georgia. *The Georgia Gazette*, 1763-1770, 1774-1775. Published at Savannah.
Maryland. *Dunlap's Maryland Gazette; or the Baltimore General Advertiser*, 1775-1776. Published at Baltimore.
——. *The Maryland Gazette*, 1763-1776. Published at Annapolis.
——. *The Maryland Journal, and the Baltimore Advertiser*, 1773-1776. Published at Baltimore.
Massachusetts. *The Boston Chronicle*, 1767-1770. Published at Boston.
——. *The Boston Evening Post*, 1763-1775. Published at Boston.
——. *The Boston Gazette, and Country Journal*, 1763-1776. Published at Boston 1763-1775 and at Watertown and Boston 1775-1776.
——. *The Boston News-Letter*, 1763. Title varies: *The Massachusetts Gazette and Boston News-Letter*, 1763-1765; *The Massachusetts Gazette*, 1765-1766; *The Massachusetts Gazette and Boston News-Letter*, 1766-1768; *The Boston Weekly News-Letter*, 1768-1769; *The Massachusetts Gazette: and the Boston Weekly News-Letter*, 1769-1776. Published at Boston.
——. *The Boston Post-Boy & Advertiser*. Title varies: *Green & Russell's Boston Post-Boy & Advertiser*, 1763; *The Boston Post-Boy & Advertiser*, 1763-1769; *The Massachusetts Gazette, and the Boston Post-Boy and Advertiser*, 1769-1775. Published at Boston.
——. *The Continental Journal, and Weekly Advertiser*, 1776. Published at Boston.
——. *The Essex Gazette*, 1768-1775. Title varies: *The New-England Chronicle, or the Essex Gazette*, 1775-1776; *The New-England Chronicle*, 1776. Published at Salem 1768-1775 and at Cambridge and Boston 1775-1776.
——. *The Essex Journal and Merrimack Packet: Or the Massachusetts and New-Hampshire General Advertiser*, 1773-1775. Title varies: *The Essex Journal or the Massachusetts and New-Hampshire General Advertiser*, 1775; *The Essex Journal or New-Hampshire Packet*, 1775-1776; *The Essex Journal or the New-Hampshire Packet, and the Weekly Advertiser*, 1776; *The Essex Journal*, 1776. Published at Newburyport.

———. *The Salem Gazette, and Newbury and Marblehead Advertiser*, 1774-1775. Published at Salem.
———. *The Massachusetts Gazette*, 1768-1769. Published at Boston.
———. *The Massachusetts Spy*, 1770-1772. Title varies: *The Massachusetts Spy Or, Thomas's Boston Journal*, 1772-1775; *Thomas's Massachusetts Spy, or American Oracle of Liberty*, 1775-1776. Published at Boston 1770-1775 and at Worcester 1775-1776.
New Hampshire. *The New-Hampshire Gazette and Historical Chronicle*, 1763-1775. Title varies: *Freeman's Journal, or New-Hampshire Gazette*, 1776. Published at Portsmouth.
New York. *The Albany Gazette*, 1771-1772. Published at Albany.
———. *The Constitutional Gazette*, 1776. Published at New York.
———. *The New York Chronicle*, 1769. Published at New York.
———. *The New York Gazette, or, The Weekly Post Boy*, 1763-1773. Published at New York.
———. *The New York Journal, or the General Advertiser*, 1766-1776. Published at New York 1766-1776 and at Kingston 1776.
———. *The New York Mercury*, 1763-1768. Title varies: *The New York Gazette and the Weekly Mercury*, 1768-1776. Published at New York 1763-1776 and at Newark and New York 1776.
———. *Rivington's New York Gazetteer; or the Connecticut, New Jersey, Hudson's River, and Quebec Weekly Advertiser*, 1773-1775. Published at New York.
———. *Weyman's New York Gazette*, 1763-1767. Published at New York.
Pennsylvania. *The Pennsylvania Chronicle, and Universal Advertiser*, 1767-1774. Published at Philadelphia.
———. *The Pennsylvania Evening Post*, 1775-1776. Published at Philadelphia.
———. *The Pennsylvania Gazette*, 1763-1776. Published at Philadelphia.
———. *The Pennsylvania Journal; and the Weekly Advertiser*, 1763-1776. Published at Philadelphia.
———. *The Pennsylvania Ledger: Or the Virginia, Maryland, Pennsylvania and New Jersey Weekly Advertiser*, 1775-1776. Published at Philadelphia.
———. *The Pennsylvania Packet, and the General Advertiser*, 1771-1773. Title varies: *Dunlap's Pennsylvania Packet, or, the General Advertiser*, 1773-1776. Published at Philadelphia.
———. *Story & Humphreys's Pennsylvania Mercury and Universal Advertiser*, 1775. Published at Philadelphia.
———. *Der Wöchentliche Pennsylvanische Staatsbote*, 1772-1774. Published at Philadelphia.
Rhode Island. *The Newport Mercury, or the Weekly Advertiser*, 1763-1776. Published at Newport.

——. *The Providence Gazette and Country Journal,* 1763-1776. Published at Providence.
South Carolina. *The South-Carolina & American General Gazette,* 1766-1776. Published at Charleston.
——. *The South Carolina Gazette,* 1763-1775. Published at Charleston.
——. *The South-Carolina Gazetteer; And Country Journal,* 1765. Title varies: *The South-Carolina Gazette; and Country Journal,* 1765-1775. Published at Charleston.
Virginia. *The Virginia Gazette,* 1775-1776. Published at Williamsburg by J. Clarkson and A. Davis.
——. *The Virginia Gazette,* 1766-1776. Published at Williamsburg by Alex. Purdie and Co. 1766; Alex. Purdie and John Dixon 1766-1775; John Dixon and William Hunter 1775-1776.
——. *The Virginia Gazette,* 1775-1776. Published at Williamsburg by Alex. Purdie.
——. *The Virginia Gazette,* 1766-1776. Published at Williamsburg by William Rind 1766-1773; Clementina Rind 1773-1774; John Pinkney 1774-1776.
——. *The Virginia Gazette, or the Norfolk Intelligencer,* 1774-1775. Published at Norfolk.

D. PAMPHLETS

Adams, John, "Novanglus: or a History of the Dispute with America from its Origin, in 1754, to the Present Time," *Works,* vol. iv, pp. 3-177.
The Association of the Delegates of the Colonies at the Grand Congress versified and adapted to Music . . . by Bob Jingle, Esq. N. p., 1774.
Authentic Account of the Proceedings of the Congress held at New-York in MDCCXV on the Subject of the American Stamp Act. London, 1767.
Bernard, F., *The Causes of the Present Distractions in America Explained in Two Letters to a Merchant in London.* London, 1774.
Boston. *Observations on several Acts of Parliament passed in the 4th, 6th, and 7th years of his present Majesty's Reign: also on the Conduct of the Officers of the Customs since those Acts were passed, and the Board of Commissioners appointed to reside in America. . . . Published by the Merchants of Boston.* Boston, 1769.
Chandler, Thomas B., *A Friendly Address to All Reasonable Americans on the Subject of our Political Confusions,* etc. New York, 1774. Ascribed also to Cooper.
Chauncy, Charles, *A Letter to a Friend. By T. W. A. Bostonian.* Boston, 1774.
The Commercial Conduct of the Province of New-York considered, and the True Interest of that Colony attempted to be shewn . . . By a Linen Draper. New York, 1767.

Cooper, Myles, *What Think Ye of Congress Now? or an Enquiry How Far the Americans are Bound to Abide by and Execute the Decisions of the Late Continental Congress.* New York, 1775. Ascribed also to Chandler and Seabury.

A Dialogue between a Southern Delegate, and his Spouse, on his Return from The Grand Continental Congress. A Fragment Inscribed To the Married Ladies of America. By . . . Mary V. V. N. p., 1774.

Dickinson, John, *The Late Regulations Respecting the British Colonies,* etc. Philadelphia, 1765.

———, *Letters from a Farmer in Pennsylvania to the Inhabitants of the British Colonies.* New York, 1768.

Drayton, W. H., "A Letter from Freeman of South-Carolina to the Deputies of North-America, assembled in the High Court of Congress at Philadelphia," Gibbes, *Documentary History,* vol. ii, pp. 11-39.

Dulany, Daniel, "Considerations on the Propriety of imposing Taxes in the British Colonies...," *Md. Hist. Mag.,* vol. vi, pp. 376-406.

Galloway, Joseph, *A Candid Examination of the Mutual Claims of Great Britain and the Colonies with a Plan of Accommodation on Constitutional Principles.* New York, 1775.

———, *The Examination of Joseph Galloway, Esq.; . . . before the House of Commons in a Committee on the American Papers,* etc. London, 1780.

———, *Historical and Political Reflections on the Rise and Progress of the American Rebellion,* etc. London, 1780.

Gray, Harrison, *A Few Remarks upon Some of the Votes and Resolutions of the Continental Congress, held at Philadelphia in September and the Provincial Congress, Held at Cambridge in November, 1774. By a Friend to Peace and good Order.* Boston, 1775.

Hamilton, Alexander, *A Full Vindication of the Measures of Congress from the Calumnies of their Enemies,* etc. New York, 1774.

———, *Full Vindication Supported; or the Farmer Refuted,* etc. New York, 1774.

Hopkins, Stephen, "The Rights of Colonies Examined," *R. I. Col. Recs.,* vol. vi, pp. 416-427.

Howard, Martin, *A Letter from a Gentleman at Halifax to his Friend in Rhode Island.* Newport, 1765.

Inglis, Charles, *The True Interest of America Impartially Stated, in Certain Strictures on a Pamphlet intitled Common Sense.* Philadelphia, 1776.

The Interest of the Merchants and Manufacturers of Great Britain in the Present Contest with the Colonies Stated and Considered. London, 1774.

Laurens, Henry, *Some General Observations on American custom house officers and Courts of Vice-Admiralty.* Charleston, 1769.

Leonard, Daniel, *Massachusettensis: or a Series of Letters, containing a faithful State of many important and striking Facts which laid the Foundation of the present Troubles in the Province of the Massachusetts-Bay,* etc. London, 1776.

Mein[?], John, *Sagittarius's Letters and Political Speculations Extracted from the Public Ledger.* Boston, 1775.

Mein, John, *State of the Importations from Great Britain into Boston, from Jan. 1769 to Aug. 17, 1769.* Boston, 1769.

Morgan, John, *Dissertation on the Reciprocal Advantages of a Perpetual Union between Great Britain and her American Colonies.* Philadelphia, 1766.

Otis, James, *The Rights of the British Colonies Asserted and Proved.* Boston, 1764.

Paine, Thomas, *Common Sense Addressed to the Inhabitants of America on the following interesting subjects,* etc. London, 1776.

The Poor Man's Advice to his Poor Neighbours: a Ballad to the Tune of Chevy Chace. New York, 1774.

Seabury, Samuel, *The Congress Canvassed: or an Examination into the Conduct of the Delegates at their Grand Convention in Philadelphia, September 1, 1774. ... By A. W. Farmer.* New York, 1774. Ascribed also to Wilkins.

——, *Free Thoughts on the Proceedings of the Continental Congress,* etc. New York, 1774.

Some Seasonable Observations and Remarks upon The State of our Controversy with Great Britain and on the Proceedings of the Continental Congress. By a Moderate Whig. America, 1775.

Thacher, Oxenbridge, *The Sentiments of a British American.* Boston, 1864.

Tucker, Josiah, Dean of Gloucester, "A Letter from a Merchant in London to his Nephew in North America," *Pa. Mag. Hist. and Biog.,* vol. xxv, pp. 307-322, 516-526; vol. xxvi, pp. 81-90, 255-264.

Watts, Stephen, *An Essay on the reciprocal Advantages of a Perpetual Union between Great Britain and her American Colonies.* Philadelphia, 1766.

West, Stephen, "The Proceedings of the Committee Appointed to examine into the Importation of Goods by the Brigantine Good Intent...," *Md. Hist. Mag.,* vol. iii, pp. 141-157, 240-256, 342-363.

Wilkins, Isaac, *An Alarm to the Legislature of New York occasioned by the present Political Disturbances in North America.* New York, 1775. Ascribed also to Cooper and Seabury.

SECONDARY SOURCES

Ambler, C. H., *Sectionalism in Virginia from 1776 to 1861.* Chicago, 1910.

Andrews, C. M., "Anglo-French Commercial Rivalry, 1700-1750: the Western Phase," *Am. Hist. Rev.*, vol. xx, pp. 539-556, 761-780.
——, "The Boston Merchants and the Non-Importation Movement," *Col. Soc. Mass. Pubs.*, vol. xix, pp. 159-259.
——, "Colonial Commerce," *Am. Hist. Rev.*, vol. xx, pp. 43-63.
——, *The Colonial Period.* New York, 1912.
——, *Colonial Self-Government.* New York, 1904.
Andrews, F. D., *The Tea-Burners of Cumberland County*, etc. Vineland, N. J., 1908.
Arnold, S. G., *History of the State of Rhode Island and Providence Plantations, 1636-1790.* 2 v. New York, 1859-1860.
Ashley, W. J., *Surveys Historic and Economic.* New York, 1900.
Baldwin, E. H., "Joseph Galloway, the Loyalist Politician," *Pa. Mag. Hist. and Biog.*, vol. xxvi, pp. 161-191, 289-321, 417-442.
Bancroft, George, *History of the United States.* 10 v.; Boston, 1834-1874. 6 v.; New York, 1883-1885.
Barry, J. S., *History of Massachusetts.* 3 v. Boston, 1855-1857.
Bassett, J. S., "The Regulators of North Carolina (1765-1771)," *Am. Hist. Assn. Rep. 1894*, pp. 141-212.
——, "The Relation between the Virginia Planter and the London Merchant," *ibid. 1901*, vol. i, pp. 551-575.
Becker, C. L., *Beginnings of the American People.* Boston, 1912.
——, *The History of Political Parties in the Province of New York, 1760-1776* (*Univ. of Wisc. Bull.*, no. 286). Madison, 1909.
Beer, G. L., *The Commercial Policy of England toward the American Colonies* (*Col. Univ. Studies*, vol. iii, no. 2). New York, 1893.
——, *British Colonial Policy 1754-1765.* New York, 1907.
Bell, H. C., "The West India Trade before the American Revolution," *Am. Hist. Rev.*, vol. xxii, pp. 272-287.
Bishop, J. L., *A History of American Manufactures from 1608 to 1860.* 3 v. Philadelphia, 1866.
Bowden, J., *The History of the Society of Friends in America.* 2 v. London, 1854.
Bradford, Alden, *History of Massachusetts.* 3 v. Boston, 1822-1829.
Bruce, P. A., *Economic History of Virginia in the Seventeenth Century.* 2 v. New York, 1896.
Bullock, C. J., *Essays on the Monetary History of the United States.* New York, 1900.
Chamberlain, Mellen, "The Revolution Impending," in *Narrative and Critical History of America*, vol. vi, pp. 1-112. J. Winsor, ed. Boston, 1888.
——, *John Adams, the Statesman of the American Revolution, with Other Essays.* Boston, 1899.
Channing, E., *History of the United States.* 4 v., in progress. New York, 1909-.

———, "The Navigation Laws," *Am. Antiq. Soc. Procs.*, New Ser., vol. vi, pp. 160-179.
Clark, V. S., *History of Manufactures in the United States, 1607-1860* (Contributions to American Economic History from the Department of Economics and Sociology of the Carnegie Institution). Washington, 1916.
Collins, E. D., "Committees of Correspondence of the American Revolution," *Am. Hist. Assn. Rep. 1901*, vol. i, pp. 243-271.
Connor, R. D. W., *Cornelius Harnett*. Raleigh, 1909.
Cushing, H. A., *History of the Transition from Provincial to Commonwealth Government in Massachusetts* (Col. Univ. Studies, vol. vii, no. 1). New York, 1896.
Davis, A. McF., *Currency and Banking in Massachusetts Bay* (*3 Am. Econ. Assn. Pubs.*, vol. i, no. 4; vol. ii, no. 1). New York, 1900-1901.
———, "The Limitation of Prices in Massachusetts, 1776-1779," *Col. Soc. Mass. Pubs.*, vol. x, pp. 119-134.
Dawson, H. B., *Westchester County, New York, during the American Revolution*. Morrisania, 1886.
Eckenrode, H. J., *The Revolution in Virginia*. Boston, 1916.
Edwards, Bryan, *The History, Civil and Commercial, of the British Colonies in the West Indies*. 2 v. London, 1793.
Farrand, M., "The Taxation of Tea, 1767-1773," *Am. Hist. Rev.*, vol. iii, pp. 266-269.
Felt, J. B., *An Historical Account of Massachusetts Currency*. Boston, 1839.
Fisher, E. J., *New Jersey as a Royal Province, 1738 to 1776* (Col. Univ. Studies, vol. xli). New York, 1911.
Fisher, S. G., *The Struggle for American Independence*. 2 v. Philadelphia, 1908,
Flick, A. C., *Loyalism in New York during the American Revolution* (Col. Univ. Studies, vol. xiv, no. 1). New York, 1901.
Ford, P. L., "The Association of the First Congress," *Pol. Sci. Quar.*, vol. vi, pp. 613-624.
Ford, W. C., "Colonial America," *Col. Soc. Mass. Pubs.*, vol. vi, pp. 340-370.
Frothingham, R., *The Rise of the Republic of the United States*. Boston, 1881.
Giesecke, A. A., *American Commercial Legislation before 1789* (Univ. of Pa. Studies). Philadelphia, 1910.
Gilbert, G. A., "The Connecticut Loyalists," *Am. Hist. Rev.*, vol. iv, pp. 273-291.
Gould, C. P., *Money and Transportation in Maryland 1720-1765* (Johns Hopkins Univ. Studies, vol. xxxiii, no. 1). Baltimore, 1915.
Greene, E. B., *Provincial America*. New York, 1905.

Haworth, P. L., *George Washington: Farmer.* Indianapolis, 1915.
Hosmer, J. K., *The Life of Thomas Hutchinson.* Boston, 1896.
———, *Samuel Adams.* Boston, 1885.
Howard, G. E., *Preliminaries of the Revolution.* New York, 1905.
Johnson, E. R., and others, *History of Domestic and Foreign Commerce of the United States* (Contributions to American Economic History from the Department of Economics and Sociology of the Carnegie Institution). 2 v. Washington, 1915.
Kimball, G. S., *Providence in Colonial Times.* Boston, 1912.
Konkle, B. A., *The Life and Times of Thomas Smith (1745-1809).* Philadelphia, 1904.
Leake, I. Q., *Memoir of the Life and Times of General John Lamb.* Albany, 1857.
Leake, J. M., *The Virginia Committee System and the Revolution* (Johns Hopkins Univ. Studies, vol. xxxiv, no. 1). Baltimore, 1916.
Lecky, W. E. H., *History of England in the Eighteenth Century.* 8 v. London, 1878-1890.
Levermore, C. H., "The Whigs in Colonial New York," *Am. Hist. Rev.*, vol. i, pp. 238-250.
Lincoln, C. H., *The Revolutionary Movement in Pennsylvania, 1760-1776* (Univ. of Pa. Pubs.). Philadelphia, 1901.
Lord, E. L., *Industrial Experiments in the British Colonies of North America* (Johns Hopkins Univ. Studies, extra vol. xvii). Baltimore, 1908.
McClellan, W. S., *Smuggling in the American Colonies at the Outbreak of the Revolution with especial Reference to the West Indies Trade.* New York, 1912.
McCrady, E., *The History of South Carolina under the Royal Government 1719-1776.* New York, 1901.
Mason, G. C., "The United Company of Spermaceti Chandlers 1761," *Mag. New Engl. Hist.*, vol. ii, pp. 165-169.
Morriss, M. S., *Colonial Trade of Maryland 1689-1715* (Johns Hopkins Univ. Studies, vol. xxxii, no. 3). Baltimore, 1914.
Osgood, H. L., *The American Colonies in the Seventeenth Century.* 3 v. New York, 1904-1907.
———, "The American Revolution," *Pol. Sci. Quar.*, vol. xiii, pp. 41-59.
Phillips, H., *Historical Sketches of American Paper Currency.* 2 v. Roxbury, 1865-1866.
Root, W. T., *The Relations of Pennsylvania with the British Government, 1696-1765* (Univ. of Pa. Pubs.). Philadelphia, 1912.
Rowland, K. M., *Life of George Mason, 1725-1792.* 2 v. New York, 1892.
Russell, E. B., *The Review of American Colonial Legislation by the King in Council* (Col. Univ. Studies, vol. lxiv, no. 2). New York, 1915.

Ryerson, E., *Loyalists of America and Their Times.* 2 v. Toronto, 1880.
Sabine, L., *Biographical Sketches of Loyalists of the American Revolution.* 2 v. Boston, 1864.
Schaper, W. A., " Sectionalism and Representation in South Carolina," *Am. Hist. Assn. Rep. 1900,* vol. i, pp. 237-463.
Schlesinger, A. M., " The Uprising against the East India Company," *Pol. Sci. Quar.,* vol. xxxii, pp. 60-79.
Sears, L., *John Hancock.* Boston, 1912.
Sharpless, I., *A History of Quaker Government in Pennsylvania.* 2 v. Vol. i: *A Quaker Experiment in Government.* Vol. ii: *The Quakers in the Revolution.* Philadelphia, 1898-1899.
Sikes, E. W., *Transition of North Carolina from Colony to Commonwealth* (Johns Hopkins Univ. Studies, vol. xvi, nos. 10-11). Baltimore, 1898.
Silver, J. A., *The Provisional Government of Maryland (1774-1777)* (Johns Hopkins Univ. Studies, vol. xiii, no. 10). Baltimore, 1895.
Smith, C. S., " The Scarcity of Salt in the Revolutionary War," *1 M. H. S. Procs.,* vol. xv, pp. 221-227.
Smith, W. R., " Sectionalism in Pennsylvania during the Revolution," *Pol. Sci. Quar.,* vol. xxiv, pp. 208-235.
——, *South Carolina as a Royal Province 1719-1776.* New York, 1903.
Sparks, J., *The Life of Gouverneur Morris,* etc. 3 v. Boston, 1832.
Staples, W. R., *Rhode Island in the Continental Congress.* Providence, 1870.
Stillé, C. J., *The Life and Times of John Dickinson, 1732-1808* (Hist. Soc. of Pa. Memoirs, vol. xiii). Philadelphia, 1891.
Trevelyan, G. O., *The American Revolution.* 4 v. New York, 1899-1912.
Tudor, W., *Life of James Otis; Containing Notices of Contemporary Characters and Events, 1760-1775.* Boston, 1823.
Tyler, M. C., *The Literary History of the American Revolution 1763-1783.* 2 v. New York, 1897.
Van Schaack, H. C., *The Life of Peter Van Schaack.* New York, 1842.
Wallace, D. D., *The Life of Henry Laurens.* New York, 1915.
Weeden, W. B., *Economic and Social History of New England.* 2 v. Boston, 1890.
——, *Early Rhode Island.* New York, 1910.
Wells, W. V., *The Life and Public Services of Samuel Adams.* 3 v. Boston, 1865.
Winsor, J., ed., *Narrative and Critical History of America.* 8 v. Boston, 1886-1889.
Woodburn, J. A., *Causes of the American Revolution* (Johns Hopkins Univ. Studies, vol. x, no. 12). Baltimore, 1892.

INDEX

Acts of trade. *Vide:* British colonial policy.
Adams, Abigail, on high cost of living, 589, 590.
Adams, John, on molasses as an ingredient of independence, 59; affairs of, interrupted by Stamp Act, 70-71; at meeting of Sons of Liberty, 72; grows tired of fighting for people's rights, 241, 254; hopes he drank smuggled tea, 244; journey of, to Philadelphia, 405-407; on diversity of interests in First Continental Congress, 409, 411; notes of, on First Continental Congress, 415; part played by, in First Continental Congress, 416, 429 n.; favors opening of trade by Second Continental Congress, 578-579.
Adams, Samuel, on execution of non-importation (1769-1770), 183; warns against dependence on merchants, 254, 345 n.; tries to keep opposition alive, 254-257; secures establishment of Boston Committee of Correspondence, 257-258; writes report of Boston Committee of Correspondence, 258-259; defect of plan of, 260-261; urges local committees in all provinces, 261; directs anti-tea riots in Boston, 283-289, 555; fails to persuade Boston merchants to adopt non-importation, 318; is present at town meeting to unseat the committee of correspondence, 321-322; says he favors an interprovincial congress, 394; leads radicals in First Continental Congress, 411; member of the Sixty-Three at Boston, 441; favors opening of trade by Second Continental Congress, 578, 580-581.

Albany, merchants of, adopt non-importation (1765), 78; merchants of, adopt non-importation (1769), 125; merchants of, rescind and renew agreement (1770), 215; merchants of, rebuke New York for abandoning agreement, 227; committee of, protests against rice exemption, 439.
Andrews, John, reaction of, to public events, 434 n.
Annapolis, non-importation agreement of inhabitants of (1769), 138; difficulties in, over price of tea, 211-212; mass meeting at, adopts non-intercourse resolutions (1774), 360-361; affair of *Peggy Stewart* at, 389-392; enforcement of non-importation in, 505.
Association. *Vide:* Continental Association; defense associations; loyalist association; non-consumption; non-exportation; non-importation; Solemn League and Covenant; Sons of Liberty.
Baltimore, merchants of, adopt non-importation (1769), 138; good faith of, suspected by Philadelphia committee, 199-200; merchants of, abandon agreement, 233-234; merchants of, limit agreement to dutied articles, 234; enforcement of non-importation (1775) in, 505-506; committee of, regulates price of salt, 585.
Boston, important as trading center, 25, 27, 314; merchants of, oppose land bank, 29; merchants of, complain regarding naval stores, 31; identity of interests of, with leading northern ports, 32; merchants of, employ Otis in writs' case, 47; bankruptcies in, 57; organization of merchants (1763) in, 59-60; non-consump-

tion agreement in, 63, 64, 76; domestic manufacturing in, 65; Stamp Act riots in, 71-72; non-importation agreement at, 78, 80; petition of merchants of, (1767), 87-88; Customs Board breaks power of smugglers in, 99, 102-104; punishment of informer in, 100; adopts non-consumption, 107-109; domestic manufacturing in, (1767-1770), 109-110, 121, 122-124; conditional non-importation agreement of merchants of, (1768), 114-115; non-importation agreements of merchants of, (1768-1770), 120-121; non-consumption of tea in, 121-122; merchants of, seek to extend agreement, 131-133; merchants of, publish *Observations*, 133-134; enforcement of non-importation in, (1769-1770), 156-183, 217; Massacre, 179-181; complaints of high prices at, 212; merchants of, boycott Rhode Island and Portsmouth, 215-216; merchants of, oppose rescinding of agreement, 219, 221, 227; merchants of, rescind agreement (1770), 232-233; merchants of, limit non-importation to dutied articles, 233; importation of dutied tea at, 246, 264-265, 282 n., 299; conservative state of public opinion in, 254-255; establishment of committee of correspondence at, 255-259, 260-261; arguments used in, to arouse opposition to shipments of East India Company, 265-277; opposition to tea shipments in, 264-265, 281-290; Tea Party, 287-288; adoption of tea non-consumption at, 300-301; passage of act for closing port of, 305; movement for non-intercourse in, 311-323; adopts circular letter (May 13, 1774), 313; problem of unemployment in, 314-315; merchants of, adopt conditional non-importation agreement, 315-316, 318; committee of correspondence of, launches Solemn League and Covenant, 319-320; merchants of, oppose Solemn League, 320-321, 322-323; efforts to unseat committee of correspondence of, 321-322; workingmen of, boycott Gage, 386-388; appoints Committee of Sixty-Three, 441; enforcement of non-consumption in, 481-482; committee of, endorses use of certificates in coast trade, 534; high prices in, 590; merchants of, depart with troops, 604.

Boston Massacre, preliminaries to, 179-180; occurrence of, 180-181; effect of, on non-importation movement in New England, 155, 181-182, 185-186, 194.

Boston Port Act, passage of, 305; presents a new issue to colonists, 306-307; crystallizes colonial opinion, 308-311, 359-360; industrial conditions in Boston as result of, 314-315; reception of, in separate colonies: Massachusetts, 311-325; Rhode Island, 325-326, 327; Connecticut, 326, 327; New Hampshire, 325, 327; New York, 327-341; Pennsylvania, 341-356; New Jersey, 356-357; Delaware, 357-358; Maryland, 360-362; Virginia, 362-370; North Carolina, 370-373; South Carolina, 373-379; Georgia, 379-386.

Boston Tea Party, preliminaries to, 281-287; occurrence of, 287-288; participants in, 288-290; approved by Philadelphia meeting, 291; effect of, on New Yorkers, 292; fails to arouse colonists generally, 298-304; second, 302 n.; official utterances of First Continental Congress concerning, 430-431.

Boycott. *Vide:* Continental Association; loyalist association; non-consumption; non-exportation; non-importation; Solemn League and Covenant.

British colonial policy, contrast in application of, in insular and continental colonies, 15; navigation act (1660) and effects, 16; regulation of colonial imports and effects, 16-17, 19; regulation of colonial exports and effects, 17-19; molasses act (1733), 19; regulation of manufactures and

INDEX 633

effects, 19-21; act for collection of debts (1732), 21, 36; prohibition of legal tender issues in New England (1751), 21-22; absence of colonial dissatisfaction with, prior to 1760, 22; measures against smuggling during Fourth Intercolonial War, 45-48; Grenville acts (1764), 50-54; colonial opposition to Grenville acts, 54-65; Stamp Act (1765), 62-63, 65-66; incidence of Stamp Act, 66-71; colonial opposition to Stamp Act, 71-82; modification of Grenville acts (1766), 82-84; reception of modifications in America, 84-90; Townshend acts (1767), 93-95; partial repeal of Townshend acts (1770), 212-213, 239; reception of partial repeal in America, 213-236, 240, 244-250; currency act to relieve New York (1770), 224; currency act (1773), 243-244; tea legislation (1767-1773), 249-251, 262-263, 270, 272; provision for paying Massachusetts judges (1772), 255; appointment of royal commission to investigate *Gaspee* affair, 253, 261; reception of tea act of 1773 in America, 264-298; coercive acts (1774), 305-306; effect of coercive acts on colonial opinion, 305-311; colonial opposition to coercive acts, 311-536; New England Restraining Act (1775), 538; General Restraining Act (1775), 539; Prohibitory Act (1775), 540, 573, 579.
Brown, William and John, merchants of Norfolk, violate non-importation (1770), 199; violate non-importation (1775), 511, 515.
Charleston, important as trading centre, 34; attitude of people of, toward Stamp Act, 73-74; non-importation in, (1765), 82; non-importation movement in, (1769-1770), 140-146, 202-208; mass meeting in, boycotts Georgia and New York, 209, 229 n.; mass meeting in, abandons non-importation, 235-236; importation of duticd tea at, 245, 246, 295; arguments used to arouse opposition to shipments of East India Company, 265; opposition to tea shipments, 295-298; formation of Chamber of Commerce of, 296-297; activity of Chamber of Commerce of, in public affairs, 375, 377; non-intercourse movement in, (1774), 374-379; appointment of General Committee, 378; enforcement of non-importation in, 525-527, 529; enforcement of non-exportation in, 574.
Coercive acts. *Vide:* Boston Port Act; British colonial policy.
Colden, Cadwallader, lieutenant governor of New York, on trade conditions, 46, 49; on attitude of merchants in 1764, 60; on New York lawyers, 69; on attitude of merchants in 1767, 92; on movement to abandon non-importation, 223; on distaste of men of property for riots, 240, 328-329; on smuggling, 247, 248, 248-249; on political apathy of rural New York, 332, 340; believes majority against non-importation, 339 n.; on attitude of merchants toward Continental Association, 448; on election of Sixty, 449; on intimidation, 454 n.; on execution of non-importation, 493; on news of Lexington fight, 544; and defense association, 545.
Commerce. *Vide:* British colonial policy; commercial provinces; Continental Association; factors; Great Britain; merchants; non-exportation; non-importation; plantation provinces; smuggling; colonies by name.
Commercial provinces, definition of term, 22-23; economy of, 23-27; dominance of merchants in, 27-28; methods of merchants in, 28-29; prevalence of smuggling in, 40-49; affected by Grenville acts, 54-55; opposition in, to Grenville acts, 55-61; affected by Stamp Act, 66; opposition in, to Stamp Act, 71-73; stages of non-importation movement in, (1767-1770), 105-106; reasons for growing discontent with non-importation (1769-1770), 209-214; effect of

INDEX

coercive acts upon merchants of, 306-311, 359; combination of workingmen of, against Gage, 386-388; instructions in, concerning non-intercourse, 398; efforts to regulate prices in, 585-589.

Committees of correspondence, system of, origin of, in Massachusetts towns (1772), 255-261; appointment of Virginia legislative committee (1773) and extension of plan elsewhere, 261-262; establishment of local committees in Rhode Island, 304; legislated against by Parliament, 306; establishment of local committees in Connecticut, 326; in New York, 331-332; in Pennsylvania, 347; in New Jersey, 357; in Maryland, 361. *Vide* also: colonies and towns by name.

Connecticut, trade of, 26; non-consumption movement in, (1767-1768), 112; non-importation movement in, (1769-1770), 150-152, 196; meetings in, boycott New York, 228-229; Assembly disapproves of Solemn League and Covenant, 325; towns of, endorse Boston circular letter, 326; committee of correspondence elects delegates to First Continental Congress, 327; ratification of Continental Association and establishment of committees in, 444-447; workings of Continental Association in, 486-488; adoption of defense association in, 542; Assembly lays embargo, 559-560; resolutions in, against exportation of flaxseed, 571-572; regulation of prices in, 486-487, 588.

Continental Association, similarity of, to Virginia Association, 368-370, 424; evolution of, in First Continental Congress, 412-421; passage of, 421-423; analysis of, 423-429; greeted by storm of protest, 435-439; ratification of, and establishment of committees in separate provinces: Massachusetts, 440-442; New Hampshire, 442-444; Rhode Island, 444; Connecticut, 444-447; New York, 447-455; New Jersey, 455; Pennsylvania, 456-460; Delaware, 460; Maryland, 461; Virginia, 461-462; North Carolina, 462-464; South Carolina, 464-469; failure of Georgia to accept, 469-472; vast importations in anticipation of, 473-475; change in character of, with outbreak of war, 475-476, 541; generalizations as to operation of, 476; workings of, in separate colonies: Massachusetts, 476-483; New Hampshire, 483-485; Rhode Island, 485-486; Connecticut, 486-488; New York, 489-493; New Jersey, 493-495; Pennsylvania, 495-502; Delaware, 502-503; Maryland, 504-509; Virginia, 509-519; North Carolina, 519-525; South Carolina, 525-529; boycott of Georgia under, 529-530, 531-533; boycott of Quebec, Nova Scotia, the Floridas *etc.*, under, 530-533; regulation of coast trade under, 534; decline of importation resulting from, 535-536; effect of, on Great Britain, 536-540; largely superseded by defense associations, 543, 546; ratification and enforcement of, in Georgia, 548, 549, 550-552; change in functions of committees of, 552-559, 563-564; amended by Second Continental Congress, 565-568; advent of non-exportation regulation of, and its enforcement, 570-575; text of, 607-613.

Continental Congress. *Vide:* First Continental Congress; Second Continental Congress.

Debts, act of Parliament for collection of, (1732), 21, 36; of planters to merchants, 36, 135; legislation of Virginia relative to, 37-38; of planters, a source of Whigism, 39, 359-360; movement in South for restrictions on, 359-360, 360-361, 366, 371; press discussion as to desirability of withholding payment of, 404-405; existence of, influences enforcement of Continental Association in plantation provinces, 504; factors in Virginia press for payment of, 511; restrictions on collection of,

in separate colonies: Maryland, 504-505; Virginia, 512; North Carolina, 522-523; South Carolina, 468, 528-529; Georgia, 549.
Declaratory Act (1766), 83.
Defense associations, adoption of, 542-546; in Georgia, 546-547, 550, 551; action of Newbern committee respecting, 559; resolution of Second Continental Congress respecting, 564; Van Schaack refuses to sign, 603 n.
Delaware, non-importation movement in, (1769-1770), 149-150, 196; convention elects delegates to First Continental Congress, 357-358; ratification of Continental Association and establishment of committees in, 460; workings of Continental Association in, 502-503; enforcement of non-exportation in, 574.
Dick, James, and Stewart, Anthony, merchants of Annapolis, own goods imported in *Good Intent*, 200-201; involved as principals in *Peggy Stewart* affair, 389-392; accede to non-importation, 505.
Dickinson, John, author of *Late Regulations*, 54-55, 67; denounces mob violence, 96; author of *Farmer's Letters*, 114; makes speech for non-importation, 118; impugns motives of Philadelphia merchants, 119-120; opposes shipments of East India Company, 269 n., 275-276; explains meaning of tea act, 272; is induced to reenter public affairs, 341-344; disapproves of Boston Tea Party, 342; is chosen chairman of Forty-Three, 346, 347; is antagonist of Galloway, 348; takes part in Pennsylvania convention (1774), 352, 354; is chosen member of First Continental Congress, 355-356, 408 n.; favors holding interprovincial congress, 394; is chosen member of Sixty-Six, 458.
Drayton, William Henry, characterization of, 202; engages in controversy with Gadsden, 202-205; leaves America as result of boycott, 203, 206; joins radical party after coercive acts, 310; favors compensation plan in South Carolina congress, 468; comments on South Carolina congress, 469; opposes landing of horses, 527.
Dulany, Daniel, author of *Considerations*, 68-69; repelled by Stamp Act riots, 92.
East India Company, efforts of, to escape bankruptcy, 250; acts of Parliament concerning tea, (1767-1773), 249-251, 262-263; becomes exporter of tea, 263-264; union of northern merchants against shipments of, 264-265; arguments used to arouse colonial opposition to, 265-277; nature of business of, 268-269; seeks to destroy china manufactory at Philadelphia, 280; opposition to shipments of, in Philadelphia, 279-281, 290-291; in Boston, 281-290; in New York, 291-294; in Charleston, 295-298; beneficiary of Boston Port Act, 305; efforts of colonists to secure compensation for, 312, 316, 317-318, 344, 353, 357, 394, 398, 407; resolutions in Virginia against, 363, 366. *Vide* also: tea.
Factors, activities of, in plantation provinces, 35-36; attitude of planters toward, 36-39, 135; opposed to mob outrages, 74-75; not inclined to sympathize with distress of northern merchants, 591-592; profits of, an argument for independence, 600-602. *Vide* also: southern provinces by name.
Fairfield County, Conn., contest of certain towns of, against ratification of Continental Association, 445-447; execution of Continental Association in, 488.
First Continental Congress, proposals for a, 326, 393-396; election of delegates to, 327, 340-341, 354-355, 357, 358, 362, 368, 372, 377-379, 396; instructions of delegates to, 339-340, 351-355, 357, 362, 369-370, 372, 377, 396-400; sources of support for holding, 393-395, 406-407 n.; factors determining policy of, 396; newspaper discussion of issues confronting, 400-405; journey of

INDEX

Massachusetts delegates to, 405-407; characterization of membership of, 407-410; proceedings of, 410-431; official utterances of, as to tea troubles, 274, 430-431; significance of radical victory in, 432-435.

Franklin, Benjamin, on incidence of Stamp Act, 68, 69-70; on reasons for colonial opposition, 83; pleased with remedial legislation of 1766, 85; urges continuance of non-importation (1770), 220; comments on reluctance of British merchants to petition Parliament, 238; disapproves of Boston Tea Party, 299-300; changes mind as to Tea Party, 309-310; gives advice as to non-exportation, 422 n.; books of, are permitted to land, 566; takes part in Second Continental Congress, 576 n., 583.

Franklin, William, governor of New Jersey, on trade conditions, 49; reports erection of slitting mill, 243; views of, on an interprovincial congress, 393, 394-395; on efficacy of Continental Association, 494.

G a d s d e n, Christopher, opposes Stamp Act, 75, 76; leads non-importation forces (1769-1770), 140, 142, 143, 145; has controversy with Drayton, 202-206; circulates agreement for tea non-importation, 296; leads movement for non-intercourse (1774), 373; economic interests of, 373 n.; is chosen delegate to First Continental Congress, 377, 378; takes part in First Continental Congress, 414, 417; seeks to have rice exemption repudiated, 464, 467, 468; opposes landing of horses, 527; takes part in Second Continental Congress, 569, 578.

Galloway, Joseph, repelled by Stamp Act violence, 92-93; writes against non-importation, 116-117; on significance of tea act (1773), 263-264; views of, prior to First Continental Congress, 347-349; takes part in election of delegates to Congress, 349-350, 354-356; approves of interprovincial congress, 393-394; leads minority in First Continental Congress, 410-415, 422-423; characterizes Samuel Adams, 411; withdraws from extra-legal activities, 433, 456; seeks to win over Assembly against measures of Continental Congress, 459-460.

Gaspee, burning of, 252-253; stirs Virginia to action, 261.

Georgia, economy of, 33-34; attitude of merchants of, toward Stamp Act, 75; boycotted by Charleston, 82; non-importation movement in, (1769-1770), 147-148, 209; non-intercourse movement in, (1774), 379-386; reasons for dependence of, on Great Britain, 379-380; conventions (1774), 381-384; failure of, to ratify Continental Association, 469-472; provincial congresses (1775), 470-472, 548-550; boycott of, 529-530, 531-533; increase of imports into, (1774-1775), 536; accedes to Continental Association, 546-551; restrictions on collection of debts, 549; establishment of committees and enforcement of Continental Association in, 550-552; enforcement of non-exportation regulation in, 574.

Good Intent, enforcement of non-importation in case of, 200-201.

Great Britain, effect of non-importation upon, (1765-1766), 82-83; effect of non-importation upon, (1769-1770), 236-239; effect of Continental Association upon, 536-540. Vide also: British colonial policy.

Grenville acts, analysis of, 50-54; colonial opinion of, 54-56; economic effects of and colonial opposition to, 56-65; Stamp Act, 62-63, 65-66; classes affected by Stamp Act, 66-71; colonial opposition to Stamp Act, 71-82; modifications of, (1766), 82-84; reception of modifications in colonies, 84-90.

Hancock, John, on trade conditions, 57, 66-67; on repeal of Stamp Act, 86; and the Liberty, 103-104; orders dutied glass, 106; visits

Dickinson, 132; vessels of, carry goods debarred by agreement 166, 167-169; entertains friends with tea, 244; permits dutied tea to be carried in his ships, 246; cools toward Samuel Adams, 254-255; declines membership in committee of correspondence, 257; part of, in tea troubles in Boston, 284, 289, 555; member of Sixty-Three, 441.

Henry, Patrick, and Parsons' Case, 38; favors non-importation in Virginia (1769), 136; influential in House of Burgesses, 363; takes part in First Continental Congress, 414.

Hopkins, Stephen, author of *Rights of Colonies*, 54; opposes powers of *Gaspee* commission, 253.

Hutchinson, Thomas, on Stamp Act riots, 71, 72 n.; alienated from merchants, 92; on merchants and non-importation, 121, 163, 172, 173, 182; relatives of, violate non-importation, 159, 164; rebukes mob, 176; seeks to stop merchants' meeting, 177; on tea smuggling, 179, 247; promotes an association against non-importation, 181; on popular excesses, 181; on observation of non-importation in Rhode Island, 195; on tea prices in England, 250; seeks to conciliate Hancock, 255; on composition of town meetings, 256; has dispute with town meeting over judges' salaries, 257; expresses opinion of committee of correspondence, 258, 259, 260; on opposition of tea traders to act of 1773, 264-265; has interest in sons' tea business, 282; conduct of, during tea riots in Boston, 281-289; on public indifference to loss of East India Company, 289-290; address to, upon departure from Boston, 316-317.

Illicit commerce. *Vide:* smuggling.

Independence, New York committee suppresses false report of, 557; opening of trade with world as a step toward, 577, 578, 580-581; passage of Prohibitory Act as incentive to, 580; Paine's *Common Sense* on, 593; criticized as visionary 594; statement of economic advantages of, requested, 595-598; economic advantages of, depicted, 598-602; course adopted by merchants upon declaration of, 602-606.

Jefferson, Thomas, on economic bondage of planters, 36; orders goods debarred by agreement, 236.

Laurens, Henry, disapproves of Stamp Act, 74; aroused by vice-admiralty regulations, 102; presides at meeting to consider abandonment of non-importation (1770), 235; weeps on hearing of Declaration of Independence, 603.

Lee, Richard Henry, favors immediate resolutions in behalf of Boston, 362; disapproves of measures adopted by House of Burgesses, 364; takes part in First Continental Congress, 414, 419, 424 n.; takes part in Second Continental Congress, 569, 576 n., 578, 582-583.

Low, Isaac, merchant of New York, characterization of, 186; works for abandonment of non-importation (1770), 225; discourages use of violence against tea shipments, 293; chairman of Fifty-One, 329, 330; takes active part in election of delegates to First Continental Congress, 334, 337, 340; takes part in First Continental Congress, 416, 419, 420; decided to continue on committees for the time, 433-434, 448; chairman of Sixty, 449; becomes loyalist, 605.

Loyalist association, in Massachusetts, 477-478; in New Hampshire, 484; in New York, 493.

McDougall, Alexander, of New York, heads public meeting favorable to non-importation (1770), 226; takes part in anti-tea agitation, 292; promises New York support to Boston, 327-328; as regarded by moderates, 328; member of Fifty-One, 329; part played by, in election of delegates to First Continental Congress, 333-336; cautions Massachusetts delegates, 406-407; member of Sixty,

450; favors relaxing of tea non-consumption, 582.
Macknight, Thomas, of Currituck County, N. C., circumstances surrounding boycott of, 523-524.
Madison, James, leads Princeton demonstration to protest against New York's defection (1770), 227; analyzes opposition to popular measures in Virginia, 364.
Manufactures, superiority of British, 16; restraints on colonial, and effects, 19-21; movement for domestic, (1764-1766), 64-65, 77; decline of, 86; movement for domestic, (1767-1770), 107, 109-111, 121, 122-124, 130-131, 146, 148, 151-152, 243; attempt of East India Company to suppress, of chinaware in Philadelphia, 280; provisions for promotion of, in Continental Association, 427, 612; movement for domestic, (1774-1776), 482-483, 484, 486, 487, 492, 495, 500-502, 517-518, 524, 528, 553-554; provisions for promotion of, by Second Continental Congress, 564.
Marblehead, merchants of, appoint committee, 60; non-importation in, (1765-1766), 80; non-importation in, (1768-1770), 121, 184-185; appoints committees of correspondence (1772), 260; endorses Boston circular letter (1774), 314; appoints committee of observation, 440-441; enforcement of non-importation in, (1774-1775), 479-480; enforcement of non-consumption in, 481-483; suppresses loyalists, 554.
Maryland, trade of, 32-33; non-importation in, (1769-1770), 139, 109-202; merchants of, capture trade of Philadelphia, 218; breakdown of non-importation in, (1770), 233-234; importation of dutied tea in, 244-245, 246, 389; county resolutions regarding non-intercourse (1774), 361; appointment of delegates to First Continental Congress in, 362; affair of *Peggy Stewart* in, 389-392; ratification of Continental Association and establishment of committees in, 461; conventions (1774), 361-362, 461, 507; increased importation into, in anticipation of Continental Association, 474 n.; workings of Continental Association in, 504-509; restrictions on collection of debts in, 360-361, 504-505; convention boycotts Georgia, etc., 531; decline of importation as result of Continental Association, 535; form of defense association in, 543; committees assist militia, 553; convention refuses to lay embargo, 560; convention favors relaxing of tea non-consumption, 583; convention encourages making of salt, 584-585. *Vide* also: Annapolis, Baltimore.
Mason, George, suggests form of non-importation for Virginia, 136; shows inner workings of House of Burgesses, 363.
Mason, Thomson, author of *British American*, 367-368.
Massachusetts, non-consumption movement in, (1767-1768), 110-111; domestic manufacturing in, (1767-1770), 122-124; enforcement of non-importation in, (1768-1770), 183-186; appointment of committees of correspondence in, (1772), 259-260; adoption of non-consumption of tea in, 301; popularity of Solemn League and Covenant in, 323-325; movement in, to boycott Gage, 387-388; election of delegates to First Continental Congress in, 396; ratification of Continental Association in, 440-442; workings of Continental Association in, 476-483; provincial congress (1774), 478; congress requires bond of coast traders, 535; congress recommends confiscation of arms, 558; congress lays embargo, 560; difficulties of, with Nantucket, 561-562. *Vide* also chief ports by name.
Mein, John, has controversy with Boston merchants over non-importation, 157, 159, 178, 179; author of pamphlet, 169-170; familiar with Drayton's views, 202.
Merchants, colonial, satisfied with

British commercial policy, 22; character of business of, in commercial provinces, 24-27, 40-45; dominant position of, 27-29; attitude of, toward England, 30-32; oppose smuggling regulations during Last Intercolonial War, 45-49; enjoy wartime prosperity, 56-57; experience hard times (1764-1766), 57-59; affected by stamp duties, 66-68, 70; partially satisfied by acts of 1766, 86-87; position of, in early 1767, 91-93; position of, after passage of Townshend acts, 95; determine upon orderly resistance, 96; methods of opposition employed by, 96-97, 105; become discontented with non-importation, 209-214; become alienated from radicals, 240-244; unite in opposition to shipments of East India Company, 264-265, 279; shocked by Boston Tea Party, 299; effect of coercive acts upon, 306-309; only eleven, in First Continental Congress, 409; effect of First Continental Congress upon, 432, 433-435; increase importations in anticipation of Continental Association, 473-475; depletion of stocks of, 579, 586, 589; accused of forestalling, 585-586; connection with revolutionary movement (1764-1775), 591-593; position of, on eve of Declaration of Independence, 593-600; decision of, when independence declared, 602-606. *Vide* also: factors; separate provinces and chief ports by name.

Middle colonies, commerce of, 26-27; importance of merchants in, 27-32.

Molasses, act of Parliament (1733), 19, 31-32, 42-43; importance of, as article of commerce, 25-26, 27, 43; smuggling of, prior to 1764, 42-49; reduction of duty on, (1764), 52-53; colonial opinion of act of 1764 concerning, 55-56, 58; as an ingredient of independence, 59; reduction of duty on, (1766), 84; effect of reduction on smuggling of, 97; reception of news of reduction on, in America, 84-85, 87; importance of duty on, as source of revenue, 131; effort of Boston merchants to have duties on, included as object of non-importation, 131-133; trade in, criticized as violation of taxation principle, 134, 191, 218, 230, 275; decline in smuggling of, 251; resolutions of First Continental Congress respecting, 421, 425, 608, 612.

Morris, Gouverneur, on rise of radicals in New York, 307-308 n.; describes election of Fifty-One, 330-331.

Murray, Robert and John, merchants of New York, involved in violation of non-importation, 491; removal of boycott against, 565.

Navigation acts. *Vide:* British colonial policy.

Newburyport, non-importation in, (1765-1766), 80, 82; appoints committee of correspondence (1772), 260; merchants of, endorse Boston circular letter (1774), 314 n.; appoints committee of observation, 440-441; enforcement of non-consumption in, 481, 483.

New England, commerce of, 24-26; importance of merchants in, 27-32; non-consumption movement in, (1767-1768), 106-114; increased importation into, in anticipation of Continental Association, 474; decline of importations into, as result of Continental Association, 535; provinces of, place militia on war footing, 542.

New Hampshire, non-importation movement in, (1770), 155, 194-195; agreements against importation of tea in, (1773), 302-303; convention elects delegates to First Continental Congress, 327; ratification of Continental Association and establishment of committees in, 442-444; workings of Continental Association in, 483-485; resolutions of provincial congress of, 556, 558-559, 589. *Vide* also: Portsmouth.

New Haven, merchants of, adopt non-importation agreement (1769), 150; meeting in, boycotts New York (1770), 228, 229; endorses Boston circular letter (1774), 326; visited by Massachusetts delegates, 406; resolves to boycott Fairfield County deputies, 446.

New Jersey, non-importation movement in, (1769-1770), 150, 196; meetings in, denounce New York for defection, 228; Assembly replies to Boston circular letter, 356-357; movement for non-intercourse in, (1774), 356-357; convention elects delegates to First Continental Congress, 357; ratification of Continental Association and establishment of committees in, 455; workings of Continental Association in, 493-495; provincial congress endorses boycott of Georgia, etc., 532; adoption of defense association in, 542; provincial congress instructs committees to apprehend deserters, 553; difficulties over prices in, 587-588, 590.

Newport, important as trading centre, 25, 27; hard times in, 58; burning of *Liberty* at, 101; adopts non-consumption agreement (1767), 112; attitude of merchants of, toward non-importation (1769-1770), 153-155, 195-196, 215-216; adopts non-importation of tea (1773), 303; endorses Boston circular letter (1774), 325-326; appoints committee of observation, 444; enforcement of non-importation in, 485; non-exportation of sheep in, 485.

New York city, important as trading centre, 26-27; identity of interests of, with leading northern ports, 32; merchants of, organize (1764), 60-61; promotion of manufacturing in, 64, 77; opposition to Stamp Act in, 73; non-consumption agreement at, (1765-1766), 76-77; non-importation agreement at, 78; merchants of, petition Parliament (1766), 87-88; punishment of informer in, 100; mass meeting adopts plan of retrenchment, 113; merchants of, adopt conditional non-importation agreement (1768), 115-116; formation of Chamber of Commerce of, 116; merchants and tradesmen adopt non-importation (1768), 124-125; merchants refuse to extend scope of agreement (1769), 133; merchants boycott Newport, 154-155, 215; enforcement of non-importation in, (1768-1770), 186-190; difficulties over price of tea, 211; breakdown of non-importation in, (1770), 217-218, 220-227; opposition to rescinding of non-importation in, 219, 220, 223; adoption of agreement against dutied articles (1770), 226-227; enforcement of tea boycott in, 246-248, 251; smuggling of tea in, 247-251; arguments used in, to arouse opposition to shipments of East India Company, 265-277; opposition to tea shipments, 291-294; movement for non-intercourse in (1774), 327-341, 406-407 n.; appointment of Fifty-One in, 329-330; Committee of Mechanics as new radical organization in, 330, 333-336, 339-340, 447, 449; Fifty-One at, answer Boston circular letter (1774), 331; contest for election of delegates to First Continental Congress in, 333-340; workingmen of, boycott Gage, 386-387; merchants in, furnish supplies to Gage, 388; Massachusetts delegates visit, 406-407; Fifty-One at, instruct departing delegates, 407; election of Sixty in, 448-450; increased importation in, in anticipation of Continental Association, 473, 474; enforcement of non-importation in, 489-491, 493; enforcement of non-exportation in, 489, 587; regulation of prices in, 491-492; enforcement of non-consumption in, 492, 581-582; promotion of manufacturing in, 492; committee boycotts Georgia, etc., 532; enforces boycott against Canada, 533; decline of importations into, as result of Continental Association, 535; appointment of One Hundred in, 454, 544-545; committee withholds weapons, 553; committee suppresses false reports, 557; prevention of exportation in, 560, 571-

INDEX 641

572; merchants petition for relaxing of tea non-consumption, 583.
New York province, act of Parliament to relieve currency shortage in, 90 n., 224; appointment of committees of correspondence in, 331-333; election of delegates to First Continental Congress in rural, 340-341; delegates of, in First Continental Congress opposed to measures adopted, 438-439, 447; establishment of committees in, 447-452, 454-455, 546; failure of Assembly to ratify Continental Association, 452-454; workings of Continental Association in, 489-493; provincial congress requires bond of coast traders, 535; decline of importations into, as result of Continental Association, 535; history of defense association in, 543-546; resolutions of provincial congress of, 554, 559, 583.

Non-consumption, in 1764-1765, 63-64, 76-77; in 1767-1768, 106-109, 111-114; in 1769-1770, 146, 181-182, 184, 185-186, 194, 196, 209; of tea (1773-1774), 300-301; in Boston (1774), 316; in Virginia, 363, 369; resolutions of First Continental Congress concerning, 414, 426, 609; enforcement of, in separate provinces: Massachusetts, 481-483; New Hampshire, 484-485; Connecticut, 486-488; New York, 492, 493, 581-582; New Jersey, 495; Pennsylvania, 500-501, 582; Delaware, 503; Maryland, 506-507, 508-509; Virginia, 516; South Carolina, 525-526, 528; Rhode Island, 581. *Vide* also: Continental Association; non-importation; Solemn League and Covenant.

Non-exportation, of tobacco suggested in Virginia, 136; of leather in South Carolina, 146; Boston circular letter proposes, 313; arguments for, in Philadelphia, 350-351; resolutions in Maryland favoring, 360-362; resolutions in Virginia favoring, 366, 369; resolutions in North Carolina favoring, 372 n.; instructions of delegates of First Continental Congress respecting, 398-399; press discussion prior to First Continental Congress concerning, 400; resolutions of First Continental Congress concerning, 415-419, 427, 609; enforcement of, of sheep, 480-481, 483, 485-486, 488, 489; of munitions at Charleston, 525; adoption of, for military purposes, 559-562; resolutions of Second Continental Congress respecting, 565-568; advent of, and its enforcement, 570-575. *Vide* also: Continental Association.

Non-importation, in 1765-1766, 77-80; as political protest, 80-81; enforcement of, 81-82; effect of, on British trade, 82-83; stages of, in commercial provinces (1767-1770), 105-106; agreement of, at Providence (1767), 111-112; efforts for league of (1768), 114-120; movement in Massachusetts (1768-1770), 120-121, 156-185; movement in New York, 124-125, 186-190; movement in Philadelphia, 125-130, 191-194; proposal of Boston merchants to extend scope of, 131-133; movement in plantation provinces (1769-1770), 134-135, 197-198; movement in separate provinces (1769-1770): Virginia, 135-138, 198-199; Maryland, 138-139, 199-202; South Carolina, 140-147, 202-208; Georgia, 147-148, 209; North Carolina, 148-149, 208-209; Delaware, 149-150; New Jersey, 150; Connecticut, 150-152; Rhode Island, 152-155, 195-196; New Hampshire, 155, 194-195, 216; difficulty of judging degree of enforcement of, 156; growth of discontent in northern provinces with, 209-214; effect of, on colonial trade, 210-212, 241-243; merchants of Albany and Rhode Island rescind and resume, 215; breakdown of, in chief ports (1770): Philadelphia, 218-220, 229-232; New York, 220-227; Boston, 232-233; Maryland, 233-234; South Carolina, 235-236; Virginia, 236; limitation of, to dutied articles, 226-227, 231,

233, 234, 235-236, 236; effect of, on Great Britain (1769-1770), 236-239; extent of enforcement of, of dutied articles, 244-251, 264-265, 282 n., 295; adoption of new agreements of, of tea (1773), 281, 285-286, 292, 296-297, 302, 303-304; execution of, of tea against East India Company (1773), 279-298; Boston circular letter (1774) proposing, 313; merchants of Boston adopt conditional, 315-316, 318; provided by Solemn League and Covenant, 319-327; arguments over, in Philadelphia, 350-351; resolutions of Pennsylvania concerning, 351-354; movement for, (1774), 311-386; instructions of delegates of First Continental Congress concerning, 398-399; press discussion concerning, (1774), 400-404; resolutions of First Continental Congress concerning, 413, 420-421, 425-426, 608, 610; enforcement of, facilitated by large advance importations, 475; enforcement of, in separate provinces (1774-1775): Massachusetts, 478-480, 534; New Hampshire, 483; Rhode Island, 485, 534; Connecticut, 486; New York, 489-491, 493; New Jersey, 494; Pennsylvania, 498-499, 502; Maryland, 505-506, 507-508, 509; Virginia, 510-511, 514-516, 519, 534; North Carolina, 520-521, 525; South Carolina, 526-527, 529; regulations concerning, in coast trade, 534-535; decline of trade resulting from, 535-536; enforcement of, in Georgia, 551; resolutions of Second Continental Congress concerning, 565-568. *Vide* also: Continental Association; Solemn League and Covenant.

North Carolina, economy of, 34; non-importation movement in, (1769-1770), 148-149, 208-209; non-intercourse movement in, (1774). 370-373; convention (1774), 372-373; election of delegates to First Continental Congress in, 372; ratification of Continental Association and establishment of committees in, 462-464; convention (1775), 463-464; enforcement of Continental Association in, 519-525; restrictions on collection of debts in, 522-523; decline of importations into, as result of Continental Association, 535; convention encourages making of salt, 584-585.

Otis, James, on writs of assistance, 47; author of *Rights of Colonies*, 54; spokesman for merchants, 54 n.; denounces mob violence, 96; fights with customs commissioner, 179; pursues reactionary course, 254; becomes chairman of Boston Committee of Correspondence, 257-258.

Paine, Thomas, author of *Common Sense*, 593.

Paper money, legal tender, prohibition of, in New England (1751), 21-22; prohibition of, in all colonies (1764), 53-54; shortage of, in Virginia and South Carolina, 73-74; absence of, a colonial grievance, 56, 83; failure of British Government to remedy stringency of, 89-90; act authorizing, in New York (1770), 224; act of Parliament concerning, (1773), 243-244; repeal of restrictions (1764) on, demanded by First Continental Congress, 430; Second Continental Congress provides boycott for refusers of continental, 564.

Parsons' Case, 37-38.

Peggy Stewart, statement of shippers regarding tea in, 245; affair of the, 389-392.

Pennsylvania, hard times in, (1764-1766), 58; establishment of committees of correspondence in rural, 347; convention (1774), 351-354; election of delegates to First Continental Congress in, 354-355; ratification of Continental Association and establishment of committees in, 456-460; workings of Continental Association in, 495-502. *Vide* also: Philadelphia.

Newspapers, colonial, printers of, affected by Stamp Act, 69-70, 71; radical activities of Bradford of

INDEX 643

Pennsylvania Journal, 73 n., 458; free advertisements in *Newport Mercury*, 112; use of, for propagandist purposes recommended, 136; *Boston Chronicle*, most enterprising of, 160, 178; radical activities of Edes of *Boston Gazette*, 72 n., 282; paper for use of, permitted to land at Wilmington, 521.

Philadelphia, important as trading centre, 26-27; merchant-aristocracy of, 28; identity of interests of, with leading northern ports, 32; merchants of, organize (1764), 61; non-consumption agreement in, 64, 76-77; opposition to Stamp Act in, 73; domestic manufacturing in, (1765-1766), 77; non-importation agreement in, 79, 81; trouble over smuggled wine at, 101; meeting in, fails to adopt non-consumption (1768), 113; merchants of, fail to adopt non-importation, 116-120; merchants of, adopt non-importation (1769), 125-130; domestic manufacturing in, (1769-1771), 130-131; merchants of, refuse to extend scope of agreement, 132-133, 230; merchants of, threaten to boycott Newport, 154-155; enforcement of non-importation in, 191-194; difficulties over price of tea in, 211; boycott of Rhode Island by, 215-216; breakdown of non-importation in, (1770), 218-220, 229-232; opposes alteration of agreement, agreement against dutied articles 222, 223; mass meeting of, boycotts New York, 227; adoption of agreement against dutied articles in, 231; observation of boycott of tea in, 246-248, 251; smuggling of tea in, 247-251; mob in, rescues detained vessel, 252; arguments used to arouse opposition to East India Company in, 265-277; opposition to tea shipments in, 264-265, 279-281, 290-291; public opinion of, veers in favor of Boston, 309-310; movement for non-intercourse in, 341-356; election of Nineteen, 344; Nineteen replies to Boston circular letter (1774), 344; election of Forty-Three, 347; election of delegates to First Continental Congress in, 349-356; merchants of, refuse supplies to Gage, 388; election of Sixty-Six, 456-458; increased importation into, in anticipation of Continental Association, 473; enforcement of non-importation in, 498-499, 502; regulation of prices in, 499-500, 586-587; promotion of manufacturing in, 501-502; enforcement of non-consumption in, 500-501; committee boycotts Georgia, etc., 531; committee enforces boycott against Newfoundland, 533; committee requires use of certificates in coast trade, 534; decline of trade in, as result of Continental Association, 535; committee erects saltpetre works, 553; committee justifies suppression of free speech, 555; alarm of merchants of, over rumor of non-exportation, 571; enforcement of non-exportation in, 572, 574, 574-575, merchants of, petition for relaxing of tea non-consumption, 583.

Plantation provinces, definition of term, 23; economy of, 32-34; leadership of planters in, 34-35; factors manage commerce of, 35-37; bankruptcy acts in, 37-38; place of planters of, in revolutionary movement, 38-39; slow to oppose Grenville acts, 62; aroused by Stamp Act, 65-66; opposition in, to Stamp Act, 73-75; non-importation movement in, (1769-1770), 134-135, 197-198; effect of coercive acts upon people of, 359-360; violent opposition to tea duty in, 388-389; instructions in, concerning non-intercourse (1774), 398-399, 409; distinctive feature of operation of Continental Association in, 504; regulation of price of salt in, 584-585; economic advantage of, assured by independence, 600-602.

Planters, leadership of, in southern provinces, 34-35; in debt to factors, 36, 39, 135; rôle of, in revolutionary movement, 38-39; take lead in non-importation (1769-

1770), 135; active in agitation against Parliament (1774), 359-360; asked to support independence on basis of self-interest, 600-602.

Portsmouth, non-importation in, (1770), 194-195, 216-217; non-importation of tea in, (1773-1774), 302-303; committee sends out Solemn League, 325; appoints Forty-Five, 443; enforcement of Continental Association in, 483-484.

Prices, regulation of, provided in Continental Association, 426, 427, 610; in Connecticut, 486-487; in New York, 491-492; in Pennsylvania, 499-500; in Maryland, 507; in Virginia, 516-517; in North Carolina, 521; in South Carolina, 525; of tea provided by Second Continental Congress, 584; of salt in plantation provinces, 584-585; of salt provided by Second Continental Congress, 585; in commercial provinces, 585-589; abandoned by Second Continental Congress, 589; results of abandonment of, 590; of salt revived by Congress, 590-591.

Providence, adopts non-importation agreement (1767), 111-112; non-importation movement in, (1769-1770), 153; rescinds and renews agreement (1770), 215-216; burning of *Gaspee* near, 252-253; endorses Boston circular letter (1774), 325-326; proposes holding of interprovincial congress, 326, 393; appoints committee of observation, 444; enforcement of non-importation in, 485, 534; enforcement of non-exportation in, 485; enforcement of non-consumption in, 486, 581; stops exportation of flaxseed, 572; regulation of prices in, 589.

Quakers of Pennsylvania, favor non-importation during Stamp Act, 191, 497; warn members against non-importation (1769), 191-192; member of, skeptical of patriotism, 212; help form slate of candidates, 346; are chief source of opposition to Continental Association, 456, 460, 495-498; oppose demonstrations against Boston Port Act, 496; oppose independence, 603-604.

Randolph, Peyton, connives at smuggling, 42; favors non-importation in Virginia, 136, 198; presides over ex-burgesses (1774), 363, 364; is chosen president of First Continental Congress, 412; thanks Williamsburg merchants, 509; answers complaint regarding mercantile credits, 511.

Rhode Island, economy of, 25-26; non-importation movement in, (1769-1770), 152-155, 195-196, 215-216; importation of dutied tea in, (1773), 303-304; establishment of committees of correspondence in, 304; towns of, object to Solemn League, 325; Assembly elects delegates to First Continental Congress, 327, 396; ratification of Continental Association and establishment of committees in, 444; increased importation into, in anticipation of Continental Association, 474; workings of Continental Association in, 485-486; resolutions of Assembly of, 559, 560.

Rice, enumerated, 18; direct shipment of, south of Georgia, 51, 57; effect of fall in price of, on non-importation sentiment (1770), 235; planters of, opposed to non-exportation in South Carolina, 374; effort in First Continental Congress to exempt, from non-exportation, 417-419, 421-422; protests against exemption of, 439; contest in South Carolina over exemption of, 464-469; non-exportation of, provided for in South Carolina, 561; exemption of, repealed by Second Continental Congress, 566.

St. John's Parish, Georgia, a centre of radicalism, 380, 469; meeting in, nominates delegate to First Continental Congress, 385-386; adoption of Continental Association in, 470; delegates of, refuse to participate in Georgia congress, 471-472; people of, seek to escape boycott, 472, 529-530; is exempted from boycott by Second Continental Congress, 532; influence of, in Georgia congress (1775), 549.

Salem, merchants of, employ Otis in writs case, 47; merchants of, appoint committee, 60; non-importation in, (1765-1766), 80; non-importation in, (1768-1770), 121, 184, 185; endorses Boston circular letter (1774), 314; appoints committee of observation, 441; enforcement of non-importation in, (1774-1775), 479, 480; enforcement of non-exportation in, 480-481; committee corrects Newport as to interpretation of Continental Association, 486; committee issues certificates, 534.

Savannah, non-importation in, (1769-1770), 147-148; importation of dutied tea in, 246; a centre of radicalism, 380; protest of inhabitants of, against provincial convention, 383-384; radicals of, differ with those of St. John's Parish, 470; caucus at, 547-548; meeting at, appoints committee of observation, 548.

Second Continental Congress, boycotts Georgia, Quebec, etc., 532, 550-551; regulates trade with Nantucket, 561-562; difficulties confronting, 562-563; becomes de facto government, 563; increases functions of committees of observation, 563-564; encourages manufacturing, 564; elaborates Continental Association, 565-566; repeals rice exemption, 566; authorizes munitions trade, 566-568; resolves to ignore parliamentary exemption, 569-570; passes resolutions respecting non-exportation, 573-574, 575; debates opening of trade with world, 576-580; opens trade with world, 580; decides to relax regulation for non-consumption of tea, 582-584, 589; provides for regulation of price of salt, 585; removes restraints on prices, 589; authorizes regulation of price of salt, 590-591.

Slaves, non-importation of, in Virginia (1769), 137; action against importation of, in South Carolina (1769-1770), 143, 146, 207; non-importation of, in Georgia, 148; action against purchase of, in North Carolina, 149; resolutions in Virginia against importation of (1774), 366-367, 369; resolutions in North Carolina against importation of, 371, 372 n.; non-importation of, provided by Continental Association, 426, 428, 608, 609; enforcement of non-importation of, 515, 521-522; non-importation of, continued by Second Continental Congress, 580.

Smuggling, prior to Last Intercolonial War, 39-44; a political error, 44-45; during Last Intercolonial War, 45-49, 50; regulations against, (1764), 52; colonial opinion of regulations on, 55, 60, 61; political influence of merchants in, 59, 60; defiance of trade laws by merchants in, 88-89; regulations against, (1767), 94-95; changed character of, 97-99; activities of Customs Board against, 99-100; defiance of trade laws by merchants in, 100-101; suppressed in Boston, 102-104; affair of *Liberty*, 103-104; chief centres of, after 1770, 247; character and extent of, after 1770, 247-253; affair of *Gaspee*, 252-253; effect of tea act (1773) upon, 263-265, 266-267; regulation of, in act of 1774, 306; merchants in, disturbers of law and order, 312; mentioned in First Continental Congress, 420, 421; merchants in, affected by non-consumption of tea, 426, 582, 583.

Solemn League and Covenant, launching of, by Boston Committee of Correspondence, 319-320; opposition of Boston merchants to, 320-323; popularity of, in rural Massachusetts, 323-325; failure of, to win favor outside of Massachusetts, 325-327.

Sons of Liberty, meeting place of, in Boston, 72; composed of unprivileged classes, 92; growing antagonism between New York merchants and, 189; of Cape Fear warn merchants to observe non-importation, 208; misconceive purpose of merchant-reformers, 210; Association of, at New York, 292; superseded by Committee of Mechanics in New York, 330.

South Carolina, economy of, 33-34; non-importation movement in, (1769-1770), 140-147, 202-208; General Committee urges South Carolina association on other provinces, 214; breakdown of non-importation in, 235-236; non-intercourse movement in, (1774), 373-374; convention (1774), 375-378; appointment of General Committee in, 378-379; delegates of, in First Continental Congress seek to protect rice and indigo interests, 417-419, 421-422; ratification of Continental Association and establishment of committees in, 464-469; congress (1775), 467-469; restrictions on collection of debts in, 527-528; enforcement of Association in, 525-529; General Committee boycotts Georgia, 529-530; decline of importations into, as result of Continental Association, 535; form of defense association in, 543; resolutions of provincial congress of, 561, 584.

Stamp Act, passage of, 62-63, 65-66; classes affected by, 66-71, 230; violent opposition to, 71-75; Congress, 23-24, 75-76; economic opposition to, 76-82; repeal of, 83.

Sugar Act (1764). *Vide:* Grenville acts.

Tea, non-consumption of, (1767-1770), 108-109, 121, 181-182, 184, 185-186, 194, 196, 209; importation of dutied, at Boston, 178; open sale of smuggled, 179; regulation of price of, (1770), 211-212; limitation of non-importation to dutied, etc., 226-227, 231, 233, 234, 235-236, 236; popular acquiescence in duty on, (1770-1773), 244-246, 264-265, 274, 282 n., 295, 389; observance of boycott of, in New York and Philadelphia, 246-247; smuggling of, after 1770, 247-251; acts of Parliament concerning, (1767-1773), 94, 97-98, 249-251, 262-263, 270, 272; effect of act of 1773 upon private trade in, 264-265; arguments used to arouse opposition to East India Company's shipments of, 265-277; opposition to shipments of, at chief ports: Philadelphia, 279-281, 290-291; Boston, 281-290; New York, 291-294; Charleston, 295-298; agreements against smuggling of, 297, 300-301; adoption of new agreements against, (1773), 281, 285-286, 292, 296-297, 300-301, 302, 303-304; defeat of motion to repeal tax on, 306; non-consumption of, (1774), 324, 363, 369; non-importation of, at Charleston, 379; and *Peggy Stewart* affair, 389-392; boycott of, provided by Continental Association, 425, 426, 608, 609; repeal of duty on, demanded by Continental Association, 425, 612; enforcement of non-consumption of, as provided by Continental Association, 481-482, 484, 485, 486, 493, 494, 495, 507, 514, 516, 525-526, 581-584; partial repeal of non-consumption of, by Second Continental Congress, 584, 589, 590. *Vide* also: East India Company.

Thomson, Charles, on repeal of Stamp Act, 86; argues for non-importation, 118-119; opposes rescinding of non-importation, 219, 231; on influence of merchants in opposition to East India Company, 279-280; induces Dickinson to re-enter public affairs, 341-344; on purpose of petition for calling Assembly, 345; clerk of Pennsylvania convention (1774), 351, 352 n.; secretary of First Continental Congress, 411; member of Sixty-Six, 458.

Timothy, Peter, chief lieutenant of Gadsden, 140, 143; assists in non-intercourse movement, 373; secretary of South Carolina General Committee, 378 n.; secretary of provincial congress (1774), 467.

Townshend acts, analysis of, 93-95; economic effects of and colonial opposition to, 95-217; only one source of mercantile discontent,

131; partial repeal of, 212-213, 239.
Virginia, trade of, 32-33; debtors' acts and Parsons' Case in, 37-38; whigism of planters of, due to debts, 39; hard times in, (1764), 62, 74; non-importation movement in, (1769-1771), 135-138, 198-199, 236; importation of dutied tea in, 246; establishment of committee of correspondence of, 261-262; public opinion of, veers in favor of Boston, 311; non-intercourse movement in, 362-370; convention (1774), 368-370; election of delegates to First Continental Congress in, 368; efforts of delegates of, in First Continental Congress to protect tobacco interests, 416-417; ratification of Continental Association and establishment of committees in, 461-462; convention (1775), 462; increased importation into, in anticipation of Continental Association, 474 n.; hostility of factors of, to Continental Association, 509-511, 513, 516-517; restrictions on collection of debts in, 512; enforcement of Continental Association in, 513-519, 534; House of Burgesses boycotts Georgia, etc., 532; decline of importations into, as result of Continental Association, 535; committees of, supervise enlistments, 553; convention passes war resolutions, 554, 560-561, 584-585; enforcement of non-exportation in, 574; economic advantages assured to, by independence, 600-602.

Washington, George, complains of poor crops, 62; works for non-importation in Virginia, 135-138; violates non-importation agreement, 197 n.

Wine, duties on, (1764), 53; smuggling of, 98, 101; importance of duties on, as source of revenue, 131; non-importation of, in South Carolina, 144, 146; non-importation of, in Georgia, 148; efforts of Boston merchants to include duties on, as object of non-importation, 131-133; trade in, criticised as violation of taxation principle, 191, 218, 230, 275; decline in smuggling of, 251; resolutions of First Continental Congress concerning, 421, 425, 426, 608, 612; enforcement of non-importation of, 499, 505.

Workingmen, colonial, dependence of, on merchants, 28; organized as Sons of Liberty, 72, 92; enter into politics in Charleston, 140; protest against Drayton's aspersions, 204; declare for continuance of non-importation at Philadelphia (1770), 219; enter into politics in Philadelphia, 280, 345, 351; discontented with high price of tea in Philadelphia, 290; combine against Gage, 386-388. *Vide* chief ports by name.

www.ingramcontent.com/pod-product-compliance
Lightning Source LLC
Chambersburg PA
CBHW020629230426
43665CB00008B/90